CALIFORNIA

ENVIRONMENTAL LAW AND POLICY

PUBLISHER'S NOTE

CALIFORNIA ENVIRONMENTAL LAW AND POLICY

A Practical Guide

SECOND EDITION

ALBERT I. HERSON, JD, FAICP

GARY A. LUCKS, JD, CPEA

CALIFORNIA

ENVIRONMENTAL LAW AND POLICY

A Practical Guide

SECOND EDITION

Solano Press Books

Post Office Box 773

Point Arena, California 95468

tel: 800 931-9373

fax: 707 884-4109

email: spbooks@solano.com

cover design: Jon Handel

interior design: Catherine Courtenaye

index: Thérèse Shere

paper: ISBN 978-1-938166-15-0

ebook: ISBN 978-1-938166-16-7

NOTICE

This book is designed to assist you in understanding environmental law and policy. It is necessarily general in nature and does not discuss all exceptions and variations to general rules. Also, it may not reflect the latest changes in the law. It is not intended as legal advice and should not be relied on to address legal problems. You should always consult an attorney for advice regarding your specific factual situation.

California Environmental Law and Policy is printed on stock comprised of 10 percent post-consumer fiber with soy-based ink formulated for minimally low VOC emissions.

PHOTO CREDITS

Page 5: Albert Herson. Page 10: bigstockphoto.com. Page 12: bigstockphoto.com. Page 28: bigstockphoto.com. Page 31: Albert Herson. Page 34: Southern California Association of Nonprofit Housing. Page 39: U.S. College Search. Page 53: Wikimedia Commons. Page 55: Wikimedia Commons. Page 62: wattsreimagined.org. Page 68: Albert Herson. Page 78: Albert Herson. Page 84: Albert Herson. Page 86: Albert Herson. Page 91: Albert Herson. Page 98: American Stock/Getty Images. Page 100: NASA. Page 130: Air Resources Board. Page 134: Sonoma County Water Agency. Page 149: Wikimedia. Page 159: City of Roseville. Page 170: Gary Lucks. Page 173: Gary Lucks. Page 181: Mendocino County APCD. Page 185: Albert Herson. Page 189: Global Water Partnership. Page 198: U.S. EPA. Page 210: Central Contra Costa Sanitary District. Page 215: Source: San Diego County Department of Environmental Health. Page 216: Washington State Department of Ecology. Page 223: U.S. EPA. Page 232: San Francisco RWQCB. Page 246: LACSD. Page 248: bigstockphoto.com. Page 251: MRWMD. Page 262: Albert Herson. Page 274: Rebecca Frick. Page 276: Albert Herson. Page 282: Gary Lucks. Page 284: NOAA. Page 287: NOAA Fisheries. Page 301: DWR. Page 311: Albert Herson. Page 327: DWR. Page 330: DWR. Page 333: Albert Herson. Page 339: U.S. Forest Service Region 5. Page 345: California Department of Fish and Wildlife. Page 357: Alex Bryceson. Page 371: Albert Herson. Page 381: Albert Herson. Page 390: U.S. Fish and Wildlife Service. Page 402: bigstockphoto.com. Page 413: bigstockphoto.com. Page 427: U.S. EPA. Page 433: U.S. EPA. Page 450: NASA. Page 454: publicdomainpictures.net. Page 461: Albert Herson. Page 467: UC Cooperative Extension

Dedication

Al Herson dedicates this book to his wife Laurie Warner Herson, who gave generous support, as always, during the writing. And to his wonderful daughters Allie Herson Jones and Michelle Herson; may they live on a sustainable planet. And lastly to the generations of dedicated federal and state environmental law and policy professionals who have devoted their careers to making the world a better place.

Gary Lucks dedicates this book to his sister, Lisa Lucks Mendel, whose loving support and guidance helped uplift him during challenging times; and to his late mother, Louise Lucks, who inspired in him a belief that with persistence, all is possible. And to his fabulous son, Dylan Gibson Lucks, for whom a sustainable planet is his birthright. It is his hope that Dylan will help innovate strategies to sustain and preserve it for the next generation and beyond.

Contents

SHORT ARTICLES

FIGURES

TABLES

Preface

BOOK OVERVIEW

The field of California environmental law is vast and ever-changing. Planners, project applicants, developers, landowners, regulatory agency staff, consultants, attorneys, environmental managers, interested citizens, and students need a survey of California environmental law written for a general, non-technical audience. This book was written to serve that need.

Ambitious in scope, *California Environmental Law and Policy* is the only book that covers the entire field of California environmental, land use, and natural resources law in a concise, user-friendly format. Written in non-technical language, the book comprehensively surveys the most important California environmental statutes and regulatory programs, as well as relevant federal environmental statutes and regulatory programs. It highlights landmark court cases and current policy issues, and provides practical tips on getting through the regulatory process successfully. To assist in more in-depth research, the book identifies sources of further information for each major program.

California Environmental Law and Policy incorporates changes to statutes and regulatory programs through 2016. The authors have thoroughly updated and added new information to the first edition's 19 chapters. In addition, the second edition adds a new Part 5, "Climate Change Law and Policy." Although the book is current through late 2016, the November 8, 2016 national election could cause major changes to some of federal environmental programs described in the book. These changes may in turn have major implications for state and local environmental programs. Readers are advised to consult environmental news resources such as legalplanet.org for the latest developments.

The legal citations in the book are selective, to promote readability. Because this book is intended for a generalist non-technical audience, procedural topics such as administrative appeals, litigation, enforcement, and remedies are addressed only briefly. Attorneys seeking more comprehensive legal citations and expanded coverage of specific topics should refer to other excellent publications identified in this book, including Solano Press titles, and the Matthew Bender treatise, *California Environmental Law and Land Use Practice*. This book is not intended to give legal advice, for which an attorney should be consulted.

BOOK OBJECTIVES, SCOPE, AND FORMAT

OBJECTIVES

The specific objectives of this book are to provide readers with:

- A comprehensive, user-friendly, concise review of California and related federal environmental law in non-technical language
- Focused information on what practicing planners, project applicants, attorneys, and other audiences need to know
- References to key publications for further research

SCOPE

The book is divided into five major parts:

- **Part 1** starts with an introduction (chapter 1), reviewing the basic framework of California environmental law. It then covers the broadest environmental programs, those related to environmental and land use planning. It includes chapters on the California Environmental Quality Act (CEQA) (chapter 2), local land use planning (chapter 3), and state and regional land use controls (chapter 4).
- **Part 2** covers specific pollution control programs. It includes chapters on air quality (chapter 5), noise (chapter 6), hazardous materials and toxic substances (chapter 7), hazardous wastes (chapter 8), solid waste (chapter 9), water quality (chapter 10), and drinking water (chapter 11).
- **Part 3** covers programs regulating the state's natural resources. It includes chapters on agriculture (chapter 12), water resources (chapter 13), fish and wildlife (chapter 14), wetlands (chapter 15), forestry (chapter 16), and surface mining (chapter 17).
- **Part 4** presents two practical guides for environmental compliance. Chapter 18 is a permitting guide designed to help project applicants navigate the complexities of environmental, land use, and natural resource permitting in California. Chapter 19 is an environmental auditing guide designed to help facility managers plan environmental compliance audits.
- **Part 5** consists of chapter 20, which integrates programs related to managing greenhouse gases and climate change adaptation.

FORMAT

The book's chapters covering individual land use or environmental regulatory programs (chapters 2 through 17 and 20) follow a common internal organization:

- Identification of key laws and agencies
- Summaries of major regulatory programs
- References to key publications
- A glossary of terms used in the chapter (major permits and approvals are indicated by an asterisk)

Acknowledgments

FIRST EDITION

The authors wish to thank the following individuals, who reviewed and provided suggestions on early drafts of various chapters:

- Mark Beuhler, Assistant General Manager, Coachella Valley Water District
- Robert A. Bray, Director, The Elm Consulting Group International LLC
- Keith Casto, Esq., Cooper White & Cooper
- Matt Haber, Senior Staff Engineer, Eastern Research Group, Inc.
- Jennifer Harder, Esq., Professor, McGeorge School of Law
- Sara Hilbrich, Esq., Attorney-Advisor, USEPA
- B. Demar Hooper, Esq., Law Offices of B. Demar Hooper
- Gary Liss, President, Gary Liss and Associates, Zero Waste Consultant
- Jon B. Marshack, D.Env., Executive Diretor, California Water Quality Monitoring Council
- Mike McCoy, Policy Advisor, Governor's Office of Planning and Research
- Dave Stein, PE, CH2MHill
- Michael J. Steel, Esq., Pillsbury, Winthrop, Shaw, and Pittman LLP
- James Stettler, Hazardous Materials Specialist, Sonoma County Department of Fire and Emergency Services
- Terry Trumbull, Esq., Trumbull Law Firm and Professor at San Jose State University
- Paul Wack, Associate Professor, California Polytechnic University, San Luis Obispo

The authors wish to thank Erin Sullivan, JD, who completed legal research and analysis and validated regulatory citations. Also, the authors appreciate the creative efforts of Tom Wyatt, who prepared illustrations for both the first and second editions to help convey the book's ideas in easy-to-understand graphic form.

SECOND EDITION

The authors also wish to thank the following individuals, who reviewed and provided suggestions on early drafts of various chapters of the second edition:

- Ken Bogdan, Esq., Senior Staff Counsel, California Department of Water Resources
- Keith Casto, Esq., Cooper White & Cooper
- Gabrielle Soto, Program Director, ERM

- Laurie Warner Herson, Owner/Principal, Phenix Environmental Planning
- Steve Wiersema, Principal, West Office
- Mark Yannett, Senior Project Manager, ERM

In addition, the authors wish to thank Catherine Courtenaye for her important roles in editing the text and designing the book.

About the Authors

Albert I. Herson, JD, FAICP, is a planner and attorney who has practiced, taught, and written about California environmental law for over 35 years. He is a recognized authority on the California Environmental Quality Act (CEQA), the National Environmental Policy Act (NEPA), and natural resources law. Al serves as the Sacramento presence for Sohagi Law Group, a full-service land use and environmental law firm representing public agencies, where he advises public agency clients on complex environmental law issues. He also maintains an independent environmental consulting practice.

Mr. Herson has devoted much of his career to making CEQA, NEPA, and natural resource laws understandable and accessible to California planners and attorneys. He is a frequent speaker and writer on California environmental law topics and on several occasions advised state agencies on revisions to the CEQA Guidelines to make them more practical and user-friendly. For over 10 years he has co-chaired CLE International's Annual CEQA Update conferences.

Mr. Herson is co-author of *The NEPA Book* (2000) and the *CEQA Deskbook* (second edition, 1999) published by Solano Press. He is co-author of the CEQA and wetlands regulation chapters in *California Environmental Law and Land Use Practice* (Matthew Bender), and a contributing editor and regular writer for *California Environmental Law Reporter*.

Mr. Herson is a member of the State Bar and a Fellow of the American Institute of Certified Planners (AICP). He is past president of the California Chapter, American Planning Association, which awarded him the Distinguished Leadership Award for a Professional Planner. He is also a past president of the California Planning Roundtable. He has served on the California State Bar Environmental Law Section Executive Committee, the California Department of Water Resources (DWR) Water Plan Advisory Committee, and the DWR Climate Change Technical Advisory Group. Mr. Herson received a J.D. from the University of the Pacific McGeorge School of Law, where he was class valedictorian, and an M.A. in Urban Planning from the University of California, Los Angeles, where he graduated *summa cum laude*.

Gary A. Lucks, JD, CPEA is a seasoned environmental attorney and scientist with deep expertise in environmental, health, and safety (EHS) law, legislative affairs, and sustainability strategy and implementation. He has over 30 years of experience advising Fortune 500 clients in clean tech, high tech, power, aerospace, biopharma, and many other industry sectors. He is a licensed attorney, a scientist, and a Certified Professional Environmental Auditor (CPEA) who has completed or overseen more than 400 major EHS compliance audits across the country. He advises clients on maintaining business continuity and license to operate while managing EHS risks.

Mr. Lucks has published extensively on environmental law, legislation, and policy. He wrote the Environmental Auditing Chapter in the California Environmental Law and Land Use Treatise and has published the lead article on new California law and policy in the California Environmental Law Reporter for over 20 years.

He served on the California State Bar Environmental Law Section's Executive Committee and has served on the Environmental Legislation Committee for over two decades. He recently completed a four-year term as an advisor to the Bay Area Air Quality Management District. He currently serves as the co-chair of the West Coast Institute of Internal Auditors.

Mr. Lucks has extensive teaching experience. He has taught courses on environmental law, auditing, sustainability, climate change, and legislation for over 25 years at the University of California Extension, for the Institute of Internal Auditors, and for industry clients.

PART 1

INTRODUCTION AND ENVIRONMENTAL/LAND USE PLANNING

CHAPTER 1

Introduction

related Solano Press titles

California Land Use and Planning Law. 35th Edition. Cecily Talbert Barclay and Matthew S. Gray. 2016.

The Open Space and Land Conservation Handbook. Jeff Loux. 2011.

in this chapter...

U.S.C. = United States Code

GPO = Government Printing Office

C.F.R. = Code of Federal Regulations

Cal. Code Regs. = California Code of Regulations

INTRODUCTION

The purpose of this chapter is to give the reader a basic understanding of the foundations of California environmental law. It first reviews the various sources of California and related federal environmental law: federal and state constitutions, statutes, and regulations; common (judge-made) law; and the public trust doctrine. It then describes the numerous California agencies responsible for environmental and resource protection, and how they are organized. The chapter concludes with a review of basic environmental law terminology and principles.

FEDERAL AND STATE ENVIRONMENTAL LAW

FEDERAL LAW

Constitutional requirements particularly relevant to environmental law include the Commerce Clause, the Fifth Amendment, and the Supremacy Clause.

Federal constitution. The federal constitution defines the powers of the executive, legislative, and judicial branches of government. Constitutional requirements particularly relevant to environmental law include the Commerce Clause, the Fifth Amendment, and the Supremacy Clause.

The Commerce Clause (Article I, § 8, Clause 3) gives the federal government the authority to regulate interstate commerce and is the constitutional basis for many federal environmental laws. The Fifth Amendment bans the taking of private property without just compensation and has been the basis for "regulatory taking" legal challenges to overly harsh environmental and land use regulations. Under the Supremacy Clause (Article 6, ¶ 2), federal law must be followed if there is conflicting state law. A conflict exists either when compliance with both federal and state law is impossible, or when a state law is an obstacle to achieving the execution of Congress' full purposes. *See Edgar v. Mite Corp.* (1982) 457 U.S. 624.

Federal statutes. For most California environmental programs, federal statutes and regulations are implemented in an integrated fashion with California laws. Federal statutes are enacted by Congress and signed by the president. A description of this process can be found at the Library of Congress website (thomas.loc.gov/home/lawsmade.toc.html). Once enacted, laws are compiled into United States Codes (U.S.C.) organized by title and subject matter. U.S. Codes are available on the Government Printing Office (GPO) website (www.gpo.gov/fdsys/browse/collectionUScode.action?collectionCode=USCODE).

Federal regulations. Federal agency regulations implementing environmental statutes may be found in the Code of Federal Regulations (C.F.R). The C.F.R is divided into titles that represent broad areas subject to federal regulation. Each volume of the C.F.R. is updated once each calendar year and is issued on a quarterly basis. The C.F.R. is available on the GPO website (www.gpo.gov/fdsys/browse/collectionCfr.action?collectionCode=CFR). Federal agency regulations and decisionmaking must comply with requirements established by the Administrative Procedure Act (5 U.S.C. § 511 *et seq.*).

Executive orders. An executive order is a presidential declaration that has the force of law, usually based on existing statutory powers, and requires no action by Congress. Examples of executive orders related to environmental law include those on wetlands (Executive Order 11990), floodplains (Executive Order 11988), and environmental justice (Executive Order 12898). Executive orders are effective during the presidential term in which they were issued unless adopted by successor presidents.

Judicial decisions. Federal courts play an important role in the implementation of environmental law in California through reviewing the constitutionality of state environmental statutes and regulations, as well as interpreting federal environmental statutes and regulations. Federal environmental cases in California are typically first brought to the relevant federal district court: Northern District, Central District, Southern District, or Eastern District. Decisions issued by these courts may be appealed to the Ninth Circuit Court of Appeals and ultimately the U.S. Supreme Court. In case citations, district court decisions are abbreviated as "Fed. Supp.," Court of Appeals decisions are abbreviated as "F. 3d.," and Supreme Court decisions are abbreviated as "U.S." or S.Ct.

STATE LAW

State constitution. The California Constitution sets forth the fundamental laws by which the state is governed. Amendments to the California Constitution require a vote of the people. All state statutes, state regulations, and local ordinances must be consistent with the California Constitution. The California Constitution (Cal. Const. Art. XI, § 7) establishes the police power under which a city or county may enact ordinances to protect public health, safety, and welfare. Also, the public trust doctrine, derived in part from the California Constitution, has been influential in the development of California environmental law and is reviewed separately below.

Most regulatory programs described in this book were established by state legislation.

State statutes. Most of the regulatory programs described in this book are established by state statute. The legislative process by which a bill becomes law is reviewed briefly below.

The California Legislature is comprised of two houses: the Senate with 40 senators and the Assembly with 80 assembly members. The Legislature, which is full time, meets in two-year sessions.

A legislator sends the idea for a new bill to the Legislative Counsel's office, which drafts the bill language. The bill is returned to the legislator for introduction in either the Senate or Assembly (house of origin). The Rules Committee of the house of origin then assigns the bill to the appropriate policy committee for its first hearing. Bills are assigned to policy committees according to the subject matter of the bill. Committees typically addressing environmental programs include the following:

CEQA = California Environmental Quality Act

OAL = Office of Administrative Law

- **Assembly.** Environmental Safety and Toxic Materials; Natural Resources; Water, Parks and Wildlife
- **Senate.** Environmental Quality; Natural Resources and Water

The policy committee votes to pass the bill, to pass the bill as amended, or to defeat the bill. Bills that require the expenditure of funds must also be heard by fiscal committees. Bills passed by committees then are voted on by the house of origin. Once the bill has been approved by the house of origin, the bill proceeds to the other house where the procedure is repeated. If a bill is amended in the second house, it must return to the house of origin for concurrence (agreement on the amendments). If agreement cannot be reached, the bill is referred to a two-house conference committee to resolve differences. If a compromise is reached, the bill is returned to both houses for a vote.

The governor can sign the bill into law, allow it to become law without signature, or veto it.

If both houses approve, the bill then goes to the governor. The governor can sign the bill into law, allow it to become law without signature, or veto it. A governor's veto can be overridden by a two-thirds vote in both houses. Almost all bills go into effect on the first day of January of the next year. Urgency measures, which require a two-thirds vote in both houses, take effect immediately after they are signed or allowed to become law without signature.

Bills passed by the Legislature and approved by the governor are assigned a chapter number by the Secretary of State. These chaptered bills (also referred to as Statutes of the year they were enacted) then become part of the California Codes. The California Codes are a comprehensive collection of laws grouped by subject matter. For example, the California Public Resources Code compiles statutes such as the California Environmental Quality Act (CEQA), state fish and wildlife laws, and state forestry laws. California codes are available at the Legislative Counsel's website (www.leginfo.ca.gov/calaw.html).

State regulations. Agencies responsible for statutory programs typically adopt detailed regulations describing the law's implementation. The state Office of Administrative Law (OAL) is responsible for reviewing regulations for compliance with the standards set forth in California's Administrative Procedure Act (Gov't Code 11340 *et seq.*; *see* OAL 2016), for transmitting these regulations to the Secretary of State, and for publishing regulations in the California Code of Regulations (CCR).

The CCR is divided into numeric titles grouping regulations by subject matter. For example, Title 14 contains regulations governing resources, and Title 22 contains regulations governing hazardous waste and drinking water. The CCR is available at the Westlaw website (government.westlaw.com/linkedslice/default.asp?SP=CCR-1000).

Executive orders. A governor's executive order is a declaration that has the force of law, usually based on existing statutory powers, and requires no action by the

Legislature. Examples of executive orders related to environmental law include those on global climate change (Exec. Order S-3-05) and streamlined approvals of water transfers (Exec. Order B-21-13).

Initiative and referendum. California has a long tradition of direct democracy, giving voters the power to enact laws without relying on the Legislature or local government. An initiative is a vehicle empowering the voters to propose and adopt state statutes and constitutional amendments (authorized by Art. II, § 8(a) of the California Constitution), and to propose and adopt local legislation (authorized by Cal. Const. Art. II, § 11). Initiatives can be amended or repealed only through another initiative, unless they state otherwise. A referendum similarly gives voters the power to approve or reject certain types of statutes (authorized by Cal. Const. Art. II, § 9).

An initiative is a vehicle empowering the voters to propose and adopt state statutes and constitutional amendments, and to propose and adopt local legislation.

The 1972 California Coastal Initiative, which established a state system for coastal zone management, was a particularly powerful use of the initiative process to enact environmental policy. At the local government level, initiatives or referenda on land use controls are common (*see* chapter 3).

Local ordinances. Ordinances are local laws passed by local agencies such as city councils and county boards of supervisors. Environmental and land use ordinances usually are based on the police power. Local agencies have individualized methods of enacting land use and environmental ordinances; the content of these ordinances often is influenced or controlled by state or federal legislation.

Judicial decisions. California courts are responsible for interpreting state and local statutes and regulations. They also establish and interpret environmental common law (*see* below). Environmental cases in California are typically first brought to one of the state's 58 trial courts, one for each county. Trial court decisions may be appealed to the appropriate Court of Appeal (there are six district courts of appeal) and ultimately to the California Supreme Court. Court of Appeal decisions are cited as "Cal. App." and Supreme Court decisions are cited as "Cal."

PRIVATE ENFORCEMENT OF ENVIRONMENTAL LAWS

Citizen enforcement. Citizens and citizen groups play a vital role in the enforcement of federal and state environmental laws. Most of these laws have citizen suit provisions, allowing citizens to sue agencies for taking actions inconsistent with statutes, regulations, and ordinances. For example, citizens having environmental concerns about a development project can make their concerns known through taking advantage of public notice and comment provisions, or filing citizen lawsuits.

Citizen enforcement of environmental laws is challenging, because many environmental laws and agencies may be involved for a particular project or environmental approval.

Unfair competition statute. Business and Professions Code § 17200 *et seq.* creates a private right of action for "unfair competition," defined to include "any unlawful, unfair or fraudulent business act or practice." By referring to unlawful acts and practices, these sections create a right to sue under environmental statutes even if the statutes themselves do not allow private enforcement. Suits may be filed on behalf of others (representative suits), but they must have suffered injury and lost money or property because of unfair competition.

ENVIRONMENTAL COMMON LAW

Common law is a system of law derived from judges' decisions arising from the judicial branch of government, rather than statutes or constitutions derived from the legislative branch of government.

Common law is a system of law derived from judges' decisions arising from the judicial branch of government, rather than statutes or constitutions derived from the legislative branch of government. Common law is an alternative legal pathway to seek relief for those injured by environmental harms.

Common law doctrines applicable to environmental claims include nuisance, trespass, negligence, strict liability, and the public trust. The term "toxic torts" means use of one of these theories of liability to remedy various types of toxic and environmental exposures. (A tort is defined as a civil wrong creating liability that does not arise from a statute or contract.)

NUISANCE

Nuisance defined and types of nuisances. A nuisance is a condition or activity interfering with the free use and enjoyment of property or the exercise of certain public rights (Civ. Code § 3479, which codifies common law), for which injunctive and damages remedies are authorized (Code Civ. Proc. § 731). Examples of environmental nuisances include air and water pollution, hazardous waste contamination, noise, odors, and violation of land use regulations. Also, certain actions are defined as nuisances either by state statute or local ordinance.

Two types of nuisances exist. Public nuisances affect an entire community, neighborhood, or population; only government attorneys may bring a public nuisance lawsuit. Private nuisances consist of all non-public nuisances; parties must own a property interest that is damaged in order to bring a private nuisance lawsuit. The classification of a nuisance as public or private may determine whether certain defenses apply and what remedies are available.

Also, nuisances are classified as permanent or continuing. A permanent nuisance is a single completed act or condition that cannot be abated, causing permanent damages that can be assessed at one time. A continuing nuisance is an ongoing act or condition that is capable of being stopped (i.e., abatable). The classification of a nuisance as permanent or continuing may determine whether a plaintiff's claim is time-barred by a statute of limitations and what remedies are available.

Defenses. To prove a nuisance, the plaintiff must show that a condition or activity resulted in substantial harm and that the use of property causing the condition or activity is unreasonable. Several defenses exist to a nuisance claim, including:

- An activity is not a nuisance if the utility of the defendant's conduct outweighs the environmental damage caused.
- Acts authorized by statute, agricultural activities, and certain other activities are declared by statute not to be nuisances.
- A plaintiff who consents to maintenance of a nuisance may not file a private nuisance lawsuit.
- An injunction may not be granted for a nuisance lawsuit against a legally permitted commercial or industrial use unless it employs unnecessary or injurious methods of operation.

However, the following are generally not valid defenses: a continuing nuisance was maintained by a prior landowner, the defendant's activity occurred first and the plaintiff "came to the nuisance," the defendant complied with relevant government regulations, or the defendant is a government agency.

Remedies. The remedies for a nuisance are injunctions and money damages. Courts can issue injunctions to abate a nuisance, both to stop the nuisance activity (mandatory injunction) or to prevent it from occurring in the future (prohibitory injunction). Money damages may consist of lost property values for a permanent nuisance, or costs of abatement for a continuing nuisance. Punitive damages are available for malicious or fraudulent acts.

TRESPASS

A trespass is an unauthorized and wrongful entry or intrusion onto land. Examples of environmental types of trespass include depositing wastes onto land, airplane overflights, and groundwater contamination or removal by neighboring landowners.

Trespass is an alternative legal theory to nuisance for environmental harms.

Trespass is an alternative legal theory to nuisance for environmental harms. Like nuisances, trespasses can be either permanent or continuing depending on whether they can be abated; this classification determines the statute of limitations for bringing a lawsuit. However, trespass has more limitations than nuisance as a legal theory. Only those who actually possess property that has been damaged may file a trespass lawsuit. Also, a trespass requires an actual physical intrusion on the plaintiff's property, so intangible intrusions such as odor and noise are not actionable.

Like nuisance actions, trespass also may allow the plaintiff to obtain injunctions or money damages. Injunctions are available to prevent a continuing or threatened nuisance. Damages typically are measured by loss of property value due to the trespass, or by the cost of restoring the property plus its rental value when it could not be used.

CERCLA = Comprehensive Environmental Response, Compensation, and Liability Act

NEGLIGENCE

Negligence is the failure to exercise the degree of care considered reasonable under the circumstances, resulting in an unintended injury to another party. Environmental harms may be remedied through a negligence lawsuit. To prove negligence, the plaintiff must show the following: the defendant had a legal duty of care to the plaintiff, the defendant breached that duty of care, the breach was a cause of the resulting injury, and actual damages resulted from the injury. Examples of negligence claims for environmental harm include improper storage, treatment, or disposal of hazardous waste, or a property owner failing to warn purchasers of property contamination.

The doctrine of "negligence per se" is often useful in environmental cases; it creates a presumption of negligence if a plaintiff violates a regulatory requirement, the violation causes personal injury or property damage, and the plaintiff is within the class of persons the regulatory requirement is intended to protect. A long-established environmental statute commonly used to impose negligence per se states that "[n]o person shall discharge...waste...in any manner which will result in contamination, pollution, or a nuisance" (Health & Safety Code § 5411). The presumption of negligence may be rebutted by the defendant proving it did what might be expected of a person of ordinary prudence, acting under similar circumstances, with a desire to comply with the law.

STRICT LIABILITY

Cropdusting is an example of an ultrahazardous activity.

Under California common law, certain uncommon activities are so inherently dangerous that they are classified as ultrahazardous (also referred to as "abnormally dangerous" activities). Defendants who conduct ultrahazardous activities, and know or should know that they could cause injury, are held strictly liable for the injury. Strict liability means that the defendant is liable even if the activity is carried out with all reasonable care.

Certain environmentally risky activities may create strict liability because they are ultrahazardous; examples include aerial application of herbicides, use of chemicals in transformers, and use of explosives near residential areas. Defenses to a strict liability lawsuit include the defendant's comparative fault (negligence), the defendant's assumption of risk, and a three-year statute of limitations for injury to real property.

Strict products liability is a related strict liability legal theory. Strict products liability applies when a product is defective due to the product's design or manufacture, or when the manufacturer fails to give appropriate warnings. Examples where this doctrine may apply include manufacture of pesticides or pollution control equipment.

STATUTES OF LIMITATIONS

In any civil action for personal injury or wrongful death due to exposure to a hazardous material or hazardous substance, the action must be brought within two years from either the date of the injury or the date the plaintiff should reasonably have been aware of the injury, the physical cause of the injury, and the wrongful acts leading to the injury (Code Civ. Proc. § 340.8). For releases of contaminants from facilities regulated by the Comprehensive Environmental Response, Compensation, and Liability Act (CERCLA), a delayed discovery rule applies, and the statute of limitations begins to run only when the plaintiff knew or reasonably should have known both the existence and the cause of the injury.

For real property damages due to contamination, the statute of limitations is three years from the contamination or when the plaintiff should reasonably have been aware of the contamination (Code Civ. Proc. § 338(b)).

PUBLIC TRUST DOCTRINE

ORIGINS OF THE PUBLIC TRUST DOCTRINE

The public trust doctrine, originated by ancient Roman law, derives from both the California Constitution and California common law. It has become a powerful tool for citizens seeking to develop a comprehensive legal approach to resource management issues.

The public trust doctrine states that certain natural resources, even those in private ownership, must be held in trust by the government for use and enjoyment by the people of the state. Constitutional provisions related to the public trust include a ban on the sale of state tidelands within two miles of an unincorporated city (Cal. Const. Art. X, § 3), the guarantee of public access to navigable waters of the state (Cal. Const. Art. X, § 4), and the right of the public to fish on public lands, including public lands sold into private ownership (Cal. Const. Art. I, § 25).

Origins of the Public Trust Doctrine

The public trust doctrine's origins are in the work of Emperor Justinian (Institutes of Justinian 2.1.1), whose statement of Roman law included the following: "[b]y law the nature of these things are common to mankind—the air, running water, the sea and consequently the shores of the sea." The state was to hold these resources in trust for the benefit of the people and to preserve their rights for commerce, fishing, and navigation.

The public trust was recognized in English common law, which formed the basis of common law in the United States. In the landmark case of *Arnold v. Mundy* (1821) 6 N.J.L. 1, a New Jersey state court found the public right to take oysters from beneath navigable waters of a coastal bay. The court held that certain types of property are unique and should not be privately owned, and that the state holds these types of properties for the benefit of all the people, but that the state may dispose of (e.g., sell or lease) portions of trust property if it furthers the public interest.

Relying on this decision, in another oyster fishing case, the U.S. Supreme Court in *Martin v. Lessee of Waddell* (1852) 41 U.S. 367 found that the state of New Jersey owned the beds of navigable waters in its sovereign capacity, to be held as a public trust for the benefit of the people and freely used by all for navigation and fishing. These principles were further interpreted in the *Illinois Central* case cited in the text. The Supreme Court in *Illinois Central* emphasized that the state may not dispose of trust lands except for public purposes.

In California, the landmark public trust case is *People v. California Fish Co.* (1913) 166 Cal. 576. In that case, the California Supreme Court ruled that state conveyance of state tideland, swamp, and overflowed lands remained subject to the public trust interest, retained by the state for the benefit of the people. The court left open the possibility of invalidating legislation that would cause the destruction of public trust uses.

In *Marks v. Whitney* (1971) 6 Cal. 3d 251, the Supreme Court expanded the public trust beyond the traditional purposes of commerce, fishing, and navigation, to include environmental and aesthetic uses. Finally, in *National Audubon Society v. Superior Court* (1983) 33 Cal. 3d 419, the Supreme Court expanded the application of the public trust doctrine to non-navigable streams and to state grants of water rights.

Mono Lake water rights were the subject of the landmark *National Audubon Society* public trust case.

California public trust case law is based on a federal Supreme Court case, *Illinois Central Railroad Co. v. Illinois* (1892) 146 U.S. 307. In that case, the Supreme Court upheld the Illinois Legislature's repeal of its earlier granting of the Chicago waterfront to a private railroad. The court held that the grant substantially impaired the public from exercising its trust rights to lands underlying navigable waters.

SCOPE OF THE PUBLIC TRUST DOCTRINE

Public uses protected by the public trust. Public uses protected by the public trust include commerce, navigation, fishing, recreation, and environmental preservation. In administering the public trust, agencies attempt to accommodate multiple uses, but have the discretion to promote one use over another.

Resources subject to the public trust. The public trust doctrine applies to the following resources:

- **Tidelands and submerged lands.** Tidelands are lands over which the tide ebbs and flows. Submerged lands include state-owned lands between the tidelands and the three-mile limit of offshore waters subject to state jurisdiction, as well as lands underlying navigable waters.
- **Navigable waters.** The beds of inland navigable waters, as defined by federal law (*see* chapter 15), and lakes are subject to the public trust doctrine.
- **Non-navigable waters and water rights.** The landmark case of *National Audubon Society v. Superior Court* (1983) 33 Cal. 3d 419 extended the public trust to non-navigable waters and to water rights. *See* chapter 13.
- **Fish and wildlife.** California's fish and wildlife resources are publicly owned in trust for the benefit of the public.

Entities administering the public trust. The agencies administering the public trust in California include:

- **Legislature.** Has ultimate responsibility for administering the State's public trust duties, either directly or through delegation to state or local agencies.
- **State Lands Commission.** Has primary jurisdiction to act as trustee for public trust lands.
- **Department of Fish and Wildlife.** Administers the public trust doctrine for fish and wildlife resources.
- **State Water Resources Control Board.** Applies the public trust doctrine to water rights decisions. See chapter 13 for a detailed discussion of the application of the doctrine to water rights.
- **Regional land use agencies.** Agencies such as the San Francisco Bay Conservation and Development Commission and the Tahoe Regional Planning Agency may apply the public trust to resources they regulate.

FIGURE 1-1
Cal/EPA Organization

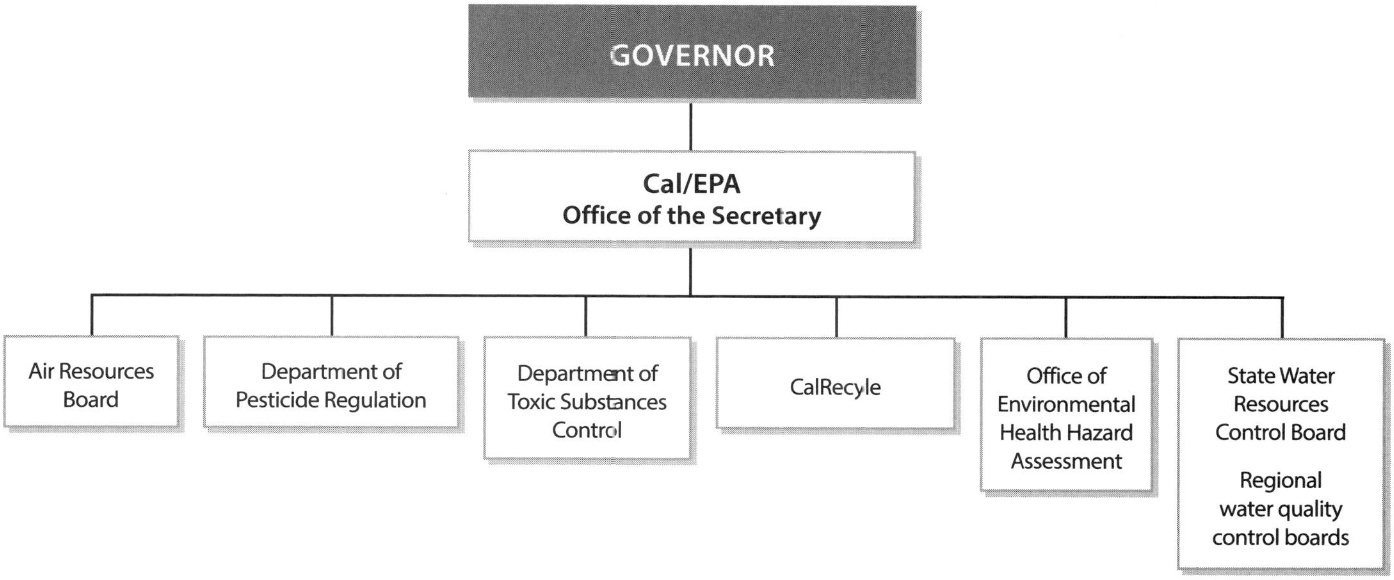

- **Local agencies.** Have been granted state sovereign lands in trust (in some cases, by the Legislature) for purposes such as port development.

Cal/EPA = California Environmental Protection Agency

These agencies have an affirmative duty to protect trust resources and have limited ability to transfer public trust resources into private ownership (*see City of Long Beach v. Mansell* (1970) 3 Cal. 3d 462).

CALIFORNIA ENVIRONMENTAL AGENCIES

The Legislature has given numerous agencies the authority to regulate and protect the state's environment and natural resources. This discussion provides an overview of state environmental agencies. Subsequent chapters discuss in more detail the roles of these agencies, as well as federal, regional, and local agencies, in implementing specific environmental programs.

The Legislature has given numerous agencies the authority to regulate and protect the state's environment and natural resources.

AGENCIES WITHIN THE CALIFORNIA ENVIRONMENTAL PROTECTION AGENCY

The California Environmental Protection Agency (Cal/EPA) was created in 1991 by an executive order. Several boards, departments, and the office of the Secretary of Cal/EPA were placed within the Cal/EPA umbrella to create a cabinet-level voice for environmental protection and to assure coordinated administration of environmental programs. Cal/EPA's mission is to "restore, protect and enhance the environment, to ensure public health, environmental quality and economic vitality."

Boards, departments, and offices. Boards, departments, and offices within Cal/EPA (*see* Figure 1-1) are the:

EJ = environmental justice

DTSC = Department of Toxic Substances Control

DPR = Department of Pesticide Regulation

- **Air Resources Board.** Regulates air pollution sources, including greenhouse gases contributing to climate change.
- **State Water Resources Control Board and regional water quality control boards.** Regulate water pollution sources, water rights, and drinking water.
- **Department of Resources Recycling and Recovery (CalRecycle).** Regulates solid waste recycling and recovery.
- **Department of Toxic Substances Control (DTSC).** Regulates hazardous waste, hazardous waste cleanup, and green chemistry.
- **Office of Environmental Health Hazard Assessment.** Protects public health and the environment by scientific evaluation of risks posed by hazardous substances.
- **Department of Pesticide Regulation.** Regulates registration, sale, and use of pesticides.
- **Office of the Secretary.** The Office of the Secretary heads Cal/EPA and is responsible for overseeing and coordinating the activities of all Cal/EPA agencies. The Secretary does not direct policies and decisions of Cal/EPA agencies. Cal/EPA agencies were created separately and operate in accordance with their own enabling authorities. Specific Office of the Secretary functions include budget review, review of personnel management, enforcement coordination, information management coordination, strategic planning, and pollution prevention.

In addition to these agency duties, the Legislature has given the Office of the Secretary several specific programmatic responsibilities. These include the Environmental Justice program and the Environmental Protection Indicators for California program.

The Legislature charged Cal/EPA with conducting its programs and enforcing environmental laws in a manner that ensures the fair treatment of people of all races, cultures, and income levels, including minority and low-income populations.

Environmental justice program. Cal/EPA's EJ program was created by Pub. Res. Code § 71110 *et seq*. The Legislature charged Cal/EPA with conducting its programs and enforcing environmental laws in a manner that ensures the fair treatment of people of all races, cultures, and income levels, including minority and low-income populations. Among other things, Cal/EPA is required to:

- Develop a model environmental justice mission statement for Cal/EPA agencies
- Convene an interagency working group composed of state agency heads, assisted by an advisory group, to develop an EJ strategy to be implemented by Cal/EPA agencies
- Ensure greater public participation in the development, adoption, and implementation of environmental regulations and policies
- Improve research and data collection on EJ issues

- Develop an agency-wide strategy for addressing gaps in existing programs or policies impeding the achievement of EJ

In 2004, Cal/EPA issued its environmental justice strategy (Cal/EPA 2004a), with the following goals:

- Ensure meaningful public participation and promote capacity-building so all communities can effectively participate in environmental decision-making processes
- Integrate EJ into the development, adoption, implementation, and enforcement of environmental laws, regulations, and policies
- Improve research and data collection to promote and address EJ issues related to the health and environment of communities of color and low-income populations
- Ensure effective cross-media coordination and accountability in addressing EJ issues

Also in 2004, the interagency working group issued an EJ Action Plan (Cal/EPA 2004b) describing short-term activities to implement these goals. To help implement the EJ program, Cal/EPA has developed and released CalEnviroScreen 2.0, a screening methodology that can be used to help identify California communities that are disproportionately burdened by multiple sources of pollution. (*See* oehha.ca.gov/ej/ces2.html.)

AGENCIES WITHIN THE NATURAL RESOURCES AGENCY

Boards, commissions, departments, and conservancies. The Natural Resources Agency is a second cabinet-level umbrella agency for agencies with authority to protect and manage natural resources. The Natural Resources Agency consists of seventeen boards and commissions and eight departments, as well as nine regional conservancies. The Natural Resources Agency mission is to "restore, protect and manage the state's natural, historical and cultural resources for current and future generations using creative approaches and solutions based on science, collaboration and respect for all the communities and interests involved."

The Natural Resources Agency mission is to "restore, protect and manage the state's natural, historical and cultural resources for current and future generations using creative approaches and solutions based on science, collaboration and respect for all the communities and interests involved."

Boards and commissions within the Natural Resources Agency are the:

- **California Coastal Commission.** Plans and regulates land use within the coastal zone.
- **California Energy Commission.** Implements the state's energy policy and programs, and administers the energy facility licensing program.
- **California State Lands Commission.** Manages state sovereign lands, and energy and minerals leasing on state lands.
- **San Francisco Bay Conservation and Development Commission.** Plans and regulates land use within San Francisco Bay, Suisun Marsh, and adjacent areas.

CERES = California Environmental Resources Evaluation System

- **Delta Protection Commission.** Plans land use within the Sacramento–San Joaquin Delta region.
- **Colorado River Board of California.** Protects California's rights and interests in the Colorado River, and represents California in negotiations regarding the Colorado River.
- **Central Valley Flood Protection Board** (formerly State Reclamation Board). Manages levees and flood control along the Sacramento and San Joaquin Rivers.
- **Board of Forestry and Fire Protection.** Regulates forest practices and oversees California Department of Forestry and Fire Protection programs.
- **Fish and Game Commission.** Regulates hunting and fishing.
- **Mining and Geology Board.** Represents the state's interests in geology, geologic and seismologic hazards, conservation of mineral resources, and surface mining reclamation.
- **Native American Heritage Commission.** Protects Native American burials from vandalism and inadvertent destruction, and provides for notification of most-likely descendants regarding the discovery of Native American remains.
- **Parks and Recreation Commission.** Approves general plans for units of the state park system, establishes general policies for the system, and recommends comprehensive recreation policies for the state.
- **State Historical Resources Commission.** Reviews applications for listing historic and archaeological resources on the National Register of Historic Places and the California Register of Historical Resources.
- **State Off-Highway Motor Vehicle Recreation Commission.** Provides policy guidance for the state's off-highway motor vehicle program.
- **California Water Commission.** Provides policy input to the Department of Water Resources.
- **California Boating and Waterways Commission.** Provides policy input to the Department of Boating and Waterways.
- **Wildlife Conservation Board.** Administers a capital outlay program for wildlife conservation and related public recreation.

Departments within the Natural Resources Agency are:

- **Department of Boating and Waterways.** Enforces the state's boating laws and helps construct state boating facilities
- **Department of Conservation.** Implements programs on mine reclamation, energy leasing, oil and gas wells, and agricultural land resource protection.
- **Department of Fish and Wildlife.** Regulates the state's fish and wildlife resources.

- **Department of Forestry and Fire Protection.** Regulates the state's forest resources and provides fire protection and emergency response services.
- **Department of Parks and Recreation.** Manages the state's park resources.
- **Department of Water Resources.** Manages the state's water resources and operates the State Water Project.
- **California Conservation Corps.** Implements a youth workforce development program that includes work in environmental conservation, fire protection, and emergency response.

The Legislature has also created nine conservancies within the Natural Resources Agency whose mission is to acquire and manage open space and conservation lands. These are:

- Baldwin Hills Conservancy
- California Tahoe Conservancy
- Coachella Valley Mountains Conservancy
- San Diego River Conservancy
- San Gabriel & Lower Los Angeles Rivers and Mountains Conservancy
- San Joaquin River Conservancy
- Santa Monica Mountains Conservancy
- Sierra Nevada Conservancy
- State Coastal Conservancy

Office of the Secretary. The Office of the Secretary for Resources serves as the Governor's spokesperson for resources policy and oversees a number of other programs, including the following:

- **California Environmental Quality Act.** The Natural Resources Agency adopts the CEQA Guidelines and certifies state environmental regulatory programs as CEQA functional equivalents. *See* chapter 2.
- **California Environmental Resources Evaluation System (CERES).** CERES is a statewide information system that facilitates access to a variety of electronic data describing California's environment.

Annual Planning Survey

Every year, OPR conducts a local government planning survey to compile the latest information on local planning activities and issues. The results, together with other reference information, are published in the *Annual Planning Survey* (formerly *The Planners Book of Lists*) (OPR 2014). The publication includes:

- An analysis of the results of the prior year's *Annual Planning Survey;*
- The results of OPR's current year *Annual Planning Survey.* The survey provides the latest information on local planning activities and special issues of statewide concern;
- A cumulative index of questions asked in previous Annual Planning Surveys; and,
- Status of local General Plans

OTHER AGENCIES

Governor's Office of Planning and Research. OPR is the statewide planning agency and also oversees CEQA implementation. See chapter 2 for OPR's CEQA responsibilities. OPR is responsible for the following other activities:

OPR = Governor's Office of Planning and Research

- Formulating long-range goals and policies for land use, population growth and distribution, urban expansion, land development, resource preservation, climate resiliency, and other factors affecting statewide development patterns

DPH = Department of Public Health

CUPA = Certified Unified Program Agency

- Assisting in the preparation of functional plans by state agencies and departments that relate to protection and enhancement of the state's environment
- Ensuring that all state policies and programs conform to the state's adopted land use planning goals and programs
- Preparing the state's environmental goals and policy report every four years
- Developing and adopting guidelines for the preparation of city and county general plans
- Providing general planning assistance to local governments, including publishing the Annual Planning Survey (*see* sidebar)

California Biodiversity Council. The California Biodiversity Council was formed in 1991 to improve coordination and cooperation between the numerous resource management and environmental protection organizations at federal, state, and local government levels. Its purpose is to discuss, coordinate, and assist in developing strategies and complementary policies for conserving biodiversity. The Council has 42 members, including 10 local governments, 20 state agencies, and 12 federal agencies.

Ocean Protection Council. The Ocean Protection Council was formed in 2004 to coordinate activities of ocean-related state agencies to improve the effectiveness of state efforts to protect ocean resources. It establishes policies to coordinate the collection and sharing of scientific data related to coast and ocean resources, recommends to the Legislature changes in law, and recommends changes in federal law and policy to the Governor and Legislature.

Department of Public Health. DPH administers a broad range of public and clinical health programs. The DPH's Environmental Health Investigations Branch controls environmental factors harmful to human health through conducting health and exposure investigations, monitoring trends in environmental exposures and health indicators, and providing public health oversight, technical assistance, and training. DPH also certifies state laboratories.

City and district attorneys' offices. Local law enforcement agencies play an important role in prosecuting violations of state and local environmental laws. Local prosecutors are particularly active in enforcing air pollution and hazardous waste laws. The Hazardous Waste Enforcement Unit within the DTSC provides information, training, and assistance for local law agencies enforcing hazardous waste laws.

Local law enforcement agencies play an important role in prosecuting violations of state and local environmental laws.

Other regional and local agencies. Numerous regional and local agencies are responsible for implementing or enforcing environmental law in California. These include regional or county air pollution control districts responsible for implementing federal and state clean air programs at the local level (*see* chapter 5). Also, certified unified program agencies (CUPAs) are designated local agencies responsible for consolidated implementation of six hazardous materials programs (*see* chapter 7).

ENVIRONMENTAL LAW AND REGULATION TERMINOLOGY AND PRINCIPLES

Many environmental regulatory programs are comprised of four common components: applicability criteria, definitions, substantive standards, and procedural requirements. This section describes these components and is intended to provide a framework for the discussions of individual programs in subsequent chapters.

Many environmental regulatory programs are comprised of four common components: applicability criteria, definitions, substantive standards, and procedural requirements.

APPLICABILITY CRITERIA

Applicability criteria define the types of activities that are regulated. Environmental regulatory programs typically apply to specified activities (e.g., filling wetlands), specified types of industries (e.g., semiconductor or aerospace manufacturing), or specified facility types (e.g., facility, owner, operator, or major air emissions source). Substantive standards will apply to these regulated categories unless they enjoy an exemption or exclusion.

Air quality programs are an example of the complexity of applicability criteria (*see* chapter 5). Certain air quality permits are required for "major" sources of air pollutants, which are distinguished from non-regulated "minor" air emissions sources. A major source is defined differently under several air quality programs. Also, a major source under the non-attainment new source review program is defined differently depending on local air district rules. Further, different definitions of "major source" are used in the Prevention of Significant Deterioration and Operating Permits programs.

KEY DEFINITIONS

It is critically important to read and understand the definitions of specific regulated activities or pollutants. Each regulatory definition is a term of art, usually having a different meaning from the same term found in Webster's dictionary. For example, although the following terms appear similar, California environmental regulations create important legal distinctions among a "hazardous waste," "toxic waste," "hazardous material," and "hazardous substance." Other terms that sound similar at first glance, such as "ignitable" and "flammable," also have specific regulatory definitions.

SUBSTANTIVE STANDARDS AND REQUIREMENTS

Environmental regulatory programs typically establish substantive standards governing regulated activities. Examples of substantive standards are emissions limitations expressed in mass loadings (e.g., pounds per day and tons per year) or concentrations (e.g., parts per million). Substantive requirements may also include specified emissions controls designed to meet emissions limits. For example, a regulated air emissions source may be required to use the best available control technology that may require use of selective catalytic reduction for certain pollutant emissions.

PROCEDURAL REQUIREMENTS

Environmental regulatory programs typically specify a variety of compliance procedures. These may include:

- Permit applications and approvals
- Compliance with permit conditions (which may be substantive or procedural)
- Monitoring
- Recordkeeping
- Payment of fees or penalties
- Notifications (e.g., accidents or spills)
- Inspections
- Design requirements
- Training
- Preparation of plans (e.g., spill prevention and emergency response plans)

for more information...

Cal/EPA, 2004a. Interagency Environmental Justice Strategy.

Cal/EPA, 2004b. Cal/EPA Environmental Justice Action Plan.

Governor's Office of Planning and Research. 2014. Annual Planning Survey Results.

Manaster, K. A. and D. P. Selmi (eds.), ND. Chapters 1, 2, 3, 10, and 12 of California Environmental Law and Land Use Practice. Matthew Bender. San Francisco, Calif.

Office of Administrative Law, 2016. California Rulemaking Law Handbook.

glossary

Common law—system of law derived from judges' decisions, rather than statutes or constitutions.

Environmental indicator—an objective measure of environmental quality used to assess the effectiveness of environmental programs.

Environmental justice—a program to ensure that environmental programs and enforcement fairly treat people of all races, cultures, and incomes, especially minority and low-income populations.

Executive Order—declaration by President or Governor that has the force of law, usually based on existing statutory powers, and requires no legislative action

Negligence—the failure to exercise the degree of care considered reasonable, resulting in unintended injury to another party.

Nuisance—a condition or activity interfering with the free use and enjoyment of property or the exercise of certain public rights.

Police power—the power of state and local governments to enact legislation to protect public health, safety, and welfare.

Public trust doctrine—enforceable doctrine by which certain natural resources are held in trust by the government for the use and enjoyment of the public.

Regulation—detailed rule adopted by a regulatory agency that implements a statute.

Sovereign lands—submerged lands, tidelands, and the beds of navigable rivers.

Statute—a law enacted by the legislative branch of government.

Statute of limitations—time limit for filing a lawsuit.

Strict liability—for certain activities, e.g., ultra-hazardous activities, a defendant is liable even if the activity is carried out with all reasonable care.

Submerged lands—includes state-owned lands between the tidelands and the three-mile limit of offshore waters subject to state jurisdiction, as well as lands underlying navigable waters.

Tidelands—lands over which the tide ebbs and flows.

Trespass—an unauthorized and wrongful entry or intrusion onto land.

CHAPTER 2

California Environmental Quality Act

in this chapter...

related Solano Press titles

CEQA Deskbook. Ronald E. Bass, Kenneth M. Bogdan, and Terry Rivasplata. 2012.

Guide to the California Environmental Quality Act. Michael H. Remy *et al*. 2007.

The NEPA Book. Ronald E. Bass, Albert I. Herson, and Kenneth M. Bogdan. 2000.

CEQA = California Environmental Quality Act

NEPA = National Environmental Policy Act

OPR = Governor's Office of Planning and Research

INTRODUCTION

The California Environmental Quality Act (CEQA) (Pub. Res. Code § 21000 *et seq.*) is California's broadest-reaching environmental law. CEQA is designed to promote informed government decisionmaking, but is not a substantive law establishing environmental standards for a particular regulated activity or medium. Rather, it sets broad environmental policies for the state, and it requires state and local agencies that carry out or approve discretionary projects to evaluate, mitigate, and publicly disclose the environmental effects of those projects before taking action. CEQA does not grant state or local agencies new powers to mitigate environmental effects of proposed projects. However, agencies may use powers granted by other laws, typically the police power, to require project mitigation or deny projects with significant adverse environmental effects.

CEQA's main objectives are to:

- Disclose to decisionmakers and the public the environmental effects of proposed projects
- Identify ways to avoid or reduce environmental damage
- Prevent environmental damage by requiring implementation of feasible alternatives or mitigation measures
- Disclose to the public the reasons for agency approval of projects with significant adverse environmental effects
- Foster interagency coordination in project review
- Enhance public participation in the planning process

This chapter reviews the key laws and agencies involved in implementing CEQA, the process for preparing CEQA documents, their contents, CEQA integration with other environmental laws, and CEQA enforcement.

KEY LAWS AND AGENCIES

STATE STATUTE AND GUIDELINES

CEQA requirements are established by the CEQA statute Pub. Res. Code § 21000 *et seq.*) and the CEQA Guidelines (Guidelines, 14 Cal. Code Regs. § 15000 *et seq.*). CEQA originally was enacted in 1970 and was modeled after the National Environmental Policy Act (NEPA), which had been enacted a year earlier. The statute has been amended frequently, and is the subject of frequent litigation.

The CEQA Guidelines are the official administrative interpretation of CEQA, and are relied upon heavily by both agencies implementing CEQA and by courts interpreting the law.

The CEQA Guidelines are the official administrative interpretation of CEQA, and are regulations that are relied upon heavily by both agencies implementing CEQA and by courts interpreting the law. The Guidelines also are amended frequently in response to new developments in case law and CEQA practice. The Governor's Office of Planning and Research (OPR) drafts amendments to the Guidelines that ultimately are adopted by the Natural Resources Agency after public review.

This chapter cites the CEQA Guidelines for authority because the Guidelines are the most commonly used CEQA reference.

CERES = California Environmental Resources Evaluation System

DFW = California Department of Fish and Wildlife

NATURAL RESOURCES AGENCY

The Natural Resources Agency is a cabinet-level agency that oversees state natural resources policy and agencies. Its CEQA responsibilities include formal rulemaking and adoption of CEQA Guidelines amendments, and certification of state regulatory programs as CEQA equivalents (*see* below).

The Natural Resources Agency also maintains the California Environmental Resources Evaluation System (www.ceres.ca.gov). CERES is an information system that facilitates access to a variety of electronic data describing California's environment. An invaluable website located within CERES (www.ceres.ca.gov/ceqa) includes an interactive CEQA flow chart, and links to the CEQA statute, CEQA Guidelines, and CEQA case law. Also, SB 122 of 2016 (Chapter 476, Statutes of 2016) gave OPR new responsibilities to establish and maintain an on-line database for CEQA environmental documents and notices.

THE GOVERNOR'S OFFICE OF PLANNING AND RESEARCH

OPR's major CEQA responsibilities include recommending changes to the CEQA Guidelines, operating the State Clearinghouse, publishing CEQA notices, publishing technical advisories on CEQA compliance, and maintaining on-line databases, including the CEQAnet database to assist agencies in CEQA implementation. OPR's CEQA technical advisories cover topics such as: public notice and review, master Environmental Impact Reports (EIRs), Mitigated Negative Declarations, and climate change. The State Clearinghouse is the single point of contact in the state government that coordinates state agency review of CEQA and NEPA documents.

OTHER STATE AND LOCAL AGENCIES

Every state and local agency in California must adopt CEQA implementation procedures consistent with CEQA and the CEQA Guidelines. Local CEQA procedures typically contain more detail that the state CEQA Guidelines, and may set forth thresholds of significance. Typically, a state or local agency plays one of two roles in CEQA implementation—as lead agency or responsible agency.

Every state and local agency in California must adopt CEQA implementation procedures consistent with CEQA and the CEQA Guidelines.

A lead agency has the principal responsibility for carrying out or approving a project, and therefore has the lead responsibility for preparing the CEQA document for that project. For private projects requiring multiple governmental approvals, the agency with general governmental powers (e.g., a city or county) is typically the lead agency. 14 Cal. Code Regs. §§ 15050, 15051.

A responsible agency is an agency other than the lead agency with responsibility for carrying out or approving a project. For example, if a development project requires a Department of Fish and Wildlife (DFW) lake or streambed alteration agreement, a city may be the lead agency and DFW the responsible

EIR = Environmental Impact Report

MND = Mitigated Negative Declaration

agency. A responsible agency must participate in the lead agency's CEQA process and must use the lead agency's CEQA document in its decisionmaking. 14 Cal. Code Regs. § 15096.

CEQA also requires lead agencies to consult with relevant trustee agencies and "agencies with jurisdiction by law" when preparing CEQA documents. Trustee agencies, such as the DFW, have jurisdiction over resources held in trust for California. Lead agencies must also consult with agencies exercising authority over the resources affected by a project. 14 Cal. Code Regs. §§ 15086, 15386.

OVERVIEW OF THE CEQA PROCESS

The CEQA process consists of three phases:

- Preliminary review to determine whether a project is subject to CEQA or exempt from CEQA
- If a project is subject to CEQA, preparation of an Initial Study to determine whether the project may have a significant environmental effect
- Preparation of an Environmental Impact Report (EIR) if the project may have a significant environmental effect, or a Negative Declaration or Mitigated Negative Declaration (MND) if no significant effect will occur

The CEQA process is illustrated in Figure 2-1.

TIMING OF CEQA PROCESS

The CEQA process must start as early as feasible in the planning process to enable environmental considerations to influence project design.

The CEQA process must start as early as feasible in the planning process to enable environmental considerations to influence project design. However, it must start late enough to provide meaningful information for environmental assessment. 14 Cal. Code Regs. § 15004. Lead agencies may not take actions that give impetus to a foreseeable project in a way that forecloses alternatives or mitigation measures. For example, in *Save Tara v. City of West Hollywood* (2008) 45 Cal. 4th 116, the "totality of the circumstances" indicated that a lead agency had prematurely approved a development project prior to completing the CEQA process.

PRELIMINARY REVIEW

IS THE ACTIVITY A PROJECT?

During preliminary review, the lead agency determines whether an activity is a "project" under CEQA, and if so, whether a statutory or categorical exemption may apply. A "project" includes (14 Cal. Code Regs. § 15378):

- An activity directly undertaken by a public agency, such as a public works project or enactment of ordinances or general plans
- An activity supported by a public agency through contracts, financial assistance, or other assistance

FIGURE 2-1
CEQA Process Flow Chart

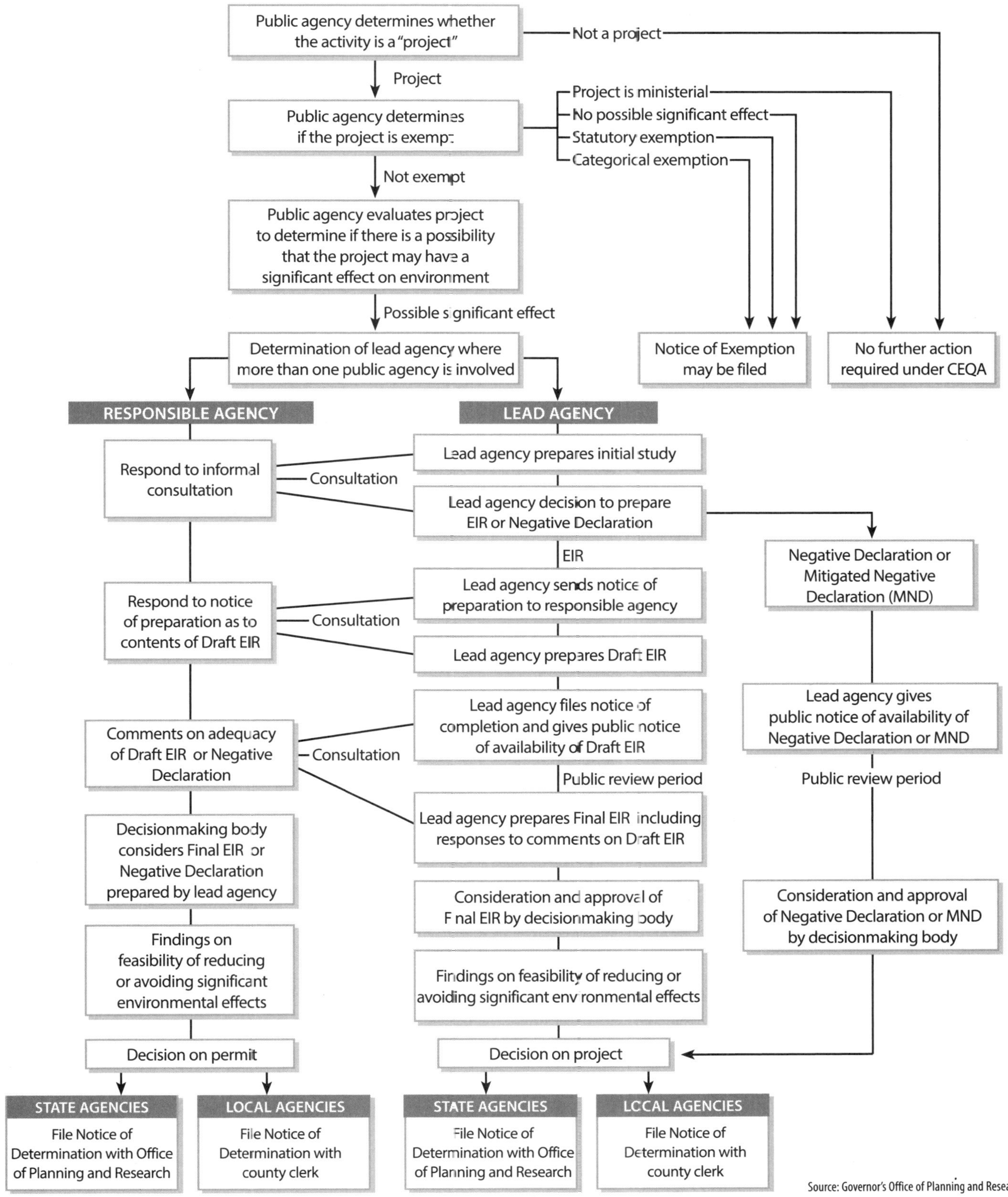

Source: Governor's Office of Planning and Research

- A public or private activity involving the issuance of a public agency permit or other entitlement, e.g., a rezoning or conditional use permit for a development project

A project includes the whole of an action with the potential for direct or indirect environmental effects. An agency generally is not allowed to piecemeal a large project into smaller pieces to evade environmental review. For example, in the landmark case *Laurel Heights Improvement Association v. Regents of the University of California* (1988) 47 Cal. 3d 376, the Supreme Court held that future development phases of a single building must be evaluated in the EIR prepared for the first phase of development, because the future phases were reasonably foreseeable and could be meaningfully evaluated. CEQA excludes certain activities from the definition of a "project," including proposals for state legislation, voter-sponsored initiatives, and funding measures not committing to specific projects with environmental impacts. 14 Cal. Code Regs. § 15378(b).

IS THE PROJECT EXEMPT?

CEQA has four main categories of exemptions: statutory exemptions, categorical exemptions, the "common sense" exemption, and certified regulatory programs.

CEQA has four main categories of exemptions: statutory exemptions, categorical exemptions, the "common sense" exemption, and certified regulatory programs.

Statutory exemptions. Statutory exemptions are created by the Legislature; if a project is statutorily exempt, no CEQA compliance is needed. Common statutory exemptions include ministerial projects, emergency projects, and feasibility or planning studies for possible future actions. 14 Cal. Code Regs. § 15260 *et seq.*

The most common statutory exemption is for ministerial projects—those requiring little exercise of judgment by the decisionmaker, such as final subdivision map approval. CEQA applies only to discretionary projects—those that require the exercise of judgment or deliberation when a decision is made. 14 Cal. Code Regs. § 15268.

Firefighting is an emergency activity that is statutorialy exempt from CEQA.

Categorical exemptions. Categorical exemptions are adopted by the Natural Resources Agency and found in the CEQA Guidelines. 14 Cal. Code Regs. § 15300 *et seq.* The most commonly applied categorical exemptions include those for operation, repair, or other minor alterations of existing facilities and for construction of new, small facilities.

Categorical exemptions represent activities that the Natural Resources Agency has determined generally do not result in significant environmental effects. However, certain exceptions to a categorical exemption may make the exemption inapplicable to an activity. 14 Cal. Code Regs. § 15300.2. For example, a categorical exemption does not apply if, due to "unusual circumstances," there is a reasonable possibility of a significant project-level or cumulative impact. In *Berkeley Hillside Preservation v. City of Berkeley* (2015) 60 Cal. 4th 1086, the Supreme Court ruled that the deferential "substantial evidence" standard of review applies to whether "unusual circumstances" exist, but the less deferential "fair argument" standard applies to whether there is a reasonable possibility of significant impact.

PSA = Permit Streamlining Act

Common sense exemption. An activity is exempt from CEQA when it can be seen with certainty that there is no possibility that the activity may have a significant environmental effect. 14 Cal. Code Regs. § 15061(b)(3).This exemption has also been termed the "common sense" exemption. Although disfavored for many years because of its strict language, this exemption may now be used more often as a result of the Supreme Court's decision in *Muzzi Ranch Co. v. Solano County Airport Land Use Commission* (2007) 41 Cal. 4th 372. In that case, the court upheld the use of the common sense exemption for a county airport land use commission's adoption of policies restricting development to currently permitted levels.

Certified regulatory programs. The Natural Resources Agency has certified certain state regulatory programs, exempting them from CEQA's requirement to prepare EIRs and Negative Declarations. A certified program must still comply with other CEQA policies, and preparation of a substitute document that is the functional equivalent of a Negative Declaration or EIR is required. Common state-certified regulatory programs include Coastal Commission certification of local coastal programs and the Energy Commission's energy facility licensing program. 14 Cal. Code Regs. § 15250 *et seq.*

INTEGRATION OF THE CALIFORNIA ENVIRONMENTAL QUALITY ACT AND THE PERMIT STREAMLINING ACT

During preliminary review, the lead agency must determine if the project is subject to the Permit Streamlining Act (PSA). Gov't Code § 65920 *et seq.* The PSA, which applies to certain private development projects requiring government approval, sets forth certain time limits for determining completeness of an application, for completion of environmental documents, and for project approval. *See* chapter 3 for a further discussion of the PSA.

PSA time limits include the following (extensions are possible for some of these time limits):

- Acceptance of application as complete—30 days from submittal of a development project application. 14 Cal. Code Regs. § 15060
- Completion of Negative Declaration—180 days from acceptance of application as complete. 14 Cal. Code Regs. § 15107
- Completion of EIR—one year from acceptance of application as complete. 14 Cal. Code Regs. § 15108
- Project approval—60 days from exemption decision or adoption of Negative Declaration; 180 days from date of EIR certification. Gov't Code § 65950 (EIR certification is a step before project approval, as described later in this chapter)

PREPARING THE INITIAL STUDY AND NEGATIVE DECLARATION

INITIAL STUDY

If an activity is a project subject to CEQA and no exemptions apply, the lead agency generally prepares an Initial Study to determine whether to prepare an EIR or a Negative Declaration.

If an activity is a project subject to CEQA and no exemptions apply, the lead agency generally prepares an Initial Study to determine whether to prepare an EIR or a Negative Declaration. A lead agency has the discretion to decide to prepare an EIR without first preparing an Initial Study.

An Initial Study is a short document containing a project description, environmental setting, potential environmental impacts, and mitigation measures for any significant effects. If the Initial Study concludes that the project will not have a significant effect, the lead agency adopts a Negative Declaration. If mitigation is needed to reduce any significant effects to less than significant levels, the lead agency adopts a Mitigated Negative Declaration. If the Initial Study shows that the project may have a significant environmental effect that cannot be mitigated, then the lead agency must prepare an EIR. 14 Cal. Code Regs. § 15063.

The Initial Study generally uses a checklist format modeled after Appendix G of the CEQA Guidelines. Each checklist answer requires a fact-based explanation to support conclusions, particularly conclusions that an impact is not significant.

DECISION TO PREPARE A NEGATIVE DECLARATION VERSUS AN EIR

An EIR must be prepared when the lead agency determines that it can be "fairly argued," based on "substantial evidence," that a project may have a significant environmental effect. This "fair argument" standard means that if project opponents have substantial evidence that a project may have a significant environmental effect, an EIR must be prepared, even if the lead agency's substantial evidence indicates lack of significant environmental effect. Thus, a low threshold exists for EIR preparation. 14 Cal. Code Regs. § 15064.

"Substantial evidence" includes facts, fact-based assumptions, and expert opinion. It does not include argument, speculation, or unsubstantiated opinion. Public controversy about a project is not considered substantial evidence, but may be used to require an EIR in marginal cases when it is unclear that substantial evidence of a significant environmental impact exists. 14 Cal. Code Regs. § 15384.

DETERMINING WHETHER ENVIRONMENTAL EFFECTS ARE SIGNIFICANT

An ironclad definition of significant effect is not possible. Instead, CEQA practice uses several tools for determining whether an environmental effect is significant, including the Initial Study checklist (CEQA Guidelines Appendix G); mandatory findings of significance; agency thresholds of significance; and special Guidelines rules for certain resources.

CEQA Guidelines Appendix G sets forth criteria or thresholds for each environmental topic (e.g., aesthetics, biological resources) to determine whether a project's environmental effects are potentially significant. A project may still have a significant environmental effect even if it does not trigger an Appendix G threshold.

The Guidelines set forth several mandatory findings of significance, requiring an EIR to be prepared when these findings are made. 14 Cal. Code Regs. § 15065. Mandatory findings of significance include substantially reducing the habitat of a fish or wildlife species, substantially reducing the number or restricting the range of an endangered or threatened species, or causing cumulatively considerable effects.

The CEQA Guidelines encourage lead agencies to voluntarily adopt thresholds of significance. 14 Cal. Code Regs. § 15064.7. A threshold of significance is an identifiable quantitative, qualitative, or performance level of a particular environmental effect that normally would be significant. Thresholds must be adopted through a public review process and supported by substantial evidence.

The Guidelines establish special rules for determining the significance of greenhouse gas impacts and impacts on "historical resources." *See* 14 Cal. Code Regs. §§ 15064.4, 15064.5.

CEQA requires that both direct and indirect (secondary) impacts of a project be evaluated for significance. An economic or social impact is not considered a significant environmental effect, but if a physical change (e.g., urban blight) is caused by an economic impact, the physical change must be evaluated for significance. 14 Cal. Code Regs. § 15064(d),(e).

The CEQA Guidelines establish special rules for the significance of impacts on "historical resources."

NEGATIVE DECLARATION PROCESS

A Negative Declaration documents the decision not to prepare an EIR. It includes a brief project description and a proposed finding of no significant impact, with the Initial Study as an attachment. 14 Cal. Code Regs. 15371. Mitigated Negative Declarations also must describe mitigation measures included in the project to avoid significant effects. OPR guidance on Mitigated Negative Declarations is available on the OPR website (www.opr.ca.gov/docs/MND_Publication_2004.pdf).

Public notice of a proposed Negative Declaration starts a 20- or 30-day public review period; the 30-day review period is required if a project requires State Clearinghouse review. 14 Cal. Code Regs. § 15073. State Clearinghouse review is required if a state agency is a lead, responsible, or trustee agency, or an agency with jurisdiction by law, or if the project is of "statewide, regional, or areawide significance," as defined by 14 Cal. Code Regs. § 15206. The State Clearinghouse, located within OPR, is responsible for sending the draft Negative Declaration to relevant state agencies and sending collated state agency comments to the lead agency. OPR guidance on circulation and notice of both Negative Declarations and EIRs is available on the OPR website (www.opr.ca.gov/docs/circulation.pdf).

The lead agency must consider comments received on the proposed Negative Declaration before adopting it and approving the project, but need not respond to comments in writing. For a Mitigated Negative Declaration, the lead agency may

MMRP = Mitigation Monitoring or Reporting Program

NOD = Notice of Determination

EIS = Environmental Impact Statement

substitute equally or more effective mitigation measures, provided this substitution is considered at a public hearing. If a Negative Declaration is "substantially revised" after public review, the lead agency must recirculate it for an additional round of public review. 14 Cal. Code Regs. §§ 15073.5, 15074, 15074.1.

When approving a Mitigated Negative Declaration, the lead agency also must adopt a Mitigation Monitoring or Reporting Program (MMRP) (*see* description under EIR section). After approving a Negative Declaration, the lead agency files a Notice of Determination (NOD) with OPR or the county clerk, and pays applicable DFW environmental review fees. 14 Cal. Code Regs. § 15075. Following adoption of a Negative Declaration, if circumstances change and the lead agency still has discretionary authority over the project, a subsequent Negative Declaration may be required. *See* rules for Subsequent and Supplemental EIRs, below.

PREPARING THE EIR

TYPES OF ENVIRONMENTAL IMPACT REPORTS AND TIERING

An EIR must be prepared if a project may have a significant environmental effect that cannot be reduced to less than significant levels through a Mitigated Negative Declaration. The CEQA Guidelines recognize several types of EIRs:

- For specific projects: project EIR, joint CEQA EIR/Environmental Impact Statement (EIR/EIS), focused EIR, staged EIR
- First-tier EIRs for plans and policies: tiered EIR, Program EIR, Master EIR, General Plan EIR
- Following EIR certification: Supplemental EIR, Subsequent EIR

Tiering refers to preparation of environmental documents using a multi-layered approach. In tiering, a first-tier EIR examines broad alternatives, mitigation criteria, and cumulative impacts, and a second-tier EIR or Negative Declaration can be focused on project-specific impacts, alternatives, and mitigation measures. For example, a first-tier General Plan EIR can analyze jurisdiction-wide alternatives, and regional impacts and mitigation measures. A second-tier EIR prepared for approval of a specific plan and rezoning can then be limited to project-specific alternatives and impacts and can incorporate by reference the general plan EIR's treatment of broader alternatives and impacts. 14 Cal. Code Regs. § 15152. Further, under CEQA streamlining procedures (14 Cal. Code Regs. § 15183), a project consistent with General Plan development policies for which an EIR was certified does not require additional environmental review, unless needed to examine site-specific impacts that are "peculiar to the parcel or site."

In tiering, a first-tier EIR examines broad alternatives, mitigation criteria, and cumulative impacts, and a second-tier EIR or Negative Declaration can be focused on project-specific impacts, alternatives, and mitigation measures.

Several types of EIRs facilitate the tiering process, as described in Appendix J of the CEQA Guidelines. The Program EIR is the most common type of first-tier EIR. 14 Cal. Code Regs. § 15168. Following preparation of the Program EIR, if a subsequent activity has effects that are within its scope, no new CEQA document is required. If the subsequent activity's effects are not within its scope, a new Negative Declaration or EIR must be prepared that focuses on project- or site-specific impacts. The Master EIR process functions similarly, but is procedurally more complex; lead agencies must re-evaluate Master EIRs after five years before approving projects within their scope, and prepare a Negative Declaration or focused EIR for subsequent projects outside their scope. 14 Cal. Code Regs. § 15175 *et seq.* OPR guidance on master EIR preparation is available on the OPR website (www.opr.ca.gov/docs/Focusing_on_Master_EIRs.pdf).

NOP = Notice of Preparation

ENVIRONMENTAL IMPACT REPORT PROCESS

Scoping. The EIR process starts with scoping, which is a process to determine the scope of environmental impacts and range of alternatives to be examined in the EIR. Scoping includes a scoping meeting (required for projects of statewide, regional, or areawide significance) and the Notice of Preparation (NOP) process. The NOP describes the proposed project and requests comments from reviewing agencies and the public. Comments responding to the NOP must be sent to the lead agency within 30 days of issuance, and the lead agency must consider these comments when preparing the EIR. 14 Cal. Code Regs. § 15082.

Scoping includes a scoping meeting (required for projects of statewide, regional, or areawide significance) and the Notice of Preparation process.

Draft Environmental Impact Report. An administrative Draft EIR is prepared for internal lead agency review, followed by publication and distribution of the public Draft EIR. The Draft EIR may be prepared by lead agency staff, another public or private entity, the project applicant, or a consultant hired by the lead agency or applicant. The lead agency is ultimately responsible for EIR content and must independently review the document prior to release. 14 Cal. Code Regs. § 15084.

Public notice of availability of the Draft EIR starts a 30- or 45-day public review period. The 45-day review period is required if a project requires State Clearinghouse review. The lead agency files a notice of completion with the State Clearinghouse at the same time it provides public notice of Draft EIR availability. Many lead agencies hold a public hearing on the Draft EIR to receive public comments, although CEQA does not require a public hearing. 14 Cal. Code Regs. §§ 15085–15087.

Final Environmental Impact Report. Following receipt of comments on the Draft EIR, the lead agency proceeds to prepare a Final EIR. The Final EIR contains comments on the Draft EIR, responses to comments, and any necessary revisions to the Draft EIR. 14 Cal. Code Regs. § 15089. If significant new information (as defined by Guidelines 15088.5(a)) is added to a Draft EIR, the lead agency must recirculate the Draft EIR and provide a second public review period.

Decisionmaking process. The lead agency must review and consider the Final EIR before acting on the proposed project. Before approving the project, in a step called EIR certification, the lead agency must certify that the Final EIR complies with

CEQA, was reviewed by the decisionmaking body, and represents the lead agency's independent judgment. The lead agency's decisionmaking body may either certify the Final EIR or delegate this responsibility to an advisory body or staff. 14 Cal. Code Regs. § 15090.

Typically, increases in jobs, housing, and tax revenues are project benefits used to override significant environmental impacts.

The lead agency may disapprove a project with significant environmental effects, or approve a project with significant environmental effects provided it adopts a statement of overriding considerations (*see* below). If the lead agency wishes to impose mitigation measures to reduce a project's significant environmental effects, it must possess the legal authority to do so independent of CEQA, and must act consistently with the constitutional prohibition on "takings" of private property. 14 Cal. Code Regs. § 15040 *et seq. See* chapter 3.

CEQA requires a unique set of findings, supported by substantial evidence, to be adopted prior to project approval. 14 Cal. Code Regs. § 15191. For each significant impact disclosed in the Final EIR, the lead agency must find one of the following:

- Changes in the project have been made (through mitigation or alternatives) to avoid or substantially lessen the impact.
- Changes to the project are within another agency's jurisdiction and have been or should be adopted.
- Specific economic, social, legal, technical, or other considerations make mitigation measures or alternatives infeasible.

If the lead agency makes the third finding, it still may approve the project, provided it adopts a statement of overriding considerations. The statement, which must be supported by substantial evidence, must set forth the specific overriding social, economic, legal, or technical benefits overriding the project's significant environmental effects. The statement of overriding considerations allows the decisionmaker to balance the benefits of a proposed project against its unavoidable environmental impacts. This process is designed to assure political accountability. Typically, increases in jobs, housing, and tax revenues are used as project benefits to override significant adverse environmental impacts. 14 Cal. Code Regs. § 15093. When adopting CEQA findings on the Final EIR, the lead agency also must adopt an MMRP. After project approval, the lead agency files an NOD with OPR or the county clerk, and pays applicable DFW environmental review fees. 14 Cal. Code Regs. §§ 15094, 15097.

Subsequent or Supplemental Environmental Impact Reports. Following project approval, if circumstances change and the lead agency still has discretionary authority over the project, a Subsequent or Supplemental EIR may be required. These documents are required if:

- Substantial changes in the project cause new or substantially increased significant impacts.
- Substantial changes in project circumstances cause new or substantially increased significant impacts.

- New information of substantial importance shows the project will have a new or substantially increased significant impact, or mitigation measures or alternatives that were unknown or thought to be infeasible are now feasible, and the project proponent declines to adopt them.

A Subsequent EIR must be prepared if the previous EIR requires substantial changes, whereas a Supplemental EIR may be prepared if changes are not major. If changed circumstances do not require a Subsequent or Supplemental EIR, the lead agency must prepare an EIR Addendum, an internal agency document explaining the minor technical EIR changes. 14 Cal. Code Regs. §§ 15162, 15163, 15164.

EIR CONTENTS

General rules. Key EIR contents include a summary, a project description, an environmental setting, significant environmental impacts, alternatives, and mitigation measures. The lead agency may present these and other required contents in any format. Although the CEQA Guidelines encourage EIRs to be written in plain language, to be from 150 to 300 pages long, and to emphasize the project's significant effects, in practice these suggestions often are not followed. The EIR's summary should be no longer than 15 pages; should summarize the project's significant effects, mitigation measures, and alternatives; and should identify areas of controversy and unresolved issues. 14 Cal. Code Regs. § 15120 *et seq.*

EIRs are often criticized as too technical and hard to read. Some simple editorial tips can help EIR preparers make EIRs more readable, as well as more defensible. *See* sidebar.

Project description. The project description must include the project objectives, project location, and project characteristics. It also must include a list of required project approvals, and related environmental review and consultation requirements. When an individual project is required for action on a larger project or commits the lead agency to a larger project, the project description must address the larger project. 14 Cal. Code Regs. § 15124. Generally, the project description need not disclose the identity of the project proponent, unless the proponent's identity creates unique environmental impacts.

Environmental setting. The EIR must describe the physical environmental conditions in the project vicinity, from both local and regional perspectives, at the time of NOP publication. The setting also must describe inconsistencies between the proposed project and applicable general and regional plans. 14 Cal. Code Regs. § 15125.

EIR Editorial Tips

- Reduce length
  - —Focus on issues most important to readers, e.g., from NOP comments
  - —Use appendices to explain technical methodologies, assumptions, and analysis results
  - —Creatively use tables and figures
  - —Delete regulatory and environmental setting information not used in impact analyses
  - —Delete repetitive descriptions of project
- Increase readability
  - —Define acronyms regularly
  - —Define technical terms
  - —Do not use a weak passive voice, e.g., "it is anticipated that"
  - —Do not overuse "potentially," as in a "potentially significant" impact
- Increase defensibility
  - —Support conclusions with facts and reasons
  - —Use consistent assumptions for each impact analysis
  - —Provide ample citations for information sources
  - —Explain impact significance conclusions using thresholds (pre- and post-mitigation)

Use the five Ws to describe mitigation measures:

- —Who
- —What
- —When
- —Where
- —Why

CEQA Documents Must Analyze Climate Change Impacts

Global climate change is the world's most critical environmental problem, but until 2006 was seldom considered in CEQA documents. In 2006, AB 32 (The Global Warming Solutions Act, *see* chapter 20) was enacted. A year later, SB 97 of 2007 (Chapter 185, Statutes of 2007) definitively established that CEQA documents are intended to address climate change impacts. It required the Natural Resources Agency to adopt CEQA Guidelines for analyzing and mitigating a project's contribution to global climate change by the end of 2009. The SB 97 Guidelines, which focus on greenhouse gas (GHG) emissions, generally give lead agencies broad discretion to select GHG impact analysis methodologies, select GHG thresholds of significance, and develop GHG mitigation measures. Lead agencies must consider whether the project increases GHG emissions compared to existing conditions, whether GHG emissions exceed an applicable threshold of significance, and whether the project complies with an applicable GHG reduction plan.

Lead agencies have been challenged to select an appropriate threshold of significance for GHG impacts. In *Center for Biological Diversity v. California Dept. of Fish and Wildlife* (2015) (popularly known as the "Newhall Ranch" case) 62 Cal. 4th 205, the Supreme Court severely limited the ability of lead agencies to using a "business as usual" (BAU) approach. Under the BAU approach, lead agencies calculate a project's GHG emission before adding discretionary GHG reduction measures, calculate the percentage reduction achieved by the GHG reduction measures, and compare that percentage to the statewide percentage reduction required under AB 32 for 2020. The Supreme Court ruled that BAU would be permissible only if the AB 32 Scoping Plan sets GHG reduction targets specific to the project type in question, which it has not for land use projects. GHG thresholds of significance that may be permissible, according to the Supreme Court, include consistency with AB 32 regulations applicable to the specific project type, consistency with a qualified GHG reduction plan, or use of numerical GHG thresholds set by air districts.

The environmental setting normally constitutes the baseline by which the lead agency determines whether an impact is significant, but a different "existing conditions" baseline may be used for fluctuating environmental resources (e.g., water resources) that historically vary from year to year. Also, a "future baseline," if supported by substantial evidence, may also be used in addition to the existing environmental setting, but cannot be the sole baseline unless use of the existing environmental setting would be uninformative or misleading. (*Neighbors for Smart Rail v. Exposition Metro Line Construction Authority* (2013) 57 Cal. 4th 439.) The CEQA Guidelines encourage the environmental setting to be no longer than necessary to support analysis of the proposed project's significant environmental effects, though in practice environmental settings are unnecessarily long.

Significant environmental impacts. CEQA requires EIRs to evaluate several types of impacts (14 Cal. Code Regs. § 15126.2):

- **Direct impacts.** Impacts caused by the project that occur at the same time and place
- **Indirect impacts.** Caused by the project, but that may occur later in time or some distance away
- **Irreversible environmental changes.** For example, use of nonrenewable resources
- **Growth-inducing impacts.** The extent to which the project directly or indirectly fosters growth, removes an obstacle to growth, taxes community services and facilities, or facilitates other activities causing significant environmental effects
- **Cumulative impacts.** Incremental impacts of the proposed project when added to other closely related past, present, or reasonably foreseeable future projects

Cumulative impact analysis is one of the most difficult tasks in CEQA document preparation. Two methods can be used for cumulative impact analysis. 14 Cal. Code Regs. § 15130. In the list approach, the lead agency identifies related projects that could add to the proposed project's environmental impacts. In the projection, or plan, approach, the lead agency relies on projections contained in an adopted planning document (e.g., a General Plan EIR) or prior environmental document. A particularly challenging cumulative impact topic is a proposed project's cumulative contribution to global climate change. *See* sidebar facing page.

CEQA sets forth special rules for analyzing impacts on particular resources:

- **Economic and social effects.** Must be related to a physical environmental change. 14 Cal. Code Regs. § 15358(b)
- **Historical resources.** A significant impact occurs if the resource is historically significant and the project would cause a substantial adverse change in the significance of the resource. 14 Cal. Code Regs. § 15064.5(a)
- **Tribal cultural resources.** A significant impact occurs if the project causes a substantial adverse change in the significance of a tribal cultural resource. Pub. Res. Code § 21084.2. This provision, as well as requirements for tribal consultation during the CEQA process, were added by AB 52 of 2014.
- **Public water system impacts.** For certain large projects, a water supply assessment, which analyzes whether sufficient reliable water supplies will be available to serve the proposed project, must be incorporated into the Draft EIR. 14 Cal. Code Regs. § 15155
- **Transportation impacts.** Under SB 743 of 2013 (Chapter 386, Statutes of 2013), OPR was required to develop transportation impact metrics that eliminate vehicle delay (e.g., as measured by level of service) as a significant impact under CEQA.
- **Impacts of the environment on the project.** Generally, CEQA is concerned about the impacts of the project on the environment, not the impacts of pre-existing environmental conditions (e.g., earthquake hazards) on a project or its residents. However, an EIR must consider the effects of the environment on a proposed project to the extent that the project exacerbates these effects. *California Building Industry Association v. Bay Area Air Quality Management District* (2015) 62 Cal. 4th 369. *See* sidebar.

When Must Effects of the Environment on a Project Be Considered?

Many CEQA observers were hoping that the Supreme Court in *California Building Industry Association v. Bay Area Air Quality Management District* (2015, 62 Cal. 4th 369) would definitively answer the following question: are CEQA documents required to consider the impacts of the environment on the project and its residents? Rather than setting forth a bright line rule, the Supreme Court's response was essentially "it depends."

The court did hold that CEQA "generally" does not require an analysis of how existing environmental conditions will affect a project's future users or residents. However, the court also held that CEQA requires a lead agency to evaluate existing conditions to determine whether a project could "exacerbate" hazards that are already present. Another exception to the general rule is that certain specific statutory provisions governing school, airport, and certain housing projects do require analysis of the effects of existing environmental conditions on a project or its residents.

Regarding the "exacerbation" exception, the issue to be worked out in future cases is the *extent* to which a project will worsen existing enviromental conditions. For example, the Court noted that if construction of a project disturbs soils that are already contaminated, the CEQA document must consider this impact of the project. On the other hand, if a coastal development project results in greenhouse gas emissions that "exacerbate" global climate change and sea level rise in a tiny way, is this enough of a cumulatively considerable impact to justify CEQA analysis of the impacts of sea level rise on the project? Future cases will have to decide.

In the meantime, CEQA does not *prohibit* a lead agency from voluntarily considering the impacts of the environment on a project. So lead agencies preparing CEQA documents for their own projects may continue their long-standing practices of considering and mitigating for the impacts of the environment on their projects, even if not required.

FIGURE 2-2
Developing a Reasonable Range of Alternatives

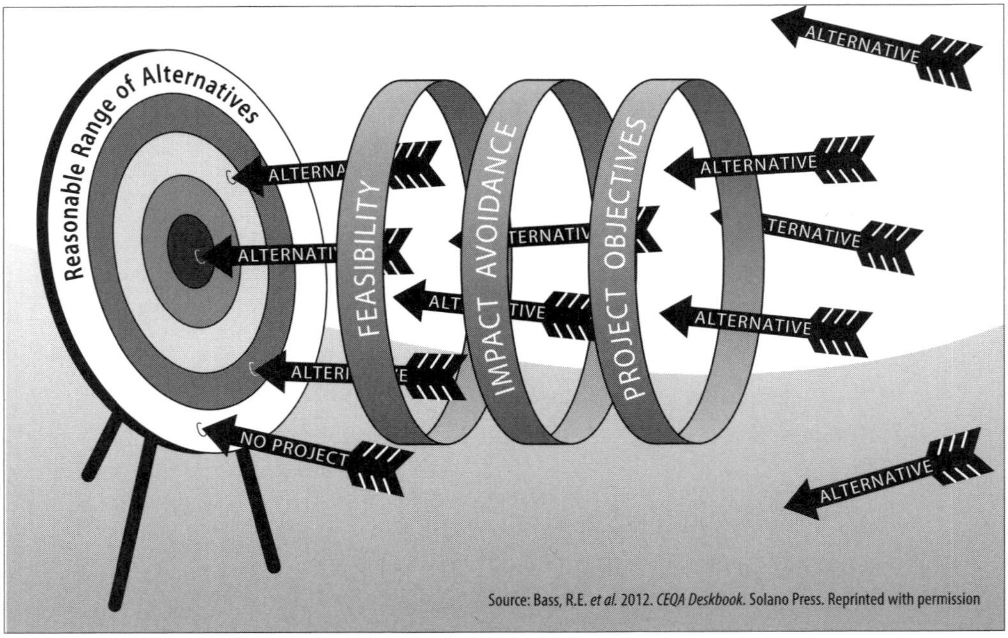

Source: Bass, R.E. *et al.* 2012. *CEQA Deskbook.* Solano Press. Reprinted with permission

Alternatives. An EIR must describe a reasonable range of alternatives that could feasibly attain most of the basic project objectives and that would avoid or substantially lessen the proposed project's significant effects. An alternative or mitigation measure is feasible when it is capable of being accomplished successfully within a reasonable time, taking into account economic, environmental, legal, social, and technological factors. The EIR must include enough information about each alternative to allow meaningful evaluation, analysis, and comparison, with quantitative analyses preferred. 14 Cal. Code Regs. § 15126.6.

The EIR must describe and evaluate the "no-project alternative" and identify an alternative other than the no-project alternative that is environmentally superior. The no-project alternative allows decisionmakers to compare the impacts of approving versus not approving the proposed project. When the proposed project is a development project at a specific location, the no-project alternative is usually the property remaining in its existing state, unless future uses of the land are predictable. When the proposed project is a revision to a plan or ongoing operation, the no-project alternative is continuation of the existing plan or operation. 14 Cal. Code Regs. § 15152.6(e).

Alternative project sites need to be evaluated when they are feasible and would avoid or substantially lessen the proposed project's significant environmental effects.

Alternative project sites need to be evaluated when they are feasible and would avoid or substantially lessen the proposed project's significant environmental effects. In the landmark case *Citizens of Goleta Valley v. Board of Supervisors* (1990) 52 Cal. 3d 553, the Supreme Court articulated several

FIGURE 2-3
Mitigation Measure Adequacy

Adequate ✓

- Avoid
- Minimize
- Rectify
- Reduce over time
- Compensate

Questionable ?

- Provide funding for
- Hire staff
- Monitor or report
- Comply with existing regulations or ordinances
- Preserve already existing natural area

Inadequate ✗

- Consult with
- Submit for review
- Coordinate with
- Study further
- Inform
- Encourage/discourage
- Facilitate
- Strive to

Source: Bass, R.E. *et al.* 2012. *CEQA Deskbook*. Solano Press. Reprinted with permission

factors for determining whether off-site alternatives are feasible, including site suitability, economic viability, infrastructure availability, general plan consistency, regulatory limitations, jurisdictional boundaries, and the applicant's control over alternative sites. Adopted regional and local plans should be used to guide the selection of feasible alternative sites. 14 Cal. Code Regs. § 15126(f).

Alternatives analysis in an EIR is typically a two-step process. First, the lead agency screens a set of preliminary alternatives to determine which alternatives meet most of the project objectives, are feasible, and reduce significant impacts. The lead agency documents the reasons for rejecting alternatives based on one or more of these factors. Second, the remaining "reasonable range" of alternatives is evaluated for environmental impacts, and these impacts are compared to proposed project impacts. Figure 2-2 illustrates the alternatives selection process.

Mitigation measures. The EIR must discuss feasible mitigation measures for each significant environmental effect that avoid the impact, minimize the impact, rectify the impact over time, reduce the impact over time, or compensate for the impact by providing substitute resources. The EIR must identify parties responsible for implementing each mitigation measure, disclose any significant side effects of implementing a mitigation measure, and explain why a particular mitigation measure was selected when several were available. 14 Cal. Code Regs. § 15126.4(a).

State legislation limits the amount of school impact fees that can be imposed as CEQA mitigation.

Mitigation measures cannot be improperly deferred to the results of future studies or regulatory agency actions. However, mitigation measures may specify performance standards that would mitigate a significant effect and that can be accomplished in several alternative ways. Figure 2-3 provides examples of mitigation measures that are adequate, inadequate, or questionable, based on the CEQA Guidelines and case law.

CEQA does not give lead agencies new authority to require mitigation, so lead agencies must use other regulatory authorities such as the police power. To avoid "regulatory taking" challenges, there must be a clear nexus between an impact and a mitigation measure, and rough proportionality between the extent of the impact and the mitigation measure imposed. 14 Cal. Code Regs. § 15126.4.

CEQA and other statutes set forth specific limitations on mitigation measures that can be used for impacts on specific resources:

- **Historical and archeological resources.** CEQA establishes cost limitations on fees, and the CEQA Guidelines define examples of adequate mitigation. Pub. Res. Code § 21082.2; 14 Cal. Code Regs. § 15126.4(b)
- **Schools.** Lead agencies may not impose fees higher than those designated by statute. Gov't Code § 65995
- **Housing.** Lead agencies may not reduce housing density as a mitigation measure unless the project has a significant impact on health or safety, and there are no feasible alternative mitigation measures. Gov't Code § 65589.5

The Supreme Court has clearly established that public universities are required to adopt feasible mitigation measures for significant off-site impacts, and that the feasibility of off-site mitigation does not depend on legislative appropriations.

Public universities have argued over the years that they are not subject to CEQA's requirement to mitigate off-site impacts when feasible. However, the Supreme Court has clearly established that public universities are required to adopt feasible mitigation measures for significant off-site impacts, and that the feasibility of off-site mitigation does not depend on legislative appropriations. *City of San Diego v. Board of Trustees of the California State University* (2015) 61 Cal. 4th 945.

Lead agencies are generally not permitted to "short circuit" the CEQA process by adding mitigation measures developed during the CEQA process to the project description. Rather, they should first describe the significance of impacts pre-mitigation, and then assess the ability of mitigation measures to reduce impacts to less than significant levels. *Lotus v. Department of Transportation* (2014) 223 Cal.App. 4th 645.

Mitigation Monitoring or Reporting Programs. When making findings on significant effects identified in an EIR, the lead agency must adopt an MMRP setting forth roles and responsibilities to assure mitigation measures are implemented. Monitoring refers to oversight of project implementation for complex mitigation measures such as wetland restoration or cultural resources recovery. Reporting refers to written mitigation measure compliance reviews.

Lead agencies use their non-CEQA authorities, e.g., the police power, to enforce mitigation measure implementation. 14 Cal. Code Regs. § 15097.

Final Environmental Impact Report contents. The Final EIR prepared after public review of the Draft EIR, includes the Draft EIR, any revisions to the Draft EIR, Draft EIR public comments or comment summaries, and lead agency responses to public comments. The responses must demonstrate good faith and be well-reasoned, and may not be conclusory. 14 Cal. Code Regs. § 15132.

Judicial review of EIR adequacy. Courts typically apply a "rule of reason" when reviewing the adequacy of EIRs. Courts require that all required contents are included in an EIR and that the EIR shows an objective, good-faith attempt at full disclosure. The scope of judicial review does not extend to the correctness of an EIR's conclusion, but only the EIR's sufficiency as an informative document for decisionmakers and the public. Disagreement among experts regarding conclusions in an EIR is acceptable, as long as the lead agency recognizes the disagreement and explains its choice of conclusions. 14 Cal. Code Regs. §§ 15003(i), 15151.

NEPA = National Environmental Policy Act

CEQ = President's Council on Environmental Quality

FHWA = Federal Highway Administration

FAST = Fixing America's Surface Transportation

The scope of judicial review does not extend to the correctness of an EIR's conclusion, but only the EIR's sufficiency as an informative document for decisionmakers and the public.

INTEGRATING CEQA WITH THE NATIONAL ENVIRONMENTAL POLICY ACT

NEPA OVERVIEW

The National Environmental Policy Act (NEPA, 42 United States Code (U.S.C.) 4321 *et seq.*) is similar to CEQA, but applies only to federal agencies. For details about NEPA implementation, *see* Bass et al. 2000.

NEPA authorizes federal agencies to carry out their activities consistent with NEPA's environmental protection policies. Its "action-forcing mechanism" is the requirement for federal agencies to prepare an Environmental Impact Statement (EIS) for major federal actions significantly affecting the quality of the human environment. The President's Council on Environmental Quality (CEQ) regulations (40 C.F.R. § 1500.1 *et seq.*) provide the basic framework for NEPA implementation.

Although federal agencies are normally responsible for NEPA implementation, there is an exception for federally funded surface transportation projects. Under 23 U.S.C. § 327, states may assume the Federal Highway Administration (FHWA) NEPA responsibilities for surface transportation projects. Through a NEPA Assignment Memorandum of Agreement, Caltrans is responsible for FHWA NEPA compliance in California, as well as FHWA compliance with Section 7 of the Endangered Species Act and Section 106 of the National Historic Preservation Act.

FONSI = finding of no significant impact

COMPARING CEQA AND NEPA

CEQA and NEPA have parallel three-step environmental review processes, as shown in Figure 2-4. CEQA and NEPA terminology differ somewhat, as shown in Table 2-1.

A major difference between the two laws is their "substantive effect." CEQA requires state and local agencies to avoid or mitigate significant environmental impacts when feasible. 14 Cal. Code Regs. §§ 15021, 15091. NEPA does not require impact avoidance or mitigation (unless mitigation is required to support a finding of no significant impact (FONSI)), but rather is essentially procedural; its requirements are satisfied when an EIS contains a good-faith disclosure of a proposed action's impacts and alternatives. *See Robertson v. Methow Valley* (1989) 490 U.S. 332.

Another major difference between the laws is the treatment of alternatives. Under CEQA, alternatives included in an EIR may be described and evaluated in less detail than the proposed project impact. Under NEPA, alternatives included in an EIS must be described and evaluated at an equivalent level of detail. 14 Cal. Code Regs. § 15126.6; 40 C.F.R. § 1502.14.

In 2015, Congress enacted the Fixing America's Surface Transportation (FAST) Act (PL 114-94). This law primarily provided transportation funding, but it also streamlined the way that major infrastructure projects are reviewed under NEPA and federal permitting programs. Certain large "covered" infrastructure projects can be reviewed under accelerated timetables using best practices for NEPA and coordinated permit processing. The Act also shortens the statute of limitations period for NEPA judicial challenges to covered projects from six to two years, and creates special exhaustion of administrative remedies and injunction limitations.

INTEGRATING CEQA AND NEPA

Lead agencies are required to integrate CEQA with other federal, state, and local environmental review requirements, of which NEPA is the most notable.

Lead agencies are required to integrate CEQA with other federal, state, and local environmental review requirements, of which NEPA is the most notable. 14 Cal. Code Regs. § 15124(d). State and local agencies are encouraged to prepare joint environmental documents; when CEQA and NEPA requirements differ, the most stringent requirement of the two laws should be followed. Further, procedures exist for using a NEPA document to satisfy CEQA requirements, provided CEQA public notice and review requirements are met. 14 Cal. Code Regs. §§ 15221, 15222. OPR and CEQ have published a useful handbook on integrating CEQA and NEPA environmental reviews. *See* www.opr.ca.gov/docs/NEPA_CEQA_Handbook_Feb2014.pdf

ENFORCING CEQA

CEQA is enforced mainly through lawsuits filed by citizens, environmental and other organizations, or public agencies. The California Attorney General also has discretionary authority to file CEQA lawsuits.

FIGURE 2-4

CEQA and NEPA Processes Compared

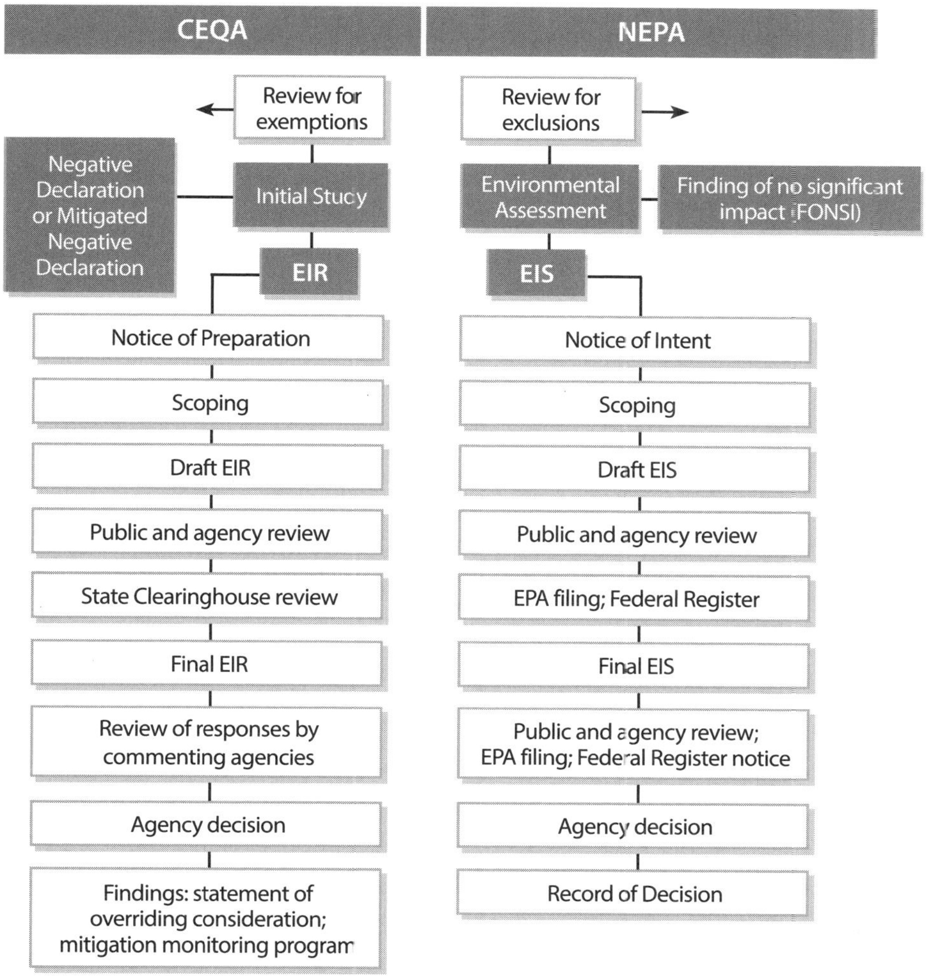

Source: Bass, R.E. *et al.* 2012. *CEQA Deskbook*. Solano Press. Reprinted with permission

Table 2-1. CEQA and NEPA Terminology Compared	
CEQA	**NEPA**
Proposed project	Proposed action
Exemptions	Categorical exclusions
Notice of Preparation	Notice of Intent
Initial Study	Environmental Assessment
Negative Declaration	Finding of no significant impact (FONSI)
Environmental Impact Report	Environmental Impact Statement
Findings	Record of Decision
Responsible agency	Cooperating agency

Challenges to Infill Projects: CEQA Streamlining Solutions

Housing advocates and planners for many years have criticized the use of CEQA lawsuits to stop infill projects with localized adverse impacts but regional environmental benefits.

These concerns have led to the development of statutory exemptions for infill housing projects. (Pub. Res. Code § 21159.24). However, the statutory infill exemptions are relatively narrow and thus seldom used. CEQA also has a categorical exemption for infill development that is used more frequently than the statutory exemptions, but it too is relatively narrow. 14 Cal. Code Regs. § 15332. CEQA also provides a partial exemption for infill and other projects that are consistent with a general plan, community plan, or zoning action for which a prior EIR has been prepared. 14 Cal. Code Regs. § 15183.

The Legislature has more recently attempted several additional approaches to streamlining CEQA compliance for infill projects, and limiting judicial challenges to infill project CEQA documents. These include:

- SB 375 (Chapter 728, Statutes of 2008), which streamlines CEQA compliance for projects consistent with a Sustainable Communities Strategy (SCS). See chapter 4 for further information on SB 375.
- SB 226 (Chapter 469, Statutes of 2011), which streamlines CEQA compliance for urban infill projects meeting certain performance standards
- SB 743 (Chapter 386, Statutes of 2013), which eliminates aesthetic impacts, parking impacts, and "level of service" traffic congestion impacts for certain infill projects, and provides a complete CEQA exemption for certain projects near transit if they are consistent with a specific plan and SCS. Many of SB 743's provisions are more widely applicable than other infill streamlining options.

The courts have played a major role in interpreting CEQA's requirements, and judicial interpretations periodically are integrated in updates of the CEQA Guidelines. CEQA has become the main vehicle for project opponents to challenge land use approvals and public agency projects, in large part because the "fair argument" standard of review applied to Negative Declaration decisions favors CEQA petitioners more than the deferential "substantial evidence" standard typically applied to agency decisionmaking.

Under the fair argument standard, if project opponents have substantial evidence that a project may have a significant environmental effect, an EIR must be prepared, even if the lead agency's substantial evidence indicates lack of significant environmental effect. Under the "substantial evidence" test, which applies to the adequacy of an EIR once one is prepared and to agency decisions under other laws, a lead agency decision will be upheld as long as it is procedurally correct and supported by substantial evidence, even if project opponents have substantial evidence that would lead to a different decision.

CEQA lawsuits challenging infill and affordable housing projects have become particularly controversial. As a result, the Legislature over the years has enacted a number of CEQA exemptions and streamlining tools to promote infill and affordable housing projects, but due to their limitations these exemptions and streamlining tools generally have not been widely applied. *See* sidebar.

Also, the Legislature has expedited the CEQA litigation process for "Environmental Leadership Development Projects." These are certain large projects certified by the Governor to meet criteria that include investment, job creation, and zero net GHG emissions. Pub. Res. Code § 21178 *et seq.*

TYPICAL CEQA CHALLENGES

Typical grounds for CEQA lawsuits include:

- Procedural violations in environmental document preparation, such as failure to prepare an EIR when one is required, or failure to provide required public notice and review
- Procedural violations in decisionmaking, such as an inappropriate finding that mitigation is infeasible, or a statement of overriding considerations not supported by substantial evidence

- Inadequate or incomplete project description
- Technical inadequacies in environmental documents, such as failure to include an adequate urban blight, water supply, or cumulative impact analysis

NOE = Notice of Exemption

BARRIERS TO JUDICIAL REVIEW

CEQA has unusually short statutes of limitation. 14 Cal. Code Regs. § 15112(c). A CEQA lawsuit must be filed within:

- 35 days after filing and posting of a Notice of Exemption (NOE)
- 30 days after filing and posting of a NOD for either a Negative Declaration or an EIR
- 180 days after the decision to carry out, approve, or start project, if no NOE or NOD has been filed

Standing refers to a petitioner's eligibility to file a lawsuit; CEQA has liberal standing rules. Most petitioners are entitled to file CEQA lawsuits, provided they exhaust their remedies by raising their CEQA objections before the close of the public hearing on the project. Pub. Res. Code § 21177(b).

ADMINISTRATIVE RECORD

Judicial review is almost always based only on evidence in the administrative record that the agency compiles prior to project approval. The administrative record includes all documents, including e-mails, related to the agency decisionmaking process in complying with CEQA. Pub. Res Code § 21167.5. Agencies may exclude certain privileged documents from the administrative record, such as attorney-client communications or documents generated during internal deliberations. To streamline CEQA litigation, legislation passed in 2016 requires a lead agency, at the request of the project applicant and with consent of the lead agency, to prepare the administrative record concurrently with the preparation of an environmental document. Pub. Res. Code § 21167.6.2.

The administrative record includes all documents, including e-mails, related to the agency decisionmaking process in complying with CEQA.

REMEDIES

A successful CEQA challenge results in a writ of mandamus (a judicial command to an official to perform a ministerial act that the law recognizes as an absolute duty and not discretionary). A court finding a CEQA violation may void the agency action, enjoin project implementation until CEQA compliance is achieved, or order the agency to comply with CEQA by preparing new environmental documents. Pub. Res. Code § 21168.9. Civil or criminal penalties are not available for CEQA violations.

for more information...

Bass, R. E., K. M. Bogdan, and T. Rivasplata, 2012. CEQA Deskbook. 3rd Edition. Solano Press. Point Arena, Calif.

Bass, R. E., A. I. Herson, and K. M. Bogdan, 2000. The NEPA Book. Solano Press. Point Arena, Calif.

Council on Environmental Quality and Governor's Office of Planning and Research, 2014. NEPA and CEQA: Integrating Federal and State Environmental Reviews.

Governor's Office of Planning and Research, 2012. State Clearinghouse Handbook.

Kostka, S. L. and M. H. Zischke, 2015. Practice under the Guide to the California Environmental Quality Act. 2nd Edition. Continuing Education of the Bar. Oakland, Calif.

Manaster, K. A. and D. P. Selmi (eds.), ND. Chapters 21–24 of California Environmental Law and Land Use Practice. Matthew Bender. San Francisco, Calif.

Remy, M. H., T. A.Thomas, J. G. Moose, and W. F. Manley, 2007. Guide to the California Environmental Quality Act. Solano Press. Point Arena, Calif.

glossary

Baseline—the starting point for determining a proposed project's significant effects, normally the same as the existing environmental setting.

Categorical exemption—CEQA exemptions for classes of projects that the Natural Resources Agency has determined do not have a significant environmental effect.

Cumulative impacts—two or more individual impacts that, when considered together, are considerable or that compound other environmental impacts.

Discretionary project—a project requiring the exercise of government judgment or deliberation.

Environmental Assessment*—brief preliminary analysis by a federal lead agency to determine whether an EIS should be prepared.

Environmental Impact Report*—a detailed statement prepared by a state or local lead agency describing a proposed project, its significant environmental effects, mitigation measures, and alternatives.

Environmental Impact Statement*—a detailed statement prepared by a federal lead agency describing a proposed action, its significant environmental effects, mitigation measures, and alternatives.

Environmental setting—the physical environmental conditions in the project vicinity.

Feasible—capable of being accomplished successfully within a reasonable period of time, taking into account economic, environmental, legal, social, and technological factors.

Findings—written conclusions prepared by a lead agency at the end of the EIR process explaining the disposition of each significant environmental effect.

Guidelines—state CEQA Guidelines, which are the state regulations interpreting and implementing CEQA.

Initial Study—preliminary analysis to determine whether a Negative Declaration or EIR should be prepared.

Lead agency—public agency having the principal responsibility for carrying out or approving a project.

Ministerial project—a government decision involving little or no personal judgment.

Mitigated Negative Declaration*—brief written statement prepared by a state or local lead agency explaining why a proposed project will not have a significant environmental effect, and therefore will not require an EIR, because the project's significant environmental effects have been mitigated.

Mitigation measure—avoiding, minimizing, rectifying, reducing, or compensating for an environmental impact.

Negative Declaration*—brief written statement prepared by a state or local lead agency explaining why a proposed project will not have a significant environmental effect, and therefore will not require an EIR.

Notice of Determination—notice filed after project approval, once a Negative Declaration or EIR has been prepared.

Notice of Exemption—optional notice filed after project approval, indicating a CEQA exemption applies.

Notice of Preparation—brief notice indicating a lead agency intends to prepare an EIR.

Project—the whole of an action with the potential for a direct or indirect physical environmental impact.

Responsible agency—public agency that uses a lead agency environmental document to carry out or approve a project.

Significant effect—a substantial or potentially substantial change in the physical environment.

Statement of overriding considerations—written explanation prepared at the end of the EIR process explaining why a lead agency approved a project notwithstanding its significant environmental effects.

Statutory exemption—an exemption created by the state Legislature.

Substantial evidence—enough relevant information and inferences that a fair argument can be made to support a conclusion. Includes facts, and reasonable assumptions and expert opinion supported by facts.

Tiering—coverage of general matters in broader environmental documents, and project-specific matters in subsequent project-specific environmental documents.

Trustee agency—state agency with jurisdiction over natural resources held in trust for the people of the state.

Writ of mandamus—a judicial command to an official to perform a ministerial act that the law recognizes as an absolute duty and not discretionary.

* equals permit or approval

CHAPTER 3

Local Land Use Planning and Regulation

related Solano Press titles

California Land Use and Planning Law. Cecily Talbert Barclay and Matthew S. Gray. 35th Edition. 2016.

Eminent Domain. 3rd Edition. Richard G. Rypinski and Alan Sozio. 2015.

Exactions and Impact Fees in California. 3rd Edition. William W. Abbott et al. 2012 with 2014 Update.

The General Plan in California. David Early. 2015.

Guide to California Planning. 4th Edition. William E. Fulton and Paul Shigley. 2012.

Ballot Box Navigator. Michael Durkee et al. 2003.

in this chapter...

COG = Council of Governments

OPR = Governor's Office of Planning and Research

OHP = Office of Historic Preservation

LAFCO = Local Agency Formation Commission

INTRODUCTION

This chapter reviews local government land use planning and regulation. City and county land use plans and regulations can play a critical role in protecting and preserving environmental quality. Following a review of key laws and agencies, this chapter reviews general plans, specific plans, and redevelopment plans; zoning law; subdivision law; the Permit Streamlining Act; historic preservation programs; takings, exactions, and development agreements; and boundary changes. State agencies such as the Coastal Commission and regional planning agencies such as councils of government (COGs) also play an important role in land use planning and regulation. These agencies and their programs are reviewed in chapter 4 (State and Regional Land Use Controls).

KEY LAWS AND AGENCIES

KEY LAWS

Police power. The police power is the legal basis for local governments (i.e., cities and counties) to regulate land use to protect public health, safety, and welfare within their boundaries. The sources of the police power are:

- The powers retained by the states (reserved powers), pursuant to the U.S. Constitution (10th Amendment)
- The California Constitution (Art. XI, § 7), which authorizes a city or county to make and enforce within its limits all local and police ordinances and regulations not in conflict with general law

State legislation. Numerous state laws create the legal framework for local government land use planning and regulation. The most important of these are:

- General plan and specific plan requirements. Gov't Code § 65100 *et seq.*
- Zoning regulations. Gov't Code § 65300 *et seq.*
- Subdivision Map Act. Gov't Code § 66410 *et seq.*
- Permit Streamlining Act. Gov't Code § 65920 *et seq.*
- The authorization of development agreements. Gov't Code § 65864 *et seq.*

KEY AGENCIES

Governor's Office of Planning and Research. State agencies play a limited role in local land use planning and regulation. Instead, the Governor's Office of Planning and Research (OPR) issues detailed General Plan Guidelines, which were revised most recently in 2017 (OPR 2017). *See* sidebar. OPR also periodically issues other land use guidance, e.g., guidelines for Native American tribal consultation, and advice on how to prepare specific plans. These publications are available on the OPR website (www.opr.ca.gov), and some are listed as sources of further information at the end of this chapter.

Department of Housing and Community Development. The Department of Housing and Community Development oversees housing element preparation. It has published guidelines on preparation of housing element updates (HCD 2012).

Office of Historic Preservation. The OHP is responsible for administering federally and state mandated historic preservation programs to protect California's historic and archaeological resources. The OHP is guided by the State Historic Preservation Officer and the State Historical Resources Commission.

Local governments. City councils and county boards of supervisors are the local government land use decisionmaking bodies. Some of their functions may be assigned to planning commissions, or to design or architectural review boards. Typically, some planning commission decisions, such as general plan amendments, are recommendations to the city council or county board of supervisors, whereas other decisions are final unless appealed, such as subdivisions and zoning variances.

Local Agency Formation Commissions. Each county has a LAFCO that is responsible for approving the formation of new local agencies and local agency boundary changes.

GENERAL PLANS AND SPECIFIC PLANS

GENERAL PLANS

Overview. Cities and counties are required to prepare general plans, which serve as the blueprints, or constitutions, for all future developments within their jurisdiction. In addition to guiding land use decisions, general plans provide the opportunity for local governments to achieve other objectives such as creating sustainable communities and efficient government operations. Prior to 1971, the general plan was considered an advisory document, but in 1971, legislation passed requiring zoning and subdivision approvals to be consistent with an adopted general plan. Gov't Code § 65860; *see* discussion of consistency requirement below.

The general plan must be a comprehensive, long-term plan for the physical development of the city or county. The general plan must include a statement of development policies, including diagrams and text, setting forth objectives, principles, standards, and plan proposals. Gov't Code § 65302. The general plan also must contain seven elements: land use, circulation, housing, conservation, open space, noise, and safety. Gov't Code § 65302(a)–(g). In addition, after 2018, a general plan must either include an environmental justice (EJ) element or integrate EJ content into other elements. *See* sidebar.

OPR General Plan Guidelines 2017 Update

For each general plan element, OPR's General Plan Guidelines Update includes statutory requirements, recommended data, recommended policies, and sample policy language. The Guidelines generally focus on efficient growth. New policy recommendations focus on several cross-element key themes:

- Climate Change: OPR's recommendations focus on how the general plan can achieve both greenhouse gas emission reductions and resiliency to climate change impacts and lead to healthier communities.
- Economics: Policy recommendations recognize that decisions regarding land use have fiscal implications, and in turn that local economies affect the health, climate, and equity of communities.
- Healthy Communities: Because general plans offer one important way to improve the community's health, OPR offers recommendations for jurisdictions interested in incorporating health-supporting policies into their general plan.
- Equitable Opportunities: OPR's policy recommendations for equity incorporate statutory requirements for environmental justice guidance (Gov't Code § 65040.12(c)), with an expanded focus on equity throughout the general plan.

Additionally, based on statewide goals, the update includes model guides and best practices related to infill development, renewable energy, and mitigation of agricultural land conversion.

SB 1000 Environmental Justice Requirements

Under SB 1000 of 2016 (Chapter 587, Statutes of 2016), a general plan must include EJ goals, policies, and objectives in either a separate element or integrated into other elements. EJ provisions must address health risks in disadvantaged communities, civil engagement, and prioritizing improvements and programs for disadvantaged communities. EJ content must be added when two or more elements are adopted or revised concurrently after January 1, 2018.

Subjects covered by the mandatory elements include the following:

- **Land use.** Designates the type, intensity, and general distribution of uses of land for housing, business, industry, open space, education, public buildings and grounds, waste disposal facilities, and other categories of public and private uses. The land use element must also address certain specific types of unincorporated communities (Gov't Code § 65302.10); OPR (2013) has issued guidance on how to do this.
- **Circulation.** Correlates with the land use element and identifies the general location and extent of existing and proposed major thoroughfares, transportation routes, terminals, and other local public utilities and facilities. The circulation element is also required to address "complete streets," so that the needs of all users, including bicyclists and pedestrians, are considered.
- **Housing.** Comprehensive assessment of current and projected housing needs for all economic segments of the community. In addition, the housing element embodies policies for providing adequate housing and includes action programs for that purpose.
- **Conservation.** Addresses the conservation, development, and use of natural resources, including water, forests, soils, rivers, and mineral deposits.
- **Open Space.** Details plans and measures for the long-range preservation and conservation of open-space lands, including open space for the preservation of natural resources, the managed production of resources, agriculture, outdoor recreation, and public health and safety.
- **Noise.** Identifies and appraises noise problems within the community and forms the basis for land use distribution.
- **Safety.** Establishes policies and programs to protect the community from risks associated with seismic, geologic, flood, and wildfire hazards, as well as other concerns such as drought. Starting in 2017, additional requirements for climate adaptation and resiliency strategies will be phased in. (SB 379 of 2015, Chapter 608, Statutes of 2015). Safety elements often implement restrictions on development in earthquake hazard zones required by the Alquist-Priolo Act (Pub. Res. Code § 2621 *et seq.*). They may integrate requirements of local hazard mitigation plans prepared under the federal Disaster Mitigation Act. Gov't Code § 65302.6.

Many cities and counties are also preparing climate action plans, which may be part of the general plan or may be a separate document linked to the general plan.

A city or county also may choose to adopt additional elements, e.g., agriculture, urban design, air quality, energy, or water supply. An air quality element is, however, mandatory for cities and counties located in the San Joaquin Valley Air Pollution Control District. Many cities and counties are also preparing climate action plans, which may be part of the general plan or may be a separate document linked to the general plan. These are discussed in chapter 20.

Point Richmond. The City of Richmond 2030 General Plan was one of the first in California to include a Community Health and Wellness element.

If a general plan does not have all the mandatory elements, if the elements do not meet statutory criteria, or if the elements are inconsistent (*see* below), then a land use decision related to the plan deficiency can be declared invalid. For example, the issuance of a conditional use permit may be beyond a county's authority if the noise element of the county's general plan does not meet the statutory criteria. *Neighborhood Action Group v. County of Calaveras* (1984) 156 Cal. App. 3d 1176. However, a city or county with an inadequate general plan may apply to OPR for a two-year extension to correct the inadequacy, during which time the city's or county's land use decisions cannot be challenged as inconsistent with the general plan. Gov't Code § 65361.

Organization. A local government may determine how its general plan will be organized, as long as the mandatory elements are included. General plan elements may be combined, as is often the case for the conservation and open space elements. Most general plans include an executive summary, a vision statement, and an implementation plan; these components are not required by state planning law.

Some larger cities and counties prepare community plans or area plans that supplement the general plan by focusing on issues relevant to a particular community. The general plan typically establishes framework policies, which are then applied to the specific circumstances and concerns of each community or area. For example, the City of Los Angeles has prepared community plans for 35 specific community plan areas. The community or area plans can either be prepared at the same time as the general plan, or later.

Internal consistency. A general plan must be integrated and internally consistent, both across elements and within each element. Gov't Code § 95300.5. For example, the land use and circulation elements must be based on the same population growth projections, and general plan diagrams of land use or circulation systems must be internally consistent with written policies and programs in the land use and circulation elements.

Consistency of land use decisions. Generally, all land use decisions must be consistent with the general plan. However, a charter city, other than the charter city of Los Angeles, is exempt from the requirement for zoning to be consistent with the general plan unless it adopts a consistency rule. Gov't Code § 55803. (In a charter city, the legal authority for the city's acts originates with a city charter, rather than from state laws. About one-fifth of California's cities are charter cities.)

A land use decision, such as a rezoning or subdivision map approval, is consistent with the general plan if, considering all its aspects, it will further the objectives and policies of the general plan and not obstruct their attainment. *Clover Valley Foundation v. City of Rocklin* (2011) 197 Cal. App. 4th 200. Courts generally defer to a city's or county's interpretation of its own general plan when reviewing consistency determinations. *See, e.g., Friends of Lagoon Valley v. City of Vacaville* (2007) 154 Cal. App. 4th 807.

A land use decision, such as a rezoning or subdivision map approval, is consistent with the general plan if, considering all its aspects, it will further the objectives and policies of the general plan and not obstruct their attainment.

HCD = Department of Housing and Community Development

RHNA = Regional Housing Needs Assessment

ALUC = airport land use commission

ALUCP = airport land use compatibility plan

General plan adoption and amendment process. The process for general plan adoption and amendment is set forth in Government Code § 63530 *et seq.* The planning commission must hold a public hearing before taking action on the general plan proposal, and then the city council or county board of supervisors must likewise hold at least one public hearing before taking action on the general plan proposal and the planning commission recommendation. A CEQA document must be prepared for the general plan proposal and considered at these hearings.

State law encourages intergovernmental coordination in general plan preparation. The general plan proposal must be referred to any county or city within or adjacent to the area covered by the proposal, to any special district that may be significantly affected by the proposal, to any school district within the area covered by the proposal, to the LAFCO, and to any affected regional planning or federal agencies. These agencies generally have 45 days to comment. Gov't Code §§ 65301, 65302.

Under Senate Bill (SB) 18 of 2004; Gov't Code §§ 65092, 65352 *et seq.*), cities and counties must send their general plan and specific plan proposals to those California Native American tribes that are on the Native American Heritage Commission contact list and have traditional lands located within the city's or county's jurisdiction. Cities and counties also must consult with these tribes prior to adopting or amending their general plans or specific plans. OPR (2005) has issued detailed guidelines for SB 18 consultation.

Housing element. Local governments must prepare housing elements consistent with the State Housing Element Guidelines prepared by the Department of Housing and Community Development (HCD). Gov't Code § 65585(a). HCD is responsible for determining regional housing needs for all income groups, and COGs (or HCD where no COG exists) are responsible for adopting a Regional Housing Needs Assessment (RHNA) that allocates a "fair share" of the regional housing need to each city and county. Gov't Code § 65584.06.

Local governments must update their housing elements every eight years and submit an annual report to OPR and HCD on the status of the general plan and housing element implementation.

Local government housing elements must meet these fair share requirements. Local governments must submit draft housing elements and proposed amendments to HCD for review and comment. They must also submit adopted housing elements and amendments to HCD. Additionally, local governments must update their housing elements every eight years and submit an annual report to OPR and HCD on the status of the general plan and housing element implementation. Gov't Code §§ 65400(b), 65588(b).

Airport land use compatibility. Airport land use commissions (ALUCs) must prepare airport land use compatibility plans (ALUCPs) for each public-use and military airport in California. Pub. Util. Code § 21675. An ALUCP contains policies and criteria that address compatibility between airports and future surrounding land uses by addressing noise, overflight, safety, and airspace protection concerns to minimize the public's exposure to excessive noise and safety hazards within the airport influence area.

FEMA = Federal Emergency Management Agency

Proposals to adopt or amend a general plan, specific plan or land use regulation affecting land uses within an ALUCP must be referred to the ALUC for a consistency determination. A local agency may override an inconsistency determination by a two-thirds vote if it finds the action is consistent with certain statutory purposes. Pub. Util. Code § 21676(b).

An ALUC has no jurisdiction over the operation of airports or over existing land uses. However, local agencies with land located within the airport influence area boundary for any of airport must amend their general plan to conform to the applicable ALUCP, unless they follow statutory procedures to override the ALUCP. Gov't Code § 65302.3)

Flood management. Legislation enacted in 2007 (AB 162, Chapter 369, Statutes of 2007) established new requirements for general plans to consider flood management. The land use element is required to identify and annually review areas subject to flooding, as identified on floodplain maps prepared by the Federal Emergency Management Agency (FEMA) or the Department of Water Resources (DWR). The conservation element must identify land and water resources that can accommodate floodwater for purposes of groundwater recharge and stormwater management. The safety element must identify flood hazard zones, and establish policies to protect the community from unreasonable risks of flooding. In Central Valley cities and counties, the revised safety element must be submitted to the Central Valley Flood Protection Board for review and comment, and local agencies must make formal findings if they reject any of the board's recommendations.

Guerneville, California flooding. Legislation enacted in 2007 required general plans to strengthen flood management policies.

SB 70 of 2007 (Chapter 367, Statutes of 2007) provides local governments with additional incentives to keep development out of the floodplains in their general plans. It requires local governments, under some circumstances, to pay their fair share of flood damages, to the extent they increase the state's exposure to liability for property damage by unreasonably approving new development in a previously undeveloped area protected by a state flood control project.

Numerous bills signed into law after 2007 further clarified these requirements. DWR has published a useful handbook compiling planning-related flood legislation and explaining how to integrate it into land use planning (DWR 2010 with 2014 Addendum). It has also issued guidance on developing general plan amendments to implement the flood legislation (DWR 2014). See chapter 4 for more information regarding California flood management.

Amendments and updates. Cities and counties must periodically review and revise the general plan. After the general plan has been adopted, the planning agency must provide an annual report to their legislative body, OPR, and HCD on the status of the plan and progress in its implementation. Gov't Code § 65400((a)(1), (2). A mandatory element of the general plan may be amended only four times a year. The housing element must be updated at least every eight years (Gov't Code § 65588(b)), but there is no statutory update requirement for the other elements.

OPR is authorized to grant extensions for general plan updates of up to two years. Gov't Code § 65361.

Good general plan examples. The California Planning Roundtable, a planning leadership organization, maintains a "Reinventing the General Plan" website with model general plans (reinventingthegeneralplan.org/). Each model highlights exemplary practices and ideas from a California general plan.

Legal challenges to general plan adequacy. When general plan adequacy is challenged, courts generally use a deferential standard of review, considering whether adoption or amendment of the general plan was arbitrary, capricious, or lacking in evidentiary support. Code Civ. Proc. § 1085; *see, e.g., Garrick Development Company v. Hayward Unified School District* (1992) 3 Cal. App. 4th 320. The court determines whether the plan substantially complies with the statutory criteria. The housing element gets closer judicial scrutiny because it has more detailed statutory requirements.

The statute of limitations for challenging a decision to adopt or amend a general plan (or specific plan) is generally 90 days. Gov't Code § 65009(c). If a general plan is found to be deficient, the court may order one or more of the following measures until the general plan deficiency has been corrected (Gov't Code § 65755):

- Suspending authority to issue building permits and other permits
- Suspending authority to issue variances
- Suspending authority to issue subdivision approvals
- Mandating approval of certain permits for housing, and certain subdivision maps, when the city's or county's ability to implement an adequate housing element will not be impaired

SPECIFIC PLANS

A specific plan implements a general plan within a smaller geographic area.

A specific plan implements a general plan within a smaller geographic area. Land use controls, such as zoning ordinances and subdivision regulations, must be consistent with adopted specific plans, as are public works projects and development agreements. Gov't Code § 65450 *et seq.* A specific plan includes text and diagrams covering the following topics (Gov't Code § 65454(a)):

- Distribution, location, and extent of land uses
- Distribution, location, extent, and intensity of infrastructure
- Standards by which development will proceed and natural resources will be managed
- Implementation measures such as regulations, public works projects, and financing measures

A specific plan must be consistent with the general plan. It is adopted using essentially the same procedures as for adoption of a general plan. Unlike general plan amendments, there is no annual limit on the number of specific plan amendments. OPR (2001) has issued guidance on specific plan preparation.

CUP = conditional use permit

ZONING AND SUBDIVISIONS

ZONING

Overview. Whereas the general plan is a long-range policy document focusing on the future, a zoning ordinance describes the immediate allowable uses on each piece of property within the city or county. Zoning divides a city or county into districts or zones, such as single-family residential, multi-family residential, commercial, industrial, and open space. Zoning regulations regulate both building standards (e.g., building heights, setbacks, and floor-to-area ratios) and the allowable uses of buildings in each of these zones.

Whereas the general plan is a long-range policy document focusing on the future, a zoning ordinance describes the immediate allowable uses on each piece of property within the city or county.

In addition to zoning applied to specific parcels, many cities or counties use overlay zones to further regulate development to address special concerns. For example, overlay zones may apply to floodplains or historic districts.

Zoning authority. Zoning authority originates from city and county police powers and from the state's Planning and Zoning Law. Gov't Code § 65000 *et seq.* This law sets minimum zoning standards for counties and general law cities (non-charter cities). Certain sections of the Planning and Zoning Law, e.g., procedures for zoning hearings, also apply to charter cities. Zoning ordinances are subject to initiatives and referenda. *See* below.

Consistency with general plans and specific plans. A zoning ordinance must be consistent with the general plan and applicable specific plans. However, a charter city, other than Los Angeles, is exempt from the requirement of zoning being consistent with the general plan unless the charter city adopts a consistency rule. Gov't Code §§ 65803, 65860. A zoning ordinance is consistent with an adopted general or specific plan if the land uses authorized by the ordinance are compatible with the plan objectives, policies, general land uses, and programs.

Zoning ordinance amendments. Most zoning ordinance amendments are subject to minimum due process requirements of notice and hearing. To enact a zoning amendment, the planning commission must hold a noticed public hearing and make its recommendation to the city council or county board of supervisors, which in turn adopts the amendment after a second noticed public hearing.

Variances and conditional use permits. Variances and conditional use permits (CUPs) provide flexibility in the application of zoning ordinances, and some cities or counties have a zoning adjustment board to grant these permits. For counties and general law cities, state law governs the issuance of variances and conditional use permits. Gov't Code § 65901 *et seq.* Charter cities may adopt different procedures.

A zoning variance is a limited exception to the usual requirements of local zoning. Gov't Code § 65906. When a city or county is asked to approve development on

Medical Marijuana Land Use Cases

The Medical Marijuana Regulation and Safety Act (AB 243, Chapter 688, Statutes of 2015) requires both a state license and local permit for medical marijuana facilities, and requires local governments to enact ordinances to regulate or ban marijuana uses. Many local governments have sought to regulate medical marijuana uses in their jurisdictions, or exclude them altogether, with various degrees of success. For example, in *City of Palm Springs v. Luna Crest Inc.* (2016) 245 Cal. App. 4th 879, a dispensary opened without seeking city permits and argued that federal law outlawing marijuana pre-empts local regulations. The court ruled there was no pre-emption because the city's regulatory program for medical marijuana dispensaries neither conflicted with federal law, nor stood as an obstacle to its purposes and objectives. The court noted that the federal Controlled Substances Act does not direct local governments to exercise their regulatory powers in any particular way, so exercising those powers to regulate medical marijuana dispensaries that meet state law requirements does not violate conflicting federal law.

In *Union of Medical Marijuana Patients v. City of Upland* (2016) 245 Cal. App. 4th 1265, the court ruled that the city's re-adoption of an ordinance banning mobile marijuana dispensaries was not a project subject to CEQA because the city had performed a CEQA analysis on the previous ordinance. But even if the ordinance did not merely restate existing law, the court observed it still would not qualify as a project under CEQA because alleged impacts were too speculative to evaluate. Speculative impacts alleged by plaintiffs included increased traffic from patients driving to other jurisdictions to obtain marijuana, and adverse environmental impacts from increased indoor marijuana cultivation.

an unusual property, the variance gives flexibility to the usual standards of the zoning ordinance. Approval of a variance allows the property owner to use property in a manner basically consistent with the zoning ordinance, with minor variations, e.g., a change in building setback requirements. Restrictions on a zoning variance must be imposed to ensure the variance will not grant special privilege to a particular landowner. For a variance to be granted, the local government must find all of the following (*Topanga Association for a Scenic Community v. County of Los Angeles* (1974) 11 Cal. 3d 506):

- There are unique physical constraints on the property
- Deprivation or hardship would result without relief
- There are disparities between the applicant's parcel and neighboring land

A CUP, sometimes called a special use permit, is issued for specified uses that are not permitted by right by a zoning ordinance, but which may still be appropriate under certain circumstances. Examples of uses requiring a CUP include community facilities, public buildings, liquor stores, churches, medical marijuana uses, and landfills. Some local zoning ordinances have special requirements for approval of certain CUPs, such as approval of neighborhood owners, or standards for proximity to sensitive uses such as schools or churches.

Regulation of medical marijuana uses has been particularly controversial and prone to litigation (*see* sidebar). Also, Proposition 64 of 2016 legalized the adult non-medical use of marijuana. It allows a city or county to regulate non-medical marijuana businesses, including completely banning them from its jurisdiction.

CUPs typically are granted with special conditions. However, state law prohibits conditions requiring either the dedication of land or the posting of a bond for public improvements not reasonably related to the conditional use. Gov't Code § 65909.

Nonconforming uses and their termination. A nonconforming use is a land use that was lawful before a zoning ordinance was adopted, but does not conform to the new zoning ordinance. *See Hill v. City of Manhattan Beach* (1971) 6 Cal. 3d 279. The concept of nonconforming uses includes nonconforming activities on undeveloped land and within structures, as well as nonconforming structures. Like a variance or conditional use permit, a legal nonconforming use is an exception from the strict application of a local zoning ordinance.

Zoning ordinances typically prohibit the expansion of a nonconforming use, starting a new nonconforming use of the property, or making the nonconforming use more permanent through structural alterations. Zoning ordinances may terminate nonconforming uses after a reasonable time period that allows the landowner to amortize his or her investment in the nonconforming use; the amortization period is proportional to the landowner's investment and the nature of the use. *See City of Los Angeles v. Gage* (1954) 127 Cal. App. 2d 577.

PUD = planned unit development

Planned unit developments. A planned unit development (PUD) is a master-planned development within a zoning district that allows multiple uses (e.g., residential, commercial, industrial). PUDs typically consist of individually owned lots and areas owned in common (e.g., greenbelts, streets) by all lot owners. A PUD permits flexibility in site planning and location of structures. The concept of a PUD is not expressly recognized by state law, but has been approved by the courts. *See, e.g., Orinda Homeowners Committee v. Board of Supervisors* (1970) 11 Cal. App. 3d 768.

Inclusionary zoning and affordable housing requirements. Inclusionary housing programs, typically implemented through zoning, require residential developers to set aside a certain percentage of new units for low-income households. Inclusionary zoning also can include density bonuses, reduced development standards, or fees to fund affordable housing production.

The state has enacted a number of statutes to prevent local governments from using zoning and land use controls to discourage affordable housing, and instead to encourage the production of affordable housing through incentives. Cities and counties are prohibited from disapproving affordable housing projects unless they make certain overriding findings. Gov't Code § 65598.5. Incentives for affordable housing are part of the state's housing policy (Gov't Code § 65915 *et seq*.).

The state has enacted a number of statutes to prevent local governments from using zoning and land use controls to discourage affordable housing, and instead to encourage the production of affordable housing through incentives.

Also, density bonuses (permission to increase project housing density) may be used as incentives for production of affordable housing. Gov't Code § 65915(a) *et seq*. Developers can request a density bonus if they include very low-, low- or moderate-income units in their development. In return for the inclusion of affordable units, the developer receives an increase in density beyond the city's maximum and can request incentives and concessions for the development

Excessive local parking requirements can be an impediment to the development of affordable housing. AB 744 of 2015 (Chapter 699, Statutes of 2015) limits minimum parking requirements for certain transit-oriented developments that include affordable housing, senior housing, or special needs housing. Local governments can require a higher parking standard if they have completed a parking study that supports the need for more parking.

Design review. Many local governments adopt design guidelines to provide more detail on desired community character than is provided in the zoning ordinance. Design standards typically address aesthetics, but can also address specific topics such as transit orientation, water conservation, and sustainability. Local design review boards often review individual projects for consistency with design standards. Design review ordinance have survived legal challenges that they are unconstitutionally vague, even when using generally-stated standards such as precluding "monotonous" development. *Novi v. City of Pacifica* (1985) 169 Cal. App. 3d 678.

Legal challenges to zoning ordinances. Adoption of a zoning ordinance is a legislative act, to which the courts typically defer, and a zoning ordinance is presumed to be constitutional. A zoning ordinance is valid if it is reasonably related to the public welfare. The California Supreme Court established the following test for determining whether a land use regulation such as a zoning ordinance is reasonably related to the public welfare (*Associated Homebuilders, Inc. v. City of Livermore* (1982) 18 Cal. 3d 582):

- What is the probable effect and duration of the land use restriction?
- What are the competing interests (e.g., affordable housing) affected by the land use restriction?
- Does the regulation, considering its probable effect, represent a reasonable accommodation of the competing interests?

Courts have permitted a substantial amount of vagueness in zoning ordinances.

A zoning ordinance is sometimes challenged on the grounds that it is too vague, thereby violating due process rights of those to which it applies. However, courts have permitted a substantial amount of vagueness in zoning ordinances. Also, zoning and other land use controls can be challenged as regulatory "takings" of private property, in violation of the Fifth Amendment to the U.S. Constitution (as is discussed later in this chapter in the takings discussion.).

First Amendment challenges to zoning ordinances. The application of zoning ordinances to adult business (e.g., adult bookstores or movie theaters), billboards, and religious land uses has generated much litigation. A zoning ordinance regulating adult businesses will be upheld as not violating the First Amendment's free speech clause, if it is content-neutral, designed to serve a substantial government interest, and allows reasonable alternative avenues of communication. *City of Renton v. Playtime Theaters, Inc.* (1986) 475 U.S. 41. The leading case on billboard regulation is *Metromedia, Inc. v. San Diego* (1981) 453 U.S. 490, in which the Supreme Court ruled that commercial interests are entitled to less freedom of speech protections than non-commercial interests, but rejected the city's billboard ordinance because it selectively banned billboards based on content. Similarly, in *Reed v. Town of Gilbert* (2015, 135 S. Ct. 2218) a town's sign code which imposed more stringent restrictions on signs directing the public to a meeting of a nonprofit group than it did on signs conveying other messages was impermissible content-based regulation of speech because the restrictions in the sign code that applied to any given sign depended entirely on the communicative content of the sign.

Land use regulation of religious uses is governed not only by the First Amendment, but also by the Religious Land Use and Institutionalized Persons Act of 2000 (42 U.S.C. § 2000cc). Under this Act, a city or county land use regulation may not impose a "substantial burden" on religious exercise unless the regulation furthers a "compelling government interest" and is the least restrictive means to further that interest. To be successfully challenged, the regulation must do more than regulate a religious institution's land use—it must actually impose a burden on religious exercise. *See, e.g., San Jose Christian College v. City of Morgan Hill* (2004) 360 F. 3d 1024, in which a city's denial of a religious college's application to rezone property from hospital use to a place of religious education did not impose a substantial burden on the exercise of religion.

SUBDIVISIONS

Overview. Dividing land for sale, lease, or financing is regulated by local ordinances based on the Subdivision Map Act (Gov't Code § 66410 *et seq.*). The Act's main goals are to encourage orderly development, ensure areas dedicated for public purposes will be properly improved, and protect public and land purchasers from fraud. The Act is implemented through local governments adopting a local subdivision ordinance. The local subdivision ordinance, together with the general plan and zoning, governs a subdivision's design, lot size, and infrastructure such as streets, water service, sewer service, and drainage facilities.

Dividing land for sale, lease, or financing is regulated by local ordinances based on the Subdivision Map Act.

Certain property divisions are exempt from the Subdivision Map Act. These include lot line adjustments, granny or second units, conveyance to or from public agencies, and condominium conversions. Gov't Code § 66412.

Typically, cities and counties impose conditions—fees or exactions—on a subdivision to meet increased public services demands caused by the subdivision's future residents. The fees or exactions are subject to constitutional and statutory limits, discussed later in this chapter. Two basic types of subdivisions exist. A parcel map is limited (with some exceptions) to divisions resulting in fewer than five lots. A subdivision map, also called a tract map, applies to subdivisions resulting in five or more lots. Gov't Code § 66426. Lot line adjustments between four or fewer existing parcels are exempt from the requirement to prepare a subdivision map. Gov't Code § 66412(d).

Subdivision processing. A city or county first approves a tentative tract map (for subdivisions of five lots or greater) after ensuring it meets the requirements of the local general plan, zoning ordinance, and subdivision ordinance, and after holding a public hearing. The applicant then typically has two years to install required infrastructure or post a bond as security, following which the city or county approves a final subdivision map, which allows the subdivision to be recorded. Gov't Code § 66424.5 *et seq.*

The Subdivision Map Act has detailed time limits for approval or denial of a tentative map application. Gov't Code §§ 66452.1, 66452.2. Also, subdivision approvals are administrative approvals that are subject to application procedures and time limits established by the Permit Streamlining Act (Gov't Code § 65920 *et seq.*). The Act's requirements are reviewed later in this chapter.

Approval of a parcel map or final map does not confer a vested right to develop. A vested right to develop occurs when actual building occurs or permits for buildings have been granted, and substantial work was performed in reliance on those permits. *Avco Community Developers, Inc. v. South Coast Regional Commission* (1976) 17 Cal. 3d 785. In 1986, the Legislature created a new form of tentative map, called the vesting tentative map, that generally confers a vested right to develop in substantial compliance with those land use polices and regulations that were in effect at the time the subdivision application is completed. Gov't Code § 66498.1 *et seq.*

A subdivision map must be disapproved if the city or county finds that its design or proposed improvements are likely to cause substantial environmental damage or are substantially and avoidably likely to injure fish, wildlife, or their habitat. Gov't Code § 66474(e). However, even if significant environmental impacts cannot be mitigated, a city or county may approve a subdivision map if it makes the appropriate CEQA findings that mitigation is infeasible. Gov't Code § 66474.01.

Enforcement. The Subdivision Map Act prohibits the sale, lease, or financing of parcels for which a subdivision map is required. Grantees or buyers may void land transactions within one year of discovering a violation of the Act. A city or county may enforce the Subdivision Map Act through seeking an injunction against a violation, or by withholding permits and approvals needed to develop a property divided in violation of the Act. Gov't Code § 66499.31 *et seq.*

REDEVELOPMENT AGENCIES AND EMINENT DOMAIN

For many decades, redevelopment agencies in California implemented redevelopment plans under the Community Redevelopment Law (Health & Safety Code § 330000 *et seq.*) using tax increment financing to promote redevelopment in blighted areas. In 2011, responding to budget pressures and reported abuses of the redevelopment process, the Legislature passed one bill that dissolved redevelopment agencies and another establishing a process for redevelopment agencies to avoid dissolution by making annual payments to local school districts, thereby offsetting much of the fiscal impact of redevelopment on the state budget (ABX1 26 and ABX1 27, Chapters 5 and 6, Statutes of 2011). In response to a legal challenge, the Supreme Court upheld the Legislature's authority to dissolve redevelopment agencies, but found the option of making payments to school districts to be unconstitutional; the decision thus effectively caused the dissolution of all redevelopment agencies in the state. *California Redevelopment Association v. Matosantos* (2011) 53 Cal. 4th 231.

Watts Re:imagined was created in 2011 after the demise of the Los Angeles Community Redevelopment Agency to help to build sustainable development projects that already have the support of local government and the community.

Each redevelopment agency has been replaced with a "successor agency" designated by the city or county whose main role is to wind down the affairs of the former redevelopment agency. A city is not required to take on a dissolved city redevelopment agency's obligations to provide affordable housing. *Macy v. City of Fontana* (2016) 244 Cal. App. 4th 1421.

Redevelopment plans were often implemented using the power of eminent domain, in which the redevelopment agency takes private property for a public use and pays the landowner just compensation. The use of eminent domain for redevelopment became controversial nationally after the Supreme Court decision in *Kelo v. City of New London* (2005) 545 U.S. 469, in which the court upheld a Connecticut city's use of eminent domain to acquire 15 homes in order for a private developer to build a commercial development.

PSA = Permit Streamlining Act

The *Kelo* decision did not fundamentally change the law in California, which generally permitted the use of eminent domain for economic development only if it is for the removal of blight. The use of eminent domain for redevelopment in California was further limited by a series of laws enacted in 2006 and following years.

PERMIT STREAMLINING ACT

PURPOSE AND APPLICABILITY

The Permit Streamlining Act (PSA, Gov't Code § 65920 *et seq.*) was passed by the California Legislature in 1977. It is intended to streamline the numerous requirements related to development projects and to expedite decisions related to such projects. The PSA requires all public agencies to follow uniform time limits and procedures for approving development projects. Although the PSA is reviewed in this chapter because it is most often encountered in local land use decisionmaking, it also applies to state agency approvals of development projects.

The PSA is intended to streamline the numerous requirements related to development projects and to expedite decisions related to such projects.

Development projects subject to the PSA include those projects requiring the issuance of "quasi-judicial" environmental and land use permits. Development projects do not include ministerial projects (non-discretionary projects requiring little judgment by the decisionmaker) such as building permits, nor do they include legislative acts such as rezoning or general plan amendments. Gov't Code § 65928.

REVIEW OF PERMIT APPLICATIONS FOR COMPLETENESS

Under the PSA, public agencies must compile one or more lists detailing the information required from any applicant for a development project. However, accepting an application as complete does not limit the permitting agency's authority to require the applicant to submit additional information for environmental evaluation of the project under CEQA. 14 Cal. Code Regs. § 15060.

Once an applicant submits an application for a development project, public agencies have 30 days to determine in writing whether the application is complete enough for processing. If the agency fails to notify the applicant of the application's completeness or incompleteness within the 30-day review period, the application is automatically deemed complete. Gov't Code § 65943.

If the agency determines that an application is incomplete, the applicant may resubmit the application. If the application is again determined incomplete, the

ND = Negative Declaration

EIR = Environmental Impact Report

applicant may appeal the decision, in which case the agency must issue a final written determination within 60 days. Again, failure to notify the applicant within this time frame constitutes acceptance of the application. Gov't Code § 65943.

TIME LIMITS FOR CEQA DOCUMENTS AND PROJECT APPROVALS

PSA time limitations are closely integrated with CEQA time limitations. Once an application is accepted as complete, the following time limits apply:

- CEQA documents (14 Cal. Code Regs. § 15100 *et seq.*):
  - 30 days from application acceptance as complete: lead agency must decide whether to prepare Negative Declaration (ND) or Environmental Impact Report (EIR)
  - 45 days from decision to prepare ND or EIR: lead agency must execute consultant contract (this time limit is seldom enforced)
  - 180 days from application acceptance as complete: lead agency must complete ND
  - One year from application acceptance as complete: lead agency must certify EIR
- Project approval (Gov't Code § 65950 *et seq.*):
  - Lead agency must approve project within 60 days after an exemption decision or adoption of an ND
  - Lead agency must approve project within six months after EIR certification
  - Responsible agency must approve project within 180 days after responsible agency accepts application as complete, or after lead agency decision, whichever is later

The PSA allows for a one-time limited extension of most of these time limits with mutual consent of the project applicant and permitting agency.

The PSA allows for a one-time limited extension of most of these time limits with mutual consent of the project applicant and permitting agency. Gov't Code § 65957. The PSA disallows any other extensions or waivers of time limits.

A seldom-used provision of the PSA states that a project may be deemed approved if the permitting agency fails to act within the time limits for project approval, provided public notice requirements have been met. Gov't Code § 65956. The deemed approved provisions do not apply to administrative permits when they are combined with applications for legislative changes, and they do not apply to approval of EIRs. *Land Waste Management v. Board of Supervisors* (1990) 222 Cal. App. 3d 950.

TAKINGS, EXACTIONS, AND DEVELOPMENT AGREEMENTS

TAKINGS

Overly restrictive land use regulations may be considered a "taking" of property without just compensation, which is prohibited by the Fifth Amendment to the U.S.

Constitution. The prohibition against takings applies not just to physical appropriation of land by the government, but also to land use or environmental regulations that are so severe their results are nearly the same as direct appropriation (i.e., regulatory takings).

To bring a takings claim in court, a property owner must first receive a "final determination" from the regulatory agency (unless there is a "facial challenge" to a statute or ordinance), and also exhaust administrative remedies. To bring a takings claim in federal court, a property owner must first seek compensation under state procedures, if available.

The U.S. and California Supreme Courts have evolved their interpretations of regulatory takings in a long and convoluted series of cases. A land use regulation is considered a "categorical taking" if it deprives the property owner of all economically viable use of the property. *Lucas v. South Carolina Coastal Council* (1992) 505 U.S. 1003. If the regulation is not a categorical taking, then courts typically employ a three-part balancing test, considering the economic impact on the property owner, whether there was interference with "investment-backed expectations," and the character of the government action (e.g., does it prevent public harm or provide broad public benefit?). *Penn Central Transportation Company v. City of New York* (1978) 438 U.S. 104; *Lingle v. Chevron USA* (2005) 544 U.S. 528.

Landowner remedies for regulatory takings include both money damages and invalidation of the unconstitutional regulation. Once a court determines that a regulatory taking has occurred, the city or county may be liable for temporary taking during the period that the regulation was in effect. *See First English Lutheran Church of Glendale v. Los Angeles County* (1987) 482 U.S. 304.

EXACTIONS AND FEES

A different line of takings cases applies to exactions and fees, which under a "heightened scrutiny" standard of review must have a nexus to the impacts of a project and be roughly proportional to those impacts. An exaction is a local government requirement to dedicate land or pay fees as a condition of development approval or construction. Exactions are designed to mitigate the impacts of a project's population and employment growth on public services and facilities. The general police power authorizes local governments to impose exactions, but overly restrictive exactions may be challenged as a regulatory taking. The nexus and rough proportionality standards apply not only to exactions involving land dedication, but also to the discretionary exaction of project-specific development fees. *See Ehrlich v. City of Culver City* (1996) 12 Cal. 4th 854.

A different line of takings cases applies to exactions and fees, which under a "heightened scrutiny" standard of review must have a nexus to the impacts of a project and be roughly proportional to those impacts.

Nollan v. California Coastal Commission (1987) 483 U.S. 825 established the nexus requirement. In that case, the Supreme Court found a regulatory taking when the Coastal Commission imposed a condition on a permit requiring the landowner's dedication of a lateral public access easement across a property's beachfront when allowing demolition and reconstruction of an existing house; a nexus did not exist between the impacts of the project and the requirement for demolition and reconstruction. *Dolan v. City of Tigard* (1994) 512 U.S. 374, established the rough proportionality requirement. In that case, the Supreme Court found a regulatory taking when a city imposed a condition on a permit allowing redevelopment of a commercial property but requiring dedication of a floodway and bicycle path; the impacts of the project alone did not justify the dedication of floodway and bicycle path facilities serving regional needs.

The *Nollan/Dolan* heightened scrutiny standard of review applies only to ad hoc exactions and fees individually imposed as a condition of development approval. It applies even if the regulatory agency denies or threatens to deny development approval because the applicant refuses to comply with the condition. *Koontz v. St. Johns River Water Management District* (2013) 530 U.S. 2588. However, the *Nollan/Dolan* standard does not apply to legislatively determined exactions or fees, e.g., those imposed through a generally applicable ordinance. In these cases, courts use the deferential "reasonable relationship to the public welfare" standard of review for a valid exercise of the police power. *Ehrlich v. City of Culver City* (1996) 12 Cal. 4th 854.

Inclusionary housing programs have sometimes been challenged as regulatory takings. However, in *California Building Industry Association v. San Jose* (2015, 61 Cal. 4th 435), the Supreme Court ruled that an inclusionary housing ordinance condition requiring 15 percent of units to be affordable was not a taking. Rather, it was an example of permissible land use regulation under the police power.

The Mitigation Fee Act requires local agencies imposing impact fees to identify the purpose of the fee and how it will be used, and show a reasonable relationship between the purpose and amount of the fee and the proposed project's impact on public facilities.

In California, the Mitigation Fee Act (Gov't Code § 66000) regulates local government imposition of impact fees. Among other things, it requires local agencies imposing impact fees to identify the purpose of the fee and how it will be used, and show a reasonable relationship between the purpose and amount of the fee and the proposed project's impact on public facilities. The Mitigation Fee Act does not apply to development agreements (*see* below).

Also, special statutory limitations apply to the imposition of school impact fees. SB 50 of 1998, Gov't Code § 65995. Under this legislation, statutory caps are placed on the amount of school fees that a school district can impose on new residential development.

In addition to the above limitations, Proposition 26 of 2010 imposed requirements for two-thirds voter approval of "regulatory fees" as taxes. The initiative applies only to new regulatory fees, and government has the burden of proof to show a levy is not tax. Voter approval is, however, not required for conditions of property development such as development impact fees.

DEVELOPMENT AGREEMENTS

If land use regulations change following project approval, a developer has no vested right to develop land for the approved use until the developer has obtained a building permit and performed substantial work in reliance on the permit. *Avco Community Developers, Inc. v. South Coast Regional Commission* (1976) 17 Cal. 3d 785. Development agreement legislation (Gov't Code § 65864 *et seq.*) is designed to give developers greater certainty against changes following project approval that might interfere with a property's development.

CEQA = California Environmental Quality Act

Under this legislation, a local government may enter into development agreements that freeze land use regulations applicable to a project and provide guidance for issuance of future project approvals. In return for this higher level of certainty, the local government can negotiate exactions higher than those allowed under the Mitigation Fee Act, as well as commitments for public facility and infrastructure financing.

Development agreements have survived legal challenges alleging that they amount to a "contracting away of the police power." *Santa Margarita Area Residents Together v. San Luis Obispo County* (2000 84 Cal. App. 4th 221). Development agreements must be consistent with the applicable general plan and zoning ordinance.

INITIATIVES AND REFERENDA

The voters of cities and counties may enact zoning ordinances and similar land use regulations under their initiative power, and via referendum they may approve or reject land use legislative acts that are approved by a legislative body. Initiatives and referenda are subject to a number of limitations, however. They cannot conflict with state law (e.g., housing element law), they must be a proper exercise of the police power, they must be consistent with the general plan, and they must be a legislative not administrative act. For example, in *Lesher Communications Inc. v. City of Walnut Creek* (1990) 52 Cal. 3d 531, the court found a traffic-based growth management initiative invalid because it was a land use regulation rather than a legislative act, and because it was inconsistent with the City's General Plan.

The voters of cities and counties may enact zoning ordinances and similar land use regulations under their initiative power, and via referendum they may approve or reject land use legislative acts that are approved by a legislative body.

So-called "ballot box zoning" has been criticized by many commentators, in part because it is not subject to CEQA review. Adoption of land use legislation proposed by the electorate through the initiative process is not a project subject to CEQA, regardless of whether the measure is placed on the ballot and approved by the voters, or is adopted by the local agency under initiative procedures described in the Election Code. *Tuolumne Jobs and Small Business Alliance v. Superior Court* (2014) 59 Cal. 4th 1029.

LOCAL AGENCY BOUNDARY CHANGES

Project applicants seeking to develop or provide services to their properties must sometimes seek to include their properties within city or special district boundaries. Such boundary changes require approval by the appropriate Local Agency Formation

LAFCO = Local Agency Formation Commission

SOI = sphere of influence

Commission (LAFCO). A LAFCO board consists of two county supervisors, two city council members, two special district members, and one at-large representative. In addition to annexations, other boundary changes approved by LAFCOs include detachment from a city or special district, incorporation of a city, or formation of a special district. OPR (2012) has issued a useful guidance document describing the relationships among LAFCOs, general plans, and annexations.

Many requirements governing LAFCOs can be found in the Local Government Reorganization Act of 2000 (Gov't Code § 56000 *et seq.*). LAFCOs implement state policies that encourage orderly development by limiting annexations to areas adjacent to existing agency boundaries and that can be served by existing or planned municipal services. A key planning tool used by LAFCOs is adoption of a sphere of influence (SOI), which is the physical boundary and service area that a local government is expected to ultimately serve. Gov't Code § 56076. The SOI requirement promotes orderly development and extension of public services. A change in a sphere of influence must be accompanied by a study called a municipal service review. Local general plans generally recognize SOI boundaries, although they are not required to do so.

In SB 244 of 2011 (Chapter 513, Statutes of 2011), the Legislature found that California has hundreds of disadvantaged unincorporated communities. Often these areas are geographically isolated islands surrounded by cities but lacking basic infrastructure. SB 244 requires LAFCOs to deny any application to annex to a city territory that is contiguous to a "disadvantaged unincorporated community" unless a second application is submitted to annex the disadvantaged community as well. It also requires LAFCOs to evaluate disadvantaged unincorporated communities in municipal service reviews. OPR (2013) has issued guidance on SB 244 compliance.

HISTORIC AND CULTURAL RESOURCES

Preservation of historic and cultural resources is governed by federal, state, and local laws and regulations.

NATIONAL HISTORIC PRESERVATION ACT

The National Historic Preservation Act protects National Register-listed historic properties.

The National Historic Preservation Act (54 U.S.C. § 470 *et seq.*) established the National Register of Historic Places, created the Advisory Council on Historic Preservation, and established the Section 106 consultation process. The Section 106 review process (36 C.F.R. § 800 *et seq.*) applies to federal agencies taking actions, including permitting and funding actions, that may affect National Register-listed or -eligible properties.

Federal agencies taking such actions are required to consult with the Advisory Council on Historic Preservation (ACHP), State Historic Preservation Officer (SHPO), local agencies, and Indian tribes, and avoid or mitigate adverse effects on National Register-listed or -eligible properties. For example, if the U.S. Army Corps of Engineers issues a Section 404 permit (*see* chapter 15) allowing filling of wetlands on a project site with historic significance, the Corps would need to initiate Section 106 consultation with the ACHP, SHPO, local agencies, and affected tribes.

ACHP = Advisory Council on Historic Preservation

SHPO = State Historic Preservation Officer

NAGPRA = Native American Graves Protection and Repatriation Act

OTHER FEDERAL LAWS

The following federal laws provide more direct protection to archeological sites:

- **Antiquities Act of 1906.** Regulates excavation of archeological sites and imposes penalties for removal or damage to archeological resources. 16 U.S.C. § 431 *et seq.*
- **Archeological Recovery Act.** Protects significant historical or archeological finds discovered during construction. 16 U.S.C. § 469 *et seq.*
- **Archeological Resources Protection Act.** Requires permits for excavation and removal of archeological resources on Native American or public lands. 16 U.S.C. § 670
- **Native American Graves Protection and Repatriation Act (NAGPRA).** This Act requires federal agencies and institutions that receive federal funding to return Native American human remains and other "cultural items" to lineal descendants and culturally affiliated Indian tribes. NAGPRA also establishes procedures for the inadvertent discovery or planned excavation of Native American cultural items on federal or tribal land
- **Section 4(f) of the Department of Transportation Act.** Prohibits the Department of Transportation from approving or funding a transportation project requiring the "use" of specified historic sites unless there is no prudent and feasible alternative, and the project includes all possible mitigation measures. 49 U.S.C. § 303

STATE LAWS

California has several laws affecting historic preservation. Pub. Res. Code § 5020 *et seq.* establishes the California Register of Historical Resources, which is to be used by local governments in their historic preservation efforts. The CEQA Guidelines (*see* chapter 2) set forth detailed procedures for determining whether impacts to "historical resources" are significant, and for mitigating significant impacts on historical resources. 14 Cal. Code Regs. §§ 15064.5, 15126.4(b). A "historical resource" under CEQA includes California Register-listed and -eligible properties, as well as locally designated historic resources. A project that causes a substantial adverse change to an historic resource creates a significant impact under CEQA, requiring mitigation when feasible. 14 Cal. Code Regs. § 15064(b).

A project that causes a substantial adverse change to an historic resource creates a significant impact under CEQA, requiring mitigation when feasible.

Under the Mills Act (Gov't Code § 50280 *et seq.*), participating local governments may enter into contracts with owners of historic properties listed on a federal, state or local register who actively participate in the restoration and

NAHC = California Native American Heritage Commission

maintenance of their historic properties. In return, property owners receive a property tax reduction.

The California Historical Landmarks Program registers sites, buildings, or features that have statewide historical, cultural, anthropological, or other significance. To be designated as an Historical Landmark by the Director of California State Parks, the resource must meet set criteria, be recommended for designation by the State Historical Resources Commission, and be approved by the property owner. Pub. Res. Code § 5020.4 *et seq*. Historical Landmarks may be eligible for property tax reduction under the Mills Act and are subject to the State Historical Building Code (Health & Safety Code § 18950 *et seq*.).

Also, as discussed previously, under SB 18 of 2004, cities and counties must consult with tribes prior to adopting or amending their general plans or specific plans. Further, AB 52 of 2014 (Chapter 532, Statutes of 2014) requires CEQA lead agencies to consult with tribes regarding impacts to "tribal cultural resources."

Regarding Native American remains, property owners must consult with the California Native American Heritage Commission (NAHC) and "most likely descendants" whenever Native American graves are found. Pub. Res. Code. § 5097.9. Also, if human remains are discovered during construction, the county coroner must be notified and must examine the remains before construction proceeds; if the coroner determines the remains are those of a Native American, the coroner must contact the NAHC by telephone within 24 hours. Health & Safety Code § 7050.5.

LOCAL LAWS

Local governments have authority under their general police power to protect historic properties. Cities and counties are authorized to place conditions on development approvals to protect historic and aesthetic values. Gov't Code §§ 25373, 37361. Typically, local governments establish a historic preservation zone or district and require property owners to seek approval before changing affected properties. Local preservation commissions often are used to administer local historic preservation regulations.

Cities and counties are authorized to place conditions on development approvals to protect historic and aesthetic values.

GROWTH MANAGEMENT AND SUSTAINABLE DEVELOPMENT

Growth management refers to local government use of a variety of measures to influence the amount, type, and location of growth. Growth management measures are often undertaken to achieve "smart growth" sustainability objectives in order to limit urban sprawl.

Growth can be managed by using the basic regulatory tools described earlier in this chapter, such as general plans, specific plans, zoning, and subdivision regulation. In addition, some local governments have imposed moratoria on growth to prevent overtaxing of public services and facilities, or created urban limit lines to control urban sprawl. Growth moratoria and urban limit lines can be imposed by voter initiative or be approved by voter referendum.

After enactment of California's climate change legislation (AB 32 of 2006, *see* chapter 20), growth management and sustainable development strategies received renewed interest by policymakers seeking to reduce greenhouse gas emissions caused by conventional development patterns. Examples of measures local governments have taken to promote sustainable development include:

- Preparation of an optional general plan sustainability element
- Revision of general plans to be consistent with regional Sustainable Communities Strategies prepared pursuant to SB 375 (*see* chapter 4)
- Preparation and implementation of local Climate Action Plans (*see* chapter 20)
- Providing CEQA streamlining for infill projects (*see* chapter 2)
- Revision of land use regulations to promote renewable energy development (*see* sidebar)

Also, AB 2722 of 2016 (Chapter 371, Statutes of 2016) established a new Strategic Growth Council (SGC) grant program for "transformative climate communities." The SGC will be awarding competitive grants for the development and implementation of neighborhood-level "transformative climate community plans" that include greenhouse gas reduction projects that benefit disadvantaged communities.

ENFORCEMENT

VIOLATION OF LOCAL LAND USE REGULATIONS

In general, cities and counties have a variety of administrative and judicial remedies available when an applicant fails to comply with a permit condition or violates a local land use ordinance. Administrative procedures include infraction or citation processes. The most common judicial remedy sought is a judicial order requiring the applicant to comply with the permit condition or ordinance.

For example, the City of Oakland zoning ordinance has the following enforcement provisions (Oakland Municipal Code § 17.152)

- **Infractions.** Any violation of the zoning regulations is an infraction, with separate infractions for each day of violation.
- **Public nuisance.** In addition, any violation of the zoning regulations is a public nuisance and may be abated as such by the city.
- **Injunction.** Any violation of the zoning is declared to be contrary to the public interest and, at the city's discretion, creates a cause of action for injunctive relief.

Removing Local Barriers to Renewable Energy Development

Many local agencies have revised their land use regulations to remove barriers to renewable energy development, often in response to state legislation. Pertinent state legislation includes:

- Limits on local permitting restrictions for wind systems outside urbanized areas (Gov't Code § 65896)
- Subdivision Map Act exemptions for solar energy projects (Gov't Code § 66412 *et seq.*)
- Limitations on local agency grounds for denying a solar project use permit, and creation of a streamlined permitting process for small solar projects (Gov't Code § 65850.5)
- CEQA exemption for solar energy projects located on rooftops over existing parking lots (Pub. Res. Code § 21080.35)
- Limits on the fees local agencies can charge for solar photovoltaic (PV) project permits (Gov't Code § 66015)

OPR (2015) has issued a Solar Permitting Guide explaining the laws governing local regulation of solar projects, and providing guidance on expedited permitting for small solar PV projects and solar water heaters.

- **Penalties.** An infraction is punishable to the maximum permitted under state law. Any violation beyond the third conviction may be prosecuted as a misdemeanor, also punishable by a fine or imprisonment to the maximum permitted under state law.
- **Liability for expenses.** In addition to the above, a violator is liable for costs and expenses incurred by the city in correction, abatement, and prosecution of the violation.

JUDICIAL CHALLENGES TO LOCAL LAND USE DECISIONS

For challenges to local land use decisions, petitioners file a writ of mandate in a "mandamus proceeding."

For challenges to local land use decisions, petitioners file a writ of mandate in a "mandamus proceeding." (CEQA cases are also mandamus proceedings—*see* chapter 2.) The writ states the petitioner's claimed bases of relief, and seeks an order directing the respondent agency to implement the remedy sought. Typically, the relief sought is for the court to vacate the local agency decision, and order the agency to take the steps necessary to comply with the law.

for more information...

Abbott, W. W. et al, 2012 (with 2014 Update). Exactions and Impact Fees in California. Solano Press. Point Arena, Calif.

Barclay, C. T. and M. S. Gray, 2016. California Land Use and Planning Law. 35th Edition. Solano Press. Point Arena, Calif.

California Department of Housing and Community Development, 2012. Housing Element Update Guidance.

California Department of Water Resources, 2010 with 2014 Addendum. Implementing California Flood Legislation into Local Land Use Planning: A Handbook for Local Communities.

California Department of Water Resources, 2014. Guidance on General Plan Amendments for Addressing Flood Risk.

Early, D, 2015. The General Plan in California. Solano Press. Point Arena, Calif.

Fulton, W.E. and P. Shigley, 2012. Guide to California Planning. 4th Edition. Solano Press. Point Arena, Calif.

Governor's Office of Planning and Research, 2001. The Planner's Guide to Specific Plans.

Governor's Office of Planning and Research, 2005. Tribal Consultation Guidelines.

Governor's Office of Planning and Research, 2012. LAFCOs, General Plans, and City Annexations.

Governor's Office of Planning and Research, 2013. Senate Bill 244: Land Use, General Plans, and Disadvantaged Communities Technical Advisory.

Governor's Office of Planning and Research, 2015. California Solar Permitting Guidebook: Improving Permit Review and Approval for Small Solar Systems.

Governor's Office of Planning and Research, 2017. General Plan Guidelines.

Manaster, K. A. and D. P. Selmi (eds.). ND. Chapters 60–65, 71, 73, 74, and 75 of California Environmental Law and Land Use Practice. Matthew Bender. San Francisco, Calif.

Rypinski, R. G. and A. Sozio, 2015. Eminent Domain. Solano Press. Point Arena, Calif.

glossary

Affordable housing—housing capable of being purchased or rented by a household with very low, low, or moderate income.

Annexation—incorporating land into an existing city or special district.

Blight—physical and economic conditions within an area that causes a reduction of, or lack of, proper utilization of that area.

California Register of Historical Resources—includes buildings, sites, structures, objects and districts significant in the architectural, engineering, scientific, economic, agricultural, educational, social, political, military, or cultural annals of California

Charter city—a city that has been incorporated under its own charter rather than under the general laws of the state.

Conditional use permit*—pursuant to a zoning ordinance, this permit authorizes uses not routinely allowed on a particular site.

Dedication*—offering by an applicant, and acceptance by the government, of private land for public use, typically imposed as a condition of development approval.

Density bonus—permission to increase a project's housing density, typically in return for production of low income housing units.

Development agreement*—a legally binding agreement between a city or county and a developer that typically prevents future changes in land use regulations from affecting a given project, in return for developer concessions.

Easement—the right to use property owned by another for specific purposes.

Eminent domain—the taking of private property by a government unit for public use.

Exaction*—land dedication or impact fee required as a condition of development approval or construction.

Final subdivision map*—map of an approved subdivision filed in the county recorder's office.

General law city—a city incorporated under the general laws of the state.

General plan—a statement of development policies, including diagrams and text, setting forth objectives, principles, standards, and plan proposals, for the future development of a city or county.

Growth management—local government use of a variety of measures to influence the amount, type, and location of growth.

Impact fee*—also known as a development fee, a monetary exaction to defray costs of public facilities related to a development project.

Inclusionary zoning—zoning programs that promote affordable housing, e.g., through requiring housing project set-asides for low-income households.

Initiative—a legislative measure that has been placed on the election ballot as a result of voter signatures.

Local agency formation commission—a countywide commission that reviews and approves city and special district boundary changes.

National Register of Historic Places—historic properties meeting eligibility criteria established by the Advisory Council on Historic Preservation.

Nexus—for purposes of this chapter, a reasonable relationship between a land use regulation and the impacts of a proposed action.

Nonconforming use—land use that was lawful before a zoning ordinance was adopted, but does not conform to the new zoning ordinance.

Overlay zone—a set of zoning requirements that is superimposed on a base zone, e.g., an historic preservation district.

Planned unit development*—a master-planned development within a zoning district that allows multiple uses (e.g., residential, commercial, industrial).

Police power—the power of state and local governments to enact legislation to protect public health, safety, and welfare.

Quasi-judicial decision—a quasi-judicial decision is one that applies policy based on factual determinations, rather than sets policy.

Redevelopment—the legally authorized process of rehabilitating or rebuilding a deteriorated section of a city.

Referendum—a ballot measure challenging a legislative action of a city or county.

Smart growth—closely related to new urbanism, a planning doctrine that discourages urban sprawl and emphasizes compact, transit-accessible, pedestrian-oriented, mixed use development patterns, and land reuse.

Specific plan*—a plan addressing land use distribution, open space availability, and infrastructure for a portion of a community.

Sphere of influence—the physical boundary and service area that a local government is expected to ultimately serve, as adopted by the LAFCO.

Subdivision—the process of dividing a larger parcel of land into smaller lots.

Taking—the appropriation by government of private land for public use, requiring just compensation under the U.S. Constitution.

Tentative subdivision map*—a map illustrating a subdivision proposal. A subdivision is complete only when conditions imposed on the tentative map have been satisfied and a final map has been certified and recorded.

Variance*—a limited waiver from the property development standards of a zoning ordinance.

Vested right—a right to develop that cannot be changed by subsequent changes in regulations.

Zoning*—a local code dividing a city or county into land use zones and specifying allowable uses in each zone.

* equals permit or approval

CHAPTER 4

State and Regional Land Use Policies

related Solano Press titles

California Land Use and Planning Law. 35th Edition. Cecily Talbert Barclay and Matthew S. Gray. 2016.

Guide to California Planning. William E. Fulton and Paul Shigley. 4th Edition. 2012.

in this chapter...

OPR = Governor's Office of Planning and Research

EGPR = Environmental Goals and Policy Report

INTRODUCTION

State and regional land use policies play an important role in California environmental protection and regulation. Although the Legislature has left land use planning and regulation largely in the control of cities and counties, over time it has adopted some comprehensive planning policies, as well as individual land use programs for sensitive areas (e.g., the coastal zone or natural hazard areas) or special project types (e.g., electrical energy facilities, medical marijuana facilities). In addition, regional planning agencies have important planning responsibilities, especially after passage of SB 375. This chapter reviews California's most important state and regional land use planning and regulatory programs.

STATE COMPREHENSIVE PLANNING

SENATE BILL 857

SB 857 of 2002 (Chapter 1016, Statutes of 2002) established the following comprehensive state planning priorities:

- To promote infill development and equity
- To protect environmental and agricultural resources
- To encourage efficient development patterns

These planning priorities are to be implemented in state agency functional plans and in the Governor's Environmental Goals and Policy Report (EGPR) (*see* below).

ENVIRONMENTAL GOALS AND POLICY REPORT

AB 2070 of 1970 (Chapter 1534, Statutes of 1970), which created the Governor's Office of Planning and Research (OPR), also called for OPR to prepare and maintain an Environmental Goals and Policy Report. The EGPR views California through a 20–30 year perspective and provides a statement of environmental goals and objectives for the state. Goals and objectives focus on land use, population growth and distribution, conservation of natural resources, and air and water quality.

"A Strategy for California @ 50 Million" considers the state's future in the context of a changing climate and a projected population of 50 million residents by 2050.

The EGPR also must include a statement of programs and policies required to implement the state's environmental goals. Few EGPRs have been prepared. The first EGPR, "An Urban Strategy for California," was adopted in 1978, and many of its goals and policies remain relevant. An updated EGPR was released in 2015 (OPR 2015). Titled "A Strategy for California @ 50 Million," the report considers the state's future in the context of a changing climate and a projected population of 50 million residents by 2050. The report provides a vision of the state's future and an overview of the state's programs and policies to achieve that vision. It establishes the following development goals:

- Reduce land consumed for development 50 percent relative to today's trend by 2050

- Reduce vehicle miles traveled per capita at least 15 percent by 2020 and 25 percent by 2040
- Prioritize the conservation of high-quality agricultural land, including rangelands

SGC = Strategic Growth Council

GHG = greenhouse gas

CZMA = Coastal Zone Management Act

NOAA = National Oceanic and Atmospheric Administration

STRATEGIC GROWTH COUNCIL

The Legislature established the SGC in 2008 (SB 732, Chapter 729, Statutes of 2008). The SGC is a cabinet-level committee that is tasked with coordinating the activities of state agencies to:

- Improve air and water quality
- Protect natural resource and agriculture lands
- Increase the availability of affordable housing
- Improve infrastructure systems
- Promote public health
- Assist state and local entities in the planning of sustainable communities and meeting AB 32 goals

The SGC plays a major role in California land use and environmental policy through its grant programs. Its historic source of grant funding, Proposition 84 of 2008, has been fully awarded. As a result of this funding, more than 250 "Sustainable Communities Planning" and "Urban Greening" projects authorized by SB 732 are completed or underway.

As a result of Proposition 84, more than 250 "Sustainable Communities Planning" and "Urban Greening" projects authorized by SB 732 are completed or underway.

The SGC implements the Affordable Housing and Sustainable Communities Program, funded by AB 32 cap-and-trade revenues established by SB 857 of 204 (Chapter 31, Statutes of 2014) (*see* chapter 20). This program funds implementation of projects that are consistent with the state planning priorities and that are included in regional plans to reduce greenhouse gas (GHG) emissions, in particular Sustainable Communities Strategies (discussed later in this chapter). By statute (Gov't Code § 75200 *et seq.*), at least 50 percent of available funds are to be directed to affordable housing and as least 50 percent of available funds must benefit disadvantaged communities. SGC 2014.

COASTAL ZONE MANAGEMENT

KEY LAWS AND AGENCIES

Coastal Zone Management Act. The key federal coastal zone law is the CZMA of 1972 (16 U.S.C. § 1451 *et seq.*). Administered by the National Oceanic and Atmospheric Administration (NOAA), the CZMA's basic purpose is to preserve coastal zones, consisting of coastal waters and adjacent coastal lands. The CZMA established a grant program to help states develop coastal programs consistent with the CZMA; NOAA must approve these programs.

ESHA = Environmentally Sensitive Habitat Area

LCP = local coastal program

CEQA = California Environmental Quality Act

California Coastal Act. California's coastal zone management started with voter approval of the 1972 Coastal Initiative, which adopted the California Coastal Zone Conservation Act of 1972. This law was superseded by the California Coastal Act of 1976. Pub. Res. Code § 30000 *et seq*. The Coastal Act defines statewide planning and management policies for the zone and establishes planning and permit programs to implement these policies. Statewide policies cover:

- Expanding public access to the coast
- Increasing coastal recreation opportunities
- Protecting the marine environment
- Protecting Environmentally Sensitive Habitat Areas and agricultural land
- Implementing standards for coastal development related to location, scenic and visual qualities, public access, and minimizing adverse effects
- Implementing standards for industrial facilities such as energy facilities

The Coastal Act empowers the Coastal Commission to protect the marine environment.

Under the Coastal Act, Environmentally Sensitive Habitat Areas (ESHAs) designated by the Coastal Commission receive special protection. ESHAs are areas in which or animal life or habitats are rare or especially valuable and could be easily distributed or degraded. Pub. Res. Code § 30007.5. ESHAs must be protected against any significant disruption of habitat values. Pub. Res. Code § 30240.

Regulation under the Coastal Act is limited to the coastal zone defined as extending seaward to the state's outer limit of jurisdiction (three miles) and inland to boundaries designated by the Legislature. Pub. Res. Code § 30103. For important natural resource areas, inland boundaries extend to the first major ridgeline or five miles from the mean high tide line, whichever is less. In developed areas, the coastal zone is much narrower, sometimes just a few blocks.

California Coastal Commission. The California Coastal Commission administers the Coastal Act and has responsibility for certifying local coastal programs and for issuing and enforcing coastal development permits. It also implements a public coastal access program. The California Coastal Commission has issued detailed regulations for Coastal Act administration. 14 Cal. Code Regs. § 13001 *et seq*.

State Coastal Conservancy. The State Coastal Conservancy is responsible for land acquisition and restoration, consistent with Coastal Act policies. Pub. Res. Code § 31100. Coastal Conservancy programs include construction of trails and other public access facilities, restoration and enhancement of wetlands and other wildlife habitat, restoration of public piers and urban waterfronts, and farmland preservation.

LOCAL COASTAL PROGRAMS

The Coastal Act gives the 76 cities and counties with land in the coastal zone the responsibility of preparing local coastal programs (LCPs) consistent with Coastal Act policies. LCPs consist of a land use plan and an implementation plan, including

EIR = Environmental Impact Report

zoning ordinances. Pub. Res. Code §§ 30108.4, 30108.5. LCP adoption is exempt from the California Environmental Quality Act (CEQA). Pub. Res. Code § 21080.9. However, local governments usually prepare CEQA documents when adopting LCPs because they usually make other discretionary decisions, such as general plan and zoning ordinance amendments, that are subject to CEQA.

The Act also requires certain ports (Hueneme, Long Beach, Los Angeles and San Diego) to prepare comprehensive port master plans consistent with Coastal Act policies, including policies in the Act that encourage port development. Pub. Res. Code § 30515 *et seq.* Local governments and ports can amend LCPs and port master plans by following the same procedures as when originally adopted. The Coastal Commission must certify or refuse certification of proposed LCP amendments, but may not approve amendments changing land use policies and development standards over the objections of the coastal city responsible for the LCP. *City of Malibu v. California Coastal Commission* (2012) 206 Cal. App. 4th 549.

The Coastal Commission is responsible for certifying both LCPs and port master plans as being consistent with Coastal Act policies. Pub. Res. Code § 30511 *et seq.* LCP certification is subject to CEQA, but also is a certified regulatory program. This means that LCP certification is exempt from CEQA's requirement to prepare a Negative Declaration or an Environmental Impact Report (EIR), but not exempt from CEQA's policy directives, e.g., to mitigate significant impacts when feasible (*see* chapter 2).

Many of the 76 coastal cities and counties have elected to divide their coastal zone jurisdictions into separate geographic segments, resulting in some 126 separate LCP segments. According to a California Coastal Commission website (www.coastal.ca.gov/lcps.html), as of 2014, approximately 73 percent of the LCP segments have been effectively certified, representing about 87 percent of the geographic area of the coastal zone.

COASTAL DEVELOPMENT PERMITS

Coastal development permits are required for the following types of activities in the coastal zone (Pub. Res. Code § 30106):

- Placement of any solid material or structure
- Change in land use density or intensity (including any land division)
- Change in the intensity of water use or access to water
- Removal of major vegetation

The Coastal Act gives local governments the responsibility of issuing coastal development permits for developments that are consistent with LCPs. Pub. Res. Code § 30600 *et seq.* Coastal development permits are not required for local nuisance abatement actions. Pub. Res. Code § 30005(b). For those areas without a certified LCP, the Coastal Commission is responsible for issuing coastal development

The Coastal Act gives local governments the responsibility of issuing coastal development permits for developments that are consistent with LCPs.

permits. In addition, the Coastal Commission retains primary permitting authority for issuing coastal development permits for certain project types: those located on tidelands, submerged lands, or public trust lands; major public works projects; and major energy facilities. Pub. Res. Code § 30519(b). The Coastal Commission imposes several standard conditions on permits, and project-specific special conditions as well. Special conditions can include mitigation fees. *Ocean Harbor House Homeowners Assn. v. California Coastal Commission* (2008) 163 Cal. App. 4th 215.

Coastal development permits are subject to the time limitations established by the Permit Streamlining Act (*see* chapter 2) and require CEQA compliance. The Coastal Act sets forth special procedures for processing emergency permits and small projects such as single-family dwellings. Pub. Res. Code §§ 30604(c), 30624(a). Certain activities, such as minor improvements to single-family residences, are exempt from permit requirements. Pub. Res. Code § 30610(a).

Local coastal development permits can be appealed administratively to the California Coastal Commission. Pub. Res. Code § 30603(a) *et seq*. The grounds for appeal are limited to whether the development conforms to certified LCP standards and to Coastal Act access policies. Pub. Res. Code §§ 30603(b), 30210 *et seq*.

Also, permit decisions by the Coastal Commission, local governments, and ports are judicially reviewable. Coastal development permits are subject to the same constitutional limitations (e.g., limitations on regulatory takings) that apply to other local land use policies, as described in chapter 3. Coastal development permits may not be granted or denied in a manner that will take or damage private property for public use, without just compensation. Pub. Res. Code § 30010.

SEA LEVEL RISE POLICY GUIDANCE

In 2015, the Coastal Commission adopted sea level rise policy guidance to guide the preparation of LCPs and coastal development permit applications.

In 2015, the Coastal Commission adopted sea level rise policy guidance to guide the preparation of LCPs and coastal development permit applications (California Coastal Commission 2015). The policy guidance addresses both protecting coastal development from the impacts of sea level rise, and considering whether sea level rise would worsen the impacts of coastal development on resources such as public access and coastal habitat. *See* sidebar.

FEDERAL AGENCY CONSISTENCY

Under the CZMA, federal agencies conducting or supporting activities or development projects directly affecting the coastal zone must ensure that their activities and projects are consistent with the approved state coastal program. Also, applicants for federal licenses or permits must certify in their applications that their proposed activity complies with and will be carried out consistent with the state coastal program. 16 U.S.C. § 1456(c); 15 C.F.R. § 930 *et seq*.

The Coastal Commission reviews the federal agency's consistency determination. If the Commission determines that the federal agency's action would not be consistent with the state's coastal program "to the maximum extent practicable," the Commission must describe alternative measures to allow the activity to be consistent. If the Commission and federal agency continue to disagree, the Secretary of Commerce may mediate the dispute, or as a last resort the state may sue in federal court to enjoin the federal activity. 15 C.F.R. § 930.42(a) *et seq.*

Special consistency requirements apply to applicants for offshore oil and gas leases under the Outer Continental Shelf Lands Act. 43 U.S.C. § 1331 *et seq.* The Coastal Act gives special recognition to the need for oil and gas (and other coastal dependent industrial) development; the Act allows these projects to be permitted even if inconsistent with certain Coastal Act policies, provided there are no feasible less damaging alternatives, and adverse environmental impacts are mitigated to the maximum extent feasible. Pub. Res. Code § 30260.

ENFORCEMENT

For violations of the Coastal Act, the Executive Director or Coastal Commission can issue cease-and-desist or restoration orders for activities undertaken without a required coastal development permit or in violation of an existing permit. The Coastal Commission generally cannot administratively order civil penalties. Rather, the Commission refers cases involving significant resource damage to the Attorney General for judicial enforcement. However, 2014 legislation enables the Commission to levy fines of up to $11,250 a day for violations of the Coastal Act public access policies. Pub. Res. Code § 30821. Violation of any provision of the Coastal Act can result

Coastal Commission Sea Level Rise Policy Guidance

The Coastal Commission 2015 sea level rise policy guidance provides detailed planning processes for addressing sea level rise in LCPs and coastal development permit applications. Major steps are summarized below.

Local Coastal Programs (LCPs)

- Step 1. Determine a range of sea level rise projections relevant to LCP planning area/segment using best-available science, which is currently the 2012 National Research Council (NRC) Report.*
- Step 2. Identify potential physical sea level rise impacts in the LCP planning area/segment, including inundation, storm flooding, wave impacts, erosion, and/or saltwater intrusion into freshwater resources.
- Step 3. Assess potential risks from sea level rise to coastal resources and development in the LCP planning area/segment, including those resources addressed in Chapter 3 of the Coastal Act.
- Step 4. Identify adaptation measures and LCP policy options to include in the new or updated LCP, including both general policies and ordinances that apply to all development exposed to sea level rise, and more targeted policies and land use changes to address specific risks in particular portions of the planning area.
- Step 5. Draft updated or new LCP for certification with California Coastal Commission, including the Land Use Plan and Implementing Ordinances.
- Step 6. Implement the LCP and monitor and re-evaluate strategies as needed to address new circumstances relevant to the area.

Coastal Development Permit Applications

- Step 1. Establish the projected sea level rise range for the proposed project's planning horizon using the best available science, which is currently the 2012 NRC Report.
- Step 2. Determine how physical impacts from sea level rise may constrain the project site, including erosion, structural and geologic stability, flooding, and inundation.
- Step 3. Determine how the project may impact coastal resources, considering the influence of future sea level rise upon the landscape as well as potential impacts of sea level rise adaptation strategies that may be used over the lifetime of the project.
- Step 4. Identify alternatives to avoid resource impacts and minimize risks throughout the expected life of the development.
- Step 5. Finalize project design and submit CDP application.

* National Research Council, 2012.

USACE = U.S. Army Corps of Engineers

FEMA = Federal Emergency Management Agency

NFIP = National Flood Insurance Program

DWR = California Department of Water Resources

in civil fines, for example, up to $15,000 per day for knowing and intentional violations. Pub. Res. Code § 30820 *et seq.*

Private parties can also maintain actions to restrain violations of the Coastal Act or to recover certain types of civil penalties for violations of the Coastal Act. Pub. Res. Code §§ 30803(a), 30805, 30822.

REGULATING REGIONAL NATURAL HAZARDS: FLOODPLAINS, EARTHQUAKES, AND FIRES

The local general plan safety element, and its implementing regulations, is the primary local government basis for protecting development against risks from flood, earthquakes, and fires.

The local general plan safety element, and its implementing regulations, is the primary local government basis for protecting development against risks from flood, earthquakes, and fires. Key state and federal programs that influence local hazard-protection requirements are described below.

FLOOD MANAGEMENT

Key laws and agencies. Many urban areas in California are located in historic floodplains. To reduce risks of loss of life and property, the federal and state governments have implemented a number of programs. Key agencies involved in flood control include:

- **U.S. Army Corps of Engineers (USACE).** Constructs and operates federal flood control projects
- **U.S. Bureau of Reclamation.** Operates several water resources projects that include flood control as a project purpose
- **National Weather Service.** Issues weather forecasts and flood warnings, and provides technical assistance to local governments
- **Federal Emergency Management Agency (FEMA).** Administers the National Flood Insurance Program (NFIP), and disaster planning and recovery programs
- **Department of Water Resources, Floodplain Management Branch.** Operates several water resources projects that include flood control as a project purpose, runs the state-federal flood operations center, carries out state floodplain management laws, conducts floodplain mapping, and coordinates implementation of the NFIP
- **Central Valley Flood Protection Board (formerly State Reclamation Board).** Coordinates with the USACE in planning, constructing, operating, and maintaining flood control projects in California's Central Valley, issues encroachment permits for development near levees
- **California Governor's Office of Emergency Services.** Provides financial assistance for disaster recovery, and administers FEMA's hazard mitigation program in California

National Flood Insurance Program. A voluntary, incentive-based program, the NFIP requires that new or replacement buildings in flood hazard areas be constructed to limit future flood damage. Local governments must regulate development in designated floodplains through the adoption of floodplain management ordinances which meet minimum NFIP requirements. Residents of participating communities meeting NFIP requirements are eligible to receive federally subsidized flood insurance. For each participating community, flood insurance rate maps are prepared that delineate areas of special flood hazards and insurance premium zones.

FEMA's Community Rating System (CRS) encourages community floodplain management activities that exceed the minimum NFIP standards. Depending upon the level of participation, flood insurance premium rates for policyholders can be reduced up to 45 percent. FEMA 2015.

Cobey-Alquist Floodplain Management Act. When a federal flood control project report designates floodway boundaries, this law provides that the state will not appropriate money to support the project unless affected local governments have enacted floodplain regulations meeting certain minimum requirements. Pub. Res. Code § 8400 *et seq.*

DWR FloodSAFE Program. The California Department of Water Resources (DWR) launched its FloodSAFE California Program in 2006. It is a multifaceted statewide program to improve flood safety through integrated flood management. In 2013, DWR and USACE (2013) issued the Flood Future Report, an initial step to assess the level of flood exposure statewide, identify flood management issues, and develop recommendations to help address California's flood risk. This report is the first product of DWR's State Flood Management Planning Program developed under the FloodSAFE Initiative to expand the focus of California's flood management planning statewide. *See* sidebar.

Assembly Bill 1602. Assembly Bill 1602 of 2007 required additional consideration of flood risk in local land use planning and regulation statewide. The general plan land use element must identify those areas that are subject to flooding, which local governments must review annually. It must also consider the locations of resources that are used for

California Responds to Major Flood Risks

The Flood Future Report (DWR and USACE 2013) is a comprehensive statewide look at flood risks and needed responses. It finds that California faces catastrophic flood risks: more than seven million people and $580 billion in assets (property, crops, and infrastructure) are at risk. Among other key findings of the report are:

- Environmental stewardship (associated with keeping floodplains natural) encounters competing regulations
- Flood management responsibilities are complex and fragmented
- Flood infrastructure does not meet current and future needs
- Funding is limited and increasingly unreliable

The report recommends an "integrated water management" approach to flood planning and implementation that combines flood management, water supply, and ecosystem actions to deliver multiple benefits. It sets forth the following recommendations:

- Tools
  — Conduct regional flood risk assessments to better understand statewide flood risk
  — Increase public and policymaker awareness about flood risks
  — Increase support for flood emergency preparedness, response, and recovery
- Plans
  — Encourage land use planning practices that reduce the consequences of flooding
  — Implement flood management from regional, systemwide, and statewide perspectives
- Actions
  — Increase collaboration among public agencies to improve flood management planning, policies, and investments
  — Establish short-term and long-term investment priorities

Weakening Sacramento River levees need repairs to provide urban levels of flood protection.

groundwater recharge and stormwater management. The general plan safety element must identify flood hazard information, and establish policies and feasible implementation measures to protect communities from unreasonable risks of flooding. Also, under AB 1602 a city or county may not approve a development agreement or permits for projects that would place residences in a flood hazard zone unless flood protection for the area has been demonstrated.

Senate Bill 5. Senate Bill 5 of 2007 (Statutes of 2007, Chapter 364) established additional flood protection requirements for the Central Valley. It required DWR to prepare updated maps of 100-year and 200-year floodplains by 2008, established a 200-year standard for Central Valley urban areas, and required adoption of building standards for construction within 200-year floodplains. The bill required that the Central Valley Flood Protection Board prepare a Central Valley Flood Protection Plan by 2012, and update it every five years. The 2017 update is expected to integrate two state-led basin-wide feasibility studies, several regional flood management plans, and a conservation strategy. (*See* www.water.ca.gov/cvfmp/.)

Senate Bill 5 also required Central Valley local governments to amend their general plans by 2014 and their land use regulations by 2015, to be consistent with the state plan, following which they may not approve inconsistent development projects unless "adequate progress" is being made towards achieving 200-year protection. *See* DWR 2010. SB 1278 of 2012 (Chapter 553, Statutes of 2012) modified the SB 5 compliance schedule, giving cities and counties until July 2, 2015 to amend their general plans, and until July 2, 2016 to update local land use regulations to be consistent with their amended general plans. *See* DWR 2014.

SEISMIC SAFETY

The Alquist-Priolo Earthquake Fault Zoning Act restricts development on the surface traces of known active earthquake faults.

Three major laws govern seismic safety in California. The Alquist-Priolo Earthquake Fault Zoning Act (Pub. Res. Code § 2621 *et seq.*) restricts development on the surface traces of known active earthquake faults. The Act requires a geological investigation before a local government can approve development projects near known earthquake faults.

The Seismic Hazards Mapping Act (Pub. Res. Code § 2690 *et seq.*) directs the state geologist to map potential hazard areas for ground shaking, liquefaction, and earthquake-triggered landslides. Local governments must inform the public about locations of all designated earthquake fault zones.

Lastly, the Unreinforced Masonry Law (Pub. Res. Code § 9975 *et seq.*) requires local governments within a certain seismic zone (Zone 4) to identify hazardous unreinforced masonry buildings and to consider regulations to abate dangerous buildings through retrofitting or demolition.

The above laws are administered through regulations adopted by the State Mining and Geology Board, an independent board that operates within the Department of Conservation. The Alfred E. Alquist Seismic Safety Commission is responsible for disseminating public information on earthquake hazards to decision-makers and the public.

SRA = state responsibility area

SLC = State Lands Commission

FIRE HAZARDS

Pursuant to Pub. Res. Code § 4125 *et seq.*, commonly known as the State Fire Responsibility Act, the State Board of Forestry and Fire Protection classifies all lands within the state to determine those areas for which the financial responsibility of preventing and suppressing fires is primarily a state responsibility. These areas are referred to as state responsibility areas (SRAs). The prevention and suppression of fires in non-SRA areas is primarily the responsibility of either local or federal agencies.

The State Board of Forestry and Fire Protection has issued SRA fire safe regulations (14 Cal. Code Regs. § 1270 *et seq.*), that set standards for design and construction of structures, subdivisions and developments in SRAs and provide for basic emergency access and perimeter wildfire protection. These regulations cover topics such as road and signage standards, minimum water supply reserves for emergency fire use, and fuel breaks around structures and subdivisions.

Also, the California Department of Forestry and Fire Protection has developed fire hazard severity zoning information for use by local governments. Gov't Code § 51175 *et seq.* The California Building Code (Cal. Code Regs. Title 24) includes a "wildland-urban interface building code," which establishes building standards for different fire hazard severity zones.

STATE LANDS COMMISSION LEASES

The State Lands Commission (SLC) may lease or otherwise manage the use of sovereign tidelands, submerged lands, and beds of navigable waters under its jurisdiction. The SLC also manages state-owned school lands and regulates marine terminals in state waters to control oil spills. The SLC's regulatory programs are established by Pub. Res. Code § 6000 *et seq.* and 2 Cal. Code Regs. § 1900 *et seq.*

The State Lands Commission may lease or otherwise manage the use of sovereign tidelands, submerged lands, and beds of navigable waters under its jurisdiction.

Those proposing to use state-owned sovereign lands must obtain a land use lease. Pub. Res. Code § 6501.1. Special SLC authorization is needed for dredging, mining, and oil, gas, or geothermal development. The SLC evaluates applications for land use leases to determine whether the proposed activity:

- Is consistent with the trusts under which the lands are held
- Is environmentally acceptable
- Will affect the value of state lands
- Will be in the best interests of the people of California

The SLC may charge rental fees, royalties, or other fees for the use of state lands. Fees may be based on a percentage of the property's appraised value, percentage of gross income, or volume of minerals extracted. Pub. Res. Code § 6503.5.

CEC = California Energy Commission

MW = megawatt

Occupation of land under SLC jurisdiction without a lease is a trespass. The Commission addresses such trespasses by working with the owners of the private structures on public lands to ensure they have the proper authorization to occupy state property, and are appropriately compensating the state.

SLC administration of lands under its jurisdiction is subject to the public trust doctrine (*see* chapter 1). SLC CEQA documents may be used to demonstrate proper consideration of public trust uses. *Citizens for East Shore Parks v. California State Lands Commission* (2011) 202 Cal. App. 4th 549.

CALIFORNIA ENERGY COMMISSION POWER PLANT CERTIFICATION PROGRAM

The analysis below focuses on land use aspects of state energy regulation, the most prominent of which are the Warren-Alquist Act and the California Energy Commission (CEC) energy facility licensing program.

KEY LAWS AND AGENCIES

Energy Policy Act of 2005. At the federal level, the Energy Policy Act of 2005 (PL 109-58) contains a number of provisions related to the siting of energy facilities. The Act clarifies the federal government's role in siting of liquefied natural gas facilities. Also, to expedite transmission line and gas pipeline permitting, the Act requires the Department of Energy, working with federal land management agencies, to designate energy corridors across the western U.S. after preparation of a programmatic environmental impact statement.

Construction of new nuclear power plants is prohibited until a satisfactory method of nuclear waste disposal has been developed.

Federal Energy Regulatory Commission. Among other responsibilities, the Federal Energy Regulatory Commission licenses hydropower projects and approves the siting of interstate natural gas facilities, including pipelines, storage facilities, and liquefied natural gas.

Warren-Alquist Act. Enacted in 1975, the Warren-Alquist Act (Pub. Res. Code § 21000 *et seq.*) establishes a streamlined "one-stop" permitting process for thermal power plants with at least 50 megawatts (MW) of generating capacity. The Act is intended to consolidate the state's responsibility for energy resources, including research and development, and the regulation of electrical generating and related transmission facilities. The Act's policies recognize that it is the state's responsibility to ensure a reliable electrical energy supply consistent with protecting public health, safety and welfare, and environmental quality.

Two provisions of the Warren-Alquist Act restrict the ability to construct new nuclear power plants in California. Pub. Res. Code §§ 25524.2, 25524.1. Construction of new nuclear power plants is prohibited until a satisfactory method of nuclear waste disposal has been developed. Also required is a case-by-case review of the adequacy of a proposed plant's nuclear waste storage capacity.

PUC = Public Utilities Commission

LORS = laws, ordinances, regulations, and standards

California Energy Commission. The Warren-Alquist Act created the CEC, which was charged with the following responsibilities (Pub. Res. Code § 25216):

- Processing applications for the licensing of thermal power plants of at least 50 MW generating capacity, and related transmission lines
- Implementing measures to reduce wasteful and inefficient use of energy
- Collecting and analyzing information on alternative ways to conserve, generate, and supply energy
- Predicting future energy demands and keeping historical data
- Developing energy technologies and encouraging renewable energy programs
- Supporting energy efficiency through appliance and building standards

Public Utilities Commission. If the CEC issues a power plant or transmission line license to a public utility, the Public Utilities Commission (PUC) must issue a certificate of public convenience and necessity, authorizing construction of the licensed facility. Also, the PUC has exclusive jurisdiction over approving, through issuing a certificate of public convenience and necessity, the siting of all transmission lines not under CEC's jurisdiction. The majority of the state's transmission lines are under PUC jurisdiction. Pub. Util. Code § 1001.

CALIFORNIA ENERGY COMMISSION LICENSING PROCESS

Overview. The CEC has exclusive certification jurisdiction over (Pub. Res. Code § 25120):

- Thermal power plants with a generating capacity of 50 MW or more
- Modifications that result in a generating capacity of 50 MW or more
- Transmission lines carrying the electricity from a power plant with a generating capacity of 50 MW or more to the interconnected grid

The CEC's jurisdiction supersedes the permit authority of other state agencies and local government land use authorities, although as discussed below, the CEC must consider state and local government policies and regulations in making siting decisions. Pub. Res. Code § 25500. Also, the CEC certification process has been determined to be a CEQA-certified regulatory program. Pub. Res. Code § 21080.5 (*see* chapter 2). The CEC's staff assessment (*see* below) serves as the functional equivalent of an EIR.

The CEC's jurisdiction supersedes the permit authority of other state agencies and local government land use authorities, although as discussed below, the CEC must consider state and local government policies and regulations in making siting decisions.

The certification process is described in CEC regulations. 20 Cal. Code Regs. § 1701 *et seq*. Useful guidance on the licensing process also can be found in a draft CEC report for energy facility developers. CEC 2000.

Consultation with other agencies. Although the CEC has exclusive jurisdiction over licensing thermal power plants of 50 MW or more in generating capacity and related facilities, the CEC is required to consult with all interested agencies

SPPE = small power plant exemption

AFC = application for certification

NOI = notice of intention

regarding applicable laws, ordinances, regulations, and standards (LORS). Typically, these issues arise in the context of local government land use requirements. 20 Cal. Code Regs. §§ 1752(k), 1755(b). The CEC must make findings on whether a proposed facility complies with LORS. The CEC is directed to consult with agencies to eliminate any non-compliance with LORS, and may not certify a non-complying project unless it finds via an "override" that the project is needed for public convenience and necessity, and that there are no more prudent feasible means to meet these needs. Pub. Res. Code § 25527.

Types of licensing proceedings. An applicant initiates the certification process by filing either a small power plant exemption (SPPE) or an application for certification (AFC). A notice of intention (NOI) also is available, and is intended to preliminarily evaluate alternative sites for complex projects such as nuclear power plants. However, NOIs have not been used frequently because many proposed projects are exempt from the NOI requirement. Pub. Res. Code § 25540.6.

Small power plant exemption. The SPPE is available for projects between 50 MW and 100 MW, provided the proposed project does not create an unmitigated significant impact on environmental resources. The CEC completes an initial study and, if approved by the CEC, the project developer is responsible for securing local, state, and federal permits to construct and operate the facility. The CEC strives to complete the SPPE review in 135 days. Pub. Res. Code § 25541; 20 Cal. Code Regs. § 1936.

Application for certification. The standard AFC process is required to be completed within 12 months of an approved AFC, but some controversial projects take longer. The AFC is a detailed description of the proposed facilities, their environmental impacts, and their compliance with LORS. When the AFC is "data adequate" (i.e., deemed complete), the CEC appoints a siting committee to oversee its processing. The staff recommendation on data adequacy must be made within 30 days of AFC filing, and the CEC must act on this recommendation within 45 days of filing. If the AFC is incomplete, the applicant is provided a written list of inadequacies to be corrected in a supplemental filing that the CEC must evaluate for adequacy within 30 days of receipt. 20 § Cal. Code Regs. 1704.

The standard AFC process is required to be completed within 12 months of an approved AFC, but some controversial projects take longer.

Staff assessment. After acceptance of the AFC, the CEC staff then prepares a preliminary and final staff assessment analyzing the environmental impacts of the proposed facilities and their compliance with the LORS. The staff assessment serves as the staff written testimony for the AFC hearing (*see* below), as well as the CEQA functional equivalent document. 20 Cal. Code Regs. § 1742 *et seq.*

Evidentiary hearing and decision. The CEC siting committee conducts an evidentiary hearing on the AFC in which the applicant has the burden of presenting sufficient evidence to support the findings required for project certification. In addition to the applicant, testimony is provided by the staff of the CEC, staff of other agencies, interveners, and the public—the CEC has a public advisor who advises the public on how to participate in CEC proceedings. After the hearing, the siting committee's presiding member prepares a proposed decision for public review and comment. 20 Cal. Code Regs. §§ 1748, 1749.

The CEC then either approves or denies the AFC, making findings on implementation of feasible mitigation measures, compliance with the LORS, and feasible alternatives. Special restrictions apply to CEC approval of sites in the coastal zone, sites within San Francisco Bay Conservation and Development Commission (BCDC) jurisdiction, and sites with recreational or environmental values such as wildlife preserves or parks. Pub. Res. Code §§ 25526, 25527.

If the AFC is approved, the CEC adopts conditions of certification (COCs) that cover topics such as implementation of mitigation measures and compliance with federal, state, regional, and local requirements. The Commission also adopts a compliance plan, which describes the procedures for post-certification monitoring of compliance with the COCs. Pub. Res. Code § 25532; 20 Cal. Code Regs. § 1770.

COC = conditions of certification

ARB = Air Resources Board

COG = Council of Governments

BCDC = San Francisco Bay Conservation and Development Commission

TRPA = Tahoe Regional Planning Agency

DPC = Delta Protection Commission

DSC = Delta Stewardship Council

MPO = Metropolitan Planning Organization

RTPA = Regional Transportation Planning Agency

RTP = regional transportation plan

Roles of other agencies in the certification process. State agencies such as the California Independent System Operator and the Air Resources Board (ARB), and federal agencies such as the Environmental Protection Agency and the U.S. Fish and Wildlife Service, often review and comment on the AFC. For facilities in the coastal zone, the Coastal Commission must comment on the AFC in a report, and the CEC must follow the report's findings and recommendations. Pub. Res. Code § 25531(c). Special procedures exist to assure that proposed facilities comply with the regulatory requirements of local air pollution control districts as well. 20 Cal. Code Regs. § 1744.5.

Judicial review of siting decisions. A CEC project certification can be reviewed only by filing a petition for review with California Supreme Court. Pub. Res. Code § 25531. These petitions for review have seldom been granted.

REGIONAL PLANNING AGENCIES

Several types of regional planning agencies exist in California, with different levels of regulatory authority over land use and environmental quality. Councils of Governments (COGs) and Metropolitan Planning Organizations are joint powers agencies established by local governments. The BCDC, Tahoe Regional Planning Agency (TRPA), Delta Protection Commission (DPC), and Delta Stewardship Council (DSC) are regional planning and regulatory agencies established by state statute.

COUNCILS OF GOVERNMENTS AND SENATE BILL 375

COGs and MPOs. COGs are joint powers agencies established pursuant to the Joint Powers Act (Gov't Code § 6500 *et seq.*) that conduct regional planning activities in most of the state. COGs do not have the authority to regulate land use or environmental quality, but are influential in establishing regional planning frameworks and guiding federal funding for transportation and housing.

COGs are joint powers agencies established pursuant to the Joint Powers Act that conduct regional planning activities in most of the state.

Transportation Planning Agencies Implementing SB 375

The following regional transportation planning agencies are required to prepare regional transportation plans that include SCSs complying with SB 375.

AMBAG = Association of Monterey Bay Area Governments

BCAG = Butte County Association of Governments

Fresno COG = Fresno Council of Governments

KCAG = Kings County Association of Governments

KCOG = Kern Council of Governments

MCAG = Merced County Association of Governments

MCTC = Madera County Transportation Commission

MTC = Metropolitan Transportation Commission*

SACOG = Sacramento Area Council of Governments

SANDAG = San Diego Association of Governments

SBCAG = Santa Barbara County Association of Governments

SCAG = Southern California Association of Governments

SJCOG = San Joaquin Council of Governments

SLOCOG = San Luis Obispo Council of Governments

SRTPA = Shasta Regional Transportation Planning Agency

StanCOG = Stanislaus Council of Governments

TCAG = Tulare County Association of Governments

TMPO=Tahoe Metropolitan Planning Organization

* SCS prepared by ABAG (Association of Bay Area Governments)

COGs allocate "fair share" regional housing needs to all cities and counties within their boundaries (*see* chapter 3). Many COGs undertake planning for growth management as well.

A main purpose of many COGs is to serve as Metropolitan Planning Organizations (MPOs) to meet federal transportation planning requirements; Regional Transportation Planning Agencies (RTPAs) can also serve as MPOs. MPOs prepare long-range regional transportation plans (RTPs) and adopt transportation improvement programs that allocate state and federal funds for highway, transit, and other surface transportation projects. In the San Francisco Bay Area, regional transportation planning is done by the Metropolitan Transportation Commission, which is a statutory planning agency. Gov't Code § 66502.

Senate Bill 375. The influence of MPOs in land use policy was substantially increased with the passage of SB 375 (Chapter 728, Statutes of 2008). SB 375 provides for a planning process to coordinate land use planning and RTPs to help California meet the GHG reductions established in AB 32 (*see* chapter 2). SB 375 has three major components: (1) using the regional transportation planning process to achieve reductions in GHG emissions from passenger vehicles (*see* chapter 20); (2) offering incentives under CEQA to encourage projects that are consistent with a regional plan that achieves GHG emission reductions (*see* chapter 3); and (3) coordinating the regional housing need allocation process with the regional transportation planning process.

Senate Bill 375 requires RTPs prepared by 18 regional transportation planning agencies—the state's largest MPOs and certain smaller RTPAs—to incorporate a Sustainable Communities Strategy (SCS) in their RTPs that demonstrates how the region would achieve regional GHG emission reduction targets for 2020 and 2035 set by ARB. *See* sidebar. An SCS must meet several requirements, including using the most recent planning assumptions; identifying general land use locations, densities, and building intensities; accommodating projected housing needs for all economic segments of the population; and considering the latest available information on agricultural lands and resource areas. Gov't Code § 65080(b)(2)(B). Transportation funding allocations must be consistent with the RTP and SCS. If the SCS cannot feasibly achieve the regional

GHG emissions reduction target, SB 375 requires MPOs to prepare another document called an Alternative Planning Strategy that could achieve the GHG emissions reduction target.

SCS = Sustainable Communities Strategy

Implementation of SB 375 SCSs by local governments is incentive-based. SB 375 does not require local governments to revise their land use policies and regulations, including their general plan, to be consistent with the SCS. Gov't Code § 65080 *et seq.*

SAN FRANCISCO BAY CONSERVATION AND DEVELOPMENT COMMISSION

Overview. The San Francisco Bay Conservation and Development Commission (BCDC) is a state agency with land use planning and regulatory authority over San Francisco Bay, Suisun Marsh, and adjacent areas. A part of the Resources Agency, BCDC was created in 1965 by the McAteer-Petris Act (Gov't Code § 66600 *et seq.*) in response to growing public concerns about the filling of San Francisco Bay. BCDC's Suisun Marsh responsibilities were established by the Suisun Marsh Preservation Act of 1977. Pub. Res. Code § 29000 *et seq.*

BCDC's responsibilities include (Gov't Code § 66630 *et seq.*):

- Regulating all filling and dredging of San Francisco Bay
- Regulating new development within the first 100 feet inland from the bay
- Protecting Suisun Marsh by administering the Suisun Marsh Preservation Act in cooperation with local governments
- Administering the CZMA within the San Francisco Bay segment of the California Coast
- Pursuing an active planning program to study bay issues

BCDC regulates filling of San Francisco Bay and new development 100 feet inland.

Regulatory program. San Francisco Bay development permits may be issued only if consistent with bay fill and public access policies in the Bay Plan adopted by BCDC. Gov't Code § 66632. Similarly, Suisun Marsh development permits may be issued only if consistent with protection policies established by the Suisun Marsh Protection Plan and certified local protection programs adopted by local governments with jurisdiction over the marsh. Pub. Res. Code § 29500.

BCDC is authorized to develop adaptation strategies for impacts of sea level rise and other climate change impacts. Gov't Code § 66646.2. It updated the Bay Plan in 2011 to deal with the expected impacts of climate change in the San Francisco Bay region.

BCDC issues several types of permits (Gov't Code § 66632):

- An administrative permit is issued for minor repair or improvement activities
- A major permit is issued for larger fills or substantial changes in use
- A regionwide permit is issued for certain activities that BCDC has determined will have no substantial impact, such as routine maintenance work

TRPA Regional Plan 2012 Update

The Tahoe Regional Plan 2012 Update had the following priorities:

- Accelerating water quality restoration and other ecological benefits by supporting environmental redevelopment opportunities and Environmental Improvement Program investments.
- Transitioning to more permitting by local governments to create one-stop shopping for homeowner improvements in order to return TRPA to the more regional role the Compact originally intended.
- Creating walkable communities and increasing alternative transportation options.

Important policies addressed by the Regional Plan Update include:

- Retaining the established regional growth control system. Under this system, overdevelopment was stopped and open spaces preserved. Most of the former policies in the Regional Plan remained in place.
- Creating a more efficient planning system that integrates TRPA requirements into the plans and permits of other government agencies.
- Encouraging property owners to transfer development rights from sensitive or outlying areas to existing town centers with the goal of restoring these lands.
- Eliminating regulatory barriers to environmental redevelopment of rundown buildings.
- Simplifying burdensome regulations for homeowners while achieving threshold gains.
- Integrating with the regional transportation plan to support sidewalk and bike trail projects that reduce automobile dependency and increase walkability and safety.
- Continuing to deliver restoration projects under the Environmental Improvement Program that achieve erosion control on roadways and restore forests and wetlands.

Source: Modified from www.trpa.org/wp-content/uploads/RPU_FactSheet_1-15-13.pdf

- An emergency permit is issued for an activity necessary to avoid an immediate danger to life, health, or property

BCDC's regulatory program is a CEQA-certified regulatory program. *See* chapter 2. CEQA's policies apply to BCDC permit decisions, but BCDC is not required to prepare CEQA environmental documents such as Negative Declarations and EIRs. 14 Cal. Code Regs. § 11500 *et seq.*

TAHOE REGIONAL PLANNING AGENCY

Interstate compact. The Tahoe Regional Planning Agency (TRPA) was established in 1969 by an interstate compact between the states of California and Nevada, approved by Congress. Public Law 91-148. The compact was substantially amended in 1980. Public Law 96-551; Gov't Code § 66800 *et seq.* Through the compact, California, Nevada and the U.S. Congress recognized Lake Tahoe's unique environmental qualities, as well as the substantial threats to Tahoe's environment posed by development and recreation activities.

Responsibilities. TRPA has the following major responsibilities (Gov't Code § 66801 *et seq.*):

- Establish environmental threshold carrying capacities for the Tahoe Region (whose boundaries are generally the hydrologic boundaries of the Lake Tahoe Basin).
- Prepare a regional plan to achieve and maintain the thresholds. Key features of the plan include regional goals and policies, and a land use element. TRPA adopted an updated regional plan in 2012 (TRPA 2012). *See* sidebar.
- Adopt the TRPA regulatory code, which sets forth regulations needed to implement the regional plan
- Prepare plan area statements and community plans for specific areas within the Tahoe Basin.
- Review and approve those development projects consistent with the regional plan and TRPA regulatory code.
- Prepare environmental impact statements (EISs) for projects that will have a significant impact on the environment. TRPA EISs are patterned after National Environmental Policy Act (NEPA) EISs, but NEPA's requirements do not apply to TRPA since it is not a federal agency.

- Implement an Environmental Improvement Program, consisting of numerous projects to improve Lake Tahoe water clarity and environmental quality.

TRPA's strict land use regulations have been the subject of a number of "takings" lawsuits. In *Suitum v. Tahoe Regional Planning Agency* (1997) 117 S. Ct. 1659, the Supreme Court held that a landowner could maintain a takings lawsuit (i.e., the lawsuit is "ripe" for decision) without first filing an application for transfer of development rights. In *Tahoe-Sierra Preservation Council, Inc. v. Tahoe Regional Planning Agency* (2002) 122 S. Ct. 1465, the Supreme Court held that a temporary development moratorium does not constitute a per se taking of property requiring compensation.

DELTA PROTECTION COMMISSION

The Delta Protection Act (Pub. Res. Code § 29700 *et seq.*) established the Delta Protection Commission (DPC) to protect the natural resources of the Sacramento-San Joaquin Delta. The DPC implementing regulations can be found at 14 Cal. Code Regs. § 20300 *et seq.*

The DPC is required to adopt a Resource Management Plan to implement the Act, and consider updating it every five years. To implement this requirement, the DPC's Land Use and Resource Management Plan was last updated in 2010.

Local governments within the "primary zone" of the Delta Region are required to amend their general plans to be consistent with the regional plan. The primary zone of the Sacramento-San Joaquin Delta includes approximately 500,000 acres of waterways, levees, and farmed lands extending over portions of five counties: Solano, Yolo, Sacramento, San Joaquin, and Contra Costa.

Local governments within the "primary zone" of the Delta Region are required to amend their general plans to be consistent with the regional plan.

DELTA STEWARDSHIP COUNCIL

The Delta Stewardship Council (DSC), a state agency performing regional planning for the Delta, was created by the Delta Reform Act of 2009 (Pub. Res. Code § 85000 *et seq.*). The DSC has adopted and is implementing the Delta Plan required by that act. *See* chapter 13 for details.

for more information...

Barclay, C. T. and M. S. Gray, 2016. California Land Use and Planning Law. 35th Edition. Solano Press. Point Arena, Calif.

California Coastal Commission, 2015. Sea Level Rise Policy Guidance.

California Department of Water Resources, 2010. Implementing California Flood Legislation into Local Land Use Planning: A Handbook for Local Governments. Addendum issued in 2014.

California Department of Water Resources, 2014. Guidance on General Plan Amendments for Addressing Flood Risk.

California Department of Water Resources and U.S. Army Corps of Engineers, 2013. California's Flood Future Report: Recommendations for Managing the State's Flood Risk.

California Energy Commission, 2000. Energy Facility Licensing Process—Developer's Guide of Practices and Procedures (draft report).

Federal Emergency Management Agency, 2015. National Flood Insurance Program Community Rating System: A Local Official's Guide to Saving Lives, Preventing Property Damage, Reducing the Cost of Flood Insurance.

Governor's Office of Planning and Research, 2015. A Strategy for California @ 50 Million: Supporting California's Climate Change Goals. The Governor's Environmental Goals and Policy Report.

Manaster, K. A. and D. P. Selmi (eds.), ND. Chapters 1, 2, 3, 10, and 12 of California Environmental Law and Land Use Practice. Matthew Bender. San Francisco, Calif.

National Research Council, 2012. Sea-Level Rise for the Coasts of California, Oregon, and Washington: Past, Present, and Future.

Strategic Growth Council, 2014. 2014 Annual Report.

Tahoe Regional Planning Agency, 2012. Regional Plan Update.

glossary

Application for certification*—an application filed by an energy facility developer seeking CEC certification of a proposed project with 50 MW or more of generating capacity.

Certificate of public convenience and necessity*—a certificate issued by the PUC to a public utility for construction of electricity facilities such as power plants and transmission lines.

Coastal development permit*—a permit for development in the coastal zone issued by a local government or the Coastal Commission.

Coastal zone—an area extending seaward to the state's outer limit of jurisdiction and inland to boundaries designated by the Legislature.

Fault trace—the line formed by the intersection of a fault and the earth's surface.

Ground shaking—ground movement resulting from the transmission of seismic waves during an earthquake.

Integrated flood management—a mix of multiple flood management strategies, including structural and nonstructural actions and approaches that enhance the ability of undeveloped floodplains to behave more naturally.

Land use lease*—a State Lands Commission lease to use state-owned sovereign lands.

Liquefaction—a process by which water-saturated granular solids transform from a solid to a liquid state during strong ground shaking.

Local coastal program—a combination of a local government's land use plans, zoning ordinances, and other implementing actions that meet the requirements of the California Coastal Act.

Sustainable communities strategy—a development pattern and associated transportation network that meet regional greenhouse gas reduction targets under SB 375.

State responsibility area—an area where fire protection is primarily a state responsibility.

* equals permits and approvals

PART 2

POLLUTION CONTROL

CHAPTER 5

Air Quality

in this chapter...

CAA = Clean Air Act

EPA = U.S. Environmental Protection Agency

ARB = California Air Resources Board

GHG = greenhouse gas

NAAQS = national ambient air quality standards

SIP = State Implementation Plan

NSR = new source review

PSD = prevention of significant deterioration

NSPS = new source performance standards

NESHAP = National Emissions Standards for Hazardous Air Pollutants

INTRODUCTION

Air quality regulation in California is based on both the federal Clean Air Act (CAA) and several state regulatory programs that implement and go further than the CAA. Key regulatory agencies include the U.S. Environmental Protection Agency (EPA), the California Air Resources Board (ARB), and 35 regional and local air quality management districts. Federal and state air quality laws create different regulatory programs for two major types of air pollution sources—stationary sources (e.g., an industrial facility like a power plant, a manufacturer, or refinery) and mobile sources (e.g., automobiles and trucks).

This chapter reviews key laws and agencies involved in air quality regulation and standards; air quality planning to attain and maintain those standards; regulatory programs for stationary sources, ozone protection, acid rain, "criteria" pollutants, air toxics, mobile sources; and enforcement of air quality regulations. This chapter touches on greenhouse gas (GHG) regulation when it is closely related to regulation of conventional air pollutants. GHG and climate change regulation are addressed in detail in chapter 20.

KEY LAWS AND AGENCIES

FEDERAL LAWS AND AGENCIES

Clean Air Act. The CAA (42 U.S.C. § 7401 *et seq.*) requires states to develop air quality plans and regulatory programs to attain and maintain federal air quality standards. Enacted in 1963, the Act was amended comprehensively in 1970, 1977, and 1990. The CAA requires the following:

- EPA must establish and enforce national ambient air quality standards (NAAQS) for criteria pollutants
- States must prepare State Implementation Plans (SIPs), approved by EPA, to attain NAAQS
- States must establish regulatory programs to attain and maintain NAAQS
- States must conduct new source review (NSR) permitting of "major sources" of air pollution in regions of the country that exceed one or more NAAQS
- EPA must administer a prevention of significant deterioration (PSD) permitting program for "major sources" of specified pollutants to assure that clean air areas meeting NAAQS remain clean
- EPA must establish new source performance standards (NSPS) for stationary sources of air pollution that fall within specified industrial categories
- EPA must administer the National Emissions Standards for Hazardous Air Pollutants (NESHAP) program, which imposes rigorous emission controls on hazardous air pollutants
- EPA must regulate mobile source emissions through regulations on motor

This photo, taken in 1956, shows the skyline of downtown Los Angeles including the city hall (center), the United States Courthouse (left) and Hall of Justice (right) obscured by smog.

vehicles, fuel, service station vapor recovery, tailpipe emissions, and clean fuel vehicles

- EPA must regulate sources of acid rain
- EPA must protect the stratosphere by prohibiting the production of chemicals that deplete the upper layer of ozone
- EPA must administer a post-construction permitting program governing air quality permits for "major sources"
- EPA must regulate sources responsible for significant visibility impairment
- EPA must regulate greenhouse gases (GHGs) (*see* chapter 20)

GHG = greenhouse gas

CAAQS = California ambient air quality standards

TAC = toxic air contaminant

VOC = volatile organic compound

Environmental Protection Agency. EPA is principally responsible for implementing and enforcing the provisions of the CAA discussed above.

STATE LAWS AND AGENCIES

Health and Safety Code and California Code of Regulations. California's air quality regulatory programs are authorized primarily by:

- Health and Safety Code. Health & Safety Code § 39000 *et seq.*
- California Code of Regulations, Title 17, Division 3. Cal. Code Regs. § 60000 *et seq.*

The Health and Safety Code establishes a broad range of rigorous state air quality regulatory programs that govern criteria pollutants, air toxics, ozone-depleting chemicals, and GHGs, requiring the ARB to:

- Adopt and enforce California ambient air quality standards (CAAQS) for California criteria pollutants
- Designate each air basin in California as either "attainment" for a given pollutant (meeting or surpassing the CAAQS for that pollutant) or "non-attainment" (failing CAAQS for a particular criteria pollutant)
- Prepare the California SIP
- Establish programs for controlling toxic air contaminants (TACs)
- Undertake a number of research and monitoring programs
- Oversee regulatory activities of regional and local air districts
- Monitor consumer products to reduce emitted volatile organic compounds (VOCs)
- Regulate GHG emissions

California Clean Air Act. The Legislature enacted the California CAA in 1988. It added an ambitious regulatory layer on top of the existing state and federal criteria pollutant programs in an effort to meet CAAQS by 2010.

The Legislature enacted the California Clean Air Act in 1988. It added an ambitious regulatory layer on top of the existing state and federal criteria pollutant programs in an effort to meet CAAQS by 2010.

Air Resources Board. The ARB is the state agency charged with regulating air pollution and implementing the CAA. It is part of the California Environmental Protection Agency (Cal/EPA) and is led by a 14-member board of directors.

OEHHA = Office of Environmental Health Hazard Assessment

APCD = air pollution control district

AQMD = air quality management district

CEQA = California Environmental Quality Act

Office of Environmental Health Hazard Assessment. OEHHA is a department within CalEPA that serves as an independent scientific advisor to CalEPA. It evaluates risks posed by hazardous substances and provides unbiased data to assist CalEPA agencies in making decisions to protect and enhance public health and the environment.

LOCAL LAWS AND AGENCIES

Local air districts. Several types of local air districts operate in California, including:

- Countywide air pollution control districts (APCDs), such as San Diego APCD
- Multi-county unified air pollution control districts, such as San Joaquin Valley Unified APCD (includes eight Central Valley counties)
- Multi-county air quality management districts (AQMDs), such as South Coast AQMD and Bay Area AQMD

Though the types of air districts have different funding and governing board compositions, their powers and duties are similar, with the exception of the South Coast AQMD and Bay Area AQMD, which have more specific powers and duties specified in the state Health and Safety Code. California's 35 air districts and their respective boundaries are shown in Figure 5-1.

Local air districts are responsible for:

- Permitting and enforcing stationary sources
- Preparing regional and local air quality attainment or maintenance plans
- Regulating TACs

The Earth's atmosphere is comprised of approximately 78 percent nitrogen and 21 percent oxygen, with trace concentrations of other gases.

Although the local air districts and ARB share responsibility for implementing the CAA, local air districts provide most of the regulatory interface in California. They also often establish California Environmental Quality Act (CEQA) thresholds of significance for air pollutant and GHG emissions.

AMBIENT AIR QUALITY STANDARDS AND AIR QUALITY PLANNING

AIR POLLUTION PRINCIPLES

The Earth's atmosphere is comprised of approximately 78 percent nitrogen and 21 percent oxygen, with the balance comprised of trace concentrations of argon, carbon dioxide, methane, and other gases. Air pollutants are divided into the following general categories: criteria pollutants, hazardous air pollutants/air toxics, and ozone-depleting chemicals, and GHGs (which are addressed separately in chapter 20). The CAA has established one or more regulatory programs to address each category of air pollutants. These pollutant categories are included in Table 5-1 following.

Criteria pollutants. A criteria pollutant is a pollutant that has had an ambient air quality standard established for it, based on the adverse effect the pollutant has on

FIGURE 5-1
California's Air Districts and Their Boundaries

Table 5-1. Federal Air Quality Programs and Regulated Pollutants

Air Quality Program	Criteria Pollutants (NSR/PSD/NSPS Programs)	Greenhouse Gases (Mandatory Reporting)***	Hazardous Air Pollutants/Air Toxics (NESHAPS)	Acid Rain	Stratospheric Ozone Depleters
Regulated Pollutants	ozone (including precursors*)	CO_2	metals	sulfuric acid	chlorofluorocarbons
	PM_{10} and $PM_{2.5}$	CH_4,	toxic organics (i.e., "VOCs"**)	nitric acid	halogens
	NO_X	N_2O	radionuclides		
	SO_2	hydrofluorocarbons			
	Pb	perfluorocarbons			
	CO	sulfur hexafluoride			
		nitrogen trifluoride			
		black carbon			

*Ozone precursors include VOCs and NO_X

**VOCs are also referred to as TOG, ROG, hydrocarbons or "total hydrocarbons minus CH_4"

***See chapter 20 for detailed discussion

PICs = products of incomplete combustion

public health and welfare. Criteria pollutants are chemicals commonly emitted in high volumes from industrial and mobile sources. Federal and state ambient air quality standards for criteria pollutants are shown in Table 5-2 on following pages. An ambient air quality standard is a concentration-based measurement of the air quality for a given criteria pollutant which is distinguished from the actual mass-based emissions from a given industrial stationary or mobile source, as illustrated in Figure 5-2.

Many criteria pollutants are generated as products of incomplete combustion (PICs) or from the oxidation of impurities bound up in fossil fuels. Complete combustion of a fossil fuel (or wood) primarily produces carbon dioxide (a GHG) and water, and no PICs.

While many criteria pollutants are generated from incomplete combustion, others are generated from fugitive gases (such as gasoline escaping from a pipe or seam, or during fueling). Ground-level ozone—the most heavily regulated criteria pollutant—typically is generated by a photochemical reaction involving NO_x (oxides of nitrogen, such as NO) and VOCs (volatile organic compounds or gases). NO_x—which is a PIC—reacts with VOCs in the presence of sunlight to create ground-level ozone. Ozone, which is present at or below the troposphere (from ground level to approximately five to nine miles high), can cause respiratory illnesses such as aggravated asthma in children and the elderly. Ground-level ozone is managed by regulating its precursor chemicals—NO_x and VOCs. NO_x is regulated both as a precursor pollutant to ozone and as a stand-alone criteria pollutant.

Other chemicals in the particulate form (either a solid or a mist) are regulated as particulate matter (PM), which is another criteria pollutant. PM (which includes

FIGURE 5-2
Ambient Air Quality Standards Are Concentration-Based

PM = particulate matter

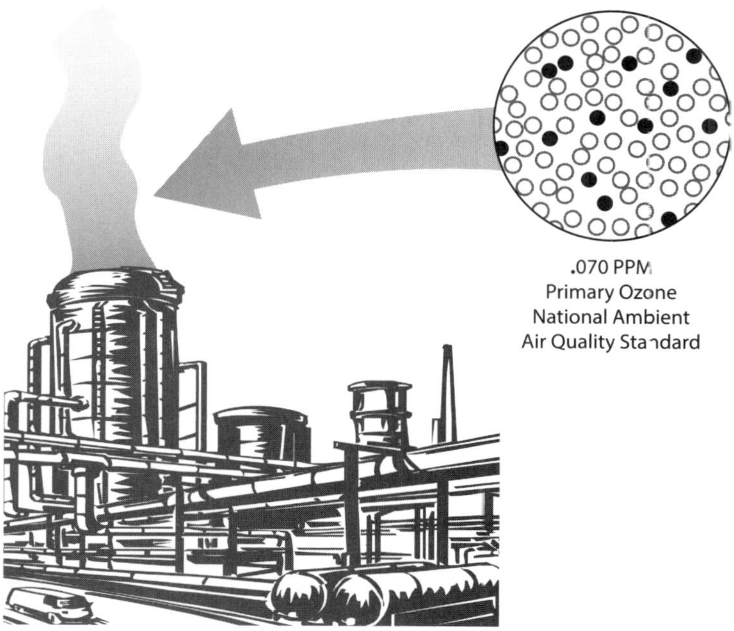

suspended dust, soot, black carbon, and more) can become embedded deeply within the lungs and cause premature death, chronic bronchitis, and aggravated asthma. EPA regulates PM_{10} and $PM_{2.5}$ (particulate matter of ten microns or less and 2.5 microns or less, respectively). Table 5-3 on the following pages displays the types of PM.

As with health problems linked to ozone, children, and the elderly are most at risk from PM emissions. Diesel PM also is an air toxic due to the presence of nickel and arsenic, along with polycyclic aromatic hydrocarbons, which are suspected carcinogens.

As with health problems linked to ozone, children, and the elderly are most at risk from particulate matter emissions.

Acid rain is another phenomenon involving two criteria pollutants. Atmospheric NO_x and SO_x chemically react with moisture in the atmosphere to create nitric acid and sulfuric acid. Most acid rain is produced from the burning of high sulfur coal (generating SO_x) and from boiler systems (generating NO_x).

Air toxics. The air toxics category of pollutants includes heavy metals, organic chemicals, pesticides, and radionuclides. Gaseous air toxics (e.g., benzene) are VOCs (a precursor chemical that forms ground-level ozone). Air toxics can cause acute and chronic illness ranging from birth defects to cancer

Ozone-depleting chemicals. The upper stratosphere (approximately seven miles above ground reaching to 25 to 31 miles high) is comprised of a gaseous layer of protective ozone molecules that screen out the sun's ultraviolet light. Millions of chemical refrigerants (such as freon, chlorofluorocarbons, and other halogenated compounds) have escaped over the last half century into the stratosphere. These

Table 5-2. Federal and State Ambient Air Quality Standards

Ambient Air Quality Standards

Pollutant	Averaging Time	California Standards[1]		National Standards[2]		
		Concentration[3]	Method[4]	Primary[3,5]	Secondary[3,6]	Method[7]
Ozone (O_3)[8]	1 Hour	0.09 ppm (180 $\mu g/m^3$)	Ultraviolet Photometry	—	Same as Primary Standard	Ultraviolet Photometry
	8 Hour	0.070 ppm (137 $\mu g/m^3$)		0.070 ppm (137 $\mu g/m^3$)		
Respirable Particulate Matter (PM_{10})[9]	24 Hour	50 $\mu g/m^3$	Gravimetric or Beta Attenuation	150 $\mu g/m^3$	Same as Primary Standard	Inertial Separation and Gravimetric Analysis
	Annual Arithmetic Mean	20 $\mu g/m^3$		—		
Fine Particulate Matter ($PM_{2.5}$)[9]	24 Hour	—	—	35 $\mu g/m^3$	Same as Primary Standard	Inertial Separation and Gravimetric Analysis
	Annual Arithmetic Mean	12 $\mu g/m^3$	Gravimetric or Beta Attenuation	12.0 $\mu g/m^3$	15 $\mu g/m^3$	
Carbon Monoxide (CO)	1 Hour	20 ppm (23 mg/m^3)	Non-Dispersive Infrared Photometry (NDIR)	35 ppm (40 mg/m^3)	—	Non-Dispersive Infrared Photometry (NDIR)
	8 Hour	9.0 ppm (10 mg/m^3)		9 ppm (10 mg/m^3)	—	
	8 Hour (Lake Tahoe)	6 ppm (7 mg/m^3)		—	—	
Nitrogen Dioxide (NO_2)[10]	1 Hour	0.18 ppm (339 $\mu g/m^3$)	Gas Phase Chemiluminescence	100 ppb (188 $\mu g/m^3$)	—	Gas Phase Chemiluminescence
	Annual Arithmetic Mean	0.030 ppm (57 $\mu g/m^3$)		0.053 ppm (100 $\mu g/m^3$)	Same as Primary Standard	
Sulfur Dioxide (SO_2)[11]	1 Hour	0.25 ppm (655 $\mu g/m^3$)	Ultraviolet Fluorescence	75 ppb (196 $\mu g/m^3$)	—	Ultraviolet Flourescence; Spectrophotometry (Pararosaniline Method)
	3 Hour	—		—	0.5 ppm (1300 $\mu g/m^3$)	
	24 Hour	0.04 ppm (105 $\mu g/m^3$)		0.14 ppm (for certain areas)[11]	—	
	Annual Arithmetic Mean	—		0.030 ppm (for certain areas)[11]	—	
Lead[12,13]	30 Day Average	1.5 $\mu g/m^3$	Atomic Absorption	—	—	High Volume Sampler and Atomic Absorption
	Calendar Quarter	—		1.5 $\mu g/m^3$ (for certain areas)[12]	Same as Primary Standard	
	Rolling 3-Month Average	—		0.15 $\mu g/m^3$		
Visibility Reducing Particles[14]	8 Hour	See footnote 14	Beta Attenuation and Transmittance through Filter Tape	No National Standards		
Sulfates	24 Hour	25 $\mu g/m^3$	Ion Chromatography			
Hydrogen Sulfide	1 Hour	0.03 ppm (42 $\mu g/m^3$)	Ultraviolet Fluorescence			
Vinyl Chloride[12]	24 Hour	0.01 ppm (26 $\mu g/m^3$)	Gas Chromatography			

Table 5-2. Federal and State Ambient Air Quality Standards *(continued)*

1. California standards for ozone, carbon monoxide (except 8-hour Lake Tahoe), sulfur dioxide (1- and 24-hour), nitrogen dioxide, and particulate matter (PM_{10}, $PM_{2.5}$, and visibility reducing particles), are values that are not to be exceeded. All others are not to be equaled or exceeded. California ambient air quality standards are listed in the Table of Standards in Section 70200 of Title 17 of the California Code of Regulations.
2. National standards (other than ozone, particulate matter, and those based on annual arithmetic mean) are not to be exceeded more than once a year. The ozone standard is attained when the fourth highest 8-hour concentration measured at each site in a year, averaged over three years, is equal to or less than the standard. For PM_{10}, the 24 hour standard is attained when the expected number of days per calendar year with a 24-hour average concentration above 150 $\mu g/m^3$ is equal to or less than one. For $PM_{2.5}$, the 24 hour standard is attained when 98 percent of the daily concentrations, averaged over three years, are equal to or less than the standard. Contact the U.S. EPA for further clarification and current national policies.
3. Concentration expressed first in units in which it was promulgated. Equivalent units given in parentheses are based upon a reference temperature of 25°C and a reference pressure of 760 torr. Most measurements of air quality are to be corrected to a reference temperature of 25°C and a reference pressure of 760 torr; ppm in this table refers to ppm by volume, or micromoles of pollutant per mole of gas.
4. Any equivalent measurement method which can be shown to the satisfaction of the ARB to give equivalent results at or near the level of the air quality standard may be used.
5. National Primary Standards: The levels of air quality necessary, with an adequate margin of safety to protect the public health.
6. National Secondary Standards: The levels of air quality necessary to protect the public welfare from any known or anticipated adverse effects of a pollutant.
7. Reference method as described by the U.S. EPA. An "equivalent method" of measurement may be used but must have a "consistent relationship to the reference method" and must be approved by the U.S. EPA.
8. On October 1, 2015, the national 8-hour ozone primary and secondary standards were lowered from 0.075 to 0.070 ppm.
9. On December 14, 2012, the national annual $PM_{2.5}$ primary standard was lowered from 15 $\mu g/m^3$ to 12.0 $\mu g/m^3$. The existing national 24-hour $PM_{2.5}$ standards (primary and secondary) were retained at 35 $\mu g/m^3$, as was the annual secondary standard of 15 $\mu g/m^3$. The existing 24-hour PM_{10} standards (primary and secondary) of 150 $\mu g/m^3$ also were retained. The form of the annual primary and secondary standards is the annual mean, averaged over three years.
10. To attain the 1-hour national standard, the three-year average of the annual 98th percentile of the 1-hour daily maximum concentrations at each site must not exceed 100 ppb. Note that the national 1-hour standard is in units of parts per billion (ppb). California standards are in units of parts per million (ppm). To directly compare the national 1-hour standard to the California standards the units can be converted from ppb to ppm. In this case, the national standard of 100 ppb is identical to 0.100 ppm.
11. On June 2, 2010, a new 1-hour SO_2 standard was established and the existing 24-hour and annual primary standards were revoked. To attain the 1-hour national standard, the three-year average of the annual 99th percentile of the 1-hour daily maximum concentrations at each site must not exceed 75 ppb. The 1971 SO_2 national standards (24-hour and annual) remain in effect until one year after an area is designated for the 2010 standard, except that in areas designated non-attainment for the 1971 standards, the 1971 standards remain in effect until implementation plans to attain or maintain the 2010 standards are approved. Note that the 1-hour national standard is in units of parts per billion (ppb). California standards are in units of parts per million (ppm). To directly compare the 1-hour national standard to the California standard the units can be converted to ppm. In this case, the national standard of 75 ppb is identical to 0.075 ppm.
12. The ARB has identified lead and vinyl chloride as "toxic air contaminants" with no threshold level of exposure for adverse health effects determined. These actions allow for the implementation of control measures at levels below the ambient concentrations specified for these pollutants.
13. The national standard for lead was revised on October 15, 2008 to a rolling three-month average. The 1978 lead standard (1.5 $\mu g/m^3$ as a quarterly average) remains in effect until one year after an area is designated for the 2008 standard, except that in areas designated non-attainment for the 1978 standard, the 1978 standard remains in effect until implementation plans to attain or maintain the 2008 standard are approved.
14. In 1989, the ARB converted both the general statewide 10-mile visibility standard and the Lake Tahoe 30-mile visibility standard to instrumental equivalents, which are "extinction of 0.23 per kilometer" and "extinction of 0.07 per kilometer" for the statewide and Lake Tahoe Air Basin standards, respectively.

Source: www.arb.ca.gov/research/aaqs/aaqs2.pdf

Table 5-3. Types of Particulate Matter

Type of PM	Size	Notes
Total Suspended Particulate	TSP <50 mm	Barely visible
PM_{10}	< 10 µm	Up to 1/20th the diameter of a human hair follicle
$PM_{2.5}$	< 2.5 µm (i.e., fine particulate matter)	Respirable
UFP	< 0.1 µm (i.e., ultrafine particulate matter)	Capable of passing through the cell wall
Black Carbon	≤ 2.5 µm (in aerodynamic diameter)	Climate pollutant which is a component of $PM_{2.5}$

highly reactive chemicals have depleted the protective layer of ozone significantly at the South Pole and other weak spots around the globe, resulting in increases in skin cancer and cataracts.

Greenhouse gases. As explained more fully in chapter 20, greenhouse gases contribute to climate change. GHGs include carbon dioxide (CO_2) methane, nitrous oxide, hydrofluorocarbons, perfluorocarbons, black carbon, and sulfur hexafluoride.

AIR QUALITY STANDARDS

Local air districts must develop plans to attain and maintain both NAAQS and CAAQS. Health & Safety Code § 40001. The CAAQS are often more strict than the NAAQS, and also establish ambient standards for three additional criteria pollutants. *See* Table 5-2 on previous pages. The CAA establishes two sets of NAAQS—primary standards (to protect human health) and secondary standards (to protect public welfare, which includes non-health considerations such as aesthetics and property). CAAQS are also generally health-based (except for visibility-reducing particles).

Local air districts must develop plans to attain and maintain both NAAQS and CAAQS.

The CAA and the California CAA (discussed below) contain specific deadlines for non-attainment areas to achieve primary NAAQS and CAAQS, respectively. The NAAQS and the CAAQS are not permitting programs; instead, they represent health-based targets that influence a number of federal, state, and local permitting programs that regulate criteria pollutants to attain and maintain these ambient air quality standards.

ATTAINMENT PLANNING

The federal CAA program and its 1990 amendments classify non-attainment air districts as marginal, moderate, serious, severe, or extreme, for the six criteria pollutants. Air districts in more severely non-attainment regions must impose stricter air quality permitting requirements on smaller stationary sources. In 2015 EPA revised its primary eight-hour average ozone standard to 0.70 ppm (80 Fed. Reg. 65292 (October 26, 2015)); this revision is expected to cause many more California air districts to be non-attainment for the ozone standard.

The federal CAA requires that each state containing non-attainment areas develop SIPs to attain the NAAQS by a specified attainment date. California's SIP, described further below, integrates non-attainment plans prepared by local air districts. Once the air quality standard is attained, air districts prepare maintenance plans to demonstrate continued maintenance of the NAAQS.

EPA's Cross State Air Pollution Rule regulates upwind emissions that contribute significantly to non-attainment or interfere with maintenance of air quality standards in downwind states. A proposed amended rule (80 Fed. Reg. 75706 (December 3, 2015)) responds to a 2015 judicial opinion that left the rule in place but ordered certain changes to be made (*EME Homer City v. Environmental Protection Agency* (DC Circ. 2015) 795 F. 3d 118).

The state CAA program, similar to but different than the federal program, classifies non-attainment air districts as moderate, serious, severe, or extreme, through the ARB. Under the state CAA (Health & Safety Code § 40910 *et seq.*), a local air district that is non-attainment for ozone, CO, SO_2, or NO_2 is required to prepare a plan to achieve attainment and maintenance of the CAAQS as expeditiously as practicable. These district attainment plans establish or modify stationary source permitting and transportation control programs to ultimately reach CAAQS attainment. Like the federal program, the stationary source and transportation control planning requirements become increasingly more strict for the more severely non-attainment air districts. Contents of district attainment plans are discussed later in this chapter.

The state CAA program, similar to but different than the federal program, classifies non-attainment air districts as moderate, serious, severe, or extreme, through the ARB.

STATE IMPLEMENTATION PLAN

The federal CAA requires a SIP to include:

- Enforceable emissions limitations and other control measures, such as economic incentives
- Timetables for compliance
- Air quality monitoring programs
- Stationary source regulatory programs
- Assurance of implementation capability
- Non-attainment area plans

The SIP, maintained by the ARB, is not a formal planning document. Rather, the California SIP is a compilation of new and previously submitted plans and programs (such as those for monitoring, modeling, permitting, air district rules, state regulations, and federal controls). Many of California's SIP elements rely on the same core set of federal control strategies, including motor vehicle emission standards and fuel regulations.

Local air districts and other agencies, such as the Bureau of Automotive Repair, prepare SIP elements and submit them to ARB for review and approval. ARB forwards SIP revisions to EPA for approval and publication in the Federal Register. 40 C.F.R. § 52.220 *et seq.* Many California submittals are pending EPA approval.

If the EPA finds a SIP or SIP revision inadequate, the EPA is authorized to prepare a Federal Implementation Plan on behalf of the state, or to impose sanctions on a state's federal transportation funding. However, the EPA has never promulgated a Federal Implementation Plan in response to California's inadequate SIP, because the state either revised its SIP before EPA took action or because legislation was passed that changed the requirements.

Section 176(c) of the Clean Air Act prohibits federal funding, permitting, or assistance to any activity that does not "conform" to the applicable SIP. EPA has issued two sets of detailed regulations specifying how federal agencies are to make

BDACT = best demonstrated available control technology

SIP conformity findings. Transportation activities are subject to special EPA transportation conformity regulations described later in this chapter. All other federal activities are subject to EPA's general conformity rule. 40 C.F.R. § 93.150 *et seq.*

FEDERAL CRITERIA POLLUTANT PROGRAMS

DEFINITION OF STATIONARY SOURCE

The CAA defines a stationary source as any building, structure, facility, or installation that emits or may emit any air pollutant subject to regulation under the CAA. Wooley and Morss 2015. A "building, structure, facility, or installation" is on one or more contiguous or adjacent properties under common ownership or control and belongs to a common industrial grouping (Standard Industrial Classification). An emissions unit is any part of a stationary source that emits or has the potential to emit regulated air pollutants. EPA 1990.

NEW SOURCE PERFORMANCE STANDARDS

A "new" source is one that is constructed after the most recent version of the NSPS for the industrial category in question. A "modified" source is any physical or operational change in an existing source that increases emissions. A "reconstructed" source involves a replacement of a component where the cost of the replacement exceeds 50 percent of the cost of constructing a comparable new facility.

The new source performance standards apply to "new," "modified," and "reconstructed" stationary sources. A "new" source is one that is constructed after the most recent version of the NSPS for the industrial category in question. If the source was constructed prior to a given NSPS, the source is grandfathered and not subject to the standards. A "modified" source is any physical or operational change in an existing source that increases emissions. A "reconstructed" source involves a replacement of a component where the cost of the replacement exceeds 50 percent of the cost of constructing a comparable new facility. 40 C.F.R. §§ 60.14 *et seq.*, 60.2, 63.41.

The NSPS vary according to the type of industrial facility. The CAA regulates over 80 types of industrial facilities (such as oil refineries, coke ovens, fossil fuel burning sources, cooling towers, volatile fuel storage, painting, and electric utility steam generating units) that contribute significantly to air pollution. 40 C.F.R. § 60 *et seq.*

The NSPS require that an owner or operator of stationary industrial sources listed in 40 C.F.R. § 60 must meet specified emissions limitations and operating standards for the criteria pollutant or pollutants that it emits, regardless of whether the source is within an attainment or non-attainment area. Stationary industrial sources must comply with emission limitations by applying the best demonstrated available control technology (BDACT). Cost, environmental impacts, and energy considerations can be considered when determining BDACT for a given industry type. BDACT includes operational standards where numerical emissions limitations are infeasible. Other air quality programs (discussed below) impose more rigorous emission control standards that give little or no consideration to costs and energy consumption.

The NSPS also include notification requirements, testing procedures, monitoring, and reporting obligations.

PTO = permit to operate

An industrial stationary source may be subject to other federal or state air quality permitting programs, in addition to NSPS, that govern toxic or other pollutants. This can result in a stationary source having several federal and state air permits with layers of controls and operating conditions. Most NSPS sources also have a permit to operate (PTO) a given source and a permit to construct new sources or modify existing sources (new source review permits).

EPA may delegate to states the authority to implement and enforce the NSPS, but maintains concurrent enforcement authority. Many California air districts have received EPA delegation. Some air districts have adopted the NSPS program and added more stringent requirements for one or more industrial sources.

EPA may delegate to states the authority to implement and enforce the NSPS, but maintains concurrent enforcement authority.

NEW SOURCE REVIEW

In the 1970 version of the CAA, a new source review permitting program was established for major sources of criteria pollutants in non-attainment areas (known as the non-attainment NSR program). The permitting program initially focused on improving the air quality in air basins designated non-attainment for one or more criteria air pollutants. Then, in 1972, the Sierra Club successfully challenged the federal NSR program because it failed to consider regulating major sources of criteria pollutants in cleaner, attainment areas. *Sierra Club v. Ruckelshaus* (D.D.C. 1972) 344 F. Supp. 253. This lawsuit spawned the PSD permitting program. Both the PSD and non-attainment NSR programs were expanded further in major amendments to the CAA in 1977 and 1990, as a result of more litigation brought in the 1970s and 1980s. The PSD program and the non-attainment NSR program are discussed separately below. The relationship between the various programs regulating major sources is shown in Figure 5-3 on the following page.

PREVENTION OF SIGNIFICANT DETERIORATION PROGRAM

The PSD program (40 C.F.R. § 52.01 *et seq.*) applies to attainment areas, and is designed to allow a level of economic growth that is consistent with preserving existing clean air resources. In addition, the PSD program is structured to preserve, protect, and enhance the air quality in national parks, national wilderness areas, national monuments, national seashores, and other areas of special national or regional natural, recreational, scenic, or historic value. 42 U.S.C. § 7470.

Program applicability. A stationary source subject to the PSD program is required to obtain a PSD permit that may include technology-oriented and operational conditions. This requirement is for a stationary source that is deemed a new major source or a major modification. The definitions of major source and major modification depend on the amount of a criteria pollutants and GHGs that *potentially* can be emitted (not *actually* emitted).

FIGURE 5-3
New Source Review Guide—NO_X Example

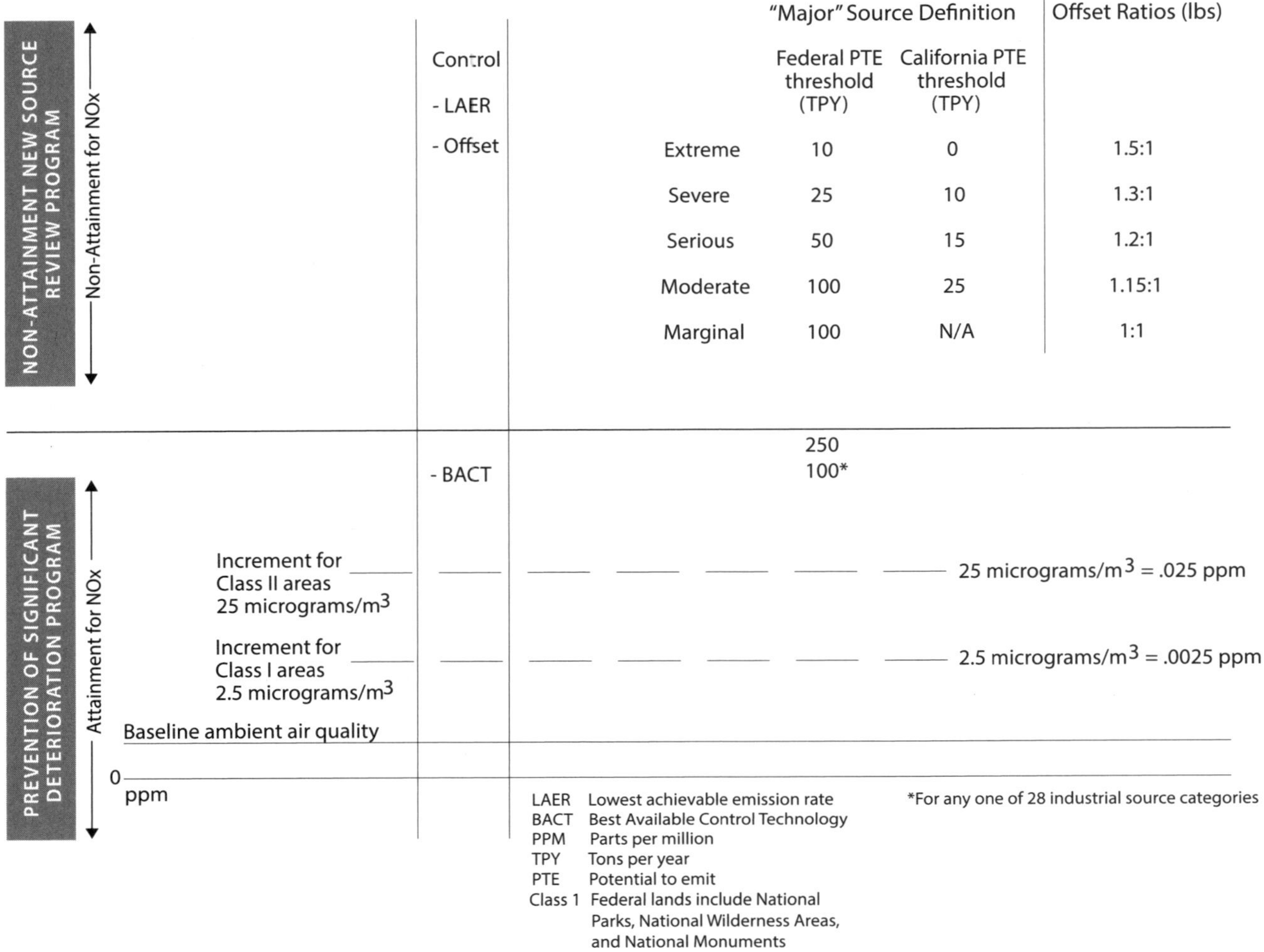

PTE = potential to emit

BACT = best available control technology

The potential to emit (PTE) is the maximum capacity of a stationary source to emit a pollutant under its physical and operational design. The following federal PTE restrictions are enforceable (EPA 1990):

- Requirements to install and operate air pollution control equipment at prescribed efficiencies
- Restrictions on design capacity utilization
- Restrictions on hours of operation
- Restrictions on the types or amount of material processed, combusted, or stored

A new stationary source is considered a major source for PSD permitting if the source is on the list of 28 industrial source categories (Table 5-4) and has a PTE threshold of 100 tons per year (TPY) of any regulated pollutant. Other new stationary sources (not on the list of 28 industrial source categories) are considered major sources for PSD permitting if the sources have a PTE of 250 TPY for any regulated pollutant. New major sources exceeding these thresholds are subject to PSD review and permitting, as are major modifications to existing major sources if modifications cause emissions of criteria pollutants to equal or exceed "significant emission rates."

Major new sources and major modifications to existing major sources that also emit GHGs (known as "anyway sources") must use BACT (see below) to control GHG emissions. *Utility Air Regulatory Group v. EPA* (2014) 134 S. Ct. 2427. See chapter 20 for further details.

Major modifications and netting out. As mentioned previously, major modifications to existing major sources are subject to PSD permitting, if modifications cause emissions of criteria pollutants to equal or exceed significant net emission rates (Table 5-5 on following page). A modification means a physical change or a change in the method of operation of the major source. In some air districts, a modification means any new equipment, even the replacement of existing equipment. A significant net emissions rate is the net PTE increase, after combining source increases and decreases. Thus, a PSD applicant may be able to "net out" of PSD review by accounting for prior emissions reductions to avoid the major modification classification.

Best available control technology requirements. Once a stationary source is subject to PSD review, the source must meet best available control technology (BACT) requirements. 42 U.S.C. § 165(a)(4); 40 C.F.R. § 52.210. BACT requirements are specific to each type of stationary source. However, determining BACT is far from straightforward. BACT results in maximum reduction for a pollutant while taking into account energy, environmental, and economic impacts, and other costs. EPA 1990. BACT is determined case-by-case using a top-down approach, where the most effective control technology feasible for the source is considered before turning to less effective control options. Each technology is evaluated for feasibility, cost-effectiveness, and other energy or environmental impacts. BACT can include a certain type of control technology, equipment design, equipment type, work practice, or operational

Table 5-4. Prevention of Significant Deterioration: "Major Source" Industrial Source Categories and Their Potential to Emit Thresholds

Industrial source category	PTE in tons per year
Any (except the sources below)	250
Fossil fuel-fired steam electric plants of more than 250 million Btu/hr heat input	100
Coal cleaning plants with thermal dryers	100
Kraft pulp mills	100
Portland cement plants	100
Primary zinc smelters	100
Iron and steel mill plants	100
Primary aluminum ore reduction plants	100
Primary copper smelters	100
Municipal incinerators capable of charging more than 250 tons of refuse per day	100
Hydrofluoric acid plants	100
Sulfuric acid plants	100
Nitric acid plants	100
Petroleum refineries	100
Lime plants	100
Phosphate rock processing plants	100
Coke oven batteries	100
Sulfur recovery plants	100
Carbon black plants (furnace plants)	100
Primary lead smelters	100
Fuel conversion plants	100
Sintering plants	100
Secondary metal production plants	100
Chemical process plants	100
Fossil fuel boilers (or combinations thereof) totaling more than 250 million Btu/hr heat input	100
Petroleum storage and transfer units with a total storage capacity exceeding 300,000 barrels	100
Taconite ore processing plants	100
Glass fiber processing plants	100
Charcoal production plants	100

Source: EPA. 1990

Table 5-5. Significant Net Emission Rates Regulated under the Clean Air Act

Criteria pollutant	Tons per year
CO	≥100
NO_x	≥40
SO_2	≥40
Particulate matter	≥25
PM_{10}	≥15
Ozone	≥40
Lead	≥0.6
$PM_{2.5}$ (direct emissions)	≥10
Fluorides	≥3
Sulfuric acid mist	≥7
Hydrogen sulfide (H_2S)	≥10
Total reduced sulfur (including H_2S)	≥10
Reduced sulfur compounds (including H_2S)	≥10

Source: 40 C.F.R. § 52.21 *et seq.*

Table 5-6. Prevention of Significant Deterioration Increments

Class I, II, and III			
Pollutant	Class I	Class II	Class III
SO_2, annual	2	20	40
SO_2, 24-hour	5	91	182
SO_2, 3-hour	25	512	700
PM_{10}, annual	4	17	34
PM_{10}, 24-hour	8	30	60
NO_2, annual	2.5	25	50
$PM_{2.5}$, annual	1	4	8
$PM_{2.5}$, 24-hour	2	9	18

Units: micrograms/meter^3

Source: 40 C.F.R. § 52.21(58)(c)

IOU = investor-owned utility

standard. An example of a non-high-tech BACT is using paints low in VOCs to minimize the generation of ozone precursor emissions.

Investor-owned utilities (IOU) or local publicly owned electric utilities are prohibited from entering into long-term contracts with power plants in Mexico that do not comply with BACT standards for controlling air emissions. Pub. Util. Code § 8350.

Prevention of significant deterioration increments. Increments of allowable air quality degradation have been established to ensure NAAQS will not be exceeded in attainment areas. Each NAAQS maximum concentration is an air quality ceiling; increments are maximum allowable fractional increases (measured in concentrations) above the existing background concentration for the attainment area. A stationary source may not be permitted if it would exceed NAAQS or completely consume the remaining increment for the attainment area.

Class I areas include national wilderness areas, national memorial parks, and national parks.

Allowable increments vary depending on whether the proposed new or modified source is to be located in a Class I, II, or III area. *See* Table 5-6. Class I areas are assigned the highest degree of protection from air quality degradation. These areas include national wilderness areas, national memorial parks, and national parks. Class I areas have small increment levels, and thus new industrial growth is limited in or near these areas. *See* Figure 5-4. Class II areas include virtually all other areas of the country. Class II areas have increments that allow reasonable, well-managed industrial growth. Class III areas have the highest increments, but EPA has not proposed to designate any areas as such.

Air quality impact analysis. In addition to meeting BACT, a PSD applicant must complete an air quality impact analysis (AQIA) demonstrating that the stationary

FIGURE 5-4

Class I Areas in California

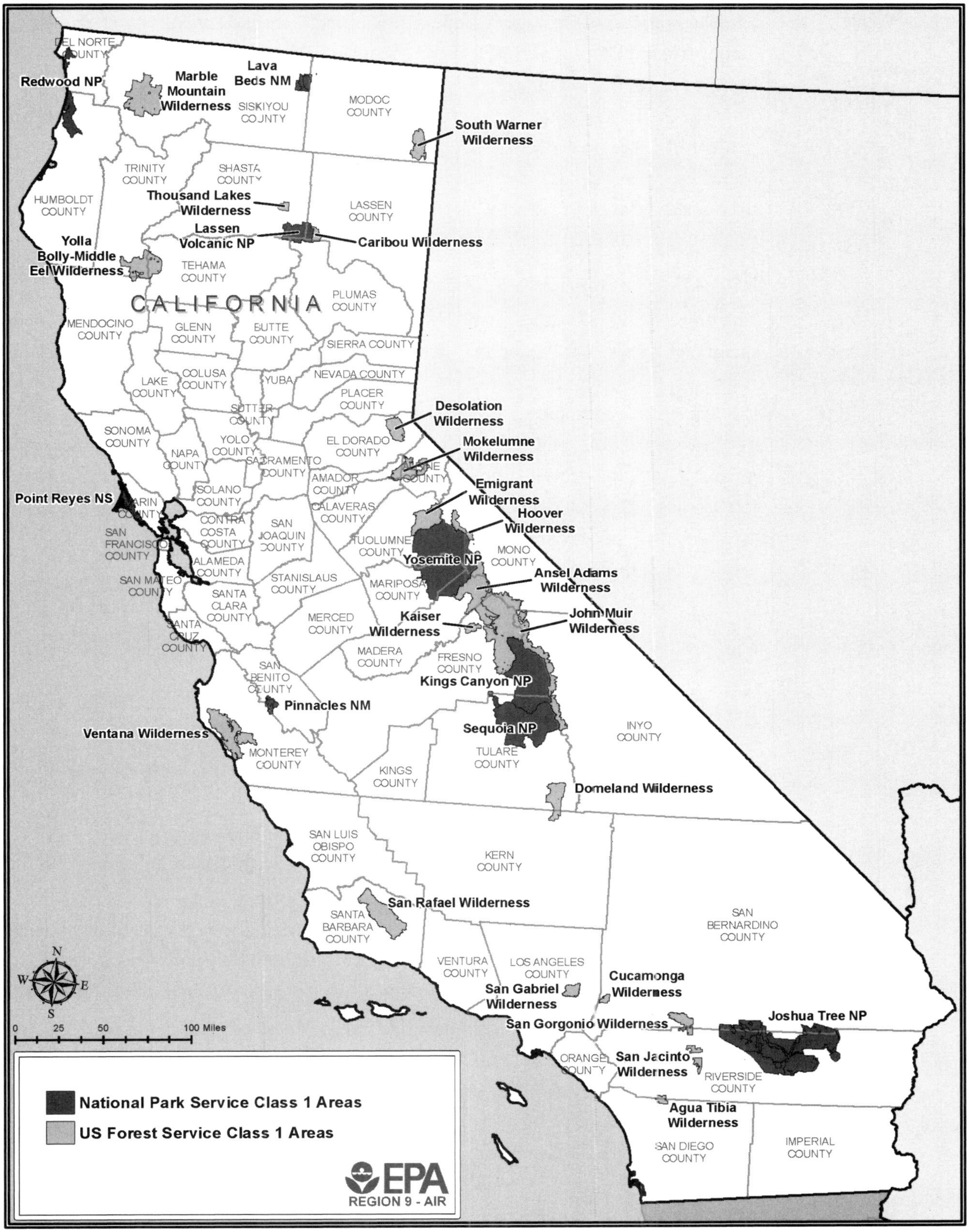

Source: https://www3.epa.gov/region9/air/maps/ca_clss1.html

AQIA = air quality impact analysis

RACT = reasonably available control technology

LAER = lowest achievable emission rate

source will not cause or contribute to a violation of NAAQS or PSD increments. This analysis considers construction, operation impacts, secondary emissions, and emissions after application of BACT. If the NAAQS or PSD increment is exceeded, a PSD permit cannot be issued.

The AQIA evaluates the existing ambient air quality level, together with the projected increased concentrations from the major new or modified source. Specifically, the AQIA uses a computer-based model to postulate the PTE from the new or modified source and adds these levels to the measured background concentrations from all existing sources in the air basin.

NON-ATTAINMENT NEW SOURCE REVIEW PROGRAM

The objective of non-attainment new source review is to achieve continuing improvement in air quality while allowing reasonable growth.

The objective of non-attainment NSR is to achieve continuing improvement in air quality while allowing reasonable growth. The non-attainment NSR program is similar to the PSD program, and only the principal differences regarding program applicability, control technology, and offsets are addressed in this section. Unlike the PSD permitting program, which allows sources to emit pollutants up to an increment of a given NAAQS, major new sources or modifications in non-attainment areas are subject to more rigorous permitting standards. The key differences between a non-attainment NSR permit and a PSD permit are (42 U.S.C. § 7503(a)(5)):

- The definition of major source
- Imposing reasonably available control technology (RACT) retrofits for existing sources with PTE of 100 TPY of ozone precursors in non-attainment areas
- Requiring the most stringent criteria pollutant control technologies available, using the lowest achievable emission rate (LAER)
- Requiring emission offsets (described below) for major new or modified major sources
- The need for applicants to certify that all major stationary sources they own or operate in the state are in compliance with CAA regulations
- The need for applicants to analyze alternative sites, sizes, production processes, and environmental control techniques demonstrating that the benefits of the proposed new source "significantly outweigh the environmental and social costs imposed as a result of its location, construction or modification"

A major new source or a major modification to an existing major source could involve simultaneous PSD and NSR permits as some emissions will be major for attainment pollutants and others may be major for non-attainment pollutants.

Program applicability. Non-attainment NSR permitting requirements apply to the non-attainment pollutants from major new or major modifications to sources. With the advent of the 1990 federal CAA Amendments, the non-attainment NSR permitting program now applies to increasingly smaller new or modified major sources. The definition of "major source" depends on the severity of an air basin's air pollution problems. Thus, a source emitting 10 TPY of NO_x or VOC is a major source in the South Coast Basin (an extreme ozone non-attainment area), but is a non-major or minor source in the San Francisco Bay Area (a marginal ozone non-attainment area). Table 5-7 on the following page presents the federal PTE thresholds and offset ratios for ozone in non-attainment air districts.

SNEI = significant net emissions increase

As with PSD permitting, when a major non-attainment source has a significant net emissions increase (SNEI) of a non-attainment pollutant, then non-attainment NSR permitting is triggered. The SNEI thresholds for ozone, PM_{10}, NO_2, SO_2, and CO appear in Table 5-8 on the following page.

Lowest achievable emission rate. LAER is the most stringent emissions limitation and is often a technology-forcing standard. Like BACT under the PSD program, LAER is specific to each type of stationary source, including fugitive emissions sources. It may not be less stringent than any applicable NSPS. LAER is determined by one of the following (whichever is more stringent) (EPA 1990):

- The most stringent emission limitation in the SIP of any state, by any source in the same industrial category (unless shown to be unachievable). In practice, LAER is often set by the South Coast AQMD, which typically has the most stringent SIP requirements in the country.
- The most stringent emission control achieved, by any source in the same industrial category. 42 U.S.C. § 7501(3); Health & Safety Code § 40405(b).
- Air districts determine whether a single measure or a combination of measures will be used to meet the LAER emissions limitation, on a case-by-case basis for a given source, without regard to cost, energy, or other environmental factors. Measures used to control emissions may consist of:
  - A change in the raw materials processed
  - A process modification
  - Add-on controls

Emissions offsets. The emissions offsets program is one of the most stringent controls for criteria pollutants emitted from major sources or major modifications. A proposed emissions increase by a major non-attainment source must be offset by an emissions decrease by existing sources within the area for the same criteria pollutant. The specific ratio of required offsets to emission increases is greater in more severe non-attainment areas, as illustrated in Table 5-7.

The emissions offsets program is one of the most stringent controls for criteria pollutants emitted from major sources or major modifications.

The units of replaced air emissions are referred to as offsets or emission reduction credits. For example, in a marginal ozone non-attainment area, if a major new source proposes to generate 100 new TPY of NO_x (after installing LAER), the source would need to provide at least 110 TPY of NO_x reductions from an existing source in the area. This can be accomplished in one of three ways:

- Pay an existing stationary source of non-attainment criteria pollutants to shut down

Table 5-7. Federal Potential to Emit Thresholds and Offset Ratios for Ozone Non-Attainment Air Districts

Non-attainment classification	Federal PTE threshold—in tons per year	Offset ratio
Marginal	100	1.1 to 1
Moderate	100	1.15 to 1
Serious	50	1.2 to 1
Severe	25	1.3 to 1
Extreme	10	1.5 to 1

Source: 42 U.S.C. § 7511

Table 5-8. Federal Significant Net Emissions Increase Thresholds for Major Non-Attainment Pollutants

Non-attainment classification	SNEI for ozone* (PTE in tons per year)	SNEI for PM_{10} (PTE in tons per year)	SNEI for NO_2 (PTE in tons per year)	SNEI for SO_2 (PTE in tons per year)	SNEI for CO (PTE in tons per year)
Marginal	40	—	40	40	100
Moderate	40	15	40	40	100
Serious	25	15	40	40	100
Severe	25**	—	40	40	100
Extreme	Any increase at an emission unit	—	40	40	100

* Including volatile organic compounds and NO_x as ozone precursors

** Please refer to statute for detailed explanation

Source: 42 U.S.C. § 7501 *et seq.*

- Pay an existing stationary source to better control existing emissions of non-attainment criteria pollutants
- Purchase offsets from an emissions bank (an emissions bank is an entity that holds emissions offsets "deposited" by stationary sources that shut down or installed better performing emission controls; offsets can be purchased and used later by other stationary sources)

Offsets must be pollutant-specific, quantifiable, surplus, permanent, federally enforceable, and voluntary.

Typical emission reductions that qualify for offsets include those that result from a source doing one or more of the following:

- Installing a control device that results in emissions control greater than required by regulation
- Agreeing to further limit actual emissions below levels required by permit or regulation
- Switching to a fuel that results in lower emissions

Offsets must be pollutant-specific, quantifiable, surplus, permanent, federally enforceable, and voluntary. Emissions reductions that result from other regulatory action do not qualify as offsets.

FEDERAL TITLE V OPERATING PERMIT PROGRAM

PTO = permit to operate

ATC = authority to construct

HAP = hazardous air pollutant

Prior to the enactment of the 1990 CAA Amendments, many state and local jurisdictions across the country did not require that a stationary source receive a permit to operate (PTO); an authority to construct (ATC) permit was all that was needed (these permits are discussed below). In these states, no mechanism existed to ensure that air emissions from a source under an ATC permit did not exceed emission limitations. To rectify this, the 1990 CAA Amendments established the Title V Operating Permits program (42 U.S.C. § 7661 *et seq.*), which is an expanded version of California's PTO program.

Under the Title V program, each state was obligated to adopt a federally enforceable operating permits program meeting specified minimum standards. 40 C.F.R. § 70. Title V consolidated all applicable federally enforceable requirements into one document for facilities meeting the definition of a major source under the Title V program. For example, a Title V operating permit serves as an umbrella document covering all relevant permit conditions for an oil refinery that hosts hundreds of stationary sources subject to a variety of permits (e.g., federal non-attainment NSR, PSD, NSPS, and NESHAP).

Local air districts implement the Title V program. Although the Title V program does not create new substantive performance standards, Title V operating permits obligate responsible officials to assure compliance at all permitted emission points. Local air district rules governing Title V permitting should be reviewed.

Although the Title V program does not create new substantive performance standards, Title V operating permits obligate responsible officials to assure compliance at all permitted emission points.

PROGRAM APPLICABILITY

The following stationary sources are considered major under Title V and thus are subject to Title V operating permit requirements:

- Sources that emit or have the potential to emit more than 100 TPY of any air pollutant
- A major source of hazardous air pollutants (includes sources with the potential to emit 10 TPY of a single hazardous air pollutant (HAP) or 25 TPY of two or more HAPs, and facilities considered area sources under the NESHAP program)
- New or modified sources required to obtain a PSD or non-attainment NSR permit
- Facilities subject to NSPS
- Power plants and other facilities subject to the acid rain program (Title IV of the 1990 CAA Amendments)
- "Anyways" Title V Source (i.e., sources subject to Title V "anyways" due to non-GHG emissions such as criteria pollutants or HAPs (these air emission sources must include GHG emission requirements).

CAM = compliance assurance monitoring

OPERATING PERMIT FEATURES

Key elements of a Title V operating permit include the permit application shield, operational flexibility, and compliance assurance monitoring (CAM).

A permit application shield is available for applicants who submit applications that are complete and timely. 42 U.S.C. § 7661c. Because the applicant may operate without a permit until the air district processes the application, the applicant may avoid (or be shielded from) additional or changed regulatory requirements not identified in the permit application.

Operational flexibility allows applicants to avoid the expense and uncertainty of a permit modification.

Operational flexibility allows applicants to avoid the expense and uncertainty of a permit modification. A permit holder may modify operations with seven days' notice to the regulating agency provided that both of the following are met (42 U.S.C. § 7661(a)):

- The modification falls within an alternative operating scenario previously identified in the permit application and approved in the permit. For example, a permit for a boiler system intended to burn natural gas could switch to fuel oil if the latter was previously approved as an alternative operating scenario.
- The emissions do not exceed the limitations established in the Title V operating permit.

Finally, the CAM rule (40 C.F.R. § 64.3) is intended to ensure that permit holders properly design and implement adequate control measures. The CAM rule is designed to ensure that control devices provide a reasonable assurance of compliance with emission limitations or standards for the anticipated range of operations at a facility.

PERMIT APPLICATIONS AND RENEWALS

New facilities must submit an initial application for an operating permit within 12 months after the source becomes subject to Title V. Generally, applications for Title V operating permits must include the following:

- Description of processes and products
- SIC code
- Description of equipment
- Description of exempt sources
- Citations of all air requirements applicable to the source(s)
- Summary of annual emissions
- Description of compliance status of all source(s)
- Compliance statement
- Compliance certification (including a statement that all fees are paid) signed by a responsible official

Title V operating permits are effective for five years. Permit renewal applications must be submitted at least six months before permit expiration. Local air districts have the discretionary authority to require renewal applications up to 18 months before permit expiration. Facilities subject to Title V operating permits must submit reports of required monitoring results every six months, certified by the responsible official.

DAP = district attainment plan

CALIFORNIA CLEAN AIR ACT PROGRAMS

Prior to the enactment of the California CAA of 1988, a number of air districts in California exceeded the CAAQS and NAAQS. At that time, a 1987 deadline to attain NAAQS had come and gone. California enacted the California CAA in response to the federal government's failure to enact tougher legislation to address non-attainment. The Act is intended to achieve and maintain the CAAQS, with an emphasis for non-attainment areas to achieve and maintain CAAQS for ozone, CO, NO_x, and SO_2. Many of the strategies in the California CAA of 1988 were adopted two years later in the federal CAA Amendments of 1990.

The California CAA classifies non-attainment areas according to the time it would take to achieve attainment. The Act imposes stringent requirements for stationary sources and expands air district authority to manage mobile and indirect sources. The Act requires that an air district designated non-attainment (whether moderate, serious, severe, or extreme) prepare and update a district attainment plan (DAP) to demonstrate how the district will attain and maintain the CAAQS by the earliest practicable date. Health & Safety Code §§ 40910–40926.

The California Clean Air Act imposes stringent requirements for stationary sources and expands air district authority to manage mobile and indirect sources.

DISTRICT ATTAINMENT PLAN

A DAP sets forth an air district's schedule for adopting rules to ensure attainment with CAAQS by specified dates. Air districts implement their DAPs by promulgating new rules that could impact existing, unpermitted stationary sources, as well as by implementing transportation control for mobile sources (discussed later in this chapter).

Basic requirements. The California CAA requires that a DAP achieves a district-wide emissions reduction of five percent per year for each non-attainment pollutant (ozone, CO, NO_x, and SO_2) or its precursors, averaged every three years. An air district may use an alternative strategy that will achieve less than a five percent reduction of non-attainment pollutants if one of the following is true:

- The alternative is demonstrated to be equal to or more effective than the five percent per year reduction
- The district is unable to achieve the five percent reduction despite use of all feasible measures

In addition, a DAP must include a permitting program designed to achieve a no-net-increase in emissions of non-attainment pollutants or precursors from all permitted new or modified sources. Health & Safety Code § 40914.

Air districts must publish an annual report summarizing progress toward meeting schedules for developing, adopting, and implementing air quality control measures. Triennially, air districts must assess the:

- Overall effectiveness of the air quality program
- Quantity of emissions reductions achieved in preceding three-year period
- Current and projected rates of population, industrial emissions, and vehicular emissions growth
- Validity of assumptions and progress toward goals in the DAP

Elimination of no-net-increase permitting requirements. AB 3319 (Health & Safety Code § 40918.5 *et seq.*) established a procedure for all air districts, except the South Coast Air Quality Management District (SCAQMD), to eliminate their no-net-increase permitting requirements within their DAPs. Although this legislation does not define "no net increase," it does state that air districts may not operate out of compliance with BACT.

An air district may petition the California ARB under this procedure if all of the following requirements are met:

- The air district has considered possible emissions growth that would occur in the absence of the no-net-increase program
- The air district has scheduled for adoption all feasible measures to achieve ambient air quality standards

Air districts responsible for or affected by emissions transported from one air basin to another must achieve attainment in both upwind and downwind air districts.

Upwind and downwind districts. Air districts responsible for or affected by emissions transported from one air basin to another must achieve attainment in both upwind and downwind air districts. The upwind districts must, at a minimum, adopt all mitigation measures established by the ARB. The downwind districts must have DAPs that contain sufficient measures to reduce local emissions below levels at which CAAQS violations occur in the absence of the transported emissions.

Non-attainment area requirements. California air districts experiencing non-attainment of the four criteria pollutants regulated by the California CAA are classified by the severity of non-attainment and must meet corresponding requirements. *See* Table 5-9. The requirements are additive—for example, an extreme non-attainment air district for a given pollutant must meet all requirements for moderate, serious, and severe non-attainment districts. Table 5-10 compares the California CAA and the federal CAA definition of a "major source" of ozone in non-attainment air districts.

Market-based incentive programs. Air districts may adopt market-based incentive programs as part of their DAPs. A market-based incentive program for stationary

Table 5-9. Non-Attainment Area New Source Review Requirements

	Non-attainment classification			
	Moderate	Serious	Severe	Extreme
Major source definition for NSR	Potential to emit is 25 TPY	PTE is 15 TPY	PTE is 10 TPY	Local NSR can be triggered by any increase over one lb/day (in the South Coast Air Quality Management District and the San Joaquin Valley Air Pollution Control District)
Control requirements	Reasonably available control technology for existing sources Best available retrofit control technology for existing larger sources (5 tons per day or 250 tons per year)	All moderate non-attainment requirements BARCT for all existing sources	All serious and moderate non-attainment requirements	All severe, serious,and moderate non-attainment requirements NSR permitting program to incorporate no-net-increase requirements
Transportation requirements	Reasonably available transportation control measures for districts with urbanized populations exceeding 50,000 Includes indirect/area source control programs	Measures to achieve the use of a significant number of low-emission motor vehicles by operators of motor vehicle fleets	Measures to achieve average weekday commuter ridership of 1.5 persons by 1999 and no net vehicle emissions after 1997 for districts with populations exceeding 250,000	Any other feasible measures that can be implemented within 10 years after an air quality plan has been adopted
Deadline requirements	Failure to meet requirements by December 31, 1997,triggers serious requirements	Failure to meet requirements by December 31, 1997,triggers severe requirements	Exposure levels must be reduced by at least 50 percent by December 31, 2000	None

Source: Health & Safety Code § 40920 *et seq.*

Table 5-10. Definition of a "Major Source" of Ozone in Non-Attainment Air Districts

Non-attainment classification	California Clean Air Act definition (PTE in tons per year)	Federal Clean Air Act definition (PTE in tons per year)
Marginal	—	100
Moderate	25	100
Serious	15	50
Severe	10	25
Extreme	0	10

Source: Health & Safety Code § 40910 *et seq.* and 40 C.F.R. § 51 App. S II A (4)(i) *et seq.*

A market-based incentive program for stationary sources can substitute for "command and control" regulations and future air quality measures, but must achieve an equivalent or greater reduction in emissions, at equivalent or less cost.

sources can substitute for "command and control" regulations and future air quality measures, but must achieve an equivalent or greater reduction in emissions, at equivalent or less cost. Health & Safety Code § 39616(c).

LOCAL PERMITTING FOR CRITERIA POLLUTANTS

There are generally two types of air quality permits for criteria pollutants under California law—a permit to construct (known as an authority to construct or ATC permit) and a permit to operate (PTO). These permits are required for a new major or major modification of a major source under the NSR permitting program (including non-attainment NSR and PSD). The criteria governing stationary source permitting, and substantive requirements for stationary sources, are detailed in local and regional air district rules and regulations. The definition of stationary source varies depending on the type of air quality permitting program and the local jurisdiction.

Authority to construct. A stationary source, unless exempt, requires an air quality permit before a device or piece of equipment is installed, constructed, or operated. ATC permits and PTOs typically are issued using the same permit application form, which must include detailed information describing the proposed equipment, along with anticipated chemicals, fuels, and operations. The ATC permit application process is intended to ensure that district requirements are considered before constructing or installing a stationary source, and to allow the applicant to make design changes in the early planning stages. Health & Safety Code § 42301. The applicant is responsible for demonstrating compliance with substantive and procedural air district requirements.

Each air district describes categories of operations and activities exempt from the ATC permit requirement. Exemptions vary from district to district. Owners of facilities claiming a permit exemption should consider drafting an internal memorandum describing the basis for reliance on the exemption.

ATC permits (as well as PTOs) may be subject to environmental review under CEQA. *See* chapter 2. Local air districts may serve as either a CEQA lead agency or a CEQA responsible agency. Some air districts have agency-specific CEQA procedures. Many districts in urban areas have adopted air quality thresholds of significance for determining whether an EIR is required, and have established standard mitigation measures to reduce air quality impacts.

Permit to operate. After the district permitting engineer issues an ATC permit and the stationary source has been installed or constructed, air district staff will inspect the stationary source to verify that the equipment meets the performance standards specified in the ATC permit. The air district then will issue a PTO, subject to payment of operating fees. The PTO may require the owner or operator to follow one or more operating conditions (e.g., specifying use of a certain fuel type, hours of operation, or use of an abatement device). Depending on the air district, PTOs are valid for one or two years and may be renewed simply by paying renewal fees. There are two major types of PTOs: individual source PTOs and site-wide PTOs under the Title V program (see previous discussion of federal Title V operating permit program).

The permit must incorporate conditions that govern specified emission limitations, fuels usage, control devices, and more. Typically, these conditions are identified through the CEQA process, as well as the NSR and air toxics permitting programs.

Air districts issue standardized permits for identical or similar air emission sources that require the same or similar information for monitoring and permit conditions. Typically, air districts maintain a list of pre-certified equipment subject to expedited permitting, such as portable internal combustion units, which require registration instead of a permit. Health & Safety Code § 42320 *et seq.*

A single facility may include several types of equipment that generate criteria pollutants and air toxics. As a result, a facility may have a number of source-specific air quality requirements. For example, typical large facilities that may require several PTOs include bulk petroleum operations, refineries, large-scale manufacturing, and power plants. Typical small businesses that may require only one PTO include dry cleaners, auto body shops, printers, and businesses with a back-up generator.

A single facility may include several types of equipment that generate criteria pollutants and air toxics. As a result, a facility may have a number of source-specific air quality requirements.

LOCAL NEW SOURCE REVIEW

Federal versus local programs. Federal non-attainment NSR programs and federal PSD programs are typically incorporated into local NSR programs; however, the emissions thresholds that require application of local BACT (equivalent to federal LAER) or offsets are considerably lower than the federal standards. As a result, a source with emissions too small to be a major source under the federal non-attainment NSR program may be subject to the local NSR program. EPA refers to the local NSR programs in California as the minor or state NSR programs. The requirements of the California CAA non-attainment NSR program are also incorporated into local rules by air districts.

Local emission control requirements. Local emission control requirements vary among air districts. Typically, the local non-attainment NSR programs apply to sources of air emissions that are subject to ATC permit and PTO requirements, and that exceed specified emission thresholds that trigger the need to comply with emissions control (e.g., local BACT) and offsets. It is important to note that the California definition for BACT is the same as LAER under the federal non-attainment NSR program.

Local emission offset requirements. Local emission offset requirements (like local emission control requirements) vary among air districts. Some air districts allow emissions banking, as described above for federal offsets. Local air district banking rules include administrative procedures that certify offsets. Typically, the rules

Table 5-11. Typical Structure of a Local Air District Rule	
Section	**Content**
General Provisions	Scope and applicability, including rule-specific exemptions
Definitions	Definitions specific to the particular rule; the same term defined in a particular rule may be defined differently in another rule
Substantive Standards	Permitting (authority to construct permits, permits to operate, and exemptions) Non-attainment new source review Prevention of significant deterioration New source performance standards (federally delegated) Operating permit program (federally delegated) Air toxics Prohibitory rules (equivalent to federal reasonably available control technology)
Administrative Procedures	Application procedures, time frames, methodologies, and other administrative requirements
Monitoring and Recordkeeping	Type and frequency of monitoring and recordkeeping
Manual of Procedures	Permitting procedures and policies, CEQA review, sample and source testing, monitoring emissions, and emission credits for mobile sources

include an application procedure and also specify which types of emissions do not qualify as offsets.

LOCAL DISTRICT RULES

Structure of local air district rules. Although local air district rules vary from district to district, each rule typically follows the structure shown in Table 5-11.

Local prohibitory rules. Local air districts establish RACT to address specified stationary sources that may not require permits. These rules, known as prohibitory rules, regulate inorganic and organic sources of emissions. Typical air district prohibitory rules regulate open burning, nuisance emissions, particulate matter emissions, organic pollutant emissions, inorganic gaseous pollutants, and hazardous air pollutants.

Open burning. The ARB has special programs regulating agricultural burning (Health & Safety Code § 41580 *et seq.*) and nonagricultural burning (Health & Safety Code § 41800 *et seq.*). ARB establishes guidelines for agricultural burning control in air basins and determines days on which agricultural burning is prohibited.

Nuisance emissions. Industrial facilities in full compliance with federal, state, and local permits and requirements may still be in violation of California's nuisance rule. California sets forth a "catchall" nuisance prohibition (Health & Safety Code § 41700) that is often used as a tool by the public to further control air emissions. For example, a paint manufacturer in full compliance with its PTO could be required to install additional controls to manage the olfactory emissions. Local air districts typically promulgate nuisance provisions similar or identical to the state nuisance rule, which reads:

> [N]o person shall discharge from any source whatsoever such quantities of air contaminants or other material which cause injury, detriment, nuisance, or annoyance to any considerable number of persons or to the public, or which endanger the comfort, repose, health, or safety of any such persons or the public, or which cause, or have a natural tendency to cause, injury or damage to business or property.

SB 1224 of 2010 (Chapter 411, Statures of 2010) was enacted to manage instances where the public lodges repeated and unsubstantiated odor complaints with an air district. SB 1224 allows air districts freedom to manage their finite enforcement resources by authorizing them to issue rules giving them discretion to ignore repeated and unsubstantiated air quality complaints or complaints made in bad faith.

Visible emissions. California has regulatory programs for visible emissions. Health & Safety § 41701. Local air districts typically adopt California regulations into local air district rules. For example, local air district rules typically state that a person may not emit any air pollutant into the atmosphere for more than three minutes during any one hour if the emissions are dark or darker in shade or opacity as designated by No. 2 on the Ringelmann Chart, as published by the United States Bureau of Mines. Health & Safety § 41701(a).

Local air districts typically adopt California regulations into local air district rules.

STRATOSPHERIC OZONE PROTECTION

Title VI of the 1990 federal CAA Amendments (42 U.S.C. § 7661 *et seq.*) was designed to implement the Montreal Protocol, which is an international treaty directing the phase-out of substances that deplete the protective ozone layer. These substances (known as ozone-depleting chemicals) include well-known refrigerants such as freons, chlorofluorocarbons (CFCs), and other halogenated compounds that aggressively react with ozone molecules in the upper stratosphere (approximately seven miles above the ground).

The program prohibits the production (with some exceptions) of carbon tetrachloride, methyl chloroform, and Class I substances (that include CFCs and halons). Production of Class II chemicals (that consist of 33 hydro-chloro-fluoro-carbons or HCFCs) were to be frozen at baseline year levels (1993) beginning January 1, 2015. After January 1, 2015, Class II substances cannot be introduced into interstate commerce unless one of the following is true:

- The substance has been used, recovered, or recycled
- The substance is used and entirely consumed in the production of other chemicals
- The substance is used as a refrigerant in an appliance manufactured before January 1, 2020

By January 1, 2030, there will be a ban on production of Class II substances.

The 1990 federal CAA Amendments (42 U.S.C. § 7401 *et seq.*) authorize the trading or production and consumption allowances between two or more persons under specified circumstances. Also, standards exist for the use and disposal of Class I and II substances during the service, repair, or disposal of industrial process refrigeration. 42 U.S.C. § 7671g(b).

Owners or operators of refrigeration and air-conditioning equipment with refrigerant charges greater than 50 pounds are required to repair leaks within 30 days when those leaks result in the loss of more than a specified percentage of the equipment's refrigerant charge. For comfort cooling (such as building chillers), leaks must be repaired when the appliance leaks at a rate that would release 15 percent or more of the charge over a year. Leaks from commercial industrial refrigeration must be repaired when leak rates are 35 percent or more. 40 C.F.R. § 82.300 *et seq.*

ACID RAIN

FEDERAL PROGRAM

The goal of the federal acid rain program is to reduce emissions of the two primary causes of acid rain: sulfur dioxide (SO_2) and nitrogen oxides (NO_x).

The goal of the federal acid rain program is to reduce emissions of the two primary causes of acid rain: sulfur dioxide (SO_2) and nitrogen oxides (NO_x). (SO_2 forms sulfuric acid, and NO_x forms nitric acid.) Authorized by Title IV of the 1990 federal CAA Amendments (42 U.S.C. § 7651 *et seq.*), the federal program reduces SO_2 and NO_x emissions in a number of ways.

First, the CAA Amendments established an SO_2 allowance trading program primarily affecting large coal-fired power plants. Under Phase I of this program, EPA issued SO_2 allowances to mostly coal-burning electric utility plants for each ton of SO_2 emitted. Allowances are transferable, allowing a utility to buy, sell, or bank its allowances as necessary. At the end of the year, the utility must have enough allowances to cover its SO_2 emissions. However, if the utility comes up short, the source will be deemed non-compliant and subject to monetary penalties. 42 U.S.C. § 7651e. Phase II of this allowance trading program began in 2000. Phase II applies to all fossil-fuel-fired utility plants and implements a permanent, collective cap of 8.95 million tons per year.

Second, in addition to limiting SO_2 emissions, the CAA Amendments also established a NO_x reduction program, with the goal of reducing annual NO_x emissions by two million tons from 1980 levels. Unlike the SO_2 program, the NO_x program focuses on emission rates rather than allowances and emission ceilings. Utility boilers may opt into the NO_x program by complying with individual emission rates or by using emission averaging, whereby utilities may average emission rates over two or more unit sources.

MACT = maximum achievable control technology

GACT = generally achievable control technology

STATE PROGRAM

The state previously established a program to control acid rain, called the Atmospheric Acidity Protection Act of 1988 (Health & Safety Code § 39900 *et seq.*). The Atmospheric Acidity Protection Program Scientific Advisory Committee issued a report concluding that pollutants that cause acid rain (such as oxides of nitrogen) have been declining since the 1970s because of other air pollution laws that reduce these emissions. Based on these results, AB 1459 of 2012 (Chapter 186, Statutes of 1012) repealed the Atmospheric Acidity Protection Act of 1988.

AIR TOXICS

FEDERAL PROGRAM

National Emissions Standards for Hazardous Air Pollutants Program. Historically, Congress and EPA emphasized control of the six federal criteria pollutants. These high volume pollutants, emitted largely from sources involving combustion, were better understood than air toxics at the time of the 1970 CAA and its major amendments in 1977.

Prior to the enactment of the 1990 federal CAA Amendments, the EPA regulated only eight hazardous air pollutants pursuant to the NESHAP program. Title III of the 1990 federal CAA Amendments dramatically expanded EPA's authority to regulate routine HAP emissions and accidental releases. Congress greatly increased the number of HAPs subject to regulation to include 189 chemicals or chemical compounds. The current list includes only 187 chemicals or chemical compounds because mercaptan and methyl ethyl ketone were since removed.

Program applicability. The NESHAP program regulates two types of stationary sources of HAPs—major sources and area sources. A major source is defined as an industrial facility or contiguous group of stationary sources under common control with a PTE of 10 TPY or more of any single HAP or 25 TPY of any combination of HAPs. A major source of HAPs that is on the list of industry source categories must comply with the maximum achievable control technology (MACT) standards. Industry-specific MACT standards that have been developed for approximately 200 industry source categories include petroleum refineries, chemical plants, aerospace manufacturers, smelting, pharmaceutical production, semiconductor manufacturing, concrete and asphalt manufacturing, auto manufacturing, publicly owned treatment works, site remediation, and hazardous waste treatment, storage, and disposal facilities.

The NESHAP program regulates two types of stationary sources of HAPs—major sources and area sources.

Area sources (sources too small to qualify as major sources) must comply with a lower performance standard known as generally achievable control technology (GACT). Area source industry categories include, among many others, commercial dry cleaners, auto body refinishing, Portland cement production, lead and copper foundries, metal fabricators, oil and natural gas production, gasoline distribution, industrial boilers, hospital sterilizers, municipal landfills, chemical manufacturing, POTWs, and pharmaceutical production.

Maximum achievable control technology. Unlike NSR programs that are premised on meeting and attaining the NAAQS, the NESHAP program does not establish ambient air quality standards for HAPs. Instead, the program requires major new or modified major sources of HAPs to comply with MACT. The NESHAP program allows EPA to later promulgate more stringent MACT for individual industrial categories that, based on health risk assessment, warrant increased control. 40 C.F.R. § 63.

MACT represents technology-based standards that require the maximum degree of emissions reduction of HAPs that EPA, after considering costs and other environmental impacts, determines is achievable. 42 U.S.C. § 7412(d). MACT standards are more stringent for new sources compared to existing sources within a given industrial category. For new stationary sources, MACT is as stringent as the control achieved in practice by the best controlled similar sources; for existing sources, MACT is the average emissions reduction of the top 12 percent of sources or the top five similar sources.

MACT standards include control equipment, process changes, material substitutions, work practices, operator trainings and certifications, and more.

MACT standards include control equipment, process changes, material substitutions, work practices, operator trainings and certifications, and more. Some MACT standards control fugitive emissions (e.g., emissions from flanges, pumps, seals, valves, and compressors), while others capture and treat emissions.

MACT is required for major new sources of HAPs or modifications to existing major sources that exceed *de minimis* thresholds of HAPs. As a practical matter, MACT typically reduces emissions of air toxics by about 95–99 percent. MACT is not required for new or modified sources that fully offset their net emission increases of HAPs below these major threshold amounts. Four major provisions govern the schedule for MACT implementation (42 U.S.C. § 7412(i)):

- Major new sources must comply with standards when beginning operations that emit HAPs.
- Major sources constructed or reconstructed after issuance of draft MACT rules, but before final MACT rules, may comply with the draft rules if the final rules are more stringent.
- After MACT rules are finalized, existing major sources must comply no more than three years after the rule is finalized.
- A qualifying major source may be granted compliance deferment under the Early Reductions Program if the facility reduces its HAP emissions by 90 percent before MACT standards are proposed.

Area sources. Generally available control technology is required for area sources. The aggregate emissions of area sources account for 90 percent of HAP emissions that pose the greatest public health risk in the majority of urban areas. In 1999, the EPA created the Urban Air Toxics Strategy to establish and prioritize the unequal risks that HAPs in urban areas have on the public health and the environment. The strategy establishes GACT standards for dry cleaners, gas stations, municipal landfills, and paint stripping operations, to name a few.

RMP = risk management plan

PSM = process safety management

ATCM = airborne toxic control measure

Accidental release program. The 1990 federal CAA Amendments (section 112(r)) also establishes a program to prevent the accidental release of "highly hazardous chemicals" such as anhydrous ammonia and gaseous chlorine. 42 U.S.C. § 7412. Facilities that manufacture, process, use, store, or handle highly hazardous chemicals exceeding threshold quantities of flammable and toxic compounds must complete hazard assessments and, in some cases, risk management plans (RMPs). These regulations apply to, among other facilities, cold storage facilities (using ammonia as a refrigerant), public drinking water systems (using chlorine gas), manufacturers, propane retailers, some wholesalers, and some service industries. RMPs must include, among other things (40 C.F.R. § 68 *et seq.*):

Facilities that manufacture, process, use, store, or handle highly hazardous chemicals exceeding threshold quantities of flammable and toxic compounds must complete hazard assessments and, in some cases, risk management plans.

- A hazard assessment, including a modeled off-site consequence analysis
- A prevention plan, including a description of the management system used to manage the risk posed by the hazard assessment
- An emergency response plan

The RMP program consists of three program tiers. Program 1 consists of an abbreviated RMP. Program 2 applies if the facility is not subject to Program 1 or 3. Finally, Program 3 requires developing and implementing an RMP with the complete set of RMP program features. Program 3 RMPs apply to processes in specific industrial facilities such as pulp mills, petroleum refineries, and petrochemical manufacturing. Program 3 RMPS are similar to a federal worker safety program that manages potential, catastrophic chemical releases in the workplace (under the OSHA process safety management [PSM] standard). 29 C.F.R. § 1910.119. However, RMPs emphasize preventing and managing potential consequences of a chemical release beyond the facility boundary.

STATE PROGRAM

Toxic air contaminants. Prior to the 1990 federal CAA Amendments, which significantly revamped the original NESHAP program, California already had established a rigorous air toxics program (Health & Safety Code § 39650 *et seq.*), often referred to as the Toxic Air Contaminants Program or "AB 1807." This program requires OEHHA to study, on an ongoing basis, the health effects of potentially harmful chemicals.

After extensive review, OEHHA is authorized to identify toxic air contaminants. Once a TAC is identified or "listed," the ARB has authority to control the TAC using airborne toxic control measures (ATCMs), which control emissions to the lowest achievable level. If it is possible to measure a specified TAC threshold level, the ATCM is designed to reduce emissions at or below that threshold. Local air districts implement ATCMs through promulgation of rules.

HRA = health risk assessment

CalARP = California Accidental Release Prevention Program

CUPAs = Certified Unified Program Agencies

T-BACT = best available control technology for toxics

TOGs = toxic organic gases

The ARB initially identified approximately 20 TACs and promulgated ATCMs for many of these chemicals. Perhaps the most common ATCM is the Phase II vapor recovery used at retail gasoline stations to control benzene (a TAC) emissions during fueling operations. The 187 HAPs are California TACs (Health & Safety § 39650 *et seq.*), so the ARB can impose ATCMs for federal HAPs. As a result, there are now more than 200 TACs.

Diesel exhaust is linked to more than 40 other cancer-causing substances. In fact, the ARB found that 70 percent of California's airborne cancer risk is due to exposures to diesel particulate matter which is found in diesel exhaust. Based on these findings, in 1998, the ARB designated diesel particulate matter as a TAC under California's Air Toxics program.

Regarding pesticides, the California Department of Pesticide Regulation (DPR) has listed only seven TAC pesticides (and one breakdown pesticide product) compared to the over 900 pesticides currently registered in California. AB 304 of 2013 (Chapter 584, Statutes of 2013) requires the Director of DPR to establish control measures for listed TACs.

The ARB is implementing an In-Use Off-Road Diesel Vehicle Regulation, which reduces diesel particulate matter emissions from existing off-road diesel vehicles used in industry.

Toxic hot spots. The California Air Toxic "Hot Spots" Information and Assessment Act (AB 2588 of 1987, Health & Safety Code § 44300 *et seq.*) is a unique procedural and substantive law designed to identify hot spots of exposure and risk and, in some cases, control them. The program applies to facilities that manufacture, formulate, use, or release one or more regulated TACs and emit or have the potential to emit specified amounts of the following criteria pollutants: toxic organic gases (TOGs) (e.g., VOCs including methane), PM, NO_X, and SO_X. Emission inventory submittal dates vary for facilities emitting or having the potential to emit over 25 TPY, between 10 and 25 TPY, and less than 10 TPY.

Appendix E of ARB's "Emission Inventory Criteria and Guidelines Report" lists classes of facilities emitting less than 10 TPY of criteria pollutants (such as wastewater treatment facilities) that are subject to the Act's requirements. In some cases, facilities are subject to the Act because they historically appeared on local air district air toxics inventories. There is a general exclusion from Appendix E for "any individual facility...which, in the judgment of the district, a health-conservative, preliminary assessment of the facility's emissions indicates that the facility's emissions would result in a prioritization score, risk level, or *de minimis* level which would qualify as a 'low level' facility for reporting purposes."

In some instances, air toxics emissions must be quantified, while in other cases only reporting of the production or other presence of chemicals is required. The air emissions inventory data must be submitted to the local air district with jurisdiction over the facility. The air district performs an assessment of the air toxics emissions inventory and determines whether the facility poses a potentially "high" health risk to the surrounding community. A prioritization score for cancer and non-cancer health effects equal to or less than one exempts the facility from reporting and fee obligations. Regulated facilities must inventory their routine air toxic emissions every four years if they have a prioritization score equal to or less than 10. Health & Safety Code § 44360 *et seq.*

Those facilities deemed to be a high risk are required to perform a health risk assessment (HRA). If the assessment concludes that the facility poses a significant health risk, the facility must notify exposed persons of this risk. As a practical matter, shortly after the Act became effective, some businesses substituted regulated toxic substances to avoid the need to perform the risk assessments that could require notification to neighbors of a significant health exposure.

Additionally, facilities that pose a significant risk must adopt an airborne risk reduction program within six months of the risk assessment. The airborne risk reduction program must reduce risks below the significance threshold discussed in the health risk assessment within five years. If risk reduction measures are technically feasible and economically practicable, the five-year timetable can be shortened. Health & Safety § 44390 *et seq.*

California Accidental Release Prevention Program. The California Accidental Release Prevention Program (CalARP, 19 Cal. Code Regs. § 2735 *et seq.*) is administered by the Governor's Office of Emergency Services and delegated to local Certified Unified Program Agencies (CUPAs) for implementation and enforcement. The goal of the program is to reduce and eliminate the accidental release of potentially harmful substances into the environment. The CalARP implements the federal Risk Management Program. However, compared with the RMP, CalARP has additional requirements under the California Health and Safety Code, such as a more inclusive list of toxic chemicals, smaller chemical threshold quantities, and performance of external event analysis (such as seismic analysis). California's legislative intent was that compliance by a regulated business or agency with CalARP would satisfy requirements of the federal accidental release prevention program. Health & Safety Chapter 6.95, Article 2. CUPAs have discretion to make a completed RMP available for public review via newspaper or CUPA's internet web site (Health & Safety Code § 25535.2).

SB 54 of 2012 (Chapter 795, Statutes of 2012) was enacted in the wake of the dramatic fire that occurred at the Chevron Richmond Refinery in the summer of 2012. This law establishes minimum skills and safety training for contractors working at chemical manufacturing and processing facilities, including refineries. Owners or operators of stationary sources engaged in petrochemical activities must ensure that their contractors and subcontractors use skilled and trained workforces paid a prevailing wage to perform on-site work on these high-hazard jobs.

Under SB 54, owners or operators of petroleum facilities subject to an RMP (governed by Section 112R of the Clean Air Act) must ensure that their contractors and subcontractors only use skilled and trained workers involving the

Revised Health Risk Assessment Methodology

In 2015, OEHHA revised its health risk assessment guidelines for the first time since 2003. The updated guidelines explicitly consider exposures to infants and children and are expected to result in higher health risk predictions. As a result, more facilities are likely to be reprioritized for submitting AB 2588 HRAs. The revised guidelines could result in more facilities exceeding public notification levels of 10-in-one-million cancer risk under AB 2588. In addition, businesses that were exempt from public notification pursuant to Proposition 65 may be required to notify employees and the public of their exposures to carcinogens and reproductive toxins.

More new or modified air emission sources are expected to exceed air toxics thresholds and will be required to deploy best available control technology for toxics (T-BACT). Finally, projects subject to CEQA with public health risks have an increased chance of exceeding significant impact levels which could require disclosures of significant health risk impacts and project mitigation measures.

building and construction trades. This applies to construction, alteration, demolition, installation, repair, or maintenance work at regulated stationary sources. Oil and gas extraction operations are exempt from these requirements.

Air Quality and Land Use Handbook. ARB has issued a guidance document for siting of sensitive receptors near sources of toxic air contaminants (ARB 2005). The handbook is intended to provide information to reduce exposure of vulnerable populations to sources of air pollution. ARB recommends that local agencies avoid siting sensitive land uses within 500 feet of a freeway or high-volume roadway, and also presents recommended distances to separate sensitive land uses from other sources of TACs, e.g., railyards, ports, and gas stations.

Air emissions from solid waste disposal sites. Solid waste disposal site owners or operators (at active and, in some cases, inactive landfills) must perform air quality tests and report on the results. Health & Safety Code § 41805(a). The ARB has issued guidelines for this testing program. Health & Safety Code § 41805.5.

High Global Warming Refrigeration Systems. Similar to the federal ODC program described above, facilities in California with stationary non-residential refrigeration systems must implement a leak detection inspection and repair program. This program applies to refrigeration systems with more than 50 pounds of high-GWP refrigerants (*see* chapter 20.)

TRANSPORTATION SOURCE REGULATION

TRANSPORTATION CONTROL MEASURES

Under the federal CAA, states such as California must require employers of 100 or more persons located in severe and extreme ozone non-attainment areas to increase average vehicle ridership by at least 25 percent by certain dates.

The California CAA requires air districts to implement transportation control measures to attain SIP requirements. Health & Safety Code § 40716 *et seq.* Transportation control measures are strategies to reduce vehicle trips, vehicle use, and vehicle miles traveled, such as employee trip reduction programs. For example, under the federal CAA, states such as California must require employers of 100 or more persons located in severe and extreme ozone non-attainment areas to increase average vehicle ridership by at least 25 percent by certain dates.

Recognizing that transportation control measures can be controversial, the Legislature has established detailed conditions that must be met before an air district may impose a trip reduction program to assure the requirement is legally necessary, is not duplicative, is feasible, and is cost-effective. Health & Safety Code §§ 40717.5, 40919. Air districts generally may not impose transportation control measures that reduce shopping trips, or on event centers such as sports arenas that meet certain average vehicle ridership. The Legislature has enacted specific restrictions on the ability of the South Coast AQMD to impose employee trip reduction programs. Health & Safety Code § 40454 *et seq.*

TRANSPORTATION CONFORMITY REGULATIONS

DOT = Department of Transportation

TIP = transportation improvement plan

Under EPA's transportation conformity regulations, regional planning agencies or Caltrans, and ultimately the U.S. Department of Transportation (DOT), are required to show that transportation plans and projects conform to the SIP. 40 C.F.R. § 93.105. The process is designed to assure that new transportation investments do not create a new air quality violation, increase the frequency or severity of an existing air quality violation, or delay timely attainment of NAAQS. The conformity requirement applies to regional transportation plans, the state transportation improvement plan (TIP), and transportation projects funded or approved by DOT.

To show SIP conformity, the modeled emissions produced by transportation activities may not exceed the SIP motor vehicle emissions "budgets." Project-level, hot-spot analysis also is required for carbon monoxide and particulates.

MOBILE SOURCE REGULATION

Overview. The federal CAA establishes control strategies for motor vehicle emissions and fuels. California's motor vehicle emission program parallels the federal program, but the state has its own motor vehicle emissions standards, certification, and enforcement programs. Mobile sources regulated by ARB include more than just motor vehicles; ARB regulates both on- and off-road sources such as passenger cars, motorcycles, trucks, buses, locomotives and railyards, heavy-duty construction equipment, recreational vehicles, marine vessels, lawn and garden equipment, and small utility engines.

California's motor vehicle emission program parallels the federal program, but the state has its own motor vehicle emissions standards, certification, and enforcement programs.

At both the federal and state levels, mobile source regulations for conventional air pollutant emissions and for GHG emissions have increasingly become integrated. For that reason, the descriptions below address both types of emissions. For further descriptions of transportation measures to reduce GHG missions, please see chapter 20.

Motor vehicle emissions standards. The CAA regulates tailpipe emissions by requiring motor vehicle manufacturers to achieve certain reductions in exhaust emissions, and as mentioned above, California has a parallel, and in many cases more stringent, program. EPA has established emissions standards for NO_x, CO, hydrocarbons, particulates, diesel smoke, and formaldehyde.

Although Section 209 of the CAA pre-empts the authority of states to regulate emissions from new motor vehicles, the CAA allows EPA waivers from pre-emption for specific standards enacted by California. In the absence of such an EPA waiver, state emissions standards can be pre-empted. For example, in *Engine Manufacturers Assn. v. South Coast AQMD* (2004) 124 S. Ct. 1756, the U.S. Supreme Court held that SCAQMD regulations controlling emissions from vehicle fleets were at least partially pre-empted by federal law.

Only new motor vehicles covered by an EPA certification of conformity may be sold or distributed in the United States. EPA enforces the emissions standards through durability testing at the time of certification, confirmatory testing, emission control system warranty and recall, and tampering provisions. The state emissions standards cover all these topics, require state certification of new motor vehicles, and include an inspection (smog check) program.

GHG emissions standards and Advanced Clean Cars Program. Assembly Bill 1493 of 2002 (Chapter 200, Statutes of 2002), also known as the Pavley regulations, required California to establish new standards for motor vehicle GHG emissions beginning in the model year 2009. Health & Safety Code §§ 42823, 43018.5. AB 1493 mandated a 30 percent reduction in motor vehicle GHG emissions by 2016. ARB adopted implementing regulations in 2005. 13 Cal. Code Regs. §§ 1900, 1961, 1961.1.

In January 2012, ARB approved a new emissions control program for model years 2017 through 2025. The program combines the control of conventional air pollutants and GHGs, and requirements for greater numbers of zero-emission vehicles, into a single package of standards called Advanced Clean Cars (13 Cal. Code Regs. §§ 1962.1, 1962.2). The Advanced Clean Cars requirements include new GHG standards for model years 2017 to 2025 vehicles.

The Charge Ahead California Initiative and other state programs promote rapid deployment of electric vehicles.

The Advanced Clean Cars Program also includes the Low Emission Vehicle (LEV) III amendments to the LEV regulations (13 Cal. Code Regs. § 1900 *et seq.*), the Zero Emission Vehicle Program, and the Clean Fuels Outlet Regulation. The Zero Emission Vehicle Program is designed to achieve California's long-term emission reduction goals by requiring manufacturers to offer for sale specific numbers of zero-emission vehicles, which include battery electric, fuel cell, and plug-in hybrid electric vehicles. The Clean Fuels Outlet regulation is intended to ensure that fuels such as electricity and hydrogen are available to meet the fueling needs of the new advanced technology vehicles as they come to market.

Charge Ahead California Initiative. SB 1275 of 2014 (Chapter 530, Statutes of 2014) establishes the Charge Ahead California Initiative. The Initiative directs ARB to establish a funding plan and programs to achieve the goals of placing in service at least one million zero-emission and near-zero-emission vehicles by 2023, establishing a self-sustaining market for these vehicles, and increasing access to these vehicles for disadvantaged, low-income, and moderate-income communities.

Heavy-duty vehicle emissions regulations. The ARB has adopted on-road heavy-duty vehicle (in-use) regulations to reduce emissions of particulates, NOx, and other criteria pollutants (13 Cal. Code Regs. § 2025 *et seq.*). These regulations require diesel trucks and buses to be upgraded to reduce emissions. Newer heavier trucks and buses had to meet particulate filter requirements beginning January 1, 2012. Lighter and older heavier trucks needed to be replaced as of January 1, 2015.

By January 1, 2023, nearly all trucks and buses are required to have 2010 model year engines or equivalent.

Also, heavy-duty vehicle regulations described in chapter 20 (13 Cal. Code Regs. § 2020 *et seq.)* reduce conventional pollutants as well as GHG emissions by improving the fuel efficiency of heavy-duty tractors that pull 53-foot or longer box-type trailers.

ARB has also adopted anti-idling regulations. With some exceptions, heavy-duty diesel vehicles with a Gross Vehicle Weight Rating (GVWR) of 10,000 lbs. or more in weight are prohibited from idling for more than five minutes. Trucks and buses must shut down their engines immediately upon arrival and leave within 30 seconds of starting the engine. 13 Cal. Code Regs. § 2485.

Lastly, ARB's Periodic Smoke Inspection Program (PSIP) requires owners of diesel and bus fleets to annually perform self-inspections to determine smoke opacity for trucks older than four years. For those trucks experiencing excessive smoke emissions, the owner is required to demonstrate compliance with the emission limit. Owners of heavy-duty diesel motor vehicles must perform smoke opacity inspections and any necessary repairs on or before December 31 of each year. 13 Cal. Code Regs. § 2180 *et seq.*

GVWR = Gross Vehicle Weight Rating

PSIP = Periodic Smoke Inspection Program

Shore power electrification and port drayage trucks. ARB's "at-berth regulation" is designed to reduce criteria air and GHG emissions associated with diesel auxiliary engines on container ships, passenger ships, and refrigerated cargo ships docked at ports in California. These ships are required to either connect to the electrically powered grid or use an alternative control that achieves equivalent emission reductions in lieu of running auxiliary engines. 17 Cal. Code Regs. § 93118.3.

Also, ARB has adopted special regulations to reduce emissions of diesel PM, NOx, and other air contaminants by setting emission standards for in-use, heavy-duty diesel-fueled vehicles that transport cargo to and from California's ports and intermodal rail facilities. 13 Cal. Code Regs. § 2027 *et seq.* Among other requirements, owners of heavy drayage trucks (over 26,000 pounds) with engine model year 2007 or newer are fully compliant until December 31, 2022 for ports and rail yards. Starting January 1, 2023, heavy trucks must have a 2010 model year or newer engine to continue entering ports and railyards. All drayage trucks must register in ARB's Drayage Truck Registry prior to port or railyard entry.

Among other requirements, owners of heavy drayage trucks (over 26,000 pounds) with engine model year 2007 or newer are fully compliant until December 31, 2022 for ports and rail yards.

Carl Moyer Memorial Air Quality Standards Attainment Program. The Carl Moyer Program provides grant funding for cleaner-than-required engines and equipment (Health & Safety Code § 44275 *et seq.*). Local air districts administer these grants and select which projects to fund. ARB works collaboratively with the districts and other stakeholders to set Guidelines. Eligible projects include cleaner on-road, off-road, marine, locomotive, lawn and garden, light duty passenger vehicles being scrapped and agricultural equipment. SB 513 of 2015 (Chapter 610,

Statutes of 2015) expanded the types of projects eligible for funding. Alternative fuel and electric infrastructure and marine vessels projects are now eligible for funding to achieve state and local air quality goals.

Regulation of vehicle fuels. ARB was required, no later than January 1, 1992, to take whatever actions were necessary, cost-effective, and technologically feasible to achieve by December 31, 2000 an emissions reduction of:

- Reactive organic gases of at least 55 percent
- NO_x from motor vehicles of at least 15 percent
- Particulate matter, CO, and TACs from vehicular sources, to the maximum feasible extent

Health & Safety Code § 43018(b)

Beginning in 1992, California required clean-burning, reformulated gasoline to be sold in the state, to reduce emissions of VOCs and toxics. ARB also regulates specifications for diesel fuel to make it cleaner burning, and has implemented an alternative diesel fuels program.

Also, pursuant to the California AB 1807 air toxics program (Health & Safety Code § 39666), local air districts regulate emissions from the distribution of gasoline. Service station vapor recovery nozzles have been required in California since the late 1970s. Vapor recovery systems also are required for cargo tanks used to haul gasoline.

Low carbon fuel standard. The LCFS program was created by Executive Order S-01-07, which sets a target of reducing the carbon intensity of California's transportation fuels by at least 10 percent by 2020. (Carbon intensity is GHG emissions per unit of motive power.) ARB adopted LCFS regulations in 2010. 17 Cal. Code Regs. § 95480 *et seq*. The regulations set forth average carbon intensity requirements and compliance schedules for gasoline, diesel fuels, and alternative fuels. See chapter 20 for further discussion of the LCFS.

Marine fuel requirements. Starting in 2014, vessels burning marine gas oil and marine diesel oil were limited to less than 0.1 percent sulfur content. These "Phase II" requirements are enforced within the California ocean-going vessel regulatory zone, which is 24 nautical miles off the coast of California, including islands. 13 Cal. Code Regs. § 2299.2.

ENFORCEMENT

FEDERAL ENFORCEMENT

Citizen suits can be filed to force EPA or the states to enforce clean air laws, and citizen suits also can be filed against violating sources.

EPA has concurrent authority, with the states, to enforce CAA permit conditions and SIP provisions. Citizen suits can be filed to force EPA or the states to enforce clean air laws, and citizen suits also can be filed against violating sources. Enforcement options include abatement orders, civil penalties, and criminal penalties. EPA can seek a monetary fine (up to $25,000 per day per violation) or an injunction against a non-complying source. EPA is alternatively authorized to pursue an administrative action without going through the Department of Justice and a trial court. CAA Section 113(d), 42 U.S.C. § 7413(d).

A Field Citation Program allows EPA to impose monetary fines of up to $5,000 per day per violation for minor violations. Alleged violators under this program can pay the fine or request an informal, administrative hearing at a place "reasonably close" to the place of business receiving the citation. 42 U.S.C. § 7413 § (d)(B)(3). The field citation program streamlines EPA's ability to enforce noncompliance enforcement without having to bring every violation to court.

Civil penalties. The maximum total civil penalty for violations under the CAA is $200,000 unless the EPA administrator and U.S. Attorney General agree that this amount is insufficient. 42 U.S.C. § 7413(d). EPA may place a violating company on a list of those ineligible for federal contracts.

Citizen suits may seek civil penalties against the EPA or a private party for violating the CAA. 42 U.S.C. § 7604(a). Also, EPA may pay $10,000 for information that leads to a criminal conviction or judicial, administrative, or civil penalty. Financial penalties from successful damage awards may be earmarked for air quality compliance activities or mitigation projects. The self-reporting obligations under the federal Title V CAM rule make compliance data available to the public, which increases the potential for EPA enforcement and citizen suits.

Criminal penalties. Felony-level sanctions or imprisonment of up to five years are authorized for individuals committing a first-time offense. Knowingly releasing any listed hazardous pollutant or substance, with knowledge that the release places another person in imminent danger, is punishable by a fine and/or imprisonment of no more than 15 years. Any organization that knowingly commits a violation under the CAA is subject to criminal fines of up to $1 million, plus imprisonment of up to 15 years. 42 U.S.C. § 7413(5)(A)(c). Penalties are determined based on business size, economic impact of the penalty, compliance history, violation duration, good faith efforts to comply, payment of penalties previously assessed for the same violation, economic benefit of noncompliance, and violation seriousness. A person can be imprisoned for up to two years for knowingly:

Knowingly releasing any listed hazardous pollutant or substance, with knowledge that the release places another person in imminent danger, is punishable by a fine and/or imprisonment of no more than 15 years.

- Omitting of material information
- Destroying, altering, concealing, or failing to maintain documents necessary for compliance
- Failing to install, or tampering with, monitoring devices

STATE ENFORCEMENT

California law establishes an enforcement program that includes administrative, civil, and criminal penalties, as well as injunctive relief. The California CAA does not allow citizen suits. Civil penalties can be brought against violators who engage in negligent, willful, or intentional acts. The more willful the violation, the higher the potential civil penalty.

Civil penalties. The negligent emission of an air contaminant can result in a fine of up to $25,000; if great bodily injury or death occurs, the fine can be up to $100,000. Each day of a violation is a separate offense. Health & Safety Code § 42402.1. The willful and intentional emission of an air contaminant can result in a fine of up to $75,000; if an unreasonable risk of great bodily injury or death occurs, the fine can be up to $125,000, and if great bodily injury or death occurs, the fine can be up to $250,000. Corporations are subject to different fines. Health & Safety Code § 42402.3. An air district may impose an administrative civil penalty of up to $500 per violation. Health & Safety Code § 42402.5. An administrative penalty cannot exceed the amount of a civil penalty or $10,000 per day of violation or a maximum of $100,000 per penalty. Health & Safety Code § 42410(a).

The negligent emission of an air contaminant can result in a fine of up to $25,000; if great bodily injury or death occurs, the fine can be up to $100,000. Each day of a violation is a separate offense.

SB 1402 of 2010 (Chapter 413, Statutes of 2010) is designed to ensure that ARB assesses penalties in a consistent fashion for similar violations. SB 1402 requires the ARB to issue a specified written communication before issuing an administrative or civil penalty for air quality violations. The written communication must state how the penalty amount was calculated and the regulatory basis supporting the penalty assessment. If the penalty pertains to a law that limits specified pollution levels, then the ARB must indicate the quantity of the pollutant alleged to have been emitted. This information along with all final settlement agreements must be publicly available.

This law also requires the ARB and the courts to consider specified factors when calculating the administrative or civil penalties connected to vehicular air pollution control laws including, among others: the extent of harm to public health, safety, and welfare caused by the violation: the nature and persistence of the violation; the compliance history of the defendant; the preventive efforts taken by the defendant; the cooperation of the defendant during the course of the investigation; and the financial burden to the defendant.

Criminal penalties. The filing of a criminal complaint requires the dismissal of any earlier civil action brought for the same offense. If civil penalties are recovered for the same offense, criminal prosecution is precluded. Health & Safety Code § 42400.4(c). Persons who violate the California air quality statutes, an air quality permit, or a rule or regulation are subject to a $1,000 fine or imprisonment in county jail for up to six months or both. Health & Safety Code § 42400(a). As with the civil penalty structure, the more willful the criminal violation, the higher the financial penalty (ranging from $25,000 to $75,000 per violation per day). Similarly, negligent emissions that cause great bodily injury or death result in fines of $100,000. Willful and intentional emissions resulting in great bodily injury or death are punishable with a fine of up to $250,000. In addition, the more willful the air quality violation, the more time a defendant can serve in jail (from nine months in county jail to up to three years in state prison). Health & Safety Code §§ 41500-42708.

SB 124 of 2009 (Chapter 561, Statutes of 2009) authorizes criminal misdemeanor penalties for violations resulting in actual injuries for violating commercial heavy-duty diesel engine idling and bus idling vehicle limits.

Variances. California law establishes a procedure for sources seeking temporary relief from permit conditions or other air district rules and regulations. The procedure includes public notice and hearing, specific findings, and a compliance deadline. A variance provides protection from state enforcement actions, but must have EPA approval as a SIP revision to provide protection from EPA enforcement.

for more information...

Air Resources Board, 2005. Air Quality and Land Use Handbook: A Community Health Perspective.

Air Resources Board, 2006. Emission Inventory Criteria and Guidelines Report: For the Air Toxics "Hot Spots" Programs.

Environmental Protection Agency, 1990. United States Environmental Protection Agency, Office of Air Quality. New Source Review Workshop Manual. North Carolina: United States EPA.

Manaster, K. A. and D. P. Selmi (eds.), ND. California Environmental Law and Land Use Practice, Chapter 40–43. Matthew Bender, San Francisco, Calif.

Wooley and Morss (eds.), 2015. Clean Air Act Handbook, 25th Edition. West Group. St. Paul, Minn.

glossary

Acid rain—a category of air emissions involving two criteria pollutants (NOx and SOx) that chemically react with moisture in the atmosphere to create nitric acid and sulfuric acid. Most acid rain is produced from the burning of high sulfur coal (generating SOx) and boiler systems (generating NOx).

Air pollution control district—a local agency responsible for monitoring air pollution.

Air quality management district—a multi-county area that administers guidelines on state and federal Clean Air Acts.

Air toxics inventory*—a "comprehensive characterization of the full range of hazardous materials that are released, or that may be released to the surrounding air from" a regulated facility.

Ambient air quality standards—allowable concentrations of atmospheric pollutants. Federal standards are adopted by EPA; state standards are adopted by the Air Resources Board.

Authority-to-construct permit*—permit to construct a new or modified stationary source of air pollution, issued by a local air pollution control district or an air quality management district.

Best available control technology—under the federal PSD program an emissions limitation based on the maximum degree of reduction for each pollutant on a case-by-case basis, taking into account energy, environmental, and economic impacts, and other costs. Under California's new source review, best available control technology is equivalent to lowest achievable emission rate under the federal nonattainment new source review program

Best demonstrated available control technology—an emissions reduction applicable to industrial source categories, based on emission standards or operational standards (where numerical limitations are infeasible) that considers cost, environmental impacts, and energy requirements.

California ambient air quality standards—ambient standards for criteria pollutants that generally are health-based. California ambient air quality standards are often more strict than national ambient air quality standards.

CAM rule—requires that properly designed and adequate control measures for emission limitations are implemented and properly operated and maintained.

Conformity process*—the process by which federal agencies show that their activities conform to the State Implementation Plan.

Criteria pollutant—a category of pollutant for which ambient air quality standards have been established based on the effect upon health and property.

District attainment plan—contains a discussion of California ambient air quality standards data and trends; a baseline emissions inventory; future-year projection of emissions, that include growth projections and adopted air emission control measures; a comprehensive control strategy of additional measures needed to reach attainment; an attainment demonstration that generally involves complex modeling; and contingency measures.

Emissions offsets—the reduction of emissions from other sources to mitigate the effect of any emissions from a proposed new or modified source.

Federal implementation plan—a plan to achieve attainment of air quality standards, used when a state is unable to develop an adequate plan.

Generally available control technology—hazardous air pollution control under National Emissions Standards for Hazardous Air Pollutants (NESHAP) imposed on sources too small to qualify as major sources.

Greenhouse gas—a gas, principally carbon dioxide, that allows sunlight to enter the atmosphere freely. When sunlight strikes the earth's surface, some of it is reflected back toward space as infrared radiation (heat). Greenhouse gases absorb this infrared radiation and trap the heat in the atmosphere.

Hazardous air pollutant—an air pollutant that poses an adverse effect and threat to human health or the environment.

Lowest achievable emission rate—a technology-forcing standard that may not be less stringent than any applicable new source performance standards. LAER is an emissions rate specific to each type of emissions unit, including fugitive emissions sources.

Major modification—a change to a major stationary source of emissions with respect to Prevention of Significant Deterioration and New Source Review under the Clean Air Act.

Maximum achievable control technology—a technology-based standard under the federal NESHAP that requires the maximum degree of reduction in emissions of hazardous air pollutants, and that EPA determines is achievable or not, after considering costs and other environmental impacts.

Mobile source—any non-stationary source of air pollution, such as an automobile or locomotive.

Modification—any physical or operational change in an existing facility that would increase emission of any air pollutant.

National ambient air quality standards—ambient standards for six criteria pollutants that are widespread and considered harmful to public health and the environment.

New source performance standards—emissions limitations for industrial source categories, adopted by EPA.

New source review rules—rules guiding authority-to-construct permits, requiring application of best available control technology and emissions offsets to new or modified major sources.

Non-attainment area—a geographic area in which the level of an air pollutant is higher than an ambient air quality standard.

Non-attainment area plan—a local air district plan for attainment and maintenance of ambient air quality standards.

Non-attainment new source review—requires stationary sources of air pollution to obtain permits before they start construction. New source review is also referred to as construction permitting or pre-construction permitting.

Ozone-depleting chemical—a compound that aggressively reacts and destroys ozone molecules in the upper stratosphere. Examples include freons, chlorofluorocarbons, and other halogenated compounds.

Particulate matter—a mixture of extremely small particles and liquid droplets that can include acids (such as nitrates and sulfates), organic chemicals, metals, and soil or dust particles. Also known as particle pollution. The size of particles is linked directly to the potential for causing health problems.

Permit by rule*—a permit in which the applicant submits a notice of intent to comply with pre-set permit conditions that are not site-specific.

Permit to operate*—an operational permit issued by an air district to a stationary air emissions source.

Potential to emit—the maximum amount of a specific pollutant that is capable of being released into the air and must be considered in equipment design.

Prevention of significant deterioration permit*—a permit for a major source of a criteria pollutant, to assure that clean air areas meeting national ambient air quality standards remain clean.

Reasonably available control technology—the lowest emissions limit that a particular existing source is capable of meeting by applying control technology that is reasonably available and technologically and economically feasible.

Reconstruction—involves replacement of one or more components where the cost of the new component(s) exceeds 50 percent of the cost of constructing a comparable new facility.

Reformulated gasoline—refined gasoline with low levels of smog-forming volatile organic compounds and low levels of hazardous air pollutants.

Risk management plan*—facilities that manufacture, process, use, store, or handle "highly hazardous chemicals" in excess of threshold quantities may be required to develop a plan that evaluates the risk of an unplanned chemical release. The risk management plan may be required to include a hazard assessment, an off-site consequence analysis, a prevention plan, and an emergency response plan.

State Implementation Plan—a detailed plan prepared by the Air Resources Board that describes the program the state will use to attain national ambient air quality standards. A State Implementation Plan is required by the federal Clean Air Act for areas with unhealthy levels of ozone, carbon monoxide, nitrogen dioxide, sulfur dioxide, and inhalable particulate matter.

Stationary source—any building, structure, facility, or installation that emits or may emit any air pollutant subject to regulation under the Clean Air Act.

Title V operating permit*—all-encompassing permit including relevant conditions for all regulated stationary source permits at a "major facility." The permit is effective for five years. Permit holders must submit compliance reports every six months that must be certified by a responsible official.

Toxic air contaminant—an air pollutant, under California law, that may cause or contribute to an increase in mortality or in serious illness, or that may pose a present or potential hazard to human health. Toxic air contaminants include substances listed as hazardous air pollutants.

Transportation control measures—strategies to reduce vehicle trips, vehicle use, and vehicle miles traveled.

Transportation improvement plan— a program for transportation projects for a specific period of time, developed by a metropolitan planning organization in conjunction with a state.

Volatile organic compound—any organic compound reacting with atmospheric photochemicals except those designated by the Environmental Protection Agency or a local air pollution control district or air quality management district as having a small photochemical reactivity. Examples include gasoline, dry cleaning solvents, and paint solvents.

* equals permits and approvals

CHAPTER 6

Noise

in this chapter...

EPA = U.S. Environmental Protection Agency

C.F.R. = Code of Federal Regulations

U.S.C. = United States Code

FAA = Federal Aviation Administration

OSHA = Occupational Safety and Health Administration

INTRODUCTION

Major sources of environmental noise include motor vehicles, aircraft, equipment, and machinery. California state and local governments have the primary responsibility for controlling noise sources. However, federal legislation has been enacted to provide a uniform approach to controlling selected noise sources among states.

This chapter reviews key laws and agencies involved in noise regulation, federal and state noise standards, and local noise regulatory programs.

KEY LAWS AND AGENCIES

FEDERAL LAWS AND AGENCIES

Noise Control Act of 1972. This Act (42 U.S.C. § 4901 *et seq.*) authorizes federal noise emission standards for products distributed in commerce. State or local governments may not set different limits on noise emissions once a federal standard has been established.

To implement the Act, the Environmental Protection Agency (EPA) has established noise emission standards for interstate rail carriers (40 C.F.R. § 201), motor carriers engaged in interstate commerce (40 C.F.R. § 202), construction equipment (40 C.F.R. § 204), and transportation equipment (40 C.F.R. § 205). Manufacturers of noise-producing products must warrant to purchasers that their products operate at noise levels at or below the EPA noise standards. The Act also requires EPA to establish labels rating the effectiveness of hearing protection products.

Manufacturers of noise-producing products must warrant to purchasers that their products operate at noise levels at or below the EPA noise standards.

Aircraft noise legislation. Federal controls on aircraft noise are established by other laws, such as:

- **Aircraft Noise Abatement Act.** Requires the Federal Aviation Administration (FAA) to establish noise standards through consultation with the EPA and apply standards in connection with issuance of civil aircraft certificates. 49 U.S.C. § 44715.
- **Airport and Airway Improvement Act.** Establishes the Airport Improvement Program to provide federal assistance for airport construction projects and to award noise mitigation grants. 49 U.S.C. § 47101 *et seq.*
- **Airport Noise and Capacity Act.** Phased out the noisiest classes of aircraft in 1999. 49 U.S.C. § 47521 *et seq.*

The FAA, in conjunction with the EPA, has full control over airport noise, preempting state and local control. *City of Burbank v. Lockheed Air Terminal, Inc.* (1973) 411 U.S. 624.

Occupational Safety and Health Act of 1970. This Act requires the Occupational Safety and Health Administration (OSHA) to develop and enforce health and safety standards, including noise exposure, for workplace activities. 26 U.S.C. § 65.

ALUC = airport land use commission

DPH = Department of Public Health

ONC = Office of Noise Control

OSHA = Occupational Safety and Health Administration

Environmental Protection Agency. In the past, the EPA coordinated all federal noise control activities through its Office of Noise Abatement and Control. However, in 1981, the Administration concluded that noise issues were best handled at the state or local government level. As a result, the EPA phased out the office's funding in 1982. Although EPA no longer plays an important role in regulating noise, its previously adopted standards and regulations remain in effect.

Federal Aviation Administration. In addition to setting aircraft noise standards as required by the Aircraft Noise Abatement Act, the FAA also has adopted regulations controlling the planning of aviation noise compatibility in and around airports. 14 C.F.R. § 150.

STATE AND LOCAL LAWS AND AGENCIES

California Noise Control Act. The California Noise Control Act of 1973 (Health & Safety Code § 46000 *et seq.*) is the main state law controlling noise; the Act establishes coordination of federal, state, and local noise regulation. Noise control enforcement is largely the responsibility of local governments, and nothing in the Act precludes the power of a local government to adopt additional noise regulations. The Act established an Office of Noise Control (ONC) within the Department of Public Health (DPH)—formerly the Department of Health Services (DHS)—to oversee the state's noise program. However, the ONC no longer exists.

The California Noise Control Act of 1973 is the main state law controlling noise; the Act establishes coordination of federal, state, and local noise regulation.

In addition to the California Noise Control Act, California has adopted regulations establishing noise standards for categories of sources such as aircraft (Cal. Code Regs. § 5000 *et seq.*) and motor vehicles (Vehicle Code § 27200 *et seq.*).

Caltrans Division of Aeronautics and airport land use commissions. The Division of Aeronautics oversees public airport planning and operation. As part of its duties, the Division administers the State Aeronautics Act (Pub. Util. Code § 21670 *et seq.*), which fosters compatible land use around airports and is implemented by county airport land use commissions (ALUCs).

NOISE STANDARDS

NOISE TERMINOLOGY

Environmental noise has a unique lexicon. The decibel (dB) is the basic unit of noise measurement. The A-weighted decibel (dbA) is a decibel scale approximating the sensitivity of the human ear. Typical noise levels are as follows:

- 5 dbA: threshold of hearing
- 45 dbA: auto at low speed
- 65 dbA: conversation
- 85 dbA: busy street
- 110 dbA: rock band
- 125 dbA: DC-10 aircraft
- 130 dbA: threshold of pain

Table 6-1. Federal Highway Administration Noise Abatement Criteria

Activity Category	L_{eq}* (dbA)	L_{10}* (dbA)	Location	Activity Description
A	57	60	Exterior	Lands on which serenity and quiet are of extraordinary significance and serve an important public need and where the preservation of those qualities is essential if the area is to continue to serve its intended purpose.
B	67	70	Exterior	Residential.
C	67	70	Exterior	Active sport areas, amphitheaters, auditoriums, campgrounds, cemeteries, day care centers, hospitals, libraries, medical facilities, parks, picnic areas, places of worship, playgrounds, public meeting rooms, public or nonprofit institutional structures, radio studios, recording studios, recreation areas, Section 4(f) sites, schools, television studios, trails, and trail crossings.
D	52	55	Interior	Auditoriums, day care centers, hospitals, libraries, medical facilities, places of worship, public meeting rooms, public or nonprofit institutional structures, radio studios, recording studios, schools, and television studios.
E	72	75	Exterior	Hotels, motels, offices, restaurants/bars, and other developed lands, properties or activities not included in A–D or F.
F	--	--	--	Agriculture, airports, bus yards, emergency services, industrial, logging, maintenance facilities, manufacturing, mining, rail yards, retail facilities, shipyards, utilities (water resources, water treatment, electrical), and warehousing.
G	--	--	--	Undeveloped lands that are not permitted.

* Either L_{eq} or L_{10} may be used on a project, but not both.

Source: 23 C.F.R. § 772, Table 1

CNEL = community noise equivalent level

dB = decibel

dbA = A-weighted decibel

L_{eq} = equivalent energy level

L_{dn} = day-night average level

L_{10} = the A-weighted noise level that is exceeded 10 percent of the time

FHWA = Federal Highway Administration

Other common noise terms are as follows:

- L_{eq} (equivalent energy level): the average acoustic energy content of noise during the time it lasts
- L_{dn} (day-night average level): the average equivalent A-weighted noise level during a 24-hour day, obtained by adding 10 decibels to noise levels between 10 pm and 7 am
- L_{10}: the A-weighted noise level that is exceeded 10 percent of the time
- CNEL (community noise equivalent level): same as L_{dn}, except 5 dB is added to noise levels between 7 pm and 10 pm

TRANSPORTATION PROJECT NOISE

The Federal Highway Administration (FHWA) has established noise standards for federally funded transportation projects and local projects requiring FHWA or Caltrans review. 23 C.F.R. § 772 *et seq*. These standards are shown in Table 6-1.

The FHWA regulations specify that in determining and abating traffic noise impacts, primary consideration is to be given to exterior areas. Abatement usually will be necessary only where frequent human use occurs and a lowered noise level would be of benefit. In those situations where there are no exterior activities to be affected by the traffic noise, or where the exterior activities are far from or physically shielded from the roadway, the interior criterion is used to determine noise impacts.

The FHWA regulations specify that in determining and abating traffic noise impacts, primary consideration is to be given to exterior areas.

HUD = U.S. Department of Housing and Urban Development

Table 6-2. California Interior and Exterior Noise Levels

Land use category	Land use	Interior*	Exterior**
Residential	Single and multifamily, duplex	45	65
	Mobile homes	—	65
Commercial	Hotel, motel, transient housing	45	—
	Commercial retail, bank, restaurant	55	—
	Office, research and development	50	—
	Amphitheater, concert hall, auditorium, movie theater	45	—
	Gymnasium (multipurpose)	50	—
	Sports club	55	—
	Manufacturing, warehousing, wholesale, utilities	65	—
Institutional/ Public	Hospital, school classroom or playground	45	65
	Church, library	45	—
Open space	Parks	—	65

*CNEL (dbA). Indoor environment excludes bathrooms, kitchens, toilets, closets, and corridors.

**CNEL (dbA). Outdoor environment limited to private yard of single-family dwellings, multiple-family private patios or balconies accessed from within the dwelling, mobile home parks, park picnic areas, school playgrounds, and hospital patios.

Source: 24 Cal. Code Regs. Part 2

EXTERIOR AND INTERIOR NOISE LEVELS

The U.S. Department of Housing and Urban Development (HUD) has established standards for exterior noise levels for HUD-supported or HUD-assisted housing projects, as follows (24 C.F.R. § 51.100 *et seq.*):

- 65 dbA L_{dn}: an acceptable zone where all projects could be approved
- 65–75 dbA L_{dn}: a normally acceptable zone where project-specific mitigation measures would be required
- 75 dbA L_{dn}: an unacceptable zone in which projects normally would not be approved

California noise regulations (24 Cal. Code Regs. Part 2) establish an interior noise standard of 45 CNEL or 45 dbA for residences, schools, and other sensitive receptors. California noise standards are shown in Table 6-2.

The regulations require that acoustical studies be prepared whenever a residential building or structure is proposed to be located near an existing or adopted freeway route, expressway, parkway, major street, thoroughfare, rail line, rapid transit line, or industrial noise source, where this source creates an exterior CNEL of 60 dbA or greater. The acoustical analysis must demonstrate that the residence has been designed to limit interior noise CNEL to 45 dbA.

AIRCRAFT NOISE

The FAA has set national standards for aircraft noise. For Stage 3 aircraft (encompassing most modern aircraft currently flying), separate standards are established for runway takeoffs and landings; these standards range from 89–106 dbA depending on the aircraft's weight and number of engines. FAA 2012; 14 C.F.R. § 36.

California has adopted the federal noise standards (Gov't Code § 65302), as well as regulations to implement those standards, requiring the airport owner, aircraft operator, local governments, and FAA to work cooperatively to reduce noise impacts. The regulations' intent is to reduce the noise impacts on communities in the vicinity of airports. 21 Cal. Code Regs. § 5000 *et seq.* Local governments and individual airports may enact stricter requirements, unless prohibited by federal law.

RAILROAD NOISE

EPA has established railroad noise standards (40 C.F.R. § 201) that are enforced by the Federal Railroad Administration. The standards apply to stationary and moving locomotives, railway cars, and car coupling activities, but do not apply to horns, whistles, or bells used as warning devices.

MOTOR VEHICLE NOISE

Interstate motor carriers. EPA has established noise standards for motor carriers engaged in interstate commerce; FHWA enforces the standards. 42 U.S.C. § 4917, 40 C.F.R. § 202. Commercial vehicles over 10,000 pounds are subject to standards for highway travel and stationary operation, but horns or sirens are not subject to standards.

California motor vehicle standards. California has established noise standards for motor vehicles that are broadly defined to include any self-propelled vehicle. The application of these standards, which are as strict as or stricter than corresponding federal standards, varies depending on the motor vehicle category, speed, age, and weight. Vehicle Code § 27200 *et seq.* Also, every vehicle subject to registration in California, as well as off-highway vehicles and motorized recreational vessels, must be equipped at all times with an adequate and continually operating muffler.

WORKPLACE NOISE

OSHA has established standards for the duration of time employees can be exposed to specific noise levels. 29 C.F.R. § 1910.95. Constant exposure may not exceed 90 dbA over eight hours. Exposure to levels higher than 115 dbA must be limited to 15 minutes within an eight-hour period. Instantaneous exposure (e.g., impact noise) may not exceed 140 dbA. If noise levels exceed these standards, employers must provide hearing protection to reduce sound levels below the standards.

OSHA has established standards for the duration of time employees can be exposed to specific noise levels.

LOCAL NOISE REGULATORY PROGRAMS

OPR = Governor's Office of Planning and Research

NOISE ELEMENT

The General Plan Guidelines (OPR 2017) set forth recommended procedures and contents for the general plan noise element. The goals of the noise element are to:

- Provide sufficient information about the community noise environment so that noise may be effectively considered in the land use planning process
- Develop strategies for abating excessive noise exposure
- Protect existing noise-sensitive areas
- Provide for local compliance for the state noise insulation standards

The noise element guidelines set forth a four-phased process for noise element preparation:

- Phase A: Noise environment definition
- Phase B: Noise-compatible land use planning
- Phase C: Noise mitigation measures
- Phase D: Enforcement

The local noise element must analyze noise levels from transportation facilities, railroads, aircraft, industrial plants, and other ground stationary sources. Gov't Code § 65302(f). Noise contours must be shown for these sources and stated in terms of either CNEL or L_{dn}. These contours are to guide land use planning, using guidelines for acceptable noise exposure for different land use categories.

The local noise element must analyze noise levels from transportation facilities, railroads, aircraft, industrial plants, and other ground stationary sources.

Figure 6-1 on the following page shows land use compatibility standards for noise exposure. These guidelines are used to develop noise element recommendations. For each land use, noise levels are classified as normally acceptable, conditionally acceptable, normally unacceptable, and clearly unacceptable.

AIRPORT NOISE

Airport land use commissions. For aircraft noise, the State Aeronautics Act (Pub. Util. Code § 21670 *et seq.*) requires the establishment of ALUCs, which are responsible for developing airport land use compatibility plans (ALUCPs) for noise-compatible land uses in the immediate proximity of a commercial or public airport. The *Airport Land Use Planning Handbook* (Caltrans 2011) establishes guidance for airport land use compatibility planning. It is intended to (1) provide information to ALUCs, their staffs, airport proprietors, cities, counties, consultants, and the public, (2) identify the requirements and procedures for preparing effective compatibility planning documents, and (3) define exemptions where applicable. Land use compatibility means that development around airports is not exposed to excessive noise levels or safety hazards.

Comprehensive land use airport plans regulate development near airports.

FIGURE 6-1

Land Use Compatibility Standards for Community Noise Environments

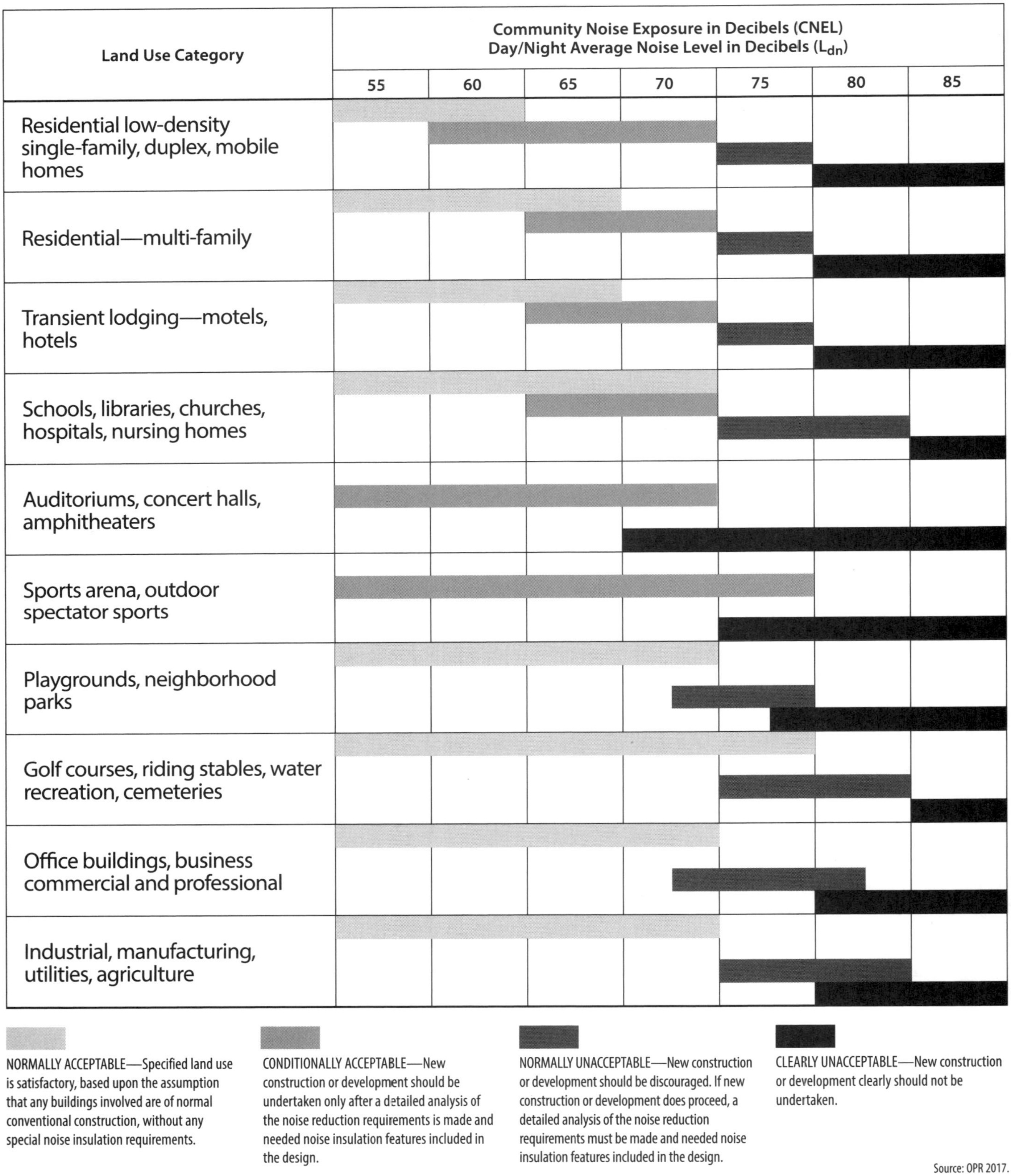

Source: OPR 2017.

ALUCP = airport land use compatibility plan

Local agencies preparing noise elements must coordinate with the appropriate county ALUC. The purposes of an ALUC are to ensure orderly expansion of public airports and to minimize land use, noise, and safety conflicts with adjacent land uses. ALUCs have two major roles:

- Preparation and adoption of airport land use compatibility plans, which address policies for both noise and safety
- Review of certain local government land use actions and airport plans for consistency with the land use compatibility plan

The ALUCP is the major tool for ALUC land use regulation. The ALUCP typically includes (Pub. Util. Code § 21675(a)):

- Height restrictions within the airport influence area
- Permissible and conditional land uses
- Soundproofing and other building standards

Local governments within the ALUCP planning boundaries must refer certain proposed land use changes (e.g., general plan amendments, specific plans, zoning ordinances) to the ALUC for a determination of consistency with the ALUCP. If the ALUC determines the proposed action is inconsistent with the ALUCP, the local government may still override this determination and approve the land use change by making certain findings. If the ALUC has not adopted an ALUCP, no consistency determination can be made, but the ALUC may nevertheless approve or disapprove the land use change if substantial progress is being made toward completion of the ALUCP. Pub. Util. Code §§ 21675.1(c), 21676.

Local governments. Cities and counties have two additional procedures for coordinating land use decisions with aircraft noise. First, a plan for airport expansion must be submitted for approval to the applicable city or county before acquisition of property for the expansion. Pub. Util. Code § 21661.6(a). Second, cities and counties may adopt airport approach zones for either public or private airports, and may establish special zoning restrictions in approach zones to prevent airport hazards, including excessive noise. Gov't Code § 50485.

ENFORCEMENT

FEDERAL NOISE CONTROL ACT

Willful or knowing violations of many provisions of the federal Noise Control Act are subject to a criminal fine of up to $25,000 per day of violation, by imprisonment of up to one year, or both. 42 U.S.C. § 4910(a)(1). These violations also may be punished civilly by fines of up to $10,000 per day of violation. Also, citizens may file civil actions against anyone alleged to be in violation of any federal noise control requirement. 42 U.S.C. § 4911(f).

Willful or knowing violations of many provisions of the federal Noise Control Act are subject to a criminal fine of up to $25,000 per day of violation, by imprisonment of up to one year, or both.

LOCAL NOISE ORDINANCES

Most cities and counties have adopted a noise ordinance to implement their noise elements and to provide a process for resolving noise complaints.

Most cities and counties have adopted a noise ordinance to implement their noise elements and to provide a process for resolving noise complaints. For example, the City of Los Angeles noise ordinance (Los Angeles Municipal Code § 116.01) provides that officers should consider the following factors, in addition to the noise level violating noise standards, in determining whether an activity violates the noise ordinance:

- Nature of the noise (usual or unusual)
- Origin of the noise (natural or unnatural)
- Level and intensity of any background noise
- Proximity of the noise to sleeping facilities
- Nature and zoning of the area
- Density of inhabitation in the area
- Time of day or night the noise occurs
- Duration of the noise
- Whether the noise is recurrent, intermittent, or constant
- Whether the noise is produced by commercial or non-commercial activity

A violation of the city's noise ordinance is a misdemeanor.

NUISANCE LAWSUITS

Property owners affected by excessive noise levels can consider filing a nuisance lawsuit as well as filing a noise complaint with local authorities. See chapter 1 for a discussion of nuisance claims.

for more information...

Caltrans, Division of Aeronautics, 2011. California Airport Land Use Planning Handbook.

Federal Aviation Administration, 2012. Noise levels for U.S. Certificated and Foreign Aircraft. Advisory Circular 36-1H.

Federal Highway Administration, 2011. Highway Traffic Noise Analysis and Abatement: Policy and Guidance.

Governor's Office of Planning and Research, 2017. General Plan Guidelines.

Manaster, K. A. and D. P. Selmi (eds.). ND. Chapter 83 of California Environmental Law and Land Use Practice. Matthew Bender. San Francisco, Calif.

glossary

CNEL (community noise equivalent level)—same as L_{dn}, except 5 dB is added to noise levels between 7 pm and 10 pm.

dB (decibel)—the unit of measurement describing the amplitude of sound.

dbA (A-weighted decibel)—a decibel scale approximating the sensitivity of the human ear.

L_{10}—the A-weighted noise level that is exceeded 10 percent of the time.

L_{dn} (day-night average level)—the average equivalent A-weighted noise level during a 24-hour day, obtained by adding 10 decibels to noise levels between 10 pm and 7 am.

L_{eq} (equivalent energy level)—the average acoustic energy content of noise during the time it lasts.

Noise contour—a line drawn about a noise source indicating equal levels of noise exposure.

CHAPTER 7

Hazardous Materials and Toxic Substances

in this chapter...

GHS = Global Harmonized Standard

OSHA = Occupational Safety and Health Administration; Occupational Safety and Health Act

MSDS = material safety data sheet

SDS = safety data sheet

EPCRA = Emergency Planning and Community Right-to-Know Act

SARA = Superfund Amendments and Reauthorization Act

INTRODUCTION

Hazardous materials (sometimes referred to as hazardous products or hazardous chemicals) are regulated under a number of state, federal, and local environmental, health, and safety regulatory programs. Generally, hazardous materials are divided into the following categories:

- Flammables (gasoline, paints, adhesives, and solvents, etc.)
- Corrosives (battery acid, chlorine, and alkaline cleaners, etc.)
- Compressed gases (acetylene, nitrogen, oxygen, helium, and argon, etc.)
- Reactives (organic peroxides, cyanides, and lithium, etc.)
- Toxics (isocyanates, benzene, lead, and methyl ethyl ketone, etc.)

This chapter reviews laws and agencies involved in hazardous materials and toxic substances regulation; programs for hazard communication, community right-to-know, chemical handling and storage, hazardous material transportation, underground storage tanks, pesticides, and other hazardous materials and toxic substances; and enforcement of hazardous materials and toxic substances regulations.

KEY LAWS AND AGENCIES

INTERNATIONAL

The GHS is an international system governing chemical classification, disclosure, labeling, hazard classification and training.

Global Harmonized Standard. The United Nations developed the GHS to harmonize the regulation of chemicals across the globe to ease the international sale, transportation, and workplace use of hazardous chemicals. The GHS is an international system governing chemical classification, disclosure, labeling, hazard classification and training. These standards address safe production, transport, handling, use and disposal of hazardous materials. The Occupational Safety and Health Administration (OSHA) adopted the GHS and in turn revised the Hazard Communication Standard and revamped the content and format of material safety data sheets (MSDS). MSDSs are now referred to as Safety Data Sheets or SDSs.

FEDERAL LAWS AND AGENCIES

Occupational Safety and Health Act. This Act (29 U.S.C. § 651 *et seq.*; 29 C.F.R. § 1900 *et seq.*), enacted in 1970, is intended to create a safe workplace. This program establishes procedures and standards for the safe handling and storage of hazardous chemicals. 29 C.F.R. § 1910.1200(c) *et seq.* In addition, an SDS containing specified information must be provided to customers, making them aware of chemical hazards to which they may be exposed.

Emergency Planning and Community Right-to-Know Act. This Act (EPCRA, 42 U.S.C. § 116 *et seq.*; 40 C.F.R. § 350 *et seq.*) also is referred to as the Superfund Amendments and Reauthorization Act of 1986, or SARA Title III. EPCRA requires facilities that store or use hazardous chemicals to submit a specified plan with copies of SDSs to the State Emergency Response Commission (SERC) and the local emergency planning committee (LEPC). Additionally, facilities must submit an annual inventory list with details on the amount, location, and storage method of regulated chemicals present at the facility. 40 C.F.R. § 370.20 *et seq.*

SERC = State Emergency Response Commission

LEPC = local emergency planning committee

RCRA = Resource Conservation and Recovery Act

UST = underground storage tank

EPA = U.S. Environmental Protection Agency

HMTA = Hazardous Materials Transportation Act

TSCA = Toxic Substances Control Act

AHERA = Asbestos Hazard Emergency Response Act

FIFRA = Federal Insecticide, Fungicide, and Rodenticide Act

Resource Conservation and Recovery Act, Subtitle I. To protect groundwater, RCRA Subtitle I establishes design, construction, and operational standards to prevent chemical releases from underground storage tanks (USTs) that are 10 percent or more beneath the ground. RCRA Subtitle I regulates USTs containing hazardous substances or petroleum. The U.S. Environmental Protection Agency (EPA) sets standards governing tank construction based on whether the tank is new or whether an existing tank is upgraded. EPA also imposes operation and maintenance procedures for UST owners and operators, and establishes reporting requirements from regulated tanks that release substances into the environment. 42 U.S.C. § 6991 *et seq.*; 40 C.F.R. § 280 *et seq.*

Hazardous Materials Transportation Act. HMTA regulates any transporter of hazardous materials or any person who manufactures, marks, repairs, or tests a package that was certified, sold, or marked for use in the transportation of hazardous materials. 49 C.F.R. § 100 *et seq.*

Toxic Substances Control Act. TSCA (15 U.S.C. § 2601 *et seq.*; 40 C.F.R. § 700 *et seq.*) enables EPA to track and restrict industrial chemicals produced or imported into the United States. EPA screens the chemicals and can require testing to determine if any pose an environmental or human health hazard. Any chemical that poses an unreasonable risk then can be regulated or banned from manufacturing or importation.

Asbestos Hazard Emergency Response Act. AHERA regulates asbestos material in school buildings, requiring schools to maintain an asbestos inventory, implement a management plan and conduct periodic inspections of the premises. 15 U.S.C. § 2641 *et seq.*; 40 C.F.R. § 763 *et seq.*

Residential Lead-Based Paint Hazard Reduction Act. This Act (42 U.S.C. § 4851 *et seq.*; 40 C.F.R. § 745.100) requires that sellers and landlords disclose known lead-based paint or lead-based paint hazards to buyers and tenants of dwelling units. The seller or landlord must provide the buyer or tenant pamphlets providing information on the hazards associated with lead and provide 10 days to inspect the premises for lead-based paint hazards.

Clean Air Act. Section 112 of the Clean Air Act requires EPA to set air toxics standards for regulating the emissions of hazardous air pollutants. The 1990 federal Clean Air Act Amendments (Section 112 (r)) establish a program designed to prevent the release of highly hazardous chemicals. *See* chapter 5.

Section 112 of the Clean Air Act requires EPA to set air toxics standards for regulating the emissions of hazardous air pollutants.

Federal Insecticide, Fungicide, and Rodenticide Act and the Federal Food, Drug, and Cosmetic Act. The use of pesticides is regulated by the EPA under FIFRA (7

ACM = asbestos-containing materials

DOT = Department of Transportation

HUD = U.S. Department of Housing and Urban Development

HSITA = California Hazardous Substances Information and Training Act

U.S.C. § 136 *et seq.*), which creates the foundation for regulation, sale, distribution, and use of pesticides in the United States. FIFRA gives EPA authority to require pesticide testing to determine potential environmental and health effects, while also requiring pesticide users to register their purchased products. EPA is authorized to review and register pesticides for particular uses. Additionally, EPA is authorized to suspend or cancel the registration of a pesticide if research shows the continued use would create an unreasonable risk. The Federal Food, Drug, and Cosmetic Act gives EPA the authority to mandate maximum residue levels or tolerances for pesticides used in or on foods, or in animal feed. 21 U.S.C. § 301 *et seq.*; 40 C.F.R. Part 180.

Environmental Protection Agency. EPA has extensive authority under several federal environmental statutory programs discussed in this chapter, including EPCRA, RCRA Subtitle I, AHERA, TSCA, NESHAP, and FIFRA. EPA regulates underground tanks, the use of asbestos-containing materials (ACM), and hazardous materials and substances, under TSCA, to reduce the risk of exposure to humans and the environment. Under TSCA, EPA has the ability to track production and importation of industrial chemicals into commerce in the United States. Based on a chemical screening process, EPA can ban or restrict specific chemicals it finds that pose an unreasonable risk to humans or the environment.

Based on a chemical screening process, EPA can ban specific chemicals it finds that pose an unreasonable risk to humans or the environment.

United States Department of Labor, Occupational Safety and Health Administration. OSHA administers and enforces the federal Occupational Safety and Health Act (also referred to as OSHA). For purposes of this chapter, OSHA implements the laws governing the Hazard Communication program and the safe handling of hazardous chemicals and products.

Department of Transportation. DOT administers the HMTA and governs the transportation of hazardous materials in commerce, including those who manufacture, mark, repair, or test packaging that was certified, sold, or marked for use in the transportation of hazardous materials.

Department of Housing and Urban Development. Effective in 1996, Congress directed the U.S. Department of Housing and Urban Development (HUD) and EPA to promulgate joint lead-based paint hazard regulations for sales and leases of older housing. While HUD is primarily responsible for enforcing the residential lead-based paint disclosure program, EPA has established standards to manage paint, dust, and soil in most "target" housing (housing constructed pre-1978, except elderly housing or zero-bedroom housing) and child-occupied facilities.

STATE AND LOCAL LAWS AND AGENCIES

California Hazardous Substances Information and Training Act. This Act (HSITA, Labor Code § 360 *et seq.*) requires manufacturers and importers of hazardous substances to assess the hazards posed by the products they introduce into commerce. They, along with distributors, are required to capture this information into SDSs that must be supplied to purchasers. Also, employers must train their staff in the safe use of hazardous products in the workplace.

HMBP= hazardous materials business plan

CUPA = Certified Unified Program Agency

CalARP = California Accidental Release Prevention program

California Hazardous Materials Release Response Plans and Inventory Law. Under this law (Health & Safety Code § 25500 *et seq.*), a handler of hazardous material is required to submit a hazardous materials business plan (HMBP) to the local emergency planning committee, the certified unified program agency (CUPA), or the local authorized administrating agency. Hazardous materials handlers must review the HMBP at least once every three years after submission. The HMBP must include an inventory of hazardous materials stored, handled, or used; emergency response plans; procedures for mitigating harm in the event of a release; evacuation plans; and employee training. Health & Safety Code § 25503.5 *et seq.*; 19 Cal. Code Regs. §§ 2729–2732.

HMBPs provide the public, local emergency responding agencies, and local government agencies information regarding potentially hazardous chemical situations in the community.

California Accidental Release Prevention program. As explained more in chapter 5, CalARP (19 Cal. Code Regs. § 2735 *et seq.*) is designed to reduce and eliminate the accidental release of harmful substances into the environment.

California underground storage tank law. California became the first state to regulate USTs. California law (Health & Safety Code § 5280 *et seq.*; 22 Cal. Code Regs. § 2630) requires a permit to operate a UST system that stores hazardous substances. Owners or operators of USTs must meet specific construction, design, and monitoring requirements, along with periodic testing and recordkeeping responsibilities.

California Asbestos Notification Act. This Act (Health & Safety Code § 25915 *et seq.*) requires owners who know their pre-1979 buildings contain asbestos to give written notice to employees working in the building. The notice must provide the specific location of asbestos-containing construction materials; the general procedures and handling restrictions necessary to limit or prevent release or exposure to the asbestos; a summary of sample analyses; and the potential health risks associated with asbestos exposure.

Lead programs. Under the Lead Hazard Reduction Enforcement Act (Health & Safety Code §§ 105250–105257), if a building contains lead hazards that are likely to endanger the health of the public or building occupants, the building owner will be in violation of the state housing law or the Health & Safety Code. The Occupational Lead Poisoning Prevention Act (Health & Safety Code § 105185 *et seq.*) creates a lead poisoning program to register and monitor laboratory reports of adult lead toxicity cases; to conduct investigation of take-home exposure cases (i.e., when lead is carried home on the worker's body, clothes, shoes, or personal vehicle); and to train employees and health experts regarding the program.

Toxic Mold Protection Act of 2001. This Act (Health & Safety Code § 26100 *et seq.*) requires sellers and landlords to disclose the presence of mold to buyers and tenants. Commercial and industrial landlords, under certain circumstances, must assess the condition of property other than real property.

BFR = brominated flame retardant

PBDE = polybrominated diphenyl ether

Proposition 65. Proposition 65 (Health & Safety Code § 25249.5 *et seq.*; 22 Cal. Code Regs. § 12000 *et seq.*), also known as the Safe Drinking Water and Toxic Enforcement Act of 1986, requires that regulated businesses not expose persons to significant concentrations of carcinogens or reproductive toxicants without providing a "clear and reasonable" warning. Additionally, regulated businesses must not discharge or release any listed carcinogens or reproductive toxicants that potentially may contact a source or potential source of drinking water.

Mercury Reduction Act of 2001. In 2001, the California Legislature pioneered a trend-setting law—the Mercury Reduction Act—which bans the manufacture, sale, or supply of mercury fever thermometers and other mercury-containing products. Pub. Res. Code § 15025 *et seq.* The Act prohibits schools from purchasing devices or materials containing mercury for use in classrooms; bans the sale of mercury thermometers; bans the sale of vehicles having mercury light switches; and prohibits the sale in California of novelty items containing mercury.

Recycled paint. Administered by CalRecycle, AB 1343 of 2010 (Chapter 420, Statutes of 2010) requires architectural paint manufacturers to establish a paint stewardship program to take back unused paint. This program is managed by a nonprofit organization (PaintCare) and is funded by an assessment on purchases of new paint sold in California.

Brominated flame retardant regulation. California law prohibits manufacturing, processing, or distributing in commerce a product or a flame-retardant part of a product that contains brominated flame retardants (BFRs), otherwise known as polybrominated diphenyl ethers (PBDEs). Health & Safety Code § 108920 *et seq.*

The Toxics in Packaging Prevention Act prohibits manufacturers and importers from selling packaging that includes lead, cadmium, mercury, or hexavalent chromium.

Toxics in Packaging Prevention Act. This Act (Health & Safety Code § 25214.11 *et seq.*) prohibits manufacturers and importers from selling packaging that includes lead, cadmium, mercury, or hexavalent chromium. Manufacturers and importers must also furnish to their purchasers a certification indicating that the package and packaging materials they offer meet the conditions of the Act.

The California Lighting Efficiency and Toxic Reduction Act. This Act restricts the sale of general purpose lighting (which include lamps, bulbs, and tubes) that contains specified hazardous substances. Health & Safety Code § 25210.9; Pub. Res. Code § 25402.5.4.

Health Tracking Act of 2003. This Act established the California Environmental Health Surveillance System, a collaborative research program led by the California Department of Public Health (DPH), the California Environmental Protection Agency, and the University of California to evaluate the potential nexus between chemicals present in the environment and chronic diseases. Health & Safety Code § 104324.25.

Pesticide regulation. California pesticide law is designed to control pesticide usage and mitigate damage incurred by pesticide usage; to protect the environment; and to protect workers who come in contact with pesticides. California law establishes product labeling standards and requires the most efficient and effective approach to pest management. The California Department of Pesticide Regulation (DPR) is the authorized agency to implement and enforce these laws and regulations. Food & Agricultural Code § 12751 *et seq.*

State Water Resources Control Board. SWRCB is principally responsible for administering the UST program. The State of California delegated day-to-day implementation and enforcement of this program to the certified uniform program agencies (CUPAs, described below).

Department of Toxic Substances Control. DTSC is the main agency that oversees compliance and enforcement of rules governing hazardous waste and green chemistry in California.

California Occupational Safety and Health Administration. Cal/OSHA administers and enforces the state's occupational safety and health program, including setting permissible exposure levels (PELs) for asbestos, as well as regulating employee exposure to and management of hazardous materials.

Department of Public Health. DPH (formerly Department of Health Services) administers the lead poisoning program, adopts PELs for mold in indoor environments, and develops standards to identify and remediate mold infestations. It also administers the Hazard Evaluation System and Information Service (HESIS), which houses data on "toxic materials and harmful physical agents" used in the workplace.

California Governor's Office of Emergency Services. OES serves as the SERC under EPCRA and receives notifications of chemical spills and releases.

Office of Environmental Health Hazard Assessment and the Attorney General. OEHHA administers the Proposition 65 program and evaluates all scientific information on substances considered for placement on the Proposition 65 list. While OEHHA administers the law, the Attorney General enforces Proposition 65.

State Fire Marshal. The Office of the State Fire Marshal is the lead agency for developing regulations to implement the Aboveground Petroleum Storage Act and requires local unified program agencies to follow these rules at the local level.

Certified unified program agencies. CUPAs administer a number of environmental regulatory programs that the state of California delegated to certified local agencies. Typically, city or county fire or health departments serve as CUPAs. CUPAs serve as the LEPC under EPCRA with authority to administer and enforce the HMBP program. CUPAs also are delegated authority to implement and enforce the UST program; the hazardous waste generator program (including the regulation of polychlorinated biphenyls (PCBs) with concentrations between 5 and 50 ppm); the on-site hazardous waste tiered treatment permitting program (*see* chapter 8); the spill prevention control and countermeasure program (*see* chapter 10); and the California Accidental Release Prevention Program (CalARP) (*see* chapter 5). Cities and counties are also eligible to oversee cleanup of USTs subject to SWRCB implementation.

DPR = Department of Pesticide Regulation

SWRCB = State Water Resources Control Board

DTSC = Department of Toxic Substances Control

Cal/OSHA = California Occupational Safety and Health Administration

PEL = permissible exposure level

DPH = California Department of Public Health

HESIS = Hazard Evaluation System and Information Service

OES = Governor's Office of Emergency Services

OEHHA = Office of Environmental Health Hazard Assessment

CUPA = Certified Unified Program Agency

PCBs = polychlorinated biphenyls

Typically, city or county fire or health departments serve as certified unified program agencies (CUPAs).

HAZCOM = written hazard communication

State Emergency Response Commission. SERCs are state agencies authorized to prepare for and to respond to potential chemical accidents. The OES carries out these duties in California and designates local emergency planning committees (LEPCs) that must develop local emergency response plans.

Local Emergency Planning Committee. LEPCs are local (typically cities and counties) community-based organizations that implement EPCRA by developing emergency response plans and provide information about hazardous materials in the community to citizens. CUPAs serve this role in California.

Department of Pesticide Regulation. DPR is principally responsible for implementing and enforcing the pesticide program in California. It manages pesticide registration, pesticide use restrictions, and licensing of pesticide applicators.

HAZARD COMMUNICATION

The federal and state governments have enacted several programs designed to inform customers and employees about the potential hazards of chemicals used in commerce and the workplace.

FEDERAL OCCUPATIONAL SAFETY AND HEALTH ACT

Safety data sheet. The federal OSHA requires manufacturers, importers, and employers to inform customers about the potential hazards of their chemical products. This information is contained in a safety data sheet. Each SDS includes, among other things, information on:

- Chemical ingredient characteristics
- Hazards
- Recommended personal protective equipment (such as specified gloves, respirator, and safety glasses)
- Fire risk management
- Disposal instructions

OSHA requires SDSs for materials that meet OSHA's definition of hazardous chemical and are "known to be present in the workplace where employees may be exposed under normal conditions or in a foreseeable emergency." 29 C.F.R. § 1910.1200(b)–(h). A hazardous chemical, under Federal OSHA, is defined as "any chemical which is a physical hazard or health hazard."

OSHA requires that employers communicate to their employees the hazards posed by the chemicals used in the workplace.

Employee communication. OSHA requires that employers communicate to their employees the hazards posed by the chemicals used in the workplace. Employers must have a written hazard communication (HAZCOM) program designed to provide information on chemical hazards to employees. The requirements for an employer are based on whether the employer manufactures, imports, or uses chemicals.

Hazard communication training. Personnel who store, handle, or use hazardous materials must receive HAZCOM training that addresses routine management

NFPA = National Fire Protection Association

FIGURE 7-1
GHS Hazard Pictograms and Exemplary Hazard Classes

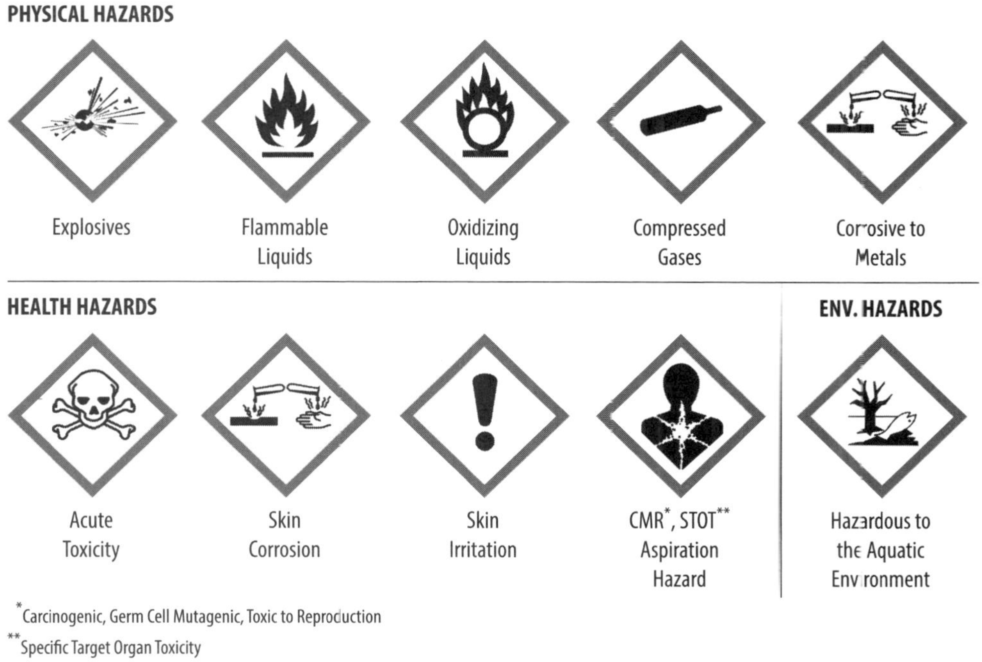

Source: www.amherst.edu/system/files/media/GHS%2520Info_0.pdf

procedures, emergency response, and how to read an SDS. Further, employees must have access to information (hard copy or electronic) on the chemicals they use in the workplace.

FIGURE 7-2
NFPA Label

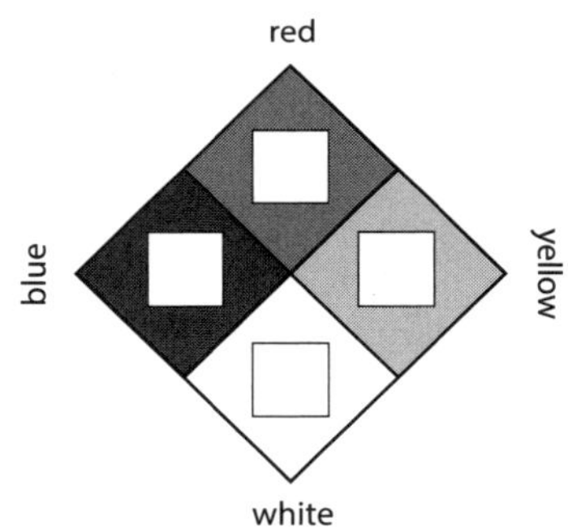

Container labels. Employers must display the chemical name and hazards on chemical containers, except on portable containers under employee control and immediate use. Employers may use any type of labeling as long as it conveys the chemical name, the responsible party (e.g., manufacturer, importer) name and address, and the hazard warnings. *See* Figure 7-1. Permissible labeling systems have included the National Fire Protection Association (NFPA) system or the Hazardous Material Identification System established by the National Paint and Coatings Association.

The NFPA diamond label shows the potential severity of the hazardous chemical, using five hazard levels (0 through 4) in relation to four color-coded hazards: health hazard (blue), fire hazard (red), reactive hazard (yellow), and specific hazard (white). *See* Figure 7-2. See Table 7-1 for NFPA severity ratings.

CALIFORNIA PROGRAMS

California's HSITA (Labor Code § 6360 *et seq.*) largely mimics federal OSHA regulations governing hazard communication. Like the federal program, the HSITA requires manufacturers and importers of hazardous substances to evaluate the hazards posed by the products they introduce into commerce. They must label their

IIPP = Injury and Illness Prevention Program

Table 7-1. Severity Ratings of the National Fire Protection Association

Hazard Levels	Health Hazard (Blue)	Fire Hazard (Red)	Reactive Hazard (Yellow)	Specific Hazard (White)
4	Deadly	Very flammable	May detonate	Oxidizer (OXY)
3	Extreme danger	Readily ignitable	Shock and heat may detonate	Acid (ACID)
2	Hazardous	Ignited with heat	Violent chemical change	Alkali (ALK)
1	Slightly hazardous	Combustible	Unstable if heated	Corrosive (COR)
0	Normal material	Will not burn	Stable	Use no water (W)

Source: Compiled from information available on the University of Wisconsin-Platteville Chemistry Department website

products to identify hazards and must prepare SDSs that explain the hazards. Distributors, along with manufacturers and importers, must supply SDSs to purchasers. Finally, employers must train their staff on the safe use of hazardous products used in the workplace.

The HSITA regulates the same hazardous substances regulated under the federal OSHA. Labor Code § 6382(d). Manufacturers, importers, and employees must develop written procedures describing how to assess hazardous substances. These procedures may be included in the employer's written hazard communication program. 8 Cal. Code Regs. § 5194(d)(2).

Employers must keep an updated inventory of SDSs for each hazardous substance used. These SDSs must be readily accessible to employees in their work areas. Labor Code § 6398(a); 8 Cal. Code Regs. § 5194(g)(1), (8). If a manufacturer does not provide the employer with SDS or other required information, California law states that the employer must request in writing within seven days that the manufacturer send a complete SDS. 8 Cal. Code Regs. § 5194(g)(12).

In California, training must be provided to any employee who receives a new or revised safety data sheet within 30 days of receipt of the SDS.

The state program is more stringent than federal requirements with regard to training. In California, training must be provided to any employee who receives a new or revised SDS within 30 days of receipt of the SDS. 8 Cal. Code Regs. § 5194(h).

SB 193 of 2014 (Chapter 830, Statutes of 2014) requires manufacturers, formulators, suppliers, distributors, and importers to provide new scientific or medical information concerning hazardous chemicals to HESIS. This law was designed to timely provide employers chemical data to facilitate alerting employees of exposures to hazards posed by the chemical product.

Injury and Illness Prevention Program. Employers must develop, implement and maintain an IIPP. An IIPP is a system to help employees maintain safe and healthy work practices. An IIPP includes, among other things, procedures to identify and evaluate workplace hazards, periodic inspections, training and retraining programs, a disciplinary program, and a system to communicate to employees matters relating to occupational safety and health. 8 Cal. Code Regs. § 3203.

COMMUNITY RIGHT-TO-KNOW PROGRAMS

EHS = extremely hazardous substance

TPQ = threshold planning quantity

FEDERAL INVENTORY AND RIGHT-TO-KNOW REQUIREMENTS

Requirements for facilities. One of the primary objectives of EPCRA is to support emergency planning at the state and local levels of government.

EPCRA (42 U.S.C. § 11001 *et seq.*) requires regulated "facilities" (defined below) that store or use any hazardous substances (defined below) or extremely hazardous substance (EHS, defined at 40 C.F.R. § 355.20) exceeding thresholds (below) to, among other things, complete an EPCRA Tier II form. The Tier II form includes information about the facility, employee contact information, and an inventory and the location of chemicals stored or used at the facility. The Tier II form must be submitted when the facility begins to handle hazardous substances at the thresholds below:

One of the primary objectives of EPCRA is to support emergency planning at the state and local levels of government.

- 10,000 pounds or greater for all "hazardous substances" present at the facility at any one time or
- 500 pounds of an extremely hazardous substance (EHS) or exceeding quantities equal to or exceeding specified amounts (known as threshold planning quantities or TPQs) of an EHS, whichever is lower
- Retail fueling stations with 75,000 gallons of gasoline and 100,000 gallons of diesel (EPCRA §§ 311, 312)

"Facilities" include stationary structures located on a single site, or located on adjacent or contiguous sites and owned or operated by the same person. These facilities must:

- Notify the LEPC of the on-site presence of EHSs in quantities equal to or exceeding TPQs. 40 C.F.R. § 355.30
- Provide information to the SERC and LEPC
- Submit to the SERC and LEPC annual chemical inventories of listed hazardous chemicals produced at or shipped to the facility. 42 U.S.C. § 11022; 40 C.F.R. §§ 370, 370.25

Toxic release inventory. Manufacturers (including importers) and processors with specified SIC and NAICS codes (such as manufacturing, electric utilities, and petroleum bulk terminals) with at least 10 full-time employees (or more than 20,000 work hours/year of full- and part-time employees), and who manufacture or process a minimum of 25,000 pounds of extremely hazardous substances, or use 10,000 pounds/calendar year, must submit an annual toxic chemical release form. There are lower reporting thresholds for persistent bioaccumulative toxic chemicals such as 10 pounds for mercury and mercury compounds and 0.1 grams of dioxins and dioxin-like compounds. This program is known as the Toxic Release Inventory. 42 U.S.C. § 11023(f); 40 C.F.R. § 372 (also known as "EPCRA § 313"). These facilities must complete a Form R summarizing the environmental

NRC = National Response Center

UPA = unified program agency

CERS = California Environmental Reporting System

fate of chemical releases. This includes technical information and the annual amounts of chemicals released to the air, water, land, underground injection wells, and off-site transfers to publicly owned treatment works. Facilities must also report to EPA information on off-site transfers for disposal, waste treatment, recycling, and energy recovery, as well as pollution prevention data addressing source reduction, recycling, and waste management activities. 42 U.S.C. § 13106.

Hazardous material inventory. Other facilities that manufacture, process, use, or store hazardous chemicals but are not required to complete a Form R must submit a hazardous material inventory report to the LEPC annually. 42 U.S.C. § 11022. The hazardous material inventory report must detail the location, amount, and storage method for chemicals at the facility.

Hazardous material inventory reports must detail the location, amount, and storage method for chemicals at the facility.

STATE INVENTORY AND RIGHT-TO-KNOW REQUIREMENTS

Requirements for businesses. All "persons" or "stationary sources" that store, handle, or use "hazardous materials" (defined below) in the quantities specified below must electronically submit an HMBP to the local "unified program agency" (UPA) (typically the CUPA) via the statewide California Environmental Reporting System (CERS) data base annually. Health & Safety Code § 25500 *et seq.;* 19 Cal. Code Regs. §§ 2729–2732. HMBPs are designed to provide advanced knowledge of the hazards posed by chemicals that could be encountered by emergency personnel responding to a fire.

The threshold quantities for on-site storage at any one time, which are much lower than those required under EPCRA, are as follows:

- 55 gallons of a liquid
- 500 pounds of a solid
- 200 cubic feet of a gas at standard temperature (68°F) and pressure
- 1,000 cubic feet of a cryogenic, refrigerated, or compressed gas; 5,000 pounds of irritants and sensitizers (solid); or 550 gallons of specified hazardous liquids (liquid)
- Combined storage capacity of oils (including mineral oil and used oil) equal to or greater than 1,320 gallons
- An extremely hazardous substance in threshold planning quantities as defined in 40 C.F.R. Part 355
- Radioactive materials in quantities for which an emergency response plan is required under federal or state regulations
- 100 cubic feet of compressed inert gases at remote, unstaffed facilities

Exemptions from HMBP requirements include:

- Consumer products (however, retail pesticide supply companies are not exempt)

- Non-flammable refrigerants used for comfort cooling, excluding ammonia in closed systems used in comfort or space cooling for computer rooms
- Hazardous materials that are in transit (e.g., hazardous material contained in any railcar or marine vessel)
- Oxygen and nitrous oxide stored at medical offices
- Less than 55 gallons of lubricating oil (excluding used oil) when the total volume of lubricating oil handled at the facility does not exceed 275 gallons at any one time
- Farms meeting specified conditions
- Unstaffed remote facilities located at least one-half mile from the nearest occupied structure are conditionally exempt from HMBP requirements

Handlers must annually submit HMBPs to the CERS by March 1 or by a date established by the CUPA. New businesses must submit an HMBP within 30 days of handling hazardous chemicals and update the hazardous materials inventory each year on or before March 1. The business must review and certify that the information in CERS is complete and accurate. In addition, the HMBP reported in the CERS must be made available to the public.

Entities required to submit HMBPs are referred to as handlers. A handler is defined as "any business that handles a hazardous material." Health & Safety Code § 25501(n). A hazardous material is defined as a substance or waste that, because of its physical, chemical, or other characteristics, may pose a risk of endangering human health or safety or of degrading the environment, and the definition includes hazardous wastes. Health & Safety Code § 25260(d).

A hazardous material is defined as a substance or waste that, because of its physical, chemical, or other characteristics, may pose a risk of endangering human health or safety or of degrading the environment, and the definition includes hazardous wastes.

Handlers must also submit the following HMBP components to the CUPA:

- Hazardous material inventory (also meets EPCRA's inventory requirements)
- List of emergency contacts
- Site plan with chemical locations

Handlers must annually review and certify the accuracy, completeness, and currency of the data supplied to the CUPA. Handlers must also report to the CUPA any changes in the quantities of chemicals stored at a facility.

Individual CUPAs may require more rigorous local requirements only upon approval of the local governing body (e.g., city council or board of supervisors). CUPAs do require submission of training and response plans along with training documentation. Handlers on leased property that already are required to develop and implement an HMBP must meet specified notification requirements. Health & Safety Code §§ 25503.6, 25505.

Guidance on Release Reporting

Unless legal counsel advises otherwise, it is prudent to "over notify" when in doubt. The principal agencies that require notification include the Governor's Office of Emergency Services (OES), the National Response Center (NRC), and the relevant CUPA and air district. OES typically will make courtesy notifications to all other state agencies, such as the DTSC and the regional water quality control board (RWQCB). Similarly, the NRC makes courtesy notifications to the appropriate federal agencies. Nonetheless, it is advisable to follow up and provide individual notifications to each agency for which a reportable quantity of a regulated chemical has been released. Failure to comply with these obligations can result in fines of several thousand dollars per day.

RWQCB = regional water quality control board

RQ = reportable quantity

CERCLA = Comprehensive Environmental Response, Compensation, and Liability Act

Release reporting. Under California law, handlers must immediately report the release of any material where there is "a reasonable basis for believing that it would be injurious to the health and safety of persons or harmful to the environment if released into the workplace or the environment." Health & Safety Code § 25507; 19 Cal. Code Regs. § 2703. Handlers must decide on a case-by-case basis whether to report; miscalculating whether a release meets the reporting criteria could result in significant penalties. Unlike the vast number of release reporting laws, this release reporting law imposes no minimum numeric reportable quantity.

If a chemical spills into the environment, a number of other federal, state, and local reporting obligations must be met, including notifying various agencies within specified time frames. For the most part, other California reporting requirements follow the federal scheme involving a specified list of chemical substances that must be reported when a hazardous substance threshold or "reportable quantity" has been exceeded.

A reportable quantity (RQ) is a quantity expressed in pounds. If a release over a 24-hour period meets or exceeds the RQ, then the notification requirements apply. Specific RQs are identified for extremely hazardous substances under CERCLA, the Comprehensive Environmental Response, Compensation, and Liability Act. The RQ for EHSs is one pound. For substances that are CERCLA hazardous substances, or are a combination of an EHS and a CERCLA hazardous substance, the RQ is listed in 40 C.F.R. § 302.4. RQs range from one pound to 5,000 pounds. RQs for releases impacting water quality have different thresholds.

Each regulatory reporting requirement is independent for compliance purposes (i.e., reporting under one law does not necessarily relieve a party from reporting under another law). For this reason, if a spill or release occurs, it is advisable to examine all federal and state release reporting requirements as applicable under one or more of the programs described above and in chapters 8 and 10. For guidance on release reporting, see sidebar.

CHEMICAL HANDLING AND STORAGE

OVERVIEW OF FEDERAL OSHA REQUIREMENTS

Federal OSHA (29 C.F.R. § 1910.1200 *et seq.*) regulates all employers (with some exceptions, such as self-employed persons and farmers who employ family members). OSHA addresses all facets of worker safety, ranging from managing electrical hazards, confined spaces, fall hazards, and chemical handling, among many other areas. This discussion only addresses those OSHA standards governing hazardous chemicals. These standards essentially codify good management housekeeping practices to prevent chemical spills, reactions, and exposures. As a general rule,

Table 7-2. Ignitable and Flammable Chemical Regulatory Classifications

Environmental Protection Agency	Federal Occupational Safety & Health Administration	U.S Department of Transportation
D001 Ignitable hazardous waste Flashpoint < 140°F	Class 1 flammable liquid Flashpoint < 73°F Boiling point ≤ 95°F	Packing Group 3, 1
	Class 2 flammable liquid Flashpoint < 73°F Boiling point ≥ 95°F	Packing Group 3, II
	Class 3 flammable liquid Flashpoint ≥ 73°F Boiling point ≤ 140°F	Packing Group 3, III
Nonhazardous waste Flashpoint > 140°F	Class 4 flammable liquid Flashpoint > 140°F Boiling point ≤ 199.4°F	Combustible Liquid, Packing Group III (DOT uses < 200°F)

OSHA standards specify where and how to store different categories of hazardous materials and hazardous waste. For example, hazardous materials and waste must be labeled to indicate chemical content, along with hazard warnings.

The federal OSHA rules specify prescriptive chemical storage standards for the following general categories of hazardous materials:

- Flammable liquids
- Corrosives
- Reactive chemicals, including compressed gases
- Toxic materials

This section addresses the "front end" risks posed by these chemicals; the "back end" risks are discussed in chapter 8, which addresses RCRA Subtitle C. California also establishes standards governing occupational exposures to hazardous chemicals in laboratories. 8 Cal. Code Regs. § 5191.

COMPATIBILITY

Chemicals must be evaluated for compatibility before storing. Incompatible substances can cause violent reactions, release toxic vapors or gases, and be explosive. Incompatible mixtures must be separated in storage by distance, or by partitions such as a dike, berm, or secondary containment. 8 Cal. Code Regs. § 5164 (a).

Chemicals must be evaluated for compatibility before storing.

FLAMMABLE LIQUIDS

Definitions. Federal OSHA rules define flammable liquids as any liquid having a flashpoint below 199.4° Fahrenheit. 29 C.F.R. § 1910.106(a)(19). Flammable liquids are subdivided into four categories as illustrated in Table 7-2, which also describes the regulatory programs and terminology used to characterize "ignitable" hazardous wastes and "flammable" materials. The handler can then determine which

U.F.C. = Uniform Fire Code

category the hazardous material falls under by consulting the SDS and referring to its flashpoint for a given hazardous material.

Flammable storage standards. The NFPA codes and standards were created to address industrial and large storage facilities that maintain large quantities of hazardous materials used for processing, manufacturing, and storage. Chapter 66 of the Uniform Fire Code (U.F.C.) establishes performance standards for flammable liquids in containers, tanks, and buildings, including:

- Design, installation, and construction of tanks and piping systems that store and transport flammable liquids
- Creation and construction of containers and portable tanks for storing such liquids

U.F.C. Chapter 67 discusses the requirements for storing, using, and handling flammable solids. U.F.C. Chapter 70 addresses the general storage, use, and handling of oxidizers and organic peroxides. Section 71.1 of the U.F.C. deals with the proper outdoor storage and handling of pyrophoric solids and liquids.

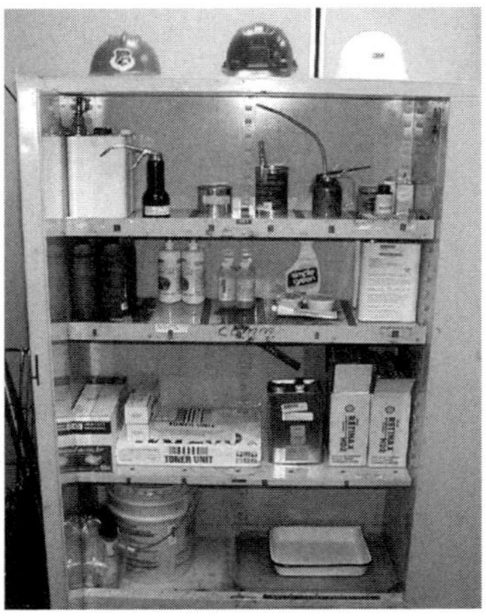

Proper storage of flammable and combustible materials.

Federal OSHA standards specify requirements for flammable liquids. 29 C.F.R. § 1910.106(d)(3) *et seq.* Storage of more than 25 gallons must be in fire-rated cabinets meeting certain specifications, including secondary containment to capture spills. No more than 60 gallons of Category I–III liquids, and no more than 120 gallons of Category IV liquids, may be stored in a flammable cabinet. Chemical containers too large to fit within a flammable cabinet, with a size of more than 60 gallons of Category I–III liquids, or more than 120 gallons of Category IV liquids, must be stored in specially equipped rooms or buildings meeting certain specifications.

The U.F.C. also contains provisions on the capacity, construction, and design of storage cabinets for flammable liquids that vary depending on the occupancy of the building. U.F.C. § 66.4.3. Additionally, the U.F.C. addresses environmental concerns associated with hazardous materials storage lockers, as well as design features necessary to meet applicable local, state, and federal regulations. U.F.C. § 66.4.6.

Whether the flammable materials are stored in a flammable cabinet or inside a storage room or building, the chemicals must meet specified storage standards. Hazardous materials must be segregated from incompatible chemicals. For example, acid cleaners (which are corrosive) must be isolated from flammable chemicals such as gasoline. In addition, flammables such as solvent-based paint must be separated from oxidizers such as lithium batteries. Further guidance on chemical compatibility may be found on the chemical's SDS.

Individual flammable containers must be kept closed, except when adding or entering contents. In addition, the containers must display the chemical hazard warnings reflected on the SDS as more fully discussed in Hazard Communication, above.

U.F.C. Chapter 43 establishes recommended or mandatory operating procedures for spraying, dipping, and coating using flammable materials, for example, performance requirements for each spray area. The U.F.C. also addresses requirements for storing, handling, and mixing flammable liquids.

CORROSIVES

Corrosive chemicals (such as strong acids and bases) can cause damage to human tissues, causing serious burns and irritation to skin and eyes. Safety showers and eye wash stations must be located near corrosive storage and activities to allow quick drenching or flushing of the eyes and body. 29 C.F.R. § 1910.151(c). See sidebar for further information on corrosives.

REACTIVE CHEMICALS, INCLUDING COMPRESSED GASES

Gases stored under pressure pose fire and explosion hazards. Federal OSHA rules require that compressed gases be stored securely to prevent tipping. Incompatible compressed gas fuel cylinders (such as propane and oxygen) must be stored separately at least 20 feet apart. The rules also establish smoking restrictions near storage areas. 29 C.F.R. §§ 1910.101, 1910.106(d)(7). California law limits the use of compressed gases for the purpose of elevating or otherwise transferring substances from one container to another. 8 Cal. Code Regs. § 3301 (e).

TOXIC MATERIALS

Toxic materials can cause chronic and acute harm, ranging from organ damage to cancer. To avoid occupational exposures, personnel should consult SDSs to learn what types of personal protective equipment to apply. U.F.C. Chapter 68 addresses the storage, use, and handling of toxic solids and liquids, and establishes standards for indoor and outdoor storage of toxic materials. Treated wood must include warnings regarding potential exposure to carcinogens and reproductive toxins pursuant to Proposition 65 along with worker safety-related personal protective equipment. Health & Safety Code § 25150.7.

GENERAL DUTY CLAUSE

Federal OSHA compliance officers have discretionary authority to cite employers who expose their employees to "recognized hazards that are likely to cause death or serious physical harm to employees" where the activity is not specifically captured in the federal OSHA regulations. Thus, an employer can be liable for exposing its employees to chemical harm even where the condition is not specifically governed by a federal OSHA standard. Federal OSHA compliance officers must demonstrate the employer had "feasible means to eliminate or materially reduce the hazard and the employer knew, or by exercising reasonable diligence could have known, of the hazardous condition." 29 U.S.C. § 654(a)(1).

Corrosive Chemicals

It is advisable to consult an SDS to determine what type of personal protective equipment (PPE) to use when handling corrosive chemicals. Corrosive chemicals should not be stored in metal drums or containers because the chemicals can corrode and compromise the container. Common acids and bases requiring special management are shown below.

Common Acids and Bases

Acids (pH 0–6)

- Hydrochloric acid
- Hydrofluoric acid
- Nitric acid
- Phosphoric acid
- Chromic acid

Bases (pH 8–14)

- Sodium hydroxide (lye)
- Sodium hypochlorite (bleach)
- Aqueous ammonia
- Potassium hydroxide (potash)
- Ammonium hydroxide

PERMISSIBLE EXPOSURE LIMITS

Federal OSHA established maximum chemical concentrations for which a worker may be exposed. These PELs have not been updated since shortly after OSHA was enacted in 1970. 29 U.S.C. § 655 (a), 29 C.F.R. § 1910.1000 (Table Z).

CAL OSHA CHEMICAL MANAGEMENT REQUIREMENTS

Cal/OSHA has established lower, more health-protective PELs which must be updated every two years (e.g., ammonia, carbon monoxide, acetone, and acetaldehyde). 8 Cal. Code Regs. § 5155 (Table AC-1).

California does not have a comparable catch-all "general duty clause." However, California employers must develop and implement a written IIPP. 8 Cal. Code Regs. § 3203. The IIPP serves as a comprehensive health and safety management program addressing all aspects of compliance with Cal/OSHA. Among other things, employers must identify workplace chemical hazards, state those hazards, inform workers of the hazards, ensure employees meet safety and health work practices, conduct training, complete periodic inspections, investigate accidents, and provide procedures to mitigate unsafe or unhealthy conditions.

Also the state cholinesterase medical supervision program requires farm workers who regularly use organophosphate and carbamate pesticides to undergo medical supervision. The monitoring is intended to determine whether the pesticides are suppressing cholinesterase levels in workers. Employers must remove from the work environment employees whose cholinesterase levels are suppressed. 3 Cal. Code Regs. § 6728.

CARCINOGENIC REPORTING

California employers whose employees handle carcinogenic substances must file a report to Cal/OSHA identifying where the regulated carcinogen is located in the workplace along with a description of each process or operation which creates exposure to the carcinogen.

Also, California employers whose employees handle carcinogenic substances must file a report to Cal/OSHA identifying where the regulated carcinogen is located in the workplace along with a description of each process or operation which creates exposure to the carcinogen. Cal/OSHA General Industry Safety Order § 5203. There is no analogous requirement under federal OSHA.

HAZARDOUS MATERIALS TRANSPORTATION

FEDERAL PROGRAM

The HMTA protects against risks to life and property from transporting hazardous materials in commerce. 49 C.F.R. § 105 *et seq.* The Act regulates any transporter of hazardous materials or any person who manufactures, marks, repairs, or tests a package that was certified, sold, or marked for use in the transportation of hazardous materials. Any person requesting transportation of hazardous materials must maintain shipping papers describing the substances to be shipped. Each person providing shipping papers must retain copies or keep an electronic image at their principal place of business for specified time periods.

STATE PROGRAM

Movement of hazardous chemicals on California roads is largely the province of HMTA; however, California law imposes commercial licensure (Civil Code § 32000.5) and training (13 Cal. Code Regs. § 1161.7).

UNDERGROUND STORAGE TANK REGULATION

FEDERAL PROGRAM

Overview. Following the pioneering policies of California, Congress enacted RCRA Subtitle I (42 U.S.C. § 6991 *et seq.*) in 1988 to regulate and manage UST risks. EPA regulations (40 C.F.R. § 280.20 *et seq.*) govern the design, permitting, operation, and closure of USTs to prevent releases of specified chemicals to the environment.

The federal program is designed to be implemented by the states, which must submit their UST programs to EPA for approval. California has not sought EPA approval yet, though the Legislature has expressed this intent. *See* Health Safety Code § 25299.7. Until the California program is approved, both federal and state requirements apply to USTs.

Applicability. RCRA Subtitle I establishes performance standards governing "UST systems" that store a "regulated substance." A "regulated substance" includes "hazardous substances" and petroleum. 40 C.F.R. § 280.12. "A hazardous substance" is a broadly defined term that includes all chemicals regulated under CERCLA (*see* chapter 8) with the exception of "hazardous waste" (which is defined under RCRA Subtitle C). "Petroleum" includes crude oil and fractions, such as motor fuels, jet fuels, distillate fuel oils, lubricants, petroleum solvents, and used oils. A "UST system" includes tanks that are 10 percent or more beneath the surface, plus underground piping, that stores a regulated substance. A regulated UST system must be constructed of nonearthen materials, such as wood, concrete, steel, and plastic. 40 C.F.R. § 280.20.

View of underground storage tank from surface.

New and upgraded underground storage tanks. Federal rules impose a number of performance requirements for new USTs and upgrades to existing USTs. 40 C.F.R. § 280.20. New USTs installed after 1988 must have been permitted and be equipped with specified secondary containment, including associated piping. For single-walled USTs, secondary containment capacity must be at least 100 percent of the primary tank. For tank systems with more than one tank, the secondary containment capacity must be at least 150 percent of the largest primary tank or 10 percent of the aggregate of all tanks (whichever is greater). For tanks with secondary containment structures exposed to rainfall, the containment capacity must be able to accommodate 24 hours of precipitation for a 25-year storm.

New USTs also must be equipped to monitor for releases into secondary containment. Specifically, UST monitoring must be able to detect releases into the

DHS = Department of Homeland Security

interstitial space that separates the primary from the secondary tank. In addition, USTs must be equipped with spill and overfill controls (e.g., automatic shutoff at 95 percent capacity and alarms) to prevent releases. Corrosion protection (e.g., cathodic protection) may be required for UST systems comprised of metal to protect the integrity of the tank. 40 C.F.R. §§ 280.20, 280.30, 280.31. For those tanks not constructed with metal, the following construction materials must be used:

- Fiberglass-reinforced plastic
- Steel with cathodic protection
- Steel fiberglass-reinforced plastic composite

Owners and operators of UST systems must monitor to ensure that regulated substances are neither released from the primary to the secondary tank nor from the secondary tank to the environment. Monitoring procedures must be described in a written routine monitoring program. 40 C.F.R. §§ 280.34, 280.45. Owners and operators must submit monthly reports and annual reports showing that data is within allowable variations. Also, owners and operators must develop and implement a response plan to address the possibility of an unauthorized release. 40 C.F.R. § 280.66.

Operating permits. UST systems must operate pursuant to a UST permit, which lasts for five years. UST system owners and operators must maintain records documenting any change in service, repairs, leak detection, monitoring, inspections, corrosion protections, agency notifications, and closure information. Each record must be maintained for a specified period of time.

UST operators. There are three classes of operators who must be trained to operate and maintain UST systems within 30 days of assuming UST responsibilities. EPA has established new training requirements which must be met by operators by October 13, 2018. 80 Fed. Reg. 41566 (July 15, 2015).

Closure. UST systems that are taken out of service temporarily or permanently must meet specified closure requirements. Different requirements apply for temporary closures of fewer than 12 consecutive months, and permanent closures of more than 12 months. 40 C.F.R. § 280.70(b), (c). An application for closure must be submitted within 30 days prior to removal from use. 40 C.F.R. § 280.71(a).

If the Department of Homeland Security determines the facility presents a potentially high risk based on a worst-case chemical screening exercise, the facility must complete a security vulnerability assessment to assist DHS in ranking these chemical facilities based on specific security concerns involving potential chemical releases off-site, chemical theft or diversion, and sabotage or contamination.

Antiterrorism requirements. The U.S. Department of Homeland Security (DHS) Chemical Facility Antiterrorism Standards requires facilities of any size to determine whether they have chemicals of interest exceeding screening threshold quantities. Facilities were required to initially screen their chemical inventory by early 2008. If the DHS determines the facility presents a potentially high risk based on a worst-case chemical screening exercise, the facility must complete a security vulnerability assessment to assist DHS in ranking these chemical facilities based on specific security concerns involving potential chemical releases off-site, chemical theft or diversion, and sabotage or contamination. Highly ranked facilities may be required to develop a site security plan to manage the risk. 6 C.F.R. Part 27.

STATE PROGRAM

Applicability. California led the nation with its groundbreaking underground storage tank policies in 1984. This program was later adopted by Congress, EPA, and other states. An underground tank system includes the tank and the underground piping that stores a "hazardous substance," is substantially or totally beneath the surface, and is constructed of nonearthen materials (e.g., wood, concrete, steel, and plastic). A "hazardous substance" is defined broadly to include hazardous wastes (as defined under California law; *see* chapter 8) and "petroleum," which includes crude oil and fractions (e.g., motor fuels, jet fuels, distillate fuel oils, lubricants, petroleum solvents, and used oils). Health & Safety Code § 25280 *et seq.*; 23 Cal. Code Regs. § 2611 *et seq.* A master list of hazardous substances can be obtained from DTSC. Health & Safety Code § 25282.

A "hazardous substance" is defined broadly to include hazardous wastes and "petroleum," which includes crude oil and fractions (e.g., motor fuels, jet fuels, distillate fuel oils, lubricants, petroleum solvents, and used oils).

For each UST system, owners and operators must operate pursuant to a permit issued by the CUPA. If there is no CUPA, the agency responsible for implementing the UST program is the local agency designated by the Secretary for Environmental Protection. Health & Safety Code §§ 25281(i), (j), (k), 25283(a), (b), 25404.3(f).

USTs may be operated only by designated operators that meet certain training and certification requirements. 23 Cal. Code Regs. § 2715. Also, owners and operators of USTs that store petroleum products must meet specified financial assurance requirements. 23 Cal. Code Regs. § 2805 *et seq.*

Exemptions. The California UST program exempts specific containers from regulation under the statute. For example, the following USTs are exempt: tanks with 1,100 gallons or less capacity that are located on a farm and used for storing motor vehicle fuel that is used primarily for agricultural purposes, or tanks storing home heating oil for consumptive use. Other exemptions apply to structures such as sumps, storm drains, catch basins, evaporation ponds, lagoons, and tanks holding hydraulic fluid for a closed loop mechanical system using compressed air or hydraulic fluid to operate lifts or other similar devices. Vaulted tanks (i.e., below-grade tanks that are not buried in the ground) that are connected to an emergency generator tank system are eligible for a conditional exemption. Health & Safety Code § 25281(y)(1)(A). In addition, storage tanks in "an underground area" are exempt where the owner or operator implements a plan to prevent and control releases. Health & Safety Code § 25270.2(o)(3).

New and upgraded underground storage tanks. The performance standards for new USTs are similar to federal standards; however, for tanks storing hazardous substances, the California standards apply to tanks installed after 1984, whereas the federal standards apply to tanks installed after 1988. Like the federal program, secondary containment for new USTs is required. The minimum volume

FIGURE 7-3
UST Performance Standards for Leak Detection

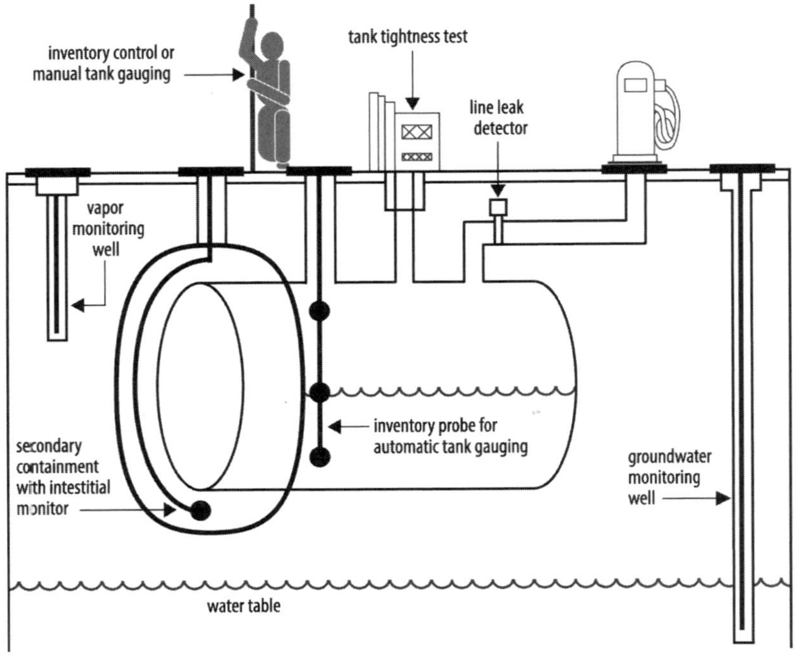

Source: National Work Group on Leak Detection Evaluations

requirements for secondary containment are the same as the federal requirements. The SWRCB offers grants to small businesses to assist in complying with testing and leak detection equipment, meeting interstitial space requirements, and integrity testing. Health & Safety Code §§ 25290.1(c)(4), (5), 25290.2 (c)(4), (5); 23 Cal. Code Regs. § 2631.

All new UST systems must be made of or lined with materials that are compatible with the substance being stored. Secondary containment systems must be tested every 36 months after initial testing. UST owners or operators must annually test the spill containment structure to show that it is capable of containing the substance if an overfilling event occurs. Owners or operators of UST systems are also required to prevent releases from overfilling during product delivery. 23 Cal. Code Regs. §§ 2631.1(a), 2637(a), 2712(k), Health & Safety Code § 25284.2. For an illustration of some required performance standards, see Figure 7-3.

UST owners or operators must annually test the spill containment structure to show that it is capable of containing the substance if an overfilling event occurs.

Since the federal deadline to upgrade or close USTs expired in 1998 (*see* below), owners and operators of USTs in California were confronted with additional state rules calling for additional performance standards. 23 Cal. Code Regs. § 2662 *et seq.* **Underground storage tank systems installed after July 1, 2004.** These tanks must be designed and constructed with a continuous monitoring system capable of detecting entry of liquid or vapor into the secondary containment from the primary containment, or detecting water intrusion. These tanks must be double-contained, with the primary and secondary containment designed to be "product tight" (impervious to liquid and vapor of the contained substance). Secondary containment must be constructed to prevent water intrusion into the UST system by precipitation, infiltration, or surface run-off. Health & Safety Code §§ 25281(o), 25290.1, 25290.2 *et seq*. Interstitial space of USTs must be maintained under constant vacuum or pressure to detect a breach in the primary or secondary containment before liquid or vapor is released to the environment. Health & Safety Code § 25290.1 *et seq*.

All secondary containment, including under-dispenser containment (e.g., gasoline dispensers), must be equipped with a continuous monitoring system that either activates an alarm or stops the flow of the product when it detects a leak. Automatic line leak detectors that restrict or shut off the flow of product through the piping must be installed on all underground pressurized piping. 23 Cal. Code Regs. § 2636(f)(1), (2).

All secondary containment, including under-dispenser containment (e.g., gasoline dispensers), must be equipped with a continuous monitoring system that either activates an alarm or stops the flow of the product when it detects a leak.

Vent lines, vapor recovery lines, and fill pipes that are beneath the surface of the ground must have secondary containment. Underground pressurized piping must be equipped with an automatic line leak detector and must be tightness tested annually. Health & Safety Code § 25290.

Installation requirements. Owners and operators of UST systems must certify that the UST and piping were installed by certified UST installers and that the CUPA approved the installation. All secondary containment systems, including piping, must comply with specified construction and performance standards similar to the federal UST program, and all secondary containment systems are required to be periodically tested. All tank and piping integrity tests must be performed or supervised by a licensed tank tester with a valid tank testing license. Finally, owners or operators of UST systems are required to notify the CUPA at least 48 hours before installing, repairing, replacing, calibrating, or certifying monitoring equipment. Health & Safety Code § 25284.4; 23 Cal. Code Regs. § 2635 *et seq*.

Monitoring, recordkeeping, and release reporting. The day-to-day operation of the UST system must follow a CUPA-approved monitoring and response program. A copy of the permit and monitoring plan must be retained either at the facility or off-site at a readily available location. The site must maintain certain records, requirements which are similar to the federal standards. Health & Safety Code §§ 25286, 25293; 23 Cal. Code Regs. §§ 2632–2634, 2636, 2711, 2712.

Unauthorized releases of hazardous substances from the secondary or primary containment (where no secondary containment exists) must be reported to the CUPA within 24 hours. UST owners or operators responsible for the unauthorized release must submit a written report to the local agency within five days. The report must describe the nature and volume of the release along with the corrective actions that were taken. Water Code §§ 13271, 13272.

Closure and cleanup. Owners or operators of USTs must notify the CUPA and receive approval before temporarily or permanently closing USTs. Owners or

TSCA = Toxic Substances Control Act

operators also must meet specified requirements for temporarily closed USTs and permanently closed USTs and must demonstrate that no unauthorized release occurred. 23 Cal. Code Regs. §§ 2670–2672.

Created in 1989, the Underground Storage Tank Cleanup Fund (Barry Keene Underground Storage Tank Cleanup Act of 1989) makes funds available to owners and operators of petroleum USTs to defray costs to clean up contaminated soil and groundwater caused from leaking USTs. Health & Safety Code § 25299.10 *et seq.* Loans or grants can be used for repair, replacement, upgrade, or removal of petroleum USTs for small businesses. The program is financed by a fee paid by UST owners and operators. To be eligible for cleanup funds, UST owners and operators must demonstrate that contamination resulted from a UST leak, and cleanup work must have been performed after 1987. The claimant also must be in compliance with UST permitting requirements and cleanup orders. The maximum reimbursement per occurrence is no more than $1.5 million.

To be eligible for cleanup funds, UST owners and operators must demonstrate that contamination resulted from a UST leak, and cleanup work must have been performed after 1987.

AB 1701 of 2012 (Chapter 536, Statutes of 2012) is designed to speed up UST cleanup and to standardize local agency oversight of these cleanup efforts. AB 1701 restructured the regulatory framework governing oversight of UST cleanup activities and replaced disparate oversight by multiple agencies. AB 1701 created a state certification process authorizing cities and counties to oversee UST cleanups.

Variances. A site-specific variance is a state-approved departure from the regulations for a particular UST system based on site-specific circumstances. Permit holders and permit applicants may apply to the appropriate regional water quality control board. Health & Safety Code § 25299.4.

OTHER HAZARDOUS MATERIALS PROGRAMS

In addition to the regulatory programs previously reviewed, there are a variety of additional federal and state programs regulating some aspect of hazardous materials and toxic substances. These miscellaneous programs are reviewed below.

TOXIC SUBSTANCES CONTROL ACT

Enacted in 1976, TSCA (15 U.S.C. § 2601 *et seq.*; 40 C.F.R. § 700 *et seq.*) is designed to protect human health and the environment by regulating chemical substances that are manufactured, processed, distributed, used, or disposed for commercial purposes. The term "chemical substance" (including mixtures) is broadly defined under TSCA to include organic and inorganic chemicals. TSCA excludes from regulation drugs, pesticides, tobacco and tobacco products, nuclear material and byproducts, food, food additives, cosmetics, and medical devices.

TSCA authorizes EPA to screen new and existing chemicals before they are introduced into commerce for their potential health or environmental effects. The Act also requires EPA to screen existing chemicals to determine if they pose an unreasonable risk of harm to human health or the environment. EPA is authorized to prohibit chemical use in commerce or to limit the volume or concentration of chemical substances if it determines the chemical poses an unreasonable risk of injury to health or the environment. 15 U.S.C. § 2605.

PMN = premanufacture notice

SNUR = Significant New Use Rule

TSCA Section 5(a) premanufacture notice. TSCA requires manufacturers, processors, or importers to notify EPA before they produce or introduce a non-exempt chemical product into commerce. 15 U.S.C.§ 2604(a). Called a premanufacture notice (PMN), it must be submitted at least 90 days prior to the activity. Upon notification, EPA has 45 days to determine whether the chemical has potential to impact human health or the environment. 40 C.F.R. § 720 *et seq.* EPA must determine that chemicals will likely meet the safety standard before being commercially manufactured or processed. TSCA Section 7. EPA is authorized to impose PMN requirements to manufactured objects (known as "articles") if EPA finds the article presents an unreasonable chemical exposure.

TSCA (15 U.S.C. 2604(h)) grants some exemptions to the PMN requirement. Specifically, upon application, manufacturers, processors, or importers of non-exempt new chemicals for test-marketing purposes are exempt from PMN. Similarly, small quantities of chemicals used solely for research and development are exempt. 40 C.F.R. §§ 720.36, 720.38.

President Obama signed significant new amendments to TSCA (known as the "Frank R. Lautenberg Chemical Safety for the 21st Century Act" or H.R. 2576) in June 2016. H.R. 2576 responded to the dearth of chemical restrictions that EPA established since the enactment of the law in 1976. TSCA Section 6 now regulates existing chemical substances that are included in the "TSCA inventory."

The Significant New Use Rule requires manufacturers, processors, or importers to notify EPA when they plan to produce, process, or use an existing chemical for a use that differs from a previously authorized use.

Significant New Use Rule. SNUR (TSCA Section 5(e)) requires manufacturers, processors, or importers to notify EPA when they plan to produce, process, or use an existing chemical for a use that differs from a previously authorized use.

Expedited chemical reviews. The TSCA amendments require EPA to develop a mandatory schedule to review and regulate the backlog of existing chemicals. By June 2018, EPA must gather chemical safety information from chemical manufacturers and processors and evaluate and prioritize the risks of existing chemicals. EPA must additionally evaluate impacts to vulnerable subpopulations (including children and pregnant women) as well as persistent bioaccumulative toxic chemicals. The TSCA amendments are designed to expedite chemical reviews by replacing the time-consuming prior cost-benefit analysis requirement with a health and environmental risk-based evaluation. At the time this book went to print (late 2016), EPA had identified five chemicals for expedited review. EPA must also develop a rule to mitigate unreasonable chemical risks in a timely manner.

State pre-emption. State laws enacted before April 22, 2016 that restrict a specific chemical are grandfathered under the TSCA amendments. States may also restrict chemicals that have not yet been regulated by EPA. These pre-emption provisions are complex and will require careful review to evaluate the degree to which the California Green Chemistry law, Proposition 65, and California's various chemical bans are affected.

Section 8(a) general reporting and recordkeeping requirements. Manufacturers, processors, and importers of listed chemical substances and mixtures must comply with various reporting and recordkeeping requirements. The Preliminary Assessment Information Rule requires manufacturers and importers to report site-specific information for each plant site at which they manufactured or imported the listed chemical. The information must include:

- The quantity of the imported or manufactured chemical
- The amount routinely lost to the environment during manufacture or importation
- The quantity of enclosed, controlled, and open releases of the chemical
- Worker exposure information

Some companies are exempt from this reporting requirement. 40 C.F.R. §§ 712.20, 712.25(a)–(c). Most chemical products manufactured for export are excluded from TSCA requirements, except for Section 8's general reporting and recordkeeping requirements. 15 U.S.C. § 2607(a); TSCA § 12 (b); 40 C.F.R. § 707.60(b).

Section 8(c) allegations of significant adverse reactions rule. Producers, processors, and distributors of regulated chemical substances must maintain a file of allegations of significant adverse reactions (to human health or the environment) and report those allegations to the EPA. Companies must keep these files for five years at their headquarters or at a centrally located site near the company's chemical operations. Not all allegations are subject to this rule. Exemptions include accusations alleging "known human effects," anonymous accusations, and any allegations directly attributable to an environmental contamination incident that has been reported to the federal government. 15 U.S.C. § 2607(c), 40 C.F.R. § 717.12(b), (d).

Section 8(e) substantial risk information requirement. Companies have a duty to report to EPA within 30 calendar days any new information they have that reasonably shows that a substance or mixture they manufacture, import, process, or distribute presents a substantial risk to human health or the environment. These notices generally include, among other things, toxicity and exposure data, and any ongoing actions that reduce potential risks to human health or the environment. *See also* 15 U.S.C. § 2607(e).

Companies have a duty to report to EPA within 30 calendar days any new information they have that reasonably shows that a substance or mixture they manufacture, import, process, or distribute presents a substantial risk to human health or the environment.

Asbestos and PCB regulation. TSCA provisions regulating asbestos and PCBs are discussed in the below sections on these substances.

ASBESTOS REGULATION

Title II asbestos regulation. The Asbestos Hazard Emergency Response Act became law in 1986 as Title II of TSCA. 15 U.S.C. § 2641 *et seq.* The Act regulates asbestos—a naturally occurring mineral substance that has been used widely for insulation (e.g., for boilers) and fireproofing (e.g., pipe lagging, floor tiles, roof shingles, and gaskets). Generally, asbestos is not a hazard unless it is inhaled. The Act prohibits the manufacture, importation, processing, and distribution asbestos-containing products *See* 40 C.F.R. § 763 Subpart I.

AHERA = Asbestos Hazard Emergency Response Act

NESHAP = National Emissions Standards for Hazardous Air Pollutants

AHERA governs the control and abatement of asbestos hazards in school buildings and requires school agencies to develop an inventory of friable (capable of being pulverized under hand pressure) and non-friable asbestos-containing materials. The schools must implement management plans that detail abatement actions they can undertake. In addition, school officials must label building materials that contain asbestos and periodically conduct facility inspections. The local school district must ensure that all staff members who work in an area with asbestos-containing building material will have at least two hours of training. 15 U.S.C. § 2643 *et seq.*; 40 C.F.R. § 763.92 (a).

AHERA was amended in 1990 by the Asbestos School Hazard Abatement Reauthorization Act. 15 U.S.C. § 2641; 40 C.F.R. § 763 *et seq.* This Act requires personnel inspecting ACM in schools and commercial and public buildings to be trained on the proper methods for handling ACM.

Asbestos fibers. When asbestos fibers are inhaled, they may get trapped in the lungs. Over time, these fibers can accumulate and cause scarring and inflammation, which can affect breathing and lead to serious health problems, including lung cancer.

Employees engaged in construction involving exposure to asbestos must monitor to ensure that PELs for asbestos are not exceeded. Regulated construction activities include, among other activities, demolition or salvage of structures, removal or encapsulation of materials, construction, alteration, repair, maintenance, or renovation. Employers must notify other employers of the activity and measures to prevent exposure. 29 C.F.R. § 1926.1101.

Occupational Safety and Health Act general industry standards. OSHA's general industry standards most typically apply to asbestos manufacturers and businesses involved in brake and clutch repairs. Specific monitoring, operational practices, and notification rules govern the construction industry for ACM demolition and removal and installation, repair, maintenance, or renovation of structures containing asbestos. 29 C.F.R. § 1926.1101(d).

National Emissions Standards for Hazardous Air Pollutants. Section 112 of the Clean Air Act created the NESHAP program with the goal of protecting the public from hazardous air pollutants. The NESHAP program (more fully described in chapter 5), among other things, regulates the release of asbestos during the demolition or renovation of all facilities, excluding residential structures with four or fewer dwelling units. Building owners and contractors must notify the local pollution control district before any processing, handling, or disposal of ACM from buildings exceeds threshold amounts. The notification must contain information such as a description of the work to be conducted, the name and location of the waste disposal site, and an estimate of the amount of regulated asbestos-containing material to be removed. Most removed material must be disposed of in either a Class II landfill that can accept "designated" wastes (*see* chapter 9) or a Class I hazardous waste landfill. *See* chapter 8. 40 C.F.R. § 61.145 *et seq.*

California asbestos program. The California Asbestos Notification Act (Health & Safety Code § 25915 *et seq.*) requires that the owner of any building constructed before 1979, who knows that the building contains asbestos, must provide written notice to employees working in the building of the following:

- Specific locations within the building of asbestos-containing construction materials
- General procedures and handling restrictions to limit, prevent release of, or prevent exposure to asbestos
- A summary of the results of any bulk sample analysis, or air monitoring, conducted for or by the owner, or within the owner's control
- Potential health risks associated with asbestos exposure

Also, Cal/OSHA imposes occupational PELs for asbestos.

LEAD REGULATION

Lead-based paint was banned from residential use in 1978, under the Residential Lead-Based Hazard Reduction Act of 1992.

Federal lead program. Lead-based paint has been extensively applied on surfaces for decades. Lead-based paint was banned from residential use in 1978, under the Residential Lead-Based Hazard Reduction Act of 1992. 42 U.S.C. § 4851 *et seq.*; 24 C.F.R. § 5 Subpart A.

The Act, also known as Title X, requires sellers and landlords of residential property built before 1978 (also known as target housing) to provide the following to property buyers and renters:

- Specified disclosures about lead
- A lead-based paint hazard pamphlet developed by the EPA, HUD, and the Consumer Product Safety Commission

Exemptions from the Act include houses built after 1978, structures with zero-bedroom units (e.g., dormitories, studio apartments), leases for less than 100 days, housing for the elderly or handicapped, rental housing found by a certified inspector to be lead-free, and foreclosure sales. 42 U.S.C. § 4851 *et seq.*; 24 C.F.R. § 35 Subpart A; 40 C.F.R. § 745.100 *et seq.*

Under the Act, sellers must allow the buyer a 10-day period to conduct a lead-based paint inspection or risk assessment, at the buyer's expense. The seller's contract must contain language of notification and disclosure about any known lead-based paint or lead-based paint hazards in the dwelling unit. Additionally, with any renovation of target housing, the renovator must provide the owner and occupant pamphlets on lead hazards before beginning such activities. 42 U.S.C. § 4852(d); 40 C.F.R. § 745.85.

California lead program. The Lead Hazard Reduction Enforcement Act (Health & Safety Code §§ 105250–105257) makes it a crime to own a residential or public building that contains lead hazards that are likely to endanger the health or the public or occupants, or to engage in an activity that creates a lead hazard. Lead hazard is defined as "deteriorated lead-based paint, lead contaminated dust, lead contaminated soil, disturbing lead-based paint or presumed lead-based paint without containment, or any other nuisance which may result in persistent and quantifiable lead exposure." 17 Cal. Code Regs. § 35037.

The Occupational Lead Poisoning Prevention Act (Health & Safety Code § 105185 *et seq.*) establishes an occupational lead poisoning prevention program to register and monitor laboratory reports of adult lead toxicity cases, to identify sources of lead poisoning through monitoring, to conduct investigations of take-home exposure cases, to train employees and health experts on prevention measures, and to recommend methods for lead poisoning prevention.

POLYCHLORINATED BIPHENYL REGULATION

PCBs are a family of over 200 aromatic chemicals that have been used pervasively due to their effective insulating properties and the fact that they are nonflammable. PCBs have been used extensively as coolants in electrical equipment (e.g., PCB-containing insulating oils in transformers and capacitors), fluorescent light ballasts, and building materials (e.g., adhesives, tile and tar coatings, caulking, paints, and inks).

PCBs contain dioxin, a probable carcinogen that also poses potentially significant health risks, including liver damage, neurological disorders, and skin hazards. PCBs are highly persistent chemicals that have a long life in the environment.

PCBs contain dioxin, a probable carcinogen that also poses potentially significant health risks, including liver damage, neurological disorders, and skin hazards.

Manufacturing ban. TSCA Section 6 (15 U.S.C. § 2601 *et seq.*) allows EPA to regulate chemicals presenting unreasonable risk. Due to the significant health and environmental hazards posed by PCBs, EPA banned PCB production in 1979. TSCA prohibits the manufacturing and use of PCBs, with some exceptions. PCBs may be used in existing equipment (such as transformers and capacitors) and in small quantities for research and development. 40 C.F.R. § 761 *et seq.*

Cradle-to-grave requirements. TSCA regulates PCB manufacturing and use, as well as storage, disposal, import, export, and spills. TSCA established a cradle-to-grave program governing the management of PCBs from the time the PCB becomes a waste to its ultimate disposal. This federal program is administered by the EPA and regulates only PCB oils and other PCB-containing equipment with concentrations above 50 parts per million (ppm). The following items, containing between 50 and 500 ppm PCB, are regulated and are subject to specified marking and labeling requirements:

- PCB capacitors
- PCB-contaminated electrical equipment
- PCB-contaminated transformers

- PCB articles (i.e., a manufactured item that contains PCBs and where the surface has been in direct contact with PCBs, such as capacitors, transformers, and electric motors)
- PCB containers (e.g., packages, cans, bottles, drums, tanks, or other package that contains PCBs, or PCB articles or equipment where the surface has been in direct contact with PCBs)
- PCB-containing light ballasts

PCB transformers that contain greater than 500 ppm PCB must be inspected once every three months. 40 C.F.R. § 761.30 (a)(1)(ix).

Key aspects of the PCB program include maintaining an annual PCB inventory (discussed below) and properly equipping long-term accumulation facilities, similar to 90-day hazardous waste accumulation facilities. *See* chapter 8. The primary difference between a 90-day hazardous waste accumulation facility and a PCB long-term accumulation facility is that the PCB bulk product waste may be stored only if the waste is piled in a manner to control dissemination by wind or any means other than water. Also, the waste must not generate leachate through decomposition or any other reaction. 40 C.F.R. § 761.65(4)(b)(1).

The primary difference between a 90-day hazardous waste storage facility and a PCB long-term storage facility is that the PCB bulk product waste may be stored only if the waste is piled in a manner to control dissemination by wind or any means other than water.

A one-year time limit exists for disposal of PCBs with concentrations of 50 ppm or more. The PCB waste must be disposed of within one year from the date the handler determines it to be a waste and decides to dispose of it. 40 C.F.R. § 761.65. PCB handlers must annually complete by July 1 of each year a log that must include an inventory of PCB items, including information on the PCB content. TSCA regulations specify disposal options that range from a TSCA-approved incinerator, a TSCA-approved chemical waste landfill, or a high-efficiency boiler.

Certain PCB items may be stored temporarily for up to 30 days from the date of their removal from service. These items include:

- Non-leaking PCB articles and equipment
- Leaking PCB articles and equipment if placed in non-leaking PCB containers
- PCB containers containing non-liquid PCBs
- PCB containers with PCB liquid concentrations of 50 ppm or more

Temporary storage is allowed only if a spill prevention, control, and countermeasure plan (*see* chapter 10) has been prepared, and if the waste is packed according to DOT hazardous materials regulations.

Similar to the hazardous waste manifest program (*see* chapter 8), PCB shipments are tracked by a PCB manifest, with copies for the PCB generator, the initial transporter, and the owner or operator of the disposal facility. Like the hazardous waste program, the generator must ensure that a signed copy of the manifest is received within 35 days of the date the PCB was accepted by the initial transporter. If the signed copy does not arrive by the 35th day, the generator immediately must contact the transporter or owner or operator of the "designated facility" to determine the status of the PCB waste. The generator must file an exception report with the EPA if the paperwork is not returned within 45 days of the date the waste was accepted by the initial transporter. Disposal facilities are required to issue a Certificate of Disposal for each shipment of manifested PCB accepted. 40 C.F.R. §§ 761.3, 761.215.

California requirements. As discussed more fully in chapter 8, PCB wastes between 5 and 50 ppm must be managed as a California-only hazardous waste. It may be necessary to manage PCB wastes with concentrations less than 5 ppm as "designated" wastes (more fully discussed in chapter 10).

TOXIC MOLD PROTECTION ACT OF 2001

This Act (Health & Safety Code § 26100 *et seq.*) requires sellers and landlords of residential, commercial, and industrial real property to disclose mold presence to buyers and tenants. Specifically, when the seller or landlord knows of mold presence that exceeds the PEL or poses a health threat, he or she must provide a written disclosure to the prospective or current buyers or tenants. Residential landlords must disclose before tenants enter into a rental agreement. These obligations only will apply after DPH sets PELs and other health standards for mold. Commercial and industrial landlords also have an affirmative duty to assess the condition of mold if they know or have received notice that the mold is present on property other than real property (such as heating, ventilation, and air conditioning systems).

PROPOSITION 65

The Safe Drinking Water and Toxic Enforcement Act of 1986 (known as Proposition 65) is a unique California law designed to minimize the public's exposure to known human carcinogens and reproductive toxicants. Health & Safety Code §§ 25249.5–25249.13. Citizens can bring actions to enforce the law when prosecutors (i.e., the Attorney General, district attorney, or city attorney) fail to sue an alleged violator after receiving a 60-day notice of the alleged violation. The law is carefully designed to ensure that only cases with merit are pursued, and that settlements between private citizens and alleged violators are brought into the open.

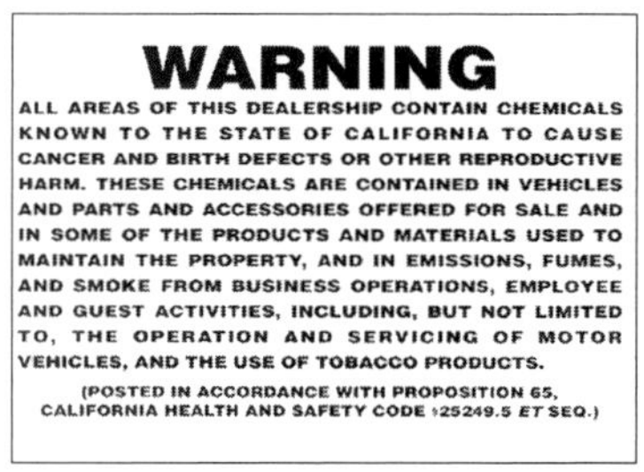

Under Proposition 65, regulated businesses must provide a clear and reasonable warning before exposing persons to listed carcinogens and toxicants.

Proposition 65 imposes two principal requirements upon businesses (local, state, and federal government entities are exempt) that have more than 10 employees. First, regulated businesses must not expose persons to listed carcinogens and reproductive toxicants without providing a "clear and reasonable" warning (known as the warning requirement). Second, regulated businesses are prohibited from discharging or releasing any listed carcinogens and reproductive toxicants (22 Cal. Code Regs. § 12000 *et seq.*) that may potentially contact a source or potential source

NSRL = no-significant-risk-level

COC = chemicals of concern

BPA = bisphenol-A

of drinking water (known as the prohibition of discharge). The list of regulated chemicals is adopted by the OEHHA.

Businesses are exempt from Proposition 65 if the exposures or discharges do not cause a significant amount of chemical to enter any drinking water source, and the exposures or discharges conform to all applicable regulations, permits, requirements, and orders. A business is exempt from the warning requirement if the exposure is not significant (known as a no-significant-risk-level). For listed carcinogens, a significant amount is defined as a lifetime exposure to the listed chemical resulting in an incremental cancer risk of more than one in 100,000. The significance threshold for reproductive toxicants is defined as a risk 1,000 times lower than the "no observable effect level." Significance levels may be determined by performing a quantitative risk assessment. 22 Cal. Code Regs. §§ 12803, 12805(a), (c). In addition, significance levels have been established for many listed chemicals by regulation.

Private or "citizen" Proposition 65 actions may not be undertaken without a certificate of merit. The plaintiff's attorney must demonstrate good cause before filing notice to sue, based on expert consultation and factual evidence.

GREEN CHEMISTRY PROGRAM

The California Green Chemistry Program (also known as Safe Consumer Product Program) is premised on the "precautionary principle" where the burden shifts to the chemical supplier to demonstrate the product is safe.

According to DTSC, notwithstanding four decades of environmental and occupational laws regulating hazardous chemicals, major health and environmental data gaps remain for most of the 83,000 chemical substances appearing in the TSCA chemical inventory. In contrast to TSCA, the California Green Chemistry program (also known as Safe Consumer Product Program) is premised on the "precautionary principle" where the burden shifts to the chemical supplier to demonstrate the product is safe.

The Safe Consumer Product Program (spawned by AB 1879 of 2008, Chapter 559, Statutes of 2008), also known as the Green Chemistry Program, establishes a comprehensive chemical policy to address the dangers of chemicals contained in consumer products. This law expands DTSC authority, which has traditionally been limited to regulating hazardous waste, and authorizes it to identify, prioritize, and evaluate chemicals of concern (COC) and their potential alternatives.

DTSC listed 165 COCs including carcinogens (e.g., lead, arsenic, cadmium), neurotoxins (e.g., mercury), reproductive and developmental toxins, endocrine disruptors such as bisphenol-A (BPA), and flame retardants. 22 Cal. Code Regs. §§ 69505.7, 69503.5. DTSC has since identified three "priority products" that contain at least one COC. This shifts the burden to the product manufacturers, importers, retailers to determine whether safer alternatives are available. This could require reformulating products, changing manufacturing processes, along with using less toxic industrial processes and safer, non-chemical alternatives. Failure to reduce the health risk could result in restrictions or required consumer warnings.

As of the writing of this book, DTSC had identified the following priority consumer products for coverage under the Safe Consumer Products Program:

- Flame retardant (TRIS) foam in children's products.
- Spray expansion isocyanate foam used as a building material.
- Methylene chloride paint strippers. This also affects children's clothing, bedding retailers, and hardware retailers.

SB 509 of 2007 (Chapter 560, Statutes of 2007) required DTSC to establish a web-based Toxics Information Clearinghouse to collect, maintain, and distribute chemical hazard traits and environmental and toxicological end-point data. It can be found at www.dtsc.ca.gov/scp/tic.cfm

CALIFORNIA CHEMICAL BANS

Various California laws ban the manufacture and/or sale of products with specified hazardous materials.

Mercury-containing products. The Mercury Reduction Act of 2001 bans the manufacture, sale or supply of mercury fever thermometers and other mercury-containing products. Pub. Res. Code § 15025 *et seq.* California law requires thermostat manufacturers to establish a mercury-added thermostat collection and recycling program. Manufacturers must provide wholesalers with bins to collect thermostats and provide government agencies that administer household hazardous waste collection facilities with collection bins, upon request by DTSC. Manufacturers are responsible for collecting the bins and providing education and outreach efforts to promote and facilitate thermostat recycling. Heating, ventilation, and air conditioning contractors and persons responsible for demolishing buildings involving the removal of mercury-added thermostats must follow these handling requirements. Health & Safety Code § 25214.8.1.

Motor vehicle brake pads. California law prohibits the sale of specified levels of cadmium, copper, chromium (VI), lead, mercury, and asbestiform fibers in motor vehicle brake pads. Health & Safety Code § 25250.51.

Glass beads. Some glass beads used to treat or otherwise strip paint from parts and materials contain dust with elevated levels of toxic heavy metals. AB 1930 of 2010 (Chapter 368, Statutes of 2010) established maximum levels of lead and arsenic to protect individuals and the environment and prohibits the manufacture or seller of glass beads containing arsenic or lead above specified limits if those glass beads will be used in blasting equipment. The law specifies labeling requirements for glass bead containers or bags.

Lighting. The California Lighting Efficiency and Toxic Reduction Act (see AB 1109 of 2007 (Chapter 534)) restricts the sale of general purpose lighting (which include lamps, bulbs, and tubes) that contain specified hazardous substances. Lighting manufacturers are prohibited from selling these products in California and must certify that their general purpose lights do not contain specified levels of hazardous substances.

Brominated flame retardants. California law bans another class of chemicals, known as BFRs, which contain PBDEs. BFRs are alleged endocrine disruptors and are found in plastic housing of electronics, computers, and textiles used in furniture. Manufacturing, processing, or distributing products, or a flame-retardant part of a product, containing one-tenth of one percent pentaBDE or octaBDE was prohibited as of January 1, 2008. Health & Safety Code § 108920 *et seq.* Manufacturers are required to mark BFRs with warnings, as well as distribution and disposal instructions, and to pay a fee for BFR sales.

Packaging. The Toxics in Packaging Prevention Act prohibits packaging containing bioaccumulative metals including lead, cadmium, mercury, and hexavalent chromium. Manufacturers, importers, agents, and suppliers are prohibited from offering for sale for promotional purposes a package or packaging component that includes these regulated metals. Each manufacturer, importer, agent, and supplier must furnish a certificate of compliance to the purchaser of a package or packaging component. Health & Safety Code § 25214.11 *et seq.* The lead content limit for glass bottles containing paint is no more than 0.06 percent by weight of lead or lead compounds.

California law prohibits the manufacture or sale of toys contaminated with specified levels of lead, antimony, arsenic, cadmium, mercury, selenium, or barium contained in paint and lacquer coatings.

Toys. California law prohibits the manufacture or sale of toys contaminated with specified levels of lead, antimony, arsenic, cadmium, mercury, selenium, or barium contained in paint and lacquer coatings Health & Safety Code § 108550 *et seq.*

California law also prohibits the use of phthalates in children's toys and baby products and requires that manufacturers use the least toxic alternative. It also prohibits manufacturers from replacing phthalates with carcinogens and reproductive toxicants as defined in the law. Health & Safety Code § 108935 *et seq.* AB 1108 of 2007 (Chapter 672, Statutes of 2007) prohibits the manufacture, sale, or distribution of toys and child care products that contain phthalates exceeding 1/10 of 1 percent beginning January 1, 2009.

Cosmetics. The California Safe Cosmetics Act of 2005 (Health & Safety Code § 111971 *et seq.*) regulates cosmetic manufacturers sold in California to provide Cal/OSHA with a list of its cosmetic products that are sold in California and containing cancer-causing or reproductive toxic ingredients. These manufactures must submit to Cal/OSHA relevant health effects data and studies. If the agency determines that a cosmetic contains any ingredient that is not safe for the specific use, this information must be displayed.

Wheel weights. Wheel weights are typically composed of a mixture of 95 percent lead and five percent antimony. When wheel weights fall from tire rims they can be drawn into stormwater systems or collected during street cleaning operations and end up in municipal landfills. SB 757 of 2009 (Chapter 614, Statutes of 2009) prohibits the manufacture, sale, or installation of wheel weights containing more than 0.1 percent lead by weight and establishes injunctive relief, civil, and administrative penalties for violation of this requirement.

PESTICIDE PROGRAMS

FEDERAL PESTICIDE PROGRAMS

FIFRA (7 U.S.C. § 136 *et seq.*) is the foundation for regulation, sale, distribution, and usage of pesticides in the U.S. EPA has been delegated the duty to review and register the use of pesticides. Without registration with EPA's Office of Pesticide Programs, a pesticide cannot be used legally. Also, EPA is authorized to suspend or cancel the registration of a pesticide when research shows that continued use would create an unreasonable risk. EPA 2016.

During the pesticide registration process, EPA must examine the product ingredients, the location or item on which the pesticide will be used, the quantity and frequency of application, and the containment and disposal procedures. In this process, EPA determines if the pesticide will have an "unreasonable adverse effect on humans, the environment and non-target species." EPA 2016. After much debate and legal proceedings, the case of *EDF v. Ruckelshaus* (1971) 439 F. 2d 584 confirmed EPA's authority to cancel pesticide registrations. In that case, EPA canceled the pesticide registration for DDT. FIFRA allows EPA to suspend a pesticide registration to thwart an imminent hazard or when there is inadequate data necessary to support re-registration. 7 U.S.C. § 136d. EPA must review pesticide registrations every 15 years. 7 U.S.C. § 136a (g)(1)(A); 40 C.F.R. §§ 160, 172; 7 C.F.R. § 110.

Both EPA and DPR strictly regulate pesticide use. Pesticide applicators require a DPR permit and may also require a county agricultural commissioner permit.

Generally, there are two types of pesticides—restricted and unrestricted. Unrestricted pesticides must be used in accordance with labeling information. Because restricted use pesticides pose public health, worker, or environmental risks, these pesticides are subject to rigorous possession and use standards. Persons who use or supervise the use of any restricted pesticide must receive a pesticide applicator certification. 40 C.F.R. § 171.11.

The Federal Food, Drug, and Cosmetic Act also gives EPA authority to mandate maximum residue levels or tolerances for pesticides used in or on foods, or in animal feed. 21 U.S.C. § 301 *et seq.*

STATE PESTICIDE PROGRAMS

All pesticides must be registered by the DPR. The Director is authorized to deny registration for pesticides having a significant adverse and unavoidable impact unless the benefit clearly outweighs the risks. 3 Cal. Code Regs. § 6158.

People in the pest control business must register with the Agricultural Commissioner and hold a pest control license issued by DPR and must be registered with the county agricultural commissioner. Applicators of some restricted use pesticides also may require a permit from the county agricultural commissioner. Food & Agricultural Code §§ 14004 *et seq.*, 15204. Licensed pest controllers, structural pest control operators, field representatives, applicators, and companies registered with the Structural Pest Control Board must notify the agricultural commissioner at least 24 hours before administering fumigants.

Employers with personnel who handle pesticides must comply with a hazard communication training and information program addressing specific risks posed by pesticide use. 3 Cal. Code Regs. § 6723 *et seq.* For guidance on storing pesticide containers and managing empty containers, see the Chemical Handling and Storage discussion above, as well as chapter 8. Registrants of agricultural- or structural-use pesticide products are required to establish a recycling program for pesticides packed in rigid, non-refillable, high-density polyethylene 55-gallon containers or smaller or demonstrate participation in a recycling program ensuring that such containers are recycled. Food & Agricultural Code § 12841.4.

ENFORCEMENT

FEDERAL ENFORCEMENT

Emergency Planning And Community Right-To-Know Act. EPA may order a facility owner or operator to comply with its obligation to notify OES that the facility has an excess of listed extremely hazardous substances or to provide an emergency plan. Violation of the order may result in a civil penalty of up to $25,000 per violation per day. Any person may commence a civil suit against a facility owner or operator, or against EPA for failing to comply with the statute. 42 U.S.C. § 11045 *et seq.*

Occupational Safety and Health Act. Any employer who willfully or repeatedly violates OSHA may face civil penalties of up to $70,000 per violation and not less than $5,000 per willful violation. An employer with either a serious violation citation or a non-serious violation citation can receive a civil penalty of up to $7,000 per violation. Employers who fail to correct a violation within the permitted period may receive a civil penalty of no more than $7,000 per day if the violation remains uncorrected. Any willful violation that results in death to any employee can result in fines of up to $10,000 or imprisonment for no more than 6 months. Convictions for violations committed after a first conviction can result in a fine of up to $20,000 or imprisonment for up to one year. 29 U.S.C. § 651 *et seq.*; 29 C.F.R. § 1910 *et seq.*

Any employer who willfully or repeatedly violates OSHA may face civil penalties of up to $70,000 per violation and not less than $5,000 per willful violation.

Resource Conservation and Recovery Act Subtitle I. Any owner of a regulated UST who knowingly fails to notify EPA of a leak or submits false information is subject to a civil penalty of up to $10,000 per violation. Additionally, EPA can issue an order against a UST owner or operator to comply with requirements within a reasonable time. Failure to comply with the order within the specified time can result in a civil penalty of up to $25,000 per day of noncompliance. 42 U.S.C. § 6991(e); 40 C.F.R. § 280 *et seq.*

Hazardous Materials Transportation Act. A person violating the HMTA is liable for a civil penalty of up to $25,000 per day or may be imprisoned for up to five years. 49 U.S.C. § 1501 *et seq.*; 49 C.F.R. § 100 *et seq.*

Toxic Substances Control Act. Any person who violates TSCA can be liable for civil and criminal penalties of up to $25,000 per day per violation, or imprisonment for up to one year. 15 U.S.C. §§ 2615, 2616(b).

Asbestos Hazard Emergency Response Act. AHERA authorizes citizen suits against EPA or the relevant state government in which the ACM-containing school building is located. Any local educational agency that fails to create management plans, fails to inspect, or submits false information can be held civilly liable for up to $5,000 per day of violation. 15 U.S.C. § 2647(a).

Contractors are civilly liable for up to $5,000 per day of violation if they fail to obtain accreditation pursuant to AHERA and then inspect for ACM, or design or conduct response actions for friable ACM in a school, public, or commercial building. Federal employees are exempt from liability. 15 U.S.C. § 2647(g).

Contractors are civilly liable for up to $5,000 per day of violation if they fail to obtain accreditation pursuant to AHERA and then inspect for ACM, or design or conduct response actions for friable ACM in a school, public, or commercial building.

Residential Lead-Based Paint Hazard Reduction Act. Any person who knowingly violates the Act by failing to disclose lead information upon transfer of residential property is subject to a civil penalty not to exceed $11,000 per violation. Persons who knowingly violate Subpart F are subject to joint and several liability to the property buyer or tenant for three times the amount of damages incurred by the buyer or tenant. 42 U.S.C. §§ 4852d(b)(1); 3545; 15 U.S.C. § 2615(a), (b); 24 C.F.R. § 30.60(a), (b); 40 C.F.R. § 745.87.

Federal Insecticide, Fungicide, and Rodenticide Act. EPA may assess a civil penalty against registrants, commercial applicators, wholesalers, dealers, retailers, or other distributors who violate any FIFRA provision. These parties are subject to up to a $50,000 criminal fine or imprisonment for up to one year for knowingly violating any FIFRA provision. Other fines apply to commercial and private applicators of restricted use pesticides who distribute or sell pesticides or who knowingly violate any FIFRA provision. 7 U.S.C. § 1361 (a)(1)(A), (B).

Chemical facilities antiterrorism standards. Non-compliance with chemical facilities antiterrorism standards requirements is punishable by a fine of up to $25,000 per day. 6 C.F.R. § Part 27.

STATE ENFORCEMENT

California Hazardous Materials Business Plan. Businesses that violate certain California Hazardous Materials Business Plan for Inventory Reporting provisions may be administratively or civilly liable for up to $2,000 per day of violation. If the violation results in or significantly contributes to an emergency, including a fire, the business also is responsible for the full cost of emergency response, as well as the cost of cleaning up and disposing of the hazardous materials. Any business that knowingly violates HMBP provisions after reasonable notification is subject to a civil penalty not to exceed $5,000 and is guilty of a misdemeanor upon conviction. Health & Safety Code § 25515(a), (b).

California Occupational Safety and Health Act penalties. Any employer convicted of certain violations is subject to a maximum civil penalty of $7,000 per violation. In certain circumstances, good faith, history, and size can be considered in determining the fine amount. 8 Cal. Code Regs. § 334(a).

Any employer who violates any standard or order that Cal/OSHA considers a serious violation (meaning that substantial probability of death or serious physical injury could occur) is subject to a civil penalty of up to $25,000 per violation. 8 Cal. Code Regs. §§ 334(c), 336.

Any employer who knowingly or negligently violates any standard under Labor Code §§ 6423–6436 may face a penalty of up to six months in county jail or a $5,000 fine or both. More stringent penalties exist for repeat violators. Labor Code § 6423 *et seq.*

Any employer convicted of a willful violation that causes death or prolonged injury to an employee will result in a fine of up to $250,000 or imprisonment for up to three years or both.

A manager who fails to report a concealed danger to affected employees and Cal/OSHA is subject to three years imprisonment and a $25,000 fine. Any employer convicted of a willful violation that causes death or prolonged injury to an employee will result in a fine of up to $250,000 or imprisonment for up to three years or both. Anyone convicted of making a false statement or certification is subject to a fine of up to $70,000 or six months imprisonment or both. Labor Code § 6425.

AB 1634 of 2014 (Chapter 497, Statutes of 2014) requires an employer to abate alleged health and safety violations pending appeal to the Occupational Safety and Health Appeals Board. The scope of this obligation is limited to serious violations, repeat serious violations, or willful serious violations. Employers may request a stay of abatement if the Department of Occupational Safety and Health determines, based on a preponderance of evidence, that the stay will not cause adverse health and safety risk to employees.

California underground storage tank law. Operators of UST systems are liable for a civil penalty of not less than $500 or more than $5,000 per UST per day of violation for any of the following:

- Operating a tank without a permit
- Violating permit requirements or conditions
- Failing to comply with monitoring, recordkeeping, reporting, or closure requirements

Owners or operators who intentionally fail to notify the SWRCB or local agency when required to do so, or who submit false information in a permit application or amendment, are liable for a civil penalty of up to $5,000 per UST. Owners or operators who falsify required monitoring records or who knowingly fail to report an unauthorized release, or who intentionally disable or tamper with an automatic leak detection system, are subject to a fine of not less than $5,000 or more than $10,000, or may be imprisoned in county jail for up to one year. Owners and operators of petroleum USTs who fail to comply with financial responsibility or corrective action requirements are subject to a civil penalty of up to $10,000 per UST per day of violation. Health & Safety Code §§ 25299.76, 25299(a)–(h).

Proposition 65. All settlements must be reported to the California Attorney General. Private parties seeking a settlement must submit a specified report to the Attorney General that includes a summary of the settlement report and the final disposition of the case.

Proposition 65's enforcement provisions are unique due to the law's bounty hunter provision. This provision allows private parties to bring an enforcement action against an alleged violator on behalf of the general public if the government fails to take action after receiving a 60-day notice. Penalties include fines of up to $2,500 per day per violation, and private enforcers may receive up to 25 percent of the penalties assessed. Health & Safety Code § 25249.7. In addition, private enforcers may be able to collect their attorney's fees.

Proposition 65's enforcement provisions are unique due to the law's bounty hunter provision.

AB 227 of 2013 (Chapter 581, Statutes of 2013) limits private citizen recovery from retail businesses (e.g., bars, restaurants, and coffee shops) that fail to publicly post Proposition 65 warnings. Penalties are capped at $500 as long as the violation is corrected and the penalty is paid within 14 days from receiving notice. This relief is limited to a one-time violation arising from the same exposure at the same location.

Mercury Reduction Act of 2001. Any person who manufactures, offers for final sale or use, or distributes for promotional purposes a mercury-added novelty, and knows or should know that the product contains mercury, is guilty of a misdemeanor punishable by a fine of up to $1,000 and imprisonment for up to one year. Pub. Res. Code § 15027(b).

Brominated flame retardants. Persons who manufacture, process, or distribute in commerce a prohibited flame-retardant product can be civilly liable for a fine of up to $5,000 per day per violation. A second offense or an offense committed with the intent to mislead or defraud, or where tableware is primarily used or marketed for children, is subject to a fine of up to $10,000 or imprisonment for up to one year or both. Health & Safety Code § 108900(a)–(h).

Lead Hazard Reduction Enforcement Act. Violations of this Act generally are punishable by a fine of up to $1,000 or imprisonment for not more than six months or both. Violations of the Act include:

- Engaging in lead construction work without a certificate
- Submitting false information to DPH
- Creating a lead hazard while performing lead-related construction work

Additionally, if DPH determines that a condition or activity is creating a lead hazard in a building, then DPH may order the owner to abate the lead hazard and may order the person whose activity is creating or created the hazard to cease and desist. Failure to obey such an order is illegal, and violations are subject to a civil penalty not to exceed $1,000. Health & Safety Code §§ 105250–105257.

Occupational Lead Poisoning Prevention Act. There are no penalties established under this Act. Health & Safety Code §§ 105185–105197. The Act establishes a program whereby employers of specific regulated industries pay an annual fee ranging from $195 to $2,232, depending on business size. The state annually allocates $100,000 to the Division of Occupational Safety and Health for the division's costs to enforce employer compliance with training and certification requirements. 17 Cal. Code Regs. § 35001 *et seq*.

The Occupational Lead Poisoning Prevention Act establishes a program whereby employers of specific regulated industries pay an annual fee ranging from $195 to $2,232, depending on business size.

Pesticide regulation. Pesticides are regulated under 3 Cal. Code Regs. § 6000 *et seq*. Violations of pesticide requirements are designated as Class A, Class B, and Class C. 3 Cal. Code Regs. § 6130(a)(A)–(C). Class A violations create an actual health or environmental hazard, are violations of a lawful order of the commissioner, or are violations that are repeat Class B violations. The fines for Class A violations range from $700 to $5,000. Class B violations pose a reasonable possibility of creating a health or environmental effect or are violations that are repeat Class C violations. The civil fines for Class B violations range from $250 to $1,000. Class C violations are violations that do not fit under either Class A or Class B. The civil fines for Class C violations range from $50 to $400.

California Asbestos Notification Act. Any owner who knowingly or intentionally fails to comply with this Act, or who knowingly or intentionally submits false or misleading information to employees or other owners, is guilty of a misdemeanor punishable by a fine of up to $1,000 or imprisonment of not more than one year in county jail or both. Health & Safety Code § 25919.7.

Toxics in Packaging Prevention Act. AB 2901 of 2008 (Chapter 575, Statutes of 2008) clarifies DTSC's authority to enforce the Toxics in Packaging Prevention Act and Lead-Containing Jewelry program. DTSC is authorized to enter locations and collect evidence to determine whether tainted products are resold. This authority gives DTSC the ability to enforce these programs without having to purchase jewelry and packaging to evaluate their metal content.

Glass bead facilities. AB 324 of 2013 (Chapter 230, Statutes of 2013) permits DTSC to inspect facilities where glass beads are manufactured and stored by obtaining consent or issuing inspection warrants.

for more information...

Environmental Protection Agency, 2016. Pesticide Registration Manual. www.epa.gov/pesticide-registration/pesticide-registration-manual, accessed May 7, 2016.

Manaster, K. A. and D. P. Selmi (eds.), ND. California Environmental Law and Land Use Practice, Chapter 58. Matthew Bender. San Francisco, Calif.

glossary

Asbestos-containing material—any material that contains more than one percent asbestos by weight.

Asbestos management plan*—a plan detailing the strategy to manage the discovery of asbestos.

Brominated flame retardants—also known as polybrominated diphenyl ethers or PBDEs. Found in plastic housing of electronics, computers, and textiles used in furniture.

Cathodic protection—a technique used to prevent corrosion of a metal surface by making it the cathode of an electrochemical cell.

Compressed gas—a gas or mixture of gases at a high pressure that can be used as a propellant.

Corrosive chemicals—chemicals that are either highly acidic or caustic and react with other substances and "burn" the other substances chemically.

Designated UST operator—one or more individuals designated by an owner of an underground storage tank facility having responsibility for training employees and conducting monthly visual inspections.

Existing underground storage tank—an under-ground storage tank installed after 1988 (under federal law) or 1984 (under California law) that was required to be upgraded to meet specified technology standards or removed by December 22, 1998.

Flammable liquid—any liquid having a flashpoint below 199.4°F.

Flashpoint—the minimum temperature at which a liquid gives off vapor within a test vessel in sufficient concentration to form an ignitable mixture with air near the surface of the liquid.

Global Harmonized Standard (GHS)—An international system of chemical classification and labeling reflecting health, physical and environmental hazards posed by chemicals.

Handler—any business that has contact with a hazardous material.

Hazardous chemical—"[a]ny chemical which is a physical hazard or health hazard," as defined under federal OSHA.

Hazardous material—a substance or waste that, because of its physical, chemical, or other characteristics, may pose a risk of endangering human health or safety or of degrading the environment.

Hazardous materials business plan*—a plan that includes an inventory of hazardous materials stored, handled, or used; emergency response plans; procedures for mitigating harm in the event of a release; evacuation plans; and employee training.

New underground storage tank—underground storage tank installed after 1988 (under federal law) or 1984 (under California law) that must have been permitted and must now be equipped with specified equipment such as secondary containment and overflow protection.

Operator—any person in control of, or having responsibility for, the daily operation of an under-ground storage tank system.

Owner—the owner of an underground storage tank.

Personal protective equipment—clothing and equipment to protect the employee from work hazards.

Primary containment—the first level of containment in an underground storage tank, such as the inner surface that comes into immediate contact with the hazardous substance being contained.

Proposition 65—requires regulated businesses to notify the public and employees of their potential exposure to chemicals that cause cancer and reproductive harm.

Regulated substances—"hazardous substances" and petroleum, under the federal underground storage tank program.

Reportable quantity—a quantity of a hazardous substance that triggers reporting under CERCLA. If the substance exceeds its reportable quantity, then the release must be reported to the National Response Center, SERC, and community emergency coordinators for areas likely to be affected.

Safety Data Sheet (SDS)—Information that manufacturers, importers, and distributors must include in chemical products addressing health, physical, environmental hazards posed during normal handling to allow employers and workers to manager safety risks in the workplace. The SDS includes information on chemical properties; physical, health, and environmental health hazards; protective measures; and safety precautions to handle, store, and transport the chemical.

Secondary containment—the level of containment external to, and separate from, the primary containment in an underground storage tank.

Toxic material—a material that has a lethal dose concentration based on one of three categories—a chemical with a median lethal dose of more than 50 milligrams per kilograms (mg/kg) but not more than 500 mg/kg of the body weight of albino rats weighing between 200 and 300 grams each; a chemical with a median lethal dose of more than 200 mg/kg but not more than 1,000 mg/kg of the body weight of albino rabbits weighing two to three kg, that is administered continuously for 24 hours; a chemical with a median lethal concentration in air of more than 200 parts per million but not more than 2,000 parts per million by volume of gas or vapor, or more than two mg/liter but not more than 20 mg/liter of mist.

Toxic release inventory*—a publicly available EPA database that contains information on toxic chemical releases and other waste management activities reported annually by regulated industry groups as well as federal facilities.

Underground storage tank—one or a combination of tanks, including associated piping used to contain industrial solvents, petroleum products, and other hazardous substances. The tank is totally or substantially (10 percent) beneath the surface of the ground.

* equals permits and approvals

CHAPTER 8

Hazardous Wastes and Hazardous Substances Cleanup

in this chapter...

EPA = U.S. Environmental Protection Agency

CERCLA = Comprehensive Environmental Response, Compensation, and Liability Act

RCRA = Resource Conservation and Recovery Act

DOT = Department of Transportation

INTRODUCTION

Manufacturing and even household activities generate a considerable amount of hazardous waste each year. In 1981, a few years after the United States Environmental Protection Agency (EPA) implemented the federal hazardous waste program, each American was producing one ton of hazardous waste each year. Since then, that number has grown dramatically.

Historically, hazardous wastes were not well managed, resulting in a legacy of over 30,000 highly contaminated properties costing billions per year to clean up. Chemical wastes from Hooker Chemical near Lake Erie found their way to Love Canal—an underground chemical trench located adjacent to a residential neighbourhood—which sparked public outrage leading to the enactment of the Comprehensive Environmental Response, Compensation, and Liability Act (CERCLA). Today, hazardous wastes are subject to rigorous requirements governing their generation, transportation, treatment, storage, and disposal. This chapter reviews these hazardous waste regulatory programs, as well as federal and state programs for cleanup of hazardous waste sites.

KEY LAWS AND AGENCIES

FEDERAL LAWS AND AGENCIES

Resource Conservation and Recovery Act. The Solid Waste Disposal Act, enacted in 1965, was designed to manage municipal solid wastes. Today, these wastes are governed by the Resource Conservation and Recovery Act (RCRA) Subtitle D and 40 C.F.R. §§ 257, 258 (see chapter 9 for more on solid waste management). Congress enacted RCRA Subtitle C in 1976 (Subtitle C 42 U.S.C. § 6901 *et seq.*) in an effort to proactively manage hazardous waste and to minimize and avoid hazardous waste contamination that today is regulated pursuant to CERCLA

Unregulated hazardous waste disposal.

RCRA Subtitle C addresses hazardous waste from cradle-to-grave, regulating the generation, transport, storage, treatment, and disposal of hazardous waste. RCRA, Subtitle I, the Hazardous and Solid Waste Amendments of 1984, expanded and clarified RCRA Subtitle C. The EPA administers RCRA Subtitle C pursuant to regulations found at 40 C.F.R. § 260 *et seq.* (primarily Parts 260–273 and Part 279) and has delegated RCRA Subtitle C implementation and enforcement within California to the state.

Hazardous Materials Transportation Act. The Hazardous Materials Transportation Act regulates transport of hazardous materials on water, rail, highways, airplanes, and pipelines, in intrastate, interstate, and foreign commerce. 49 U.S.C. § 1801 *et seq.* The Department of Transportation (DOT) administers the Act, pursuant to 49 C.F.R. § 100 *et seq.* The Hazardous Materials Transportation Uniform Safety Act of 1990 clarifies the maze of conflicting state, local, and federal regulations by encouraging uniformity among various state and local highway regulations regarding (49 U.S.C. § 5101 *et seq.*; 49 C.F.R. § 171 *et seq.*):

- Criteria for issuance of permits to hazardous materials carriers
- Transport of radioactive materials
- Training, packaging, and placarding requirements

HWCL = Hazardous Waste Control Law

HSAA = Carpenter-Presley-Tanner Hazardous Substance Account Act

NPL = National Priorities List

DTSC = Department of Toxic Substance Control

RWQCB = regional water quality control board

Comprehensive Environmental Response, Compensation, and Liability Act. CERCLA, also known as Superfund, establishes procedures to identify and clean up chemically contaminated sites posing a significant environmental health threat. 42 U.S.C. § 9601 *et seq.* The program also establishes an elaborate and heavily litigated liability process that governs which party or parties are responsible for the enormous costs of cleanup. Under CERCLA, the EPA is authorized to clean up contaminated sites and seek reimbursement from liable individuals for expenses incurred during the cleanup process. 42 U.S.C. § 9606(a). EPA administers CERCLA. 40 C.F.R. § 300 *et seq.*

Environmental Protection Agency. RCRA authorizes the EPA to develop regulations identifying certain hazardous wastes and to issue permits for facilities that treat, store, and dispose of hazardous waste. Additionally, RCRA authorizes EPA to bring suit against any individual who contributes to an "imminent and substantial endangerment to health or the environment." 42 U.S.C. § 6973(a).

RCRA authorizes the EPA to develop regulations identifying certain hazardous wastes and to issue permits for facilities that treat, store, and dispose of hazardous waste.

STATE LAWS AND AGENCIES

Hazardous Waste Control Law. The Hazardous Waste Control Law (HWCL) is the principal state law regulating hazardous waste. Health & Safety Code § 25100 *et seq.*; 22 Cal. Code Regs. § 66260 *et seq.* The state regulations, sometimes referred to as "Title 22" follow a numerical order that aligns regulatory sections with their federal counterpart sections—however, the state sections are preceded by "66." For example, 40 C.F.R. § 262 corresponds to 22 Cal. Code Regs. § 66262. In many cases, the state statutes and regulations are more stringent than the federal rules.

Carpenter-Presley-Tanner Hazardous Substance Account Act. The Carpenter-Presley-Tanner Hazardous Substance Account Act (HSAA) establishes a state Superfund program to clean up contaminated sites not listed on the National Priorities List (NPL). The HSAA authorizes the Department of Toxic Substance Control (DTSC) to initiate remedial and removal actions, and to enter into enforceable agreements with potentially responsible parties to investigate and remediate contamination. Health & Safety Code § 25300 *et seq.*

California corrective action program. This program (22 Cal. Code. Regs. § 66264.550 *et seq.*) establishes a Superfund-like program governing the cleanup of hazardous waste releases from solid waste management units.

Porter-Cologne Water Quality Control Act. This Act (Water Code § 13000 *et seq.*) authorizes the regional water quality control boards (RWQCBs) to order cleanup of chemical contamination not classified as hazardous.

CUPA = Certified Unified Program Agency

SWRCB = State Water Resources Control Board

Department of Toxic Substances Control. EPA delegates authority to implement and enforce the law to DTSC; however, EPA retains oversight authority. DTSC administers both RCRA Subtitle C and the HWCL (22 Cal .Code Regs. § 66260 *et seq.*). DTSC often serves as the lead agency overseeing hazardous waste contamination under specified circumstances. DTSC can order responsible parties to conduct short-term cleanup efforts and can require an owner of a solid waste management unit to clean up hazardous wastes releases from such units.

Certified unified program agencies. State authority to regulate the management of hazardous waste is delegated primarily to city and county departments of health and fire. These local agencies are collectively referred to as certified unified program agencies (CUPAs). Health & Safety Code § 25404 *et seq.*; 27 Cal. Code Regs. § 15100 *et seq.* CUPAs apply statewide standards governing hazardous waste generation and treatment on behalf of DTSC. DTSC retains primary oversight over permitted treatment, storage, and disposal facilities.

State Water Resources Control Board. The State Water Resources Control Board (SWRCB) governs the cleanup and abatement of discharges to groundwater containment zones.

Regional water quality control boards can issue cleanup and abatement orders to parties who have discharged wastes into waters of the state.

Regional water quality control boards. Regional water quality control boards can issue cleanup and abatement orders to parties who have discharged wastes into waters of the state. RWQCBs are the lead agency overseeing contaminated property where the source of contamination is leaking underground storage tanks, agricultural operations, or inactive mines. In addition, RWQCBs become the lead agency when the contamination:

- Primarily affects surface water
- Is from a non-RCRA surface impoundment
- Is from a landfill not regulated by DTSC

MAJOR HAZARDOUS WASTE REGULATIONS

OVERVIEW OF STATE AND FEDERAL REGULATIONS

An overview of state and federal regulations that govern hazardous waste is presented in Table 8-1.

DEFINING HAZARDOUS WASTE

Generators of waste must (at the point of waste generation prior to any diluting or mixing) determine whether their wastes meet the definition of hazardous waste by:

- Using knowledge of the chemicals and processes involved (a strategy known as process knowledge)
- Laboratory testing of representative samples of routine, predictable waste streams

Table 8-1. Overview of State and Federal Regulations

Brief Description	State Regulation	Federal Regulation
Definitions	22 Cal. Code Regs. § 66260 *et seq.*	40 C.F.R. § 260 *et seq.*
Defines hazardous waste	22 Cal. Code Regs. § 66261 *et seq.*	40 C.F.R. § 260 *et seq.*
Describes standards governing generators of hazardous waste	22 Cal. Code Regs. § 66262 *et seq.*	40 C.F.R. § 262 *et seq.*
Contains standards applicable to transporters of hazardous waste	22 Cal. Code Regs. § 66263 *et seq.*	40 C.F.R. § 263 *et seq.*
Includes requirements governing facilities that treat, store, or dispose of hazardous wastes	22 Cal. Code Regs. § 66264 *et seq.*	40 C.F.R. § 264 *et seq.*
Includes requirements for interim status facilities known as treatment, storage, and disposal facilities (TSDFs)	22 Cal. Code Regs. § 66265 *et seq.*	40 C.F.R. § 265 *et seq.*
Addresses standards applicable to recycling hazardous waste and waste managed in boilers and industrial furnaces	22 Cal. Code Regs. § 66266.1 *et seq.*	40 C.F.R. § 266 *et seq.*
Sets forth treatment standards for waste that is to be sent to land disposal units (land disposal requirements)	22 Cal. Code Regs. § 66268 *et seq.*	40 C.F.R. § 268 *et seq.*
Sets forth the issuance and administration requirements for hazardous waste permits	22 Cal. Code Regs. § 66270 *et seq.*	40 C.F.R. § 270 *et seq.*
Presents a set of more relaxed management requirements for a subset of hazardous wastes known as universal wastes	22 Cal. Code Regs. § 66273 *et seq.*	40 C.F.R. § 273 *et seq.*
Describes requirements governing the characterization, accumulation, storage, recycling, and disposal of used oil	Primarily California Health & Safety Code § 25250 *et seq.*, as well as 22 Cal. Code Regs. § 66279 *et seq.*	40 C.F.R. § 279 *et seq.*

Source: 22 Cal. Code Regs. § 66260 *et seq.*; 40 C.F.R. § 260 *et seq.*

Using process knowledge is typically more practical for evaluating routine, predictable waste streams; laboratory testing is more suited for complex waste streams.

TSDF = treatment, storage, and disposal facility

The generator must first determine if the waste material meets the federal definition of "solid waste," which includes solids, semi-solids, liquids, and gases. A material is considered a waste if it is abandoned, recycled, or inherently waste-like. The primary criterion is whether the material is discarded. Examples of solid wastes include abandoned materials such as waste paint or spent solvents (spent material is no longer fit for use, as a result of contamination, without being regenerated, reclaimed, or otherwise processed). Waste also can include materials kept in storage that are no longer useable and cannot be reclaimed or recycled, such as a drum of solvent that has degraded and is unsuitable for its intended purpose.

Once a waste is determined to be a solid waste, the next step is to determine whether it is a "hazardous waste," first under federal law and then under California law. The waste generator must determine whether the waste appears on a specified list of hazardous wastes or whether it meets one or more of the following hazardous characteristics: ignitable, corrosive, reactive, or toxic. If a waste is on one or

Once a waste is determined to be a solid waste, the next step is to determine whether it is a "hazardous waste," first under federal law and then under California law.

FIGURE 8-1

Hazardous Waste Determination Flow Chart

STEP 1. DETERMINE IF THE WASTE IS A WASTE 22 Cal. Code Regs. § 66261.2

STEP 2. DETERMINE IF THERE ARE ANY REGULATORY EXCLUSIONS
22 Cal. Code Regs. § 66261.4; Health & Safety Code § 25143 *et seq.*; 40 C.F.R. § 261.4

STEP 3. DETERMINE IF THE WASTE IS A LISTED HAZARDOUS WASTE

A. RCRA List of Non-Specific Source Wastes — "F" List 40 C.F.R. § 261.31
B. RCRA List of Specific Source Wastes — "K" List 40 C.F.R. § 261.31
C. RCRA List of Discarded Commercial Chemical Products, Off-Specification Species, Container Residue, or Spill Residue Contained on the Acute Hazardous Waste List — "P" List 40 C.F.R. § 261.33
D. RCRA List of Discarded Commercial Chemical Products, Off-Specification Species, Container Residue, or Spill Residue Contained on the Chronic Hazardous Waste List — "U" List 40 C.F.R. § 261.31
E. Used Oil — non-RCRA Health & Safety Code §§ 25250–25250.25

STEP 4. DETERMINE IF THE WASTE IS SUBJECT TO THE "MIXTURE" OR "DERIVED FROM" RULES
22 Cal. Code Regs. § 66261.3(a)(2)(E), (F); 22 Cal. Code Regs. § 66261.3(c); 40 C.F.R. § 261.3(c)

STEP 5. DETERMINE IF THE WASTE IS A CHARACTERISTIC HAZARDOUS WASTE

A. Ignitability →
i. Ignitable Liquids
ii. Ignitable Non-Liquids
iii. Ignitable Compressed Gas
iv. Oxidizers
22 Cal. Code Regs. § 66261.21

B. Corrosivity →
i. Aqueous Wastes
ii. Liquid Wastes
iii. Non-Aqueous Wastes (Solid Wastes) (non-RCRA only)
iv. Non-liquid Wastes (non-RCRA only)
22 Cal. Code Regs. § 66261.22

C. Reactivity
i. Normally Unstable
ii. Water Reactivity
iii. Potentially Explosive Mixtures with Water
iv. Generates Toxic Gases When Mixed with Water
v. Cyanide or Sulfide Bearing Waste
vi. Capable of Explosive Reaction at Standard Temperature and Pressure
vii. Class "A" or "B" Explosive
22 Cal. Code Regs. § 66261.23

D. Toxicity 22 Cal. Code Regs. § 66261.24(a) →
i. Toxicity characteristic (as measured by the TCLP) 22 Cal. Code Regs. § 66261.24(a)(1)
ii. Inorganic Persistent and Bioaccumulative Toxic Substances (STLCs (as measured by the Waste Extraction Test)) and TTLCs)) 22 Cal. Code Regs. § 66261.24(a)(2)
iii. Organic Persistent and Bioaccumulative Toxic Substances (STLCs (as measured by the Waste Extraction Test)) and TTLCs)) 22 Cal. Code Regs. § 66261.24(a)(2)
iv. Acute Oral Toxicity (LD50) 22 Cal. Code Regs. § 66261.24(a)(3)
v. Acute Dermal Toxicity (LD50) 22 Cal. Code Regs. § 66261.24(a)(4)
vi. Acute Inhalation Toxicity (LC50) 22 Cal. Code Regs. § 66261.24(a)(5)
vii. Acute Aquatic Toxicity (LD50) 22 Cal. Code Regs. § 66261.24(a)(6)
viii. Listed Carcinogens 22 Cal. Code Regs. § 66261.24(a)(7)
ix. General Toxicity 22 Cal. Code Regs. § 66261.24(a)(8)

E. Extremely Hazardous Waste Criteria
i. Acute Oral Toxicity (EH)
ii. Acute Dermal Toxicity (EH)
iii. Acute Inhalation Toxicity (EH)
iv. Listed Carcinogens (EH)
v. General Toxicity (EH)
vi. Water Reactivity (EH)
vii. Persistent and Bioaccumulative Substances (EH) 22 Cal. Code Regs. § 66261.21

more lists or fails one or more of the characteristic tests, the waste is considered to be a hazardous waste. Hazardous waste generators must identify each hazardous listing and each hazardous characteristic that causes the waste to be hazardous. Figure 8-1 illustrates the process of making a hazardous waste determination under federal and California law.

The definition of hazardous waste in California is very complex (Health & Safety Code § 25141 *et seq.*; 22 Cal. Code Regs. § 66261.20 *et seq.*) and subject to detailed exemptions. Hazardous waste in California includes all wastes considered hazardous waste under federal law (RCRA Subtitle C), as well as additional materials known as

FIGURE 8-2
California and Federal Hazardous Wastes Compared

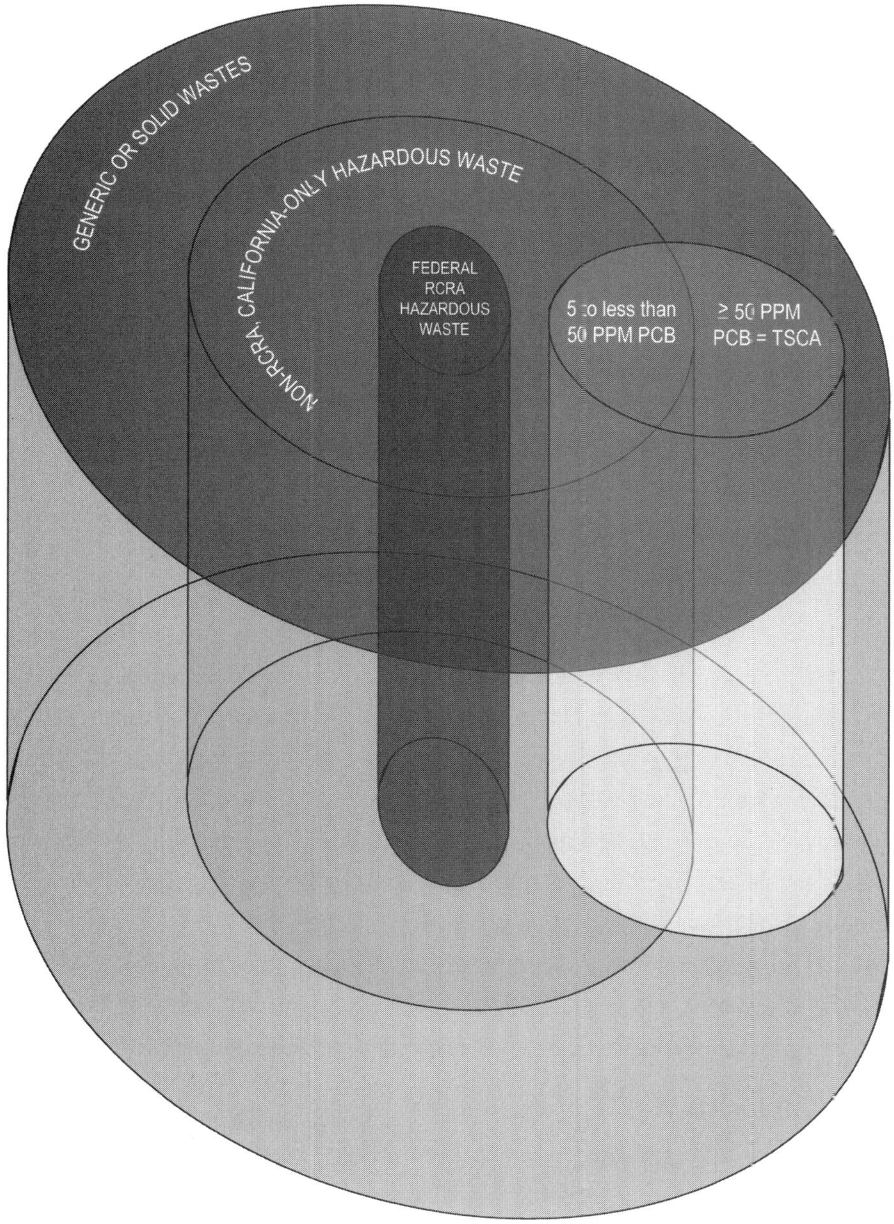

non-RCRA (or California-only) hazardous wastes. In many instances a solid waste will pass the federal test, but fail the more rigorous California definition.

Figure 8-2 illustrates the relationship between federal and California hazardous wastes. The outer rim represents the universe of all wastes including non-hazardous wastes. The inner circle captures the subset of all wastes that meet the federal definition. The middle ring depicts wastes that would pass the federal definition of hazardous waste (and thus not be considered hazardous waste under federal law) but which would be considered hazardous waste under the broader California definition.

NPDES = National Pollutant Discharge Elimination System

Table 8-2. Relationship Among Listed Wastes, Process Wastes, and Non-Process Wastes

Type of waste	Listed waste nomenclature
Process wastes	
Signature waste streams from specified industry categories (e.g., refineries, and metal smelting)	K-listed hazardous waste
Spent solvents	F-listed hazardous waste
Wastewater treatment sludges	F-listed hazardous waste
Spent plating solutions	F-listed hazardous waste
Still bottoms from the recovery or recycling of spent solvents	F-listed hazardous waste
Non-process wastes	
Off-specification products (i.e., a chemical product that remained in stock too long and is no longer efficacious for its intended purpose)	U- or P*-listed hazardous waste
Unused chemical product and container residues	U- or P*-listed hazardous waste
Spilled, unused chemical product	U- or P*-listed hazardous waste

* Refers to acutely hazardous wastes

Source: 40 C.F.R. § 261 *et seq.*

Exemptions. Some materials that are solid waste are exempt from regulation as a hazardous waste. For example, exemptions include wastes generated from the extraction, beneficiation, or processing of ores and minerals as well as industrial waste discharged pursuant to a National Pollutant Discharge Elimination System (NPDES) surface water permit. *See* chapter 10. If a waste is exempt, it may still be managed either as a non-hazardous municipal solid waste (*see* chapter 9), a biohazardous waste (*see* chapter 9), or a designated waste (*see* chapter 10). A business may petition EPA to "delist" from regulation the waste it generates if it can demonstrate the waste does not possess dangerous properties.

DTSC may grant a variance from classification of a material as a hazardous waste if the waste is a non-RCRA hazardous waste, poses an insignificant hazard to health or the environment, or is effectively regulated by another agency.

Variances. DTSC may grant a variance from classification of a material as a hazardous waste if the waste is a non-RCRA hazardous waste, poses an insignificant hazard to health or the environment, or is effectively regulated by another agency.

TYPES OF HAZARDOUS WASTES

Listed hazardous wastes. As depicted in Figure 8-3, listed hazardous wastes are mostly process wastes (i.e., generated from an industrial process) or non-process wastes (wastes that include unused commercial chemicals, container residues, spill residues, and expired chemicals). Both are further subdivided and described below.

Process wastes are generated from industrial activities. Some are industry-specific (e.g., refineries, metal smelting) and are classified as K-listed hazardous wastes. Examples include industry-specific waste streams such as slop oil emulsion solids from the refining industry (K-049). Non-industry-specific process wastes are classified as F-listed hazardous wastes. Examples include spent solvents, wastewater treatment sludges, and spent plating solutions.

FIGURE 8-3
Characteristic and Listed Hazardous Wastes

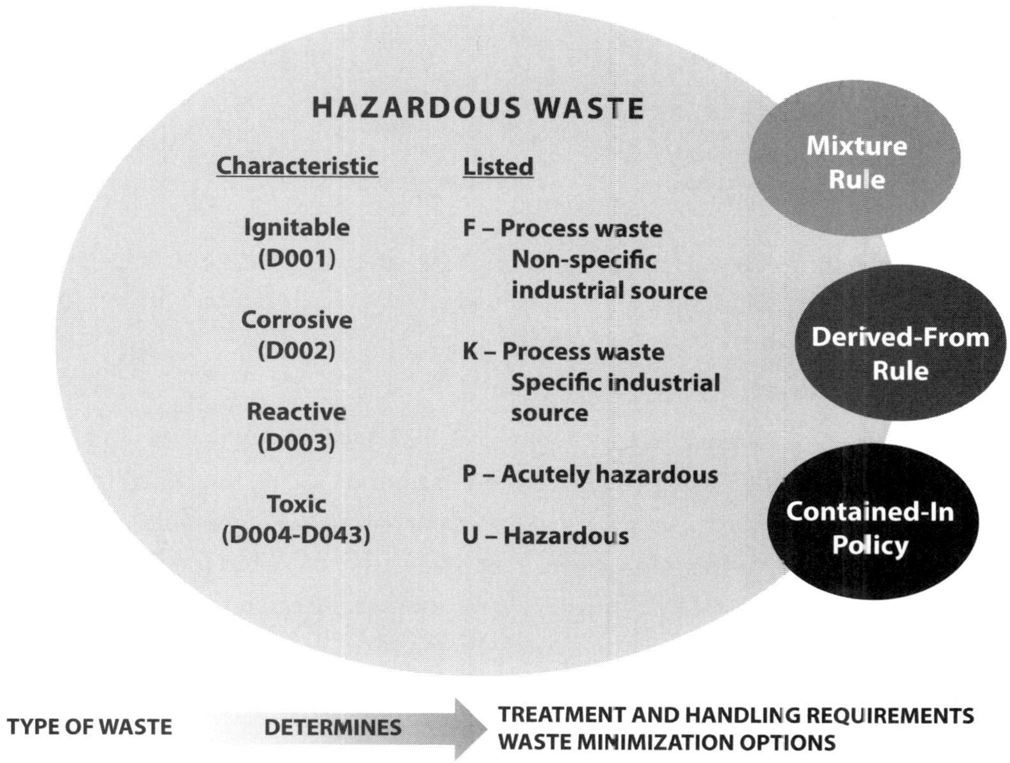

Non-process wastes are not industry-specific. Acutely hazardous non-process wastes are classified as P-listed hazardous wastes. Those that are not acutely hazardous are classified as U-listed hazardous wastes. U- and P-listed wastes become hazardous wastes due to spills (i.e., spill residue), unused chemicals (i.e., container residues), or are off-specification products.

The relationship between listed, process, and non-process wastes is illustrated in Table 8-2.

Listed wastes are further categorized as:

- Industry-specific process hazardous wastes: K-listed hazardous wastes
- Non-industry-specific process hazardous wastes: F-listed hazardous waste
- Non-industry-specific, non-process hazardous wastes: U-listed hazardous waste
- Non-industry-specific, non-process, acutely hazardous wastes: P-listed hazardous waste

These four listed hazardous waste categories are divided by four key distinguishing characteristics, as shown in Table 8-3 on the following page. Additionally, California law regulates a somewhat larger category of listed hazardous wastes by including:

LDR = land disposal requirement

Table 8-3. K-, F-, U-, and P-Listed Wastes Compared				
Waste classification	Industry-specific waste	Process waste	Non-process waste	Acutely hazardous waste
K	X	X		
F*		X		
U			X	
P			X	X

*Some F codes correlate with specific industries, e.g., F037 waste is petroleum refinery waste.

- Used oil that exceeds minimum standards set by the American Society for Testing and Materials and specified levels of lead, arsenic, chromium, cadmium, total halogens, and PCBs
- Mercury switches

Characteristic hazardous wastes. Figure 8-3 illustrates characteristic and listed hazardous wastes. If a waste is not listed as a hazardous waste, the generator must determine whether it exhibits a hazardous characteristic (i.e., ignitable, corrosive, reactive, or toxic) by using knowledge of the waste as depicted in the figure below. This can be accomplished by consulting a safety data sheet and determining, for example, whether the pH fails the corrosivity standard or whether the flashpoint for a liquid is below the ignitability threshold. Alternatively, the generator can determine if the waste exhibits one or more characteristics by performing specified laboratory tests using a California-certified environmental testing laboratory. This laboratory test measures the degree to which toxic constituents are liberated from the laboratory sample. The California definition for toxicity is considerably more expansive than the federal definition. As a result, a waste that may pass the federal definition for toxicity could fail under one of the many California toxicity tests and thus be characterized as a toxic hazardous waste. See sidebar for a description of the federal and state hazardous waste characteristics.

A California-certified environmental testing laboratory measures the degree to which toxic constituents are liberated from the laboratory sample.

Additional waste categories. California law regulates several other categories of hazardous wastes:

- **Restricted wastes.** These wastes include all hazardous wastes that must meet specified pretreatment standards before being disposed of in land-based disposal facilities (e.g., landfills, surface impoundments, waste piles, injection wells, and land treatment facilities). These requirements, known as land disposal restrictions (LDRs), apply to hazardous waste generators who dispose of (i.e., place) waste on-site to land-based units or ship waste off-site from land-based units.
- **Extremely hazardous wastes.** These wastes pose an extreme hazard to public health. A waste is considered to be an extremely hazardous waste if it exceeds specified toxicity levels expressed as either a lethal dose or a lethal concentration, carcinogenic chemicals exceeding 1000 ppm,

Federal and State Hazardous Waste Characteristics

Ignitable. A waste is ignitable if a representative sample is easily combustible or flammable. Ignitable waste includes:

- A liquid with a flashpoint equal to or less than 140°F
- A non-liquid capable under standard temperature and pressure of causing fire by means of friction, absorption, moisture, or spontaneous chemical changes and that when ignited burns so vigorously and persistently that it creates a hazard
- An ignitable compressed gas, as defined in the Department of Transportation regulations
- An oxidizer, as defined in DOT regulations

An ignitable waste is assigned the EPA Hazardous Waste Number D001. 40 C.F.R § 261.21; 22 Cal. Code Regs. § 66261.21.

Ignitable is distinguished from combustible and flammable. Combustible refers to a hazardous material (not a hazardous waste) which has a flashpoint above 100°F, while flammable refers to a hazardous material with a flashpoint under 100°F. 29 C.F.R. § 1910.106(a)(18).

Corrosive. A waste is corrosive if a representative sample dissolves metals and other materials or burns the skin or eye on contact. A waste is corrosive if:

- It is aqueous (i.e., contains water) and has a pH equal to or less than 2.0 or greater than 12.5.
- It is a liquid and corrodes steel (SAE 1020) at a rate greater than 6.35 mm (0.250 inch) per year at a test temperature of 55°C (130°F).
- It is not aqueous (typically a solid) and, when mixed with an equivalent weight of water, produces a solution having a pH less than or equal to 2 or greater than or equal to 12.5.
- It is not a liquid and, when mixed with an equivalent weight of water, produces a liquid that corrodes steel (SAE 1020) at a rate greater than 6.25 mm (0.25 inch) per year at a test temperature of 55°C (130°F).
- California has a corrosive test for solids (e.g., powder NaOH).
- A corrosive waste is assigned the EPA Hazardous Waste Number D002. 40 C.F.R. § 261.22; 22 Cal. Code Regs. § 66261.22.

Reactive. A waste is a reactive hazardous waste if it is unstable or undergoes rapid or violent chemical reactions, such as exploding, catching fire, or giving off fumes (when exposed to or mixed with water, air or other materials). A reactive waste meets one of the following criteria:

- Is normally unstable and readily undergoes violent change without detonating
- Reacts violently with water
- Forms potentially explosive mixtures with water
- When mixed with water, generates toxic gases, vapors or fumes in a quantity sufficient to present a danger to human health or the environment
- Is a cyanide or a sulfide which, when exposed to pH conditions between 2 and 12.5, can generate toxic gases
- Is capable of detonation or explosive reaction if it is subject to a strong initiating source or if heated under confinement
- Is readily capable of detonation or explosive decomposition or reaction at standard temperature and pressure
- Is a forbidden explosive per DOT regulations (40 C.F.R. § 173.51). *See* 40 C.F.R. § 261.23; 22 Cal. Code Regs. § 66261.23.

A reactive waste is assigned the EPA Hazardous Waste Number D003. 40 C.F.R. § 261.23; 22 Cal. Code Regs. § 66261.23.

Toxic. A waste is toxic if it is on a list of toxic substances (22 Cal. Code Regs. § 66261.24) and exceeds a specified regulatory level. If the waste is on the list, or the toxicity thresholds for the waste are unknown, generators must use their knowledge of the waste or test the waste to determine if it exceeds the total threshold limit concentration (TTLC)

- If the waste does exceed the TTLC, then the waste is a California Hazardous Waste.
- If the waste does not exceed the TTLC, then do the following:

  —If the TTLC value for the waste is 10 times the soluble threshold limit concentration (STLC, known as the Waste Extraction Test or WET test), then determine if it exceeds STLC limits. If so, the waste is a California Hazardous Waste.

  —If the TTLC value is 20 times the federal toxic characteristic leaching procedure (TCLP), then analyze the waste using TCLP (40 C.F.R. § 261.24) to determine if the waste is a federally regulated hazardous waste under RCRA Subtitle C. If limits are exceeded, the waste is a federal hazardous waste.

  —If the waste is not subject to the TCLP test (i.e., it is not listed in 22 Cal. Code Regs. § 66261.24) and does not exceed the listed regulatory level, then conduct an aquatic bioassay test. If the waste fails this test, it is a California Hazardous Waste. If it does not fail the test, the waste is nonhazardous unless it fails specified acute oral, dermal, and inhalation toxicity tests (40 C.F.R. § 261.24; 22 Cal. Code Regs. § 66261.24).

The federal and state solubility tests (i.e., TCLP and STLC) expose a representative sample of waste to a weak acid and then measure the amount of regulated constituent that leaches out. If the leachate exceeds specified regulatory thresholds, the waste is a hazardous waste for the characteristic of toxicity. The TTLC test completely digests the representative sample to determine the total amount of regulated substance bound within the sample. As a result, the TTLC results in a higher yield of regulated substance than the TCLP or the STLC, for the same sample.

SQH = small quantity handler

LQH = large quantity handler

TWW = treated waste wood

chemicals exhibiting water reactivity, and persistent and bioaccumulative toxic substances.

- **Universal wastes.** Federal and state regulations relax requirements for a subset of hazardous wastes that are universally generated in society regardless of whether they come from industrial or commercial facilities. The California universal waste program includes batteries (except lead acid batteries), pesticides (suspended, canceled, or unused), thermostats, cathode ray tubes (from computers or televisions), mercury-containing equipment (e.g., fluorescent bulbs and mercury-containing thermostats), aerosol cans, and non-empty electronic devices. There are two types of generators of universal wastes: small quantity handlers (SQH) and large quantity handlers (LQH). SQHs do not accumulate more than 5,000 kg (or 11,000 pounds) of universal waste at any time while LQHs accumulate more than 5,000 kg at any time. 22 Cal. Code Regs.§ 66273 *et seq*.
- **Non-empty aerosol cans.** Non-empty aerosol cans are not regulated as universal wastes under federal law. A steel aerosol can that does not contain a significant amount of liquid is considered "scrap metal" (40 C.F.R. § 261.1(c)(6)) and is exempt from RCRA if it is recycled. Under California law, universal waste handlers may puncture universal waste aerosol cans if they follow specified handling requirements which include, among other duties, following written operating procedures; delivering safety training; and puncturing the cans in a well-ventilated area. The universal waste handler must also notify the CUPA of the activity. Health & Safety Code § 25201.6. The removed chemicals (e.g., liquids or contained gases) may be considered hazardous waste and the activity may also be subject to local air quality requirements.

A steel aerosol can that does not contain a significant amount of liquid is considered "scrap metal" and is exempt from RCRA if it is recycled.

- **Mercury-containing thermostats.** AB 2347 of 2008 (Chapter 572, Statues of 2008) requires manufacturers to collect and recycle mercury-added thermostats when they are removed from service. People servicing heating, ventilation, and air conditioning contractors and those responsible for demolishing buildings involving the removal of mercury-added thermostats must follow specified handling requirements. (See chapter 7 for additional information.)
- **Treated waste wood management standards.** Generators of spent telephone poles, railroad ties, wood pallets and other treated wood may optionally manage this "treated waste wood" (TWW) pursuant to more relaxed requirements than other hazardous waste generators. Businesses generating TWW incidental to the normal course of business must segregate TWW from other materials. Generators may accumulate TWW for extended time frames (up to 1,000 pounds for up to 30 days), and transport them without a hazardous waste manifest to a Class II landfill (accepting "designated" waste). These generators must comply with

specified labeling requirements, and transport the TWW to the Class II landfill. Businesses engaged in activities expected to routinely accumulate 1000 pounds of TWW in 30 days (e.g., construction/demolition contractors) are subject to additional requirements. 22 Cal. Code Regs. § 67386.1 *et seq*.

ERM = excluded recyclable material

- **Special wastes.** These wastes include, among other things, bag house and scrubber waste, cement kiln dust, dewatered sludge from industrial process water treatment, sand from sandblasting, foundry casting, and coal gasification. These wastes may be disposed of in nonhazardous waste Class II facilities (accepting designated wastes) or Class III facilities (accepting nonhazardous, municipal solid wastes).
- **Metal shredder waste.** Metal shredder waste includes the glass, rubber, plastics, and heavy metal residue from scrapped vehicles and appliances. Prior to 2015, this category of special waste was subject to a conditional exemption under the HWCL. SB 1249 of 2014 (Chapter 756, Statutes of 2014) responded to a DTSC study that concluded that treated and untreated metal shredder waste exceeded toxicity thresholds for lead, zinc and cadmium and thus would constitute a hazardous waste. Similar to TWW, DTSC is required to develop an alternative set of hazardous waste management standards governing metal shredder waste.
- **Recyclable wastes.** Recyclable wastes (e.g., batteries and used oil filters) must be managed as hazardous wastes. However, recyclable wastes that are recycled and managed consistent with certain standards are considered "excluded recyclable material" (ERM), unless otherwise subject to a variance. ERM is excluded from classification as a waste altogether and so is managed as a hazardous "material."

Recyclable wastes (e.g., batteries and used oil filters) must be handled as hazardous wastes.

- **Other excluded recyclable material.** ERM includes non-RCRA materials used as an ingredient in an industrial process to make a product (if the material is not being reclaimed). Materials used as a safe and effective substitute for commercial products (if the material is not being reclaimed) are also considered ERM. Materials returned to the original process from which they were generated, without first being reclaimed, and used as a substitute for raw material feedstock, are also considered ERM. (Health & Safety Code § 25143.2(b),(d)). ERM must be held in a labeled container or tank, and the owner or operator must implement a hazardous materials business plan or HMBP (*see* chapter 9) (Health & Safety Code § 25143.9). ERM is not excluded from the definition of hazardous substances in Health & Safety Code § 25316(g).
- **Used oil.** Federal regulations presume that "used oil" will be recycled; a used oil generator that ships used oil off-site in volumes greater than 55 gallons must obtain an EPA identification number. Under California law, used oil destined for recycling is not ERM; however, it is eligible for a qualified exemption from the HWCL. Regardless, generators must manage

VSQG = very small quantity generator

used oil on-site as a hazardous waste. Generators of used oil must notify DTSC and CUPA if they claim that the oil does not need to be regulated as a hazardous waste. Used oil is exempt from off-site hazardous waste management requirements (e.g., manifesting).

Example of household hazardous waste collection facility.

- **Household hazardous waste.** California law prohibits disposal of household hazardous waste (HHW) in the trash, down the sink, or via abandonment. HHW can include batteries, pesticides, electronics, cell phones, fluorescent lamps, solvents, cleaners, used oil and filters, and latex- and oil-based paint. HHW must be disposed of in accordance with a local government HHW program. In most instances local agencies manage the door-to-door collection of HHW and the permanent household hazardous waste collection facilities. Health & Safety Code § 25218 *et seq*.
- **Recyclable paints.** AB 408 of 2011(Chapter 603, Statutes of 2011) allows businesses to more easily dispose of recyclable paints under the HWCL. Businesses may dispose of oil-based paint and recyclable latex as long as the paint is 1) collected pursuant to an architectural paint stewardship plan; 2) received incidental to owning or maintaining a place of residence or a very small quantity generator (VSQG); and 3) remains in its closed and clearly labeled original container as a liquid.
- **Banned, unregistered, or outdated agricultural wastes.** This category is defined as a hazardous waste, including extremely hazardous waste, containing a pesticide for which EPA or the California Director of Pesticide Regulation has canceled or suspended its registration. This waste must be prepackaged according to the DOT and include the appropriate shipping papers. Health & Safety Code §§ 25207.1(a), 25207.6.

Mixed hazardous waste. When hazardous wastes are mixed with nonhazardous wastes, the entire mixture must be managed as a hazardous waste, subject to some exceptions. An exception is made when a characteristic hazardous waste is mixed with a nonhazardous waste and the resulting mixture is diluted enough to pass the test for ignitability, corrosivity, or reactivity. However, a mixed hazardous waste that exhibits the characteristic of toxicity or is acutely toxic must be managed as a hazardous waste regardless of the concentration of the toxic constituent. Deliberately diluting a mixed hazardous waste is not permitted.

Even if a mixed hazardous waste satisfies the exemption criteria, the waste must be pretreated before being disposed to a land management unit. The generator must consult land disposal restriction standards that specify pretreatment for the underlying hazardous constituents.

Under federal law, specified wipes that are mixed with specified categories of solvents are subject to a conditional exemption from the hazardous waste mixture rule when cleaned, reused or disposed. This conditional exemption applies to wipes containing specified halogenated and non-halogenated solvents (with one or more F001-F005 listed solvents) or the specified listed solvents exhibiting a hazardous characteristic (listed in 40 C.F.R. § 261.33 such as acetone, benzene, and toluene). C.F.R. § 261.4(a)(26) and 40 C.F.R. § 261.4(b)(18). In addition, wipes containing non-listed solvents that exhibit the characteristic of ignitability are also conditionally exempt. The solvent wipe conditional exemption has not yet been adopted in California.

California law provides a conditional exemption from the hazardous waste mixture rule for contaminated textile materials (e.g., solvent-soaked rags), which are reusable due to laundering or other cleaning. Laundry facilities seeking the conditional exemption must meet specified management procedures to ensure that the materials are appropriately managed. Health & Safety Code § 25144.6.

The hazardous waste debris rule offers relief from the hazardous waste mixture rule for hazardous debris (defined as a solid material exceeding 60 mm or 2.5 inches in particle size). A mixture of listed hazardous waste and hazardous debris is not considered mixed hazardous waste as long as it meets the pretreatment LDR standards. Hazardous debris that is treated and that no longer exhibits a hazardous characteristic after treatment is not a hazardous waste and does not need to be managed as such. However, if the debris exhibits a hazardous characteristic after treatment, it must be regulated as hazardous waste. Furthermore, any residuals from the treatment must be separated from the treated debris and managed as hazardous waste.

Empty containers. Completely empty containers (such as a 55-gallon drum) are not considered hazardous wastes. However, containers with residual hazardous waste, in specified amounts, are hazardous waste and must be managed in accordance with hazardous waste generator requirements discussed below. Under federal rules, small containers (with a capacity of 119 gallons or less) are considered empty only if no more than one inch or three percent of the total weight of the container's contents remain in the container. Large containers (capacity greater than 119 gallons) are considered empty if they have less than 0.3 percent by weight of the chemical residue. Additionally, under DTSC regulations, it must not be possible for any hazardous waste residue to be removed by scraping, chipping, or pouring. Aerosol cans and compressed gas cylinders are not empty unless the container has reached atmospheric pressure.

Containers with residual hazardous waste, in specified amounts, are hazardous waste and must be managed in accordance with hazardous waste generator requirements.

Empty containers greater than five gallons no longer intended for use on-site must be sent to be reclaimed for scrap value (for metal recovery), reconditioned, or remanufactured. Empty containers with a capacity of five gallons or less also may be disposed of at an appropriate, permitted solid waste facility. Before choosing to dispose of empty containers, generators should consider potential liability under CERCLA (discussed below).

Contained-in policy. A generator who manages contaminated environmental media (such as groundwater, soil, water, or solid sediments) may be subject to hazardous waste requirements. DTSC has authority to regulate environmental media

Table 8-4. Types of Hazardous Waste Generators

Type of generator	Applicability criteria	Federal accumulation time limits	California accumulation time limits
Very small quantity generator (VSQG)	≤100 kg (i.e., 220 lbs.) per month of non-acute hazardous waste ≤1 kg (i.e., 2.2 lbs.) per month of acute hazardous waste ≤100 kg (i.e., 220 lbs.) per month acute hazardous waste cleanup residue	No accumulation time limits	Same as SQG after collecting first 100 kg (or 220 lbs.) of non-acute hazardous waste except for household generators of hazardous waste
Small quantity generator (SQG)	No more than between 100 kg (i.e., 220 lbs.) per month and less than 1,000 kg (i.e., 2,200 lbs.) per month of non-acute hazardous waste ≤1 kg (i.e., 2.2 lbs.) per month of acute hazardous waste ≤100 kg (i.e., 220 lbs.) per month acute hazardous waste cleanup residue	No more than 180 days (270 days if hazardous waste must be transported more than 200 miles to a TSDF). Subject to a DTSC-approved 30-day extension. No more than 6,000 kg (i.e., 13,200 lbs. on-site at any time)	Same as federal
Large quantity generator (LQG)	≥1,000 kg (i.e., 2,200 lbs.) per month of non-acute hazardous waste >1 kg (i.e., 2.2 lbs.) per month of acute hazardous waste >100 kg (i.e., 220 lbs.) per month acute hazardous waste cleanup residue	No more than 90 days. Subject to a DTSC-approved 30-day extension	Same as federal

Source: 40 C.F.R. §§ 261.5, 262.13; 22 Cal. Code Regs. § 262.34

LQG = large quantity generator

SQG = small quantity generator

that contain hazardous waste pursuant to EPA's "contained-in" policy. Under this policy, soil and other environmental media must be managed as hazardous wastes so long as they contain listed hazardous waste or exhibit a characteristic of hazardous waste. The contained-in policy was upheld by the D.C. Circuit Court of Appeals in *Chemical Waste Management v. EPA* (1989) 869 F. 2d 1526.

Contaminated environmental media are no longer considered to be hazardous waste once the hazardous constituents are removed by treatment, or when DTSC determines by risk assessment that the waste no longer poses a threat to human health and the environment. A contaminated medium that contains a hazardous waste listed solely for a characteristic no longer needs to be managed as hazardous waste when it no longer exhibits that characteristic.

Derived-from rule. Residues derived from the treatment, storage, or disposal of hazardous waste are considered to be hazardous waste. These residues include sludge, spill residue, ash, emission control dust, and leachate. These highly concentrated wastes are considered hazardous unless the waste does not exhibit a characteristic of hazardous waste, or if the waste is delisted. 40 C.F.R. § 261.3(c)(2).

HAZARDOUS WASTE GENERATOR AND ACCUMULATION REQUIREMENTS

Overview. The HWCL imposes a number of rigorous responsibilities, referred to as the generator requirements, on hazardous waste generators. The hazardous waste

Table 8-5. Hazardous Waste Generator Requirements				
Requirement	Federal very small quantity generator (federal VSQG)	Federal small quantity generator (federal SQG)	Federal large quantity generator (federal LQG)	Very small quantity generator (state VSQG)
Waste characterization	X	X	X	X
Obtain EPA identification number		X	X	X
Manifesting		X	X	X
Land disposal requirements notification		X	X	X
Exception reporting		X	X	X
Tank labeling		X	X	X
Personnel training		X	X	X
Personnel training program			X	
Contingency plan			X	
Weekly inspections		X	X	X
Post emergency information		X	X	X
Emergency equipment		X	X	X
Container management		X	X	X
Tank management		X	X	X
Accumulation facility closure			X	
Biennial report			X	
Hazardous waste prevention (California only)			X	
Short-term waste accumulation limit (i.e., satellite accumulation)*		Up to 55 gallons of hazardous waste and one quart of acutely hazardous waste*	Up to 55 gallons of hazardous waste and one quart of acutely hazardous waste*	Up to 55 gallons of hazardous waste and one quart of acutely or extremely hazardous waste*
Long-term waste accumulation limit*		180 Days	90 Days	180 Days
50-foot buffer			For long-term accumulation of ignitable and reactive wastes	

* California law prohibits storing wastes for more than one year from collection of the first drop or particle at a satellite accumulation point regardless of whether 55 gallons have been accumulated at the SAP.

Source: 40 C.F.R. § 262.34; 22 Cal. Code Regs. § 66262.34

generator has the primary responsibility for determining whether material generated is classified as a hazardous waste.

Generators of hazardous waste fall into one of three categories, depending on the amount of hazardous waste generated by weight. These weight thresholds are based on monthly values and the cumulative quantity (by weight) stored at any one time. Criteria for the various types of generators, and federal and state requirements for each, are compared in Table 8-4. Table 8-5 shows separate requirements for the different types of hazardous waste generators under federal and state law.

Small quantity and large quantity generators of RCRA hazardous waste must obtain an identification number issued by EPA for RCRA wastes (40 C.F.R. § 261.5).

SAP = satellite accumulation point
SAA = satellite accumulation area
IAP = initial accumulation point

The EPA identification number is site-specific and connects to the generator's business address. Generators of only non-RCRA hazardous waste, or VSQGs of RCRA hazardous waste, must obtain a California identification number from DTSC.

Hazardous waste accumulation. Determining how long wastes can be accumulated on-site is complex. There are two categories of hazardous waste accumulation: satellite accumulation points (SAPs) and long-term accumulation.

SAPs initially accumulate hazardous wastes at or near the point of generation, and are under the control of the generator. (SAPs are alternatively referred to as satellite accumulation areas (SAAs) or initial accumulation points (IAPs).) These initial accumulation points are referred to as satellite accumulation points because they are like a satellite orbiting a larger celestial body (i.e., the long-term storage area). Typically, one or more SAPs are in place at industrial and commercial facilities.

As depicted in Figure 8-4, VSQGs and SQGs may not accumulate hazardous waste for more than 180 days after receipt from the SAP. For LQGs, hazardous waste must not be stored for more than 90 days after receipt from the SAP. Generators storing hazardous wastes beyond these time limits must obtain a long-term storage permit. 22 Cal. Code Regs. § 66270.

A generator may accumulate up to 55 gallons of hazardous waste (or one quart of acutely [RCRA] or extremely [California-only, non-RCRA] hazardous waste) at a SAP. A generator may accumulate more than one type of hazardous waste in an SAP.

To qualify as a SAP, hazardous wastes must be accumulated at or near the point of generation, provided that the waste is within the control of the generator. When hazardous waste is accumulated "in excess" of the 55 gallon limit of hazardous waste (or one quart of acutely or extremely hazardous waste), the excess must be marked with the date the threshold was exceeded and the excess container must be moved (within three days) to one of the following:

- On-site to a designated long-term accumulation area (either a 90-day or 180-day accumulation area depending on whether it is a LQG or SQG)
- To a licensed treatment, storage, and disposal facility

Once the first drop or particle of hazardous waste is accumulated at the SAP, a one-year clock begins. Under California law, the generator must ensure that the hazardous waste is ultimately moved off-site to a permitted TSDF within one year, regardless of whether 55 gallons of hazardous waste (or one quart of acutely or extremely hazardous waste) is accumulated at the SAP. This one-year time limit is more strict than the federal standard, which allows a generator to accumulate hazardous waste at a SAP indefinitely as long as no more than 55 gallons (or one quart of acutely or extremely) hazardous waste is accumulated. 22 Cal. Code Regs. § 66262.34(e)(1)(B); 40 C.F.R. § 262.15.

Once the first drop or particle of hazardous waste is accumulated at the SAP, a one-year clock begins.

Although not required by law, hazardous waste generators often affix labels to containers indicating "full" and "arrival date," to demonstrate compliance with time

FIGURE 8-4

Hazardous Waste Generator/Accumulator Timeline

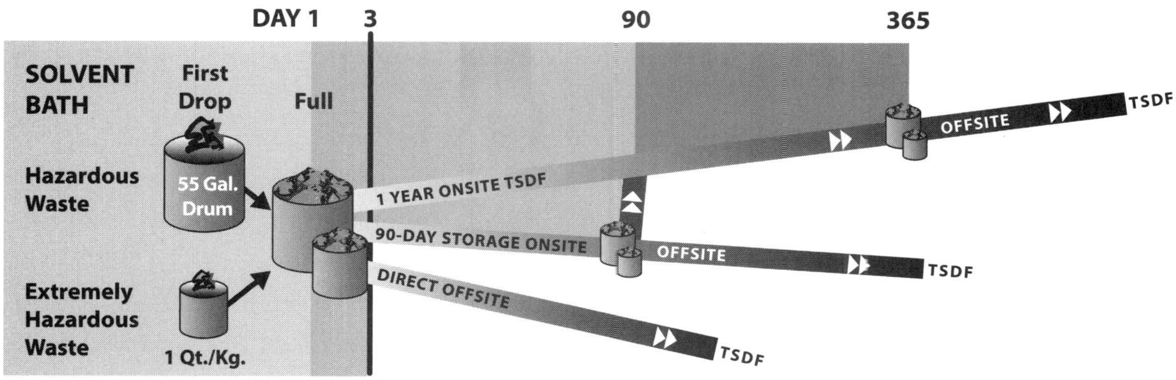

TSDF = Treatment, Storage or Disposal Facility

frames. By using this approach, a hazardous waste generator can demonstrate meeting three different time frames as follows:

- **Initial accumulation date.** The date that the first drop or particle enters the container at the SAP, which starts the one-year clock for accumulation.
- **Full date.** The date that the drum at the SAP is full (up to 55 gallons of each type of hazardous waste or one quart of each type of acutely or extremely hazardous waste), which starts the three-day clock for moving wastes from the SAP to the long-term accumulation area. 40 C.F.R. § 262.15; 22 Cal. Code Regs. § 66262.34 (e)(3).
- **Arrival date.** The date on which the full drum arrives at the long-term accumulation area starts the 180- or 90-day clock for accumulating waste after receipt from the SAP.

Although not required at SAPs, it is advisable to accumulate liquid hazardous waste drums or containers within secondary containers, to collect potential spills and prevent releases to the environment.

Containers and labeling. Hazardous waste containers must be labeled with:

- The composition of the waste
- Its physical state (liquid, solid, or gas)
- Its hazardous properties (e.g., reactive, ignitable)
- Contact information of the person producing the waste (i.e., name, address, telephone number, and EPA identification number of the facility)
- The date waste was first placed into the container

Hazardous waste label.

Hazardous wastes must be collected in containers compatible with the wastes accumulated, approved by the U.S. DOT. Hazardous wastes collected at SAPs also must be segregated from incompatible wastes such as acids and bases or ignitables and acids. Additionally, large quantity generators of volatile hazardous wastes (e.g., solvents) must prevent fugitive releases from containers and tanks located at long-term accumulation areas. Containers must be kept securely closed at all times, except to add or remove wastes. 40 C.F.R. §§ 262.34(j)(3), 264.1030(b)(1-3). Hazardous waste generators of volatile emissions can satisfy these requirements by implementing a relevant air quality permit.

Requirements for accumulation areas. SAPs and hazardous waste 180-day and 90-day accumulation areas must be equipped with specified equipment, including a telephone, alarm, portable fire extinguishers, fire control equipment, and spill control and decontamination equipment. 40 C.F.R. §§ 262.250 *et seq.*, 262.16(b)(8). (At the time of book publication, California had not approved equipment requirements for SAPs.) The generator must inspect the 90-day hazardous waste accumulation facility weekly to ensure that the containers and tanks are in good condition (free of corrosion and not leaking), that accumulation storage time frames have not been exceeded, and that containers are securely closed.

LQGs must write and implement a hazardous waste contingency plan that, among other things, describes actions to be taken to respond to fires, explosions, or unplanned releases of hazardous waste. Additionally, the contingency plan must describe arrangements the generator has made with local police, fire, hospitals, response contractors, and emergency response teams to manage emergency response scenarios. 22 Cal. Code Regs. § 66264.51 *et seq.* LQGs and LQGs must not accumulate ignitable and reactive hazardous wastes within 50 feet of the property line.

Universal waste label.

Universal waste handler requirements. Universal waste handlers have more relaxed management requirements, including simpler staging requirements. Both LQGs and SQHs of universal wastes may accumulate wastes for up to one year, but need not follow requirements associated with satellite accumulation discussed above. Universal waste handlers must accumulate wastes in closed, non-leaking containers to ensure that the wastes are not released to the environment, and may transport universal wastes using a bill of lading.

Training. LQGs must ensure that employees receive initial training within six months of receiving or changing a job assignment involving the management of hazardous waste. The training must address the handling, storage, and emergency response considerations of managing hazardous waste. LQGs must ensure that personnel receive annual refresher training. Also, LQGs must establish a training program that assigns different levels of hazardous waste training curricula for a range of job categories. Hazardous waste training records must be maintained for at least three years. 22 Cal. Code Regs. §§ 66262.34(a)(3), 66265.16. SQGs of hazardous waste are subject to reduced training requirements. 22 Cal. Code Regs. § 66262.34(d)(2).

Handlers of universal waste have reduced training requirements compared to generators of hazardous waste. SQHs of universal waste must ensure that employees who handle or have responsibility for managing universal wastes are apprised of proper handling and emergency procedures. LQHs must make sure that all employees are thoroughly familiar with proper waste handling and emergency procedures, relative to their responsibilities during normal facility operations and emergencies. 22 Cal. Code Regs. § 66273.36.

Recordkeeping. Hazardous waste generators and universal waste handlers must retain the following records for at least three years:

- 90-day accumulation facility inspections on-site (for LQGs)
- Copies of each signed hazardous waste manifest (for LQGs and SQGs)
- Biennial reports (for LQGs)
- Manifest exception reports (for LQGs and SQGs)
- All test results, waste analyses, or other hazardous waste characterization determination data (for LQGs and SQGs)
- Training records (for LQGs)
- Records of each shipment of universal waste received by or sent from their facilities (for LQHs of universal wastes)

WASTE MINIMIZATION

Pollution Prevention Act of 1990. This federal Act (42 U.S.C. § 13101 *et seq.*; 40 C.F.R. §§ 370, 372) establishes a national policy to reduce or prevent pollution at the source. Each owner or operator of a facility is required to file (with EPA) an annual toxic chemical release report. This report must describe toxic chemical source reduction and recycling initiatives for the previous calendar year, including the quantity of the chemical entering any waste stream before it is recycled, treated, or disposed of, and the percentage change from the previous year.

Each owner or operator of a facility is required to file (with EPA) an annual toxic chemical release report.

Hazardous Waste Source Reduction and Management Review Act. This state Act (commonly known as SB 14 or the Pollution Prevention Act, Health & Safety Code § 25244.12, 22 Cal. Code Regs. § 67100 *et seq.*) is intended to encourage businesses that generate large quantities of hazardous waste to decrease the amount of waste they produce. Specifically, SB 14 is designed to reduce the generation of hazardous waste at its source, reduce releases to the environment of chemicals that have adverse health or environmental effects, and document hazardous waste management information and make that information available.

SB 14 applies to LQGs who routinely generate more than 12,000 kg (or 26,455 pounds) of hazardous waste or more than 12 kg (or 26.4 pounds) of extremely hazardous waste during a reporting year. For purposes of determining SB 14 applicability, the law excludes a number of waste streams from the aggregate hazardous waste total, including universal wastes, non-routine wastes, motor vehicle fluids, and household hazardous wastes. Health & Safety Code § 25244.12 *et seq.*

SB 14 provides a framework for companies to evaluate site-specific pollution prevention practices to minimize generation of hazardous waste without mandating specified waste reduction levels. In general, SB 14 requires LQGs to detail their waste generation processes as well as their goals and methods to decrease the amount of hazardous waste generated. Pollution prevention reports must be completed every four years but need not be submitted to DTSC; however, they must be made available for review by DTSC or the CUPA. *See* DTSC 2010.

HAZARDOUS WASTE TRANSPORTATION

Generators of hazardous waste must use registered haulers of hazardous waste and complete a hazardous waste shipping document known as a manifest.

Generators of hazardous waste must use registered haulers of hazardous waste and complete a hazardous waste shipping document known as a manifest. 22 Cal. Code Regs. § 66263.10 *et seq*. When signing a manifest, the generator certifies that a waste minimization program is in place. In order to sign the manifest, the generator must be current with hazardous waste training, including DOT training. Although the DOT regulations do no directly state that the DOT training is required to sign a manifest, DOT training is required to handle hazardous materials (which includes "hazardous wastes"). 49 C.F.R. § 172.704.

Generators of hazardous waste must take steps to ensure that hazardous wastes leaving the facility ultimately arrive at the TSDF. Generators must receive a signed copy of the manifest from the TSDF within 35 days; otherwise, generators must contact the transporter and/or the TSDF owner or operator. If the generator does not receive a copy of the signed manifest within 45 days, the generator must submit an exception report to DTSC explaining its efforts to locate the missing hazardous waste. 22 Cal. Code Regs. § 66262.42(B).

If a TSDF rejects a shipment of hazardous waste, the TSDF may use the original manifest to return the hazardous waste load. The generator who receives the rejected shipment may accumulate the rejected hazardous waste on-site for up to 90 days, provided it is labeled indicating that the load was rejected and the date it was received by the generator.

Generators and operators responsible for loading hazardous waste must verify the transporter's class of driver's license and hazardous materials endorsements.

Hazardous waste transporters must:

- Obtain an EPA identification number and DTSC registration
- Submit a disclosure statement and undergo background checks
- Use properly equipped vehicles passing annual inspections by the California Highway Patrol
- Complete hazardous waste manifests
- Comply with Highway Patrol regulations on packaging, labeling, and other matters
- Report to DTSC if hazardous wastes of concern (e.g., explosives, poisons) become missing during transport

Transporters that handle hazardous wastes of concern are required to submit a disclosure statement to DTSC and submit to a background check. In addition,

WMU = waste management unit

WDR = waste discharge requirement

FIGURE 8-5
WMU Classification

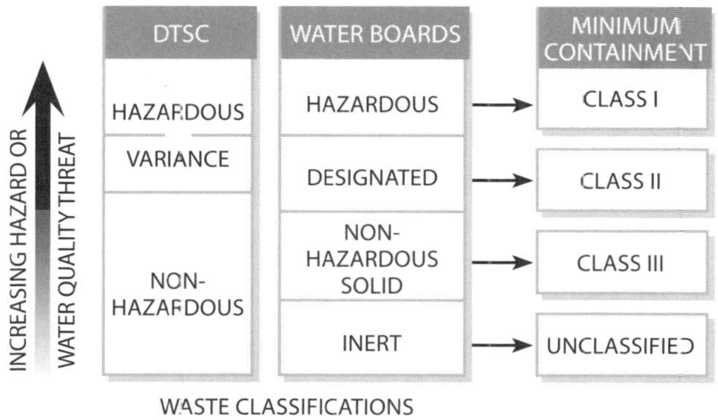

Source: Jon Marshack. Reprinted with permission

they must contact DTSC within 24 hours and file a report when they discover that hazardous wastes of concern are missing or appear unusual. Health & Safety Code § 25169.5.

HAZARDOUS WASTE FACILITIES

Regulatory requirements. The HWCL imposes a number of particularly rigorous requirements on facilities that own or operate hazardous waste treatment (such as neutralization, incineration, and bioremediation), storage, transfer, recycling, and disposal (such as landfills and surface impoundments) facilities. The rules establish a complex and cumbersome set of requirements for permitting several types of these waste management units (WMUs). WMUs include containers, tanks, landfills, surface impoundments, land treatment, waste piles, incineration units, and miscellaneous units.

In addition to hazardous waste permitting requirements, facilities that dispose of hazardous wastes are also regulated under the Porter-Cologne Water Quality Control Act pursuant to waste discharge requirements (WDRs) (discussed in chapter 10). Class I WDR permits are issued to waste units that collect hazardous wastes. Class II WDR permits govern waste units that collect designated wastes (which include wastes that pass the definition for hazardous wastes but that exceed the beneficial uses for water quality). Finally, Class III permits are required for municipal solid waste landfills, which collect non-hazardous wastes. *See* chapter 9. WMU classification is illustrated in Figure 8-5.

Facilities that dispose of hazardous wastes are also regulated under the Porter-Cologne Water Quality Control Act pursuant to waste discharge requirements.

Waste management unit requirements. The HWCL imposes a number of responsibilities on the operation of hazardous waste facilities, including WMU-specific requirements and requirements applicable to all WMUs. Owners or operators of all Class I facilities must (22 Cal. Code Regs. § 66264 *et seq.*):

- Develop a waste analysis plan to identify testing and sampling methods to be used, among other things
- Meet certain general facility standards, e.g., for worker safety and accident prevention
- Meet emergency preparedness and prevention requirements, including preparation of an emergency contingency plan
- Implement a hazardous waste manifest system and retain records
- Implement air quality and water quality monitoring programs
- Meet financial responsibility requirements
- Take corrective action in the event of release of hazardous waste from the facility
- Develop and implement a training plan
- Develop and implement a site security plan
- Develop and implement facility inspections
- Notify DTSC when reportable quantities of hazardous wastes of concern (i.e., poisons and explosives) have been released or are missing
- Handle hazardous wastes generated from cleanup activities pursuant to Corrective Action Management Unit regulations
- Prepare a facility closure plan and provide post-closure monitoring

In addition to RCRA facility standards, the HWCL establishes standards for facilities that treat, store, or dispose of non-RCRA, California-only hazardous waste.

Different requirements for Resource Conservation and Recovery Act and California-only hazardous waste. In addition to RCRA facility standards, the HWCL establishes standards for facilities that treat, store, or dispose of non-RCRA, California-only hazardous waste. TSDFs are grouped into tiers in descending order of regulatory stringency:

- **Tier 1.** RCRA Subtitle C-equivalent permits that are required for treatment, storage, and disposal of all RCRA hazardous waste
- **Tier 2.** Facility permits (known as standardized permits) for off-site facilities that treat and store (but do not dispose) California-only hazardous wastes
- **Tier 3.** "Permit by rule" governing specified on-site treatment (but facilities do not store or dispose) specified methodologies and specified California-only hazardous waste categories
- **Tier 4.** Conditional authorization for on-site facilities that treat (but do not store or dispose) other types of waste with low hazardous chemical concentrations
- **Tier 5.** Conditional exemption for on-site treatment of certain low-risk waste or *de minimis* amounts of certain waste

Treatment, storage, and disposal facility permit applications. Hazardous waste TSDF permit applications consist of two parts. Part A of the application includes a description of the hazardous waste management processes and facilities and of the hazardous waste itself. Part B of the application is known as the operations plan, and includes detailed contingency plans in case of accidental releases.

The HWCL allows for expedited approval of off-site hazardous waste facilities. The process includes:

- Complying with applicable laws
- Soliciting public comment
- Having an appeal process regarding local agency decisions denying a land use permit for a TSDF
- Requiring counties to develop county hazardous waste management plans to identify locations within the county suitable for building or expanding upon TSDFs. Cities and counties are required to appoint a local assessment committee with certain specified membership, to advise the local agencies on permit terms and conditions to make the facility acceptable to the community. Health and Safety Code § 25199 *et seq.*

Applicants for TSDFs and tiered permits, and applicants seeking authorization to transport hazardous wastes, must issue a disclosure statement to DTSC and undergo background checks. In addition, applicants for TSDFs must provide fingerprint images to DTSC.

OTHER HAZARDOUS WASTE REGULATIONS

Surface impoundments and land treatment. The Toxic Pits Cleanup Act of 1984 (Health & Safety Code § 25208 *et seq.*) regulates the cleanup of surface impoundments containing liquid hazardous waste, where structures once thought to contain hazardous leachates had proved insufficient. This Act mandates that all such impoundments meet specified requirements, such as a double lining and being located a certain distance from drinking water supplies. Discharge of hazardous waste is prohibited into land treatment units that are unequipped with liners, leachate collection and removal systems, a groundwater monitoring system, and a vadose zone monitoring system.

Discharge of hazardous waste is prohibited into land treatment units that are unequipped with liners, leachate collection and removal systems, a groundwater monitoring system, and a vadose zone monitoring system.

More stringent state requirements were enacted under the Toxic Injection Well Control Act of 1985 (TIWCA) (Health & Safety Code §§ 25159.10–25159.25). TIWCA prohibits injection of hazardous wastes into an underground well unless the following criteria are satisfied:

- The well may not be within 0.5 mile of a source of drinking water
- No discharge is allowed into or above a formation that contains a source of drinking water
- The well must be permitted as a hazardous waste facility

Hazardous waste properties and border zone properties. A hazardous waste property (where a hazardous waste deposit poses a hazard to public health or safety) may not be used for any new use, other than modification of certain existing industrial or manufacturing facilities on the property. A border zone property (a property located within 2,000 feet of a hazardous waste deposit) designated by DTSC (*see* Health & Safety Code § 25220 *et seq.*) may not be used for human habitation, a hospital, a school, or a day care center. Requests for DTSC determination of whether a property is a hazardous waste or border zone property may be made by certain owners, lessors, or lessees, or by cities or counties with jurisdiction over the property.

ENFORCEMENT

EPA delegated the federal RCRA program to California in 1992. Although the state of California is authorized to adopt more stringent rules, EPA retains authority to enforce the RCRA program.

DTSC and local authorized health officers may employ a broad range of enforcement mechanisms for violations of California hazardous waste laws. Potential enforcement mechanisms include facility inspections and corrective action orders, permit revocation, injunctions, civil penalties, and criminal fines and imprisonment.

DTSC inspectors may, at any time, enter and inspect facilities where hazardous wastes are stored, handled, processed, disposed of, or treated. Permits may be suspended without a hearing if violations threaten "imminent and substantial danger to the public health or safety of the environment." If orders for corrective action are ignored, DTSC may outsource the enforcement work and bill the violator up to $100,000. Health & Safety Code § 25187.5(b).

DTSC inspectors may, at any time, enter and inspect facilities where hazardous wastes are stored, handled, processed, disposed of, or treated.

DTSC is authorized to prosecute civil and administrative enforcement cases against alleged violators who intentionally or negligently store or treat hazardous wastes at unlicensed hazardous waste facilities. Those taking reasonable steps to determine that a hazardous waste transporter is properly licensed or a storage facility is authorized to accept hazardous wastes are exempt. DTSC is required to prioritize enforcement in the "most impacted environmental justice communities." Health & Safety Code § 25180.2.

Civil penalties depend on the type and severity of the violation. Minor violations are those that (Health & Safety Code § 25117.6):

- Do not present a significant threat to human health or safety
- Do not impede waste being properly disposed of
- Do not cause the release of waste
- Do not impede release detection
- Do not compromise cleanup

- Are not chronic, committed by a recalcitrant violator
- Are not knowing, willful, or intentional

Minor violations do not immediately result in individual civil penalties, but are aggregated and can incur penalties up to $25,000 per day if corrective action orders are ignored. Civil penalties for almost all other violations (known as Class II violations) incur up to $25,000 per day per violation. A select group of knowing, wilful, and intentional violations may trigger penalties up to $100,000 per day, or $250,000 per day and imprisonment if violations cause serious bodily injury or death. Health & Safety Code § 25189.5. In addition to civil penalties, violators may be subject to criminal misdemeanor charges, punishable by up to $1,000 in fines and up to 6 months imprisonment. Health & Safety Code § 25190.

FEDERAL CLEANUP PROGRAMS

COMPREHENSIVE ENVIRONMENTAL RESPONSE COMPENSATION AND LIABILITY ACT

Overview. CERCLA (42 U.S.C. § 9601 *et seq.*), also known as "Superfund," imposes a retroactive, strict liability process assigning responsibility for cleanup of contaminated property. In addition, the law establishes a process for investigation and cleanup of contaminated sites and determination of cleanup levels. 40 C.F.R. § 300 *et seq.*

Heavy equipment is often used to clean up contaminated soils.

CERCLA governs a release or threat of a release of a "hazardous substance, pollutant, or contaminant" (which is expansively defined to include all regulated chemicals under the major federal statutes except for petroleum and natural gas) into the "environment" (which is also broadly defined), where it may present imminent and substantial danger. The liability process imposes strict, joint, and several retroactive liability at multiparty sites. This means that regardless of the care taken to prevent a spill or release into the environment, a "person" is potentially liable for cleanup costs if the person is one of the following:

- The current owner or operator of the facility
- The historic owner or operator of the facility, when disposal of the hazardous substance occurred
- The person who "by contract, agreement or otherwise arranged for disposal or treatment" of the hazardous substance (e.g., a hazardous waste generator who made arrangements to send hazardous waste to a licensed TSDF that leaks)
- The person who accepted the hazardous substance for transport, disposal, or treatment

These persons are called potentially responsible parties (PRPs). CERCLA broadly defines persons to include individuals, business entities, and state,

PRP = potentially responsible party

federal, and local government agencies. Corporate officers and employees who participated actively in the challenged conduct are also considered persons, and can be held liable as PRPs. *United States v. NEPACCO* (1986) 810 F. 2d 726, *cert. denied*, 484 U.S. 848, 1987. EPA is exempt from the person definition when acting in its regulatory or remedial capacity. Lenders may be exempt when they involuntarily acquired a contaminated site through means such as acquisition of security interests.

Potentially responsible party liability. CERCLA imposes liability on a PRP who is responsible for a hazardous substance release even when the party was not negligent or at fault, or the PRP's actions were consistent with standard industry practices at the time. Current owners may be liable even if they have not actively participated in the management of the facility or contributed to the hazardous substance release, while former owners are liable only if disposal occurred at the time of ownership or operation. PRPs may be held jointly and severally (i.e., separately) liable for the government's cleanup costs, and may seek contribution from other responsible parties. If other PRPs cannot be found or cannot pay their proportional liability, the PRP may be responsible for the entire cleanup cost. 42 U.S.C. § 9607(a).

Current owners may be liable even if they have not actively participated in the management of the facility or contributed to the hazardous substance release, while former owners are liable only if disposal occurred at the time of ownership or operation.

PRPs may be required to reimburse EPA for response costs (costs associated with cleanup) unless the investigation and cleanup activities are inconsistent with standards in National Contingency Plan (NCP) regulations. 40 C.F.R. § 300 *et seq.* PRPs are presumed liable for response costs unless evidence of inconsistency with the NCP standards (defined below) can be demonstrated, effectively contending that the response costs were not cost-effective.

Potentially responsible party defenses. CERCLA liability can be avoided if a PRP did not know and had no reason to know of a hazardous substances disposal at the site prior to acquisition. If a PRP engages in "all appropriate inquiries" into the previous use of the property in accordance with specified due diligence standards (such as a phase one or two property assessment), one of three defenses under CERCLA may be asserted—the innocent landowner, bona fide prospective purchaser, and contiguous property defenses.

"All appropriate inquiries" means that a PRP must do the following:

- Interview past and present owners, operators, and occupants
- Review historical sources of information
- Conduct a visual inspection of the facility
- Review government records
- Search for environmental cleanup liens
- Assess any specialized knowledge of the prospective owner
- Assess purchase price in comparison to the fair market value of the property if it was not contaminated

- Obtain commonly known or reasonably ascertainable information

The brownfields program (discussed below) clarifies what actions property owners or operators must undertake to satisfy the "all appropriate inquiries" defense under CERCLA. These inquiry criteria apply to land that is contaminated solely due to a release from a contiguous or similarly situated property owned by someone else, if the owner or operator:

- Did not cause or contribute to the release or threatened release
- Is not potentially liable or affiliated with any other person potentially liable
- Exercises appropriate care regarding the release
- Provides full cooperation, assistance, and access to persons authorized to undertake the response action and natural resource restoration
- Complies with all land use controls and does not impede the performance of any institutional controls
- Conducted all appropriate inquiry at the time of purchase and did not know or have reason to know of the contamination (ASTM E1527-13)

CERCLA also exempts from liability "bona fide prospective purchasers," including their tenants. All disposals must have taken place before the purchase, and the person must have made all appropriate inquiries exercising appropriate care with respect to any release.

A PRP is exempt from CERCLA liability if less than 110 gallons of liquid or 200 pounds of solid hazardous substance were generated and disposed of before April 1, 2001, and these *de micromis* volumes are the sole reason for liability. Also, municipal waste contributors (e.g., residential property owners, small businesses, and non-profits) also are exempt from CERCLA liability.

Cleanup process. CERCLA establishes standards for two types of cleanup activities—removal actions and remedial actions. A removal action is a straightforward cleanup effort requiring immediate attention to stabilize the release or threat of a release of a hazardous substance (e.g., controlling surface water runoff, pumping, leaking ponds, or removing bulk containers of hazardous substances). A remedial action involves a contaminated property that cannot be readily cleaned up without a lengthy and sophisticated investigation, and which typically requires expensive treatment technologies to remedy the contaminated site.

CERCLA establishes standards for two types of cleanup activities—removal actions and remedial actions.

Tens of thousands of properties are either underutilized or too dangerous to occupy due to contamination. These sites include leaking landfills, Department of Defense installations, operating and abandoned industrial facilities, and more. The NCP guidelines establish criteria for prioritizing which sites are eligible for government clean up funds (i.e., the Superfund) when one or more PRPs cannot be located or are insolvent. These prioritized sites appear on the National Priorities List and must follow NCP cleanup standards. The NCP is composed of a two-step process

FIGURE 8-6
CERCLA Remedial Response Process

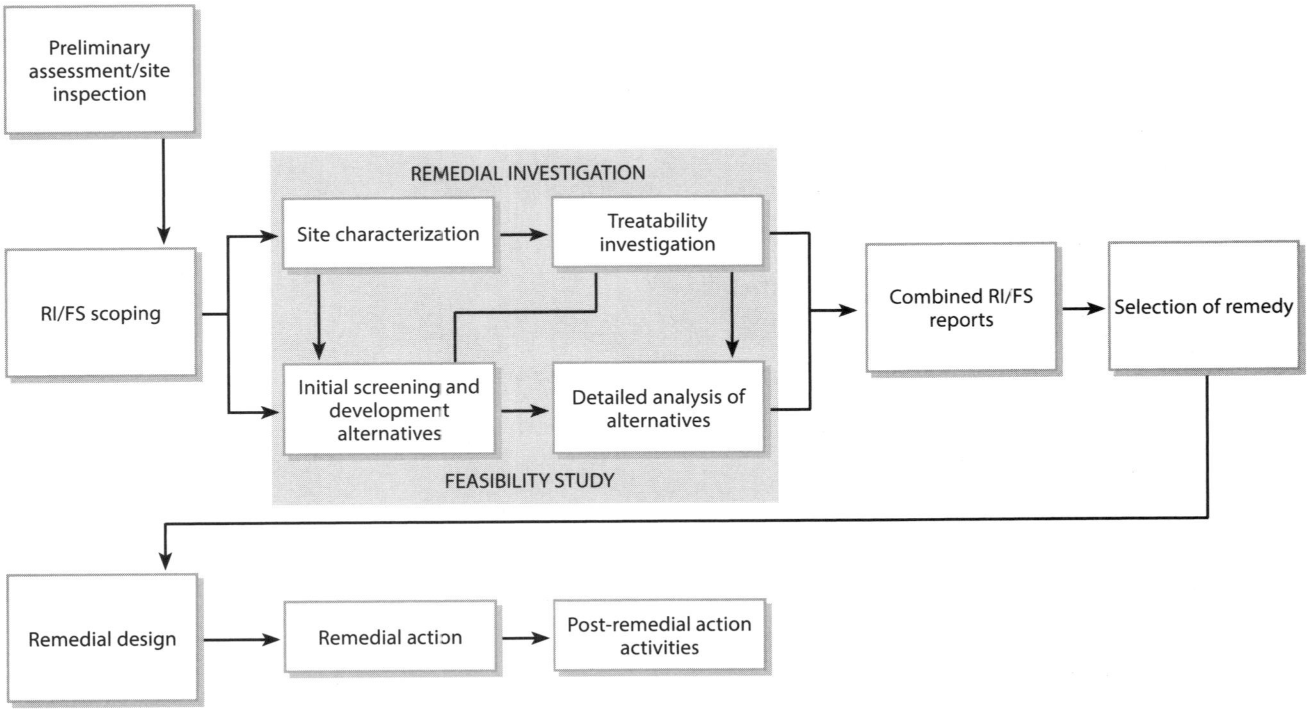

RI = remedial investigation

FS = feasibility study

that includes conducting a remedial investigation (RI) and a feasibility study (FS). This process is illustrated in Figure 8-6.

The RI/FS process is an elaborate set of procedures that determines the nature and extent of contamination and that governs site remediation. Prior to commencing the RI, a preliminary assessment/site investigation (PA/SI) typically is performed to gather information to support an informed risk management decision on the appropriate remedy.

The RI characterizes site conditions and identifies the source and extent of contamination to determine whether and to what extent a contaminant plume is migrating. In addition, the RI determines the extent to which human populations and the environment are exposed to the contaminants. The data collected from the RI are used to develop and evaluate remedial alternatives that are considered in the FS stage. Remedial action remedies are adopted at the conclusion of the FS.

The FS process is informed by a variety of criteria designed to balance the protection of human health and the environment (typically based on a risk assessment) with compliance with "applicable or relevant and appropriate requirements" (ARARs) for environmental health and safety. These threshold criteria must be balanced against the long-term effectiveness and permanence of the proposed cleanup remedy, compared with the technical administrative ease and cost-effectiveness of implementing the cleanup remedy. The NCP guidelines show a strong preference for on-site treatment instead of off-site disposal. The ultimate cleanup remedies must be documented in a Record of Decision (ROD), which is available for public comment in the Federal Register.

ARAR = applicable or relevant and appropriate requirement

ROD = Record of Decision

IDW = investigation-derived waste

Throughout the RI/FS process, ARARs govern investigation and remedial activities. ARARs also influence the clean up standard (i.e., how clean is clean?). ARARs must be met for both remedial actions and, to the extent feasible, for removal actions. Examples of ARARs, among many others, include RCRA Subtitle C land disposal restrictions and Clean Water Act stormwater standards.

During field investigating activities under CERCLA, wastes (known as investigation-derived waste or IDW) are generated that can pose a public or environmental health risk. IDW is created during sampling and investigation to determine the nature and extent of contamination. IDW includes drilled muds, soil cuttings, and purge water from well installation and sample collection. Under EPA guidance, IDW must be disposed of immediately or managed through an interim process. Site managers must choose an option that protects human health and the environment and complies with or qualifies for a waiver from ARARs. EPA 1992.

Waste characterization is necessary to determine which ARARs may apply. Characterization determines whether the waste is a RCRA hazardous waste, a regulated waste under other laws, or non-hazardous. For example, characterizing an IDW as an RCRA hazardous waste determines if land disposal restrictions are applicable, whether the waste can be managed on-site, or whether the waste must be disposed of in a TSDF.

Waste characterization determines whether the waste is a RCRA hazardous waste, a regulated waste under other laws, or non-hazardous.

RESOURCE CONSERVATION AND RECOVERY ACT

RCRA, Subtitle C (40 C.F.R. § 264.550 *et seq.*) establishes a program to clean up releases of hazardous waste or hazardous waste constituents from permitted TSDFs. A release is broadly defined to include any spill, leaking, pouring, emitting, emptying, discharging, injecting, pumping, escaping, leaching, dumping, or disposing of hazardous waste or constituents into the environment. The RCRA corrective action program requires TSDF owners and operators to investigate and clean up hazardous waste releases from permitted waste management units (e.g., surface impoundments or landfills). A release from a regulated TSDF sets in motion a prescriptive site assessment and cleanup process similar to the CERCLA RI/FS process; however, the RCRA corrective action program uses different terminology. See Table 8-6 on the following page for a comparison of terms.

An owner or operator required to implement corrective action has the following responsibilities:

Table 8-6. Comparison of Terms Between the Comprehensive Environmental Response, Compensation, and Liability Act and the Resource Conservation and Recovery Act

Type of Term	CERCLA	RCRA
Process initiation	Release or threat of release of a hazardous substance into the environment or a release of any pollutant or contaminant that may present an imminent and substantial danger to public health or welfare	Hazardous waste treatment, storage, and disposal facility permit action or RCRA enforcement order
Record search	Preliminary assessment (PA)	RCRA facility assessment (RFA) (conducted by EPA/state)
Sampling to confirm or refute	Site inspection (SI)	No direct equivalent
		However, an optional phase known as Phase I RFI (or release assessment) can be used to determine whether interim/stabilization measures are needed or focus should be on the RFI
		(Occasionally, sampling occurs during RFA)
Site scoring	Hazard ranking system	No equivalent
	National Priorities List	
Determine nature and extent of contamination	Remedial investigation (RI)	RCRA facility investigation (RFI)
Interim action (can occur at any point in the process)	Time critical removal action or non-time critical removal action	Interim stabilization measure
Evaluate alternatives	Feasibility study	Corrective measures study (CMS)
Proposed action	Proposed plan	Statement of basis
Decision document	Record of Decision (ROD)	Permit modification
Action implementation	Remedial design/Remedial action (RD/RA)	Corrective measures implementation

Source: Adapted from U.S. Army Corps of Engineers. 2001. CERCLA/RCRA Remediation Process Workshop Manual

PA = preliminary assessment

SI = site inspection

CMS = corrective measures study

RD/RA = remedial design/remedial action

RFA = RCRA facility assessment

RFI = RCRA facility investigation

- Ensuring that regulated units are in compliance with groundwater protection standards
- Implementing a program that prevents hazardous constituents from exceeding concentration limits at the compliance point by removing the hazardous waste constituents or treating them in place
- Beginning a corrective action within a reasonable time period after the groundwater protection standard is exceeded
- Establishing and implementing a groundwater monitoring program to show the effectiveness of the corrective action program
- Conducting a corrective action program to remove any hazardous constituents that exceed concentration limits in groundwater
- Continuing corrective action measures during the compliance period to ensure that groundwater protection standards are not exceeded
- Writing and submitting a semiannual report to EPA describing the effectiveness of the corrective action program
- Submitting a permit modification application within 90 days to make changes to the program, if the corrective action program is no longer applicable

FEDERAL BROWNFIELDS PROGRAM

HSAA = Hazardous Substances Account Act

The Brownfields Revitalization and Environmental Restoration Act of 2001 (42 U.S.C. § 9604(k)) authorizes up to $200 million per year to support assessment and cleanup of brownfields. A brownfield is real property where development may be complicated by the potential presence of a hazardous substance, pollutant, or contaminant (except property subject to a planned or ongoing CERCLA removal action, listed or proposed for the NPL, or subject to specified orders and consent decrees under CERCLA). The Act authorizes grants of up to $200,000 per site to investigate and plan for cleanup.

STATE CLEANUP PROGRAMS

CALIFORNIA HAZARDOUS SUBSTANCES ACCOUNT ACT

Overview. The California HSAA establishes a state Superfund program to clean up contaminated sites not listed on the NPL. The California HSAA authorizes DTSC to initiate remedial and removal actions and to enter into enforceable agreements with PRPs to investigate and remediate contamination. Health & Safety Code § 25355.5(a)(1)(C).

The California HSAA authorizes DTSC to initiate remedial and removal actions and to enter into enforceable agreements with PRPs to investigate and remediate contamination.

Differences from the Comprehensive Environmental Response, Compensation, and Liability Act. The state and federal Superfund programs are fundamentally the same, except for terminology and a few substantive differences. Differences include:

- **Retroactive liability.** Unlike CERCLA, the California HSAA does not impose retroactive liability for activities that occurred on or before January 1, 1982.
- **Definition of hazardous substance.** California's HSAA definition of hazardous substance is more expansive than in CERCLA and includes California hazardous waste and extremely hazardous waste (as defined in Health & Safety Code §§ 25115 and 25117). The California HSAA definition also excludes petroleum and natural gas, but includes "non-toxic, non-flammable, non-corrosive stormwater runoff drained from underground vaults, chambers, or manholes into gutters or storm sewers."
- **Liability defense.** The California HSAA provides an additional liability defense for special districts, entities, or organizations holding a specified conservation easement for properties acquired on or after January 1, 1995, and where there is no evidence of a hazardous substances release. The California HSAA also offers a defense to "innocent owners" of single-family residences located on five acres or less, and also presumes no liability against owners of common areas within residential common interest developments.
- **Orphan shares.** The California Orphan Share Reimbursement Trust Fund underwrites the investigation and cleanup of listed sites associated with

MOA = memorandum of agreement

RAP = remedial action plan

orphan shares (i.e., the portion of liability attributable to defunct or insolvent persons).

Release reporting. New and past releases of hazardous substances must be reported to DTSC unless subject to exemption. Any release of a reportable quantity of hazardous substances must be reported to DTSC within 30 days of discovery. Reportable quantity includes volumes below federal thresholds for reporting if the hazardous substance may pose a significant threat to public health and safety or the environment. Release means "any spilling, leaking, pumping, pouring, emitting, emptying, discharging, injection, escaping, leaching, dumping, or disposing into the environment." Health & Safety Code § 25359.4.

Cleanup process. DTSC serves as the lead agency for overseeing cleanup of hazardous waste sites where no responsible party is identified. When there is a responsible party, DTSC serves as the lead agency if the site is on the EPA's NPL, or when it is deemed appropriate to expend state Superfund money. Additionally, DTSC becomes the lead agency when the contamination is primarily confined to soil or when a release stems from a TSDF. If the contamination is primarily airborne, DTSC must consult with the appropriate air district.

A responsible party may petition Cal/EPA to designate a particular agency as lead agency under the Unified Agency Review Law. Health & Safety Code § 25262. To prevent developers from choosing a lead agency, Cal/EPA (2005, www.calepa.ca.gov/Brownfields/MOA/MOA3_05.pdf) issued a memorandum of agreement (MOA) among DTSC, the SWRCB, and the nine RWQCBs. The MOA:

- Establishes procedures for determining whether DTSC or a RWQCB will serve as lead agency
- Calls for a single, uniform site assessment procedure to be used by both agencies

All cleanups must address the requirements of both agencies. DTSC and each RWQCB must provide ample opportunity for public involvement in the cleanup decisions. Finally, both agencies must coordinate and communicate on brownfield sites.

DTSC can order responsible parties to conduct removal actions to "prevent, minimize, stabilize, mitigate, or eliminate the release or threat of release" of a hazardous substance. DTSC requires development of a full remedial action plan (RAP) for removal actions unless the total cost is less than $2 million, and DTSC determines that an abbreviated RAP provides equivalent protection of human and environmental health. (A federal ROD is the counterpart to a California RAP.) Typically, responsible parties (or a DTSC contractor) prepare draft RAPs according to the RI/FS process (discussed above). Draft RAPs must be made available for public comment. Health & Safety Code § 25323.

DTSC can order responsible parties to conduct removal actions to "prevent, minimize, stabilize, mitigate, or eliminate the release or threat of release" of a hazardous substance.

When the remedial action results in residual contamination, DTSC may issue land use restrictions such as easements, covenants, restrictions, servitudes, and other institutional controls.

Also, the Expedited Remedial Action Reform Act is a pilot program that expedites cleanups of hazardous substances while allowing increased flexibility. Health & Safety Code § 25396 *et seq.*

CALIFORNIA WATER QUALITY CLEANUP PROGRAMS

Regional water quality control board cleanup and abatement orders. The RWQCBs can require cleanup of chemical contamination that would not otherwise be classified as hazardous under state or federal hazardous laws. RWQCBs can issue cleanup and abatement orders to parties who have discharged waste into waters of the state. RWQCBs are the lead agencies overseeing contaminated property where the source of contamination is leaking underground storage tanks, agricultural operations, or inactive mines. In addition, RWQCBs become the lead agency when the contamination:

- Primarily impacts surface water
- Is from a non-RCRA surface impoundment
- Is from a landfill not regulated by DTSC

Containment-zone policy. This SWRCB policy allows certain contaminated sites to be cleaned up at levels higher than background. The policy ensures that when applicable water quality objectives cannot be reasonably achieved due to technological or economic infeasibility, risk-based assessments may be used to guide groundwater cleanup efforts in lieu of traditional, standard-based cleanup goals. Dischargers may petition RWQCBs to designate a containment zone if the zone is limited in size; human health and safety and the environment are protected; and a violation of water quality objectives beyond the containment zone is not expected.

CALIFORNIA CORRECTIVE ACTION PROGRAM

Corrective action may be required if the DTSC or CUPA determines that a hazardous waste facility released hazardous waste into the environment. 22 Cal. Code Regs. § 66264.550 *et seq.* For facilities required to have a permit, DTSC can seek remedies, such as the issuance of a corrective action order, before seeking legal remedies, with the following exceptions:

Corrective action may be required if the DTSC or CUPA determines that a hazardous waste facility released hazardous waste into the environment.

- The responsible party voluntarily requests in writing that DTSC issue a corrective action order
- The responsible party is unable to pay for the corrective action
- The responsible party is unwilling to take a corrective action
- The release is part of a regional or multi-site groundwater contamination problem that cannot be addressed fully using available legal remedies

SWMU = solid waste management unit

RFA = RCRA facility assessment

RFI = RCRA facility investigation

QPO = qualifying property owner

VCP = Voluntary Cleanup Program

CLEAN = Cleanup Loan and Environmental Assistance to Neighborhoods

- A corrective action order was issued previously against the responsible person who has agreed to address the required cleanup

Under California's Corrective Action Program, the first step is to conduct a RCRA facility assessment, performed by DTSC, to identify solid waste management units (SWMU) located at a given facility while obtaining information on potential releases from those units. Absent any releases, DTSC prepares a memo in lieu of the RCRA facility assessment (RFA). If a release is discovered, DTSC issues a corrective action order or permit condition to require the owner or operator to conduct further investigative work; this process is called RCRA facility investigation (RFI). When the RFI indicates release levels that threaten the health of humans or the environment, then the owner or operator must conduct a corrective measures study to determine possible remedies to address the SWMU releases.

CALIFORNIA BROWNFIELDS PROGRAMS

San Pablo brownfields site. After cleanup, market-rate homes, low-income rental units, and a day care center were constructed on the seven-acre project site.

Throughout California, thousands of properties have been abandoned or underdeveloped because of contamination. The objective of brownfields programs is to provide incentives to developers, lenders, and prospective property purchasers to rehabilitate properties.

The Private Site Manager Program Act allows a private site manager certified as a Class II environmental assessor to independently supervise a cleanup effort. The private site manager is authorized to undertake a site investigation and submit recommendations to DTSC. If the private site manager recommends a response action, the project proponent may request DTSC to approve a private site management team to administer the response action. The management team must prepare a RAP, and when the remediation effort is completed, must file a request for a certificate of completion.

California law establishes other mechanisms to promote cleanup of brownfields sites, by reducing liability. The California Land Reuse and Revitalization Act of 2004 (Health & Safety Code § 25395.60 *et seq.*) protects innocent landowners, bona fide purchasers, and contiguous property owners by providing immunity from liability for response costs or damage claims under common law and statutory schemes. A property owner can qualify for immunity by meeting the standards of a qualifying property owner (QPO) and by entering into an agency agreement committing the QPO to perform a property site assessment.

DTSC also promotes redevelopment of brownfields in other ways, including the establishment of a prospective purchaser policy, which provides assurances against future liability. DTSC 1996. Prospective purchaser agreements include covenants not to sue, contribution protection, and voluntary cleanup agreements. Broad eligibility criteria includes sites under DTSC's Voluntary Cleanup Program (VCP), described below. The Cleanup Loan and Environmental Assistance to Neighborhoods (CLEAN) account established a now defunct account to provide low-interest loans for cleanup of underutilized brownfield properties. RWQCBs and, in some cases local agencies, can serve as the lead agency under the CLEAN loan program. The state also established an environmental insurance program, known as FAIR (Financial Assurance and Insurance for Redevelopment), to provide cleanup loan guarantees for smaller redevelopment programs. Health & Safety Code § 25395.20 *et seq.*

FAIR = Financial Assurance and Insurance for Redevelopment

CLRRA = California Land Restoration and Reuse Act

The California Land Restoration and Reuse Act (CLRRA) authorizes municipalities to compel landowners to complete investigations of brownfields that are less than five acres (including larger contiguous sites under the same ownership that meet specified conditions). Subject to DTSC approval, cities and counties are authorized to start remedial and removal actions for sites on the state Superfund list. Health & Safety Code §§ 25401 *et seq.*, 25351.2. The CLRRA allows innocent land owners, bona fide purchasers, and contiguous property owners not responsible for causing or contributing to a chemical release a qualified immunity from response costs.

The Polanco Redevelopment Act (as modified by AB 440 of 2014 (Chapter 588, Statutes of 2014)) authorizes "local agencies" (counties, cities, or housing authorities) to investigate and clean up releases or spills within their jurisdiction and provides immunity from liability to local agencies and parties entering into an agreement to develop the property including future property owners. These local agencies are authorized to recover cleanup costs from the responsible party. DTSC, a RWQCB, or a local agency must approve the local agency's RAP before starting cleanup. Health & Safety Code § 33459 *et seq.*

The Polanco Redevelopment Act authorizes "local agencies" (counties, cities, or housing authorities) to investigate and clean up releases or spills within their jurisdiction and provides immunity from liability to local agencies and parties entering into an agreement to develop the property including future property owners.

The VCP allows responsible parties, with DTSC oversight, to investigate and remediate contaminated sites that are not on the NPL or the state Superfund list. Program participants agree to pay DTSC's costs for overseeing site characterization and cleanup. DTSC 1995. The VCP allows participants the freedom to conduct the cleanup in accordance with their own schedules. Ultimately, project participants receive "no further action" letters or remedial-action certifications from DTSC that specify acceptable land uses, deed restrictions, and other requirements.

DTSC administers another VCP that permits a responsible party to request that cleanup be supervised by a local officer, that is, by a county or city health officer or a county director of an environmental health program. A local officer who has enough staff and resources to supervise the remedial action may enter into a remedial action agreement. This process is not available for state Superfund sites, NPL sites, sites subject to RWQCB cleanup and abatement orders, or hazardous waste facilities subject to a corrective action or corrective action order.

AB 42 of 2007 (Chapter 597, Statutes of 2007) harmonizes aspects of the site assessment program involving the California Superfund and brownfields program. Regardless of which agency serves as the lead agency (DTSC, SWRCB, or RWQCB), a human health or ecological risk assessment must be completed to evaluate

VOC = volatile organic compound

volatile organic compound (VOC) exposures. The exposure assessment must be prepared in conjunction with a response action that evaluates the reasonable maximum indoor estimates of VOC that could enter structures that are located on the contaminated site or proposed to be constructed. The SWRCB and RWQCBs must require either a screening level or site-specific assessment for those involved in cleaning up a brownfield site. With some exceptions, this applies only to cleanup orders issued by the SWRCB or a RWQCB on or after January 1, 2008.

METHAMPHETAMINE CLEANUP

California adopted the first health-based clean-up standards for methamphetamine.

As a result of the methamphetamine manufacturing process, chemicals such as ether (starting fluid), toluene (paint thinner), and sulfuric acid can contaminate carpeting, wallboard, ceiling tile, fabric furniture, and draperies. California adopted the first health-based clean-up standards for methamphetamine. OEHHA established an externally peer-reviewed methamphetamine cleanup standard for surface contamination to be 1.5 g/100 cm^2. California Health & Safety Code § 25354.5.

for more information...

Cooke, S. M. (ed), 2003. The Law of Hazardous Waste: Management, Clean up, Liability, and Litigation. Matthew Bender. San Francisco, Calif.

Department of Toxic Substances Control, 2013. Departmental Procedures Memorandum DPM-CR-01, Cost Recovery: Administrative Site Management.

Department of Toxic Substances Control, 1995. EO-95-006-PP, Policy and Procedure for Managing Voluntary Site Mitigation Projects.

Department of Toxic Substances Control, 1996. EO-96-005, Prospective Purchaser Policy.

Department of Toxic Substances Control, 2010. Guidance Manual for complying with the Hazardous Waste Source Reduction and Management Review Act of 1989.

Environmental Protection Agency, 1992. Guide to Management of Investigation-Derived Wastes. Publication 9345.3-03FS.

Manaster, K. A. and D. P. Selmi (eds.), ND. California Environmental Law and Land Use Practice, Chapters 50–57. Matthew Bender. San Francisco, Calif.

glossary

Acutely hazardous waste—a waste that EPA has determined to be very dangerous, even in minute quantities.

Applicable or relevant and appropriate requirement—a promulgated or legally enforceable federal or state requirement used to govern investigation and remedial actions throughout the RI/FS process. These requirements also influence the cleanup standard (i.e., how clean is clean).

Biennial Report*—all large quantity generators of hazardous waste must annually report (by March 1 of each even-numbered year) summarizing waste shipments for a two-year period.

Border zone property—a property located within 2,000 feet of a hazardous waste deposit designated by DTSC and which may not be used for human habitation, a hospital, a school, or a day care center.

Brownfield—a "real property" whose development may be complicated by the potential presence of a hazardous substance, pollutant, or contaminant (except property subject to a planned or ongoing CERCLA removal action, listed or proposed for the NPL, or subject to specified orders and consent decrees under CERCLA).

California-only hazardous waste—a non-RCRA hazardous waste that meets California's more stringent hazardous waste definition.

Characteristic waste—a waste that has one or more of the following characteristics: ignitability, corrosivity, reactivity, or toxicity.

Conditional authorization*—a type of "permit by rule" authorizing on-site treatment of "California-only," non-RCRA hazardous wastes. Hazardous waste generators of low concentrations of hazardous waste are authorized to use specified treatment technologies.

Contained-in policy—a policy that requires that soil, sediment, and other environmental media must be managed as hazardous wastes so long as the mixture contains listed hazardous wastes or exhibits a characteristic of hazardous wastes.

Corrosive hazardous waste—a waste that dissolves metals and other materials or burns the skin or eye on contact. A waste is corrosive if it fails any one of a number of tests such as aqueous wastes with a pH equal to or less than 2.0 or greater than 12.5.

County hazardous waste management plan conformity*—applicants for an off-site hazardous waste treatment, storage, or disposal facility must demonstrate that the facility will be located in accordance with siting criteria specified in a County HWMP. For example, a facility may not be located in a flood plain or a seismically unsafe zone.

Derived-from rule—a rule that classifies solid waste generated from the treatment of a hazardous waste as a hazardous waste.

Empty container—under federal rules, a container with no residual hazardous waste (e.g., no more than one inch remaining in a particular-sized container).

EPA identification number*—a number assigned to a facility that generates hazardous waste, a business that transports hazardous waste, or a business that operates a facility that recycles, treats, stores, or disposes of hazardous waste.

Extremely hazardous waste—a waste that exceeds specified toxicity levels expressed as either a lethal dose or a lethal concentration, or if the chemical appears on a list of pesticides or heavy metals, or is a PCB that exceeds a specified concentration in milligrams per kilogram.

F-listed hazardous waste—a type of process waste (i.e., generated from industrial activity) that is non-industry-specific and is hazardous. Examples include spent solvents, wastewater treatment sludges, and spent plating solutions.

Feasibility study—an analysis of the practicability of a proposal; a description and analysis of potential cleanup alternatives for a contaminated property appearing on the National Priorities List. The feasibility study is used to inform decisionmakers on cost-effective cleanup alternatives. The feasibility study usually starts as soon as the remedial investigation is underway; together, they commonly are referred to as the RI/FS.

Hazardous waste generator—a person or facility whose processes and actions create hazardous waste.

Hazardous substance—broadly defined for CERCLA purposes to include all regulated chemicals, except for petroleum and natural gas, under the major federal statutes.

Ignitable hazardous waste—a waste that is easily combustible or flammable. Ignitable hazardous waste includes a liquid with a flashpoint equal to or less than 140°F; a non-liquid capable under standard temperature and pressure of causing fire by means of friction, absorption, moisture, or spontaneous chemical changes and that when ignited burns so vigorously and persistently that it creates a hazard; an ignitable compressed gas, as defined in the Department of Transportation (DOT) regulations; or an oxidizer, as defined in DOT regulations.

K-listed hazardous waste—a type of process waste (i.e., generated from industrial activity) that is industry-specific (e.g., refineries, metal smelting) and is hazardous. Examples include industry-specific waste streams such as slop oil emulsion solids from the refining industry (e.g., K-049).

Large quantity handler—a person or facility that accumulates more than 5,000 kg of universal waste.

Listed hazardous waste—a process waste (i.e., generated from an industrial process) or a non-process waste (includes unused commercial chemicals, container residues, pill residues, and expired chemicals).

Manifest—a shipping document that tracks hazardous waste from the time it leaves its place of origin until it reaches an off-site treatment, storage, and disposal facility (TSDF).

Mixed hazardous waste—a waste that results from the combination of a nonhazardous waste and a hazardous waste and that exhibits a hazardous waste characteristic. There are exceptions to this definition, such as when a characteristic hazardous waste is mixed with a nonhazardous waste and the resulting mixture is diluted enough to pass the test for ignitability, corrosivity, or reactivity. However, a mixed hazardous waste that exhibits the toxicity characteristic must be managed as a hazardous waste regardless of the concentration of the toxic constituent.

National Priorities List—a list of highly contaminated sites that EPA prioritizes for cleanup and access to Superfund monies.

P-listed hazardous waste—a type of non-process waste that is non-industry-specific and is acutely hazardous.

Permit by rule*—a permit in which the applicant submits a notice of intent to comply with pre-set permit conditions that are not site-specific.

Potentially responsible party—any individual or business—including owners, operators, transporters, or generators—potentially responsible for, or contributing to, a spill or other contamination at a Superfund site. Whenever possible, through administrative and legal actions, EPA requires cleanup of hazardous sites by potentially responsible parties.

RCRA Part B TSDF permit*—"Part B" is the portion of a hazardous waste TSDF permit application (known as the "operations plan") that provides details governing operation of the TSDF along with a detailed contingency plan in the event of an accidental release of hazardous waste.

Reactive hazardous waste—a waste that is unstable or that undergoes rapid or violent chemical reactions, such as exploding, catching fire, or giving off fumes (when exposed to or mixed with water, air, or other materials).

Record of Decision*—a public document that explains the cleanup alternative(s) to be followed.

Recyclable waste—material that is removed or separated from other residential, commercial, or industrial garbage for the purpose of reuse or reprocessing.

Release—broadly defined under RCRA to include any spill, leaking, pouring, emitting, emptying, discharging, injecting, pumping, escaping, leaching, dumping, or disposing of hazardous waste or constituents into the environment.

Remedial action—the actual construction or implementation phase of a Superfund site cleanup that follows remedial design.

Remedial action plan*—a state plan to restore or clean up a site.

Remedial investigation—an in-depth study to gather data needed to determine the nature and extent of contamination at a Superfund site, to establish site cleanup criteria, to identify preliminary alternatives for remedial action, and to support technical and cost analyses of alternatives. The remedial investigation is usually done with the feasibility study. Together they commonly are referred to as the RI/FS.

Removal action—a straightforward cleanup effort requiring immediate attention to stabilize the release or threat of a release of a hazardous substance (e.g., controlling surface water runoff, pumping leaking ponds, or removing bulk containers of hazardous substances).

Restricted waste—a hazardous waste that must meet special requirements before being disposed of in land-based disposal facilities.

Satellite accumulation point—a location where hazardous waste is accumulated at the point of generation. No more than 55 gallons of a hazardous waste, or one quart of an acutely hazardous or extremely hazardous waste, may be accumulated at each SAP.

Small quantity handler—a person or facility that accumulates no more than 5,000 kg (or 11,000 pounds) of universal waste at any time.

Solid waste—garbage, refuse, sludge and other discarded material including solid, liquid, semisolid or contained gaseous material resulting from industrial, commercial, mining and agricultural operations and from community activity.

Special waste—items such as auto shredder waste, bag house and scrubber waste, cement kiln dust, dewatered sludge from industrial process water treatment, sand from sandblasting, foundry casting, and coal gasification.

Standardized permit*—in the context of hazardous waste regulation, governs treatment and storage of "California-only," non-RCRA hazardous wastes.

Superfund—the program operated under the legislative authority of CERCLA and SARA that funds and carries out EPA solid waste emergency and long-term removal and remedial activities. These activities include establishing the National Priorities List, investigating sites for inclusion on the list, determining their priority, and conducting and/or supervising cleanup and other remedial actions.

Surface impoundment—a ditch constructed primarily of earthen materials used for treating, storing, or diluting liquid hazardous waste.

Tiered permit*—a permit program based on regulatory requirements matched against the risks associated with a facility's activities.

Toxic hazardous waste—a waste that appears on a list that exceeds a specified regulatory level.

Treatment, storage, and disposal facility—a regulated facility that treats, stores, or disposes of hazardous wastes.

U-listed hazardous waste—a type of non-process waste that is non-industry-specific and is hazardous.

Underground storage tank—one or a combination of tanks, including associated piping used to contain industrial solvents, petroleum products, and other hazardous substances. The tank is totally or substantially (10 percent) beneath the surface of the ground.

Universal waste—a hazardous waste that is not fully regulated as a hazardous waste. Examples include batteries, thermostats, lamps, cathode ray tube material, aerosol cans, mercury-containing motor vehicle and non-automotive light switches, dental amalgam wastes, mercury-containing pressure or vacuum gauges, mercury counterweights and dampers, mercury dilators and weighted tubing, mercury-containing rubber flooring, mercury-added novelties, and mercury gas flow regulators.

Waste discharge requirements*—permit issued by a RWQCB for discharge of waste into waters of the state.

Waste management unit—containers, tanks, landfills, surface impoundments, land treatment facilities, waste piles, incineration units, and miscellaneous units used for hazardous waste treatment.

* equals permits and approvals

CHAPTER 9

Solid Wastes

in this chapter...

SWDA = Solid Waste Disposal Act and Resource Conservation and Recovery Act

RCRA = Resource Conservation and Recovery Act

EPA = Environmental Protection Agency

C.F.R. = Code of Federal Regulations

INTRODUCTION

Not long ago, Californians earned the dubious distinction of being the largest generators of solid waste, per capita, in the country. The Legislature responded by enacting several laws to promote waste reduction and encourage recycling and reuse. Additionally, the Legislature passed other laws to encourage businesses to convert wastes into products. Wastes are broken into the following categories:

- Nonhazardous "solid waste" (covered in this chapter)
- Hazardous waste (*see* chapter 8)
- Universal waste (*see* chapter 8)
- Electronic waste (covered in this chapter)
- Used oil (*see* chapter 8)
- Household hazardous waste (covered in this chapter)
- Designated waste (*see* chapter 10)
- Medical waste and unused pharmaceuticals (covered in this chapter)
- Special waste (*see* chapter 8)
- Tire waste (covered in this chapter)
- Asbestos (*see* chapter 7)
- Appliances (covered in this chapter)
- Plastics
- Carpets
- Mattresses

The Legislature has enacted several laws to promote waste reduction and encourage recycling and reuse.

This chapter reviews key laws and agencies involved in solid waste management, federal landfill requirements, California solid waste management programs, and enforcement of solid waste management laws.

KEY LAWS AND AGENCIES

FEDERAL LAWS AND AGENCIES

Solid Waste Disposal Act and Resource Conservation and Recovery Act. Congress enacted the Solid Waste Disposal Act (SWDA, 42 U.S.C. § 6901 *et seq.*) in 1965 to manage municipal solid wastes. This Act was later amended by the Resource Conservation and Recovery Act (RCRA), Subtitle D. Environmental Protection Agency (EPA) regulations implementing Subtitle D are found at 40 C.F.R. §§ 257 and 258.

Subtitle D led to the promulgation of regulations in Part 258. Subtitle D governs nonhazardous "solid waste," defined as:

> [A]ny garbage, refuse, sludge from a waste treatment plant, water supply treatment plant, or air pollution control facility and other discarded

MSWLF = municipal solid waste landfill

IWMA = Integrated Waste Management Act

WTE = waste to energy

SWAT = solid waste assessment test

RWQCB = regional water quality control board

> material including solid, liquid, semisolid or contained gaseous material resulting from industrial, commercial, mining and agricultural operations and from community activity.

Subtitle D establishes provisions governing municipal solid waste landfills (MSWLFs), which collect and dispose of "household wastes." Medical waste, if determined to be hazardous, is regulated by RCRA under Subtitle J.

Environmental Protection Agency. EPA administers RCRA Subtitle D. This program is delegated to CalRecycle (officially known as the Department of Resources Recycling and Recovery, or DRRR) for implementation and enforcement. 42 U.S.C. § 6941 *et seq.*

STATE LAWS AND AGENCIES

Integrated Waste Management Act of 1989. The IWMA (Pub. Res. Code § 40000 *et seq.*) is the principle state statutory authority governing solid waste planning and management. (IWMA also is known as Assembly Bill 939.) The Act is implemented by regulations found at 14 Cal. Code Regs. Division 7 *et seq.* Among other things, the IWMA establishes a hierarchy of actions that local governments must follow to manage waste, including reducing waste at the source, recycling, composting, transformation, and landfilling. Each city and county must develop plans to divert solid waste from landfills by 50 percent compared to the amount of wastes disposed of in 1990. Pub. Res. Code § 41780.

The IWMA establishes a hierarchy of actions that local governments must follow to manage waste, including reducing waste at the source, recycling, composting, transformation, and landfilling.

Integrated Solid Waste Management Act of 1989. This Act establishes the permitting program for solid waste facilities, including landfills, transfer stations, and waste to energy (WTE) facilities. Pub. Res. Code §§ 43020, 43021; Health & Safety Code § 4250. It is implemented by regulations found at 14 Cal. Code Regs. § 17600 *et seq.* and 27 Cal. Code Regs. § 21600 *et seq.*

Solid Waste Assessment Test Program. This program (Health & Safety Code § 41805.5; Water Code § 13273) requires owners and operators of active or closed landfills to complete a solid waste assessment test (SWAT) program to evaluate the potential risk of a release or discharge from a MSWLF. Regional water quality control boards (RWQCBs) administer this program. SWATs do the following:

- Evaluate the potential air emissions liberated from an MSWLF
- Potentially mitigate the emissions liberated from an MSWLF
- Evaluate the potential release of hazardous wastes from MSWLFs to the soil, surface, or groundwater

California Beverage Container Recycling and Litter Reduction Act. Passed in 1986, this Act establishes recycling rates for certain beverage containers. Pub. Res. Code § 14500 *et seq.*

LEA = local enforcement agency

WDR = waste discharge requirement

APCD = air pollution control district

Cell Phone Recycling Act of 2004. Effective July 1, 2006, this Act makes it illegal for retailers to sell cell phones to a consumer unless the retailers implement a system for their collection, reuse, and recycling. Pub. Res. Code § 42490 *et seq.*

Electronic Waste Recycling Act of 2003. Effective January 1, 2005, this Act is designed to reduce the amount of hazardous substances used in certain products sold throughout California. Pub. Res. Code § 42460 *et seq.* This reduction is accomplished primarily through a funding system to collect and recycle electronic wastes.

California Lighting Efficiency and Toxics Reduction Act. This Act is designed to promote energy efficient lighting by prohibiting the sale or manufacturing of incandescent and other lighting that contains hazardous substances prohibited by the European Union under the RoHS (Restriction of Hazardous Substances in electrical and electronic equipment) Directive. Health & Safety Code § 25210.9.

California Medical Waste Management Act. This Act established a program governing the cradle-to-grave management of medical wastes. Health & Safety Code § Health & Safety Code § 117600 *et seq.*; 22 Cal. Code Regs. § 65600 *et seq.* The program sets forth on-site generator, treatment, storage, and disposal requirements administered at the county level.

CalRecycle. EPA delegated authority to implement and enforce RCRA Subtitle D to CalRecycle in September 1993; however, EPA retains oversight authority regarding implementation and enforcement of federal requirements. CalRecycle is charged with implementing the IWMA. CalRecycle must concur with the issuance of a solid waste facility permit prior to issuance by the local enforcement agency (LEA). Each LEA is responsible for processing solid waste facility permits and for conducting inspections of permitted solid waste facilities. Landfills and transfer/processing stations that accept solid waste also must obtain waste discharge requirement (WDR) permits from RWQCBs governing discharge to a Class III landfill (*see* chapter 10) and permits from local air pollution control districts (APCDs). CalRecycle also implements the Beverage Container Recycling Act through enforcement, audits, education, technical assistance, and certification of recycling centers, curbside programs, and beverage container processors.

Local enforcement agency. Cities and counties serve as LEAs and have primary authority to implement and enforce solid waste facility programs and CalRecycle rules. LEAs process solid waste facility permits, together with RWQCBs and local APCDs. Before the LEA may issue a final solid waste facility permit, CalRecycle must have an opportunity to concur or object to the proposed permit. Pub. Res. Code § 43101(c).

Cities and counties serve as LEAs and have primary authority to implement and enforce solid waste facility programs and CalRecycle rules.

Air pollution control districts. Local APCDs are authorized to implement the SWAT program and issue air quality permits for solid waste facilities.

Regional water quality control boards. RWQCBs and LEAs jointly review applications for solid waste facilities. In addition, RWQCBs implement the SWAT program and issue WDR permits for solid waste facilities.

FEDERAL REQUIREMENTS FOR LANDFILLS

EPA promulgated revised regulations governing MSWLFs in 1993 (58 FR 51536; October 9, 1993) under RCRA Subtitle D. These Subtitle D rules govern the design, construction, operation, and permitting of landfills and transfer/processing stations (facilities that temporarily store solid wastes prior to ultimate disposal) accepting municipal solid waste. These regulations apply to approximately 6,000 landfills nationwide. Prior to the Subtitle D regulatory programs, many landfills functioned as unlined open dumps that collected refuse along with household hazardous wastes (such as paints, solvents, pesticides, and other household chemical waste products). Wastes disposed in these landfills could leak into the surrounding soil and groundwater, causing significant contamination. A number of current and former landfills are listed on the National Priorities List of Superfund sites (*see* chapter 8) and are subject to multi-million dollar cleanup efforts.

A number of current and former landfills are listed on the National Priorities List of Superfund sites and are subject to multi-million dollar cleanup efforts.

A MSWLF unit is a discrete area of land or an excavation that receives household waste and that is not a land application unit, surface impoundment, injection well, or waste pile. 40 C.F.R.§ 257.2. A MSWLF unit also may receive RCRA Subtitle D wastes, such as commercial solid waste, nonhazardous sludge, conditionally exempt small quantity generator waste, and industrial solid waste.

Criteria exists for the classification of solid waste disposal facilities and practices (40 C.F.R. § 257), as well as for MSWLF units (40 C.F.R. § 258). New MSWLFs must be located away from hazardous or unsuitable areas, including flood plains, seismic impact zones, wetlands, airports, and unstable areas. Permitted landfills must be equipped with specified liners and leachate collection systems and must meet groundwater monitoring and corrective action requirements. 40 C.F.R. § 258.40. Landfill owners and operators must semiannually monitor for 15 heavy metals and 47 volatile organic constituents. If the monitoring results yield statistically significant increases, the owner or operator must monitor for an expanded list of 213 organic and inorganic constituents. 40 C.F.R. §§ 258.40, 258.54.

Landfill owners and operators must commit to specified closure, post-closure, and financial assurance requirements, and also must establish procedures to exclude acceptance of hazardous waste. Additionally, landfills must comply with specific criteria addressing:

- Daily cover requirements
- Disease vector control
- Explosive gases control
- Air criteria
- Access control requirements
- Liquids restrictions
- Run-off and run-on control systems (to prevent stormwater flow into and from the landfill)

EMSW = engineered municipal solid waste

- Surface water requirements
- Record keeping requirements

In 2002, EPA delegated authority to the states to implement "bioreactor" landfills. These are the next generation of landfilling being promoted by industry. Bioreactor landfills add water in a regulated environment to accelerate decomposition of materials landfilled. Pilot facilities have begun operating in California and may expand to more operations in the future.

CALIFORNIA SOLID WASTE PROGRAMS

SOLID WASTE PLANNING AND WASTE MINIMIZATION

By focusing on reducing waste, the Legislature expected less demand for landfilling and hoped to preserve the remaining landfill capacity.

Source reduction and recycling elements. Prior to enactment of the IWMA in 1989, approximately 90 percent of California solid waste was disposed of in landfills. Approval for new landfills or expanded capacity for existing ones was increasingly difficult to obtain due to the prevalence of the "not in my backyard" attitude. Predictions suggested that landfill space in California would be exhausted by 2000—a mere decade away. With this backdrop, the Legislature approved the IWMA, which was designed to fundamentally shift from landfilling and incinerating municipal solid waste to reducing wastes through source reduction, recycling, and composting. By focusing on reducing waste, the Legislature expected less demand for landfilling and hoped to preserve the remaining landfill capacity.

Largely implemented by cities and counties, the IWMA requires local governments to divert solid waste from landfills by reducing waste at the source (source reduction or reuse), by recycling, by composting, and by implementing environmentally safe "transformation" and land disposal. Ultimately, municipal solid wastes that are not reduced at their source, recycled, or composted can be either landfilled or incinerated.

The Act required cities and counties to divert 25 percent of all solid waste from landfill or transformation facilities (i.e., environmentally safe incineration that includes "incineration, pyrolysis, or distillation, or biological conversion other than composting and does not include composting or gasification") by January 1, 1995, through source reduction, recycling, and composting. It required a similar diversion of 50 percent by January 1, 2000. Up to 10 percent of these targets can be met via transformation. Pub. Res. Code § 40201.

AB 1126 of 2013 (Chapter 411, Statutes of 2013) was introduced to address the dearth of landfill capacity in California and the challenges of siting and permitting new disposal sites for municipal solid waste. AB 1126 exempts the "engineered municipal solid waste" (EMSW) to energy process from the definition of "transformation" thereby creating a "clear permitting pathway" for this waste-to-energy process. The residual ash and other products of conversion are not considered hazardous waste. In order to enjoy the exemption, the facility must not convert more than 500 tons per day of EMSW and it must remove chlorinated plastics and materials from the EMSW prior to conversion.

SRRE = source reduction and recycling element

Local governments implement the 50 percent diversion target by developing and implementing source reduction and recycling elements (SRREs) that establish, among other things, the waste management hierarchy described above. Each city and county was required to develop and implement its own SRRE by 1991 which outlines its strategy to achieve its diversion targets. Each SRRE must have the following components:

- **Waste composition.** Analysis of types and quantities generated
- **Source reduction.** Analysis of generator incentives to reduce quantities and increase recyclable and reusable materials and products
- **Recycling.** Analysis of curbside recycling, zoning, rate structures, etc., to encourage recycling
- **Solid waste facility capacity.** Projection of disposal capacity
- **Household hazardous waste.** Description of collection and disposal plan for household hazardous waste
- **Composting.** Development of a program and implementation schedule describing the types of materials to be composted
- **Education and public information.** Description of how the city or county will increase public awareness of, and participation in, source reduction, recycling, and composting
- **Funding.** Description of costs, revenues, and revenue sources used to implement the SRRE
- **Special waste.** Description of existing waste handling and disposal practices and identification of proposed programs

Since the enactment of the IWMA, California has diverted 66 percent of non-hazardous, solid waste from landfills by recycling, composting, and "transformation."

Statewide waste reduction goal. AB 341 (Chapter 476, Statutes of 2011) established a statewide goal to reduce, recycle, or compost at least 75 percent of solid waste by 2020. Unlike the IWMA, this initiative is a statewide recycling goal, not a diversion goal. This initiative emphasizes source reduction, recycling and composting and does not include "transformation." Waste-to-energy, alternative daily or intermediate cover do not count toward the goal.

The statewide waste reduction goal emphasizes source reduction, recycling and composting and does not include "transformation."

One-third of the non-hazardous, solid waste stream is comprised of organic green waste. AB 1826 of 2014 (Chapter 727, Statutes of 2014) helps achieve state waste reduction goals by diverting organic materials from landfills which release seven millions tons of CO_2 equivalent annually. California businesses that generate

IWMP = Integrated Waste Management Plan

HHWE = household hazardous waste element

NDFE = non-disposal facility element

four cubic yards or more of commercial solid waste weekly must arrange for organic waste recycling services.

In addition, SB 1383 of 2016 (Chapter 395, Statutes of 2016) established the following goals: a 50-percent reduction in the level of the statewide disposal of organic waste from 2014 levels by 2020, and a 75-percent reduction in the level of the statewide disposal of organic waste from 2014 levels by 2025. This bill also authorized CalRecycle to adopt regulations, to take effect on or after January 1, 2022, to achieve these targets.

Zero waste and other waste reduction goals. CalRecycle adopted a strategic plan in 2001 that included zero waste as one of its goals to:

> Promote a "zero-waste California" where the public, industry, and government strive to reduce, reuse, or recycle all municipal solid waste materials back into nature or the marketplace in a manner that protects human health and the environment and honors the principles of California's Integrated Waste Management Act.

In addition, many local governments have adopted Urban Environmental Accords developed by the United Nations for World Environment Day in 2005 in San Francisco. One of the Urban Environmental Accords establishes a zero waste policy by 2040. Many communities are developing sustainability goals and policies and working to reduce greenhouse gases. These communities are now recognizing that landfills are a significant source of greenhouse gas emissions—especially methane.

Many communities are developing sustainability goals and policies and working to reduce greenhouse gases.

As part of these efforts, communities that had adopted zero waste as a goal as of 2016 include:

- Alameda
- Berkeley
- Burbank
- Castro Valley
- Culver City
- Del Norte County
- El Cajon
- Fresno
- Los Angeles
- Marin County
- Mountain View
- Novato
- Oakland
- Oceanside
- Palo Alto
- Pasadena
- Sacramento
- San Diego
- San Francisco City and County
- San Jose
- San Luis Obispo County
- Santa Cruz County
- Santa Monica
- San Ramon
- Sonoma County
- Sunnyvale

Countywide Integrated Waste Management Plans. In addition to submitting an SRRE to CalRecycle, counties must submit an Integrated Waste Management Plan (IWMP). The IWMP consists of a household hazardous waste element (HHWE), a city and county non-disposal facility element (NDFE), and a county-wide siting element (CSE). These plans, described further below, can be submitted for approval individually or as a package.

CSE = county-wide siting element

RDSI = report of disposal site information

The HHWE sets forth the municipality's program to safely collect, recycle, treat, and dispose of hazardous wastes generated from households. The city or county NDFE must describe the current and future facilities available to implement the SRRE. These facilities must be capable of recovering materials for reuse or recycling, but cannot include disposal or transformation facilities. The NDFE must describe those recovery facilities located within the municipality and those facilities outside the county that it plans to utilize. Pub. Res. Code § 41733; 14 Cal. Code Regs. § 18753.

To better predict and plan for future municipal solid waste management capacity, each county must develop a CSE. Pub. Res. Code § 41700 *et seq*. Each CSE must include:

To better predict and plan for future municipal solid waste management capacity, each county must develop a CSE.

- The 15-year estimated landfill and transformation capacity
- The capacity currently available
- Identification of areas for new facilities

If existing capacity will be consumed within 15 years, then the CSE must identify new areas for transformation or disposal that are consistent with the city or county general plan. Pub. Res. Code § 41701; 14 Cal. Code Regs. § 18755 *et seq*.

SOLID WASTE FACILITIES REGULATION

Landfills. In 1967, California completed a study uncovering dangerous conditions that existed at disposal sites throughout the state. The study highlighted the fire and safety hazards as well as the vector, air, and water pollution problems present at these facilities. This study led to the state's current permit programs, which rigorously manage solid waste facilities in California.

Applicants must complete a permit application called a report of disposal site information (RDSI) if they propose to handle, process, transport, store, or dispose of solid wastes (including household garbage, trash, refuse, paper, rubbish, ashes, industrial wastes, construction debris, abandoned vehicles, discarded appliances, manure, and other discarded wastes). Applicants must submit the RDSI to the LEA; it must include:

- Proposed manner of operation
- Types and quantities of wastes to be received
- Capacity
- Life expectancy
- Site location (disposal site standards are in 14 Cal. Code Regs. § 17600 *et seq.*)

Like a MSWLF under the federal program, solid waste landfills (also known as Class III landfills, as further described in chapter 10) must be located in accordance

SWRCB = State Water Resources Control Board

CEQA = California Environmental Quality Act

SWD = solid waste disposal

DTSC = Department of Toxic Substances Control

with the State Water Resources Control Board's (SWRCB's) siting and design criteria. 27 Cal. Code Regs. § 20260. The applicant also must obtain a WDR permit from the RWQCB (*see* chapter 10) and air quality permits from the APCD (*see* chapter 5). New or expanded solid waste facilities must conform to CSEs. In addition, the California Environmental Quality Act (CEQA) likely will apply to the project.

California is required to ensure that its solid waste permitting program for solid waste disposal facilities are at least as stringent as federal MSWLF standards. EPA is authorized to enforce its MSWLF requirements should California fail to implement these standards. 42 U.S.C. § 6945(c)(1)(B).

Puente Hills landfill. About 135 acres of this 1,365-acre closed landfill are proposed to be converted to a Los Angeles County park.

Landfill closure. Owners and operators of solid waste landfills are required to plan for and fund "post-closure maintenance financial assurance" for 30 years after closure for the purpose of managing the environmental risks from closed landfills. Common post-closure maintenance activities include leachate collection and treatment, groundwater monitoring, inspection and maintenance of the final landfill cover, and monitoring of landfill gases. 27 Cal. Code Regs. § 21090 *et seq.*

Solid waste assessment tests. MSWLFs have the potential to release dangerous air emissions (e.g., dust, odor, smoke, and gases such as methane and other toxic chemicals) and to discharge water pollution (chemical leachate) to the soil and surface and groundwater. The Legislature responded to this risk by enacting a law, sometimes referred to as the Calderon Act (Health & Safety Code § 41805.5; Water Code § 13273), that requires owners and operators of active or closed landfills to complete a SWAT to evaluate the potential risk of a release or discharge from the MSWLF.

On or before July 1, 1987, owners and operators of active Class III landfills, referred to as solid waste disposal (SWD) sites, were obligated to complete an air-SWAT for submission to the local APCD. Health & Safety Code § 41805.5; 23 Cal. Code Regs. § 2510 *et seq.* On or before November 1, 1986, owners and operators of inactive SWD sites were obligated to complete a preliminary screening questionnaire and submit it to the APCD for review. Based on the results of these submittals, the local APCD is authorized to determine whether the air pollutant releases pose a health risk or an environmental threat to sensitive populations including schools, hospitals, and residences. The APCD has authority to impose mitigation measures to reduce or minimize those impacts that pose a health risk to human beings or a threat to the environment. Health & Safety Code § 41805.5(g).

To evaluate SWD sites for hazardous waste leakage to the subsurface, the SWRCB ranked all SWD sites based on the threat they may pose to water quality. The first 150 SWD operators were to submit water-SWATs by January 1, 1987; the next 150 SWD operators were to submit water-SWATS by July 1, 1988. Water Code § 13273. If the SWRCB determines that hazardous waste has migrated into the water, it must notify the Department of Toxic Substances Control (DTSC) and CalRecycle and take appropriate remedial action. Water Code § 13273(3).

Transfer stations. Transfer processing stations are temporary locations for the transfer of materials from smaller collection vehicles onto larger, higher-volume vehicles (e.g., trucks, barges, and trains) for transport to ultimate destinations. The final destination for solid waste is generally a landfill or transformation facility. California requires permits for the design and operation of transfer stations and has recordkeeping requirements. 14 Cal. Code Regs. § 17400 *et seq.* Transfer stations also must be permitted by the LEA, RWQCB, and local APCD. Permitting and operations standards differ for small versus large transfer stations. A medium transfer station is one that receives less than 100 tons/day. 14 Cal. Code Regs. § 17402(a)(11).

DOC = California Department of Conservation

California requires permits for the design and operation of transfer stations and has recordkeeping requirements.

Waste-to-energy facilities. Waste-to-energy facilities burn municipal refuse or other waste to produce electricity or steam. These facilities must comply with specified permitting standards for solid waste facilities, air quality standards (*see* chapter 5), and CEQA review requirements (*see* chapter 2). WTE facilities with a thermal generating capacity of 50 megawatts or more must comply with specific permitting requirements under the Warren-Alquist Act (Pub. Res. Code § 25500 *et seq.*), which is discussed in chapter 17. 14 Cal. Code Regs. § 17225.58; Health & Safety Code § 39050.5.

Waste tire facilities. Owners or operators of facilities that store or dispose of tires must obtain a permit issued by CalRecycle. Each waste tire facility permit establishes specified storage and disposal standards ranging from fire protection and security to vector controls. Solid waste facilities that accept for transfer, or discard up to, 150 tires per day require a waste tire facility permit. People who transport waste tires to tire facilities must operate pursuant to a permit. Pub. Res. Code § 42800 *et seq.*

Construction and demolition debris facilities. The LEA also issues permits for facilities that receive, store, handle, transfer, or process construction and demolition debris and inert debris, which includes lumber and wood, gypsum wallboard, glass, metal, roofing material, tile, carpeting and floor coverings, window coverings, plastic pipe concrete, fully cured asphalt, heating ventilation and air conditioning systems and their components, lighting fixtures, appliances, equipment, furnishings, and fixtures. 14 Cal. Code Regs. § 18223.

Scrap metal recycling. AB 844 of 2008 (Chapter 731, Statutes of 2008) is designed to reduce sales of stolen metal. This law imposes identification, recordkeeping and reporting requirements upon junk dealers and recyclers (known as "core recyclers") when they purchase specified nonferrous materials (i.e., copper, copper alloys, stainless steel, and aluminum, excluding beverage containers).

CALIFORNIA BEVERAGE CONTAINERS RECYCLING AND LITTER REDUCTION ACT

The California Department of Conservation (DOC) is principally responsible for implementing this Act, also known as the California Bottle Bill or "AB 2020" (Pub.

RPPC = rigid plastic packaging container

HDPE = high-density polyethylene

NPDES = National Pollutant Discharge Elimination System

Res. Code § 14500 *et seq.*). The Act establishes a redemption value on specific categories of beverage containers (such as beer, wine, coffee, tea, fruit drinks, and soft drinks, in aluminum, glass, plastic, and bi-metal containers). This law is designed to ensure that no less than 65 percent of specified beverage containers are recycled. The redemption value assigned to each regulated beverage container can fluctuate to a higher level whenever the redemption rate drops below 65 percent.

California has experienced a drop in the historically high recovery rate of beverage containers as more and more plastic containers are introduced into the marketplace. The Legislature responded by increasing the California redemption value of containers, now $.05 for small bottles and $0.10 for larger beverage containers. Pub. Res. Code § 14575. AB 1778 of 2008 (Chapter 733 of 2008) responded to underground businesses with organized crews and large trucks seeking refund money by prohibiting "junk dealers" and "recyclers" from paying the California redemption value for containers unless the junk dealer or recycler collects identifying information including the address of the seller.

SUPPLY CHAIN PROGRAMS

Rigid plastic packaging container program. 14 Cal. Code Regs. § 17900 *et seq.* This law was enacted to reduce the amount of plastic waste disposed in California landfills and to increase the use of recycled postconsumer plastic. Rigid plastic packaging containers (RPPCs) made entirely of plastic meeting other specifications that are sold or distributed in California must meet, among other standards, postconsumer material content (at least 25 percent) or a specified recycling rate, or be reusable. Product manufacturers must calculate their container compliance using the formulas developed by CalRecycle.

RPPCs destined for shipment outside California are exempt from the Act. In addition, RPPCs that contain drugs, medical devices, cosmetics, food, medical food, or infant formula, toxic or hazardous products (regulated under the federal Insecticide, Fungicide, and Rodenticide Act) are also exempt. Businesses can petition CalRecycle for a 12-month waiver for "newly introduced products sold in California." 14 Cal. Code Regs. § 17943 *et seq.*

California law requires that cities and counties meet source reduction and recycling targets.

Plastic packaging and bags. AB 3025 of 2008 (Chapter 471, Statutes of 2008) prohibits expanded polystyrene loose fill packing material (i.e., "peanuts") wholesalers or manufacturers from selling or offering for sale in California unless the material is comprised of 100 percent recycled material on and after January 1, 2017. SB 1723 of 2008 (Chapter 533, Statutes of 2008)) requires those who first sell specified pesticide or agricultural product packaging to either establish a recycling program or participate in such a program to ensure that HDPE (high density polyethylene) containers are recycled. This program applies to persons that sell packaging in rigid, non-refillable, HDPE containers for agricultural or structural use pesticides up to 55 gallons in capacity.

The SWRCB, pursuant to the Preproduction Plastic Debris Program (AB 258, Statutes of 2008), establishes conditional exemptions from National Pollutant Discharge Elimination System (NPDES) permitting for the plastics industry. Plastic manufacturing, handling, or transportation facilities must submit a no-exposure certification to claim exemption (*See* chapter 10).

SB 1749 of 2004 (Chapter 619, Statutes of 2004) prohibits the sale of plastic bags and plastic food and beverage containers labeled as "biodegradable," "compostable," "degradable," or "marine degradable" unless the plastic meets the American Society for Testing and Materials standards for the term used on the label. In addition, manufacturers of compostable bags must ensure that the compostable plastic bag is readily and easily identifiable from other plastic bags. Manufacturers must also abide by the Federal Trade Commission Guides for the Use of Environmental Marketing Claims and may not sell or distribute compostable plastic bags that display a recycling symbol (e.g., a chasing arrow). More recently, local agencies have adopted plastic bag ordinances. *See* sidebar.

Extended producer responsibility. EPP or "manufacturer take-back" programs require manufacturers to manage the end-of-life of the products they produce. California law establishes EPP for manufacturers of products ranging from pharmaceuticals to cell phones. In addition, several local ordinances place the primary responsibility for drugs on pharmaceutical companies.

OTHER SUPPLY CHAIN AND RECYCLING PROGRAMS

Mattresses and carpets. SB 254 of 2013 (Chapter 388, Statutes of 2013) establishes the Used Mattress Recovery and Recycling Act which requires mattress manufacturers and retailers to recover and recycle used mattresses and reduce illegal dumping of wastes. CalRecycle administers a "mattress recycling charge" which is included in the purchase price of a mattress. Mattress manufacturers, retailers, and renovators must register with the mattress recycling organization. In a similar fashion, AB 2398 of 2010 (Chapter 681, Statutes of 2010) establishes infrastructure to collect and process waste carpet. Carpet manufacturers in California must submit to CalRecycle a carpet stewardship plan that sets forth product design, use, and end-of-life management strategies for carpet. In addition, a carpet manufacturer must add a $0.05 per square yard assessment on the purchase price for carpet sold in California. Retailers and wholesalers are obligated to add this assessment to the purchase price.

History of the Plastic Bag Ban

Close to 80 percent of marine debris found on beaches and in the oceans is generated from the land—90 percent of which is plastic. Plastic debris such as plastic bags and cigarette filters impact the health of marine life that often confuses the debris for food.

California residents and businesses generate approximately 19 billion disposable plastic bags each year, which results in over 147,000 tons of waste. Approximately 60 percent of these non-biodegradable bags are generated by grocery stores.

In 2006, AB 2449 responded by requiring most large grocery stores and other retailers to establish recycling programs to collect and recycle plastic bags. By July 1, 2008, supermarkets and retail stores (with more than 10,000 feet of retail space and an associated pharmacy) were required to maintain an on-site plastic bag take-back and recycling program. Among other things, stores must establish conspicuous and easily accessible collection bins for bags. Retailers must also make available for purchase reusable bags and manufacturers must implement a public education program designed to encourage reduction, reuse, and recycling of plastic carry-out bags.

Many cities and counties have adopted plastic bag ordinances. SB 270 of 2014 (Chapter 850, Statutes of 2014) established a statewide prohibition on the sale or distribution of single-use carryout plastic bags in grocery stores and pharmacies, convenience food stores, and food marts. Retailers must charge customers at least 10 cents to buy a recycled paper bag or reusable grocery bag. A referendum to repeal this law failed in the November 2016 election.

Mercury devices. As more fully discussed in chapter 7, California law bans the manufacture and sale of mercury fever thermometers and other mercury-containing products. California law also prohibits the sale of specified levels of cadmium, chromium (VI), lead, mercury and asbestiform fibers in motor vehicle brake pads (Health & Safety Code § 25250.51). Finally, California law requires thermostat manufacturers to establish a mercury-added thermostat collection and recycling program. Health and Safety Code § 25214.8.10 *et seq*.

Paint stewardship. Waste latex and oil-based paints generated by consumers in California represent the largest source of household hazardous waste for consumers. With only five percent of California households using HHW programs, AB 1343 of 2010 (Chapter 420, Statutes of 2010) established an architectural paint recovery program to recover and properly manage leftover paint. This program requires paint manufacturers or a designated stewardship organization to develop and implement an architectural paint stewardship plan. The plan must be designed to recover and reduce the generation of and promote the reuse of postconsumer architectural paint. The manufacturer or its stewardship organization must submit the plan to the CalRecycle for review and approval. Manufacturers or retailers are prohibited from selling or offering for sale architectural paint unless the manufacturer is listed on CalRecycle's website as meeting the requirements of this law. Failure to comply could subject a violator to civil penalties.

Manufacturers or retailers are prohibited from selling or offering for sale architectural paint unless the manufacturer is listed on CalRecycle's website as meeting the requirements of this law.

Pharmaceutical management. Approximately one million Californians inject medications at home or otherwise outside medical facilities. SB 1305 of 2006 (Chapter 64, Statutes of 2006) prohibits disposal of home-generated sharps waste into commercial and residential solid waste collection containers. It also requires that sharps be managed only at licensed household hazardous waste or medical waste facilities and transported only in approved sharps containers. Pharmaceutical manufacturers that sell or distribute self-injected medications (e.g., hypodermic or pen needles) are required to develop a collection and disposal plan. The plan must provide for safe collection and proper disposal; educate consumers about safe management and collection opportunities; and support efforts by retailers, pharmaceutical distributors, manufacturers, health care organizations, solid waste service providers through safe collection and proper disposal of waste devices. Pub. Res. Code §§ 47115–47116 .

Consumers are free to dispose of waste pharmaceuticals in the trash as a household hazardous waste which is exempt from classification as hazardous waste (RCRA 40 C.F.R. § 261.4(b)) and as medical waste (Health & Safety Code § 117700). In practice, unused drugs often are improperly flushed to the sanitary sewer and discarded as refuse. The Alameda County Board of Supervisors approved the first-in-the-nation Environmentally Preferable Purchasing program for drugs to prevent unintentional poisonings due to these disposal practices. The Alameda County Safe Drug Disposal Ordinance program shifted the cost of disposal from taxpayers to

CED = covered electronic device

drug companies. This ordinance requires pharmaceutical "producers" who manufacturer, sell or distribute drugs within Alameda County to fund the collection and disposal of unused medications, excluding over-the-counter drugs. Each producer must either operate a Product Stewardship Program or have an agreement with a product stewardship organization to operate on their behalf. Each Product Stewardship Program must have a Product Stewardship Plan which, among other things, describes the method that allows for the convenient collection of drugs in all areas of the county along with a description of how the drugs will be safely and securely tracked to their final disposal.

In *PhRMA v. County of Alameda* (9th Cir. 2014) 768 F. 3d 1037, the court upheld the ordinance against a dormant commerce clause challenge. The City and County of San Francisco and San Mateo County have approved similar ordinances.

Appliances: AB 1447 of 2007 (Health & Safety Code § 25211.1 *et seq.*) is designed to ensure that major appliances (e.g., refrigerators, freezers, washers, dryers, microwaves, air conditioners, and furnaces) manage the risk of releasing hazardous materials (e.g., mercury, chlorofluorocarbon, used oil, and polychlorinated biphenyls) from these appliances. This program permits appliance service technicians and certified appliance recyclers to remove refrigerants from major appliances.

Cell Phone Recycling Act of 2004. Californians throw away thousands of cell phones each day. Cell phones often contain hazardous amounts of materials such as lead, arsenic, and cadmium. Once in the landfill, the toxins ultimately may be released into groundwater.

The Cell Phone Recycling Act of 2004 (Pub. Res. Code § 42490 *et seq.*) requires that cell phone retailers establish a system to collect, reuse, and recycle cell phones. Retailers must inform consumers about cell phone recycling opportunities, and California agencies that purchase or lease cell phones must require bidders to certify compliance with the provisions described above. Further, the Act requires that DTSC provide online information on cell phone recycling rates.

Electronic Waste Recycling Act of 2003. The Electronic Waste Recycling Act of 2003 (Pub. Res. Code § 42460 *et seq.*) requires manufacturers to phase out the use of heavy metals in electronic devices and to increase the use of recycled materials. The Act also imposes a ban on the sale of covered electronic devices (CEDs) if those devices would be prohibited from sale in the European Union due to the presence of heavy metals. The ban conditionally took effect January 1, 2007.

California's Electronic Waste Recycling Act of 2003 established comprehensive programs to promote recycling of covered electronic devices.

The Act also requires that retailers of CEDs collect from consumers an electronic waste recycling fee of $6 to $10 depending on the size of the screen. These fees are to be paid to authorized CED recyclers who must provide free and convenient collection, consolidation, and transportation of CED wastes. Exporters of electronic waste to foreign destinations must meet standards adopted by the Organization for Economic Cooperation and Development. The Act also requires CED manufacturers to label equipment with the manufacturer's brand label.

Additionally, manufacturers must provide information to consumers describing where and how to return, recycle, and dispose of CEDs. Manufacturers are required to report annually on the:

- Number of CEDs sold in the state
- Amount of recycled materials used in CED manufacture
- Efforts to design CEDs for recycling
- Goals to increase CED recycling

CalRecycle must annually establish and update statewide electronic waste recycling goals. Cities and counties were required to revise their IWMPs by January 1, 2004, to ensure that the household hazardous waste element articulates actions necessary to promote the collection, consolidation, recovery, and recycling of covered electronic waste.

California Lighting Efficiency and Toxics Reduction Act. The California Lighting Efficiency and Toxic Reductions Act bans (on and after January 1, 2010) the sale or manufacture of incandescent and other lighting that contains hazardous substances prohibited by the European Union pursuant to the RoHS Directive. DTSC and CalRecycle are required to develop a strategy to collect and recycle general purpose lights. Health & Safety Code § 25210.9.

California Tire Recycling Act. Californians generate approximately 40 million waste tires while about 30 million of these tires are diverted from landfills for reuse, retreading, and combustion. The California Tire Recycling Act collects a fee on the sale of new tires. This fee supports the regulation of waste tire facilities and hauler and recycling activities. In addition, people who haul tires to an approved waste facility must register with CalRecycle. Pub. Res. Code § 42860 *et seq*.

Laws promoting recycled product markets. As millions of tons of materials are diverted from landfills each year, more and more resources are available for other productive uses. California law leverages the enormous marketing power of its procurement system by requiring that the Department of General Services purchase products made with post-consumer materials where fitness and quality are equal. State law promotes development of markets for recycled goods by requiring that state agencies purchase minimum percentages of post-consumer content of the following recycled products: paper, compost, glass, oil, plastic, solvents, paint, rubberized asphalt concrete, returned plastic concrete (otherwise known as "recycled concrete") and tires. Companies that fail to meet the required minimum post-consumer content are banned ("debarred") from state contracts. Pub. Contracts Code § 12200 *et seq*.

California law leverages the enormous marketing power of its procurement system by requiring that the Department of General Services purchase products made with post-consumer materials where fitness and quality are equal.

In addition to these procurement policies, commercial printers and publishers must ensure that at least 50 percent of newsprint contains a minimum of 40 percent post-consumer paper fiber. Pub. Res. Code § 42760.

CALIFORNIA MEDICAL WASTE MANAGEMENT ACT

This Act (Health & Safety Code § 117600 *et seq.*) significantly reformed the management of medical waste in California. Prior to this Act, medical waste was regulated as a California-only, non-RCRA hazardous waste. Medical waste means waste that meets both of the following requirements (Health & Safety Code §§ 117635, 117690, 117755):

- "Biohazardous waste" (such as blood or infectious agents) or "sharps waste" (such as a syringe)
- Waste that is generated or produced as a result of the diagnosis, treatment, or immunization of human beings or animals, in research or in the production of or testing of vaccines, antigens, and other "biologicals"

The Act imposes a cradle-to-grave program on the generation, treatment, storage, and disposal of medical wastes. The level of program rigor depends on quantities of medical wastes generated. A large quantity generator generates 200 pounds or more per month of medical waste. A small quantity generator generates less than 200 pounds per month.

The California Medical Waste Management Act imposes a cradle-to-grave program on the generation, treatment, storage, and disposal of medical wastes.

Generators of medical wastes must meet specified registration and labeling requirements. In addition, they must meet specified hold times and complete a medical waste management plan. Health & Safety Code § 117935. Wastes must be labeled with the words "Biohazardous Waste" or the international biohazard symbol, and the word "BIOHAZARD." Sharps waste must be labeled "sharps waste" or the international biohazard symbol, and the word "BIOHAZARD." In addition, onsite accumulation areas must display specified labels.

Bags containing biohazardous wastes must be tied to prevent leakage. Health & Safety Code § 118280(a). Generators of medical wastes are subject to different accumulation and holding requirements that depend on the amount of medical waste generated monthly and whether the waste is refrigerated. Health & Safety Code § 118280. Sharps waste must be stored in rigid containers and taped or closed with a tight lid. Health & Safety Code § 118285.

Medical wastes may be incinerated, steam sterilized, or microwaved. Liquid and semi-liquid medical wastes may be chemically disinfected.

Also, AB 1442 of 2012 (Chapter 689, Statutes of 2012) authorizes transportation by common carrier for outdated or otherwise unsalable non-creditable pharmaceutical waste (i.e., medical waste). These wastes can alternatively be transported by the generator or health care professional as long as the generator, health care professional, and the facility receiving the medical wastes maintains specified records.

ENFORCEMENT

FEDERAL ENFORCEMENT

The SWDA authorizes any person including the United States or any other governmental agency to enforce the Act. Additionally, EPA and CalRecycle are authorized to issue formal administrative orders to ensure compliance with the SWDA. 42 U.S.C. § 7002; 40 C.F.R. § 254.1.

STATE AND LOCAL ENFORCEMENT

California has delegated authority to implement rules governing solid waste facilities. LEAs are required to inspect all solid waste facilities and sites at least once each month and, if any violations are found, a notice of violation must be sent to the operator. Pub. Res. Code § 43218; 14 Cal. Code Regs. § 18083.

Facilities with chronic violations of state minimum standards have their names published on CalRecyle's Inventory list.

Facilities with chronic violations of state minimum standards have their names published on CalRecyle's Inventory list. These facilities must develop a compliance schedule to prove they are diligently working to comply with the standards. Pub. Res. Code § 44106.

Violation of any LEA order may result in a civil penalty not greater than $5,000 per day of noncompliance. The intentional or negligent violation of a facility's permit may subject the owner or operator to civil penalties of no more than $10,000 per day of violation. Pub. Res. Code §§ 45011, 45023.

LEAs can:

- Issue cease and desist orders for solid waste facilities that operate without a permit. Pub Res. Code §§ 44002, 44005
- Issue injunctions and penalties to any person failing to comply. Pub.Res. Code § 45014
- Issue an enforcement order requiring a facility or site to comply within a given time frame
- Suspend or revoke a facility permit
- Enforce violations for plastic bag labeling standards

AB 1398 of 2013 (Chapter 509, Statutes of 2013) responds to occasional confusion arising with the jurisdiction of LEAs to implement and enforce the Integrated Waste Management Act. AB 1398 clarifies that an LEA remains independent from the local governing body (e.g., county) when implementing and enforcing state law.

A Superior Court can issue an injunction to any person failing to comply with a final order (Pub. Res. Code § 45014), and LEAs are authorized to issue administrative civil penalties to operators who fail to comply by the deadline in a final notice and order. Penalties can range up to $5,000 per day per violation, with no limit on the total fine amount. Owners and operators who intentionally or negligently violate the terms of a solid waste facility permit are subject to civil penalties of up to $10,000 per day of violation. Pub. Res. Code § 45023.

CalRecycle enforces compliance with the Integrated Waste Management Act, the RPPC, and the California Tire Recycling Act. If CalRecycle determines a jurisdiction has not implemented its SRRE, CalRecycle may issue an order of compliance with a specific schedule for achieving compliance. If the jurisdiction subsequently fails to meet the compliance schedule, CalRecycle has authority to fine a city or county up to $10,000 per day. Pub.Res. Code § 41850. Senate Bill 1016 of 2007 (Chapter 343, Statutes of 2007) authorizes CalRecycle to issue an order of compliance if it finds that a city or county failed to make a good faith effort to implement its SRRE or its household hazardous waste element. CalRecycle also has authority to assess penalties of up to $5,000 for any violation of the RPPC up to a cumulative total of $100,000.

CalRecycle also has authority to assess penalties of up to $5,000 for any violation of the RPPC up to a cumulative total of $100,000.

CalRecycle can issue similar penalties and injunctive relief for violations of the waste tire storage and disposal requirements. Pub. Res. Code § 42850 *et seq.*

In addition, "illegal dumping enforcement officers" are authorized to enforce laws prohibiting illegal waste dumping or littering, and have arresting authority as peace officers. Penal Code § 830.7(j). The courts are authorized to impose a fine of either $100 for an infraction and $200 for a misdemeanor for a defendant convicted of littering and illegal dumping offenses.

for more information...

Manaster, K. A. and D. P. Selmi (eds.), ND. California Environmental Law and Land Use Practice. Chapters 90–91. Matthew Bender. San Francisco, Calif.

glossary

Biohazardous waste—"laboratory wastes" such as human and animal specimen cultures, human surgery specimens or tissues removed at surgery contaminated with infectious agents, blood, fluid blood products, containers, or equipment containing blood.

Construction and demolition debris facility permit*—a permit governing facilities that receive, store, handle, transfer, or process construction and demolition debris and inert debris such as lumber, wallboard, glass, metal, roofing material, tile, carpeting, and materials.

Household hazardous waste—means any hazardous waste generated incidental to owning or maintaining a place of residence. Household hazardous waste does not include any waste generated in the course of operating a business concern at a residence.

Local Enforcement Agency—Solid waste local enforcement agencies (LEAs) are certified by CalRecycle to implement and enforce the Integrated Waste Management Act. LEAs are typically comprised of a local environmental health department. Under the oversight of CalRecycle, LEAs are authorized to inspect and permit solid waste facilities.

Medical waste—waste that meets both of the following requirements: (1) biohazardous waste or sharps waste, and (2) waste that is generated or produced as a result of the diagnosis, treatment, or immunization of human beings or animals, in research, in the production or testing of biologicals, or in the accumulation of properly contained home-generated sharps waste.

Municipal solid waste landfill unit—a discrete area of land or an excavation that receives household waste and that is not a land application unit, surface impoundment, injection well, or waste pile.

Municipal solid waste transfer station—a solid waste management facility that temporarily stores municipal solid waste before being shipped to a permitted municipal solid waste landfill for disposal.

Report of Disposal Site Information*—a report filed with the LEA if an applicant proposes to handle, process, transport, store, or dispose of solid wastes.

Sharps waste—any device having acute rigid corners, edges, or protuberances capable of cutting or piercing, including, but not limited to, hypodermic needles, broken glass, and any item capable of cutting or piercing that is contaminated with trauma scene waste.

Solid waste—garbage, refuse, sludge and other discarded material including solid, liquid, semisolid or contained gaseous material resulting from industrial, commercial, mining and agricultural operations and from community activity.

Solid waste assessment test—method to determine the potential risk of a release or discharge from a municipal solid waste landfill. SWATs are designed to evaluate the potential air emissions liberated and water discharged from a municipal solid waste landfill and to potentially mitigate the releases.

Source reduction—any action that causes a net reduction in the generation of solid waste. Source reduction includes, but is not limited to, reducing the use of non-recyclable materials, replacing disposable materials and products with reusable materials and products, reducing packaging, reducing the amount of yard wastes generated, establishing garbage rate structures with incentives to reduce waste tonnage generated, and increasing the efficiency of the use of paper, cardboard, glass, metal, plastic, and other materials.

Source reduction and recycling elements—a municipality's approach to managing solid waste, including all feasible source reduction, recycling, and composting programs while identifying the landfill and transformation capacity necessary for solid waste that cannot be reduced, recycled, or composted.

Transfer station—a permitted facility that receives, handles, separates, converts, or otherwise processes solid waste.

Transformation—incineration, pyrolysis, distillation, or biological conversion other than composting. Transformation does not include composting, gasification, or biomass conversion.

Waste discharge requirements*—permit issued by a RWQCB for discharge of waste into waters of the state.

Waste tire facility permit*—authorizes owners or operators of facilities to store or dispose of tires subject to standards ranging from fire protection and security to vector controls.

* equals permits and approvals

CHAPTER 10

Water Quality

related Solano Press title

California Water II, Arthur L. Littleworth and Eric L. Garner. 2007.

in this chapter...

CWA = Clean Water Act

NPDES = National Pollutant Discharge Elimination System

TMDL = total maximum daily load

SPCC = spill prevention control and countermeasure

INTRODUCTION

The industrial fire that erupted on the Cuyahoga River in Cleveland, Ohio in 1969 shined a spotlight on the nation's damaged water systems. Before Congress enacted the federal Clean Water Act (CWA) of 1972, a vast majority of watersheds in the United States were polluted. The CWA was enacted to restore and maintain water quality levels that protect fish, wildlife, and recreational uses.

This chapter reviews the key laws and agencies involved in water quality regulation, water quality planning and standards, permit programs for point and nonpoint sources, ocean protection programs, oil management programs, water quality release reporting, and enforcement of water quality laws.

KEY LAWS AND AGENCIES

FEDERAL LAWS AND AGENCIES

The Clean Water Act protects the water quality of jurisdictional surface waters.

Clean Water Act of 1972. The CWA (33 U.S.C. §§ 1251–1376) protects the water quality of jurisdictional surface waters. The CWA revamped the Federal Water Pollution Control Act (enacted in 1948), to restore and maintain the "chemical, physical, and biological integrity of the Nation's waters."

The CWA created the following programs to achieve and maintain water quality:

- **National Pollutant Discharge Elimination System (NPDES).** To grant permits for point source discharges of industrial and municipal wastewater to waters of the United States (33 U.S.C. § 1342; 40 C.F.R. §§ 122–125, 403), including specialized requirements for general permits, stormwater, concentrated animal feeding operations (CAFOs), and pretreatment
- **Total maximum daily loads (TMDLs).** To specify waste load allocations for both point and nonpoint source discharges for impaired waters (waters that do not meet water quality standards). 33 U.S.C. § 1313(d) (otherwise known as CWA § 303(d))
- **Nonpoint source grants.** To enable states to address nonpoint source pollution via management programs. 33 U.S.C. § 1329
- **Spill prevention control and countermeasure (SPCC) program.** To regulate the discharge of oil and hazardous substances, and to report releases of oil and "hazardous substances." 33 U.S.C. § 1321; 40 C.F.R. §§ 116, 177; 40 C.F.R. § 112 *et seq.*
- **Permits for discharge of dredged or fill material into waters of the United States.** 33 U.S.C. § 1344; 40 C.F.R. §§ 230, 232 (*see* chapter 15)
- **Administrative, judicial, and citizen enforcement.** 33 U.S.C.§§ 1319, 1365, 1369; 40 C.F.R. § 135

Under the CWA, EPA sets national effluent standards based on industry-specific criteria. EPA also approves state receiving water quality standards to protect specific uses of waters of the U.S.

Safe Drinking Water Act. The federal SDWA (42 U.S.C. § 300(f) *et seq.*) protects groundwater aquifers by regulating discharges of waste to deep and shallow underground geological formations. The Act establishes permitting requirements governing injection of wastes known as the underground injection control (UIC) program; the Act additionally regulates sole source aquifers with the goal of protecting drinking water systems from contaminants that could jeopardize public health. 40 C.F.R. § 149. Finally, the Act also regulates drinking water. *See* chapter 11.

SDWA = Safe Drinking Water Act

UIC = underground injection control

EPA = U.S. Environmental Protection Agency

WDR = waste discharge requirement

SWRCB = State Water Resources Control Board

Marine Protection, Research, and Sanctuaries Act. The Marine Protection, Research, and Sanctuaries Act has two basic aims: to regulate intentional ocean disposal of materials, and to authorize related research. Permit and enforcement provisions of the law are often referred to as the Ocean Dumping Act.

The Marine Protection, Research, and Sanctuaries Act has two basic aims: to regulate intentional ocean disposal of materials, and to authorize related research.

Environmental Protection Agency. EPA administers the federal CWA and SDWA programs. EPA also has authority to administer NPDES permits. 33 U.S.C. § 1251 *et seq.* Authority to administer NPDES permits may be delegated to states and Native American tribal governments.

STATE LAWS AND AGENCIES

Porter-Cologne Water Quality Control Act. The Porter-Cologne Act (Water Code § 13000 *et seq.*) implements and augments federal protections under the CWA via regulation of the "waters of the state," which include surface, ground, and ocean water as well as point sources and nonpoint sources. To protect waters of the state, the Act implements the federal NPDES permitting program and the California waste discharge requirement (WDR) permitting program.

Oil Spill Prevention and Response Act (Lempert-Keene-Seastrand Act). This Act (Gov't Code § 8670 *et seq.*) establishes spill contingency plan requirements and other programs to protect marine waters from oil spills.

The California Marine Invasive Species Act. This Act establishes ballast water management standards governing vessels that operate in waters of the state designed to prevent or minimize the introduction of nonindigenous species to California waters. Pub. Res. Code § 71200 *et seq.*

State Water Resources Control Board. The SWRCB is authorized by EPA to implement and enforce the surface water permitting and TMDL programs and has adopted federal regulations under the Porter-Cologne Act. The SWRCB implements and ensures compliance with the Porter-Cologne Act, including the adopted federal standards, and the CWA. The SWRCB is comprised of a board with members who represent a variety of water quality and water supply interests and who serve staggered terms. The SWRCB has both administrative rulemaking and adjudicatory powers.

RWQCB = regional water quality control board

DOGGR = Division of Oil, Gas, and Geothermal Resources

WQS = water quality standards

The SWRCB is responsible for creating and implementing a statewide plan that establishes policies to protect waters of the state. It also issues statewide general NPDES permits. The SWRCB also administers the state's water rights program. *See* chapter 13.

Regional water quality control boards. The nine RWQCBs implement state water policy on a regional basis and establish regional water quality standards and policy. Regional boards are established along major drainages within the state, as depicted in Figure 10-1. RWQCBs implement and ensure compliance with the Porter-Cologne Act, including adopted federal standards, and the CWA. RWQCBs are comprised of a board with members who serve staggered terms. The Boards have both administrative rulemaking and adjudicatory powers.

RWQCBs are responsible for creating and implementing regional water quality control plans, also called basin plans.

RWQCBs are responsible for creating and implementing regional water quality control plans, also called basin plans. Regionally, each basin plan is tailored to the unique characteristics of that watershed and provides a scientific and regulatory basis for each regional board's water protection efforts.

The boards issue and enforce WDRs, including NPDES permits. Specifically, RWQCBs issue facility-specific WDR and NPDES permits within their regions, as well as general WDRs and NPDES permits to regulate similar waste discharges within each region. RWQCBs, as well as the SWRCB, implement water quality monitoring and reporting programs and have authority to issue enforceable orders.

The SWRCB and the nine RWQCBS are collectively referred to as the "Water Boards."

Ocean Protection Council. This council is authorized to protect coastal water habitat. The Council is comprised of the Resources Agency, the California Environmental Protection Agency, and the chair of the State Lands Commission. It is required to establish a science advisory team to incorporate the best available science into the council's decisions.

Governor's Office of Emergency Services. This office plans for statewide disasters and receives notifications and reports of chemical spills in the environment.

California Department of Conservation. The Department of Conservation's Division of Oil, Gas, and Geothermal Resources (DOGGR) oversees the federal UIC program for discharge of oil and gas wastes, and implements the state regulatory program for stimulation of oil and gas wells ("fracking").

Department of Fish and Wildlife. This agency oversees oil contingency plans and other prevention programs to manage oil spills in marine waters.

WATER QUALITY PLANNING AND STANDARDS

FEDERAL REQUIREMENTS

Water quality standards (WQS) serve to protect the public health or welfare, and also enhance the quality of water. They reflect "the limits or levels of water quality

FIGURE 10-1
California Regional Water Quality Control Boards

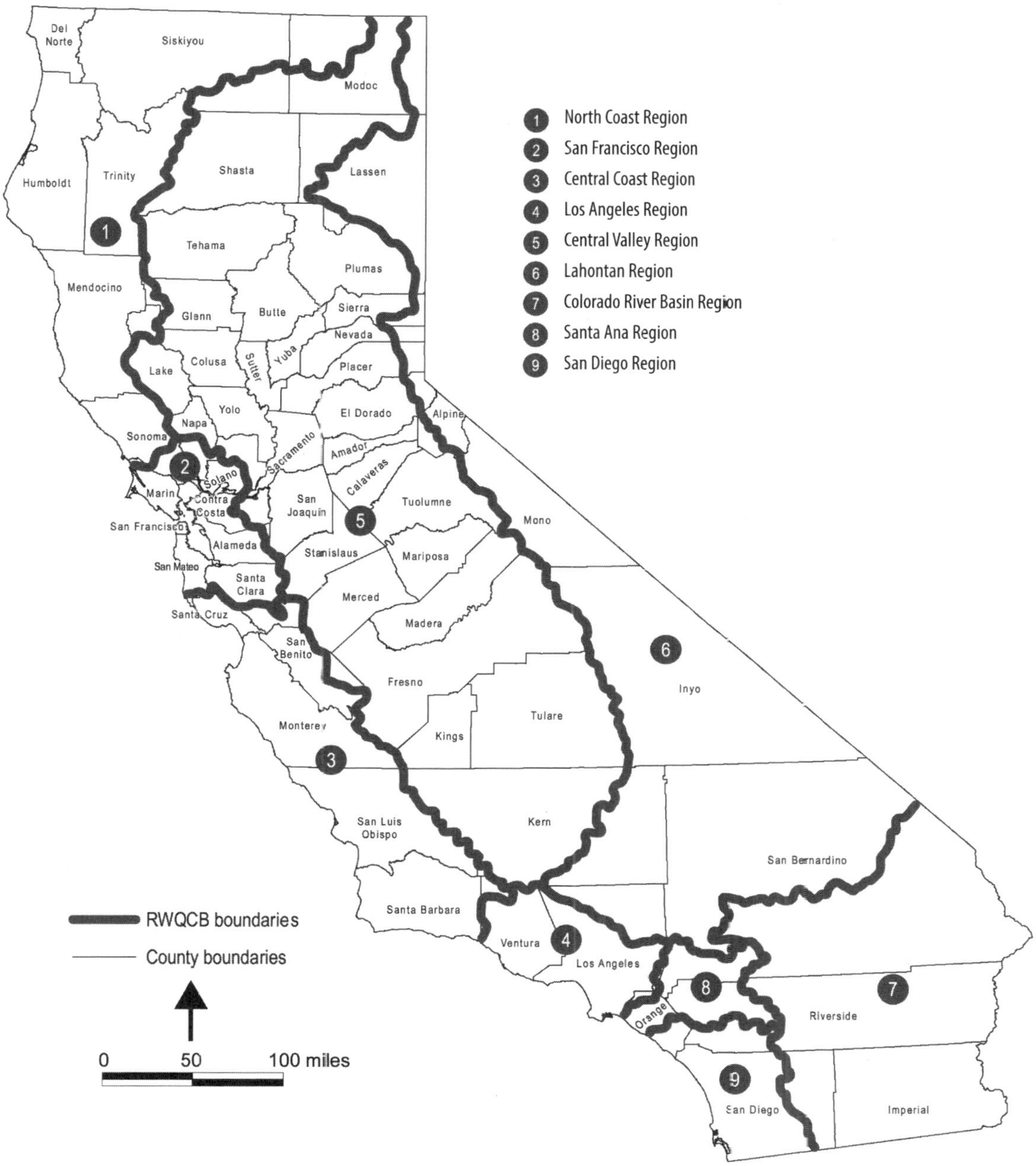

Source: State Water Resources Control Board

constituents or characteristics which are established for the reasonable protection of beneficial uses of water or the prevention of nuisance within a specific area." 40 C.F.R. §§ 130.2(d), 131.3(i). WQS include two components: beneficial uses of water, and water quality criteria to protect those uses. The CWA mandates that each state specify beneficial uses for each of its water bodies.

CTR = California toxics rule

STATE REQUIREMENTS

The state's water quality planning process consists primarily of developing, adopting, reviewing, and updating a variety of statewide water quality control plans and regional water quality control plans (basin plans). The SWRCB adopts statewide water quality plans, and the RWQCBs adopt basin plans. WQS contained in these plans are translated into effluent limitations written into NPDES permits and WDRs.

The SWRCB has adopted a number of statewide water quality control plans and policies, including:

Basin plans set forth water quality objectives for beneficial uses such as contact recreation.

- Statement of Policy with Respect to Maintaining High Quality of Waters in California (antidegradation plan)
- Ocean Plan
- Enclosed Bays and Estuaries Plan
- Inland Surface Water Plan
- Thermal Plan (temperature control in coastal and interstate waters and in enclosed bays and estuaries)
- Bay-Delta Plan (Sacramento-San Joaquin Delta and Suisun Marsh)
- Lake Tahoe Basin Water Quality Plan
- Sources of drinking water policy

California toxics rule. States are required to adopt numeric water quality criteria for priority toxic pollutants if there is a reasonable chance that the pollutant could interfere with the designated beneficial uses of the state's water. In April 1991, California adopted numeric criteria for priority toxic pollutants. However, two of the state's water control plans (the Inland Surface Water Plan and the Enclosed Bays and Estuaries Plan) were rescinded by a 1994 state court decision, leaving the state without numeric water quality criteria for many toxic pollutants. EPA responded by issuing a final rule known as the California toxics rule (CTR). 33 U.S.C. § 1313. CTR criteria, along with beneficial use designations in California's basin plans, constitute WQS for priority toxic pollutants in California inland and estuarine surface waters.

Originally published in 1997, the CTR became effective on May 18, 2000. 65 C.F.R. § 31681. The CTR establishes ambient aquatic life criteria for 23 priority toxic pollutants, as well as ambient human health criteria for 57 priority toxic pollutants. The rule also authorizes the state to conditionally issue compliance schedules for new or revised NPDES permit limits based on the federal criteria. Until the state re-adopts its own numeric criteria for toxics, the federal criteria apply to the state's inland surface waters, enclosed bays, and estuaries, in addition to state-adopted water quality standards contained in the basin plans.

WQO = water quality objective

Table 10-1. Examples of Beneficial Uses

General category	Beneficial uses
Supply	Municipal and domestic supply, agricultural supply, industrial process supply, industrial service supply, groundwater recharge, freshwater replenishment, navigation, hydropower generation, aquaculture, commercial fisheries, shellfish harvesting
Recreation	Water contact recreation, non-contact water recreation, sport fishing
Wildlife protection	Freshwater habitat, saline water habitat, estuarine habitat, marine habitat, wildlife habitat, endangered species habitat, aquatic organism migration, spawning, areas of special biological significance

Beneficial uses. In its basin plan, each RWQCB identifies desired beneficial uses for specified surface and groundwaters located within that region (e.g., waters for spawning, fishing, recreation). Examples of beneficial uses are presented in Table 10-1.

Water quality objectives. In California, water quality criteria adopted to protect uses of water ("beneficial uses") are called water quality objectives (WQOs). Basin plans establish WQOs, in numeric and narrative form, for specified water bodies and for particular segments of water bodies. Numeric WQOs serve as the upper limits for specified pollutants allowed in receiving waters for permits, while narrative WQOs are translated into appropriate numerical permit limits where feasible. Establishing such numerical limits may involve reviewing the maximum contaminant levels under the state or federal Safe Drinking Water Acts (*see* chapter 11) or evaluating ambient water quality criteria, cancer risk estimates, or health advisories. SWRCB 2016.

In California, water quality criteria adopted to protect uses of water ("beneficial uses") are called water quality objectives.

For example, the San Francisco Bay RWQCB's basin plan establishes WQOs for the following constituents and parameters:

- Bacteria
- Bioaccumulation
- Biostimulatory substances
- Color
- Dissolved oxygen
- Floating material
- Oil and grease
- Population and Community Ecology
- pH
- Radioactivity
- Salinity
- Sediment
- Settleable material
- Sulfides
- Taste and Odors
- Suspended material
- Temperature
- Toxicity
- Turbidity
- Un-iodized ammonia

Sources of drinking water policy. This policy (SWRCB Resolution No. 88-63) implements the Safe Drinking Water and Toxic Enforcement Act of 1986 (otherwise known as Proposition 65). This policy provides that all surface and groundwater of the state must be protected as existing or potential sources of municipal and domestic supply, unless the water body meets certain conditions.

The antidegradation policy provides that existing high water quality (exceeding water quality standards) can be "degraded" only if it can be demonstrated to the SWRCB or RWQCB that any such change is in the best interest of the people of California.

Antidegradation policy. Another important policy for water quality control is the antidegradation policy (SWRCB Resolution No. 68-16), which is derived from EPA's antidegradation policy (40 C.F.R. § 131.12). The antidegradation policy provides that existing high water quality (exceeding water quality standards) can be "degraded" only if it can be demonstrated to the SWRCB or RWQCB that any such change is in the best interest of the people of California. Specifically, the degradation must:

- Be consistent with the maximum benefit to the people of the state
- Not unreasonably affect present or probable future beneficial uses of such water
- Not result in water quality less than prescribed in state policies

The antidegradation policy must be considered when arriving at numerical water quality limits in water quality permits.

POINT SOURCE AND GROUNDWATER PERMIT PROGRAMS

FEDERAL POINT SOURCE PROGRAMS

Applicability. The CWA prohibits the discharge of any pollutant by any person to waters of the United States, except pursuant to the NPDES permitting program. 40 C.F.R.§ 122. The NPDES program requires permits for discharge:

- Of "pollutants"
- From a "point source"
- Into "waters of the United States"

The CWA's definition of "pollutant" (adopted by reference in California) includes:

- Dredged spoil
- Solid waste
- Incinerator residue
- Filter backwash
- Sewage
- Garbage
- Sewage sludge
- Munitions
- Chemical wastes
- Biological materials
- Radioactive materials (except those regulated under the Atomic Energy Act of 1954, as amended (42 U.S.C. § 2011 *et seq.*)
- Heat
- Wrecked or discarded equipment
- Rock
- Sand
- Cellar dirt
- Industrial, municipal, and agricultural waste discharged into water

Excluded from the CWA definition of pollutant is sewage from vessels, and some water and materials associated with oil or gas production. 40 C.F.R. § 122.2.

A "point source" is defined by federal regulations "as any discernible, confined, and discrete conveyance." This includes any pipes, ditches, channels, tunnels, conduits, wells, vessels, and more. 40 C.F.R. § 122.2. The Sixth Circuit Court of Appeals invalidated the long-standing exclusion for agricultural return flows and stormwater runoff from the definition of point source (see *National Cotton Council, et al. v. EPA* (6th Cir. 2009) 553 F.3d 927). The court determined that point source discharges of biological pesticides and chemical pesticides leave a residue in "waters of the U.S." and are thus pollutants under the CWA. EPA responded by issuing an NPDES "pesticides general permit" for point source discharges arising from pesticide applications.

A "point source" includes any pipes, ditches, channels, tunnels, conduits, wells, vessels, and more.

Under California law, agricultural sources are covered under a conditional waiver that allows RWQCBs to waive WDRs for a certain type of discharge based on specified criteria (*see* below). In addition, the Ninth Circuit Court of Appeals has narrowed this exception and found that aerial spraying constitutes a point source that requires an NPDES permit. *League of Wilderness Defenders/Blue Mountain Diversity Project et al. v. Forsgren et al.* (9th Cir. 2002) 309 F. 3d 1181.

The term "waters of the United States" is defined to include (40 C.F.R. § 122.2):

- Waters used in interstate or foreign commerce
- All interstate waters
- Intrastate waters where use, degradation, or destruction could affect interstate commerce
- Impoundments of any of the above
- Tributaries of any of the above
- The territorial sea
- Wetlands adjacent to any of the above

The courts, mostly in the context of wetlands regulation, have interpreted the term "waters of the United States" extensively. *See* chapter 15 ("Wetlands") for a discussion of recent judicial interpretations and regulatory attempts to more clearly define "waters of the United States." Groundwater is not a water of the United States unless there is a known direct conduit from the groundwater to surface water.

Key features of the NPDES and related programs are summarized in Table 10-2 on the following page.

Technology-based effluent limitations. Effluent limitations are NPDES permit limits on the quality of wastewater that may be discharged from point sources. There are two types of effluent limitations. Technology-based limitations are

Table 10-2. National Pollutant Discharge Elimination System Permitting Summary

Clean Water Act program	Program features	CWA regulatory citation
NPDES permitting	Addresses requirements for standard permits, general permits, and municipal separate storm sewer systems (MS4s)	40 C.F.R. Part 122
State authorization	Outlines EPA procedures for approving, revising, and withdrawing state NPDES programs (California has been delegated authority to implement the NPDES program)	40 C.F.R. Part 123
Permit approval provisions	Establishes procedures to evaluate NPDES permit applications and to issue NPDES permits	40 C.F.R. Part 124
NPDES technology-based treatment requirements	Establishes criteria and standards for technology-based treatment requirements	40 C.F.R. Part 125
Toxic pollutants	Provides toxic "priority pollutant" effluent standards and prohibitions	40 C.F.R. Part 129
Effluent limitation guidelines	Provides technology-based effluent guidelines and standards for existing and new sources based on certain industrial classifications	40 C.F.R. Part 401, 405–499
Water quality standards	Describes requirements and procedures for state development and approval of water quality standards; additional specific requirements are in 40 C.F.R. § 131.37	40 C.F.R. Part 131
Pretreatment requirements	Establishes pretreatment standards for pollutants passing through publicly owned treatment works	40 C.F.R. Part 403

Source: 40 C.F.R .§§ 112, 123–125, 129, 131, 401, 405, 499

POTWs = publicly-owned treatment works

ELGs = effluent limitation guidelines and standards

established industry-by-industry and apply nationwide. Water quality-based limitations are derived for individual water bodies. For an individual NPDES permit, the stricter of the two limitations applies.

Technology-based effluent limitations serve as a minimum level of effluent water quality control. These limitations apply uniformly to industry categories, regardless of where the discharge occurs or the quality of the surface water receiving the discharge. For example, the standards for a semiconductor plant may be different than for a power plant. Nonetheless, standards will be the same for all semiconductor facilities, whether the facility is in San Francisco discharging into the San Francisco Bay or in New York City discharging into the Hudson River. Similarly, all publicly-owned treatment works (POTWs) are required to provide a minimum of secondary wastewater treatment.

General requirements for technology-based water quality limitations are in 40 C.F.R. § 125.3; industry-specific requirements known as categorical effluent limitation guidelines and standards (ELGs) are in 40 C.F.R. §§ 405–499. These categorical effluent limitations are established for conventional, nonconventional, and toxic pollutants, as well as new sources and indirect discharges for the following industrial categories (40 C.F.R. Part 122):

BOD = biochemical oxygen demand

- Adhesives and sealants
- Aluminum forming
- Auto
- Battery manufacturing
- Coal mining
- Coil coating
- Copper forming
- Electrical and electronic components
- Electroplating
- Explosives manufacturing
- Foundries
- Gum and wood chemicals
- Inorganic chemicals manufacturing
- Iron and steel manufacturing
- Leather tanning and finishing
- Mechanical products manufacturing
- Nonferrous metals manufacturing
- Ore mining
- Organic chemicals manufacturing
- Paint and ink formulation
- Pesticides
- Petroleum refining
- Pharmaceutical preparations
- Photographic equipment and supplies
- Plastics processing
- Plastic and synthetic materials manufacturing
- Porcelain enameling
- Printing and publishing
- Pulp and paper mills
- Rubber processing
- Soap and detergent manufacturing
- Steam electric power plants
- Textile mills
- Timber products

The ELGs for each industrial category must meet specific standards for three types of pollutants: conventional, nonconventional, and toxic. Conventional pollutants consist of the following typical, higher volume pollutants found in municipal wastewater (40 C.F.R. § 401.16):

- Biochemical oxygen demand (BOD)
- Fecal coliform
- pH
- Oil and grease

Nonconventional pollutants consist of all pollutants other than conventional and toxic pollutants, and include:

- Chemical oxygen demand
- Total organic carbon
- Nitrogen
- Phosphorus
- Ammonia
- Sulfide

Table 10-3. Effluent Limitation Guidelines by Pollutant Source

Pollutant source	Level of treatment
Conventional	BCT/BPT
Non-conventional	BAT/BPT
Toxic	BAT/BPT

Table 10-4. Examples of Effluent Limitation Guidelines by Industrial Category

Industry	Effluent limitation guidelines
Battery manufacturing	BPT, BAT, NSPS, PSES, PSNS
Dairy products processing	BPT, BCT, NSPS, PSES, PSNS
Electrical and electronic components	BPT, BCT, BAT, NSPS, PSES, PSNS
Explosives manufacturing	BPT
Inorganic chemicals manufacturing	BPT, BAT, NSPS, PSES, PSNS (limited BCT)
Organic chemicals manufacturing	BPT, BCT, BAT, NSPS, PSES, PSNS
Petroleum refining	BPT, BCT, BAT, NSPS, PSES, PSNS
Pharmaceutical manufacturing	BPT, BCT, BAT, NSPS, PSES, PSNS
Pulp and paper mills	BPT, BCT, BAT, NSPS, PSES, PSNS
Steam electric power plants	BPT, BAT, BCT, NSPS, PSES, PSNS
Timber products processing	BPT, BCT, BAT, NSPS, PSES, PSNS

Source: 40 C.F.R. Part 400 *et seq.*

BCT = best conventional pollutant control technology

BAT = best available technology economically achievable

BPT = best practicable control technology currently available

NSPS = new source performance standards

PSES = pretreatment standards for existing sources

PSNS = pretreatment standards for new sources

SIC = Standard Industrial Classification

Toxic pollutants consist of 65 specified pollutant categories commonly categorized as heavy metals, organics, and pesticides. 40 C.F.R. § 401.15.

The ELGs for conventional pollutants are based on a "best conventional pollutant control technology" (BCT) standard, which considers what controls are technologically and economically achievable in relation to the benefits. The ELGs for nonconventional and toxic pollutants are based on a "best available technology economically achievable" (BAT) standard, which considers what controls are technologically and economically achievable but does not balance the cost of attainability against the potential benefit. Additionally, a "best practicable control technology currently available" (BPT) standard may be used where the BCT or BAT standard is equivalent to the BPT (an older standard), or where the BCT or BAT standard has not yet been promulgated. Effluent limitation guidelines by pollutant source are summarized in Table 10-3.

The ELGs for new dischargers are the "new source performance standards" (NSPS), which represent state-of-the-art treatment technology. The ELGs for indirect dischargers (into publicly owned treatment works, discussed in further detail below) include "pretreatment standards for existing sources" (PSES) and "pretreatment standards for new sources" (PSNS).

A given industrial source type or category typically shares similar wastewater discharge characteristics, and accordingly is subject to industry-specific ELGs defined by Standard Industrial Classification (SIC) code. Each ELG sets forth the following: applicability criteria, definitions, effluent limitations, process procedures, operating methods, and pretreatment requirements. ELG examples for some industrial categories are shown in Table 10-4.

WQBEL = water quality-based effluent limitation

DMR = discharge monitoring report

An applicant for an NPDES permit must, at a minimum, meet the nationwide, industry-specific, technology-based ELG for the conventional, nonconventional, and toxic pollutants they discharge. Where no ELGs are established, a best professional judgment standard must be applied by the permitting authority on a case-by-case basis. 33 U.S.C. § 1342.

Water quality-based effluent limitations. Where technology-based ELGs are not sufficient to meet a state or federal water quality standard, EPA or the state is required to establish more stringent water quality-based effluent limitations (WQBELs). WQBELs also may be developed for discharges that are not subject to categorical effluent limitations. WQBELs may be derived from water quality standards or TMDLs, where TMDLs have been established.

NPDES permitting process. The NPDES permit application must be completed and submitted at least 180 days before commencing the discharge. 40 C.F.R. § 122.21. Permit applications must include:

- General facility information
- Expected effluent characteristics
- Effluent flow rate
- A proposed treatment system

A final NPDES permit will set forth, among other requirements, effluent limitations, monitoring, and reporting obligations. In addition, NPDES permits often include standard terms and conditions addressing, among other things, proper operation of treatment systems, prohibitions against bypass, and what to do if a treatment system upset occurs. NPDES permits must be renewed every five years. Stormwater discharges today are regulated by special NPDES programs (discussed later in this chapter).

NPDES permits often include standard terms and conditions addressing, among other things, proper operation of treatment systems, prohibitions against bypass, and what to do if a treatment system upset occurs.

National Pollutant Discharge Elimination System monitoring. An essential element of an NPDES permit is the monitoring of discharges and the submittal of discharge monitoring reports (DMRs). Typical NPDES monitoring requirements are in Table 10-5 on the following page.

Pretreatment permitting. Some industrial facilities do not directly discharge wastewater into surface waters. Rather, they indirectly discharge their wastewater via a sanitary sewer to a POTW. These indirect dischargers, both new and existing sources, are subject to specified pretreatment discharge limitations prior to discharging wastewaters to the sanitary sewer system. In this case, the POTW or municipality, in lieu of the RWQCB, serves as the permitting authority for those facilities discharging to its sanitary sewer system. In California, municipalities typically incorporate relevant pretreatment requirements into their ordinances.

Among other things, pretreatment standards are designed to prevent the introduction of pollutants to the POTW that would interfere with operations and to

Table 10-5. Typical Monitoring Requirements of the National Pollutant Discharge Elimination System Program

Parameter/Constituent	Units	Sampling type	Sampling frequency	Reporting frequency
Flow	million gallons per day	N/A	Daily/monthly	Quarterly
Biochemical oxygen demand	lbs/day	24-hour composite	Daily/monthly	Quarterly
Total suspended solids	lbs/day	24-hour composite	Daily/monthly	Quarterly
pH	pH	Grab	Daily/monthly	Quarterly
Settleable material	mL/L	Grab	Daily/monthly	Quarterly
Bioassay	% survival	24-hour composite	Weekly	Quarterly
Temperature	degrees	Grab	Daily	N/A
Metals	mg/L	24-hour composite	Quarterly	Quarterly

SIU = significant industrial user

prevent pollutants incompatible with the POTW from passing through. Effluent limitation guidelines for indirect dischargers are based upon requirements in CWA § 307. 33. U.S.C. § 1317.

Federal pretreatment standards have been established for the following classes of pollutants:

- Flammability
- pH
- Obstruction (viscosity)
- BOD
- Temperature
- Petroleum oils lubricants
- Toxic gases, fumes, vapors
- Trucked pollutants

The federal pretreatment standards depend on whether the indirect discharger is a new or existing discharger and whether it is a "significant industrial user" (SIU). An SIU has throughput exceeding 25 kilograms of process wastewater daily or greater than five percent hydraulic or organic flow of a POTW, or where the discharge could result in the reasonable potential to cause pass through and compromise the POTW. Some SIUs are subject to categorical pretreatment requirements.

Local POTWs may require the discharger to develop a plan to control the fats, oils and greases discharged to the treatment system as well as a slug discharge control plan.

Local POTWs may impose more stringent pretreatment standards. POTWs will sometimes issue individual, site-specific pretreatment permits governing discharges while others will publish ordinances which function like a "permit-by-rule." Local POTWs may require the discharger to develop a plan to control the fats, oils and greases discharged to the treatment system as well as a slug discharge control plan. Slug discharge control plans are intended to prevent accidental spills or batch discharges to a sanitary sewer.

TMDL = total maximum daily load

WLA = waste load allocation

UIC = Underground Injection Control

Total maximum daily loads. Section 303(d) of the CWA requires each state to develop a list of impaired water bodies (segments of surface waters that do not meet WQS). The list must be based on "all existing and readily available water quality-related data and information," must identify specific pollutant(s) causing impairment, and must be ranked by priority. 33 U.S.C. § 1313(d).

States must then develop total maximum daily loads (TMDLs) to restore the § 303(d)-listed water bodies. TMDLs calculate the maximum amount of a pollutant that a water body can receive from both point and nonpoint sources (its loading capacity) and still attain WQS. TMDLs may include more than one water body and more than one pollutant. (For example, see San Francisco Bay RWQCB's TMDL for diazinon and pesticide-related toxicity in Bay Area urban creeks.)

Each TMDL uses the loading capacity, in conjunction with a margin of safety, to allocate pollutant loadings among point and nonpoint sources. These allocations are called waste load allocations (WLAs) and load allocations, respectively. If WLAs are more stringent than other WQBELs, or more stringent than technology-based limitations, the WLAs are incorporated into NPDES permits. EPA issued controversial rules that require waste load allocations for nonpoint sources of pollution. 40 C.F.R. § 130.

In the 1990s, California, along with other states, failed to submit its list of impaired waters to EPA as required by the CWA. Environmental advocacy groups then compelled California to prepare its list of impaired waters and to prepare TMDLs, resulting in a number of TMDLs driven by consent decrees. In 2002, the SWRCB identified and EPA approved a list of more than 600 impaired stream segments, river segments, lakes, and estuaries. At the time of book publication, the most current list of impaired waters was available at www.waterboards.ca.gov/water_issues/programs/tmdl/integrated2012.shtml.

Thermal discharges. Many industrial facilities take in large volumes of surface water to cool their facilities. This can result in killing and injuring fish and fish eggs from heat, physical stress, or by chemicals used to clean cooling systems. Thermal rules require dischargers, such as large power plants and new offshore and coastal oil and gas extraction facilities, to comply with location, design, construction and capacity requirements for cooling water intake structures, and to meet BAT to minimize adverse environmental impacts. CWA § 316(b).

Many industrial facilities take in large volumes of surface water to cool their facilities that can result in killing and injuring fish and fish eggs from heat, physical stress, or by chemicals used to clean cooling systems.

FEDERAL GROUNDWATER PROGRAMS

Underground injection control wells. The Underground Injection Control (UIC) program (40 C.F.R. § 144) established under the federal SDWA protects drinking water in underground aquifers. The program regulates over 400,000 wells that pump waste fluids into the ground (i.e., in soils and porous rock formations above the water table, in groundwater aquifers, in deep geological formations) (safewater.zendesk.com/hc/en-us/articles/211398248-How-many-of-each-type-class-of-underground-injection-control-UIC-wells-are-in-the-United-States-In-each-state-). The SDWA specifically

Table 10-6. Underground Injection Control Well Classifications by Agency		
Type of discharge	**UIC well classification**	**Agency**
Deep wells	Class 1	Environmental Protection Agency
Oil and gas injection wells	Class 2	California Department of Conservation
Mining wells	Class 3	Environmental Protection Agency
Shallow hazardous and radioactive injection wells	Class 4	Environmental Protection Agency
Shallow injection wells	Class 5	Environmental Protection Agency

Source: 40 C.F.R. Part 144

exempts hydraulic fracturing (i.e., "fracking") from these requirements. The UIC program regulates discharges of:

- Hazardous wastes
- Wastes from oil and gas exploration and production (i.e., the re-injection of briny waters)
- Fluid injection for mineral extraction
- On-site disposal systems (e.g., stormwater drainage wells, cesspools, and septic system leach fields) are used by individuals and businesses to discharge non-hazardous fluids into septic systems and leach fields (known as Class V wells).

Table 10-6 depicts UIC well classifications and the agencies responsible for managing individual classes of UIC wells.

Sole source aquifer protection program. The EPA defines a sole source aquifer as a "principal source aquifer which supplies at least 50 percent of the drinking water consumed in the area overlying the aquifer." The sole source aquifer protection program is authorized under the SDWA and allows EPA to determine whether an aquifer is the sole or principal source of drinking water for an area. Under the program, EPA reviews federally financed projects that are proposed for an aquifer area and determines whether there is a possibility of source contamination. The sole source aquifer demonstration program creates procedures for developing, implementing, and evaluating demonstrations to protect critical aquifer protection areas. 42 U.S.C. § 300h-c; 40 C.F.R. § 149.

STATE PERMITTING REQUIREMENTS

Waste discharge requirements. The Porter-Cologne Act governs discharges of waste that could affect the quality of the waters of the state. The Act regulates individual dischargers of both point sources (e.g., an industrial discharge from a pipe to surface water) and nonpoint sources (e.g., potential releases from landfills). Waters of the state include both surface waters and groundwater in California.

Waters of the state include both surface waters and groundwater in California.

Where waste discharges could affect the quality of the waters of the state, the discharger must obtain a WDR permit. In California, an individual NPDES permit is technically a type of WDR granted by RWQCB order. Therefore, every individual NPDES permit applicant must fill out a state Report of Waste Discharge form (basically, an application form) in addition to the standard NPDES permit application forms. The RWQCB then issues either a combined NPDES permit/WDR or just a WDR. A WDR sets limits on discharge by specifying effluent limits, receiving water limits, prohibitions, or best management practices, or a combination of these. The SWRCB issues a statewide or general permit for stormwater (discussed below). Water Code §§ 13260(a)(1), 13263(a).

A WDR sets limits on discharge by specifying effluent limits, receiving water limits, prohibitions, or best management practices, or a combination of these.

Like NPDES permits, complete WDR applications must be submitted to the RWQCB within 180 days of the proposed discharge. While NPDES permits last for five years, WDRs can last for longer than five years. Complete renewal applications must be submitted within 180 days prior to the expiration date.

Permitting process. The water quality permitting process in California begins with determining whether a pollutant:

- Potentially could threaten a designated beneficial use of water
- Will be released to surface water (thus requiring an NPDES permit and a WDR)
- Will be released to groundwater (thus requiring a WDR)
- Will be treated, stored, or disposed of in a waste management unit, thus requiring a WDR (*see* below)

Next, the applicant must determine whether the proposed activity could impair present or probable future beneficial uses by consulting the WQOs for those uses, or whether it could cause nuisance. Finally, the concentrations of the projected constituents must be compared against the narrative and numerical WQOs and anti-degradation policies.

General WDRs. The SRWCB and RWQCBs via General Orders have issued General WDRs governing certain categories of discharges. If a discharger complies with the terms and conditions of a General WDR, a project-specific Report of Waste Discharge may not be required. Examples of General WDRs include those adopted for small domestic wastewater systems (SWRCB) and for existing dairies (Central Valley RWQCB).

Water reclamation requirements for recycled water use. In 2016, the SWRCB adopted General Order WQ 2016-0068-DDW, which establishes a separate permitting program for recycled water use. Under this approach, new recycled water uses can be authorized by a single permit that can be used across RWQCB boundaries if certain water reclamation requirements are met. The permitting program governs non-potable uses of treated municipal wastewater, for example landscape and crop irrigation, dust control, and industrial and commercial cooling.

SWPPP = stormwater pollution prevention plan

MS4 = municipal separate storm sewer system

NONPOINT SOURCE PERMIT PROGRAMS

Despite a quarter century of rigorous water quality control many surface waters in the United States remain impaired for their beneficial uses. Much of this remaining impairment is due to diffuse nonpoint sources, which represent significant exceptions carved out of the definition of point source. For example, agricultural runoff and irrigation return flows, and most silvicultural activities, were and continue to be outside of the CWA's definition of point source.

STORMWATER PERMIT PROGRAMS

Nonpoint sources are managed through a national program established by Section 319 of the CWA (33 U.S.C. § 1329). Major elements of the stormwater program include:

- Individual NPDES permits (which are also WDRs and administered in California by the RWQCBs)
- General NPDES permits (for industrial discharges, construction activities, and municipalities) (which are also WDRs and administered in California by RWQCBs)
- Stormwater pollution prevention plans (SWPPPs)
- Effluent Limitations (for specified industrial dischargers)
- Training (and certification in California)
- Monitoring
- Annual reporting

The Clean Water Act regulates urban runoff via stormwater permit programs.

The CWA amendments of 1987 required EPA to develop a regulatory program to manage stormwater. 33 U.S.C. § 1342(p). This program requires large and small municipalities to seek NPDES permits to regulate stormwater; it also requires certain industrial facilities and construction sites to obtain NPDES stormwater permits. 40 C.F.R. § 122.26.

Municipal stormwater. Urban stormwater runoff is a nonpoint source, but becomes a point source when collected in a storm sewer pipe. When discussing stormwater discharges, it is useful to distinguish between two types of municipal sewer systems:

- Sanitary sewer systems, which receive domestic sewage and industrial wastewaters that typically route to a POTW
- Municipal separate storm sewer systems (MS4s) that collect stormwater precipitation (e.g., from rain, snow, sleet, and freezing rain)

Stormwater is discharged in either a separate municipal separate storm sewer system, or in a combined sanitary and stormwater sewer system. Figure 10-2 shows the two types of sewer systems and illustrates that stormwater in an MS4 is not

FIGURE 10-2
Sanitary and Stormwater Sewer Systems Compared

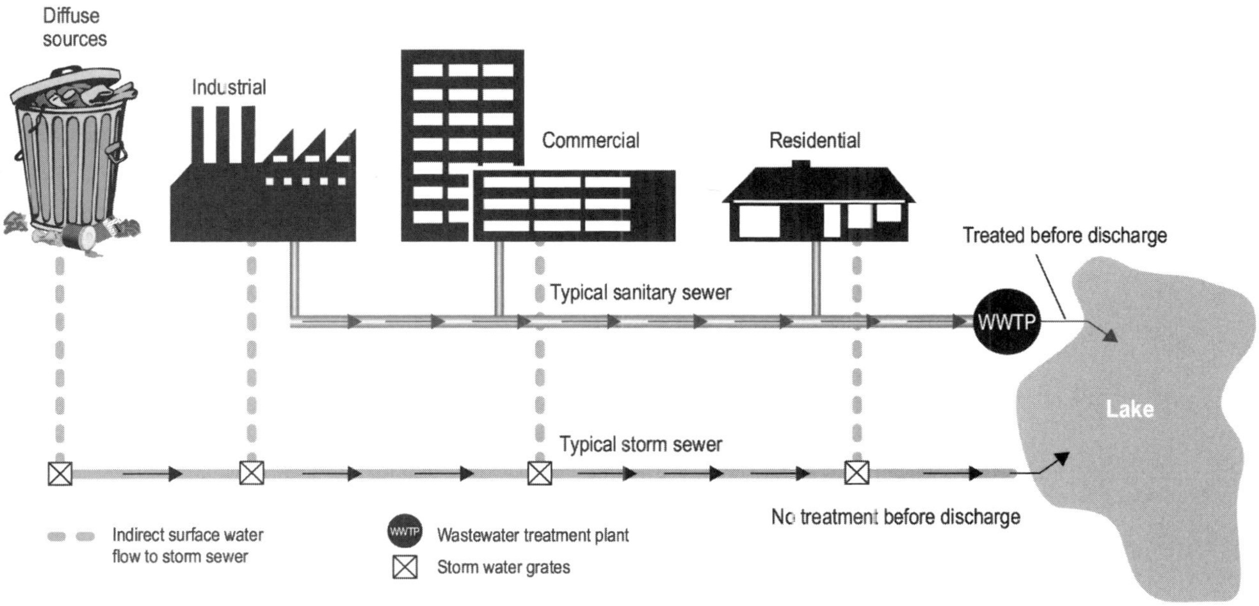

BMP = best management practice

treated, unlike stormwater in a sanitary sewer system or a combined storm/sanitary system.

Municipalities serving large populations (over 100,000) are subject to Phase I MS4 permit requirements. An MS4 is "a conveyance or system of conveyances (including roads with drainage systems, municipal streets, catch basins, curbs, gutters, ditches, man-made channels, or storm drains)." Municipalities must control stormwater pollution to the "maximum extent practicable." 33 U.S.C. § 1342(p). In addition, municipalities must implement, at a minimum, the following best management practices (BMPs): public education and outreach, public participation and involvement, illicit discharge detection and elimination, construction site run-off control, post-construction run-off, and pollution prevention and good housekeeping measures.

Municipalities must obtain renewed permits from the RWQCB every five years. NPDES regulations require that all MS4 permits incorporate a monitoring program in order to evaluate run-off and water received. The monitoring program creates an evaluation process for environmental risks associated with stormwater discharges that include identifying the types and quantity of pollutants, the possible sources of pollutants, and the effectiveness of permit requirements and stormwater management plans.

Municipalities serving small populations (less than 100,000) are subject to a "small MS4 General Permit (known as "Phase II") that includes municipal governments and non-traditional municipalities (e.g., state and federal facilities,

SMARTS = Stormwater Multiple Application and Report Tracking System

NAL = numeric action level

IGP = Industrial General Permit

universities, and military bases). On February 5, 2013 the Phase II Small MS4 General Permit was adopted; it became effective on July 1, 2013. Permittees obtain coverage under this General Permit by filing an electronic notice of intention (NOI) through the SWRCB's Stormwater Multiple Application and Report Tracking System (SMARTS) and by mailing the appropriate permit fee to the SWRCB. This General Permit specifies the actions necessary to reduce the discharge of pollutants in stormwater to the maximum extent practicable in a manner designed to achieve compliance with water quality standards and objectives.

Industrial stormwater. Federal stormwater regulations require industrial facilities included in one of 11 listed categories to acquire an NPDES stormwater permit:

- Category one. Facilities with effluent limitations
- Category two. Manufacturing
- Category three. Mineral, metal, oil and gas
- Category four. Hazardous waste, treatment, or disposal facilities
- Category five. Landfills
- Category six. Recycling facilities
- Category seven. Steam electric plants
- Category eight. Transportation facilities
- Category nine. Treatment works
- Category ten. Construction activity of one acre or more
- Category eleven. Light industrial activity

BMPs are required for construction activities.

Stormwater discharges associated with oil and gas exploration, production, or processing are also exempt from NPDES permits under the Energy Policy Act of 2005. 42 U.S.C. § 13201 *et seq.*

In California, an Industrial General Permit was initially adopted in 1997, and it was substantially revised in 2014. Significant changes from the 1997 permit include an increase in monitoring, sampling and reporting requirements; numeric action limits (NALs) for certain pollutants; new or improved best management practices associated with an exceedance of the NALs; the elimination of conditional exemptions, thereby increasing the number of covered facilities; and additional requirements for facilities that discharge to an impaired water body.

The 2014 Industrial General Permit (Order 2014-0057-DWQ, also known as the "IGP"), regulates operators of facilities discharging stormwater associated with industrial activity. To qualify for coverage under California's general industrial stormwater permit, a discharger must electronically submit an NOI through the SWRCB's SMARTS. Industrial stormwater discharges are conditionally excluded from the California IGP if there is no exposure of industrial activities and materials to stormwater runoff. Dischargers can avoid most of the IGP requirements by issuing a No Exposure Certification (NEC) completed by a Qualified Industrial Stormwater Practitioner (QISP) which must be annually recertified. Dischargers may also claim that the IGP does not apply by issuing a notice of non-applicability (i.e., NONA) if they are not the legal owner of the facility, the facility is closed, or an incorrect SIC Code was assigned to the facility. To be eligible, a California-licensed professional engineer must certify and electronically submit in SMARTS a NONA Technical Report supporting the "No Discharge" eligibility determination.

NEC = No Exposure Certification

QISP = Qualified Industrial Stormwater Practitioner

ERA = Exceedance Response Action

PRD = Permit Registration Document

NONA = notice of non-applicability

Facility operators must eliminate unauthorized non-stormwater discharges (NSWDs) and implement a set of minimum BMPs (mostly non-structural BMPs) and advanced BMPs (mostly structural, such as treatment and exposure reduction BMPs). Operators must arrange to have a trained staff member (i.e., a QISP) or delegate a QISP contractor to implement the IGP.

The California IGP requires dischargers (or their delegate) to visually monitor stormwater and collect samples for comparison to applicable NALs or "benchmark values."

Operators discharging pollutants to impaired waters (pursuant to CWA Section 303(d)) must also monitor for those parameters. Samples must be collected during scheduled facility operating hours. Facilities discharging through outfalls to the ocean must develop and implement a monitoring plan in line with the California Ocean Plan.

Operators must develop and implement an Exceedance Response Action (ERA) when they exceed an NAL, which includes annual and instantaneous maximum NALs. The discharger must evaluate and, where necessary, revise BMPs for a first-time NAL exceedance and submit a report prepared by a QISP. Upon a second exceedance for the same parameter, the discharger must submit a Level 2 ERA Action Plan and a Level 2 ERA Technical Report.

Dischargers must certify and submit permit-related compliance documents via SMARTS including Permit Registration Documents (PRDs), NOIs, NECs, and SWPPPs, annual reports, notices of termination, ERA reports and technical reports.

Under the IGP, the discharger also must prepare an SWPPP, which is intended to identify potential sources of stormwater pollution and to establish a program to minimize or eliminate pollutants that could be discharged during a storm event. When stormwater pollution cannot be avoided, treatment may be warranted before discharging the polluted stormwater. Typical requirements of an SWPPP include:

- Establishing a pollution prevention team to implement the SWPPP
- Identifying and inventorying significant materials that could come in contact with stormwater
- Delineating stormwater drainages

ILRP = Irrigated Lands Regulatory Program

- Developing BMPs to minimize or prevent pollution of stormwater by minimizing exposure of raw, final, or waste materials to rain, snow, snowmelt, and runoff
- Identifying cross-connections of piping to the storm sewer system, which could result in unpermitted discharges of process or non-process wastewater
- Developing procedures to review and update the SWPPP

BMPs are the heart of SWPPPs. BMPs can include managerial practices (e.g., good housekeeping and inspections) and structural measures (e.g., berming, covers, oil/water separators, grassy swales, rock-lined ditches, and detention ponds). EPA has developed a guidance manual to assist in developing and implementing SWPPPs for industrial facilities (EPA 2007).

Construction stormwater. The California Construction General Permit for stormwater (2009-0009-DWQ amended by 2010-0014-DWQ and 2012-0006-DWQ) governs construction or demolition activity (e.g., clearing, grading, grubbing, or excavation) involving one or more acres. It also regulates similar activity involving small linear underground and overhead projects disturbing at least one acre and less than five acres (including trenching and staging areas). Construction activity that disturbs less than one acre is governed by the general permit where the activity is part of a larger common development plan or sale of one or more acres. Small construction sites greater than one acre in size and less than five acres may seek a waiver by self-certifying that soil conditions result in low rainfall erosivity.

Dischargers must electronically file PRDs to obtain coverage under the general construction stormwater permit. The PRD must include, among other items, a NOI and SWPPP before commencing construction. EPA has developed a guidance manual to assist in developing and implementing SWPPPs for construction sites (EPA 2009).

Construction SWPPPs must include minimum BMPs and be developed by a Qualified SWPPP Developer and implemented by a Qualified SWPPP Practitioner. These stormwater practitioners must meet specified training and certifications.

A given construction project must be evaluated for its overall risk in terms of project sediment risk.

A given construction project must be evaluated for its overall risk in terms of project sediment risk (the relative amount of sediment that can be discharged given the project and location details) and the receiving water risk (the risk sediment discharges pose to the receiving waters). There are three risk levels presented in Figure 10-3.

Dischargers must conduct effluent monitoring and reporting for pH and turbidity involving stormwater discharges to evaluate whether NALs and numeric effluent limitation for active treatment systems are exceeded. Failure to take corrective action in light of an NAL exceedance may result in a violation.

The risk level for a given project dictates the rigor of stormwater effluent monitoring required. Risk Level 1 dischargers must analyze for any parameters

FIGURE 10-3
Combined Risk Level Matrix

<table>
<tr><th rowspan="2">Receiving Water Risk</th><th colspan="3">Sediment Risk</th></tr>
<tr><th>Low</th><th>Medium</th><th>High</th></tr>
<tr><td>Low</td><td>LEVEL 1</td><td colspan="2">LEVEL 2</td></tr>
<tr><td>High</td><td colspan="2">LEVEL 2</td><td>LEVEL 3</td></tr>
</table>

indicating the presence of pollutants identified in the pollutant source assessment. Risk Level 2 and 3 dischargers have greater monitoring and planning requirements.

Agricultural discharges. Water discharges from agricultural operations in California include irrigation runoff, flows from tile drains, and stormwater runoff. These discharges can affect water quality by transporting pollutants, including pesticides, sediment, nutrients, salts (including selenium and boron), pathogens, and heavy metals from cultivated fields into surface waters.

To prevent agricultural discharges from impairing the waters that receive these discharges, the state's Irrigated Lands Regulatory Program (ILRP) regulates discharges from irrigated agricultural lands. This is done by issuing WDRs or conditional waivers of WDRs (Orders) to growers. These Orders contain conditions requiring water quality monitoring of receiving waters and corrective actions when impairments are found. As of 2016, about six million acres of agricultural land and 40,000 growers were enrolled in the ILRP (www.swrcb.ca.gov/water_issues/programs/agriculture/).

In California's highly productive Central Valley, the Central Valley RWQCB has adopted a series of geographically-based WDRs for discharges from irrigated lands, to protect both surface water and groundwater. The WDRs replace earlier interim regulatory requirements under a conditional waiver of WDRs.

ADDITIONAL STATE NONPOINT SOURCE PROGRAMS

Discharges of waste to land: hazardous waste and nonhazardous solid waste. RWQCBs issue WDRs for indirect discharges of waste to land that have

Construction Stormwater Rules Largely Affirmed

The California Building Industry Association, the Building Industry Legal Defense 2009-0009-DWQ amended by 2010-0014-DWQ & 2012-0006-DWQ Foundation, and the California Business Properties Association (petitioners) challenged Order No. 2009-0009-DWQ in *California Building Industry Association et al. v. State Water Resources Control Board.* On December 27, 2011, the Superior Court issued a judgment and writ of mandamus ruling in favor of the SWRCB on almost all of the issues the petitioners raised. However, the court invalidated the numeric effluent limitations for pH and turbidity for Risk Level 3 and LUP Type 3 sites and suspended compliance storm event provisions and receiving water monitoring at Risk Level 3 and LUP Type 3 sites.

All sites not covered by a Phase I or Phase II MS4 NPDES permit must comply with runoff reduction performance standards and manage post-construction stormwater runoff impacts. Legally responsible parties must file a Notice of Termination with the RWQCB when construction is complete and final stabilization has been achieved or ownership has been transferred. Projects enrolled for more than one continuous three-month period must annually certify that the site complies with the general stormwater permit.

WMU = waste management unit

DTSC = Department of Toxic Substances Control

the potential to impair the quality of state waters. One set of regulations (often called Chapter 15 regulations) addresses the indirect discharge of hazardous waste to land; another set governs the treatment, storage, processing, or disposal of non-hazardous "solid waste" (includes refuse and "designated" wastes, nonhazardous solid wastes, and inert wastes, as discussed below) to land.

These regulatory programs set forth standards for locating, constructing, monitoring, closing, and post-closure maintenance of RCRA-type waste management units (WMUs), such as surface impoundments, landfills, and waste piles (see chapter 8 for a discussion of WMUs). State law allows alternatives to these standards where an engineering alternative is demonstrated to protect water quality. Water Code § 13172; 23 Cal. Code Regs. §§ 2510–2601 (dealing with hazardous waste); 27 Cal. Code Regs. § 20200 (governing nonhazardous waste). The regulatory programs regulate potential nonpoint sources of pollution by managing WMUs to prevent wastes from accidentally or indirectly discharging wastes to waters of the state.

The nonhazardous waste classification is further subdivided into designated waste, nonhazardous solid waste, or inert waste, based on the potential threat to beneficial uses of groundwater and surface water.

The Department of Toxic Substances Control (DTSC) is authorized to classify wastes as either hazardous waste (*see* chapter 8) or nonhazardous waste (*see* chapter 9). The nonhazardous waste classification is further subdivided into designated waste, nonhazardous solid waste, or inert waste, based on the potential threat to beneficial uses of groundwater and surface water.

Designated waste can be non-hazardous or hazardous waste. Designated waste that is non-hazardous waste consists of or contains pollutants that, under ambient environmental conditions at the WMU, could be released at concentrations exceeding applicable WQOs; designated waste that is hazardous waste is subject to a hazardous waste variance. Non-hazardous solid waste includes municipal solid waste or refuse with a significant proportion of degradable material. Inert waste includes paving fragments and non-degradable construction debris. 23 Cal. Code Regs. §§ 2521, 2523, 2524; 27 Cal. Code Regs. §§ 20210, 20220, 20230.

Each of the four waste classifications (hazardous, designated, non-hazardous solid, inert) has a corresponding minimum WMU classification, as shown in Figure 8-5, chapter 8. Important waste and WMU distinctions include:

- **Hazardous wastes.** May be treated, stored or disposed ("discharged") only to Class I WMUs. These heavily regulated units must be equipped with both natural geologic and engineered containment structures to ensure that the wastes will be not released to surface or groundwaters. Hazardous wastes may be "discharged" to a less protective Class II WMU pursuant to a hazardous waste variance granted by DTSC.
- **Designated wastes.** Must be discharged either to a Class II or optionally to **a Class I WMU.**

- **Nonhazardous solid wastes.** Must be discharged to Class III WMUs (although these waste units do not provide complete containment, but rather are designed to protect beneficial uses of water) or optionally in a Class I or Class II WMU.
- **Inert wastes.** May be discharged to "unclassified units" (which must be in a location and have equipment that prevents wastes from entering drainage courses) or optionally in a Class I, II, or III WMU.

UST = underground storage tank

Discharges of waste to land: underground injection, underground storage tanks, and septic systems. Discharges of waste to land also can occur through USTs and septic systems. Important regulatory program elements for these discharges include:

- California is delegated the authority by EPA to implement and enforce the injection of oil and gas wastes into underground wells. 14 Cal. Code Regs. § 1724. Discharge of other wastes into UIC wells is largely the domain of the federal SDWA (discussed above). California regulates new and existing USTs that store petroleum products and "hazardous substances." *See* chapter 7.
- California establishes minimum statewide standards that require the SWRCB to adopt minimum regulations for septic systems. Regulations address the construction, replacement, major repair of systems, and pooling or discharging to the surface. Water Code § 13290 *et seq.*

Regulation of fracking. SB 4 of 2013 (Chapter 313, Statutes of 2013) establishes a California regulatory program for well stimulation ("fracking") by amending multiple sections of the Public Resources Code and the Water Code. Among other things, SB 4 requires the Division of Oil, Gas, and Geothermal Resources (DOGGR, which is a division within the Department of Conservation) to adopt rules and regulations specific to well stimulation. *See* 14 Cal. Code Regs. § 1780 *et seq.* The regulations required by SB 4 govern the construction of stimulation wells and well casings; disclosure of the composition and disposition of well stimulation fluids; and procedures for DOGGR to issue well stimulation permits if certain conditions are met. SB 4 also requires the SWRCB to develop groundwater monitoring criteria, and implement a groundwater monitoring program for the state's oil and gas fields. Water Code § 10783.

SB 1281 of 2014 (Chapter 561, Statutes of 2014) expands this framework and requires DOGGR to compile data on unlined oil and gas field sumps. SB 1281 also requires well owners to collect and report the amount of water consumed as a result of oil and gas field activities.

Special landfill requirements. Landfill owners and operators must implement a water quality testing program to determine the water quality impacts of disposal sites. California requires the SWRCB to rank all active and inactive disposal sites based on the threat posed to water quality. Water Code § 13273. Current operators

Landfill owners and operators must implement a water quality testing program to determine the water quality impacts of disposal sites.

NOAA = National Oceanic and Atmospheric Administration

Cal/EPA = California Environmental Protection Agency

must complete a solid waste assessment test to evaluate the threat to groundwater and submit it to the RWQCB.

Toxic Pits Cleanup Act. The TPCA bans use of new surface impoundments that store or dispose of liquid hazardous wastes within one-half mile of potential sources of drinking water. Preexisting surface impoundments were required to be removed by June 30, 1988. Health & Safety Code § 25208 *et seq.*

OCEAN PROTECTION PROGRAMS

FEDERAL REGULATION OF OCEAN DUMPING

Prior to the Marine Protection, Research, and Sanctuaries Act of 1972 (P.L. 92-532), U.S. marine waters had been used extensively as a convenient alternative to land-based sites for the disposal of various wastes such as sewage sludge, industrial wastes, and pipeline discharges and runoff. The Act has two basic aims: to regulate intentional ocean disposal of materials, and to authorize related research. Title I of the Act, which is often referred to as the Ocean Dumping Act, contains permit and enforcement provisions for ocean dumping. Research provisions are contained in Title II; Title IV authorizes a regional marine research program; and Title V addresses coastal water quality monitoring.

Oil tanks are subject to SPCC requirements.

The basic provisions of the Act have remained virtually unchanged since 1972; however, many later authorities have been added. These later parts include (1) research responsibilities for EPA; (2) specific direction that EPA phase out the disposal of "harmful" sewage sludge and industrial wastes; (3) a ban on ocean disposal of sewage sludge and industrial wastes by December 31, 1991; (4) inclusion of Long Island Sound within the purview of the act; and (5) inclusion of medical waste provisions.

Four federal agencies have responsibilities under the Ocean Dumping Act: EPA, the U.S. Army Corps of Engineers, the National Oceanic and Atmospheric Administration (NOAA), and the Coast Guard. EPA has primary authority for regulating ocean disposal of all substances except dredged spoils, which are under the authority of the Corps of Engineers. NOAA is responsible for long-range research on the effects of human-induced changes to the marine environment, while EPA is authorized to carry out research and demonstration activities related to phasing out sewage sludge and industrial waste dumping. The Coast Guard is charged with maintaining surveillance of ocean dumping.

CALIFORNIA OCEAN PROTECTION ACT

The Legislature enacted the California Ocean Protection Act (Pub. Res. Code § 35500 *et seq.*) in response to several studies, including the Pew Oceans Commission Report (2003), which found the ocean habitat along California's 1,100-mile coastline to be in failing health. The Act establishes the Ocean Protection Council, comprised of the Secretaries of the Resources Agency and Cal/EPA, and the chair of the State Lands Commission. The Council is authorized to protect the state's coastal waters and ocean ecosystems.

The Act also establishes the California Ocean Protection Trust Fund, which is authorized to issue grants and loans for projects that:

- Eliminate or reduce threats to coastal and ocean ecosystems, habitats, and species
- Foster sustainable fisheries
- Improve coastal water quality
- Allow increased public access to oceans and coastal resources
- Improve management, conservation, and protection of coastal waters and ocean ecosystems
- Provide monitoring and scientific data to improve conservation and protection of ocean resources

MARINE PLASTIC POLLUTION

Stormwater is a leading cause of pollution along the California coast and in the ocean. Close to 80 percent of marine debris found on beaches and in the oceans is generated from the land—a significant proportion of which is plastic.

Close to 80 percent of marine debris found on beaches and in the oceans is generated from the land—a significant proportion of which is plastic.

Due to the small size of some of the plastics, conventional storm catch basins fail to capture this pollution. Aside from an aesthetic problem, plastic debris such as cigarette filters, plastic bags, and "preproduction plastic" impact the health of marine life that often confuse the debris for food.

The plastic patches in the world's oceans collect plastic carried as storm runoff. This plastic waste that does not end up in landfills or recycled collects as marine debris in the ocean. Most of the plastic marine debris originating from California ends up in the North Pacific Central Gyre.

AB 258 of 2007 (Chapter 735, Statutes of 2007) requires the SWRCB and RWQCBs to develop a fee-based monitoring program to reduce the discharges of preproduction plastics (such as resin pellets and powdered coloring for plastics) that enter the marine environment. The program addresses waste discharge, monitoring, and reporting requirements for plastic manufacturing, handling, and transportation facilities, and specified minimum BMPs. The program establishes criteria that warrant a "no exposure" certification that allow conditional exemptions for plastics manufacturers, handlers, and transportation facilities.

Marine invasive species. The California Marine Invasive Species Act establishes ballast water management standards governing vessels that operate in waters of the state designed to prevent or minimize the introduction of nonindigenous species to California waters. Public Resources Code § 71200 *et seq.* Vessels over 300 gross registered tons, capable of carrying ballast water must follow standards to minimize the uptake and the release of nonindigenous species to waters of the state. The Act also requires regular removal of "hull fouling organisms" from the submerged portions of a vessel and regular cleaning of the ballast tanks to remove fouling organisms. Visiting vessels must maintain records of vessel activities including dry docking, in-water cleaning of the submerged portion of the vessel, and antifouling paint applications.

OIL MANAGEMENT PROGRAMS

FEDERAL REQUIREMENTS: SPILL PREVENTION CONTROL AND COUNTERMEASURE PROGRAM

Overview. In 1973, EPA first issued regulations designed to prevent oils from reaching waters of the United States. 40 C.F.R. § 112 *et seq*. These regulations require specified facilities to prepare an SPCC plan. The SPCC plan is intended to minimize a facility's potential for an oil spill and to implement measures to correct the cause of an oil spill. Generally, the SPCC plan establishes engineering and management procedures and equipment standards to prevent oil from entering surface waters. Each plan must document site-specific spill prevention and control measures to manage facility structures, procedures, and equipment.

Collapsed aboveground storage tank.

A facility must prepare an SPCC plan if it:

- has an aggregate aboveground storage capacity greater than 1,320 gallons counting containers greater or equal to 55 gallons (40 C.F.R. § 112.1(d)(2)) or
- a completely buried storage capacity greater than 42,000 gallons; and
- has a reasonable expectation that discharge will enter navigable waters of the United States or adjoining shorelines.

EPA has discretion to regulate facilities it sees as a threat even if the oil capacity of the facility is below applicability thresholds.

Several classes of oil containers are exempt from SPCC requirements including hot-mix asphalt containers, residential heating oil containers used solely at single-family residences, pesticide application containers, intra-facility gathering lines regulated by DOT, and produced water containers that do not contain oil in harmful quantities.

EPA modified the definition of "facility" to clarify that contiguous or non-contiguous buildings, properties, parcels, leases, structures, installations, pipes, or pipelines may be considered separate facilities. This revision allows owners or operators to separate or aggregate containers to determine the facility boundaries for purposes of SPCC rule applicability. Owners and operators have discretion to consider factors including ownership or operation of property boundaries, buildings, structures, containers, and equipment on the site, as well as the activities being conducted. 40 C.F.R. § 112.2.

Applicability to non-transportation-related onshore facilities. "Oil" is broadly defined to include "petroleum, fuel oil, sludge, oil refuse, and oil mixed with wastes other than dredge spoil." Thus, in addition to crude oil, gasoline, and diesel fuel, "oil" includes waste oils and waste fuels, and non-petroleum oils (such as turpentine, animal fats such as tallow and lard, and vegetable oils). "Oil" does not include compressed gases or liquefied natural gas. 33 U.S.C. § 1321(a)(1); 40 C.F.R. § 112.2.

SPCC plans are required for non-transportation-related onshore and offshore facilities that could reasonably be expected to discharge oil into navigable waters of the United States or adjoining shorelines. These facilities include those that drill, produce, gather, store, use, process, refine, transfer, distribute, or consume oil and oil products. 40 C.F.R. § 112.1(b). Non-transportation-related facilities are found in such industries as oil drilling and production, oil refining and storage, agriculture, and oil treatment.

SPCC plans are required for non-transportation-related onshore and offshore facilities that could reasonably be expected to discharge oil into navigable waters of the United States or adjoining shorelines.

Transportation-related vessels, such as oil tankers, are subject to another set of specific SPCC requirements. This section focuses on non-transportation-related onshore facilities that, due to their locations, could be reasonably expected to discharge harmful quantities of oil into or upon surface waters or adjoining shorelines. 40 C.F.R. §§ 112.1 and 112.2. This "reasonably expected" determination:

- Is based on land features (e.g., topographic contours with respect to drainage) and related factors (e.g., facility proximity to navigable waters or adjoining shorelines)
- Must not consider equipment (e.g., shut-off valves and catchment basins) designed to prevent oil from reaching navigable waters or adjoining shorelines

A non-transportation-related onshore facility is subject to an SPCC plan and related requirements if the facility meets one of the following "oil" volumes:

- The total unburied (essentially aboveground) storage capacity of the facility is greater than 1,320 gallons (only counting containers greater than or equal to 55 gallons). 40 C.F.R. § 112.1(d)(2). Thus, a standalone 2,000-gallon aboveground tank storing oil could trigger SPCC plan requirements.
- Completely buried underground storage tanks (USTs) with combined capacity of greater than 42,000 gallons (except for completely buried tanks meeting UST regulations; see chapter 7 for a discussion of UST regulatory requirements)

Containers and tanks are broadly defined to include:

- Units that are owned and operated, such as units used by tenants
- Mobile oil units, such as units used for aircraft ground equipment, waste oils (presumed also to be hazardous waste under California law), polychlorinated biphenyl oils (may be inside transformers along with other operational tanks such as manufacturing equipment and hydraulic equipment), and fuel trucks.

AST = aboveground storage tank

There are three types of non-transportation-related facilities subject to varying levels of SPCC requirements. Facilities meeting the minimum levels of oil storage described above must comply with the full set of SPCC plan requirements unless they are eligible as a "qualified facility." There are two types of qualified facilities that may be subject to more streamlined requirements. A Tier 1 qualified facility may have oil storage capacity up to 10,000 gallons of aboveground oil capacity in aggregate with maximum individual aboveground oil container storage capacity not exceeding 5,000 gallons. A Tier II qualified facility is one with individual oil container storage capacity greater than 5,000 gallons but no more than 10,000 gallons capacity in total. Both types of qualified facilities must not have experienced a reportable oil discharge in the prior three years.

Facilities meeting the SPCC applicability requirements must prepare and implement an SPCC plan prior to operation.

Plan requirements. Facilities meeting the SPCC applicability requirements must prepare and implement an SPCC plan prior to operation. 40 C.F.R. § 112.3(a)(1). The SPCC plan must include, among other things:

- Each container's type of oil and storage capacity. 40 C.F.R. § 112.7(a)(3)(i)
- Spill response systems (e.g., emergency coordinator, arrangements with local emergency agencies and local emergency response contractors). 40 C.F.R. § 112.7(a)(3)(vi)
- Emergency prevention and response equipment and procedures. 40 C.F.R. § 112.7(a)(3)(iii)–(v); 40 C.F.R. § 112.7(a)(4)–(5)
- Reasonable potential for equipment failure. (40 C.F.R. § 112.7(b))
- Corrosion protection for buried metallic storage tanks. 40 C.F.R. § 112.8(c)(4)
- Written inspection procedures. 40 C.F.R. § 112.7(e); 40 C.F.R. § 112.8(c), (d)
- Integrity testing of above-ground storage tanks (ASTs) on a regular schedule, and whenever repairs are made. 40 C.F.R. § 112.8(c)(6)
- Secondary containment systems or diversionary structures for all tanks, piping, and loading and unloading areas (such as dikes, berms, and curbs). 40 C.F.R. § 112.7(a)(3)(iii), (c)
- Security measures (such as fencing and locked gates). 40 C.F.R. § 112.7(g)

The SPCC plan, along with technical amendments, must be reviewed by a professional engineer. Unlike most environmental plans, the SPCC plan need not be submitted to EPA or other state or local agencies. 40 C.F.R. §§ 112.3, 112.5(c). Additionally, owners and operators must instruct their staff how to operate and maintain spill control equipment to prevent discharges. Owners and operators also must annually schedule and conduct briefings for staff to ensure familiarity and understanding of the facility's SPCC plan. 40 C.F.R. § 112.7(f).

The owner or operator of the non-transportation-related onshore facility must amend the SPCC plan within six months of a change in facility design, construction, operation, or maintenance that materially affects the facility's potential for the discharge of oil (e.g., installation of new piping systems or changes in volume of oil). 40 C.F.R. § 112.5. The amended plan must be implemented as soon as possible and no later than six months following the amendment. Additionally, the owner or operator must review and evaluate the plan every five years. 40 C.F.R. § 112.5(b).

FRP = facility response plan

Release reporting. A reportable spill is a discharge greater than 1,000 gallons of oil or two discharges of more than 42 gallons of oil each in any 12-month period. If an owner or operator experiences a reportable spill, the facility must submit specified information to EPA regarding details of the discharge and corrective measures taken. 40 C.F.R. § 112.4(a).

FEDERAL REQUIREMENTS: THE OIL POLLUTION ACT OF 1990

Overview. This Act was passed in response to the 1989 catastrophic release of more than 11 million gallons of oil from the Exxon Valdez, which killed about 500,000 birds, more than 4,000 sea otters, 300 seals, and dozens of killer whales. It has been reported that the Exxon Valdez resulted in the death of more wildlife than any other environmental disaster in U.S. history.

The 1989 Exxon Valdez oil spill was the second worst in U.S. history, exceeded only by the Deepwater Horizon drilling rig blowout in 2010.

This Act (3 U.S.C. § 2701 *et seq.*; 40 C.F.R. § 112.20):

- Prohibits the discharge of oil into waters of the U.S. by tank vessels and marine transportation
- Establishes the National Oil Spill Liability Trust Fund
- Requires facilities that "could reasonably be expected to cause substantial harm to the environment by discharging oil into or on the navigable waters or adjoining shorelines" to prepare and submit a facility response plan (FRP)

Applicability. As noted above, an FRP is required for substantial harm facilities, defined as a non-transportation-related onshore facility that "because of its location, could reasonably be expected to cause substantial harm to the environment by discharging oil into or on navigable waters or adjoining shorelines." 40 C.F.R. § 112.20(a). A substantial harm facility must complete an FRP if the facility meets one of the following substantial harm criteria:

- Has a total oil storage capacity greater than or equal to 42,000 gallons and transfers oil over water to or from vessels
- Has a total oil storage capacity greater than or equal to one million gallons and the facility lacks sufficient secondary containment to contain the amount of oil that could be released from the largest AST plus sufficient freeboard to allow for precipitation

OES = Office of Emergency Services

- Has a total oil storage capacity greater than or equal to one million gallons and, due to the facility's location, a discharge could injure fish and wildlife and sensitive environments
- Has a total oil storage capacity greater than or equal to one million gallons and, due to its location, a discharge would shut down a public drinking water intake (as per 40 C.F.R. § 143.2(c))
- Has a total oil storage capacity greater than or equal to one million gallons and the facility has had a reportable oil discharge in an amount greater than or equal to 10,000 gallons within the past five years (40 C.F.R. § 112.20(f)(1))

The FRP must document how the facility would respond to a worst-case discharge of oil and to a substantial threat of such a discharge. Among other things, the FRP must include a flow diagram and must specify quantity limits and types of locations with potential for substantial harm. 40 C.F.R. § 112.20(h).

STATE REQUIREMENTS

Aboveground Petroleum Storage Act. In 2008, major revisions to the state's Aboveground Petroleum Storage Act (APSA, Health & Safety Code § 25270 *et seq.*), which was first enacted in 1991, became effective. Responsibility for the implementation, enforcement, and administration of the APSA was transferred from the SWRCB to CUPAs. The Act applies to either tank facilities subject to 40 C.F.R. § 112, or to facilities storing petroleum with an aggregate storage capacity of at least 1,320 gallons. These facilities must prepare and implement an SPCC plan in accordance with 40 C.F.R. § 112. Health & Safety Code §§ 25270.3, 25270.5.

Each owner or operator of a tank regulated by the APSA must file an annual tank facility statement (referred to as a "tank facility statement" or a "storage statement") with the CUPA specifying the tank facility's name, address, contact person, and total storage capacity. The submission of a hazardous materials business plan (*see* chapter 7) to the CUPA satisfies the tank facility statement requirement. For each tank exceeding 10,000 gallons capacity and that holds a substance containing at least five percent petroleum, the statement must contain additional information: the tank's location on the facility, size, age, and contents. Health & Safety Code § 25270.6(a).

Each owner or operator of a tank regulated by the APSA must file an annual tank facility statement with the CUPA specifying the tank facility's name, address, contact person, and total storage capacity.

Each owner and operator of an AST must pay an annual fee to the CUPA. Owners and operators are required to notify the Governor's Office of Emergency Services (OES) and the CUPA when there is a spill or release of at least one barrel (42 gallons) of petroleum. Health & Safety Code § 25270.8.

At least once every three years, the CUPA must inspect each AST, or a representative sample of ASTs, at tank facilities with a storage capacity of at least 10,000 gallons of petroleum. The purpose of the inspection is to determine whether the tank's owner or operator is in compliance with the SPCC plan. Health & Safety Code § 25270.5.

RQs = reportable quantities

Lempert-Keene Act. The Lempert-Keene Act is designed to prevent and respond to oil spills into marine waters along the California coast. The Department of Fish and Wildlife has developed an oil spill contingency plan describing how to respond to potential oil spills using "best achievable protection" of marine waters and the coast. In addition, operators of vessels, and owners and operators of marine facilities, must develop and implement contingency plans addressing preparation for and response to oil spills. The Act further requires that ports along the California coast develop harbor safety committees and plans for safe navigation of vessels within the port jurisdiction. The Act further governs loading and unloading of oil tankers. Gov't Code §§ 8670.23.1, 8670.29, 8670.31, 8670.56; 14 Cal. Code Regs. § 851 *et seq.*

WATER QUALITY RELEASE REPORTING

The Porter-Cologne Act and CWA (42 U.S.C. § 311) require agency reporting for releases of specified quantities (i.e., reportable quantities or RQs) of hazardous substances and oil or petroleum products. Not all discharges exceeding the RQ must be reported. Only those discharges that reach or probably will reach surface and groundwaters must be reported. The reportable quantity depends on whether the release is of petroleum or of other hazardous chemicals.

Only those discharges that reach or probably will reach surface and groundwaters must be reported.

Discharges exceeding the RQ and that could reach or probably reach surface and groundwaters must be reported to State Office of Emergency Services (OES) and to either the SWRCB or the RWQCB "as soon as the discharge is discovered and notification can be provided without substantially impeding cleanup or emergency measures." Immediate notification to the appropriate federal agency complies with California Water Code reporting provisions. 42 U.S.C. § 311; Water Code §§ 13271, 13272.

Any person, regardless of intent or negligence, who permits or causes the discharge of sewage or waste in or on waters of the state is required to notify the local health officer or director of environmental health as soon as the person learns of the release, regardless of whether the person has already notified OES. Water Code § 13271.

ENFORCEMENT

STATE VERSUS FEDERAL ENFORCEMENT

The SWRCB and RWQCBs are the principal state agencies responsible for regulating water quality. Water Code § 13001. This role includes enforcing statutes and regulations (including the Porter-Cologne Act and TPCA) to prevent and mitigate impacts

CAO = Cleanup and abatement order

to the state's waters. The Boards may exercise their authority via any one or more of the following:

- Cleanup and abatement orders (CAOs)
- Cease and desist orders
- Administrative civil liability (fines)
- Referral to the Attorney General for injunctive or civil action or both
- Criminal penalties

Although EPA's regulations authorize (and require) states with NPDES programs to enforce violations of the CWA, EPA is not precluded from also utilizing its enforcement authority in such cases. In fact, EPA explicitly retains the authority "to commence enforcement actions to the extent that State judgments or settlements provide penalties in amounts which EPA believes to be substantially inadequate." 40 C.F.R. § 123.27.

EPA policy dictates that the agency will utilize its enforcement authority to support and strengthen state programs. EPA policy generally limits "overfiling" to four types of cases—the state has requested EPA action, local enforcement has not been timely or appropriate, important legal or programmatic precedents are involved in the case, or there has been a violation of an EPA order or consent decree.

VIOLATIONS OF THE CLEAN WATER ACT AND PORTER-COLOGNE ACT

If the SWRCB determines that there is a continual violation of any CAOs, or if any person fails to achieve compliance, civil enforcement allows for fines of up to $10,000 per day of violation. Water Code § 13300 *et seq*. Passed in 1999, the California Clean Water Enforcement Act established mandatory minimum penalties of $3,000 for every "serious" violation—any waste discharge that exceeds permitted levels for a hazardous pollutant by 20 percent or more, or a nonhazardous pollutant by 40 percent or more. These minimum penalties also will be assessed for facilities that commit four or more ongoing violations in a six-month period, including exceeding numeric effluent limitations, failing to file a permit application, filing an incomplete application, exceeding chronic or acute toxicity limitations, violating compliance schedules, or (for a POTW) failing to enforce pretreatment requirements.

If the SWRCB determines that there is a continual violation of any CAOs, or if any person fails to achieve compliance, civil enforcement allows for fines of up to $10,000 per day of violation.

For criminal penalties, persons who knowingly or negligently violate a WDR, a CAO, or a CWQ requirement, or introduce pollutants into a sewer system, can be fined at least $5,000 for each day of violation, with maximum penalites of up to $2 million in fines and 30 years in prison. Water Code §§ 13268, 13271, 13387.

In addition to Water Board enforcement, violations of effluent limitations under the CWA may be enforced by civil "citizen suits." 33 U.S.C. § 1365(a). Such suits are generally brought by environmental organizations.

SUPPLEMENTAL ENVIRONMENTAL PROJECTS

SEP = supplemental environmental project

Dischargers may mitigate civil penalties by up to half by agreeing to fund and implement supplemental environmental projects (SEPs). An SEP is a pollution prevention effort that exceeds the existing statutory obligations of the discharger and achieves an environmental benefit. SEPs include anything from wetlands preservation projects to educational efforts. Water Code § 13385 (h)(i).

for more information...

California State Water Resources Control Board, 2016. A Compilation of Water Quality Goals, 17th Edition.

Environmental Protection Agency, 2007. Developing Your Stormwater Pollution Prevention Plan: A Guide for Construction Sites.

Environmental Protection Agency, 2009. Developing Your Stormwater Pollution Prevention Plan: A Guide for Industrial Operators.

Manaster, K. A. and D. P. Selmi (eds.). ND. California Environmental Law and Land Use Practice. Chapters 30–33. Matthew Bender. San Francisco, Calif.

glossary

Basin plan—a RWQCB basin plan sets forth WQS for surface and groundwaters within a particular water body or portion thereof and implementation plans to achieve the WQS. Designed to protect water quality within specified hydrological units.

Best available technology economically achievable standard—considers the controls that are technologically and economically achievable, but does not balance the cost of attainability against the potential benefit for ELGs for nonconventional and toxic pollutants.

Best conventional pollutant control technology standard—considers the controls that are technologically and economically achievable in relation to the benefits for ELGs for conventional pollutants.

Best management practices—methods determined to be the most effective, practical means of preventing or reducing pollution from nonpoint sources.

Best practicable control technology—allows industries to emit higher than normal pollution levels with equipment that uses the best practicable means available.

Categorical effluent limitation guidelines and standards—includes ELGs for conventional, nonconventional, and toxic pollutants, as well as new sources and indirect discharges.

Concentrated animal feeding operations—agricultural facilities that house and feed a large number of animals in a confined area.

Construction general permit*—requires development of a stormwater pollution prevention plan describing best management practices to prevent stormwater pollution associated with construction activities disturbing soil of one acre or more.

Conventional pollutants—typical, higher volume pollutants that include biochemical oxygen demand, total suspended solids, fecal coliform, pH, and oil and grease.

Designated waste—nonhazardous waste that consists of or contains pollutants that, under ambient environmental conditions at the waste, management unit could be released at concentrations exceeding applicable WQOs; designated waste that is hazardous waste is subject to a hazardous waste variance.

Effluent limitations—limitations on discharge in an NPDES permit (the more stringent of either technology-based or water quality-based limitations).

Facility response plan*—a comprehensive spill response and contingency plan designed to prevent the discharge of oil from vessels and land-based oil storage facilities that could reasonably be expected to cause substantial harm to the environment by discharging oil into or on navigable waters or adjoining shorelines.

General industrial permit*—an NPDES permit that regulates stormwater discharges associated with ten broadly described industrial activities. Among other things, the permit requires the development of a stormwater pollution prevention plan designed to implement best management practices to prevent stormwater contamination.

Municipal separate storm sewer system—a conveyance (that can include roads with drainage systems, municipal streets, catch basins, curbs, gutters, ditches, built channels, or storm drains) designed to collect or convey stormwater, but is not a combined sewer or part of a POTW.

Municipal separate stormwater permit*—governs stormwater discharges from municipalities serving over 100,000 people. The site-specific NPDES permit must incorporate a monitoring program to evaluate runoff and water received.

National Pollutant Discharge Elimination System permit*—a permit that controls water pollution by regulating point sources that discharge pollutants into surface waters defined as "waters of the United States."

Numeric Action Level (NAL)—a numeric action level under the California industrial stormwater program for total suspended solids, and oil and grease.

New source performance standards—emissions limitations for industrial source categories, adopted by EPA.

Nonconventional pollutants—all pollutants other than conventional and toxic pollutants, and including but not limited to chemical oxygen demand, total organic carbon, nitrogen, phosphorus, ammonia, and sulfide.

Nonhazardous solid waste—municipal solid waste or refuse that has a significant proportion of degradable material or "inert" waste (such as paving fragments and non-degradable construction debris).

Nonpoint source pollution—diffuse sources of pollution (i.e., without a single point of origin or not introduced into a receiving stream from a specific outlet). The pollutants are generally carried off the land by stormwater. Common nonpoint sources are agriculture, forestry, urban, mining, construction, dams, channels, land disposal units, saltwater intrusion, and city streets.

Oil—broadly defined to include petroleum, fuel oil, sludge, oil refuse, and oil mixed with wastes other than dredge spoil, including non-petroleum oils such as vegetable oil.

Point source—any discernible, confined, and discrete conveyance, including pipes, ditches, channels, tunnels, conduits, wells, vessels, and more.

Pollutant—dredged spoil, solid waste, incinerator residue, filter backwash, sewage, garbage, sewage sludge, munitions, chemical wastes, biological materials, radioactive materials (except those regulated under the Atomic Energy Act of 1954, as amended (42 U.S.C. 2011 et seq.)), heat, wrecked or discarded equipment, rock, sand, cellar dirt, and industrial, municipal, and agricultural waste discharged into water.

Pretreatment standards—standards designed to prevent the introduction of pollutants to publicly owned treatment works that would interfere with operations and to prevent pollutants incompatible with the POTW from passing through.

Priority toxic pollutant—129 specified pollutants commonly subdivided into heavy metals, organic compounds, and pesticides.

Qualifying Storm Event (QSE)—Pursuant to the California industrial stormwater program, a precipitation event that produces a discharge for at least one drainage area, and is preceded by 48 hours with no discharge from any drainage area.

Sole source aquifer—a principal source area that supplies at least 50 percent of the drinking water consumed in a specific area overlying the aquifer.

Spill prevention control and countermeasure plan*—establishes engineering and management procedures and equipment standards designed to prevent oil from entering surface waters. Each plan must document site-specific spill prevention and control measures to manage facility structures, procedures, and equipment.

Stormwater—precipitation that flows over a surface, or urban runoff or melted snow that flows into the storm drain system or otherwise into surface waters.

Stormwater pollution prevention plan*—identifies pollution sources that affect the quality of stormwater discharges from a site and requires implementation of best management practices to reduce pollutants in stormwater discharges.

Supplemental environmental projects—pollution prevention efforts that exceed the existing statutory obligations of dischargers and achieve an environmental benefit.

Technology-based effluent limitation—a minimum level of effluent control that uniformly applies to industry categories, regardless of where the discharge occurs or the quality of the surface water receiving the discharge.

Total maximum daily load—specifies waste load allocations for point and nonpoint sources that discharge into an impaired water body (i.e., a water body that does not meet one or more established beneficial uses specified for that water body).

Underground injection control program—the program, under the federal Safe Drinking Water Act, that regulates the discharge of wastes into underground injection wells.

Waste discharge requirements*—permit issued by a RWQCB for discharge of waste into waters of the state.

Waste management unit—an area of land, or a portion of a waste management facility, at which waste is discharged. The term includes containment features and ancillary features for precipitation and drainage control and for monitoring.

Water quality objective—an area of land, or a portion of a waste management facility, at which waste is discharged. The term includes containment features and ancillary features for precipitation and drainage control and for monitoring.

Water quality standards—composed of two parts: (1) the designated uses of water and (2) criteria to protect those uses. Water quality standards are enforceable limits in the bodies of water for which they have been established.

Water quality-based effluent limitation—an effluent limitation applied to dischargers when technology-based limitations have the potential to cause violations of water quality standards.

Waters of the United States—all waters used or susceptible to use in interstate or foreign commerce, or that could affect interstate or foreign commerce. Waters of the United States include lakes, rivers and coastal waters, as well as all adjacent "other waters"

* equals permits and approvals

CHAPTER 11

Drinking Water

related Solano Press title

California Water II. Arthur L. Littleworth and Eric L. Garner. 2007.

in this chapter...

SDWA = Safe Drinking Water Act

PWS = public water system

EPA = U.S. Environmental Protection Agency

Thanks to improved water quality during the 20th century, health and life expectancy have improved dramatically.

INTRODUCTION

Californians take for granted that clean water flows from the tap. Waterborne disease used to be the primary killer of babies and young children and still is in some developing countries. Thanks to improved water quality during the 20th century, health and life expectancy have improved dramatically. Chlorination and other drinking water treatments began in the early 1900s and became widespread public health practices, further decreasing the incidence of waterborne diseases. Since 1900, the average lifespan has increased approximately 30 years in the United States, with improved water quality playing a critical role in this advance.

KEY LAWS AND AGENCIES

FEDERAL LAWS AND AGENCIES

Safe Drinking Water Act. The SDWA regulates public water systems (PWSs) that supply drinking water. 42 U.S.C. § 300(f) *et seq.*; 40 C.F.R. § 141 *et seq.* The principle objective of the federal SDWA is to ensure that water from the tap is potable (safe and satisfactory for drinking, cooking, and hygiene). The main components of the federal SDWA are to:

- Ensure that water from the tap is potable
- Prevent contamination of groundwater aquifers that are the main source of drinking water for a community
- Regulate the discharge of wastes into underground injection wells pursuant to the Underground Injection Control program (*see* 40 C.F.R. § 144 and chapter 10)
- Regulate distribution systems that convey treated water to homes, businesses, and factories

The Public Health Security and Bioterrorism Preparedness and Response Act of 2002. This Act, also called the Bioterrorism Act (Pub. Law 107–188, 42 U.S.C. § 300hh, *et seq.*), was enacted in response to September 11, 2001. Title IV of the Act requires a PWS serving more than 3,300 people to perform a vulnerability assessment of its water system. The vulnerability assessment evaluates the risk of a terrorist attack or other intentional acts intended to substantially disrupt the ability of the system to provide a safe and reliable drinking water supply.

Environmental Protection Agency. The EPA implements the federal SDWA by:

- Establishing levels of contaminants (e.g., inorganics, organics, pesticides, fecal coliform, and radionuclides) that must not be exceeded in drinking water
- Delegating duties to the states

Public water supply systems must ensure that specified levels of contaminants are not exceeded. PWSs accomplish this via treating, monitoring, and reporting on their performance in achieving drinking water quality standards.

Food and Drug Administration. Bottled water is regulated as a food product under the federal Food and Drug Administration standards.

DWR = Department of Water Resources

SWRCB = State Water Resources Control Board

PWS = public water system

MCL = maximum contaminant level

Cal/EPA = California Environmental Protection Agency

OEHHA = Office of Environmental Health Hazard Assessment

STATE LAWS AND AGENCIES

Water as a Human Right. State law establishes that Californians have a right to clean, affordable and accessible water adequate for human consumption, cooking, and sanitary purposes water without discrimination. California agencies, including the Department of Water Resources (DWR) and the State Water Resources Control Board (SWRCB), are required to consider this mandate when establishing or modifying state policy and funding for human uses of water. Water Code § 106.3 *et seq.*

California Safe Drinking Water Act. The California SDWA (Health & Safety Code § 116270 *et seq.*; 22 Cal. Code Regs. § 64400 *et seq.*) regulates drinking water more rigorously than the federal law. Like the federal SDWA, California requires that primary and secondary maximum contaminant levels (MCLs) be established for pollutants in drinking water; however, some California MCLs are more protective of health. The Act also requires the SWRCB to issue domestic water supply permits to PWSs.

The SWRCB enforces the federal and state SDWAs and regulates more than 7,500 PWSs across the state. (Implementation of the federal SDWA is delegated to the state of California.)

The SWRCB's Division of Drinking Water oversees the state's comprehensive Drinking Water Program (DWP). The DWP consists of three branches: the Northern California Field Operations Branch, the Southern California Field Operations Branch, and the Programs Management Branch. The DWP is the agency authorized to issue PWS permits.

Office of Environmental Health Hazard Assessment. The California Environmental Protection Agency's (Cal/EPA) Office of Environmental Health Hazard Assessment (OEHHA) informs state and local regulatory agencies of important toxicological and medical information relevant to decisions involving public health. OEHHA is primarily responsible for developing procedures and practices for performing health risk assessments to determine healthy levels of exposure to pollutants. These assessments help risk managers determine California MCLs.

OEHHA is primarily responsible for developing procedures and practices for performing health risk assessments to determine healthy levels of exposure to pollutants.

Bottled Water Consumer Right-to-Know. Under California's right-to-know legislation (SB 220 of 2007, Health & Safety Code § 111070 *et seq.*) water bottling plants and water-vending machines must provide water quality information to consumers. Bottles of water sold in California must label both the source of the water and two ways for consumers to contact the company for a water quality report.

MCLG = maximum contaminant level goal

DRINKING WATER PROGRAMS: THE BASICS

DEFINITION OF PUBLIC WATER SYSTEM

A public water system is defined as a system for providing the public with piped water for human consumption that has 15 or more service connections or regularly serves at least 25 individuals daily at least 60 days out of the year.

The key provisions of the federal and state SDWAs apply to PWSs that supply drinking water to the public. A PWS is defined as a system for providing the public with piped water for human consumption that has 15 or more service connections or regularly serves at least 25 individuals daily at least 60 days out of the year. 42 U.S.C. § 300(f)(4); Health & Safety Code § 116275(h). PWSs collect water either from groundwater or surface water and then treat, store, and distribute the water for use. There are four types of PWSs:

- **Community PWS.** A PWS that regularly serves at least 15 service connections to year-round residents or regularly serves at least 25 year-round residents.
- **Non-community PWS.** A PWS that is not a community water system. (This includes all other water systems meeting the PWS definition.)
- **Non-transient, non-community PWS.** A PWS that is not a community water system and regularly serves at least 25 of the same people over six months of the year. (This is aimed at school and workplace water supplies that cause long-term exposure.)
- **Transient, non-community PWS.** A PWS that is not a community system and does not regularly serve at least 25 of the same people over six months of the year. (This includes rest stop areas, campgrounds, restaurants, and motels.)

DRINKING WATER STANDARDS

Primary drinking water standards. EPA establishes primary drinking water standards (also known as MCLs) that are mandatory and enforceable health-protective standards. 40 C.F.R. § 141 Subparts B, G. EPA establishes a primary MCL for a specified contaminant by:

- Determining a preliminary level where no adverse health effects appear and including a margin of safety; this figure is known as a maximum contaminant level goal (MCLG). 40 C.F.R. § 141 Subpart F
- Setting the MCL as close to the MCLG as possible while taking into account technological feasibility and costs. 42 U.S.C. § 300(g)(b)(4)(B)

Primary MCLs are established for:

- Inorganic contaminants (e.g., metals)
- Organic contaminants (e.g., benzene)
- Synthetic organic contaminants (e.g., pesticides)
- Trihalomethanes (THMs if disinfectant has been added)

- Microbial contaminants (e.g., fecal coliforms, viruses, *giardia,* and *crypto-sporidium*)
- Radioactivity
- Corrosivity
- Turbidity (i.e., a measure of the amount of particles in water, and that can be caused by microbial or non-microbial sources)

The greatest public health risk related to drinking water is microbial contamination, causing waterborne disease. Potential microbes in water supplies (prior to treatment) include bacteria such as cholera and *salmonella*, viruses such as polio and Norwalk virus, and protozoans such as *cryptosporidium* and *giardia*. Surface waters are filtered to remove most of these pathogens. Groundwater is less vulnerable to these pathogens because the soil acts as a natural filter. All surface water and most groundwater in California must be disinfected to reduce microbial risk. Common disinfectants include chlorine, chloramines, and ozone.

The greatest public health risk related to drinking water is microbial contamination, causing waterborne disease.

Secondary drinking water standards. EPA also establishes secondary drinking water standards (another set of MCLs) that are not federally enforceable, but are enforced by the state in California. 22 Cal. Code Regs. § 64449 *et seq*. Secondary MCLs protect aesthetic qualities (taste, odor, color) of drinking water. 40 C.F.R. § 143. Thus far, EPA has issued secondary MCLs for 15 contaminants, including color, odor, pH, total dissolved solids, fluoride, iron, and manganese.

DRINKING WATER STANDARDS AS BENCHMARKS FOR CLEANUP

Primary and secondary MCLs are often used as benchmarks for acceptable cleanup standards for contaminated groundwater. (*See* chapter 8.)

MONITORING REQUIREMENTS: WATER QUALITY

Frequency and contaminants. PWSs must monitor the water quality leaving their water systems to ensure that concentrations do not exceed MCLs. Typically, all contaminants on the MCL list initially are tested at a given PWS. Afterwards, the frequency of monitoring and the contaminants to be monitored are based on (40 C.F.R. § 141 Subpart C):

- The contaminant group
- The type of drinking water facility
- The number of people served
- The water source (i.e., groundwater or surface water)
- Whether any MCLs have been exceeded

Each PWS is also subject to nine-year monitoring cycles, divided into three-year compliance periods, to demonstrate compliance with scores of MCLs. During the initial period, a PWS must monitor contaminants using a state-certified lab to conduct the analyses. Should the PWS exceed one or more MCLs, the PWS must complete more frequent monitoring and commit to corrective measures. 40 C.F.R. § 141. During each compliance period, a PWS is obligated to collect samples from groundwater supply systems, as well as surface water supply systems after treatment.

Monitoring plan. A PWS must write a monitoring plan, and the SWRCB must approve the plan. Monitoring programs vary by PWS type and size and include sampling for the following:

- Inorganic contaminants
- Organic contaminants (including synthetic organic contaminants)
- Total trihalomethane
- Radioactivity
- Turbidity
- Chlorinated compounds
- Disinfectant residuals (e.g., chlorine, chloramines)
- Microbial contaminants
- Miscellaneous contaminants (e.g., sulfate, sodium, corrosivity, general minerals, pH)

PWSs must also sample for microbial activity by collecting microbial samples at representative locations throughout the distribution system. The sampling strategy and plan is captured in a written sampling plan that is approved by the SWRCB. The sampling frequency is determined by the population served. If a microbial sample is positive for coliform, the SWRCB must be notified within 24 hours if further testing reveals the presence of fecal coliform or *E. coli.* 40 C.F.R. § 141.21; 22 Cal. Code Regs. § 64421 *et seq.*

PWSs must immediately notify EPA within 24 hours where there is the potential for immediate impact to human health and the public.

PWSs must immediately notify EPA within 24 hours where there is the potential for immediate impact to human health and the public. For those instances where an exceedance does not pose an immediate risk to human health, the PWS must notify its customers as soon as possible and no later than 30 days from the violation. For those instances where an MCL violation does directly impact human health, the PWS may include the notice in its consumer confidence report. 40 C.F.R. § 141.20 *et seq.*

CONSUMER CONFIDENCE REPORTS

PWSs are required to report annually on the water quality served to their users. 40 C.F.R. § 141 Subpart O. Each report must, at a minimum, provide consumers with the following information about their drinking water:

- **Water system information.** Name and phone number of PWS contact person; public meetings and hearings; information for non-English speaking populations (if applicable).

- **Water source.** Type (i.e., groundwater or surface water); common name; location; availability of source water assessment; summary of potential sources of contamination.
- **Definitions.** Key definitions such as MCL and MCLG.
- **Detected contaminants.** Tabular summary of regulated and unregulated contaminants that were detected during sampling; known or likely source of each detected contaminant; potential health effects; cryptosporidium information (if applicable).
- **Compliance with drinking water regulations.** Explanation of violations; compliance with other drinking water rules.
- **Required educational information.** Explanation of contaminants and their presence in drinking water; information on nitrate, arsenic, lead, and total THM (if applicable); EPA's drinking water hotline number.

Like other federal drinking water regulations, states may set their own regulations for PWS reports. California has established its own requirements for consumer confidence reports that parallel the federal requirements to ensure that consumers' right-to-know is respected by all water suppliers. Health & Safety Code § 116470.

California has established its own requirements for consumer confidence reports that parallel the federal requirements to ensure that consumers' right-to-know is respected by all water suppliers.

In order to reduce disease incidence associated with disease-causing microorganisms in drinking water, the EPA "groundwater rule" establishes a risk-based approach to target groundwater systems that are vulnerable to fecal contamination. This rule applies to all systems that use groundwater as a source of drinking water. Groundwater systems that are identified as being at risk of fecal contamination must take corrective action to reduce potential illness from exposure to microbial pathogens. 40 C.F.R. Parts 141 and 142.

Filtration and disinfection are required for PWSs that use surface water or groundwater that is under the influence of surface water. 40 C.F.R. § 141 Subpart H. PWSs using surface water supplies must sample for turbidity and disinfectant residuals nearly continuously, typically once every four hours. 40 C.F.R. § 141.22. Low turbidity and the presence of a chlorine residual ensure that water does not contain pathogenic microbes such as bacteria, viruses, and protozoans.

Water system operators must be certified to treat, distribute, and monitor drinking water at community and non-transient non-community PWSs. 17 Cal. Code Regs. § 63750 *et seq.*

Lead and copper. A PWS must monitor for lead and copper levels at the tap, to ensure that its distribution system does not add unacceptable levels of lead and copper to tap water. 40 C.F.R. § 141 Subparts E, I. If a representative lead or copper action level is exceeded (i.e., if at least 10 percent of tap water samples exceed the lead or copper MCL), the PWS must implement a corrosion control program and treat the source water. If the MCL is still exceeded after corrective measures are

Flint, Michigan Water Contamination

In April 2014, the Flint Michigan PWS switched water sources and allegedly failed to apply corrosion control to protect lead in older pipes from leaching into the water supply. Up to 12,000 children were exposed to elevated levels of lead, which is a heavy metal neurotoxin. Several lawsuits were filed against government officials, including criminal charges.

implemented, then the PWS must replace lead service lines. Pipes, solder, flux, and water coolers installed after June 19, 1986, must be lead-free. Lead contamination of drinking water in Flint, Michigan focused national attention on problems associated with older lead pipes. *See* sidebar.

Backflow. No federal programs regulate backflow; however, the state does regulate backflow through the SWRCB's Division of Drinking Water. 17 Cal. Code Regs. §§ 7583–7605; Health & Safety Code § 116800 *et seq*. The SWRCB and local health agencies implement and enforce backflow prevention programs (also known as cross-connection programs).

A PWS owner or operator is required to protect the system from backflow-related contamination by implementing a cross-connection control program. 17 Cal. Code Regs. § 7584. Backflow prevention devices are designed to ensure that contaminants, especially pathogens, are not back-siphoned into a potable water system. A PWS program must include, at a minimum, the following elements:

- Operating rules or ordinances to implement a backflow prevention program
- Surveys to identify locations where cross-connections are likely to occur
- Provisions of backflow protection by the water-user at all connections where a cross-connection hazard has been identified
- At least one person trained in cross-connection control to carry out the cross-connection program
- A procedure for testing backflow preventers, with a semiannual to biannual frequency. 17 Cal. Code Regs. § 7605
- Records of locations, tests, and repairs of backflow preventers

Water suppliers (i.e., owners or operators of PWSs) also must evaluate the potential health hazard created by conditions on the water user's premises. 17 Cal. Code Regs. § 7585. Water users, not water suppliers, are responsible for abatement of cross-connections.

RECORDS

Owners or operators of PWSs are also responsible for complying with reporting and recordkeeping requirements

Owners or operators of PWSs are also responsible for complying with reporting and recordkeeping requirements. 40 C.F.R. § 141 Subpart D; 22. Cal. Code Regs. § 64453. PWSs must maintain records of:

- Bacteriological analyses, for at least five years
- Chemical analyses, for at least 10 years. 40 C.F.R. § 141.33
- Corrective measures taken for violations of primary drinking water regulations, for at least three years
- Water quality complaints and corrective measures taken, for at least five years (state requirement)

Federal and state law requires PWSs to provide timely notification to EPA and the SWRCB, respectively, of failure to meet applicable drinking water standards.

PHG = public health goals

MORE ON CALIFORNIA DRINKING WATER PROGRAMS

PRIMARY AND SECONDARY MAXIMUM CONTAMINANT LEVELS

Although the state adopted the federal primary and secondary MCLs, the state also adopted (22 Cal. Code Regs. § 64449):

- Some primary MCLs that are lower (more health-protective) than the federal MCLs (e.g., arsenic, perchlorate, and 1,4 dichlorobenzene). 22 Cal. Code Regs. §§ 64441–64444; 22 Cal. Code Regs. § 64670 *et seq.*
- Some primary MCLs for which there are no federal MCLs (e.g., bentazone and perchlorate). California has adopted an MCL of 0.006 mg/l for perchlorate. Perchlorate is a widespread drinking water contaminant, especially in Southern California, derived primarily from rocket fuel propellants
- Some secondary MCLs that are lower (more health-protective) than the federal MCLs (e.g., methyl tertiary butyl ether or MTBE)
- Some secondary MCLs for which there are no federal MCLs (e.g., manganese and the herbicide thiobencarb). 22 Cal. Code Regs. § 64449

A SWRCB-approved laboratory must analyze samples used to determine MCL compliance in California. SB 385 of 2015 (Chapter 272, Statutes of 2015) authorizes the SWRCB to allow PWSs up to five years to achieve the more health-protective MCL for hexavalent chromium.

RISK ASSESSMENTS

OEHHA performs risk assessments that are used to set public health goals (PHGs). Like the federal MCLGs that serve as a starting point for setting federal MCLs, the PHGs are used by the SWRCB to set California MCLs. PHGs represent levels of contaminants in drinking water that do not pose a significant health risk to consumers. Health & Safety Code § 116365(c). For each contaminant, the risk assessment assumes that an individual consumes contaminated water daily for a lifetime and does not experience a one in one million incremental cancer risk. PHGs are based solely on scientific and public health considerations without regard to economic considerations. On the other hand, the state's primary MCLs must consider economics and technical feasibility and be set as close as feasible to the corresponding PHG while placing primary emphasis on protecting public health. Health & Safety Code § 116365(a).

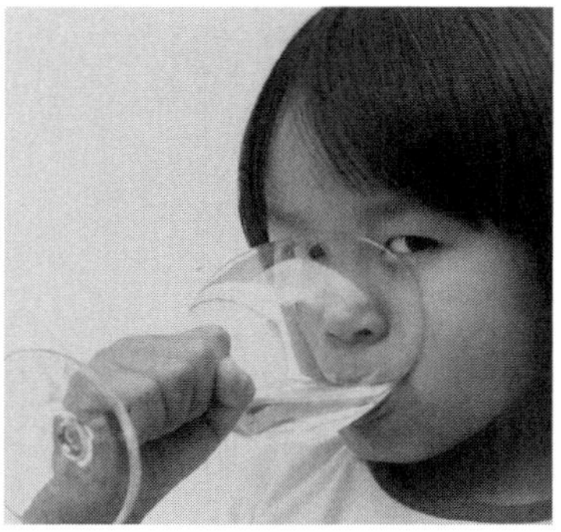

OEHHA performs risk assessments that are used to set public health goals for drinking water contaminants.

DOMESTIC WATER SUPPLY PERMITS

No person may operate a PWS without having secured a domestic water supply permit from SWRCB. As mentioned above, the California SDWA defines a PWS as any

ANSI = American National Standards Institute

VA = vulnerability assessment

entity that serves drinking water to at least 25 persons for at least 60 days out of the year, or that services domestic water to 15 or more service connections. SWRCB (2007) has issued detailed instructions to applicants for a domestic water supply permit. If a community water system serves at least five but fewer than 15 service connections, it is called a state small water system, and is regulated by the local health department rather than SWRCB. Health & Safety Code §§ 116525, 116530, 116540, 116550.

Lead-free Plumbing. AB 1953 of 2006 (Chapter 853, Statutes of 2006) requires use of only lead-free plumbing to convey or dispense water for human consumption. SB 1395 of 2008 (Chapter 581, Statutes of 2008) requires the DTSC to monitor and test lead plumbing for compliance with these standards. In addition, DTSC must annually select up to 75 drinking water faucets (or other drinking water plumbing fittings and fixtures) from publicly accessible wholesale or resale locations to test and evaluate compliance with the lead limits.

SB 1334 of 2008 (Chapter 580, Statutes of 2008) is intended to help prevent consumers from unknowingly purchasing water faucets and fixtures that fail to meet the lead-free standards established under AB 1953 (above). SB 1334 requires all plumbing products to be certified by an independent American National Standards Institute (ANSI)-accredited third party for compliance with existing lead standards. Certification must meet the lead-free requirements described above.

The SWRCB is authorized to grant a small PWS (serving up to 3,300 people) a variance from meeting primary MCLs if it can demonstrate it cannot afford to comply. The PWS may use technology capable of removing contaminants to the maximum extent that is affordable and protective of public health. 42 U.S.C. § 1415(e)(3).

SECURITY MEASURES

The Bioterrorism Act is intended to protect the nation's water supplies and systems against harmful disruptions.

Under the Bioterrorism Act (42 U.S.C. § 300hh *et seq.*), community drinking water systems that service more than 3,300 people must conduct vulnerability assessments (VAs), evaluating their vulnerability to attack (e.g., terrorist attack, vandalism, and insider sabotage). The Act is intended to protect the nation's water supplies and systems against harmful disruptions. EPA and PWSs are the primary entities responsible for ensuring a safe and reliable supply of drinking water, and are charged with developing response measures for potential threats to the nation's water supplies and systems.

Under the Bioterrorism Act, a community water system serving more than 3,300 people must:

- Conduct a vulnerability assessment
- Certify and submit a written copy of the VA to the EPA administrator
- Prepare or revise an emergency response plan that incorporates VA results

- Certify to the EPA administrator, within six months of completing the VA, that an emergency response plan has been completed or revised
- Maintain a copy of the emergency response plan for five years

The Bioterrorism Act prohibits states from reviewing PWS VAs. 42 U.S.C. § 300i-2. Therefore, SWRCB cannot require a copy of the completed VA.

ENFORCEMENT

FEDERAL ENFORCEMENT

Under the federal SDWA, EPA can bring a civil action against a violator, and the court can impose a civil penalty of up to $25,000 per day of violation. 42 U.S.C. § 300(g) *et seq.*; 42 U.S.C. § 1414(b). EPA also can collect the following:

Under the federal SDWA, EPA can bring a civil action against a violator, and the court can impose a civil penalty of up to $25,000 per day of violation.

- A maximum penalty of up to $25,000 for violation of an administrative order. 42 U.S.C. § 1414(g)(3)
- Up to $5,000 per violation per day of an emergency order. 42 U.S.C. § 1431(b)
- Up to $50,000 for tampering with a PWS. 42 U.S.C. § 1432(c)
- Up to $20,000 for attempting to or threatening to tamper with a PWS. 42 U.S.C. § 1432(c)
- Up to $25,000 for failing to keep or make appropriate records. 42 U.S.C. § 1445(c)

STATE ENFORCEMENT

Civil penalties. Under California law, SWRCB can assess the following civil penalties:

- $5,000 per day per violation, from any person who knowingly makes a false statement or representation in a record, report, application or other submitted document. Health & Safety Code § 116725
- $25,000 per day per violation, from any person who violates a schedule of compliance for a primary MCL other than turbidity
- $5,000 per day per violation, from any person who violates any order under the Health and Safety Code. (The fine is larger, and prison time can be imposed, if violating the order creates a substantial likelihood of imminent danger to the health of people; *see* paragraph below)

Criminal penalties. A person may be fined up to $25,000 per day of violation or imprisoned in county jail for up to one year or both, if convicted of knowingly committing any of the following (Health & Safety Code § 116730):

- Making a false representation or statement on any record, report, or application
- Altering any record currently in the individual's possession that is required to be maintained under the Health and Safety Code

- Destroying or concealing any record
- Withholding information about an imminent and substantial danger to the public health or safety, if the information has been requested by SWRCB
- Violating an order that creates a substantial likelihood of imminent danger to the health of people
- Operating a PWS without an SWRCB-issued permit

A person may be fined up to $30,000 for tampering with a PWS or imprisoned for three to five years (a felony) or both. Health & Safety Code § 116750.

for more information...

State Water Resources Control Board, 2007. Domestic Water Supply Permit Applicant Instructions.

Manaster, K. A. and D. P. Selmi (eds.), ND. California Environmental Law and Land Use Practice, Chapter 33. Matthew Bender, San Francisco, Calif.

glossary

Consumer confidence report—annual report, written by public water suppliers who serve community water systems, that summarizes information about drinking water sources used (rivers, lakes, reservoirs, aquifers, etc.), detected contaminants, and other educational information. To be delivered to customers by July 1 of each year.

Domestic water supply permit*—a permit issued by SWRCB for a PWS that supplies domestic water.

Maximum contaminant level goal—a non-enforceable concentration of a drinking water contaminant, set at the level at which no known or anticipated adverse effects on human health occur and that allows a margin of safety. The MCLG is usually the starting point for determining the enforceable maximum contaminant level.

Potable water—tap water that is safe and satisfactory for drinking and cooking.

Primary maximum contaminant level—a mandatory and enforceable standard (federal and state) that is protective of human health.

Public health goal—contaminant level in drinking water that does not pose a significant health risk to consumers and is based solely on scientific and public health considerations without regard to economic considerations.

Public water system—system that provides the public with piped water for human consumption, and has 15 or more service connections or regularly serves 25 individuals daily at least 60 days out of the year.

Secondary maximum contaminant level—a mandatory and enforceable standard (state only) that protects aesthetic qualities of drinking water, such as taste, odor, and color.

Underground injection control program—the program, under the federal Safe Drinking Water Act, that regulates the discharge of wastes into underground injection wells.

Vulnerability assessment—an evaluation conducted by community drinking water systems that service more than 3,300 people, that evaluates vulnerability to attack (e.g., terrorist attack, vandalism, insider sabotage) and identifies actions to reduce the threat risk.

* equals permits and approvals

PART 3

REGULATION OF NATURAL RESOURCES

CHAPTER 12

Agricultural Land

related Solano Press titles

California Land Use and Planning Law. Cecily Talbert Barclay and Matthew S. Gray. 35th Edition. 2016.

The Open Space and Land Conservation Handbook. Jeff Loux. 2011.

in this chapter...

CEQA = California Environmental Quality Act

NRCS = Natural Resources Conservation Service

DLRP = Division of Land Resource Protection

DOC = Department of Conservation

RCD = resource conservation district

LAFCO = Local Agency Formation Commission

AFT = American Farmland Trust

INTRODUCTION

California is the leading agricultural producer and exporter in the United States. In 2013, the State's 77,900 farms and ranches received $46.4 billion for their output. (U.S. Department of Agriculture 2015)

In addition to its major contributions to the California economy, agricultural land in California provides other important public benefits, including open space and aesthetics. Urban growth and water supply shortages, however, have been steadily reducing the acreage of California farmland in production. The Legislature has recognized that farmland preservation is in the public interest and has enacted several farmland preservation programs. (Local land use planning and zoning, reviewed in Chapter 3, also play an important role in agricultural land preservation.) This chapter reviews key laws and agencies involved in agricultural land preservation, the role of the California Environmental Quality Act (CEQA), the Williamson Act, conservation and open space easements, right-to-farm ordinances, and other agricultural land preservation programs. Nonprofits such as the American Farmland Trust also play a key role in agricultural land preservation. *See* sidebar on facing page.

KEY LAWS AND AGENCIES

KEY LAWS

The Williamson Act offers agricultural landowners reduced property tax assessments if they contract with counties or cities to voluntarily restrict their land to agricultural and open space uses.

Williamson Act. The Williamson Act, also called the California Land Conservation Act (Gov't Code § 51200 *et seq.*), is California's oldest agricultural land preservation program, dating back to 1965. The Williamson Act offers agricultural landowners reduced property tax assessments if they contract with counties or cities to voluntarily restrict their land to agricultural and open space uses. In return, restricted parcels are assessed for property taxes at rates consistent with their actual uses, rather than potential market value. Revenue & Taxation Code § 423 *et seq.*

Coastal Act. The Coastal Act includes a policy to maintain in agricultural production the "maximum amount of prime agricultural land" within the coastal zone. Pub. Res. Code § 30241. The policy is implemented in Local Coastal Plans and coastal development permitting.

KEY AGENCIES

Natural Resources Conservation Service. The NRCS, formerly the Soil Conservation Service, is within the United States Department of Agriculture. It operates the Farm and Ranch Lands Protection Program, a voluntary conservation easement program authorized by the Farm Security and Rural Investment Act of 2002. 16 U.S.C. § 3830 *et seq.* NRCS also operates other programs that promote farmland preservation, including programs for technical assistance, environmental improvement, and resource assessments.

California Department of Conservation. Through its Division of Land Resource Protection (DLRP), the DOC operates four programs related to agricultural land preservation: the Farmland Mapping and Monitoring Program, the Resource Conservation District Assistance Program, the Williamson Act Program, and the California Farmland Conservancy Program. The first two programs are described below, and the latter two programs are described in detail later in this chapter.

The Farmland Mapping and Monitoring Program produces maps and statistical data used for analyzing impacts on California's agricultural resources. Agricultural land is rated according to soil quality and irrigation status; the best quality land is called prime farmland. Maps are updated every two years using aerial photographs, a computer mapping system, public review, and field reconnaissance.

DLRP provides support to Resource Conservation Districts (RCDs), which are special districts involved in conservation of both agricultural and non-agricultural land (*see* below). This support includes financial assistance through an RCD grant program and technical assistance.

California Department of Food and Agriculture. The DFA plays an indirect role in agricultural land preservation by promoting a strong agricultural industry. DFA's goals are to:

- Ensure that only safe and quality food reaches the consumer
- Protect against invasion of exotic pests and diseases
- Promote California agriculture and food products both at home and abroad
- Ensure an equitable and orderly marketplace for California's agricultural products
- Build coalitions supporting the state's agricultural infrastructure to meet evolving industry needs

Resource conservation districts. RCDs emerged during the 1930s as a way to prevent the soil erosion problems of the Dust Bowl from recurring. Formed as independent local liaisons between the federal government and landowners, RCDs always have worked closely with NRCS. RCDs are California special districts locally governed by locally appointed or elected boards of directors. Pub. Res. Code § 9001 *et seq*. There are currently over 100 RCDs in California implementing agricultural land resource conservation projects and programs, including agricultural land preservation.

Local Agency Formation Commissions. LAFCO decisions on spheres of influence and boundary changes (*see* Chapter 4) are guided by state policies encouraging preservation of prime agricultural land. Gov't Code § 56377.

American Farmland Trust Plays Key Role in Agricultural Land Preservation

The American Farmland Trust (AFT) is a nonprofit organization established in 1980 to conserve agricultural resources. The AFT has undertaken a number of programs to conserve California farmland. For example, it has outlined a new framework for farmland conservation in the San Joaquin Valley (AFT 2013) with six objectives, and established performance measures for each:

- Avoid development of high quality farmlands
- Minimize farmland loss with more efficient development
- Ensure stability at the urban edge
- Minimize rural residential development
- Mitigate the loss of farmland with conservation easements
- Encourage a favorable agricultural business climate

LESA = California Agricultural Land Evaluation and Site Assessment

CALIFORNIA ENVIRONMENTAL QUALITY ACT ROLE IN AGRICULTURAL LAND PRESERVATION

CEQA APPENDIX G

The California Environmental Quality Act plays an important role in agricultural land preservation. Appendix G of the CEQA Guidelines sets forth an initial study checklist used to determine whether a project's impacts are potentially significant. *See* chapter 2.

Under Appendix G, a project would have significant effects on agricultural resources if the project would:

- Convert prime farmland, unique farmland, or farmland of statewide importance, as shown on DLRP maps, to non-agricultural use
- Conflict with existing agricultural zoning or a Williamson Act contract
- Involve other environmental changes that could result in the conversion of farmland to non-agricultural use

The LESA model evaluates factors such as soil resource quality, water resource availability, amount of surrounding agricultural lands, and amount of surrounding protected resource lands.

Appendix G also states that the California Agricultural Land Evaluation and Site Assessment (LESA) model may be used to assess agricultural land impacts. The LESA model quantifies the relative importance of agricultural land resources based upon specific measurable features. The model evaluates factors such as soil resource quality, water resource availability, amount of surrounding agricultural lands, and amount of surrounding protected resource lands.

FARMLAND DEFINITIONS

Department of Conservation definitions of farmland classifications used in Appendix G are as follows:

- **Prime farmland.** Farmland with the best combination of physical and chemical features able to sustain long-term agricultural production. This land has the soil quality, growing season, and moisture supply needed to produce sustained, high yields. Land must have been used for irrigated agricultural production at some time during the four years prior to the mapping date.
- **Farmland of statewide importance.** Farmland similar to prime farmland but with minor shortcomings, such as greater slopes or less ability to store soil moisture. Land must have been used for irrigated agricultural production at some time during the four years prior to the mapping date.
- **Unique farmland.** Farmland of lesser quality soils used for production of the state's leading agricultural crops. This land usually is irrigated, but may include nonirrigated orchards or vineyards as found in some climatic zones in California. Land must have been cropped at some time during the four years prior to the mapping date.

CONSERVATION EASEMENTS AS CEQA MITIGATION

Conservation easements (*see* below) sometimes are proposed as mitigation measures for significant agricultural land impacts. Even though they do not result in "no net loss" of agricultural land, but rather seek to preserve existing agricultural land, the courts have recognized conservation easements as valid CEQA mitigation. *See, e.g., Masonite Corporation v. County of Mendocino* (2010) 208 Cal. App. 4th 230; *Save Panoche Valley v. San Benito County* (2013) 210 Cal. App. 4th 504.

WILLIAMSON ACT

OVERVIEW

The Williamson Act, also called the California Land Conservation Act (Gov't Code § 51200 *et seq.*), is California's oldest agricultural land preservation program, dating back to 1965. The purposes of the Williamson Act are to preserve the maximum amount of agricultural land to maintain the state's agricultural economy, to discourage premature and unnecessary conversion of agricultural land to urban uses, to discourage discontinuous urban development, and to preserve the open space and aesthetic values of agricultural land. The DLRP is responsible for interpretation and enforcement of the Williamson Act.

The Williamson Act establishes certain rules for uses compatible with the agricultural, recreational, or open spaces uses of land in an agricultural preserve.

AGRICULTURAL PRESERVES

City and county participation in the Williamson Act is voluntary. The first step for a city or county to participate in the Williamson Act is to establish an agricultural preserve. Only land within an agricultural preserve is eligible for a Williamson Act contract. The city or county establishes the agricultural preserve boundary and adopts rules restricting land uses within the preserve to ensure it is maintained for agricultural and open space uses. Gov't Code §§ 51231, 51237. An agricultural preserve must consist of at least 100 acres (with local exceptions possible), in one or more ownerships. Once an agricultural preserve is established, the city or county must file a map and a resolution creating the preserve with the county recorder.

The Williamson Act is California's oldest agricultural land preservation program.

The Williamson Act establishes certain rules for uses compatible with the agricultural, recreational, or open spaces uses of land in an agricultural preserve. Gov't Code § 51238.1. Local compatibility rules may be more restrictive than those required by the Act. The Act discourages public agencies from placing federal, state, or local public improvements or public utility improvements in agricultural preserves; it establishes special procedures that must be followed if public agencies acquire land under Williamson Act contract.

CONTRACTS

The Williamson Act offers agricultural landowners reduced property tax assessments if they contract with counties or cities to voluntarily restrict their land to

FSZ = Farmland Security Zone

In addition to land used for agriculture, recreational areas, scenic highway corridors, wildlife habitat, salt ponds, managed wetlands, and submerged areas may be included in an agricultural preserve and be eligible for a Williamson Act contract.

agricultural and open space uses. In return, restricted parcels are assessed for property taxes at rates consistent with their actual uses, rather than potential market value for urban uses. Revenue & Taxation Code § 423 *et seq.* In addition to land used for agriculture, recreational areas, scenic highway corridors, wildlife habitat, salt ponds, managed wetlands, and submerged areas may be included in an agricultural preserve and be eligible for a Williamson Act contract.

Historically, the Department administered a subvention program to partially reimburse local governments for property tax revenues foregone as a result of Williamson Act participation. This program was created by the Open Space Subvention Act of 1972 to provide for the partial replacement of local property tax revenue foregone as a result of participation in the Williamson Act and other enforceable open space restriction programs (Gov't Code § 16140 *et seq.*). However, subvention payments were discontinued in 2010 due to budget issues, and as of 2015 had not been resumed. An alternative funding option allows participating counties to recapture a portion of the foregone property tax revenue by decreasing the duration of Williamson Act and Farmland Security Zone (*see* below) contracts by one and two years, respectively. Gov't Code § 51244.

As of the 2013, approximately 16.4 million acres of the state's 30 million acres of farm and ranch land currently were protected under the Williamson Act. California DOC 2015. As of 2013, 52 of the state's 58 counties offered Williamson Act contracts.

TERM OF CONTRACT

A Williamson Act contract has a minimum 10-year rolling term. Unless either party files a notice of nonrenewal, the contract automatically is renewed annually for an additional year. An optional program within the Williamson Act allows landowners of certain lands to petition a county to create a Farmland Security Zone (FSZ) with a 20-year rolling contract. Gov't Code §§ 51244, 51296. As of 2013, the FSZ program had been adopted by 25 counties, with a reported 875,000 acres of land under FSZ contract. Once an agricultural preserve is established, the city or county must file a map and a resolution creating the preserve with the county recorder and must keep this information current. Gov't Code § 51237.

NONRENEWAL AND CANCELLATION

Nonrenewal, rather than cancellation, is the preferred termination method for Williamson Act contracts. *See* sidebar. A notice of nonrenewal starts a nine-year nonrenewal period, during which the annual tax assessment gradually increases until the property is taxed at its full market value by the time the contract expires. The goal of this process is to achieve fair taxation as the Williamson Act restriction is eliminated over time. Revenue & Taxation Code § 426.

Alternatively, a landowner can petition to cancel a Williamson Act contract if "extraordinary circumstances" exist. Gov't Code § 51280. To approve a contract cancellation, a county or city must make findings that the cancellation is consistent with the Williamson Act or in the public interest. An opportunity for another use is not a sufficient reason for cancellation, nor is, by itself, the uneconomic character of an existing agricultural use. Upon cancellation, the landowner must pay a cancellation fee of 12.5 percent of the unrestricted current fair market valuation of the property. Gov't Code § 51283.

SOLAR USE EASEMENTS

The parties, after an eligibility determination and management plan review conducted by the Department of Conservation, may rescind a Williamson Act contract in order to simultaneously enter into a "solar-use easement." This provision, added by 2011 legislation, is intended to encourage the development of utility-scale solar photovoltaic facilities on marginally productive or physically impaired farmland. A solar-use easement requires that the land be used for solar photovoltaic facilities for a term of 20 years, or if the landowner requests, for a term of not less than 10 years. Gov't Code § 51190 *et seq.*; 14 Cal. Code Regs. § 3100 *et seq.*

ENFORCEMENT

Williamson Act contracts are binding on successors in interest of the owner, with special provisions for transfers among immediate family members. If a landowner fails to comply with the terms and conditions of a contract, the local government or DOC may seek an injunction to enforce the contract. Structures permitted or built after January 1, 2004, that exceed 2,500 square feet and are not permitted by the contract terms, are considered material breaches of the contract and may be subject to penalties equal to 25 percent of the value of the affected land and 25 percent of the value of any improvements. Gov't Code § 51250(a).

CONSERVATION AND OPEN SPACE EASEMENTS

CONSERVATION EASEMENTS

A statutory conservation easement is a recorded deed restriction voluntarily executed by a landowner with the purpose of retaining land "predominantly in its natural scenic, historical, agricultural, forested, or open space condition." Civ. Code § 815.1. Conservation easements may be held by state and local governments authorized to hold real property, by tax-exempt nonprofit organizations, and by California Native American tribes.

Conservation easements "run with the land," meaning they are binding on all current and future owners of the property. Violations may be enforced through injunctions and money damages.

California Farmland Conservancy Program Act. Funding for agricultural conservation easements is available under the California Farmland Conservancy Program (CFCP) Act. Pub. Res. Code § 10200 *et seq.* Agricultural conservation easements are

Supreme Court Interprets Williamson Act in Landmark Case

In *Sierra Club v. City of Hayward* (1981) 28 Cal. 3d 840, the Supreme Court firmly established that nonrenewal of a Williamson Act contract is the preferred method of termination. The court ruled that cancellation can occur only in "extraordinary circumstances," when the difficult findings required by the Act can be made by a city or county.

The case dealt with the City of Hayward's cancellation of a 93-acre parcel under Williamson Act contract. The court first held that local government Williamson Act cancellation decisions are judicially reviewable and should be construed narrowly to achieve the purposes of the Act. The court then proceeded to invalidate some of the City of Hayward's cancellation findings as unsupported by substantial evidence.

CFCP = California Farmland Conservancy Program

created specifically to support agriculture and prevent development on the agricultural parcels subject to the easements. Easements funded by the CFCP must be of a size and nature suitable for viable commercial agriculture. Although other benefits (e.g., scenic) may result from the land not being developed, the primary use of the land under easement must be agricultural. The placement of an agricultural conservation easement on land may provide income, property tax, and estate tax benefits.

Agricultural land easements funded by the CFCP may be held by land trusts or local governments, which are responsible for enforcing the terms of the easement. The easement may be donated to the easement holder, purchased, or both.

Several non-profit organizations provide technical assistance for establishing conservation easements. These include the American Farmland Trust and Land Trust Alliance.

Farm and Ranch Lands Protection Program. The Farm and Ranch Lands Protection Program, operated by the NRCS, provides funding for conservation easements, working through state, tribal, or local governments that acquire the easements. Participating landowners agree not to convert their land to non-agricultural uses and to implement a conservation plan for any highly erodible land. To qualify for this program, the land must meet a number of requirements, including the requirements to contain prime, unique, or other productive soil, or historical or archeological resources; and to be included in a pending offer for a state, tribal, or local farmland protection program. 7 C.F.R. § 1491.

Local agricultural mitigation programs. As of 2015, about a dozen counties and cities had adopted agricultural mitigation programs. (Yolo County 2015.) These programs typically require off-site agricultural conservation easements to be purchased as a condition of development approval, typically at a 1:1 mitigation ratio (one acre of land under easement for every acre of land developed). They also typically allow fees to be paid in lieu of easements, often for smaller sized development projects. Local agricultural mitigation programs requiring agricultural conservation easements to be purchased as a condition of development approval have been upheld by the courts as a valid exercise of the police power and valid CEQA mitigation. *See, e.g., Building Industry Association of Central California v. County of Stanislaus* (2010) 190 Cal. App. 4th 582.

OPEN SPACE EASEMENTS

Open space easements authorized by the Open Space Easement Act of 1974 (Gov't Code § 510070 *et seq.*) also may be used for agricultural land preservation. Open space easements may be held only by cities, counties, or nonprofit organizations, and must have at least a rolling 10-year term. An open space easement can be approved by a city or county only if preservation of the land as open space is consistent with the general plan and is in the best interest of the city or county. Building permits may not be issued if inconsistent with the easement.

Open space easements may be held only by cities, counties, or nonprofit organizations, and must have at least a rolling 10-year term.

An open space easement can be terminated through nonrenewal, similar to a Williamson Act contract. Alternatively, a landowner may seek abandonment of the easement by filing a petition; the relevant city or county must approve the petition through making certain findings.

RIGHT-TO-FARM ORDINANCES

Right-to-farm ordinances seek to reduce the opposition of urban neighbors to agricultural operations through requiring disclosure of the potential adverse impacts of agricultural operations to purchasers of nearby property. First enacted in the 1980s, they were encouraged by passage of Civil Code § 3482.5, which declares that a farm in operation for more than three years is not considered a nuisance due to changed circumstances, such as urbanization, in the area. The right to farm law also includes commercial agricultural processing facilities.

Ordinances typically contain the following provisions:

- **Statement of purpose.** For example, to preserve agricultural operations as an important part of the local economy, or to promote a good neighbor policy between farm and other landowners
- **Nuisance.** A reference to Civil Code § 3482.5, although some ordinances reduce the time of operation from three years to one year
- **Disclosure.** A requirement that potential purchasers or developers of property near farming operations be notified of the potential adverse impacts of agricultural operations
- **Grievance procedure.** A process for resolving complaints against agricultural operations

OTHER AGRICULTURAL LAND PRESERVATION PROGRAMS

In addition to the programs described, local governments can implement a number of additional tools to preserve agricultural land. These include:

- General plan policies encouraging agricultural land preservation (sometimes captured in a General Plan Agricultural Element; *see* sidebar)
- Urban growth boundaries
- Agricultural zoning
- Purchase of agricultural land conservation easement programs
- Agricultural land mitigation banks
- Ordinances requiring notices to property purchasers near agricultural operations
- Development agreements
- Encouraging formation of local land trusts

Yolo County General Plan Agricultural Element

Yolo County has been a statewide leader in agricultural land preservation. Its innovative General Plan Agriculture and Economic Development Element (adopted in 2009) establishes a comprehensive framework for not just preserving the County's agricultural land, but also strengthening the agricultural economy. It addresses agricultural issues throughout Yolo County through goals and related policies on six topics:

- Preservation of agriculture
- Natural resources for agriculture
- Healthy farm economy
- Education and awareness
- Local preference
- Delta agriculture

for more information...

American Farmland Trust, 2013. Saving Farmland, Growing Cities: A Framework for Implementing Effective Farmland Conservation Policies in the San Joaquin Valley.

Barclay, C. T. and M. S. Gray, 2016. California Land Use and Planning Law. 35th Edition. Solano Press. Point Arena, Calif.

California Department of Conservation, 2015. The California Land Conservation Act 2014 Status Report.

Manaster, K. A. and D. P. Selmi (eds.). ND. Chapter 70 of California Environmental Law and Land Use Practice. Matthew Bender. San Francisco, Calif.

U.S. Department of Agriculture, 2015. California Agricultural Statistics, 2013 Crop Year.

Yolo County, 2015. Yolo County Agricultural Mitigation Program—Policy Options for Increased Mitigation Ratios.

glossary

Conservation easement—a recorded deed restriction voluntarily executed by a landowner with the purpose of retaining land predominantly in its natural scenic, historical, agricultural, forested, or open space condition.

Subvention—as used in the Williamson Act, the granting of funds from state government to local governments to partially compensate for foregone property tax revenues when land is placed under contract.

Williamson Act contract—a voluntary contract entered into between a landowner and a local government in which the landowner receives reduced property tax assessments in return for restricting land to agricultural and open space uses.

CHAPTER 13

Water Resources

related Solano Press titles

California Water II. Arthur L. Littleworth and Eric L. Garner. 2007.

Water and Land Use: Planning Wisely for California's Future. Karen E. Johnson and Jeff Loux. 2004.

in this chapter...

INTRODUCTION

California water law is a very complex field with a long history, and this chapter can do no more than provide a basic outline. For further general reading, the Water Education Foundation's "Layperson's Guides" provide an excellent, easy-to-understand introduction to California water law and policy. The California Water Plan Update provides a much more detailed compendium of state water law, policy, and data, as well as a long-term strategic plan for managing the state's water resources.

A key to understanding California water law is to understand the various state, federal, and local water projects that have been constructed over the years to solve a fundamental distribution problem: most of the state's water is located in northern California, whereas most of the demand is located in the southern two-thirds of the state. Figure 13-1 shows the location of major federal, state, and local water project facilities in California.

This chapter reviews key laws and agencies involved in California water resources management, California water resources background information, water rights law, water supply planning, Delta planning, and wild and scenic river systems. Flood risk management, a related topic, is addressed in chapter 4, and water quality is discussed in chapter 10.

San Joaquin River Restoration Program

In 1988, a coalition of environmental groups, led by the Natural Resources Defense Council (NRDC), filed a lawsuit, *NRDC, et al., v. Kirk Rodgers, et al.*, challenging the renewal of long-term water service contracts between the United States and the CVP Friant Division. In 2006, after more than 18 years of litigation, the parties entered into a Settlement Agreement. In 2009, Congress passed the San Joaquin River Settlement Restoration Act (part of PL 111-11) to implement the Settlement Agreement.

The Settlement Agreement establishes goals of restoring flows to the San Joaquin River from Friant Dam to the confluence of Merced River and restoring a self-sustaining Chinook salmon fishery in the river, while at the same time reducing or avoiding adverse water supply impacts from restoration flows. The first water releases from Friant Dam in support of the SJRRP, called interim flows, began October 1, 2009. Restoration flows began January 1, 2014.

KEY LAWS AND AGENCIES

FEDERAL LAWS AND AGENCIES

U.S. Bureau of Reclamation. The federal government has played a major role in developing California's water resources. The U.S. Bureau of Reclamation was created by the Reclamation Act of 1902 to reclaim western lands, mainly for agricultural development. This agency owns and operates two large water supply projects serving California—the Central Valley Project (CVP) and the Colorado River facilities.

Central Valley Project. The CVP was authorized in 1937 and was largely completed in 1951. The CVP is comprised of 20 dams and reservoirs, 11 power plants, and 500 miles of major canals as well as conduits, tunnels, and related facilities. It manages 9 million acre-feet of water, historically delivering about 7 million acre-feet annually for agriculture, urban, and wildlife use. It also dedicates 800,000 acre-feet per year to fish and wildlife and their habitat and 410,000 acre-feet to state and federal wildlife refuges and wetlands pursuant to the Central Valley Project Improvement Act of 1992 (CVPIA, 34 U.S.C. § 3401 *et seq.*). More recently, the Bureau of Reclamation began implementing the San Joaquin River Restoration Program pursuant to a litigation Settlement Agreement. *See* sidebar.

Colorado River facilities. The Colorado River is a highly regulated river that passes through seven states. California, Arizona, and Nevada are the lower basin states. The U.S. Bureau of Reclamation built a series of major dams, reservoirs, and aqueducts on the lower Colorado River. Facilities serving California include:

FIGURE 13-1
Major Water Project Facilities in California

Source: Littleworth and Garner. 2007. *California Water II*. Solano Press. Reprinted with permission.

CVP = Central Valley Project

FERC = Federal Energy Regulatory Commission

USACE = U.S. Army Corps of Engineers

DWR = California Department of Water Resources

SWP = State Water Project

SWRCB = State Water Resources Control Board

- **Colorado River Aqueduct.** Operated by the Metropolitan Water District of Southern California
- **All-American Canal, Imperial Dam, and Yuma Project.** Operated by the Imperial Irrigation District
- **Coachella Project.** Operated by the Coachella Valley Water District
- **San Diego Project.** Operated by the San Diego County Water Authority

Federal Energy Regulatory Commission. Pursuant to the Federal Power Act (16 U.S.C. § 791 *et seq.*), FERC issues licenses for hydroelectric projects using navigable waters or federal land. The FERC licensing process balances hydropower needs with other objectives such as water supply, recreation, and environmental protection. Many public and private multi-purpose water projects are subject to FERC licensing.

U.S. Army Corps of Engineers. USACE is the primary federal flood control agency. *See* chapter 4. USACE constructs flood control projects and operates multi-purpose projects that provide water supply, such as New Melones Dam and Reservoir.

STATE LAWS AND AGENCIES

California Department of Water Resources. DWR operates and maintains the State Water Project (SWP), including the California Aqueduct. DWR also provides dam safety and flood management services, assists local water districts in water management and conservation activities, promotes recreational opportunities, and plans for future statewide water needs.

The California Water Commission provides a public forum for discussing water issues and advises DWR.

California Water Commission. The California Water Commission consists of nine members appointed by the Governor and confirmed by the State Senate. The Commission provides a public forum for discussing water issues and advises DWR. Statutory duties include approving certain rules and regulations, and monitoring and reporting on the construction and operation of the SWP.

State Water Project. The SWP, authorized in 1960, is the nation's largest state-built water and power development and conveyance system. It includes facilities—pumping plants, power plants, reservoirs, canals, and pipelines—to capture, store, and convey water to 29 water agencies. Major facilities include Oroville Dam and Reservoir, with a storage capacity of 3.5 million acre-feet, and the North Bay, South Bay, and California Aqueducts, serving major urban and agricultural users.

State Water Resources Control Board. The mission of the SWRCB's Division of Water Rights is to establish and maintain a stable system of water rights in California to best develop, conserve, and utilize in the public interest the water resources of the state, while protecting vested rights, water quality, and the environment. The SWRCB's major water rights responsibility is to issue permits and licenses for water appropriation. *See* below.

DSC = Delta Stewardship Council

The Water Commission Act of 1913 (Statutes of 1913, Chapter 586) created the agency that later evolved into the SWRCB, and granted it the authority to administer permits and licenses for California's surface water. The Act was the predecessor to today's Water Code provisions (Water Code § 1200 *et seq.*) governing appropriation.

In addition to issuing permits and licenses, the SWRCB conducts statutory adjudications; statutory adjudication is a process by which the comprehensive determination of all water rights in a stream system is made. Also, the SWRCB can act as referee or fact-finder in court cases involving water rights.

Delta Stewardship Council. The DSC was created by the Delta Reform Act of 2009 (Pub. Res. Code § 85000 *et seq.*). The council has adopted and is implementing the Delta Plan required by that Act.

Delta Conservancy. The Delta Conservancy was also created by the Delta Reform Act of 2009 to implement Delta ecosystem restoration activities.

Colorado River Board of California. This agency's mission is to protect California's rights and interests in the resources provided by the Colorado River and to represent California in discussions and negotiations regarding the Colorado River and its management.

REGIONAL AND LOCAL LAWS AND AGENCIES

California has thousands of regional and local water agencies (including city water departments and various types of special districts) with varying responsibilities for the development, wholesaling, or retailing of water supplies. Regional and local agencies may be formed through either a general district or a special district act. See Department of Water Resources (1994) for a general comparison of water district acts. Several regional or local water agencies have developed their own large water supply projects, including the City of San Francisco (Hetch Hetchy project), the East Bay Municipal Utility District (Mokelumne River Aqueduct System), the City of Los Angeles (Owens Valley project), and the Imperial Irrigation District (Colorado River projects).

California has thousands of regional and local water agencies (including city water departments and various types of special districts) with varying responsibilities for the development, wholesaling, or retailing of water supplies.

BACKGROUND INFORMATION ON CALIFORNIA WATER RESOURCES

California's water resources management history is long and complex. California's water history can roughly be divided into five eras (Johnson and Loux 2004):

- **The early years (1769–1900).** Includes local development of water supplies and the Gold Rush
- **First importation projects (1900–1930).** Includes construction of Los Angeles Aqueduct from Owens Valley
- **Era of great importation projects (1930–1970).** Includes construction of the CVP, Colorado River project, and SWP

- **Environmental transition (1970–1990).** Includes passage of major federal and state environmental laws, changing water projects and water use
- **Towards collaboration and water management (1990–present).** Initiation of regional collaborative and integrated water management programs

Today, the state's water system faces many challenges. These include increasingly unreliable water supplies due to multi-year drought, declining ecosystems and related regulatory restrictions on water deliveries, competing water demands, increasing flood risk, groundwater depletion and related land subsidence, Sacramento-San Joaquin Delta vulnerabilities, and aging infrastructure. The remainder of this chapter explores some of the legal mechanisms and emerging polices to address many of these challenges.

WATER RIGHTS LAW

OVERVIEW

Water use and supplies in California are controlled and managed under a complex system of common law principles, constitutional provisions, state and federal statutes, court decisions, and water contracts. The summary below of California water rights is derived largely from descriptions in prior versions of California Water Plan Updates. DWR 2005.

GENERAL PRINCIPLES

The principle of reasonable and beneficial use can limit water rights because it prohibits the waste, unreasonable use, unreasonable method of use, or unreasonable diversion of water.

Principle of reasonable and beneficial use. Article X, Section 2 of the California Constitution requires that all uses of the state's water be reasonable and beneficial. This principle can limit water rights because it prohibits the waste, unreasonable use, unreasonable method of use, or unreasonable diversion of water. This requirement applies to all California water rights, including riparian rights, appropriative rights, and groundwater rights.

Article X, Section 2 requires fact-specific balancing of uses. The meaning of reasonableness changes as conditions change, and the reasonableness of one use is relative to other uses. In determining whether a use is reasonable and beneficial, the following factors are important (*in re Waters of Long Valley Creek Stream System* (1979) 25 Cal. 3d 339, 354):

- Other beneficial uses to be made of the water
- Social, economic, cultural, environmental, and other benefits and costs associated with competing water uses
- Whether there is a "physical solution" available by which the needs of competing users can be met
- The technical, hydrologic, engineering, economic, and environmental feasibility of competing uses

Public trust doctrine. The public trust doctrine imposes responsibilities on state and local agencies, as trustees, to protect trust resources associated with California's waters, such as navigation, fisheries, recreation, and ecological preservation. See chapter 1 for a review of the origins and scope of the public trust doctrine. The importance of the public trust doctrine in guiding state water planning and allocation was affirmed in the landmark case *National Audubon Society v. Superior Court of Alpine County* (1983) 33 Cal. 3d. 419 (*see* sidebar).

The public trust doctrine and water rights law developed independently and, in some ways, are inconsistent. A water right is an estate in real property; water rights holders need to rely on certainty of water rights to make investments and to be economically productive.

To resolve this inherent conflict, the Supreme Court in *National Audubon* announced the principle of accommodation, under which the public trust and private ownership are to be balanced, and the public trust protected where "feasible." Although the Supreme Court did not elaborate on the meaning of feasibility, the concept is generally thought to encompass environmental, economic, legal, technical, and social considerations.

Public Trust Doctrine Limits Water Rights

The public trust doctrine has its origins in ancient Roman law and was introduced to California through federal and state judicial decisions, as well as through the influential writings of Professor Joseph Sax. Sax 1970 (*see* chapter 1). A series of judicial decisions prior to *National Audubon* placed limits on the government's ability to dispose of trust resources, but the issue of whether the public trust doctrine applied to water rights was unresolved.

In *National Audubon Society v. Superior Court of Alpine County* (1983) 33 Cal. 3d 419, the California Supreme Court found that the public trust doctrine applied to the tributary streams of Mono Lake. The court prohibited the Los Angeles Department of Water and Power (LADWP) from exercising its vested right to divert these streams if public trust values would be harmed. Past LADWP diversions had decreased the level of Mono Lake, causing harm to a large breeding colony of California Gulls.

The court recognized that the state may have to approve water appropriations despite foreseeable harm to public trust use. However, the court required the state as a trustee to consider the effect of water appropriations on the public trust, and to avoid or minimize harm to public trust interests if feasible. Further, the court held that even after an appropriation has been approved, the state may reconsider the allocation decision if it failed to adequately weigh and consider public trust uses.

SURFACE WATER RIGHTS

California has a dual system of surface water rights, recognizing both riparian and appropriative rights. Prescriptive rights are a third type of surface water right and are described later in this chapter.

Riparian rights. A riparian right entitles landowners to use a share of the water flowing past their property. Unlike an appropriative right, a riparian right is not quantified. Rather, it is a "correlative right" to use a portion of the natural flow of water in common with other riparian users.

Riparian rights do not require government approval, but they apply only to the water that would naturally flow in the stream. Riparian rights do not entitle a water user to divert water to storage in a reservoir for use in the dry season or to use water on land outside of the watershed. Riparian rights remain with the property when it changes hands, although parcels severed from the adjacent water source generally lose their right to the water.

When riparian land is divided and sold, a parcel that is no longer contiguous to the river may or may not lose its riparian rights. The general rule is that courts examine the intent of the parties under all of the circumstances; one factor may be the nature and purpose of the conveyance. For example, conveyance of an easement or right-of-way typically would not result in a severance of riparian rights.

Appropriative rights. An appropriative water right has certain fundamental characteristics: amount of water claimed, priority of the right, point of diversion, place of use, purpose of use, and season of diversion. Water right priority has long been the central principle in California water law; the more senior right holders take water before junior right holders in times of shortage.

As noted above, a riparian right can be used only on the riparian parcel, generally on the parcel adjacent to the river. The appropriative system developed to allow the user to convey water for use on non-riparian parcels. Under the "first in time, first in right" principle, the first appropriator had the most senior priority, regardless of whether subsequent users were upstream or downstream of the first appropriator. Subsequent appropriators "lined up" in priority behind the first appropriator based on the same principle. In times of shortage, the most recent (junior) right holder must be the first to discontinue use of water.

The doctrine of progressive development is balanced by the "use it or lose it" doctrine, under which water rights may be forfeited through non-use.

The doctrine of progressive development allows a water user to claim an amount greater than could immediately be put to use, to allow for the orderly construction of facilities and growth. The doctrine of progressive development is balanced by the "use it or lose it" doctrine, under which water rights may be forfeited through non-use. The courts or the SWRCB may declare a water right forfeited after five years of non-use, assuming that water was available. Water Code § 1240 *et seq.*

California recognizes two categories of appropriative surface water rights—those acquired prior to 1914, and those acquired after 1914, the effective date of the Water Commission Act.

Pre-1914 appropriative rights. Before 1872, an appropriative water right could be acquired simply by posting notice and putting the water to beneficial use. In 1872, a provision was added to the Civil Code to allow appropriators to record notice with the county clerk. Pre-1914 water rights are subject to the jurisdiction of the courts, but generally not to the permitting jurisdiction of the SWRCB. The SWRCB may, however, exercise jurisdiction over pre-1914 rights if necessary to decide an issue that is within its jurisdiction, to enforce the prohibition against waste and unreasonable use in Article X, Section 2, or to enforce the public trust doctrine.

Also, water users with pre-1914 appropriative rights, as well as riparian rights, are required to file a Statement of Water Diversion and Use with the SWRCB. Water Code § 5100 *et seq.* The purpose of filing these statements is to make a public record of all surface diversions not already on file with or known to the SWRCB. Failure to file the statements can result in penalties, and willful misstatements are subject to misdemeanor prosecution. Water Code §§ 5107, 5108.

Valid pre-1914 rights are senior to post-1914 rights. Riparian rights are generally senior to pre-1914 rights, unless the date of appropriation occurred prior to the date that the riparian owner acquired the patent for the land.

Post-1914 appropriative rights and the State Water Resources Control Board water rights process. The Water Commission Act of 1913 established the current water rights permitting and licensing process, and created the agency that later evolved into the SWRCB. After 1914, only the SWRCB had the authority to issue new appropriative rights for surface water and subterranean streams. Water Code § 174 *et seq.*

SWRCB water right permits establish the amounts, conditions, and construction timetables for a proposed project. Only unappropriated waters are available for appropriation. Water Code § 1202. Before the SWRCB issues a permit, it must take into account all prior rights and the availability of water in the basin. The SWRCB also considers the flows needed to preserve instream uses such as recreation and fish and wildlife habitat. The SWRCB process for obtaining appropriative water rights is illustrated in Figure 13-2 on the following page.

SWRCB water right permits establish the amounts, conditions, and construction timetables for a proposed project. Only unappropriated waters are available for appropriation.

To obtain a permit, an applicant must first file an application to divert water. Water Code § 1252. The application specifically describes the proposed project's source, place of use, purpose, point of diversion, and quantity to be diverted. Following resolution of any protests, to issue a permit the SWRCB must find that unappropriated water is available to supply the applicant, and the appropriation is in the public interest. Conditions typically placed on permits include construction completion dates, and when water use is to be completed. Water Code § 1330 *et seq.*; 23 Cal. Code Regs. § 650 *et seq.*

When the water project is completed, the terms of the permit have been met, and water under the permit is put to beneficial use, the SWRCB issues a license to the appropriator. The license is the final confirmation of the water right and remains effective as long as its conditions are fulfilled and beneficial use continues. Water Code § 1395 *et seq.*

The SWRCB has the authority to enforce the conditions of both permits and licenses, and can revoke them if conditions are not met. Other, less severe enforcement actions, such as cease-and-desist orders, can be taken to ensure compliance with permit terms. Water Code § 1831; 23 Cal. Code Regs. § 820 *et seq.*

If the appropriation includes construction or enlargement of a dam or reservoir, the applicant also may need to obtain a Certificate of Approval from DWR's Division of Safety of Dams. Water Code § 6000 *et seq.* The Division has jurisdiction over dams that are at least 25 feet high or have an impounding capacity of at least 50 acre-feet or more. Any dam shorter than six feet, regardless of storage capacity, or that has a storage capacity less than 15 acre-feet regardless of height, is not considered jurisdictional. In addition to approving new dams, the Division also inspects operating dams to ensure they are adequately maintained.

Changes in appropriative rights. The point of diversion, place of use, and purpose of use for a water right may be changed as long as the change does not injure other water right holders, whether junior or senior, or unreasonably affect fish and wildlife. For example, a water user with an appropriative right may decide to divert water from a different location on a stream, use water on other lands than originally designated, or change the purpose of use from agricultural to urban.

The method of change and enforcement of the no-injury rule differs between

FIGURE 13-2
Process for Obtaining Appropriative Water Rights

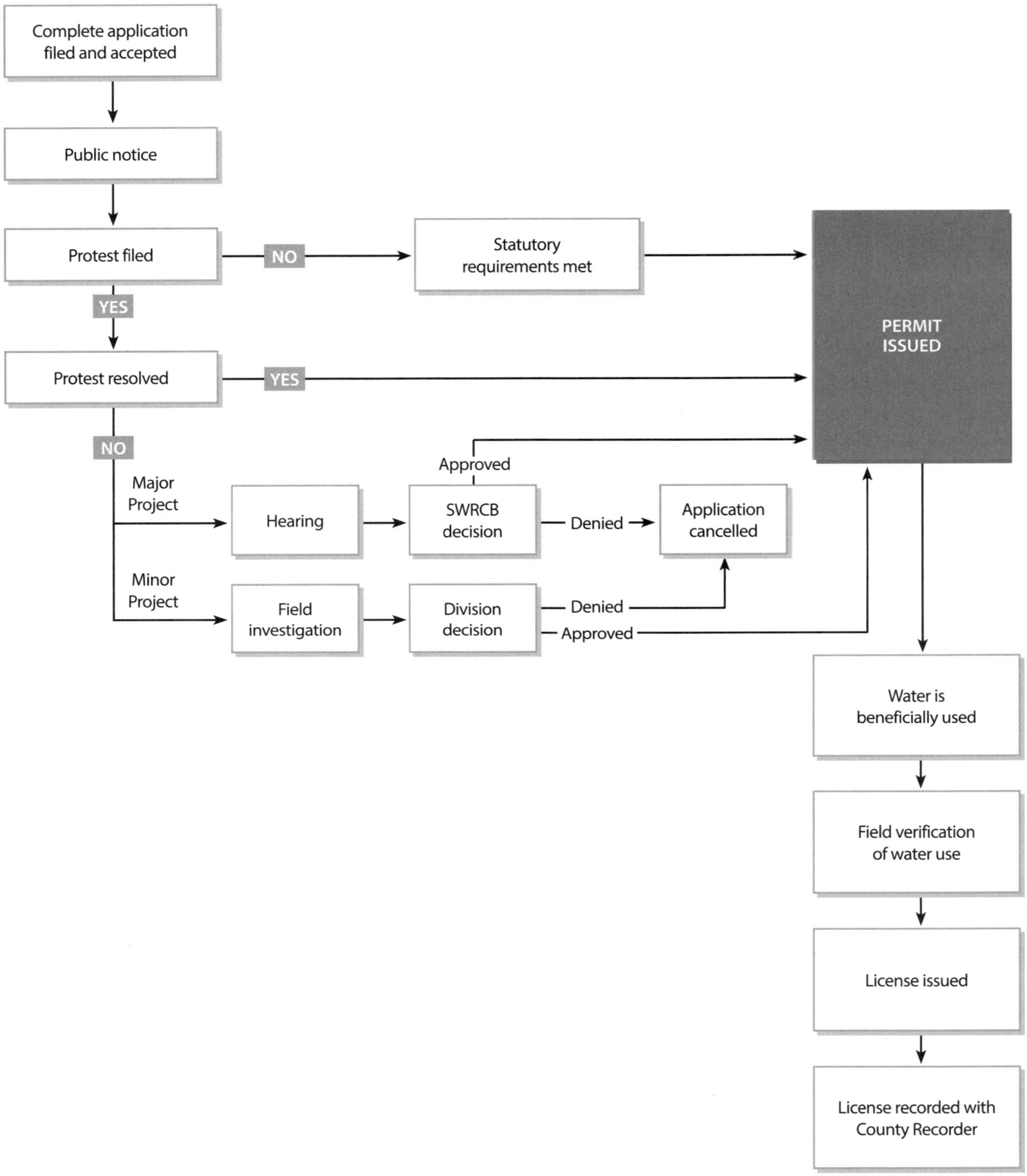

Source: State Water Resources Control Board

pre-1914 and post-1914 rights. For pre-1914 rights, a user may change any of these variables without notice to others or the state, and any challenges based on injury must be affirmatively filed and are generally heard only by the courts.

MAF = million acre-feet

For post-1914 rights, a user must file a petition with the SWRCB before undertaking the change. The SWRCB will issue public notice of the request and will evaluate claims of injury to other right holders or public trust values. Typically, a water right holder cannot increase the amount of water claimed (but can progressively develop the amount claimed) or change the season of diversion. 23 Cal. Code Regs. § 791 *et seq.*

LOSS OR SEVERANCE OF SURFACE WATER RIGHTS

Historically, a prescriptive right could be obtained by "open, notorious, continuous, and adverse use" (each term is a legal term of art) for the prescriptive period, which in California is five years. Essentially, a prescriptive right is the right to prevent another water user from objecting to one's own water use. A right held by a public entity, including the federal or state government, may not be lost by prescription. Civ. Code § 1007. Prescriptive rights today are difficult to establish in the absence of an SWRCB adjudication or court proceeding.

Abandonment. Appropriative water rights can be permanently lost through abandonment. Abandonment requires both relinquishment of possession and the permanent intent to abandon the water.

Forfeiture. An appropriative water right may be lost when water is not put to a reasonable, beneficial use. For post-1914 rights, an appropriative right may be lost by five years of non-use. An SWRCB hearing is required prior to forfeiture. Water Code §§ 1240, 1241.

PERSPECTIVES ON WATER RIGHTS

The Bureau of Reclamation holds the most water rights in California, 112 million acre-feet (MAF), mainly for delivery through the federal CVP. Second to this are the water rights held by Imperial Irrigation District (44 MAF), serving mainly farms in the Colorado River region. Water rights exceed actual total water volume availability on almost all river systems in the state. This in part reflects the fact that water may be reused as it runs off farms or may be returned to the river after use for a "non-consumptive" diversion purpose such as energy production. In some cases, however, water rights are "oversubscribed," meaning that they exceed actual water availability. (LAO 2009.)

Shasta Lake is a key component of the federal CVP. It is the state's largest reservoir, with a capacity of 4.5 million acre feet.

GROUNDWATER RIGHTS

Correlative rights. In contrast to surface water use, California has limited regulatory authority over groundwater use. In 1903, the California Supreme Court, in *Katz v. Walkinshaw* (1903) 141 Cal. 3d 116, established the doctrine of correlative rights for groundwater, under which every landowner overlying a groundwater

In contrast to surface water use, California has limited regulatory authority over groundwater use.

SGMA = Sustainable Groundwater Management Act

basin has a right to extract and use groundwater correlative with the rights of other overlying landowners. An overlying right is analogous to a riparian right. Groundwater cannot be appropriated for use on nonoverlying lands unless it is surplus to the needs of overlying landowners.

If groundwater is used on nonoverlying lands, or is used to provide water for municipal purposes, the right is appropriative rather than overlying and in a shortage water is allocated according to priority. All overlying rights are typically senior to all appropriative rights, except perhaps during overdraft (see discussion of adjudication below).

Underground streams and underflow. Water under the ground is classified either as percolating groundwater, as a subterranean stream that flows in a known and definite channel in an underground water course (an underground stream), or as underflow. Percolating groundwater water is subject to groundwater law rather than surface water law. Percolating groundwater is defined as all underground water other than underground streams and underflow. Water Code §§ 1200, 2500. In contrast, underground streams and underflow are subject to surface water law and potentially to SWRCB jurisdiction.

Proof of the existence of an underground stream requires a demonstration that water is flowing through a defined, relatively impermeable underground channel whose course can be determined by reasonable inference

Proof of the existence of an underground stream requires a demonstration that water is flowing through a defined, relatively impermeable underground channel whose course can be determined by reasonable inference. The underflow of a surface stream consists of the water in the soil, sand, and gravel in the bed of a stream in its natural state and essential to its existence; the underflow may include lateral extensions of the stream on each side of the surface channel if its movement and location can be determined. Water Code § 1200.

Groundwater regulation prior to the Sustainable Groundwater Management Act (SGMA). Groundwater provides about 40 percent of the state's water supply in an average year and can provide close to 60 percent of the supply during a drought. Despite the importance of groundwater to California's water supplies, until 2014, California did not have a statewide regulatory program for groundwater use. Groundwater management is generally the responsibility of local agencies; 13 groundwater management agencies have been directly authorized by state legislation.

Many local agencies voluntarily have prepared Assembly Bill 3030 groundwater management plans pursuant to state legislation (AB 3030 of 1992, Water Code § 10750 *et seq.*). Also, nearly half of California's counties have adopted groundwater management ordinances intended to sustain groundwater as a viable local resource and which may regulate export of groundwater from the county. These ordinances typically require an export project proponent to show that the project will not cause groundwater depletion, groundwater degradation, or subsidence.

Adjudication is also an important aspect of groundwater management. An adjudication typically takes the form of a lawsuit filed where groundwater levels are declining over a long period of time, called overdraft. The goal of an adjudication is to define the relative pumping rights of groundwater users and to allocate those rights in a way that ensures the basin will no longer experience overdraft. In an adjudication, appropriators may be assigned senior pumping rights that otherwise would belong to users overlying the basin if the court concludes that prescription has occurred. Adjudications often involve development of a supplemental water supply via a physical solution. Courts typically appoint a watermaster to manage the physical solution and the basin after an adjudication has concluded.

CASGEM = California State Groundwater Elevation Monitoring Program

GSAs = Groundwater Sustainability Agencies

GSP = Groundwater Sustainability Plan

In 2009, legislation was passed (SB X7-6, Water Code § 10920 *et seq.*) mandating a statewide groundwater elevation monitoring program to track seasonal and long-term trends in groundwater elevations in California's groundwater basins. To achieve that goal, collaboration between local monitoring entities and DWR is required to collect groundwater elevation data. DWR publishes the results of the California State Groundwater Elevation Monitoring Program (CASGEM) online.

Sustainable Groundwater Management Act. In 2014, SGMA (Water Code § 10720 *et seq.*) was enacted. SGMA built upon pre-existing groundwater management provisions established by AB 3030, SB X7-6 and other legislation, and established a new system for managing California's groundwater. SGMA establishes a state policy that groundwater resources be managed sustainably for long-term reliability and multiple economic, social, environmental benefits for current and future beneficial uses.

SGMA requires the formation of locally-controlled Groundwater Sustainability Agencies (GSAs), which must develop Groundwater Sustainability Plans (GSPs) in groundwater basins or subbasins that DWR designates as medium or high priority. SGMA defines sustainable groundwater management as the management and use of groundwater in a manner that can be maintained without causing undesirable results. "Undesirable results" include chronic lowering of groundwater levels and significant and unreasonable reduction of groundwater storage, seawater intrusion, degraded water quality, land subsidence, or effects on beneficial uses of interconnected surface water.

SGMA defines sustainable groundwater management as the management and use of groundwater in a manner that can be maintained without causing undesirable results.

SGMA requires those high and medium priority basins, identified under the CASGEM program as those that are subject to critical conditions of overdraft, to be managed under a groundwater sustainability plan (GSP) by January 31, 2020. It requires all other groundwater basins designated as high or medium priority basins to be managed under a GSP by January 31, 2022. The GSP must achieve groundwater basin sustainability within 20 years of plan implementation and maintain sustainable yield for the following 50 years. The planning deadlines have been criticized by some as too long, given the severity of existing groundwater overdraft and land subsidence conditions in many groundwater basins, many of which reached historic lows in elevation caused by increased groundwater pumping during ongoing drought conditions.

DWR has designated 127 of California's 515 groundwater basins and subbasins

Enacted in 2014, SGMA estabished a new statewide program for managing California's groundwater resources.

as high and medium priority. Mostly located in the Central Valley and the Los Angeles area, these basins account for 96 percent of California's annual groundwater pumping and supply 88 percent of the population residing over groundwater basins. DWR 2014.

Local agencies can request that DWR modify the boundaries of a groundwater basin or subbasin, or create new subbasins. Water Code § 10722.2. DWR regulations specify the processes for requesting, reviewing, and approving groundwater basin boundary modifications. 23 Cal. Code Regs. § 340 *et seq.*

SGMA provides for financial and enforcement tools to carry out effective local sustainable groundwater management through formation of GSAs. SGMA also expands the role of DWR to support local implementation of sustainable groundwater management, and allows for state intervention (by the SWRCB) at discrete points throughout the process if local agencies are not willing or able to manage groundwater sustainably.

It is anticipated that adjudication will continue to play a role in groundwater management post-SGMA. In 2015 California enacted a number of laws intended to streamline the adjudication process and to ensure that SGMA and adjudications work together to achieve sustainable groundwater levels (*see* next section).

"Comprehensive groundwater adjudications" were designed to streamline the costly and time-consuming process for groundwater adjudications.

Comprehensive groundwater adjudications. Legislation enacted in 2015 established the methods and procedures for "comprehensive groundwater adjudications;" it was designed to streamline the costly and time-consuming process for groundwater adjudications. "Comprehensive groundwater adjudications" are defined as actions filed in superior court to comprehensively determine the rights to extract groundwater within a basin. The court's final judgement may declare each element of a groundwater user's rights, including priority, amount, purpose and place of use, and location of pumping. The court may issue injunctions if there is long-term groundwater overdraft, and may also implement a physical solution. Code Civ. Proc. § 830 *et seq.*

A court conducting a comprehensive groundwater adjudication may not interfere with timely completion and implementation of a GSP under SGMA. A comprehensive groundwater adjudication may not substantially impair the ability of a GSA to comply with SGMA. Water Code § 10737 *et seq.*

FEDERAL AND TRIBAL RESERVED RIGHTS

When the federal government reserved land from the public domain for uses such as Native American reservations, national parks, and national forests, it also implicitly reserved sufficient water to fulfill the uses of reservations at the time they were established. Federal and tribal reserved rights are often senior in priority to water rights established under California law. In *United States v. New Mexico* (1978) 438 U.S. 690, the U.S. Supreme Court ruled that reserved rights apply only to the extent necessary to accomplish the primary purposes for which a land reservation was made, thereby limiting expansion of use. Federal courts in California have also recognized a right to water based on uses that pre-date U.S. occupancy of Native American lands, sometimes called aboriginal rights, which have a priority of time immemorial. *United States v. Adair* (9th Cir. 1983) 723 F. 2d 1394.

EIR = Environmental Impact Report

COLORADO RIVER WATER RIGHTS: LAW OF THE RIVER

The so-called Law of the River, consisting of numerous compacts, judicial decisions, contracts and other instruments, governs the management and operation of the Colorado River; *Arizona v. California* (1963) 373 U.S. 546 is a seminal case. Under the Law of the River:

- The upper basin and lower basin states are entitled to 7.5 million acre-feet per year (MAFY).
- Of this amount, California's apportionment is 4.4 MAFY.
- Mexico must receive 1.5 MAFY.

California's Colorado River water use historically exceeded the 4.4 MAFY apportionment. California's Colorado River water users entered into a Quantification Settlement Agreement in 2002, which established a program to limit water use to achieve the 4.4 MAFY apportionment.

WATER CONTRACTS

State Water Project. DWR has entered into long-term water supply contracts with 29 agricultural and urban water districts. Most SWP water goes to urban users. DWR has established the maximum amount of water that contractors can request each year, but DWR has never completed the SWP facilities needed to deliver the maximum amounts to all water contractors.

DWR has entered into long-term water supply contracts with 29 agricultural and urban water districts.

In 1994, SWP contracts were restructured under the terms of an agreement named the "Monterey Agreement" (now "Monterey Amendment"), named after the location where the agreement was reached. *Planning and Conservation League v. Department of Water Resources* (2000) 83 Cal. App. 4th 89. The Monterey Agreement EIR was deemed inadequate in part because it failed to properly evaluate a realistic no-project alternative based on realistic SWP deliveries. In 2003, a settlement agreement was reached that called for preparation of a new Environmental Impact Report (EIR), which was released in 2009. Additional litigation challenging the 2009 EIR as well as actions in the Monterey Amendment was being heard by the trial court at the time this book was written in 2016.

Central Valley Project. The CVP supplies water to more than 250 water contractors under contracts with the U.S. Bureau of Reclamation. Most CVP water goes to agricultural uses. CVP contracts call for a maximum annual delivery of 9.3 MAFY. Contracts allocate both 4.8 MAFY of "project water" and 4.5 MAFY of "settlement water" (water covered in agreements with water rights holders whose diversions existed before the CVP was constructed). In 2005, the CVP delivered 7 MAFY to

DFW = California Department of Fish and Wildlife

agricultural users and 600,000 acre-feet per year (AFY) to urban users. U.S. Bureau of Reclamation 2005.

Racanelli decision. The SWRCB has jurisdiction over both water rights and water quality (*see* chapter 6), but the ability of the SWRCB to regulate operation of the CVP and SWP based on water quality objectives was unclear until the Racanelli decision. In *United States v. SWRCB* (1986) 182 Cal. App. 3d 82 (decided by Judge Racanelli), the court held that the SWRCB could impose water-quality based restrictions on both the CVP and the SWP, without regard to their water right priorities. The court ruled that the SWRCB has the power to determine the proper balance between water quality interests and the effects of water diversions in determining whether a water use is "reasonable."

WATER TRANSFERS

Water transfers are an increasingly common way to provide flexibility in water use. Usually, transfers are from agricultural to urban uses, and the transfers can substitute for additional surface water diversions by urban water agencies.

For post-1914 water rights, the SWRCB is authorized to approve short-term and long-term water transfers of water or appropriative rights. Most water transfers have been short-term (one year or less). Short-term transfers may be either temporary urgency changes (Water Code § 1435) or temporary changes (Water Code § 1724 *et seq.*); temporary urgency changes have expedited processing procedures. For long-term transfers—lasting more than one year—the SWRCB must provide an opportunity for a hearing. To approve either a short-term or long-term water transfer, the SWRCB must find that the transfer will not injure any legal user of water and will not unreasonably affect fish, wildlife, or other instream beneficial uses.

AB 1755 of 2016 (Chapter 506, Statutes of 2016) brings greater transparency to the water transfer market. It requires DWR, SRWCB and the Department of Fish and Wildlife (DFW) to integrate existing water and ecological data. These agencies are required to develop water data protocols to promote open-source platforms and decision support tools.

AREA OF ORIGIN PROTECTIONS

The Legislature has sought to protect the water rights of areas of origin, watersheds from which water projects obtain water for exporting outside the watershed, so that water will be available to these areas of origin when needed.

The Legislature, through several statutes, has sought to protect the water rights of areas of origin, watersheds from which water projects obtain water for exporting outside the watershed, so that water will be available to these areas of origin when needed. Protected areas include:

- Certain specified areas of origin, e.g., lands within the Sacramento and San Joaquin River systems, which may not be deprived of water by means of appropriations after 1985. Water Code § 1215 *et seq.*
- Northern California counties in which water for the SWP and CVP originates, which may not be deprived of water by means of state-filed applications. Water Code §§ 10505, 10505.5

- Watersheds of origin, which may not be deprived of water through operation of the SWP and CVP. Water Code § 11460 *et seq.*

The area of origin laws have seldom been interpreted by the courts, and many uncertainties about the scope of these laws remain. Two meaningful appellate court discussions interpreting these statutes can be found in *SWRCB Cases* (2006) 136 Cal. App. 4th 67 and *Tehama-Colusa Canal Authority v. U.S. Department of the Interior* (9th Cir. 2013) 721 F. 3d 1086. In the *Tehama* case, the Ninth Circuit held that a water user in the watershed of origin that had entered into a CVP contract in lieu of exercising its area of origin rights was not entitled to preferential deliveries of CVP water during shortage.

REMEDIES

A wide variety of remedies is available to enforce water rights. Administrative and statutory procedures are available, but final jurisdiction lies with the courts. *See* Littleworth and Garner, 2007. Remedies include injunctions, "physical solutions" (water allocations that may involve increase in supply and allocation of costs based on priority, often judicially developed), and adjudication of water rights through judicial or statutory procedures.

The SWRCB has exclusive jurisdiction over the issuance of permits and licenses. Claims that the SWRCB has exceeded its authority or acted arbitrarily in denying or issuing a permit or license are subject to judicial review, but such review is rare.

WATER SUPPLY PLANNING

CALIFORNIA WATER PLAN AND GOVERNOR'S WATER ACTION PLAN

DWR publishes and updates the California Water Plan every five years. The plan provides a statewide overview of water supplies, demands, and management strategies, and provides detailed assessments for each of the state's hydrologic regions. The latest version of the California Water Plan (at the time of book publication) was issued for 2013. Department of Water Resources 2013. The Plan advances three critical themes in a long-term strategic plan: commit to integrated water management, strengthen government agency alignment, and invest in innovation and infrastructure.

DWR publishes and updates the California Water Plan every five years.

In 2014, Governor Brown adopted a five-year Water Action Plan (updated in 2016) that helps implement the California Water Plan. The Water Action Plan was developed to meet three broad objectives: more reliable water supplies; the restoration of important species and habitat; and a more resilient, sustainably managed water resources system. It calls for the following ten actions:

1. Make conservation a California way of life
2. Increase regional self-reliance and integrated water management

UWMP = Urban Water Management Plan

3. Achieve the co-equal goals (water supply reliability and ecosystem protection) for the Delta
4. Protect and restore important ecosystems
5. Manage and prepare for dry periods;
6. Expand water storage capacity and improve groundwater management
7. Provide safe water for all communities
8. Increase flood protection
9. Increase operational and regulatory efficiency
10. Identify sustainable and integrated financing opportunities.

URBAN WATER MANAGEMENT PLANS

The Urban Water Management Planning Act (Water Code § 10610 *et seq.*) calls for large water purveyors (those serving 3,000 acre-feet per year or serving 300 urban connections) to prepare an Urban Water Management Plan (UWMP) that evaluates water supplies and demands for a 20-year period. UWMPs took on increased importance with the passage of SB 610 and SB 221 of 2001, which rely on these plans for local development project reviews (*see* below).

UWMPs must be submitted to DWR for approval every five years. DWR issued a new Guidebook for preparation of UWMPs in 2015. DWR recommends that UWMPs consist of 10 standard chapters. Required contents include an assessment of 20-year water supply reliability during normal, single dry years, and multiple dry years, as well as a water shortage contingency plan. Starting in 2020, UWMPS must also include a seismic risk assessment and mitigation plan. Water Code § 10632.5.

WATER CONSERVATION

California has made great progress in water use efficiency over the past several decades. However, with tighter environmental constraints on the Sacramento-San Joaquin Delta (Delta), increasing population, and the necessity of adapting to climate change, even greater efficiencies will be needed, and are achievable (DWR 2013a).

The Water Conservation Act of 2009 (SB X7-7, Water Code § 10608 *et seq.*), was enacted as part of a five-bill package aimed at improving the reliability of California's water supply and restoring the ecological health of the Delta. SB X7-7 has multiple urban and agricultural water use efficiency provisions. The key urban conservation measure established a statewide goal of reducing urban per-capita water use by 20 percent by 2020. Meeting this statewide goal of a 20 percent decrease in demand would result in a reduction of just over 2 million acre-feet (maf) of urban water use in 2020. Under SB X7-7, each urban water supplier is required to set water use targets based on its historical water use, the local climate, and locally implemented conservation programs.

The key urban conservation measure of the Water Conservation Act of 2009 established a statewide goal of reducing urban per-capita water use by 20 percent by 2020.

SB X7-7 also requires agricultural water suppliers providing water to at least

10,000 irrigated acres to adopt a water management plan with specified components, and implement cost-effective efficient water management practices. However, any agricultural water supplier providing water to less than 25,000 irrigated acres is exempt unless funding has been provided to implement the law's requirements. These requirements were adjusted by a drought-response Executive Order in 2015.

CEQA = California Environmental Quality Act

WSA = water supply assessment

In response to the state's severe multi-year drought that started in 2011, the Governor issued a series of Emergency Proclamations and Executive Orders. At the time this book was written, the latest of these was EO B-37-16 (May 2016). This EO required the SWRCB to adjust its emergency water conservation regulations through January 27, 2017, and develop new water use targets for urban water agencies. These targets would achieve the 20 percent reduction in urban water use called for by SB X7-7. The EO also required the SWRCB to permanently prohibit practices that waste potable water, such as hosing off sidewalks and driveways. In addition, it set forth measures to strengthen local drought resilience and improve agricultural water use efficiency. Also, SB 814 of 2016 (Statues of 2016) prohibits excessive use by individual residential customers during drought emergencies, and requires water agencies to establish fines for such excessive water users.

In response to the state's severe multi-year drought that started in 2011, the Governor issued a series of Emergency Proclamations and Executive Orders.

Also, to encourage water conservation, state law requires water utilities to meter all municipal and industrial customers by 2025, and charge customers based on the amount of water delivered. Water Code § 527, Pub. Util. Code § 781. SB 7 of 2016 (Chapter 623, Statute of 2016) extends these requirements to multi-family housing by requiring owners of multi-unit rental properties constructed after January 1, 2018 to install "submeters" for individual dwelling units. Residents' water bills must then be based on water usage.

STORMWATER AND RECYCLED WATER

The state continues to encourage the expanded use of stormwater and recycled water as water supplies, to reduce reliance on conventional surface and groundwater resources. For example, SB 985 of 2014 (Chapter 555, statutes of 2014) authorizes public agencies to develop stormwater resource plans for using publicly owned lands to capture and reuse stormwater. Also, the SWRCB (2013) has adopted policies strongly encouraging the expanded use of recycled water as a water supply, and has streamlined permitting of recycled water facilities. General Order WQ 2016-0068-DDW.

SB 610 AND SB 221

Senate Bill 610 of 2001 (Water Code §§ 10631, 10656, 10910, 10912, 10915, 10657) requires California Environmental Quality Act (CEQA) documents to incorporate water supply assessments (WSAs) for certain large development projects, e.g., residential projects exceeding 500 units. WSAs are prepared by local water suppliers and can be based on information in the latest applicable UWMP. The WSA

DSC = Delta Stewardship Council

must determine whether sufficient water supplies will be available to serve the proposed project in normal, dry, and multiple dry years, after taking into account a 20-year projection of demands from existing and other planned water users.

Senate Bill 221 of 2001 (Gov't Code § 66473) creates analogous but stricter requirements for local government approval of subdivision maps for subdivisions over 500 units. Water suppliers must prepare a water supply verification, verifying that a sufficient reliable water supply will be available to serve the proposed project in normal, dry, and multiple dry years, after taking into account a 20-year projection of demands from existing and other planned water users. A final subdivision map may not be approved unless a sufficient reliable water supply is available.

CEQA AND WATER SUPPLY PLANNING

Many CEQA cases have considered the adequacy of water supply impact analysis in CEQA documents prepared for development and other water-using projects. *See* sidebar. In the landmark case *Vineyard Area Citizens for Responsible Growth v. City of Rancho Cordova* (2007, 40 Cal. 4th 412), the Supreme Court held that an EIR for a specific plan was inadequate because it failed to disclose specific long-term water supplies, and the impacts of developing those supplies. To be adequate, the Court ruled that a CEQA water supply impact analysis must identify long-term supplies, assess their impacts, assess likelihood that the long-term supplies will actually be available, and if availability is uncertain, identify additional supplies and analyze the impacts of the project not having sufficient water.

DELTA PLANNING

DELTA PLAN

The Sacramento-San Joaquin River Delta is the heart of California's water supply system, and due to deteriorating conditions has been the subject of much water resource management planning and litigation. (*See* sidebar page 338.) In the 1990s, federal and state agencies collaborated in an effort known as CALFED to develop actions for ecosystem restoration, water use efficiency, and water supply. In the mid-2000s, the Delta Vision Process built on the CALFED framework, and CALFED programs eventually transitioned to the Delta Stewardship Council (DSC), which was created by the Delta Reform Act of 2009 (Pub. Res. Code § 85000 *et seq.*).

The Delta Reform Act established that it is the policy of the state to reduce reliance on the Delta for future water supply needs (Water Code § 85021). The Delta Reform Act required the DSC to adopt a Delta Plan meeting the Act's requirements, which the DSC did in 2013. The Delta Plan is designed to achieve the co-equal goals of providing a more reliable water supply for California, and protecting, restoring, and enhancing the Delta ecosystem. These goals must be achieved while protecting

The Delta Plan is designed to achieve the co-equal goals of providing a more reliable water supply for California, and protecting, restoring, and enhancing the Delta ecosystem.

Selected CEQA Cases on Water Supply Impacts of Development Projects

Stanislaus Natural Heritage v. Stanislaus County (1996) 48 Cal. App. 4th 182. Programmatic EIR prepared for large master-planned community was inadequate because it failed to evaluate water supply impacts, and deferred such evaluation to second-tier EIRs.

Save Our Peninsula Committee v. Monterey County Board of Supervisors (2001) 87 Cal. App. 4th 99. EIR for a residential project was inadequate because the lead agency used an incorrect environmental baseline for evaluation of water supply impacts and related mitigation measures.

Napa Citizens for Honest Government v. Napa County Board of Supervisors (2001) 91 Cal. App. 4th 342. EIR for specific plan was inadequate because it failed to describe secondary sources of water supply in the event the primary designated sources were not available.

Santa Clarita Organization for Planning and the Environment v. County of Los Angeles (2003) 106 Cal. App. 4th 715. EIR for residential development was inadequate because it did not present an accurate analysis of available water supply to serve the project, relying on SWP entitlements ("paper water") versus realistic SWP deliveries.

California Oak Foundation v. City of Santa Clarita (2005) 133 Cal. App. 4th 1219. EIR for industrial development was inadequate because it tiered from EIRs found to be inadequate and because water supply analysis relied on SWP "paper water."

Vineyard Area Citizens for Responsible Growth v. City of Rancho Cordova (2007) 40 Cal. 4th 412. In landmark case, EIR for specific plan was inadequate because it failed to disclose specific long-term water supplies, and the impacts of developing those supplies. To be adequate, a CEQA water supply impact analysis must identify long-term supplies, assess their impacts, assess likelihood that the long-term supplies will actually be available, and if availability is uncertain, identify additional supplies and analyze the impacts of the project not having sufficient water.

Santa Clarita Organization for Planning and the Environment v. County of Los Angeles (2007) 157 Cal. App. 4th 149. EIR for residential development (previously challenged in 2003 case) was adequate because water supply analysis showed that water supplies were reasonably certain.

Watsonville Pilots Association v. City of Watsonville (2010) 183 Cal. App. 4th 1059. EIR water supply impact analysis was adequate because EIR was not required to solve regional groundwater overdraft problem.

Cherry Valley Pass Acres and Neighbors v. City of Beaumont (2010) 190 Cal. App. 4th 316. EIR water supply impact analysis was adequate because it used the proper baseline and established a reasonable likelihood the project would have sufficient water supplies.

Clover Valley Foundation v. City of Rocklin (2011) 197 Cal. App. 4th 200. EIR water supply impact analysis was adequate because water supplier verification established that long-term water supplies were virtually certain to be available.

Preserve Wild Santee v. City of Santee (2012) 210 Cal. App. 4th 260. EIR for development project was inadequate because it failed to recognize uncertainty associated with delivery of imported water supplies.

Habitat and Watershed Caretakers v. City of Santa Cruz (2013) 213 Cal. App. 4th 1277. EIR water supply impact analysis was adequate, but EIR was rejected because it failed to include an alternative with limited water supply.

The Sacramento-San Joaquin Delta: A System in Crisis

The Sacramento-San Joaquin Delta (Delta) is a vast ecosystem that supports hundreds of aquatic and terrestrial species, many of which are threatened or endangered. Located at the crux of two major watersheds that capture runoff from approximately 40 percent of the land in California, the Delta is also at the core of CVP and SWP.

It is generally acknowledged that the Delta is in a state of deepening crisis. Several threatened and endangered fish species, including Delta smelt and winter-run Chinook salmon, have experienced the lowest population numbers in their recorded history. Meanwhile, Delta levees and the infrastructure they protect are at risk from earthquake damage, continuing land subsidence, and rising sea level.

At the same time, the amount of water available for human use south of the Delta has decreased, independent of drought conditions, due to regulatory actions by the Fish and Wildlife Service (FWS), the National Marine Fisheries Service (NMFS), and the DFW. Applying federal and state endangered species laws (*see* chapter 14), these entities have required the DWR and the Bureau of Reclamation to alter operations of the SWP and CVP, resulting in reduced water deliveries to water contractors and adverse economic impacts.

Many current problems stem from the location of SWP and the CVP intake facilities, including pumps, which are located at the far southern edge of the Delta, near the City of Tracy. Because of their far southerly location and their elevation above sea level, these pumps create "reverse flows" that pull river water southward ("upstream") towards the intakes, rather than allowing it to flow downstream towards San Francisco Bay and the Pacific Ocean. These reverse flows adversely affect fish species such as Delta smelt, which are pulled towards the pumps, where adverse conditions, such as the presence of predator species, await them. The reverse flows also adversely affect salmon migration patterns. However, the relative importance of SWP and CVP operations in causing declining endangered fish populations, relative to other factors such as drought, climate change, and other water diversions, has been intensely debated.

(Modified from DWR and Bureau of Reclamation 2015)

and enhancing the unique cultural, recreational, natural resource, and agricultural values of the Delta as an evolving place.

The Delta Plan accomplishes this through 14 enforceable regulatory policies and 73 non-binding regulations. DSC (2013) summarizes the Delta Plan as asking California to do the following:

- In order to improve and secure our water supply, while taking pressure off the Delta, use water more efficiently in cities and on farms, and develop alternative, usually local, water sources
- Get much better at capturing and storing the surplus water that nature provides in the wettest years, building reserves that can be drawn on in dry ones
- To revitalize the Delta ecosystem, provide adequate seaward flows in Delta channels, on a schedule more closely mirroring historical rhythms—what the Plan calls natural, functional flows
- Bring back generous wetlands and riparian zones in the Delta for the benefit of fish and birds
- To preserve the Delta as a place, restrict new urban development to those peripheral areas already definitely earmarked for such growth, while supporting farming and recreation in the Delta's core
- Floodproof the Delta, as feasible, mainly by improving levees and by providing more overflow zones where swollen rivers can spread without doing harm

BAY DELTA CONSERVATION PLAN

The BDCP was a voluntary approach undertaken by Bay-Delta system water users to reduce impacts of Delta water exports on endangered species, improve water supply reliability and improve the Delta ecosystem. DSC will incorporate the BDCP, once it is approved by state and federal lead agencies, into the Delta Plan provided it meets certain conditions outlined by the Delta Reform Act.

BDCP was initially designed to both construct new conveyance facilities to increase water supply reliability, and to attain endangered species incidental take coverage under a Habitat Conservation Plan (HCP, for federally listed species) and Natural Communities Conservation Plan (NCCP, for state listed species). (See chapter 14 for descriptions of HCPS and NCCPs.) In 2013, the Draft BDCP proposed a "twin tunnels" conveyance facility under the Delta as a conservation measure within the HCP/NCCP.

Subsequently, in 2015 DWR decided to separate BDCP's proposed conveyance facility and habitat conservation measures into two separate efforts: California WaterFix and California EcoRestore. California WaterFix includes the twin tunnels, three new water intakes with a capacity of 9,000 cubic feet per second (cfs), and habitat restoration and protection mitigation measures to be funded by water users. California EcoRestore includes more than 30,000 acres of additional Delta habitat restoration and protection to be publicly funded. DWR and Bureau of Reclamation 2015.

BDCP = Bay Delta Conservation Plan

HCP = Habitat Conservation Plan (federal)

NCCP = Natural Communities Conservation Plan (state)

cfs = cubic feet per second

WILD AND SCENIC RIVERS

FEDERAL WILD AND SCENIC RIVERS ACT

This Act (16 U.S.C. § 1271 *et seq.*) designates, and provides for further designations of, rivers that possess extraordinary scenic, historical, wildlife, geological, or other similar values. It requires designated rivers to be maintained in free-flowing conditions and requires management plans for designated rivers. River segments are classified as "wild," "scenic," and "recreational," with different management objectives for each classification. In California, the federal system designates river segments totaling almost 2,000 miles. Designated rivers are as follows:

- Amargosa River
- American River, Lower
- American River, North Fork
- Bautista Creek
- Big Sur River
- Black Butte River
- Cottonwood Creek
- Eel River
- Feather River, Middle Fork
- Fuller Mill Creek
- Kern River
- Kings River
- Klamath River System
- Merced River
- Owens River Headwaters
- Palm Canyon Creek
- Piru Creek
- San Jacinto River, North Fork
- Sespe Creek
- Sisquoc River
- Smith River
- Trinity River
- Tuolumne River

The Eel River is a federal- and state-designated wild and scenic river.

Federal agencies are prohibited from licensing or permitting hydroelectric dams or major diversions on designated rivers. In addition, federal agencies are prohibited from assisting any water resource projects that may directly affect designated rivers.

The Secretaries of Agriculture and the Interior are directed to carry out suitability studies and recommend to Congress possible additions to the wild and scenic rivers system. The Act establishes a river corridor boundary averaging about one-quarter mile on each side of the river, and requires federal agencies to manage the public lands in the corridor to protect the river's free-flowing character and outstanding values. In addition, the managing federal agency for federally designated rivers is required to develop and implement a management plan that will ensure the river's protection. 36 C.F.R. §§ 251, 297; 43 C.F.R. § 8350.

CALIFORNIA WILD AND SCENIC RIVERS ACT

This Act (Pub. Res. Code § 5093.50 *et seq.*) was passed in 1972 to preserve designated rivers possessing extraordinary scenic, recreation, fishery, or wildlife values. Patterned after the federal act, the state act declares that certain rivers that possess these extraordinary values must be preserved in their free-flowing state, together with their immediate environments. The Act prohibits impoundments and diversions on designated rivers (with a few exceptions), but these prohibitions are not applicable to federal agencies.

Patterned after the federal act, the state act declares that certain rivers that possess these extraordinary values must be preserved in their free-flowing state, together with their immediate environments.

The Act initially protected segments of the Smith River and tributaries, Klamath River and tributaries, Scott River, Salmon River, Trinity River, Eel River, Van Duzen River, and American River. The state system was subsequently expanded by the Legislature to include the East Carson and West Walker rivers in 1989, the South Yuba River in 1999, the Albion and Gualala rivers in 2003, and Cache Creek in 2005. In addition, segments of the McCloud River, Deer Creek, and Mill Creek were protected under the Act in 1989 and 1995 respectively, although these segments were not formally designated as components of the system.

The state act is more limited than the federal act in that it does not establish a one-quarter mile corridor or require management plans for state-designated rivers. The state act provides protection only to the first line of permanent riparian vegetation.

The state act requires state and local agencies to exercise their existing powers consistent with the Act's policies and provisions. Pub. Res. Code § 5093.61. The Act does not, however, change the land use regulatory powers or authorities of state and local agencies granted by other laws.

for more information...

Department of Water Resources, 1994. General Comparison of Water District Acts, Bulletin 155–94.

Department of Water Resources, 2015. The State Water Project Delivery Capability Report.

Department of Water Resources, 2005. California Water Plan Update 2005.

Department of Water Resources, 2013a. California Water Plan Update 2013: Investing in Innovation and Infrastructure.

Department of Water Resources, 2013b. California's Groundwater Update 2013.

Department of Water Resources, 2014. CASGEM Groundwater Basin Prioritization.

Department of Water Resources, 2015. Urban Water Management Plan Guidebook.

Department of Water Resources and Bureau of Reclamation 2015. Partially Recirculated Draft EIR/ Supplemental Draft EIS for Bay-Delta Conservation Plan.

Delta Stewardship Council, 2013. The Delta Plan.

Johnson, K. and J. Loux, 2004. Water and Land Use: Planning Wisely for California's Future. Solano Press. Point Arena, Calif.

Legislative Analyst's Office, 2009. Water Rights: Issues and Perspectives.

Littleworth, A. and E. Garner, 2007. California Water II. Solano Press. Point Arena, Calif.

Sax, J. 1970. The Public Trust Doctrine in Natural Resource Law: Effective Judicial Intervention. Volume 68, Michigan Law Review, 471.

State Water Resources Control Board, 2013. Policy for Water Quality Control for Recycled Water.

Water Education Foundation, 2008. Layperson's Guide to California Water.

glossary

Acre-foot—325,851 gallons or enough water to cover an acre of land one foot deep.

Adjudication—the judicial proceeding in which a priority is assigned to water rights and a decree is issued.

Anadromous fish—a fish species, such as salmon, that migrates from freshwater streams to the ocean and back to complete its cycle.

Appropriative right—a water right based on physical control and beneficial use of water (pre-1914), or based on a permit or license for its beneficial use (post-1914).

Beneficial use—use of an amount of water that is reasonable and appropriate under efficient practices to accomplish, without waste, the purpose for which a diversion is made.

Certificate of approval*—a certificate issued by DWR for construction of certain dams.

Conjunctive use—combined use of surface and groundwater supplies.

Correlative right—in the context of riparian rights, the right to use a portion of the natural flow of water in common with other riparian users. Similar doctrine also applies in the context of groundwater rights, where overlying land-owners must share rights to groundwater.

Desalination—treatment of seawater or brackish water to reduce salt levels, making the water useful for potable or non-potable supplies.

FERC license*—a license for a hydroelectric project using navigable waters or federal land.

Firm yield—the dependable annual water supply that could be available in all years, without exceeding specified shortages in agricultural deliveries during droughts.

Groundwater—water that is seeped beneath the earth's surface and is stored underground.

Instream use—the beneficial use of water within a stream, such as for fisheries habitat.

Integrated water management—a collection of policies, practices, and tools applied to water resources planning and management to achieve multiple objectives and enhanced outcomes. Integrated water management integrates planning for water supply, water quality, flood risk management, and land use.

Law of the River—numerous compacts, judicial decisions, contracts, and other instruments, governing the management and operation of the Colorado River.

Long-term transfer*—a transfer of water or water rights lasting more than one year.

Overdraft—a groundwater basin in which the amount of water withdrawn exceeds the amount of water replenishing the basin.

Paper water—water entitlements under water contract that may never be delivered.

Percolating groundwater—all underground water other than underflow or under-ground streams.

Prescriptive right—a water right obtained by "open, notorious, continuous, and adverse use" (each of these terms is a legal term of art) for the prescriptive period, which in California is five years.

Public trust doctrine—enforceable doctrine by which certain natural resources are held in trust by the government for the use and enjoyment of the public.

Recycled water—treated wastewater that is reused for beneficial purposes such as agricultural and landscape irrigation, industrial processes, toilet flushing, and replenishing a groundwater basin.

Riparian right—a water right based on the ownership of land bordering a river or waterway.

Stormwater—rain or melting snow that "runs off" the land instead of seeping into the ground. It generally consists of water that washes off impervious surfaces such as driveways, rooftops, parking lots, and roads.

Temporary change*—a short-term (one year or less) water transfer involving a change in point of diversion, place of use, or purpose of use.

Temporary urgency change*—a short-term (one year or less) water transfer to meet an urgent need involving a change in point of diversion, place of use, or purpose of use.

Underflow—the water in soil, sand, and gravel in the streambed of a stream in its natural state, and essential to its existence.

Underground streams—groundwater that flows in a known and definite channel in a subterranean water course.

Water banking—storage of surface water in groundwater basins in times of surplus, for withdrawal during times of shortage. Can also involve the use of surface water in lieu of groundwater to enable groundwater recharge.

Water right—a legal entitlement authorizing water to be diverted from a specified source and put to beneficial, nonwasteful use. Water rights are property rights, but their holders do not own the water itself—they possess the right to use it.

Water right license*—an SWRCB license issued when a permitted water project is completed, the permit terms have been met, and water is put to beneficial use.

Water right permit*—an SWRCB permit required for a post-1914 appropriative water right.

Water transfer—marketing arrangement that can include the permanent sale or lease of a water right by the water right holder, or the sale or lease of a contractual right to a quantity of water.

Watermaster—a court-appointed person or agency given the authority to regulate the quantity of water to be extracted from a designated basin or river system.

Watershed—the area from which water drains to a single point.

* equals permits and approvals

CHAPTER 14

Fish and Wildlife

related Solano Press title

California Land Use and Planning Law. Cecily Talbert Barclay and Matthew S. Gray. 35th Edition. 2016.

in this chapter...

ESA = Endangered Species Act

CESA = California Endangered Species Act

NCCPA = Natural Communities Conservation Planning Act

USFWS = U.S. Fish and Wildlife Service

NOAA Fisheries = National Oceanic and Atmospheric Administration Fisheries Service

HCP = habitat conservation plan

ITP = incidental take permit

INTRODUCTION

This chapter covers federal and state regulation of biological resources, focused on protection of endangered, threatened, and other sensitive species. The federal Endangered Species Act (ESA) is the main federal regulatory program for protecting these species. At the state level, the California Endangered Species Act (CESA) and Natural Communities Conservation Planning Act (NCCPA) play major roles.

KEY LAWS AND AGENCIES

FEDERAL LAWS AND AGENCIES

Endangered Species Act. The federal ESA (16 U.S.C. § 1531 *et seq.*), reviewed in detail later in this chapter, is considered one of the most comprehensive wildlife conservation laws in the world. Enacted in 1973, the Act is administered by the U.S. Fish and Wildlife Service (USFWS) and the National Oceanographic and the Atmospheric Administration (NOAA) Fisheries Service ("NOAA Fisheries," formerly National Marine Fisheries Service). (In this chapter, USFWS and NOAA Fisheries are jointly referred to as "the Services.")

The purpose of the ESA is to conserve and recover endangered and threatened species, and the ecosystems upon which they depend.

The purpose of the ESA is to conserve and recover endangered and threatened species, and the ecosystems upon which they depend. The ESA requires all federal agencies to protect listed species and preserve their habitats. The law:

- Sets forth a process for listing species as endangered or threatened, for designating critical habitat for listed species, and for preparing recovery plans for listed species (Section 4)
- Requires federal agencies to consult with the Services to ensure their actions do not jeopardize listed species (Section 7)
- Prohibits the "take" of a listed species (Section 9)
- Allows non-federal entities that prepare a habitat conservation plan (HCP) to obtain an incidental take permit (ITP) allowing development projects to proceed (Section 10)
- Sets forth enforcement and penalty provisions (Section 11)

Regulations for implementing the ESA are found at 50 C.F.R. § 17. Also, at the time this book was being written, the Services were developing a new ESA compensatory policy to shift from project-by-project to landscape-scale mitigation approaches. 81 Fed. Reg. 61032 (September 2, 2016).

Other federal laws protecting fish and wildlife. Other federal laws protecting fish and wildlife include:

- **Fish and Wildlife Coordination Act.** Requires federal agencies, when approving or implementing an action to modify a water body, to consult with the Services and the relevant state wildlife agency. 16 U.S.C. § 661 *et seq.*

CESA = California Endangered Species Act

DFW = California Department of Fish and Wildlife

- **Convention on International Trade in Endangered Species.** Regulates trade in endangered species and is implemented via the ESA. Regulations are found at 50 C.F.R. § 23.
- **Marine Mammal Protection Act.** Lists protected marine mammals and establishes a moratorium on taking of listed marine mammals, with some exceptions. 16 U.S.C. § 1361 *et seq.* This Act is administered by the Services. Permits may be issued to authorize take, with the permit process differing depending on whether the species also is listed under the ESA. Regulations are found at 50 C.F.R. § 18.
- **Migratory Bird Treaty Act.** Prohibits the taking, killing, or possessing of migratory birds (birds that migrate across state and national borders). 16 U.S.C. § 703 *et seq.* Regulations are found at 50 C.F.R. § 21.
- **Bald Eagle and Golden Eagle Protection Act.** Prohibits the taking or possession of and commerce in bald and golden eagles, with a few exceptions. 16 U.S.C. § 668. Regulations are found at 50 C.F.R. § 22.
- **Magnuson-Stevens Fishery Conservation and Management Act.** Regulates ocean fishing and allows NOAA Fisheries to designate Essential Fish Habitat within coastal rivers and streams. 16 U.S.C. § 1801 *et seq.* The Act creates eight regional fishery management councils that work in partnership with NOAA Fisheries to manage marine fish stocks. Federal agencies must consult with NOAA Fisheries on activities that may affect Essential Fish Habitat. Regulations are found at 50 C.F.R. § 600.
- **Lacey Act.** Makes it a federal crime to import, export, transport, sell, receive, acquire, possess, or purchase any fish, wildlife, or plant taken, possessed, transported, or sold in violation of any federal, state, foreign, or Indian tribal law, treaty, or regulation. 16 U.S.C. § 1855. Regulations are found at 50 C.F.R. §16.

The bald eagle was de-listed because recovery efforts were successful.

U.S. Fish and Wildlife Service. Under the ESA, USFWS has jurisdiction and permitting authority over terrestrial wildlife, freshwater fish, and some marine species. USFWS also has responsibility for implementing many of the other laws listed above, as well as operating a system of national wildlife refuges. USFWS general permit procedures, covering implementation of many of these laws, are found at 50 C.F.R. § 13.

NOAA Fisheries. Under the ESA, NOAA Fisheries (also known as the National Marine Fisheries Service) has jurisdiction and permitting authority over marine species, including anadromous fish species such as salmon and steelhead. NOAA Fisheries also has responsibility for implementing the Marine Mammal Protection Act and the Magnuson-Stevens Fishery Conservation and Management Act.

STATE LAWS AND AGENCIES

California Endangered Species Act. CESA (Fish & Game Code § 2050 *et seq.*), reviewed in detail later in this chapter, is similar but less comprehensive than the federal ESA. Administered by the Department of Fish and Wildlife (DFW), CESA establishes a state policy to conserve, protect, enhance, and restore endangered and threatened species and their habitats. Like the federal ESA, CESA establishes a state listing process, prohibits unauthorized "take," and provides for incidental take permits.

CESA emphasizes early consultation to avoid potential impacts to endangered and threatened species, and to develop appropriate mitigation planning to offset impacts to listed species populations and their essential habitats. State and local agencies consult with DFW through the California Environmental Quality Act (CEQA) process, prior to taking actions that may affect listed species; there is no separate consultation process analogous to the federal ESA's Section 7 consultation process.

Natural Community Conservation Planning Act. The NCCPA (Fish & Game Code § 2800 *et seq.*), reviewed in detail later in this chapter, encourages voluntary, broad-based planning to provide effective wildlife protection and allow appropriate development through preparation of natural community conservation plans (NCCPs). The focus of the initial NCCP effort in the 1990s was to protect the coastal sage scrub habitat of Southern California, home to the California gnatcatcher and approximately 100 other potentially threatened or endangered species. Many NCCPs have now been prepared or are underway statewide.

Fully protected species. State law (Fish & Game Code §§ 3511, 4700, 5050, and 5515) designates 37 species of fish and wildlife as "fully protected." DFW may not issue permits authorizing take of fully protected species, except for collecting these species for necessary scientific research (*see* sidebar) or relocation of birds (e.g., fully protected raptors) for the protection of livestock, or in association with implementing an NCCP. Thus project proponents must assure their project will not result in take of a fully protected species. Similarly, DFW is unable to authorize the incidental take of five types of birds listed in Fish & Game Code § 3505, or the incidental take of unlisted raptors or the destruction of their nests or eggs. Fish & Game Code § 3503.5.

Take of Fully Protected Species

The scientific research exception allowing take of fully protected fish species includes efforts to recover these species. Fish & Game Code § 5515. However, in *Center for Biological Diversity v. Department of Fish and Wildlife* (2015) 62 Cal. 4th 204, the Supreme Court ruled that DFW may not authorize, as a CEQA mitigation for a development project, actions that would protect a fully protected species from harm even though these measures would assist in its recovery.

Other state and local laws protecting fish, wildlife, and plants. Other state and local laws protecting fish, wildlife, and plants include the following:

- **Native Plant Protection Act.** Establishes a listing process and protections for "rare" or "endangered" plants. Fish & Game Code § 1900 *et seq.* When CESA was enacted in 1984, the list of endangered plants from the Native Plant Protection Act was included in CESA's list of endangered plants. Rare plants receive no CESA protection. Plants are no longer proposed for listing under the Native Plant Protection Act, and the Act today has little regulatory effect compared to CESA.
- **California Desert Native Plants Act.** Regulates the harvesting of certain desert plants in specified counties. Food & Agriculture Code § 80001 *et seq.*

CEQA = California Environmental Quality Act

DFW = California Department of Fish and Wildlife

DFW enforces the Act, but county agricultural commissioners and sheriffs are authorized to issue harvesting permits.

- **Marine Life Protection Act.** Establishes a network of marine protected areas to protect marine life and habitats, marine ecosystems, and marine natural heritage. Fish & Game Code § 2850 *et seq.* Marine protected areas include marine reserves, marine parks, and marine conservation areas.
- **Orca Protection Act.** Phases in a prohibition on holding an orca in captivity for any purpose, including entertainment, with certain specific exceptions as described in the law. Fish & Game Code § 4502.2
- **Local programs (cities and counties).** Establish policies for protection of fish, wildlife, and plants through the general plan conservation element. In addition, some cities and counties have enacted regulations for the protection of specified resources such as riparian vegetation, wetlands, or heritage trees.

Department of Fish and Wildlife. DFW regulates activities related to fish, wildlife, and plants in California. DFW is responsible for administering CESA and the other state laws mentioned above. DFW also manages the California Natural Diversity Database, an inventory of the reported locations of listed species and species of special concern. Data in the database are available to the public digitally or as hard copy.

To locally administer fish and wildlife laws, DFW is divided into seven regions: Northern California–North Coast, Sacramento Valley–Central Sierra, Central Coast, San Joaquin Valley–Southern Sierra, South Coast, Eastern Sierra–Inland Deserts, and Marine.

Fish and Game Commission. The Commission is composed of up to five members, appointed by the governor and confirmed by the Senate. The Commission meets at least 11 times each year to publicly discuss various proposed regulations, permits, licenses, management policies, and other subjects within its areas of responsibility. Major Commission responsibilities include making listing decisions under CESA and formulating general policies to administer DFW. The Commission also decides hunting seasons, bag limits, and methods of take for game animals and sport fish.

FEDERAL ENDANGERED SPECIES ACT

SPECIES LISTING

A species is "endangered" when it is in danger of extinction throughout all or a significant portion of its range. 16 U.S.C. § 1532(6). A species is "threatened" if it is likely to become endangered within the foreseeable future throughout all or a significant part of its range. 16 U.S.C. § 1532(20).

A species is "endangered" when it is in danger of extinction throughout all or a significant portion of its range. A species is "threatened" if it is likely to become endangered within the foreseeable future throughout all or a significant part of its range.

Endangered species are entitled to all the ESA's protections, whereas threatened species may receive less protection from "take," as identified at the time of listing under "a Section 4(d) rule." ESA Section 4(d) (16 U.S.C. § 1533(d)) authorizes the Services to define the exact activities constituting take of a threatened species.

In 2014, the Services adopted a policy to interpret the term "significant portion of its range." 79 Fed. Reg. 37578 (July 1, 2014). The policy clarifies that the Services can list a species if it is endangered or threatened in a "significant portion of its range," even if that species is not endangered or threatened throughout all of its range. A portion of the range of a species is defined as "significant" if the species is not currently endangered or threatened throughout all of its range, but the portion's contribution to the viability of the species is so important that, without the members in that portion, the species would be in danger of extinction, or likely to become so in the foreseeable future, throughout all of its range.

All species of plants and animals, except pest insects, may be listed as endangered or threatened. The Services list species on the basis of the best scientific and commercial data available, considering solely the species' biological status and threats to their existence. The term "species" is defined broadly to include "subspecies" and, for fish and wildlife, any "distinct population segment" of a vertebrate fish or wildlife species. 16 U.S.C. § 1532(16). The Services have adopted a distinct population segment policy which considers both the discreetness and the significance of the population segment. 61 Fed. Reg. 4722 (February 7, 1996).

The Services list species on the basis of the best scientific and commercial data available, considering solely the species' biological status and threats to their existence.

Listings can be justified by one or more of the following factors (16 U.S.C. § 1533(a)(1)):

- Present or threatened destruction, modification, or curtailment of the species' habitat or range
- Over-utilization for commercial, recreational, scientific, or educational purposes
- Disease or predation
- Inadequacy of existing regulatory mechanisms
- Other natural or anthropogenic factors affecting the species' survival

The Services, through a formal rulemaking process lasting 12 months, can list species either independently or in response to a citizen petition following development of a listing proposal. 16 U.S.C. § 1533(b). The Services may not consider economic impacts when deciding to list a species.

A complete catalog of all listed species can be found on the USFWS website (www.fws.gov/endangered/species/us-species.html). The Services also maintain a list of "candidate" species. Candidate species are those with enough information to be proposed for listing, but for which the Services have not yet developed a listing proposal. 50 C.F.R. § 424.02(b). Candidate species are not protected by ESA, but they may be protected in HCPs.

At the end of the 12-month review process, the Services decide whether a listing is warranted, not warranted, or "warranted but precluded." If listing is warranted, the Services publish a notice and final listing rule in the Federal Register. If a listing is warranted but precluded, the species is assigned candidate status and its status is reviewed annually for possible later listing. 16 U.S.C. § 1533(b)(3)(B). In the early 2000s, the number of warranted-but-precluded findings had outpaced the number of listings; the backlog of precluded candidate species had grown to 251 as of 2010. In 2011, the Services entered into settlement agreements requiring them to meet strict deadliness for submitting either a warranted or not warranted finding for all 251 species. *See In re* Endangered Species Act Section 4 Deadline Litigation (D.C. Cir. 2013) 704 F. 3d 972, 974. In 2016, the Services published a new framework for prioritizing status reviews, giving the highest priority to critically imperiled species. 81 Fed. Reg. 49248 (July 27, 2016).

The Services also may de-list species using a process similar to the listing process, if successful recovery efforts warrant this change. 16 U.S.C. § 1533(c). For example, the bald eagle has been de-listed because nesting pairs of bald eagles have risen nationwide to 7,066, compared to a low of 417 in 1963 when high levels of the insecticide DDT were damaging their eggs. 71 C.F.R. § 8238.

The Services must perform status reviews of listed species every five years to determine whether, based on current best available science, each listed species should have its status changed (i.e., either lowered from endangered to threatened or raised from threatened to endangered) or have its status removed because protection is no longer justified. 16 U.S.C. § 1533(c)(2).

CRITICAL HABITAT

The ESA requires designation of critical habitat for listed species when prudent and determinable. Critical habitat designation affects federal agencies, but does not directly affect private landowners. Federal agencies, under the Section 7 consultation process, must protect critical habitat when undertaking federal actions. *See* below.

Critical habitat is a formally designated specific geographic area that contains those physical or biological features essential to the conservation of a listed species, and that may require special management or protection. Critical habitat may include areas not occupied by the species at the time of listing, but essential to conservation of the species. In designating critical habitat, the Services must consider the best scientific data available, as well as the probable economic and other impacts of making the designation. Critical habitat may be reduced in acreage if economic effects of designation would be severe. 16 U.S.C. §§ 1532, 1533(b). In 2013, the Services published a regulation governing how economic effects of designating critical habitat are to be evaluated. 50 C.F.R. § 424.19. Regulations adopted in 2016 provide guidance on which areas the Services will include and exclude when designating critical habitat. 81 Fed. Reg. 7414 (February 11, 2016).

Critical habitat is a formally designated specific geographic area that contains those physical or biological features essential to the conservation of a listed species, and that may require special management or protection.

EIS = Environmental Impact Statement

The Services are required to designate critical habitat at the time of listing if prudent, but no later than one year after listing. 16 U.S.C. § 1533(a)(3), (b)(6)(C). Budget and administrative constraints have prevented the Services from meeting the one-year deadline for many species, leading to lawsuits by environmental groups to force critical habitat designation. On the other hand, once the Services do designate critical habitat, affected landowners often file lawsuits challenging the designations.

In California and other states in the Ninth Circuit, the Services are not required to conduct a NEPA review prior to designating critical habitat. *Bear Valley Mutual Water Company v. Jewell* (2015) 790 F. 3d 977,994.

RECOVERY

The Services are required to prepare recovery plans for listed species describing the actions needed to encourage the species' overall health and viability, such that ESA protection is no longer needed.

The ESA's ultimate goal is to "recover" species so they no longer need the Act's protection. The Services are required to prepare recovery plans for listed species describing the actions needed to encourage the species' overall health and viability, such that ESA protection is no longer needed. 16 U.S.C. § 1533(f)(1). Recovery plans are advisory and have no legal effect. The pace of recovery plan preparation has been slowed by lawsuits and competing priorities.

SECTION 7 CONSULTATION

The ESA is implemented mainly through two processes: Section 7 consultation and the Section 10 incidental take permit process. Section 7 prohibits federal agencies from undertaking actions that are likely to jeopardize the continued existence of a listed species or that result in the destruction or adverse modification of designated critical habitat. 16 U.S.C. § 1536(a)(2).

Regulations adopted in 2016 define "destruction or adverse modification" as a direct or indirect alteration that appreciably diminishes the value of critical habitat for the conservation of a listed species. Such alterations may include, but are not limited to, those that alter the physical or biological features essential to the conservation of a species or that preclude or significantly delay development of such features. 81 Fed. Reg. 7214 (February 11, 2016).

Federal actions requiring Section 7 consultation include federal funding, permits, leases, or other entitlements issued to private or local and state government applicants. 50 C.F.R. § 402.02. However, Section 7 consultation is required only for discretionary federal actions for which there is federal control and responsibility. *National Association of Homebuilders v. Defenders of Wildlife* (2007) 551 U.S. 644. Section 7 consultation is not required for non-discretionary actions. *See Grand Canyon Trust v. U.S. Bureau of Reclamation* (9th Cir. 2012) 691 F. 3d 1008.

The Services have issued detailed regulations on Section 7 consultation (50 C.F.R. § 402), as well as a detailed handbook (USFWS and NOAA Fisheries 1998) explaining the Section 7 consultation process. Under the Section 7 regulations, the "scope of the action" subject to consultation is broad. The scope of the action consists of the "action area" and the "effects of the action." The effects of the action include indirect effects, and effects of other activities that are "interrelated" or "interdependent" with the action. The Services use a "but for" test in deciding whether activities are interrelated or interdependent. *See* sidebar.

Under Section 7, federal agencies must consult with the Services to ensure that actions they authorize, fund, or carry out will not "jeopardize" listed species; jeopardize means appreciably reducing the likelihood of both the survival and recovery of a listed species in the wild by reducing the reproduction, numbers, or distribution of the species. Federal agencies and applicants may not make any irreversible or irretrievable commitment of resources during the consultation process. 16 U.S.C. § 1536(a)(2). In Section 7 consultations, the action agency and the Services must use the best available scientific and commercial information.

The Section 7 process typically starts with "informal consultation," during which the federal agency (or a designated non-federal representative such as an applicant) communicates with the Services to determine which listed or proposed species and critical habitats are in the federal action area, and whether the action may affect these species or critical habitats. The informal consultation process is illustrated in Figure 14-1 on the following page.

For "major construction activities," the federal agency must prepare a biological assessment if there may be an effect on a listed species or critical habitat; a major construction activity is an action that significantly affects the quality of the human environment and thus would trigger an Environmental Impact Statement (EIS) under the National Environmental Policy Act (NEPA, 16 U.S.C. § 1536(c); 50 C.F.R. § 402.02).

The biological assessment must be based on the best scientific and commercial data available. 50 C.F.R. § 402.14(d). It must consider the direct, indirect, and cumulative effects of the federal agency action. After preparation of the biological assessment, the action agency must conclude that the proposed action has one of three effects on listed species and critical habitat: "no effect," "not likely to adversely affect," or "likely to adversely affect." If the action agency concludes that the proposed action is not likely to adversely affect a listed species or critical habitat, and the Services concur with this determination, no further consultation is required.

If the action agency concludes that the proposed action is likely to adversely affect a listed species or critical habitat, then formal Section 7 consultation is required. Under formal consultation, the Services determine whether a proposed action, alone or taken together with cumulative effects, will "jeopardize" the species or result in destruction or adverse modification of critical

"Interrelated and Interdependent" Actions

In *Sierra Club v. BLM* (9th Cir. 2015) 786 F. 3d 1219, the court upheld a Section 7 consultation and EIS prepared for a road right-of-way that would connect to a private wind project. Regarding ESA compliance, the court ruled that Section 7 consultation could be limited to the direct effects of a BLM road project because the wind project was not a federal action, but rather was developed by a private party on private land. Further, the wind project was not an indirect effect of the BLM road project requiring consultation. The road project did not cause the wind project or bring it into existence. Finally, the wind project required no consultation because it was not an action that was "interrelated" or "interdependent" with the road project; the wind project could have been completed without the road, and the road project had independent utility even if the wind project were not built. The projects thus failed the "but for" causation test required to establish interrelated or interdependent actions for purposes of Section 7 consultation.

FIGURE 14-1
Section 7 Informal Consultation Process

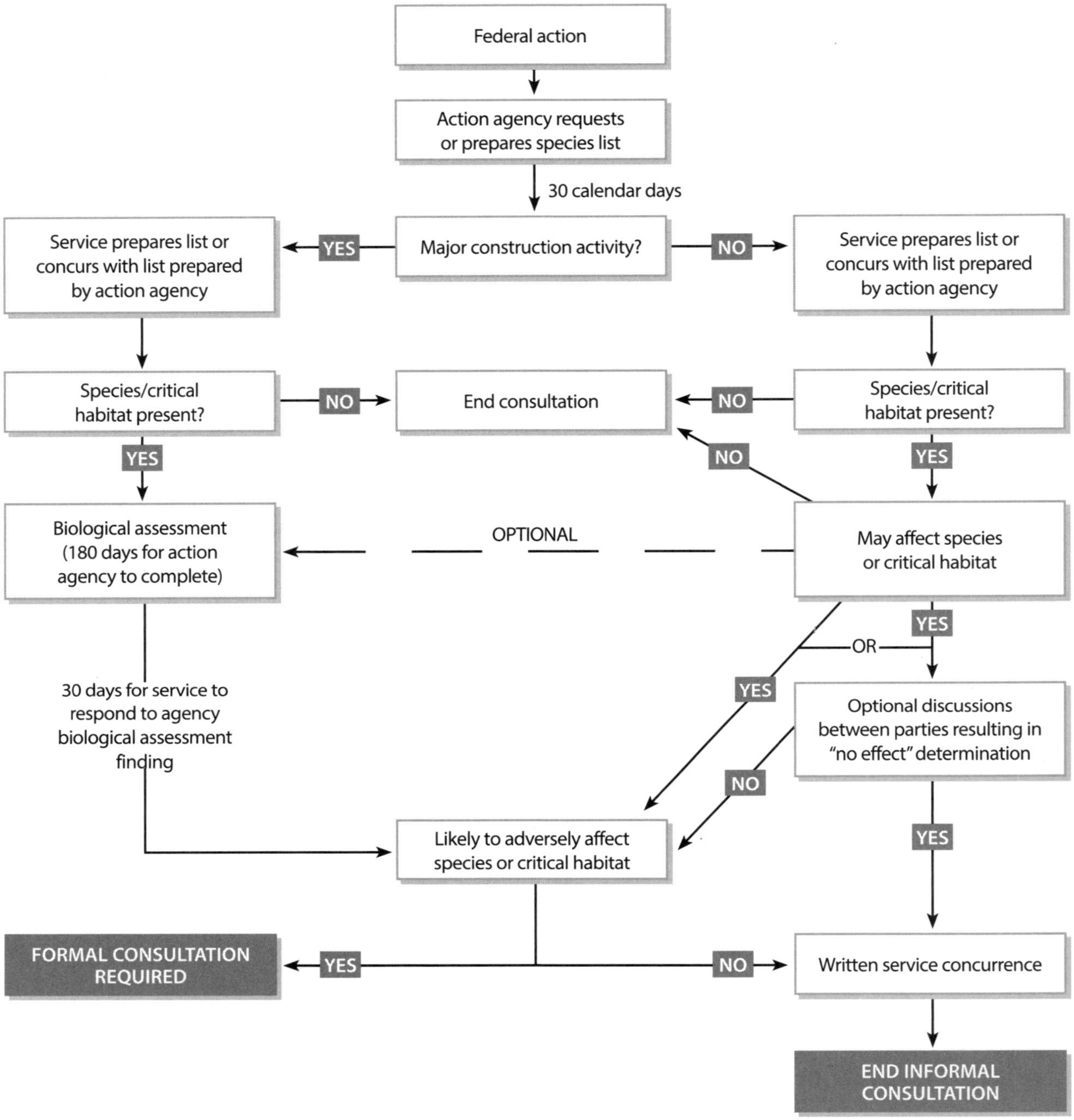

Source: U.S. Fish and Wildlife Service and NOAA Fisheries. 1998. Endangered Species Consultation Handbook

FIGURE 14-2
Section 7 Formal Consultation Process

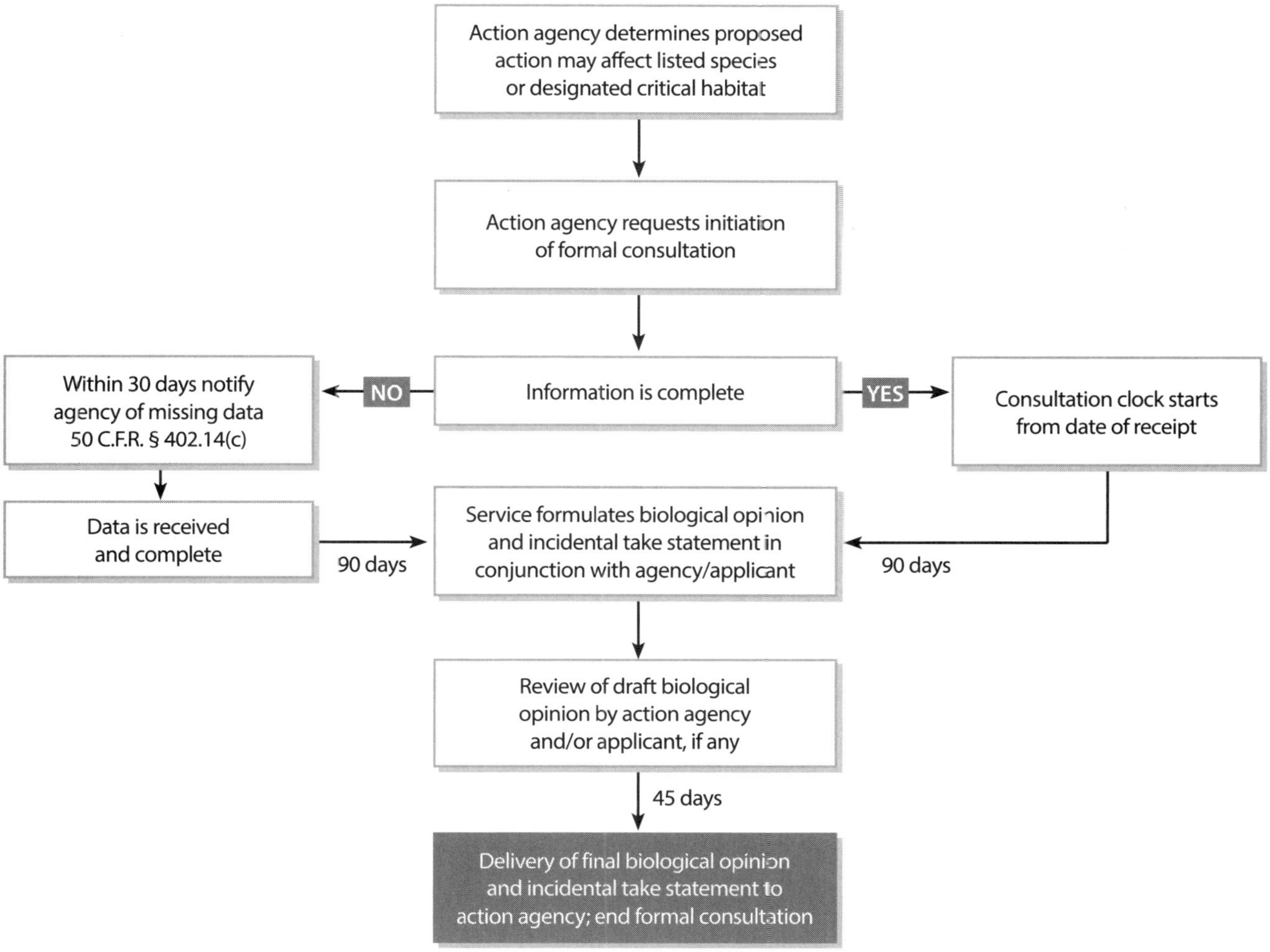

Source: U.S. Fish and Wildlife Service and NOAA Fisheries. 1998. Endangered Species Consultation Handbook

habitat. "Jeopardize" means that an action would be expected to reduce appreciably the likelihood of both the survival and recovery of a listed species in the wild. "Destruction or adverse modification of critical habitat" means an alteration that appreciably diminishes the value of critical habitat for both the survival and recovery of a listed species. 50 C.F.R. § 402.02. (*See* Figure 14-2.)

If the action would result in jeopardy then the Services issue a jeopardy opinion, which offers "reasonable and prudent alternatives" to avoid jeopardy. A federal agency is prohibited (with very narrow exemptions) from implementing the action if it would jeopardize the species or eliminate critical habitat. Following issuance of a jeopardy opinion, the federal agency must notify the Services of its final decision on the project, and either adopt one of the reasonable and prudent alternatives identified in the biological opinion, deny the action, or apply for an exemption (the exemption process is highly complex and almost never pursued). In the Ninth Circuit, courts apply a deferential standard of review when reviewing challenges to jeopardy opinions. *See* sidebar on following page.

If the Services issue a non-jeopardy opinion, the opinion often includes an incidental take statement setting forth "reasonable and prudent measures" to minimize the impacts of any incidental take of a listed species. The federal agency must implement these measures as a condition of approval of the action in order to obtain incidental take coverage.

Once Section 7 consultation is completed, it may need to be reinitiated if the action agency retains discretionary control over the action and certain circumstances change. For example, reinitiation of consultation is required if new information reveals that impacts on listed species or habitat would be worse than previously identified. 50 C.F.R. § 402.16.

Court Defers to Services in Water Project Biological Opinions

In 2014, the Ninth Circuit upheld controversial Biological Opinions issued by the Services which found that the combined operations of the Central Valley Project and the State Water Project would jeopardize endangered Delta smelt and salmonid species. *San Luis & Delta-Mendota Canal Water Authority v. Jewell* (9th Cir 2014) 747 F. 3d 581; *San Luis & Delta-Mendota Canal Water Authority v. Locke* (9th Cir 2014) 776 F. 3d 971. The court recognized the "enormous practical implications" these decisions would have in reducing federal and state water project deliveries, but nevertheless applied a very deferential standard of review to the Services' determinations. It also observed that "people need water, but so do fish."

The court found that each of the Services' findings and decisions were reasonable and supported by substantial evidence in the administrative record. It also ruled that the district court exceeded the scope of its review by admitting expert testimony outside the administrative record, and relying on this testimony rather than on the Services' substantial evidence.

TAKE PROHIBITION AND AUTHORIZATION

Prohibition against take. Section 9 of the ESA makes it unlawful for a person to "take" a listed fish or wildlife species, as well as to possess, transport, deliver, or sell a listed species. The take prohibition does not apply to listed plants, which are protected from transport and sale, and from removal, damage, or destruction only on federal lands. 16 U.S.C. § 1538(a)(1), (2).

"Take" means to "harass, harm, pursue, hunt, shoot, wound, kill, trap, capture, or collect" a listed species, or to attempt such conduct. Controversial regulations (50 C.F.R. §§17.3, 222.102) define the term "harm" as including "significant habitat modification or degradation" if it actually kills or injures wildlife by significantly impairing essential behavioral patterns such as nesting or reproduction. *See* sidebar on facing page.

Take authorizations. Section 10 of the ESA (16 U.S.C. § 1539) authorizes the Services to issue several types of take authorizations. These include:

- **Scientific take permit.** Allows take for scientific purposes or to enhance the affected species
- **Safe harbor agreement.** Provides incentives for landowners to manage their land to maintain or enhance species. 64 C.F.R. § 32717
- **Candidate conservation agreement with assurances.** Promotes the conservation of candidate species, proposed species, or proposed critical habitat. 68 C.F.R. § 37170
- **Incidental take permit.** Authorizes incidental take by non-federal entities (*see* below)

Incidental take permits and habitat conservation plans. ITPs were added to Section 10 of the ESA in 1982 as a practical solution for private landowners, state agencies, and local agencies whose activities, even if mitigated, might result in the incidental take of a listed species. "Incidental take" means the take of a listed species that results from, but is not the purpose of, otherwise lawful activity. 16 U.S.C. § 1539(a)(2). Issuance of a Section 10 incidental take permit requires preparation of both an HCP and a NEPA document.

Habitat conservation plans vary in complexity depending on the number of "covered species" and the number of "covered activities." An HCP is required to address impacts on listed species only. However, many applicants voluntarily include conservation measures for candidate species, to avoid having to amend the HCP if they become listed in the future. Typically, HCPs cover multiple species and multiple activities, and are costly and time-consuming to prepare.

Useful guidance for HCP preparation includes the USFWS and NOAA Fisheries Habitat Conservation Planning and Incidental Take Permit Processing Handbook (USFWS and NOAA Fisheries 2016), and USFWS and NOAA Fisheries regulations. 50 C.F.R. §§ 17.22, 17.32. An HCP must include the following information (16 U.S.C. § 1539(a)(2)(A)):

- Impacts likely to result from the take
- Steps undertaken by the applicant to monitor, minimize, and mitigate these impacts
- Funding assurances to implement conservation measures
- Procedures to address unforeseen circumstances
- Alternatives considered that would not result in take, and why they were not adopted
- Additional measures the Services identify as necessary or appropriate

A controversial aspect of ITPs and HCPs is the "no surprises rule" Under the no surprises rule, incidental take permittees are assured that if "unforeseen circumstances" arise, the Services will not require the commitment of additional land, water, financial compensation, or additional restrictions on land or water use, beyond that agreed to in the HCP to address "changed circumstances." The Services will honor these assurances as long as the permittee is implementing the terms and conditions of the HCP and permit in good faith. However, under the "Permit Revocation Rule," an ITP may be revoked if permittee actions would put a species in jeopardy. 50 C.F.R. §§ 17.22(b)(5), 17.32(b)(5), 222.307(g).

"Take" Includes Significant Habitat Modification

In *Babbit v. Sweet Home Chapter of Communities for a Great Oregon* (1995) 515 US 687, the U.S. Supreme Court upheld the regulatory definition of "harm" (and thus "take") as including significant habitat modification. In *Babbitt*, a group supporting timber harvesting in northern spotted owl old-growth habitat challenged this regulatory definition. The Supreme Court observed that the term "harm" is linked specifically to activities causing death or injury to listed species, and that the USFWS regulation interpreting "harm" to include significant habitat modification leading to death or injury to listed species was reasonable.

However, there must be *some* connection between habitat modification and death or injury to a listed species in order to find a take. Mere modification of suitable habitat may not be sufficient to constitute a take.

In *Arizona Cattle Growers' Association v. USFWS* (2001) 273 F. 3d 1229, the Ninth Circuit in a leading case invalidated, as arbitrary and capricious, incidental take statements in a biological opinion issued pursuant to Section 7 consultation. The biological opinion was issued for proposed federal agency grazing permits, but there was no evidence that the listed fish species of concern was present on the federal lands. USFWS included mitigation measures in the incidental take statements intended to regulate grazing activity because it was possible that listed fish species could return to the federal lands in the future. However, the court held that the ESA was not intended to regulate all parcels of land that are merely capable of supporting a listed species.

FIGURE 14-3
ITP Process

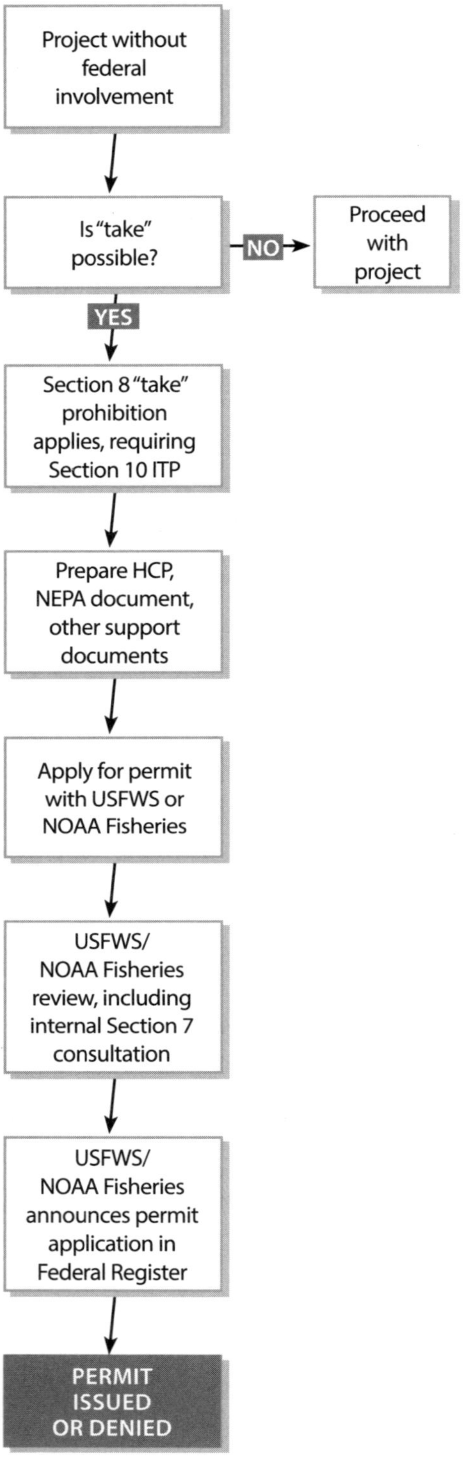

The ITP process is illustrated in Figure 14-3. An applicant is responsible for deciding whether to pursue an ITP. The applicant is responsible for submitting a completed permit application, an HCP, an implementation agreement (if required), and a draft NEPA analysis. While processing the permit application, the Services complete the NEPA analysis and also write a biological opinion under an "internal" ESA Section 7 consultation.

ENFORCEMENT AND PENALTIES

The ESA authorizes "citizen suits" to enforce certain of its provisions. These are suits seeking to enjoin any entity alleged to be in violation of the ESA or its regulations, suits to compel the Services to enforce the ESA's prohibitions, and suits to compel the Services to perform certain nondiscretionary duties. 16 U.S.C. § 1540(g). Plaintiffs may also bring an ESA action under the Administrative Procedure Act.

Section 11 of the ESA (16 U.S.C. § 540) sets forth civil and criminal penalties and authorizes injunctions for violations of any portion of the Act. The Law Enforcement Division of the Services typically brings lawsuits.

Criminal penalties include a fine of up to $50,000 per violation or imprisonment for one year, for knowing violations of the Section 9 "take" prohibition. All other knowing violations are subject to a fine of up to $25,000 per violation or imprisonment up to six months. 16 U.S.C. § 1540(b). In addition to or in lieu of criminal penalties, civil penalties include a fine of up to $25,000 per violation for knowing ESA violations, and a fine of up to $500 per violation for inadvertent violations. 15 U.S.C. § 1540(a).

CALIFORNIA ENDANGERED SPECIES ACT

CESA is patterned generally after the federal ESA, but has some notable differences. As discussed below, the prohibition against take applies to both endangered and threatened species, and species proposed for listing are afforded greater protection. On the other hand, the state definition of "take" does not include habitat modification, and there is no state-level equivalent to the Section 7 consultation process.

LISTING

Individuals, organizations, or DFW can submit petitions to the Fish and Game Commission requesting that a species, subspecies, or variety of plant or animal be added to, deleted from, or changed in status on the state lists of rare, threatened, or endangered species. Factors considered in determining the need to list a species include the present or threatened modification or destruction of habitat, competition, predation, disease, overexploitation by collectors, other natural occurrences, or human-related activities. Fish & Game Code § 2071 *et seq.*

SSC = species of special concern

The Fish and Game Commission must accept a petition for consideration if there is sufficient information to conclude there is a substantial possibility that the requested listing could occur. *Center for Biological Diversity v. Fish & Game Comm'n* (2008) 166 Cal. App. 4th 597. If the petition is accepted and the species becomes a candidate species, a 12-month review period starts, during which time the candidate species receives the same CESA protection as a listed species. DFW recommends to the Commission whether the species should be listed based on the best scientific information available to DFW. Fish & Game Code § 2071 *et seq.*

DFW compiles updated lists of state and federally listed species on the agency website (www.dfg.ca.gov/wildlife/nongame/t_e_spp/). DFW also maintains a list of "species of special concern" (SSC). SSC status applies to animals not listed under the federal ESA or CESA, but which nonetheless are declining at a rate that could result in listing, or which historically occurred in low numbers and known threats to their persistence currently exist. SSC are considered during the CEQA review process and in preparation of conservation plans. Lists of SSC are available at the DFW website.

To protect California's imperiled species, the Legislature initially enacted CESA in 1970. Major CESA amendments were enacted in 1984 and 1997.

CESA, unlike the federal ESA, does not require formal designation of critical habitat or preparation of recovery plans (other than a pilot program for the greater sandhill crane) for listed species. Fish & Game Code § 2105 *et seq.*

TAKE PROHIBITION AND AUTHORIZATION

Prohibition against take. Section 2080 of the Fish & Game Code prohibits "take" of any species that the Commission determines to be an endangered species or a threatened species. Because of an ambiguity in CESA, it is unclear whether the take prohibition applies to listed plants.

Take is defined as "hunt, pursue, catch, capture, or kill, or attempt to hunt, pursue, catch, capture, or kill." Fish & Game Code § 86. Unlike the federal ESA, this definition does not encompass harm, harassment, or habitat modification, but rather includes only acts leading to the death of a listed species.

Incidental take authorization. Fish & Game Code Section 2081 allows for take incidental to otherwise lawful development projects. A flow chart of the Section 2081 permit process is shown in Figure 14-4 on the following page. Regulations governing incidental take permits (also known as Section 2081 permits) are found at 14 Cal. Code Regs. § 783 *et seq.*

A Section 2081 permit is not available to authorize take of fully protected species. The Section 2081 program is a certified regulatory program under CEQA (see

FIGURE 14-4
Section 2081 Permit Process

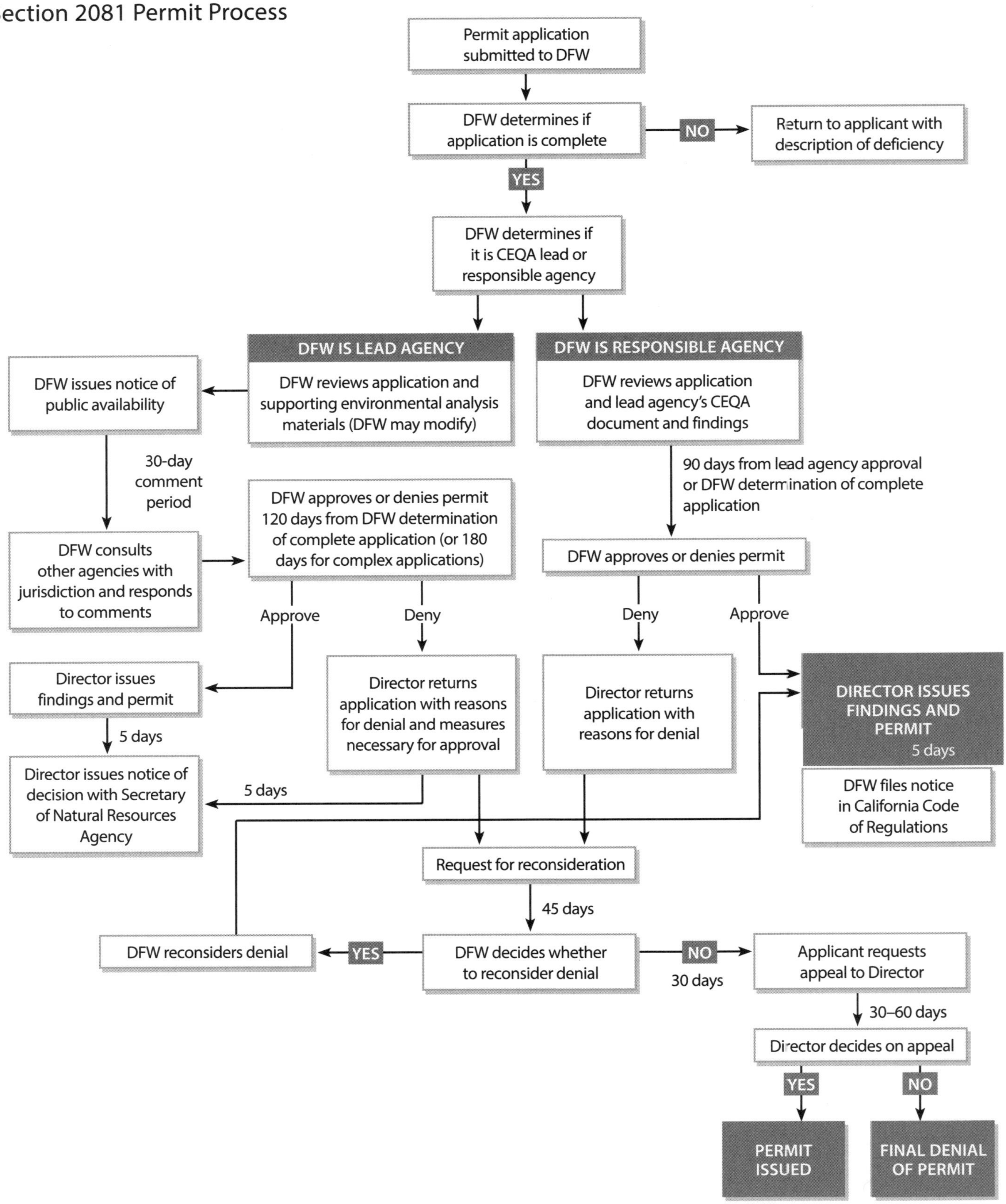

chapter 2), so DFW does not need to prepare a separate CEQA document when serving as a lead agency approving a Section 2081 permit. Section 2081 permit CEQA procedures can be found at 14 Cal. Code Regs. § 783.3.

A Section 2081 permit may be issued if the following criteria are met (Fish & Game Code § 2081(b)):

- The authorized take is incidental to an otherwise lawful activity
- The impacts of the authorized take are minimized and fully mitigated
- The measures required to minimize and fully mitigate impacts are roughly proportional to the impact of the taking on the species, maintain the applicant's objectives to the greatest extent possible, and are capable of successful implementation
- Adequate funding is provided to implement the required minimization and mitigation measures and to monitor compliance with and the effectiveness of the measures
- Issuance of the permit will not jeopardize the continued existence of a state-listed species

Measures to minimize the take of species covered by the permit (covered species) and to mitigate the impacts caused by the take are set forth in one or more attachments to the permit. This attachment generally is a mitigation plan (e.g., an HCP) prepared and submitted by the permittee in coordination with DFW staff.

Special streamlining procedures apply if a project will result in take of a species that is both federally and state listed. For such jointly listed species, CESA compliance can be achieved through formal Section 7 consultation or through the Section 10 incidental take process; note however that the federal "no surprises" policy for a Section 10 ITP does not apply to a state Section 2081 incidental take permit (*EPIC v. Cal. Dep't of Forestry* (2008) 44 Cal. 4th 459). The applicant must consult with DFW during these federal ESA processes, and DFW must concur with the mitigation measures proposed by the Services. Also, the Section 7 consultation or Section 10 ITP must comply with other CESA requirements, including full mitigation of impacts and financial assurances to carry out required mitigation. Fish & Game Code § 2080.1.

Special streamlining procedures apply if a project will result in take of a species that is both federally and state listed.

SB 839 of 2016 (Chapter 340, Statutes of 2016) required DFW to establish a graduated application fee schedule for Section 2081 permits.

Scientific collecting permit. Through permits or memoranda of understanding, the DFW also may authorize individuals, public agencies, universities, zoological gardens, and scientific or educational institutions to import, export, take, or possess any endangered species, threatened species, or candidate species of plants and animals for scientific, educational, or management purposes. Fish & Game Code § 1002.

Santa Clara Valley Habitat Plan

The Santa Clara Valley Habitat Plan is a good example of a modern regional multi-species joint HCP/NCCP, covering about 520,000 acres and 18 listed and non-listed species. (*See* http://scv-habitatagency.org/178/Final-Habitat-Plan). The Plan provides a framework for promoting the protection and recovery of natural resources, including endangered species, while streamlining the permitting process for planned development, infrastructure, and maintenance activities. The Plan allows the permittees—the County of Santa Clara, the Santa Clara Valley Water District, the Santa Clara Valley Transportation Authority (VTA) and the cities of Gilroy, Morgan Hill, and San Jose—to receive 50-year incidental take permits for activities and projects they conduct and those under their jurisdiction.

A primary goal of the plan is to obtain authorization for incidental take of covered species under the ESA and the NCCP Act for covered activities, which fall into seven general categories.

- Urban development
- In-stream capital projects
- In-stream operations and maintenance
- Rural capital projects
- Rural operations and maintenance
- Rural development
- Conservation strategy implementation

The plan's conservation strategy was designed to mitigate impacts on covered species and to contribute to the recovery of these species. The conservation strategy includes biological goals and objectives developed specifically for the Plan, and conservation actions to achieve them. The heart of the conservation strategy is the creation of a Reserve System that will protect about 47,000 acres for the benefit of covered species, natural communities, biological diversity, and ecosystem function.

Total costs of plan implementation were estimated to be about $658 million. Funding sources include private and public development fees as well as other local, state, and federal funding sources.

Agricultural activities. CESA allows DFW to authorize local voluntary programs for routine and ongoing agricultural activities on farms and ranches that encourage habitat for candidate and listed species and wildlife in general; implementing regulations are found at 14 Cal. Code Regs. § 786.0 *et seq.* Activities performed under these approved programs are exempt from the prohibition on take. Fish & Game Code § 2086 *et seq.*

ENFORCEMENT

CESA states that an intentional taking of a listed species is prosecuted as a misdemeanor. Fish & Game Code §§ 12002, 12003.1. SB 839 of 2016 (Chapter 340, Statutes of 2016) increased the penalty for illegal taking of an endangered, threatened, or candidate species to a fine of not less than $25,000 or more than $50,000, imprisonment for not more than one year, or by both fine and imprisonment. Also, the Penal Code § 653(o) *et seq.* prohibits importing or selling the dead bodies of certain listed species. For Penal Code violations, maximum criminal penalties are $5,000 per violation or one year imprisonment; maximum civil penalties are $10,000 per violation. Fish & Game Code §§ 2582, 2583, 12008.

NATURAL COMMUNITY CONSERVATION PLANNING ACT

The NCCPA (Fish & Game Code § 2800 *et seq.*) establishes a voluntary comprehensive planning approach that balances fish and wildlife protection with community development. NCCPs prepared pursuant to the Act are often combined with HCPs to provide coverage for both state and federally listed and sensitive species. *See* sidebar.

The NCCP process begins with a planning agreement signed by DFW and plan participants. The planning agreement outlines the geographic planning area, species, and natural communities to be addressed, processes for scientific and public input, and an interim process for project review. Fish & Game Code § 2810.

To approve an NCCP, DFW must find that the NCCP (Fish & Game Code § 2815):

- Protects habitat, natural communities, and species diversity on a landscape or ecosystem level

- Includes a reserve system and conservation measures meeting certain ecological requirements
- Identifies activities allowed within reserves
- Includes specific conservation measures for covered species
- Includes monitoring and adaptive management programs
- Includes an implementation schedule and funding provisions

An NCCP Implementation Agreement must be prepared. The Implementation Agreement is a binding contract describing the roles and responsibilities of all parties, including plan oversight, establishment of reserves or other conservation measures, monitoring and adaptive management, and funding. Fish & Game Code § 2821.

Once an NCCP and associated CEQA documents have been approved, DFW may provide take authorization for all of the NCCP's covered species. Covered species include both CESA-listed and CESA-non-listed species conserved under the NCCP, as well as fully protected species. The NCCP is thus an efficient alternative to obtaining individual Section 2081 incidental take permits for each species affected by a proposed plan or project. Fish & Game Code § 2835.

Similar to the federal ESA "no surprises rule," an NCCP also may include "long-term assurances" that unforeseen circumstances will not trigger additional conservation or funding requirements. DFW must suspend or revoke take authorization if the continued take of the species would jeopardize the species' continued existence. Fish & Game Code §§ 2820(f), 2835.

DFW must suspend or revoke take authorization if the continued take of the species would jeopardize the species' continued existence.

for more information...

Barclay, C. T. and M. S. Gray, 2016. California Land Use and Planning Law. Solano Press. Point Arena, Calif.

Manaster, K. A. and D. P. Selmi (eds.), ND. Chapter 81 of California Environmental Law and Land Use Practice. Matthew Bender. San Francisco, Calif.

U.S. Fish and Wildlife Service, 2013. Permits for Native Species Under the Endangered Species Act.

U.S. Fish and Wildlife Service and National Marine Fisheries Service, 2016. Habitat Conservation Planning and Incidental Take Permit Processing Handbook.

U.S. Fish and Wildlife Service and National Oceanic and Atmospheric Administration Fisheries, 1996. Habitat Conservation Planning and ITP Processing Handbook.

U.S. Fish and Wildlife Service and National Oceanic and Atmospheric Administration Fisheries, 1998. Endangered Species Act Consultation Handbook.

glossary

Anadromous fish—a fish species, such as salmon, that migrates from freshwater streams to the ocean and back to complete its cycle.

Biological assessment—a document prepared for Section 7 consultation to determine whether a proposed federal major construction activity is likely to adversely affect a listed species, proposed species, or designated critical habitat.

Biological diversity—the variety of life and its processes, including the variety of living organisms, the genetic differences among them, and the communities and ecosystems in which they occur.

Biological opinion*—a document stating the opinion of USFWS or NOAA Fisheries on whether a federal action is likely to jeopardize the continued existence of a listed species or result in destruction or adverse modification of its critical habitat.

California Natural Diversity Database—an inventory of the reported locations of listed species and species of special concern.

Candidate species—a plant or animal species for which enough information is known concerning biological vulnerability and threats to support a proposal to list as endangered or threatened.

Conserve, conserving, and conservation—the use of methods and procedures necessary to bring any listed species to the point at which measures under the ESA are no longer necessary.

Critical habitat—a formally designated specific geographic area that contains those physical or biological features essential to the conservation of a listed species and that may require special management or protection.

Ecosystem—a dynamic and interrelated complex of plant and animal communities, and their associated environment.

Endangered species—a species in danger of extinction throughout all or a significant portion of its range.

Formal consultation—the required process under ESA Section 7 when a proposed federal action is likely to adversely affect a listed species or critical habitat, used to determine in a biological opinion whether the proposed action is likely to jeopardize the continued existence of the species or adversely modify critical habitat.

Fully protected species—a species for which DFW may not issue a take permit, except for scientific purposes.

Habitat—the place or environment where a plant or animal lives naturally.

Habitat conservation plan*—a plan prepared under ESA Section 10(a) that outlines ways of maintaining, enhancing, and protecting a habitat type needed to protect a listed species.

Harass—to intentionally or negligently create the likelihood of injury to wildlife by annoying it to such an extent as to significantly disrupt normal behavior patterns such as breeding, feeding, or sheltering.

Harm—to perform an act that kills or injures wildlife; may include significant habitat modification or degradation when it kills or injures wildlife by significantly impairing essential behavioral patterns such as nesting or reproduction.

Incidental take—take of a listed species that results from, but is not the purpose of, otherwise lawful activity.

Incidental take permit*—a permit issued by USFWS or NOAA Fisheries under the federal ESA Section 10(a), or DFW under CESA Section 2081, authorizing take of a listed species.

Informal consultation—a process under ESA Section 7 prior to or in lieu of formal consultation that includes all interactions between USFWS or NOAA Fisheries and a federal agency or its designated non-federal representative such as an applicant.

Jeopardize—appreciably reducing the likelihood of both the survival and recovery of a listed species in the wild by reducing the reproduction, numbers, or distribution of the species.

Listing—the formal process by which USFWS or NOAA Fisheries under the federal ESA, or the Fish and Game Commission under CESA, adds species to the list of endangered and threatened wildlife and plants.

Migratory birds—birds that migrate across state and national borders.

Natural community conservation plan*—a regional plan prepared under the NCCPA that provides measures necessary to conserve and manage natural biological diversity within the plan area while allowing compatible and appropriate economic development, growth, and other human uses.

No surprises rule—under the federal ESA and the NCCPA, assurances given to incidental take permittees that unforeseen circumstances will not result in additional conservation or funding requirements.

Range—the geographic area a species is known or believed to occupy.

Reasonable and prudent alternative—a recommended alternative action identified in a biological opinion that is feasible, can be implemented consistent with the purpose of the action, is consistent with the federal agency's legal authority and jurisdiction, and would avoid jeopardy.

Reasonable and prudent measure—an action necessary to minimize the impacts of incidental take of a listed species that is anticipated to result from implementing a project with a non-jeopardy opinion.

Recovery—the process by which decline of a listed species is stopped or reversed, or threats to its survival neutralized, so that its long-term survival in the wild can be ensured.

Recovery plan—a document serving as the guide for activities to recover or conserve a listed species.

Section 4(d) rule—a regulation that establishes prohibitions on take necessary and advisable to provide for conservation of a threatened species.

Section 7 consultation*—the process by which a federal agency consults with USFWS or NOAA Fisheries under the federal ESA to determine whether any activity authorized, funded, or carried out by the agency may affect a listed species or designated critical habitat.

Section 2081 incidental take permit*—DFW permit authorizing take of state-listed species incidental to otherwise lawful development projects.

Species of special concern—animals not listed under the federal ESA or CESA, but that nonetheless are declining at a rate that could result in listing, or that historically occurred in low numbers and known threats to their persistence currently exist.

Take—under the federal ESA, to harass, harm, pursue, hunt, shoot, wound, kill, trap, capture, or collect a listed species, or to attempt such conduct; under CESA, to hunt, pursue, catch, capture, or kill a listed species, or to attempt such conduct.

Threatened species—a species likely to become endangered within the foreseeable future throughout all or a significant part of its range.

* equals permits and approvals

CHAPTER 15

Wetlands

related Solano Press titles

California Land Use and Planning Law. Cecily Talbert Barclay and Matthew S. Gray. 35th Edition. 2016.

Wetlands, Streams, and Other Waters. Paul Cylinder et al. 2004.

in this chapter...

CWA = Clean Water Act

USACE = U.S. Army Corps of Engineers

EPA = U.S. Environmental Protection Agency

The heightened societal awareness of wetlands values, and significant long-term declines in wetland acreage, have caused federal, state, and local governments to implement programs to regulate and protect wetlands.

INTRODUCTION

Wetlands are areas of land that are wet seasonally or permanently, and support special types of adapted vegetation. Wetlands were once thought of as useless swamps and marshes requiring draining and filling, but are now recognized as providing flood control, fish and wildlife, and water quality benefits.

The heightened societal awareness of wetlands values, and significant long-term declines in wetland acreage, have caused federal, state, and local governments to implement programs to regulate and protect wetlands. This chapter reviews key laws and agencies involved in wetlands regulation, and federal, state, and regional wetlands regulation programs. It also covers regulation of activities in waters of the state under Fish & Game Code § 1600 *et seq.*

KEY LAWS AND AGENCIES

FEDERAL LAWS AND AGENCIES

Clean Water Act. Section 404 of the federal Clean Water Act (CWA, 33 U.S.C. § 1244) requires private and governmental entities to obtain a U.S. Army Corps of Engineers (USACE) permit prior to discharge of dredged or fill material into waters of the United States, which include adjacent wetlands. (This chapter focuses on Section 404 permitting for wetlands fills, but it should be noted throughout that the same permitting requirements apply to all waters of the United States, as defined below.) Section 404 authorizes the USACE permit program, requires the Environmental Protection Agency (EPA) together with USACE to issue guidelines governing the permit program, and authorizes EPA to veto permits. As explained in detail below, the Section 404 program has evolved into a highly complex and pervasive regulatory scheme.

Rivers and Harbors Act of 1899. This Act (33 U.S.C. § 4501 *et seq.*) is the legislative origin of the Section 404 program. Section 10 permits under the Rivers and Harbors Act are required for any obstruction or alteration of any navigable water of the United States, including placement of structures in, dredging of, or disposal of dredged material into navigable waters.

USACE regulatory authority under the Rivers and Harbors Act is limited to traditional "navigable waters." Traditional "navigable waters" regulated by Section 10 are waters that are, could be, or were once used to transport interstate or foreign commerce. In contrast, "waters of the United States" regulated under Section 404 also include "other waters" such as wetlands that could affect interstate commerce. 33 C.F.R. § 328.3. The lateral extent of jurisdiction under Section 10 and Section 404 is shown in Figure 15-1.

In practice, USACE regulatory authority under the Rivers and Harbors Act has been integrated with regulatory authority under the CWA, and USACE uses one permit application for both types of permits.

MOA = memorandum of agreement

USFWS = U.S. Fish and Wildlife Service

NOAA = National Oceanic and Atmospheric Administration

DFW = California Department of Fish and Wildlife

ESA = Endangered Species Act

FIGURE 15-1

Lateral Extent of Jurisdiction under Section 404 and Section 10

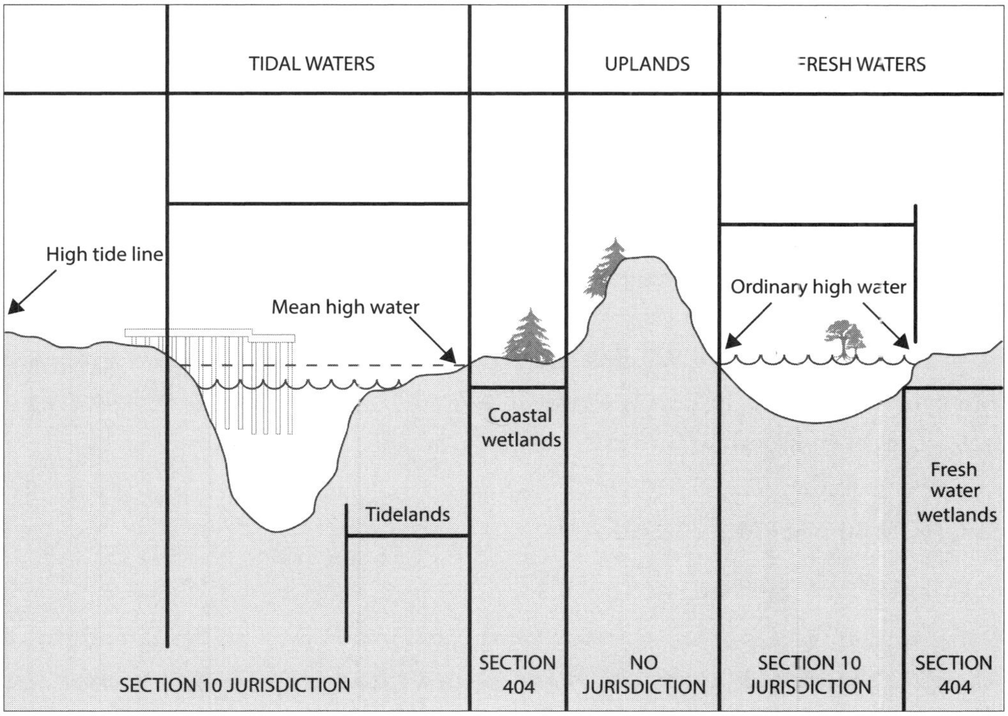

Source: U.S. Army Corps of Engineers, Sacramento District

U.S. Army Corps of Engineers. USACE is primarily responsible for implementing the Section 404 program. USACE is organized geographically into eight divisions and 41 subordinate districts. Three district offices are responsible for administering California's Section 404 program—San Francisco, Sacramento, and Los Angeles. They are all located within the USACE South Pacific Division.

USACE regulations implementing the Section 404 program are found at 33 C.F.R. § 320 *et seq.* Other important sources of Section 404 requirements include Regulatory Guidance Letters issued by the Chief of Engineers and published District-specific policies.

Environmental Protection Agency. EPA is responsible for Section 404 program oversight. EPA and USACE have issued several memoranda of agreement (MOAs), including one that defines each agency's roles more specifically. USACE and EPA 1989.

Other federal agencies. U.S. Fish and Wildlife Service (USFWS) and National Oceanic and Atmospheric Administration (NOAA) Fisheries review and comment on Section 404 applications, and USACE must give full consideration to comments of those agencies and the Department of Fish and Wildlife (DFW). If a Section 404 permit may affect a listed threatened or endangered species, then consultation under Section 7 of the Endangered Species Act (ESA) is required (*see* chapter 14).

WOTUS = waters of the United States

SWRCB = State Water Resources Control Board

RWQCB = regional water quality control board

WDR = waste discharge requirement

STATE LAWS AND AGENCIES

State Water Resources Control Board and regional water quality control boards. Section 401 of the CWA requires applicants for a federal permit resulting in a discharge to jurisdictional waters, such as a USACE 404 permit, to provide the USACE with a state certification stating the discharge will comply with the state's water quality plan and standards. The State Water Resources Control Board (SWRCB) and regional water quality control boards (RWQCBs) are responsible for issuing Section 401 certifications for Section 404 permits. RWQCBs also have the authority to issue waste discharge requirements (WDRs) permits for discharge of dredged or fill materials into waters of the state, including wetlands.

Department of Fish and Wildlife. DFW enters into lake or streambed alteration agreements pursuant to Fish & Game Code § 1600 *et seq.* These agreements regulate activities in lakes and the beds, channels, and banks of rivers and streams.

SECTION 404 PERMIT PROGRAM

REGULATED WATERS AND ACTIVITIES

Definition of waters of the United States. Section 404 jurisdiction extends to all waters of the United States, which are defined expansively to include all waters used or susceptible to use in interstate or foreign commerce. Waters of the United States include lakes, rivers, estuaries, and coastal waters, as well as all adjacent wetlands. 40 C.F.R. § 328.3.

Wetlands are defined as those areas inundated or saturated by surface water or groundwater at a frequency to support, and that under normal circumstances do support, a prevalence of vegetation adapted to saturated soil conditions.

Wetlands are defined as those areas inundated or saturated by surface water or groundwater at a frequency to support, and that under normal circumstances do support, a prevalence of vegetation adapted to saturated soil conditions. "Adjacent" wetlands subject to Section 404 jurisdiction are those that are bordering, contiguous, or neighboring to other waters of the United States. 33 C.F.R. § 328.3(b).

Section 404 jurisdiction does not apply to "isolated" intrastate waters and wetlands. In the controversial *SWANCC* decision (*Solid Waste Agency of Northern Cook County v. U.S. Army Corps of Engineers* (2001) 531 U.S. 159), the U.S. Supreme Court held that Section 404 jurisdiction does not extend to non-navigable, isolated waters, at least when based solely on the fact that these waters are used as habitat by migratory birds.

The Supreme Court again took up the regulation of isolated wetlands in its opinion on two consolidated appeals in *Rapanos v. United States* (2006) 126 S. Ct. 2208. In a highly divided opinion, the controlling test was articulated by Justice Kennedy in a concurring opinion. Under this test, waters of the United States include tributaries to, and wetlands adjacent to, navigable waters, if there is a "significant nexus" to waters that are or were navigable in fact. *See* sidebar.

Methods for determining jurisdictional wetlands and other waters. Project applicants are typically responsible for delineation of jurisdictional wetlands and other waters in the U.S. on their property. USACE is then responsible for verifying the applicant's delineation.

Wetlands are delineated using the 1987 USACE Wetlands Delineation Manual (USACE 1987), together with applicable regional supplements. The 1987 manual uses a three-parameter test: if a site has positive indicators of hydrophytic (water-loving) vegetation, hydric soils, and wetlands hydrology, it is normally considered a jurisdictional wetland. In "disturbed" or "abnormal" circumstances (e.g., when wetland vegetation has been artificially removed from a wetland), all three factors need not be present. This approach addresses situations where an applicant attempts to eliminate the need for a Section 404 permit by intentionally destroying hydrophytic vegetation.

Also, the USACE has issued an Arid West Regional Supplement to the 1987 manual to provide more current knowledge and practice in this region, which includes most of California. (USACE 2008a).

Because of the *SWANCC* and *Rapanos* cases, wetlands delineations should document hydrologic connections between the wetland and waters of the United States. Also, "special aquatic sites" that receive special protection during the Section 404 permitting process should be identified in delineations. In addition to wetlands, special aquatic sites include sanctuaries and refuges, mudflats, vegetated shallows, coral reefs, and riffle and pool complexes. 40 C.F.R. § 230.40 *et seq.*

In 2007, USACE and EPA issued guidance on wetlands delineations to implement the requirements of the *Rapanos* case. USACE and EPA 2007a. USACE and EPA (2007b) also issued a memorandum on coordinating jurisdictional determinations in light of both the *SWANCC* and *Rapanos* decisions.

In June 2015, the USACE and EPA issued a final rule defining waters of the U.S. that attempted to integrate the

Supreme Court Interprets "Waters of the United States"

In *Solid Waste Agency of Northern Cook County v. U.S. Army Corps of Engineers* (2001, 531 U.S. 159) (*SWANCC*), a solid waste agency proposed to develop a waste disposal facility on a 533-acre site that was an abandoned sand and gravel mine. About 17 acres of the site was covered by permanent and seasonal ponds created by former excavations. USACE determined that it had jurisdiction over these ponds under the "Migratory Bird Rule" because migratory birds used them, even though the ponds were isolated and not adjacent to any navigable waters. The Supreme Court held that isolated seasonal ponds do not fall under the definition of waters of the United States subject to Section 404 jurisdiction merely because they serve as habitat for isolated birds. The case also has been interpreted to stand for the broader proposition that no other Commerce Clause connection (e.g., use by interstate or foreign travelers) can justify regulation of intrastate isolated waters.

The Supreme Court again took up the regulation of isolated wetlands in its opinion on two consolidated appeals in *Rapanos v. United States* (2006) 126 S. Ct. 2208. The Supreme Court issued five separate opinions with no single majority opinion, thus creating considerable confusion in how to apply the case. Justice Kennedy's concurring opinion to Justice Scalia's more conservative plurality opinion was generally the most influential in subsequent court decisions and regulatory practice. His plurality opinion held that CWA jurisdiction applies to traditional navigable waters (e.g., rivers and lakes) and all other waters (including intermittent waters) with a "significant nexus" to a traditional navigable water. A "significant nexus" is established when the tributaries or wetlands significantly affect the chemical, physical, and biological integrity of waters that are or were navigable in fact. Many commentators criticized the "significant nexus" test as requiring costly and time-consuming case-by-case determinations of CWA jurisdiction, rather than creating easy-to-apply categorical rules.

2015 Final Rule Defining Waters of the United States

Scope. The controversial final rule defining "waters of the United States" (80 Fed. Reg. 3705, (June 29, 2015)) defines this term for all CWA purposes, including not just Section 404 permitting, but also Sections 303 (water quality standards), 401 (state water quality certification), and 402 (National Pollutant Discharge Elimination System permits). The rule (enjoined at the time of book publication) recognizes jurisdiction for three basic categories: waters that are jurisdictional in all instances, waters that are excluded from jurisdiction, and additional "other waters," including a narrow category of waters subject to case-by-case analysis to determine whether they are jurisdictional.

Automatically Jurisdictional Waters. The final rule defines the following waters as automatically jurisdictional:

- Traditional navigable waters, interstate waters, territorial seas, and impoundments of waters that otherwise qualify as jurisdictional
- Certain "tributaries:" water bodies with a defined bed and banks, and an ordinary high water mark, that contribute flow to traditional navigable waters, interstate waters, or territorial seas
- Certain "adjacent" wetlands and waters: wetlands and waters adjacent to jurisdictional waters within the 100-year floodplain and within 1,500 feet of the ordinary high water mark, or within 100 feet of the high water mark of a jurisdictional water, or within 1,500 feet of the high tide line of a tidally influenced water

Automatically Excluded Waters. The final rule is intended to create greater certainty in wetlands permitting by creating an integrated list of waters automatically excluded from CWA jurisdiction, including:

- Waste treatment systems
- Stormwater control features
- Wastewater recycling and groundwater recharge facilities
- Certain erosional features, including gullies, rills and other ephemeral features
- Certain ephemeral ditches
- Certain artificially created or maintained waters

Additional "Other Waters"

- Specific regional waters that are "similarly situated." These consist of five sets of regional waters which are under the definition of WOTUS where they have a significant nexus; western vernal pools (seasonal wetlands that dry out in summer) are of most importance in California.
- On a case-by-case basis, additional "other waters" may be jurisdictional if there is a "significant nexus" to jurisdictional waters. These are waters within the 100-year floodplain of a traditional navigable water, interstate water, or territorial sea, as well as waters within 4,000 feet of jurisdictional waters. A significant nexus exists if the functions performed by a water contribute significantly to the physical or biological integrity of jurisdictional water.

SWANCC and *Rapanos* decisions, as well as the latest wetlands science. 80 Fed. Reg. 37054 (June 29, 2015). *See* sidebar. This rule was also intended to replace prior USACE and EPA guidance interpreting these cases, and reduce reliance on the 1987 wetlands delineation manual and regional supplements. However, in October 2015, implementation of the final rule was enjoined nationwide, and further litigation had not been concluded are the time this book was written; readers of this book should consult the USACE or EPA for the latest legal status of these regulations.

Definition of discharge of dredged or fill material. A Section 404 permit is required for the "discharge" of "dredged or fill material" into waters of the United States. Under the CWA, discharge of a pollutant is the addition of any pollutant to waters of the United States from any point source (*see* chapter 6 for further discussion of the CWA). "Dredged material" means materials that were removed from waters of the United States, typically during dredging. "Fill materials" are materials such as dirt and rock that replace an aquatic area with dry land or raise its elevation. 33 U.S.C. §§ 1344(a), 1362.

The application of Section 404 permits to certain types of activities affecting wetlands has been particularly controversial:

- Dredging or excavation activities per se are not regulated under Section 404, even if they cause "incidental fallback" into waters of the United States, but they are regulated under Section 404 if the redeposit is more than incidental fallback. *National Mining Association v. Army Corps of Engineers* (1998) 145 F. 3d 1399; 40 C.F.R. § 232.3

- Tractors conducting deep ripping of agricultural land are regulated under Section 404. *Borden Ranch Partnership v. USACE* (2001) 261 F. 3d 810
- Draining wetlands is not regulated under Section 404 unless there is a discharge of dredged or fill material, or unless the draining is part of land clearing for land use conversion. *Avoyelles Sportsmen's League, Inc. v. Marsh* (1983) 715 F. 2d 897
- The placement of pilings is regulated under Section 404 when it would have the effect of a discharge, e.g., when pilings are placed so closely together that they increase sedimentation. 33 C.F.R. § 323.2(d)(1)

NEPA = National Environmental Policy Act

Exemptions. The following activities are exempt from Section 404 regulation (33 U.S.C. § 1344(f)(1)):

- "Normal" farming, silviculture (forestry), and ranching that was currently in use as of December 23, 1985
- Constructing or maintaining stock or farm ponds and irrigation ditches, or maintaining drainage ditches
- Constructing or maintaining farm, forest, or mining roads, or temporary roads for moving mining equipment
- Maintaining or reconstructing structures that are currently serviceable
- Construction of temporary construction sedimentation basins
- Activities regulated by an approved best management practices program authorized by Section 208(b)(4) of the CWA

These exemptions are subject to a "recapture" provision, and are not exempt under certain circumstances. They are not exempt if the activity would violate toxic effluent standards or if the activity has the purpose of bringing an area within jurisdictional waters into a new use that impairs the flow, circulation, or reach of waters. USACE often applies this recapture provision when agricultural land is converted to a different use such as urban development. 33 U.S.C. § 1344(f)(2).

Also, a narrow Section 404(r) exemption exists for specific congressionally authorized construction projects invoking that exemption. Before authorizing funding, the federal agency must prepare an Environmental Impact Statement pursuant to the National Environmental Policy Act (NEPA) that includes consideration of EPA's Section 404(b)(1) Guidelines. *See* below. 33 U.S.C. § 1344(r).

Section 404 jurisdiction extends to all waters of the United States, which are defined expansively.

SECTION 404 PERMIT PROCESS: OVERVIEW

There are two broad types of Section 404 permits. "Standard" permits include individual permits, and when applicable, letters of permission. *See* below. "General"

NWP = nationwide permit

JD = jurisdictional determination

permits include nationwide permits (NWPs), regional general permits, and programmatic general permits. General permits are intended to authorize activities that USACE has determined would have minimal adverse effects on aquatic resources (individually or cumulatively), and that would require minimal USACE review time.

Individual permits and NWPs are the two most common types of Section 404 permits. The individual permit process is summarized in Figure 15-2, and the NWP process is summarized in Figure 15-3 following.

The permit process typically is initiated by a jurisdictional determination that the proposed activity would occur in wetlands or other waters of the United States.

The permit process typically is initiated by a jurisdictional determination (JD) that the proposed activity would occur in wetlands or other waters of the United States. The project applicant typically prepares a wetlands delineation report that documents the extent of jurisdictional waters, and submits the report to USACE, requesting verification. USACE then sends the applicant a JD that verifies the jurisdictional boundaries. The verification letter is valid for five years. 33 C.F.R. § 320.1(a). In the Ninth Circuit, approved JDs may not be challenged in court, since they are not final agency actions. *Fairbanks North Star Borough v. U.S. Army Corps of Engineers* (9th Cir. 2008) 543 F. 3d 586. However, the Eighth Circuit held the opposite in *Hawkes Co., Inc. v. U.S. Army Corps of Engineers* (2015), and in late 2015 the Supreme Court granted review to resolve the split among the circuits. (Supreme Court No. 15-290).

To expedite the wetlands permitting process, the USACE has developed procedures for landowners to obtain a "Preliminary JD" (USACE 2008b). A Preliminary JD is a "non-binding" document that presumes federal jurisdiction over all potential wetlands and other waters that may be subject to Section 404 jurisdiction.

INDIVIDUAL PERMITS

The individual permit process is shown in Figure 15-2. Individual permits typically are issued before a discharge occurs, but USACE can also issue "after-the-fact" permits allowing fill to remain in place if certain conditions are met. The individual permit process is intended to take 60–120 days once a permit application is submitted, but in practice usually takes longer. 33 C.F.R. §§ 325.2(a), 326.3(e).

Pre-application process. The pre-application process includes USACE verification of jurisdictional waters, and a pre-application meeting or meetings. Relevant agencies such as USFWS are invited to the pre-application meeting to share their views about the proposed project.

Permit application. Individual permit applications must include (33 C.F.R. § 325.1), among other things:

- The project description, purpose, and need
- The purpose of activities involving discharge of dredged or fill materials, and type and quantity of material to be discharged
- Acreage of wetlands or other waters to be filled

FIGURE 15-2

Individual Permit Process for a Section 404 Permit

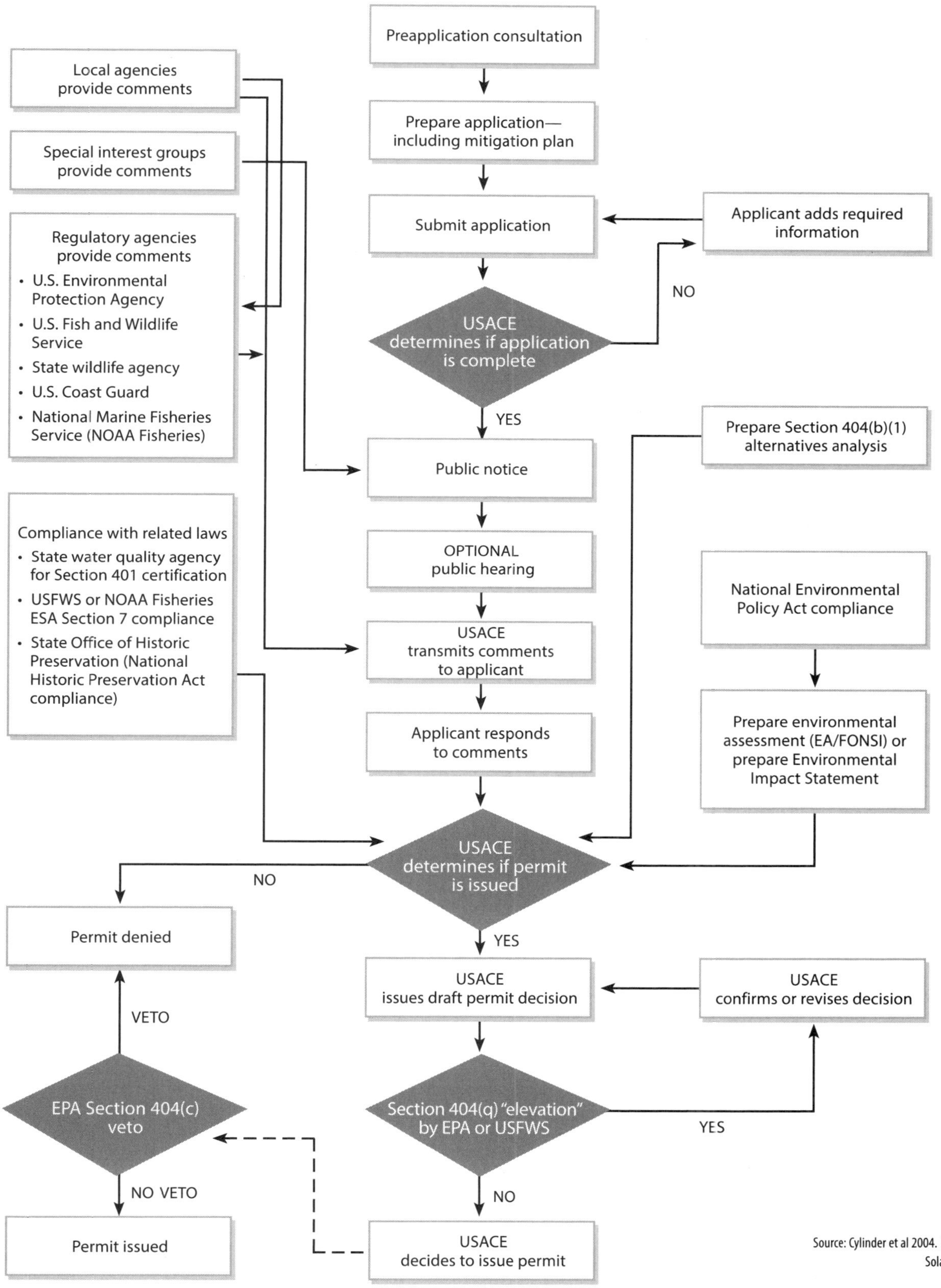

Source: Cylinder et al 2004. *Wetlands, Streams, and Other Waters.* Solano Press. Reprinted with permission

FIGURE 15-3
Nationwide Permit Process

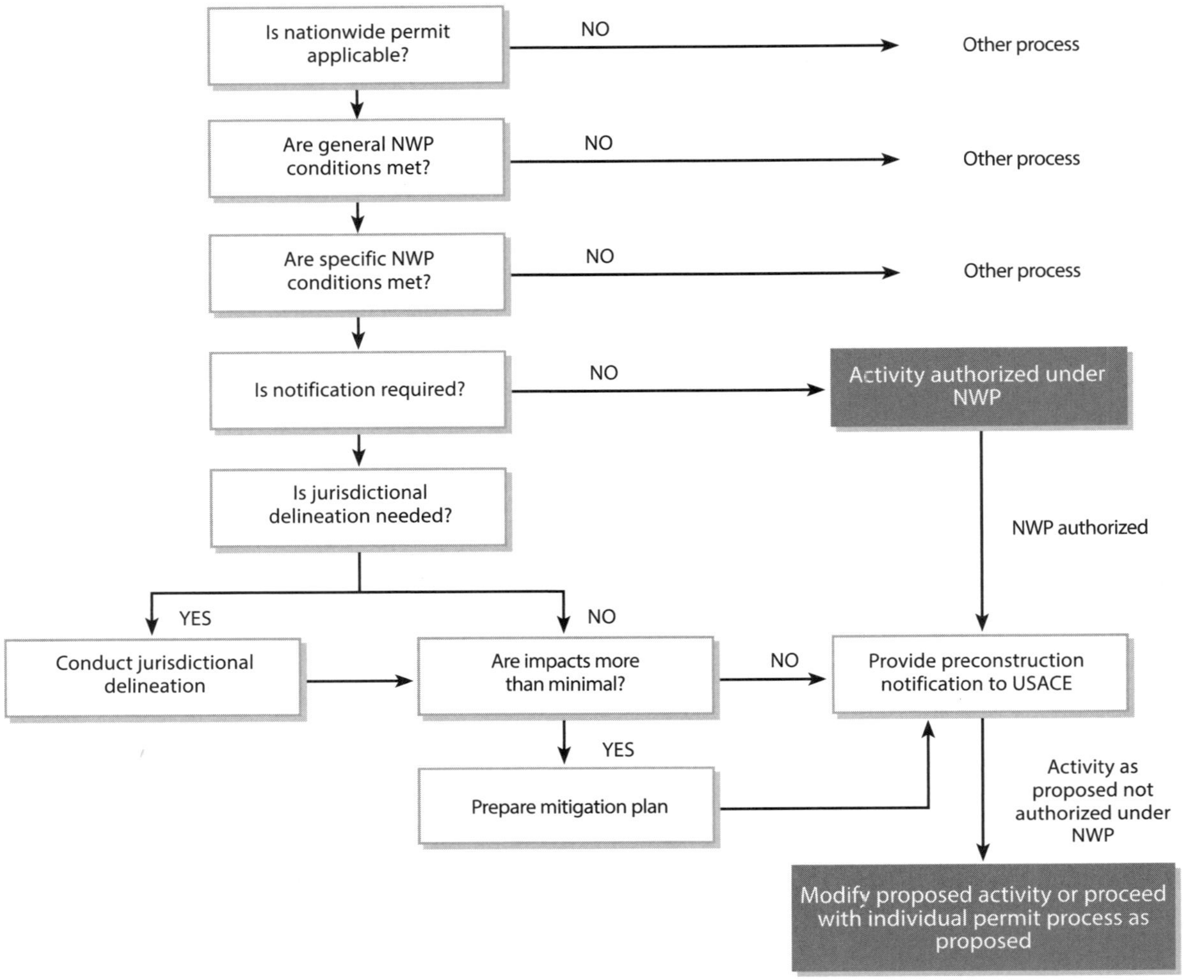

Source: Cylinder et al. 2004. *Wetlands, Streams, and Other Waters.* Solano Press. Reprinted with permission

- Drawings or plans sufficient for public notice
- Federal, state, and local authorizations required for the work

In addition, applicants often include a Section 404(b)(1) alternatives analysis and a mitigation plan together with the permit application. These documents, described below, can speed the permit process when submitted with the permit application.

Following submittal of the permit application, USACE issues a public notice of the permit application and solicits comments during a 30-day review period. A public hearing is sometimes held, if requested. Public comments are submitted to the applicant for response. 33 C.F.R. § 25(a)(2).

404(b)(1) Guidelines. The USACE permit decision is based on whether the proposed activity complies with EPA's Section 404(b)(1) Guidelines, and whether issuance of a permit is in the public interest. The Guidelines (40 C.F.R. § 230 *et seq.*) state that USACE may not issue a permit if there is a less environmentally damaging practicable alternative to the proposed discharge that would have less effect on the aquatic ecosystem, and not have other significant adverse environmental consequences. The Guidelines also restrict permitting of activities that (40 C.F.R. § 230.10(b), (c)):

- Violate water quality or toxic effluent standards
- Jeopardize the continued existence of a species listed under the ESA
- Violate marine sanctuary protections
- Cause "significant degradation" to waters of the United States

When a proposed activity that is not "water-dependent" involves discharge into a special aquatic site such as wetlands, the Guidelines presume other practicable alternatives are available that do not involve discharge into special aquatic sites, unless it can be clearly demonstrated otherwise. An activity is water-dependent if it could not meet the basic project purpose unless located in a special aquatic site; a marina is an example of a water-dependent activity. 40 C.F.R. § 230.10(a).

An activity is water-dependent if it could not meet the basic project purpose unless located in a special aquatic site; a marina is an example of a water-dependent activity.

Also, the Guidelines require the applicant to prepare a mitigation plan that mitigates the effects of the discharge, and compensates for wetlands impacts that cannot be avoided or minimized. Under the USACE/EPA mitigation policy, mitigation is to be sequenced, with avoidance and minimization of wetlands impacts preferred, and compensation considered only if avoidance and minimization are not feasible (*see* the discussion of mitigation below). 40 C.F.R. § 230.10(d).

The project applicant is typically responsible for preparing the Section 404(b)(1) alternatives analysis, which is often submitted as part of the permit application.

Public interest review. If a permit meets the Section 404(b)(1) Guidelines, USACE may still deny the permit if it is determined to be contrary to the public interest. The public interest review balances the project benefits against its reasonably foreseeable detriments. Factors considered in the public interest review include conservation, economics, aesthetics, environmental quality, historic values, fish and wildlife values, flood control, land use, navigation, recreation, water supply and quality, energy needs, safety, and food production. A presumption exists that an activity is not in the public interest if it involves a discharge into wetlands performing functions important to the public interest, such as wetlands providing flood control benefits. 33 C.F.R. § 320.4(a), (b)(4).

Compliance with related environmental laws. To issue a Section 404 permit, USACE must demonstrate compliance with:

- CWA § 401 certification (*see* discussion later in this chapter)
- NEPA (*see* chapter 2 and sidebar)

NEPA Review of Section 404 Permits

The scope of NEPA review of Section 404 permits has been controversial. USACE "small federal handle" regulations state that the NEPA analysis should evaluate the impacts of the specific activity over which there is sufficient federal control and responsibility. 33 C.F.R. § 325, App. B. Ninth Circuit decisions applying the "small federal handle" doctrine have ruled that:

NEPA review of a Section 404 permit for a golf course parking lot need not evaluate the impacts of a related resort development because each could exist without the other. *Sylvester v. U.S. Army Corps of Engineers* (9th Cir. 2008) 884 F. 2d 384.

NEPA review of a 16-acre wetland fill needed to construct a 600-acre mixed use project need not evaluate impacts of upland development, because uplands could be developed in the absence of a Section 404 permit. *Wetlands Action Network v. U.S. Army Corps of Engineers* (9th Cir. 2000) 222 F. 3d 1105.

NEPA review of filling jurisdictional washes running through a proposed development project had to consider impacts of developing the entire property, including uplands, because developing the site was either not possible or was not economically feasible without filling jurisdictional waters. *Save our Sonoran v. Flowers* (9th Cir. 2005) 408 F. 3d 1113; *White Tanks Concerned Citizens v. Strock* (9th Cir. 2009) 563 F. 3d 1033.

- ESA Section 7 (*see* chapter 14)
- Section 106 of the National Historic Preservation Act (*see* chapter 3)

Elevation and veto of permit decisions. Under CWA § 404(q) (33 U.S.C. § 1344(q)), USACE has entered into MOAs with EPA, USFWS, and NOAA Fisheries to elevate disputes with USACE districts, and resolve these disputes expeditiously. To be elevated, permit decisions must involve discharges that have a substantial and unacceptable impact on aquatic resources of national importance.

Under CWA § 404(c) (33 U.S.C. § 13444(c)), EPA may veto a Section 404 permit issued by USACE if it determines that the discharge would have unacceptable adverse impacts on water supplies or fishing, wildlife, or recreation areas. EPA seldom exercises this veto authority, but the threat of an EPA veto may cause changes in proposed projects.

There is no temporal limit on EPA's veto authority. EPA has the authority to veto a Section 404 permit even several years after it has been issued by the USACE. *Mingo Logan Coal Co. v. U.S. Environmental Protection Agency* (D.C. Cir. 2013) 714 F. 3d 608.

Appeals of permit decisions. USACE regulations establish procedures for administrative appeals of permit applications denied with prejudice and declined individual permits. 33 C.F.R. § 333.1 *et seq.* Requests for appeal must be submitted within 60 days.

LETTER OF PERMISSION

The LOP process is an expedited individual permit process not requiring a public notice. Activities eligible for an LOP (e.g., habitat restoration) typically have the purpose of benefiting environmental resources. An LOP still requires agency coordination and compliance with the Section 404(b)(1) Guidelines, and compliance with related environmental laws such as the ESA. 33 C.F.R. § 325.5(b)(2).

Each USACE district lists categories of activities proposed to be authorized under LOP procedures. The district must provide public notice and an opportunity to comment on its proposed list of activities.

GENERAL PERMITS

General permits are intended to streamline the Section 404 permitting process for certain types of activities. General permits apply to categories of activities that are similar in nature and will cause only minimal individual and cumulative adverse environmental effects. Activities meeting conditions of a general permit may proceed without the need for an individual permit, though many require pre-construction notification (PCN) to USACE. USACE reviews general permits every five years, and may reissue, modify, or revoke a general permit following this review. 33 U.S.C. § 1344(e)(1). Types of general permits include regional general permits, programmatic general permits, and the most common type, nationwide permits.

LOP = letter of permission

PCN = pre-construction notification

Regional and programmatic general permits. Regional general permits are issued by a USACE district or division, for a specific geographic region. They cover activities for similar projects within that region that have minimal impacts, such as levee repair and maintenance, and are not covered by another general permit. To adopt a regional general permit, USACE must provide a public notice and comment period, and coordinate with resource agencies. To be authorized by a general permit, a proposed activity must fit within the general permit's defined activities, and meet all general permit conditions, which may require PCN. 33 C.F.R. § 325.2(e)(2).

Programmatic general permits are issued by a USACE district or division, for federal, state, or local wetlands protection programs that meet or exceed the objectives of the Section 404 program. The agency holding the permit may become the permitting authority, with USACE no longer involved in reviewing each use of the permit. 33 C.F.R. § 325.5(c)(3).

Nationwide permits. NWPs are the most common type of general permit. They must be reissued every five years. The latest categories of NWPs at the time of book publication were adopted in 2012. *See* Table 15-1 on the following page. The full text of the NWPs, and any conditions, should be consulted for complete descriptions. At the time this book was written, USACE planned to reissue all 52 of the 2012 NWPs in 2017 with some modifications, and add two more. 81 Fed. Reg. 35186 (June 1, 2016).

Commonly used NWPs include those for small fills associated with residential development, minor road crossings, outfall structures, bank stabilization, wetland restoration, and utility line activities. USACE regulations (33 C.F.R. § 330.5) set forth detailed requirements for the issuance, modification, suspension, and revocation of both NWPs and USACE written authorizations to proceed under NWPs. NWPs offer project applicants a streamlined and time-saving approach to Section 404 compliance for qualifying activities.

Commonly used NWPs include those for small fills associated with residential development, minor road crossings, outfall structures, bank stabilization, wetland restoration, and utility line activities.

All NWPs are subject to general national conditions, which include compliance with the ESA, the National Historic Preservation Act (NHPA), and state water quality standards (*see* Section 401 certification below). NWP permits require mitigation of wetlands impacts following USACE/EPA requirements (*see* below). USACE districts are authorized to add regional conditions and modify, suspend, or revoke an NWP. 33 C.F.R. § 330.1(d).

The NWP process is shown in Figure 15-3. Many of the NWPs require a PCN prior to undertaking an activity. Once an applicant submits a PCN, USACE has 30 days to determine whether the notification is complete. If a project requiring a PCN results in loss of more than one-half acre of waters of the United States, USACE must immediately provide the PCN to EPA, USFWS, NOAA Fisheries, SWRCB, and the State Historic Preservation Officer. Within 45 days of receipt of a complete

Table 15-1. 2012 Nationwide Permits			
No.	Activity	No.	Activity
1	Aids to navigation	27	Wetland and riparian restoration and creation activities
2	Structures in artificial canals	28	Modifications of existing marinas
3	Maintenance activities	29	Single-family housing
4	Fish and wildlife harvesting, enhancement, and attraction devices and activities	30	Moist soil management for wildlife
5	Scientific measurement devices	31	Maintenance of existing flood control facilities
6	Survey activities, including core sampling and seismic exploratory activities	32	Completed enforcement actions
7	Outfall structures	33	Temporary construction, access, and dewatering
8	Oil and gas structures	34	Cranberry production activities
9	Structures in fleeting and anchorage areas	35	Maintenance dredging at existing basins
10	Mooring buoys	36	Boat ramps
11	Temporary recreational structures	37	Emergency watershed protection and rehabilitation
12	Utility line discharges	38	Cleanup of hazardous and toxic waste
13	Bank stabilization	39	Residential, commercial, and institutional developments
14	Linear transportation projects	40	Agricultural activities
15	U.S. Coast Guard-approved bridges	41	Reshaping existing drainage ditches
16	Return water from upland, contained disposal areas	42	Recreational facilities
17	Hydro-power projects	43	Stormwater management facilities
18	Minor discharges	44	Mining activities
19	Minor dredging	45	Repair of uplands damaged by discrete events
20	Oil spill cleanup	46	Discharges in ditches
21	Surface coal mining activities	47	Reserved
22	Removal of vessels	48	Existing commercial shellfish aquaculture activities
23	Approved categorical exclusions	49	Coal remining activities
24	State-administered Section 404 programs	50	Underground coal mining activities
25	Structural discharges	51	Land-based renewable energy generation facilities
26	Reserved	52	Water-based renewable energy generation pilot projects

PCN, USACE must notify the applicant that the activity is authorized under the NWP or requires an individual permit. When a PCN is required, USACE may add conditions to its authorization to ensure the activity complies with the NWP terms and conditions, and results in only minimal individual and cumulative impacts on the aquatic environment. 33 C.F.R. § 330.1(e).

MITIGATION OF WETLANDS IMPACTS

Overview. USACE and EPA have a national goal of no net loss of wetlands, to be applied to each permit decision. In measuring no net loss, USACE primarily will consider loss of wetlands values and functions. USACE and EPA have issued detailed guidance on methods for mitigating impacts to wetlands and other waters of the United States. Mitigation for both individual and general permits must follow this guidance. Mitigation guidance may be found in a USACE and EPA 1990 MOA (USACE and EPA 1990), and more recently in USACE and EPA 2008 regulations for compensatory mitigation.

USACE and EPA have a national goal of no net loss of wetlands, to be applied to each permit decision.

The USACE and EPA 1990 MOA establishes the basic mitigation sequencing framework. Wetlands impacts can be mitigated through avoidance, minimization, or compensation. Avoidance by selecting a non-wetlands site, and minimization of impacts through project modifications and permit conditions, should be implemented prior to compensation.

Compensatory mitigation regulations. USACE and EPA issued comprehensive regulations governing compensatory mitigation in 2008 (73 Fed. Reg. 19594 (April 10, 2008)) in response to studies showing that the compensatory mitigation program needed improvement. The regulations establish performance standards and criteria for compensatory mitigation and mitigation banks. They account for regional variations in aquatic resource types, and emphasize a "watershed approach" to compensatory mitigation. They also require permittees to submit detailed mitigation plans that must be approved by the USACE.

The regulations emphasize the use of wetlands mitigation banks under appropriate circumstances, and simplify the process for establishing mitigation banks. Mitigation banks are a unique form of compensatory mitigation, in which off-site wetlands are enhanced, created, or restored to mitigate impacts on wetlands resources affected by individual projects. A credit system is then used to purchase compensation credits. Each credit is a unit of restored or created wetlands that can be withdrawn to offset impacts of an individual project.

The regulations establish a strong preference for mitigation banks over other types of mitigation due to greater certainty of successful large-scale wetlands mitigation. In-lieu fee programs are second in preference; in-lieu fee programs, like mitigation banks, offer good opportunities for successful large-scale wetlands mitigation. In these programs, permittees pay a fee which is used to fund off-site mitigation projects carried out by others. The National Fish and Wildlife

Sackett v. EPA: EPA Goes Too Far

In a rare unanimous decision in an environmental law case, the U.S. Supreme Court ruled that property owners may bring a pre-enforcement civil action under the Administrative Procedure Act (APA) to challenge the issuance of an EPA compliance order directing restoration of alleged wetlands that have been filled. *Sackett v. EPA* (2012) 132 S. Ct. 1367.

The Sacketts were individual property owners who filled alleged wetlands in order to construct one house on a small lot. The EPA alleged an illegal wetlands fill, and ordered the Sacketts to either restore the site (at what would be considerable expense); if they did not, they would face large ($75,000/day) CWA fines for noncompliance. The Sacketts disputed that the property contained jurisdictional wetlands, asked EPA for a hearing, were denied, brought an action in district court alleging they were denied Fifth Amendment due process, and were denied relief by both the district court and the Ninth Circuit, before their claim was heard by the Supreme Court.

The majority opinion was narrow in scope, and limited to statutory interpretation. The court first decided that EPA's administrative compliance order constituted "final agency action" subject to judicial review under the APA. The court then ruled that the CWA does not preclude such pre-enforcement review under the APA. The court was not asked to and did not rule on the broader due process claims brought in the lower courts; a decision that the Sacketts were denied constitutional due process would have had broader ramifications for the enforcement programs of many other federal environmental laws.

Importantly, the Court decided only the issue of whether landowners receiving an EPA administrative compliance order can judicially challenge EPA's authority to regulate their land under the CWA. The decision did not address whether, at this pre-enforcement stage, landowners can also judicially challenge the terms of such a compliance order.

Foundation operates an in-lieu fee program for projects in the USACE Sacramento District.

The lowest priority for mitigation is "permittee-responsible" mitigation directly carried out by permittees, either on-site or off-site. If mitigation ratios are used, they should be at least 1:1 (in acreage or linear feet), with higher ratios when necessary, e.g., to reflect mitigation success uncertainty.

ENFORCEMENT

CLEAN WATER ACT ENFORCEMENT

EPA and USACE share authority for enforcing Section 404. Also, under Section 505 of the CWA (33 U.S.C. § 1365), citizen suits can be filed against alleged violators of Section 404, or against USACE or EPA for failing to perform nondiscretionary duties under the CWA.

EPA and USACE enforcement responsibilities are defined in a 1989 MOA (USACE and EPA 1989). In most cases, USACE conducts initial investigations and uses its enforcement authority. Enforcement techniques include administrative orders and referrals for judicial enforcement.

Administrative orders may require compliance with Section 404 permit conditions, or take the form of cease-and-desist orders for unauthorized discharges. Compliance orders are final agency actions that may be challenged in court. *Sackett v. Environmental Protection Agency* 132 S. Ct. 1367. *See* sidebar.

USACE and EPA have the authority to assess administrative penalties for violations of Section 404 permit conditions and for unpermitted discharges of dredged or fill material, respectively. Maximum fines range from $37,500 to $187,000. 33 C.F.R. § 326.6; 40 C.F.R. § 19.

For judicial enforcement, referrals are made to the Justice Department, which files the lawsuits. USACE and EPA may recommend criminal or civil actions to obtain penalties for violations, compliance with administrative orders, and other relief. Negligent violations can result in misdemeanor penalties of $2,500 to $25,000 per day, and imprisonment for up to one year. Knowing violations can result in felony penalties of $5,000 to $50,000 per day, and imprisonment for up to three years. 33 U.S.C. § 1319(c)(1), (2).

REGULATORY TAKINGS

Permit denials may be subject to takings claims under the Fifth Amendment to the U.S. Constitution, which prohibits the taking of private property without just compensation (*see* chapter 3). An applicant whose permit is denied and who has a takings claim of $10,000 or more must file suit in the U.S. Court of Federal Claims to determine whether a regulatory taking has occurred and just compensation should be awarded. 28 U.S.C. § 1295(a)(3).

STATE AND REGIONAL PROGRAMS

STATE REGULATORY PROGRAMS

Lake or streambed alteration agreements. Fish & Game Code § 1600 *et seq.* requires any person, state or local government agency, or public utility to notify DFW before beginning any activity that will:

- Substantially obstruct or divert the natural flow of a river, stream, or lake
- Substantially change or use any material from the bed, channel, or bank of a river, stream, or lake (a "bank" is defined by the outer edge of riparian vegetation)
- Deposit or dispose of debris, waste, or other material containing crumbled, flaked, or ground pavement where it may pass into a river, stream, or lake

DFW regulation of lakes and streambeds applies to all perennial, intermittent, and ephemeral rivers and streams in the state, often to the outer edge of the floodplain, a larger area than is subject to Section 404 jurisdiction. Also, the regulatory program covers substantial diversions of water from a stream, even if the streambed itself is not altered or damaged. *Siskiyou County Farm Bureau v. Department of Fish and Wildlife* (2015) 237 Cal. App. 4th 411.

DFW has not promulgated regulations to implement Fish & Game Code § 1600 *et seq.*, so all program requirements are found in statute or on the program website (www.wildlife.ca.gov/conservation/LSA). After receiving a complete notification package, DFW will determine whether a Lake or Streambed Alteration Agreement ("agreement") is needed for the activity. An agreement will be required if the activity could substantially adversely affect an existing fish and wildlife resource. If an agreement is required, DFW will conduct an on-site inspection if necessary, and within 60 days submit a draft agreement to the applicant. If DFW fails to submit the draft agreement within 60 days of receiving a complete application, the agreement is automatically approved. DFW has the authority to impose appropriate mitigation measures for fish and wildlife impacts, including off-site mitigation measures, as conditions to the agreement. The applicant then negotiates a final agreement, using an arbitration panel if necessary. Fish & Game Code § 1603.

A DFW streambed alteration agreement is needed to alter the bed of banks or rivers.

CEQA = California Environmental Quality Act

DFW signs the final agreement when it receives the appropriate notification fee and after it complies with the California Environmental Quality Act (CEQA). Usually, DFW is a CEQA responsible agency for lake or streambed alternation agreements, with a state or local government agency serving as lead agency.

There are three types of agreements:

- **Standard Agreement:** For activities expected to take place within a five-year time frame.
- **Standard Long-Term:** For activities expected to continue past a five-year time frame.
- **Master Agreement:** An agreement for a duration longer than five years' duration that is similar to a programmatic agreement. This agreement covers a large, multi-phased project consisting of smaller specific projects for which detailed project plans are not prepared at the time of application for the agreement.

DFW may suspend or revoke the agreement at any time if it finds the applicant is in noncompliance. Violations of Section 1600 *et seq.* may be corrected through administrative order, and are subject to civil penalties of up to $25,000 per violation. Fish & Game Code §§ 1612, 1615. For certain limited types of emergency work, no agreement is required, but DFW notification is required 14 days before beginning work. Fish & Game Code § 1610.

Section 401 certification. CWA § 401 requires applicants for Section 404 permits in California to obtain certification from the SWRCB or RWQCB that the discharge will not violate state water quality standards. 40 C.F.R. § 230.10(b)(1). Generally, the RWQCB issues Section 401 certifications, but RWQCB decisions may be appealed to the SWRCB, which has ultimate authority over Section 401 certifications. The SWRCB must certify hydropower projects requiring a Federal Energy Regulatory Commission permit, and projects that must secure a state water right permit.

The RWQCB or SWRCB may deny certification, issue certification without conditions, or issue certification with conditions to ensure compliance with water quality standards.

The RWQCB or SWRCB may deny certification, issue certification without conditions, or issue certification with conditions to ensure compliance with water quality standards. 23 Cal. Code Regs. § 3855 *et seq.* Section 401 certifications are discretionary projects under CEQA, and the RWQCB or SWRCB typically serves as a CEQA responsible agency.

For activities undertaken pursuant to an NWP, the SWRCB has pre-certified several NWPs if those activities comply with conditions in the certification; in some cases, pre-discharge notification to the RWQCB or SWRCB is still required. The SWRCB has denied certification to several NWPs, preventing the use of these NWPs in California. For NWPs that are neither pre-certified nor denied certification, project-specific 401 certifications are required.

Coastal Zone Management Act certification. To issue a Section 404 permit, the applicant must certify that the proposed activity complies with the state's Coastal

Zone Management Program, and the Coastal Commission must concur with the certification or waive its right to do so. 33 C.F.R. § 325.2(b)(2).

State regulation of waters of the state. RWQCBs may regulate wetlands under WDRs issued pursuant to the Porter-Cologne Act (*see* chapter 10), if dredging, filling, or excavation activities affect the quality of waters of the state, which include wetlands. The SWRCB and RWQCBs have taken particular interest in prioritizing WDRs for activities affecting isolated waters no longer subject to federal regulation after the *SWANCC* decision.

SWRCB has adopted general WDRs for certain discharges to non-federal waters. Activities authorized are limited to discharges not greater than one-fifth of an acre and 400 linear feet (for fill and excavation) or 50 cubic yards (for dredging). Applicants must submit a notice of intention, a mitigation plan to avoid and minimize impacts, and a compensation plan for unavoidable permanent impacts to wetlands and headwater streams.

In 2016, the SWRCB issued proposed Procedures for Discharges of Dredged or Fill Material to Waters of the State. The proposed Procedures consist of three elements: 1) a statewide wetland area definition; 2) wetland delineation procedures; and 3) regulatory processes. The SWRCB developed these procedures to strengthen protection of waters of the state that are no longer protected under Section 404 due to U.S. Supreme Court decisions, and to establish uniformity among RWQCBs in wetlands permitting procedures. Readers should monitor the future implementation status of these procedures (www.waterboards.ca.gov/water_issues/programs/cwa401/wrapp.shtml).

Conservation/mitigation banks. The Natural Resources Agency and DFW distinguish between conservation banks (for mitigated impacts to endangered species) and mitigation banks (for impacts to wetlands), and have developed similar policies for both. Conservation/mitigation banks are a viable alternative to requiring piecemeal mitigation for individual project impacts, and provide incentives to private landowners to practice conservation. Additionally, landowners using conservation/mitigation banks can take advantage of economies of scale otherwise unavailable for individual mitigation projects.

Conservation/mitigation banks are a viable alternative to requiring piecemeal mitigation for individual project impacts, and provide incentives to private landowners to practice conservation.

In 1995, Cal/EPA and the Natural Resources Agency published the state's official policy on conservation banks, which provided formal policy guidance on appropriate locations, mechanisms for permanent protection of the habitat, and basic elements needed for DFW to approve a conservation/mitigation bank. In 2012, SB 1148 (Chapter 565, Statutes of 2012) established a new process for DFW review and approval of mitigation and conservation bank applications and new fees for program services, administration, and oversight by DFW. The legislation recognized that mitigation and conservation banking is an important conservation mechanism in California because banks provide regulatory efficiencies, environmental benefits, and economic advantages.

BCDC = San Francisco Bay Conservation and Development Commission

The legislation also acknowledged a desire for greater transparency to ensure mitigation requirements are fully met when employing banks, and that the monitoring of banks to ensure long-term conservation of species and habitats is needed. SB 1148 also imposed new fees to cover the administrative and regulatory costs incurred by DFW in providing banking program services, administration and oversight. In 2014, DFW issued detailed conservation and mitigation banking guidelines to implement the relevant portions of SB 1148 (Fish & Game Code § 1797 *et seq.*).

STATE PROGRAMS FOR PROTECTING THE COASTAL ZONE AND SUISUN MARSH WETLANDS

Under the Coastal Act, wetlands are defined as "lands within the coastal zone which may be covered periodically or permanently with shallow water and include saltwater marshes, fresh water marshes, open or closed brackish water marshes, swamps, mudflats, and fens."

Coastal Act. Under the Coastal Act (*see* chapter 4), wetlands are defined as "lands within the coastal zone which may be covered periodically or permanently with shallow water and include saltwater marshes, fresh water marshes, open or closed brackish water marshes, swamps, mudflats, and fens." Pub. Res. Code § 30121. This definition includes isolated wetlands not regulated under Section 404.

Local coastal programs and coastal development permits must comply with wetlands policies of the Coastal Act, and with the Coastal Commission's interpretive guidelines for wetlands. In general, these policies allow wetlands to be filled only for water-dependent activities when no feasible upland alternatives exist. They also require wetland impacts to be avoided or minimized. The Coastal Commission has also issued more detailed guidance on evaluation of wetlands mitigation proposals. California Coastal Commission 1995.

Suisun Marsh. Suisun Marsh is a unique and valuable wetlands area subject to special state and regional regulation. The Suisun Marsh comprises approximately 85,000 acres of tidal marsh, managed wetlands, and waterways in southern Solano County. Suisan Marsh is the largest remaining wetland near San Francisco Bay, and includes more than 10 percent of California's remaining wetland area. The Marsh is also a wildlife habitat of nationwide importance.

The Legislature directed the San Francisco Bay Conservation and Development Commission (BCDC) and the DFW to prepare a Suisun Marsh Protection Plan "to preserve the integrity and assure continued wildlife use" of the Suisun Marsh. The Suisun Marsh Preservation Act (Pub. Res. Code § 2900 *et seq.*) was enacted in 1977 to incorporate the findings and policies contained in the plan into state law. The Act creates a primary management area that includes all wetlands in the marsh, and a secondary management area (or buffer zone) that includes most of the adjacent agricultural upland areas surrounding the marsh. The Act requires local governments to develop protection plans for both the wetland and upland areas to further ensure the integrity of the marsh.

for more information...

Barclay, C. T. and M. S. Gray, 2016. California Land Use and Planning Law. 35th Edition. Solano Press. Point Arena, Calif.

California Coastal Commission, 1994. Procedural Guidance for the Review of Wetland Projects in California's Coastal Zone.

California Coastal Commission, 1995. Procedural Guidance for Evaluating Wetland Mitigation Projects in California's Coastal Zone.

California Department of Fish & Wildlife, 2014. Conservation and Mitigation Banking Guidelines.

Manaster, K. A. and D. P. Selmi (eds.), ND. California Environmental Law and Land Use Practice, Chapter 69. Matthew Bender. San Francisco, Calif.

U.S. Army Corps of Engineers, 1987. Corps of Engineers Wetlands Delineation Manual. Technical Report Y-87-1.

U.S. Army Corps of Engineers, 2008a. Regional Supplement to the Corps of Engineers Wetland Delineation Manual: Arid West Region. Version 2.0.

U.S. Army Corps of Engineers, 2008b. Regulatory Guidance Letter No. 08-02.

U.S. Army Corps of Engineers and Environmental Protection Agency, 1989, as amended in 1993. MOA Between the Department of The Army and The Environmental Protection Agency Concerning Determination of the Geographic Jurisdiction of the Section 404 Program and the Application of Exemptions Under Section 404(f) of the CWA.

U.S. Army Corps of Engineers and Environmental Protection Agency, 1990. MOA Between The Department of the Army and The Environmental Protection Agency Concerning the Determination of Mitigation Under the Clean Water Act Section 404(b)(1) Guidelines.

U.S. Army Corps of Engineers and Environmental Protection Agency, 2007a. Clean Water Act Jurisdiction Following the U.S. Supreme Court's Decision in *Rapanos v. United States* and *Carabell v. United States.*

U.S. Army Corps of Engineers and Environmental Protection Agency, 2007b. Memorandum: Coordination on Jurisdictional Determinations under Clean Water Act Section 404 in Light of the *SWANCC* and *Rapanos* Supreme Court Decisions.

glossary

Adjacent wetlands—wetlands that are bordering, contiguous, or neighboring to other waters of the United States.

Compensatory mitigation—mitigation to offset wetlands impacts that cannot be offset through avoidance or minimization.

Delineation—the identification and mapping of wetlands and other waters of the United States.

Dredged material—material removed from waters of the United States.

Fill material—any material used for the primary purpose of replacing an aquatic area with dry land or changing the bottom elevation of a water body.

General permit*—a Section 404 permit for a class of activities precluding the need for a project-specific Section 404 permit.

Headwaters—the point on a nontidal stream above which the average annual flow is less than 5 cubic feet per second (cfs).

Hydrophytic vegetation—plants that can grow in wetland conditions.

Individual permit*—a project-specific Section 404 permit.

Isolated waters—nontidal waters not part of a surface tributary system to interstate or navigable waters of the United States, and not adjacent to such tributaries.

Jurisdictional determination—the final USACE decision on its jurisdiction over a site under Section 404.

Lake or Streambed Alteration Agreement*—an agreement negotiated between DFW and an applicant for activities involving alteration of a lake or stream zone.

Letter of permission*—a Section 404 permit issued through an abbreviated process that includes agency coordination and public interest review, but not public notice.

Mean high water—the average position of the high water mark.

Mitigation banking—use of a site via a credit system for enhancement, restoration, or creation of wetlands, for mitigation of impacts on wetlands at other sites.

Mudflats—periodically inundated and exposed unvegetated areas such as tidal coastal areas and the edges of inland lakes, ponds, and rivers.

Nationwide permit*—a type of general permit that applies nationally.

Navigable waters—waters that are, could be, or were used to transport interstate or foreign commerce.

Ordinary high water mark—the line on the shore established by fluctuations of water and indicated by physical characteristics such as a clear natural line impressed in the bank.

Pre-construction notification—notification made to USACE of an intent to perform fill activities authorized by a nationwide permit.

Programmatic general permit*—permit issued by a USACE district or division where another agency's program provides equivalent protection to the Section 404 program.

Public interest review—USACE evaluation of whether a Section 404 permit is in the public interest, using specific criteria.

Regional general permit*—a Section 404 permit issued by a USACE district or division authorizing a class of activities within a geographic region that has minimal environmental impacts.

Riffle and pool complexes—high quality fish and wildlife habitat where a rapid current flowing over a coarse substrate results in turbulence (riffles) and a slower moving current in deeper areas results in smooth flow (pools).

Section 10 permit*—USACE permit issued pursuant to the Rivers and Harbors Act for activities that involve obstruction of, excavation in, or filling of navigable waters.

Section 401 certification*—RWQCB or SWRCB certification that a Section 404 permit is consistent with state water quality standards.

Section 404 permit*—a USACE permit issued pursuant to the Clean Water Act for the discharge of dredged or fill materials into waters the U.S.

Section 404(b)(1) alternatives analysis—an analysis prepared consistent with the Section 404(b)(1) Guidelines to determine whether a practicable alternative to a proposed discharge exists that has less adverse effect on the aquatic ecosystem.

Special aquatic sites—specific types of waters of the United States for which mitigation requirements are more stringent under Section 404(b)(1) Guidelines.

Standard permit*—in the context of wetlands regulation, a project-specific permit (either a general permit or letter of permission) issued after the formal Section 404 permit review process.

Vegetated shallows—periodically inundated sites with rooted, submerged vegetation.

Waste discharge requirements*—permit issued by a RWQCB for discharge of waste into waters of the state.

Waters of the United States—all waters used or susceptible to use in interstate or foreign commerce.

Wetlands—under the Section 404 program definition, those areas that are inundated or saturated by surface or groundwater at a frequency and duration sufficient to support, and that under normal circumstances do support, a prevalence of vegetation typically adapted for life in saturated soil conditions.

* equals permits and approvals

CHAPTER 16

Forestry

in this chapter...

related Solano Press title

Guide to the California Forest Practice Act and Related Laws. Sharon E. Duggan and Tara Mueller. 2005.

U.S.C. = United States Code

FPA = Forest Practice Act

INTRODUCTION

This chapter reviews California law related to forestry regulation. The discussion of forestry regulation focuses on commercial timber harvesting on private forest lands, as opposed to public lands, given the intensity of regulation of timber harvesting on private land.

KEY LAWS AND AGENCIES

FEDERAL LAWS AND AGENCIES

U.S. Forest Service and U.S. Bureau of Land Management. The U.S. Forest Service and U.S. Bureau of Land Management manage extensive forests on federal lands in California. These agencies manage federal forests to achieve multiple use objectives pursuant to the National Forest Management Act (16 U.S.C. § 471(a) *et seq.*), the Multiple-Use Sustained-Yield Act of 1960 (16 U.S.C. § 528 *et seq.*), the Forest and Rangeland Renewable Resources Planning Act of 1974 (16 U.S.C. § 1600 *et seq.*), and regulations implementing these laws. Management of federal forests is coordinated with state and local policies for adjacent lands.

STATE LAWS AND AGENCIES

The Forest Practice Act governs harvesting of non-federal timberland in California.

Z'berg-Njedly Forest Practice Act of 1973 and Forest Practice Rules. The FPA (Pub. Res. Code § 4511 *et seq.*) governs harvesting of non-federal timberland in California. The Act's goals are to restore, enhance, and maintain timberland productivity and to achieve the maximum sustained production of high-quality timber products while giving consideration to other environmental and economic values.

To implement the FPA, the Board of Forestry and Fire Protection has adopted specific forest practice rules (14 Cal. Code Regs. § 906 *et seq.*) for three districts: the Coast Forest District, the Northern Forest District, and the Southern Forest District. Within each district, the Forestry Board has created subdistricts and special treatment areas subject to more specific rules. The Forestry Board also has passed rules for Coastal Commission Special Treatment Areas and for five individual counties: Monterey, Santa Cruz, San Mateo, Santa Clara, and Marin. 14 Cal. Code Regs. §§ 921 *et seq.*, 924 *et seq.*

Forest practice rules cover the following topics (14 Cal. Code Regs. § 895.1):

- Silvicultural systems (planned programs of forest stand treatments during the life of a stand) and regeneration areas
- Harvesting practices and erosion control
- Site preparation
- Watercourse and lake protection
- Hazard reduction
- Insect and disease protection

- Bird and nesting site protection
- Logging roads and landings
- Archeological and historical resource preservation
- Sensitive species classification
- Sensitive watersheds
- Late succession forest stands

TPZ = timberland production zone

CAL FIRE = California Department of Forestry and Fire Protection

SRA = state responsibility area

California Forest Legacy Program Act. This Act (Pub. Res. Code § 12200 *et seq.*) allows owners of private forest lands or woodlands (forest lands composed mostly of hardwood species such as oak) meeting certain criteria to voluntarily protect significant forest resources by selling or donating conservation easements. Easements may be held by federal, state, or local agencies, or by non-profit land trusts.

Timberland Productivity Act. This Act (Gov't Code 51100 *et seq.*) implements a state policy to keep timberlands in production, rather than converted to other uses. Similar to the Williamson Act, the Timberland Productivity Act provides that if land is placed within a timberland production zone (TPZ), property assessments must be based on the value of the land when restricted to timber growing. Uses of land within TPZs are limited to those compatible with timberland production, as defined by local ordinance. TPZ zoning lasts for a rolling 10-year period, and if rezoning is proposed prior to the end of 10 years, increased taxes and a tax recoupment fee must be paid.

The Timberland Productivity Act provides that if land is placed within a timberland production zone, property assessments must be based on the value of the land when restricted to timber growing.

Board of Forestry and Fire Protection. The Forestry Board is responsible for developing forest practice rules and regulations to implement the FPA.

The Forestry Board has the following general powers (Pub. Res. Code § 730(a)):

- Developing an adequate state forest policy
- Representing state interests in federal forestry issues
- Setting policy for the California Department of Forestry and Fire Protection (CAL FIRE)
- Overseeing forest management information and research

The Forestry Board has the following specific powers (Pub. Res. Code §§ 760, 4516 *et seq.*):

- Overseeing CAL FIRE 's fire protection system
- Setting minimum standards for firesafe development in state responsibility areas (SRAs), in which the financial responsibility of preventing and suppressing wildfires is primarily the responsibility of the state
- Licensing of professional foresters
- Setting regulations for forest practices, state forest management, insect and disease control, and forest improvement and vegetation management projects

THP = timber harvest plan

California Department of Forestry and Fire Protection. CAL FIRE oversees enforcement of California's forest practice regulations that guide timber harvesting on private lands. Pub. Res. Code § 4570 *et seq*. CAL FIRE reviews an average of 600 timber harvest plans (THPs) and conducts over 6,500 site inspections each year. CAL FIRE also conducts major firefighting activities statewide, including providing emergency services in SRAs in 36 counties through contracts with local governments. Also, CAL FIRE conducts the Forest and Resource Assessment Program, which periodically assesses the status and trends of the state's forests and rangelands. Lastly, CAL FIRE implements the California Forest Legacy Program by acquiring conservation easements from owners of private forest land to protect forest resources. Pub. Res. Code § 12200 *et seq*.

Counties. The FPA generally prohibits counties from requiring permits for conducting timber harvest operations. Counties, however, may recommend to the Forestry Board additional rules and regulations governing timber operations that address local needs. A county also may request a public hearing on a THP at a location within the county.

TIMBER HARVEST REGULATION

ACTIVITIES REGULATED

The FPA applies to "timber operations" on "timberland." Timber operations include cutting of timber for commercial purposes or for incidental work, such as construction and maintenance of roads, fuel breaks, stream crossings, skid trails, fire hazard abatement, and site preparation. Timberland is defined as non-federal land available for and capable of growing a crop of trees of any commercial species used to produce lumber and other forest products. Exemptions for emergencies and for minor harvesting operations are available, including a one-time conversion of less than three acres of timberland to non-timber use, and harvesting of Christmas trees. Also exempt are the cutting or removal of trees within 150 feet of structures in order to reduce flammable materials and maintain a fuel break, and certain forest thinning activities under the Forest Fire Prevention Pilot Project Exemption. Pub. Res. Code § 4584.

Timber harvest plans must be prepared for timber harvest on non-federal land.

Timber operator licenses from the Forestry Board are required for any person engaging in timber operations. Pub. Res. Code § 4571(a).

RESOURCE CONSERVATION STANDARDS

To ensure an adequate cover of trees is maintained or established after timber operations, the FPA establishes resource conservation standards for minimum stocking, soil erosion control, and stream protection. Pub. Res. Code § 4561 *et seq*. Minimum stocking standards are met if, within five years after timber operations, certain minimum tree counts or densities are met. Soil erosion standards specify permissible levels of soil loss in timber operations. Stream protection standards prevent unreasonable impacts to beneficial uses of waters of the state by regulating activities such as construction of logging roads and stream crossings, and removal of riparian vegetation.

RPF = registered professional forester

DFW = California Department of Fish and Wildlife

RWQCB = regional water quality control board

CEQA = California Environmental Quality Act

PHI = pre-harvest inspection

TIMBER HARVEST PLAN

A THP must be prepared by a registered professional forester (RPF) for any proposed timber harvest on non-federal land. Among other contents, the THP describes the site to be harvested, the silviculture methods to be applied, reforestation methods, road building, and mitigation measures to avoid soil erosion and other environmental damage. Pub. Res. Code § 4582.

Certain minor timber harvesting operations may be exempt from THP requirements. Pub. Res. Code § 4584; 14 Cal. Code Regs. § 1038(a). Also, under certain specified emergency conditions, operations may begin without an approved THP. Pub. Res. Code § 4592; 14 Cal. Code Regs. § 1052 *et seq.*

A timber harvest plan must be prepared by a registered professional forester for any proposed timber harvest on non-federal land.

THP process. Figure 16-1 on the following page illustrates the generalized THP review process. Upon receipt of a THP, the following process is followed (14 Cal. Code Regs. § 1037 *et seq.*):

- Copies are distributed to all state and federal reviewing agencies.
- A notice of intention is sent to the landowners within 300 feet of the THP, to the office of the county clerk within the THP county, and to the local CAL FIRE unit headquarters.
- A first review of the THP is performed by a multi-agency team that includes CAL FIRE, the Department of Fish and Wildlife (DFW), the regional water quality control board (RWQCB), the California Geological Survey, and other agencies as needed. This first review assesses whether the THP is complete. Incomplete applications are returned for revision to the RPF who prepared the THP.
- Once all review team concerns are clarified and the THP is deemed complete, it is officially "filed," and a notice of filing is issued. The public may submit comments to CAL FIRE on a filed THP.

Within 10 days of the notice of filing, the review team may conduct a preharvest inspection (PHI) to examine the proposed logging site. 14 Cal. Code Regs. § 1037.5(g) (2). Almost all plans receive a PHI. Within 20 days of the PHI, the review team meets to discuss the PHI reports and to finalize any changes needed for the THP.

The public comment period ends 30 days after the PHI. The public comment period may be extended to allow time for agencies involved in the THP process to complete their reviews, or for additional study of a specific THP issue. 14 Cal. Code Regs. § 1037.3(c).

FIGURE 16-1
Review Process for Timber Harvest Plan

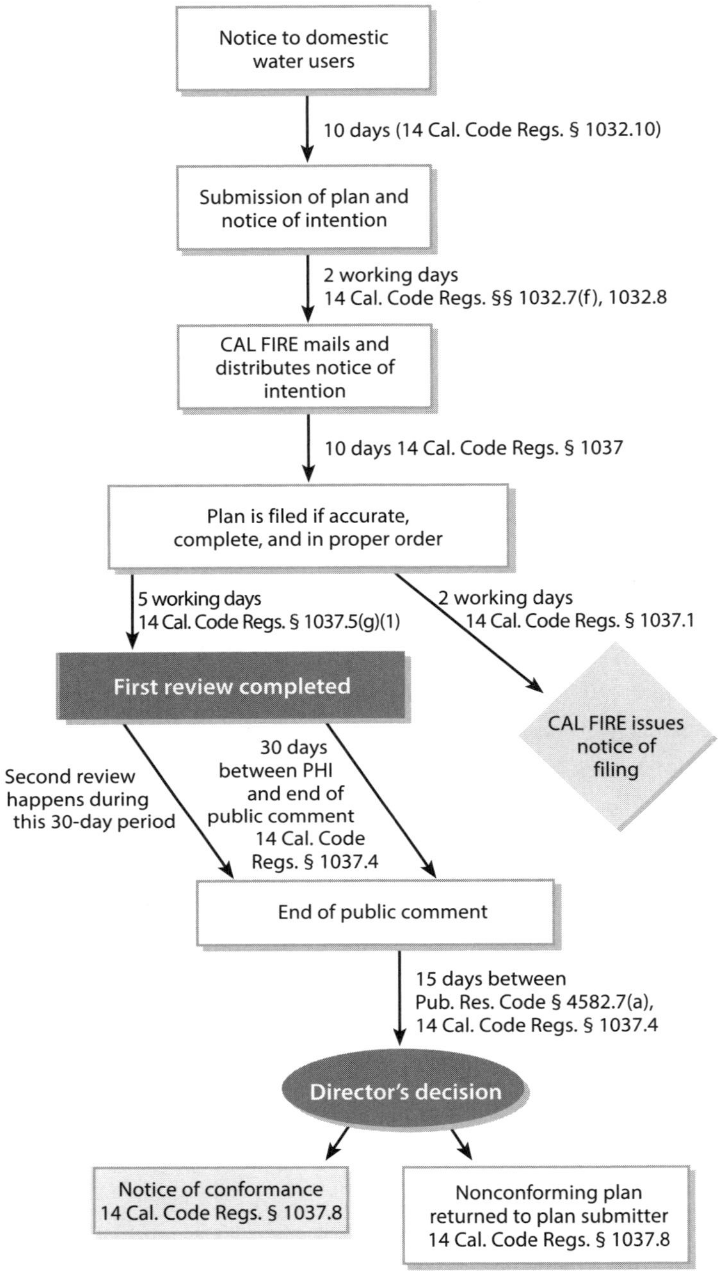

Source: Duggan, S.E. and T. Mueller. 2005. *Guide to the Forest Practice Act and Related Laws*, p. 113. Solano Press. Reprinted with permission.

The review team's final recommendations are sent to the RPF for response. After the RPF's response is received and the public comment period closes, the THP goes to the CAL FIRE director, or the director's representative, who has 15 working days to approve or deny the THP. The director considers all Forestry Board rules, the review team's recommendations, and any public comments that were submitted concerning the proposed timber operation before making a decision to approve or deny the THP. Pub. Res. Code § 4582.7(a).

WDR = waste discharge requirement

If the THP is denied, the applicant may appeal by requesting a public hearing before the Forestry Board. If the THP is approved, the SWRCB (State Water Resources Control Board) and DFW may appeal the approval to the Forestry Board if they participated in an on-site inspection with CAL FIRE and in multidisciplinary reviews of the THP. Pub. Res. Code §§ 4582.7(c), 4582.9.

A THP is effective for a maximum of three years, unless extended by an amendment. Once a THP is approved, CAL FIRE inspectors periodically will inspect the logging operation to ensure compliance with the approved THP and applicable regulations. When a THP operation has been completed, the timber owner has the responsibility for submitting a completion report to CAL FIRE. CAL FIRE then inspects the area to certify that all rules were followed. The landowner must restock the area to meet minimum standards. A stocking report must be filed with CDF to certify that these requirements were met. 14 Cal. Code Regs. § 1037.5; Pub. Res. Code § 4585(a).

Once a THP is approved, CAL FIRE inspectors periodically will inspect the logging operation to ensure compliance with the approved THP and applicable regulations.

Water quality regulation. Timber operations under the FPA are exempt from RWQCB waste discharge requirements (WDRs) if certain conditions are met. However, this exemption currently is not in effect because one condition has not been met: the Environmental Protection Agency and SWRCB must first certify that provisions of the FPA constitute best management practices for silvicultural nonpoint source discharges. Should these agencies in the future make this certification, then the FPA's WDR exemption would become effective unless one of the following occurs (Pub. Res. Code § 4514.3):

- The Forestry Board requests issuance of WDRs
- The SWRCB finds that the Forestry Board's water quality regulatory process does not constitute best management practices
- The SWRCB finds that compliance with best management practices would result in less water quality protection than required by the relevant basin plan

Although the RWQCBs have the authority to issue WDRs for timber operations, some RWQCBs have adopted waivers of the WDR requirement, provided certain conditions protecting water quality are met. Further, water quality is protected by the RWQCB's veto authority over THP approval if the timber operations cause a discharge to a water body that is classified as "impaired" due to sediment, and the discharge will contribute to a violation of the regional water quality control plan. Pub. Res. Code § 4582.71.

Once a THP is approved, the RWQCB still has the authority to impose water quality monitoring requirements if it believes the THP's water quality monitoring program is not adequate. *Pacific Lumber Company v. SWRCB* (2006) 37 Cal. 4th 574. Although the FPA is intended to streamline permitting and regulation of timber

CEQA Litigation on THPs is Extensive

The Forest Practice Act is the most litigated CEQA functional equivalent program. Major cases include those listed below.

Environmental Protection Information Center, Inc. v. Johnson (1985) 170 Cal. App. 3d 604. THP for old-growth redwood logging failed to consider cumulative erosion, aesthetics, and recreational impacts of past logging activities combined with impacts of proposed harvest. Also, CAL FIRE failed to consult with the Native American Heritage Commission on cultural resources impacts, as required by CEQA.

Laupheimer v. State of California (1988) 200 Cal. App. 3d 440. THP for proposed timber harvest operation failed to adequately analyze cumulative impacts.

Sierra Club v. State Board of Forestry (1994) 7 Cal. App. 4th 1215. THP failed to provide information on old-growth dependent wildlife species.

Friends of the Old Trees v. Department of Forestry and Fire Protection (1997) 52 Cal. App. 4th 1383. THP for old-growth redwood logging failed to analyze cumulative impacts on water supply and should have analyzed alternatives, such as preserving some old growth areas on project site or logging other sites.

Schoen v. Department of Forestry and Fire Protection (1997) 58 Cal. App. 4th 556. Cumulative impact analysis in THP that complies with FPA's cumulative impact requirements must also comply with CEQA's cumulative impact requirements.

Ebbetts Pass Forest Watch v. Department of Forestry and Fire Protection (2008) 43 Cal. 4th 936. THP cumulative impact analysis complied with FPA procedures, and THP herbicide impact analysis was adequate.

Environmental Protection Information Center, Inc. v. Department of Forestry and Fire Protection (2008) 44 Cal. 4th 459. A Sustained Yield Plan cumulative impact analysis was required to consider relevant prior activities, and was upheld as adequate.

operations, it has a "savings clause" stating that the FPA does not limit the authority of other resource agencies to administer or enforce their laws.

Modified THP for fuel hazard reduction. A "Modified THP for fuel hazard reduction" may be submitted for a project area to utilize intermediate and special prescriptions to create fire-resilient conditions and reduce fuel. The project area for this plan may not exceed 2,500 acres (subject to several conditions), and an average of at least 40 percent overstory must be retained. 14 Cal. Code Regs. § 1051.3 *et seq.*

California Environmental Quality Act and THPs. The application of CEQA to THP approval was affirmed in *Natural Resources Defense Council, Inc. v. Arcata Nat. Corp.* (1976) 59 Cal. App. 3d 959. In response, the timber harvest planning process and Forestry Board rulemaking process became certified regulatory programs under CEQA. CEQA's policies and substantive requirements apply to these programs, but the programs are exempt from the requirement to prepare CEQA documents such as Environmental Impact Reports (EIRs). *See* chapter 2.

The application of CEQA to the THP process has been the subject of extensive CEQA litigation, much of which has been related to either logging of old-growth redwood forests, cumulative impacts of forestry operations, or effects of forestry operations on endangered species. In fact, the THP process has by far been the most litigated CEQA certified regulatory program. *See* sidebar.

OTHER FORESTRY PROGRAMS

Program Timber Harvest Plan. A PTHP may be prepared for ownerships in which a Program Timber Environmental Impact Report (PTEIR) has been prepared. 14 Cal. Code Regs. § 1092 *et seq.* The PTEIR and PTHP provide an alternative to the functional equivalent process normally associated with THPs. A PTEIR analyzes significant impacts and identifies mitigation measures as required by CEQA for timber operations within one or multiple ownerships. The PTHP must be within the scope of the analysis contained in the PTEIR. The PTHP must be limited to areas with reasonably similar environmental characteristics that constitute a logical harvesting unit.

Legislation enacted in 2014 authorized CAL FIRE to enter into agreements and make grants for the purpose of preparing a PTEIR for projects that demonstrate potential to increase carbon sequestration, decrease atmospheric carbon levels, and reduce the potential for large wildland fires on land owned by smaller nonindustrial landowners. Pub. Res. Code § 4598 *et seq*.

Sustained yield plan. An SYP is a plan to achieve sustainable levels of timber harvest. SYPs supplement the THP process by addressing long-term issues and cumulative effects of timber operations in defined management units. In an SYP, the landowner selects sustainable harvest yields that support the production of high-quality timber products. CAL FIRE evaluates the SYP and approves a defined level of "long-term sustained yield" that must conform to the Forest Practice Rules. Pub. Res. Code § 4513(b); 15 Cal. Code Regs. §§ 913.11, 933.11, 953.11.

"Sustained yield" is defined as the yield of commercial wood that an area of commercial timberland can provide continuously at a given intensity of management consistent with required environmental protection, and which is professionally planned to achieve a balance between growth and removal. "Long-term sustained yield" is defined as the average growth sustainable by an inventory predicted at the end of a 100-year planning period. 14 Cal. Code Regs. §§ 895.1, 1091.14.

SYPs have a maximum duration of 10 years and are subject to a continuous monitoring process. Individual THPs rely on SYP analyses of sustained timber production, watershed impacts, and fish and wildlife issues. Each THP submitted for an area covered by an SYP must demonstrate consistency with the SYP and must include mitigation measures included in the SYP. 14 Cal. Code Regs. §§ 1091.2, 1091.3.

Nonindustrial timber management plan. Nonindustrial tree farmers (owners of timberland less than 2,500 acres not primarily engaged in the manufacture of forest products) may file a nonindustrial timber management plan. This plan has the objectives of a managed, uneven-aged timber stand and sustained yield. Pub. Res. Code § 4593 *et seq*.

Working forest timberlands. The Legislature established another program for nonindustrial forest management in 2013. A "working forest landowner" may prepare a "working forest management plan" for working forest timberlands of less than 15,000 acres. These plans have the objectives of maintaining, restoring, or creating uneven-aged managed timber stands, achieving sustained yield, and promoting forestland stewardship. Pub. Res. Code § 4597 *et seq*.

Timberland conversion. The FPA requires an owner of timberland intending a "conversion" to non-timber uses to apply to the Forestry

Climate Change and Forestry in California

According to the Air Resources Board,* the goals of the California Global Warming Solutions Act (AB 32) have focused renewed attention on California forests and the role they play in the carbon cycle. There is a need to understand how much carbon dioxide California forests are currently producing and sequestering, and how much they could sequester in the future. There is also a need to understand how management practices could increase carbon sequestration and decrease GHG loss without compromising the host of other ecosystem functions forests provide.

The Forest Climate Action Team (FCAT) is an interagency working group dedicated to achieve the carbon sequestration goals of California's forests as set forth in the AB 32 Scoping Plan Update. A Forest Carbon Plan was scheduled for completion in 2016.

Under the AB 32 cap-and-trade program, ARB has adopted GHG compliance offset protocols for U.S. forest projects and for urban forest projects. These offset protocols are controversial and have been challenged in court, unsuccessfully. Challengers unsuccessfully argued that the offset protocols rely on GHG emission reductions that are not "additional" to reductions that would otherwise occur, and therefore do not result in real net GHG emission reductions. *Our Children's Earth Foundation v. California Air Resources Board* (2015) 234 Cal. App. 4th 870.

* www.arb.ca.gov/cc/forestry/forestry.htm

SYP = sustained yield plan

EIR = Environmental Impact Report

PTEIR = Program Timber Environmental Impact Report

PTHP = Program Timber Harvest Plan

Board for a timberland conversion permit. For lands within a TPZ, any immediate rezoning (i.e., rezoning prior to the expiration of the rolling 10-year period for reduced property taxes) is considered a conversion. For TPZ land, the Forestry Board may approve the application if (Pub. Res. Code § 4621(a)):

- The conversion is in the public interest
- The conversion would not have a substantial and unmitigated effect on other timberland
- Soils, slopes, and watershed conditions would be suitable for the proposed new uses

Removal of trees for subdivision development is exempt from this requirement if a local government has approved a tentative subdivision map and issued a subdivision use permit. The exemption must be consistent with FPA purposes and is not applicable to lands designated within a TPZ. Pub. Res. Code § 4628.

Climate change and forestry. California's climate policy recognizes the important role of forests in sequestering carbon. The state has created greenhouse gas emissions offsets for certain types of forest projects. *See* sidebar.

ENFORCEMENT

Enforcement of timber harvesting regulations starts with a CAL FIRE inspection report describing violations observed and corrections needed.

Enforcement of timber harvesting regulations starts with a CAL FIRE inspection report describing violations observed and corrections needed. If corrections are not made, CAL FIRE may take corrective action and charge costs to the responsible person. Failure to make corrections may result in warnings, civil actions, suspension or revocation of timber operator licenses, or misdemeanor prosecutions.

Violation of most FPA procedural rules or regulations generally is punishable as an infraction with a fine of up to $250 per violation; infraction penalties are not applicable if environmental damage is caused or if requirements for THP submission or licensing are violated. Pub. Res. Code § 4601.5(a). Knowing or negligent violations of the FPA can result in a civil penalty of up to $10,000 per violation. Pub. Res. Code § 4601.1(a)(1). Criminal penalties for violations include misdemeanor fines of up to $1,000 or imprisonment for six months. Pub. Res. Code § 4601.

for more information...

Duggan, S. E. and T. Mueller, 2005. Guide to the California Forest Practice Act and Related Laws. Solano Press. Point Arena, Calif.

Manaster, K. A. and D. P. Selmi (eds.), ND. Chapter 80 of California Environmental Law and Land Use Practice. Matthew Bender. San Francisco, Calif.

glossary

Long-term sustained yield—the average growth sustainable by an inventory predicted at the end of a 100-year planning period.

Nonindustrial tree farmer—owner of timberland less than 2,500 acres not primarily engaged in the manufacture of forest products.

Program Timber Environmental Impact Report—an Environmental Impact Report prepared for a Program Timber Harvest Plan.

Program Timber Harvest Plan*—a timber harvest plan prepared for single or multiple ownerships in which CEQA compliance is achieved through a Program Timber Environmental Impact Report.

Rangeland—land used primarily for livestock grazing and occupied by a few tree species usually not harvested for lumber products.

Silvicultural system—a planned program of forest stand treatments during the life of a stand.

Special treatment area—an area designation by the Coastal Commission according to Coastal Act criteria, such as scenic view corridors, wetlands, and significant habitats.

State responsibility area—an area where fire protection is primarily a state responsibility.

Sustained yield—the yield of commercial wood that an area of commercial timberland can provide continuously at a given intensity of management consistent with required environmental protection, and that is professionally planned to achieve a balance between growth and removal.

Sustained yield plan—a plan to achieve sustainable levels of timber harvest; supplements the THP process by addressing long-term issues and cumulative effects of timber operations in defined management units.

Timber harvest plan*—under the FPA, a plan prepared by a registered professional forester (RPF) for any proposed timber harvest on non-federal land. Among other contents, the THP describes the site to be harvested, the silviculture methods to be applied, reforestation methods, road building, and mitigation measures to avoid soil erosion and other environmental damage.

Timber operation—under the FPA, an operation that includes cutting of timber for commercial purposes or for incidental work, such as construction and maintenance of roads, fuel breaks, stream crossings, skid trails, fire hazard abatement, and site preparation.

Timberland—under the FPA, non-federal land available for and capable of growing a crop of trees of any commercial species used to produce lumber and other forest products.

Timberland conversion permit*—a permit issued by the Forestry Board authorizing conversion of timberland to non-timber uses.

Woodlands—forest lands composed mostly of hardwood species such as oak.

* equals permits and approvals

CHAPTER 17

Surface Mining

related Solano Press title

California Surface Mining Law. A Guide to Federal, State and Local Requirements. Derek F. Cole. 2007.

in this chapter...

SMARA = Surface Mining and Reclamation Act

SWRCB = State Water Resources Control Board

SMGB = State Mining and Geology Board

DOC = Department of Conservation

INTRODUCTION

This chapter reviews California law related to surface mining. The discussion of mining focuses on environmental regulation of mining operations under the Surface Mining and Reclamation Act (SMARA). State Water Resources Control Board (SWRCB) regulation of mining wastes is addressed in chapter 10. This chapter and book do not address regulation of oil and gas mining.

In 2013, California ranked eighth among the states in non-fuel mineral production, accounting for approximately 4.2 percent of the United States total. There were approximately 700 active mines in the state, and the total market value of production was $3.3 billion. In terms of value, the top five non-fuel minerals produced in 2013 were construction sand and gravel, portland cement, boron minerals, crushed stone, and gold. (Clinkenbeard 2013.)

KEY LAWS AND AGENCIES

KEY LAWS

SMARA recognizes the importance of mineral extraction to the California economy and that reclamation of mined lands is needed to protect the environment, and public health and safety.

Surface Mining and Reclamation Act. SMARA (Pub. Res. Code § 2710) recognizes the importance of mineral extraction to the California economy and that reclamation of mined lands is needed to protect the environment, and public health and safety. Administered by the State Mining and Geology Board (SMGB), the Act's goals are to:

- Prevent or minimize environmental effects
- Ensure that mined lands are reclaimed to a useable condition adaptable for various uses
- Encourage the production and conservation of minerals, while considering environmental values
- Eliminate residual hazards to public health and safety

SMARA has two main regulatory programs: mineral conservation and surface mine reclamation. It also requires every operator to obtain a city or county permit, typically a conditional use permit, before conducting surface mining operations. Regulations implementing the Act are found at 14 Cal. Code Regs. § 3500 *et seq.*

KEY AGENCIES

State Mining and Geology Board. The SMGB serves as a regulatory, policy, and appeals body representing the state's interests in geology, geologic and seismologic hazards, and conservation of mineral resources and reclamation of lands following surface mining activities. SMARA requires the SMGB to set state policy for reclaiming mined lands. The Board operates within the Department of Conservation (DOC).

Office of Mine Reclamation. This office, also within DOC, is responsible for administering SMARA implementation. It also includes an Abandoned Mines Land Unit to address research and policy on abandoned mines issues.

California Geological Survey. The CGS provides staff to the state geologist and is also within DOC. It provides the public with information and advice to protect life and property from natural hazards, and to promote a better understanding of the state's geologic environment. CGS is responsible for classifying the state's mineral resources and inventorying the state's non-fuel mineral resources.

Lead agencies. Under SMARA, cities and counties are designated as lead agencies, and given the responsibility for administering and enforcing SMARA.

CGS = California Geological Survey

ND = Negative Declaration

MRMP = mineral resource management policy

MINERAL CONSERVATION

Although SMARA is mostly known for its regulation of surface mine regulation, it also plays an important role in preventing mineral resources from being lost through incompatible urban development. The Act requires the DOC, using input from CGS, to classify those areas of the state that contain "significant mineral deposits" that are subject to urban expansion or other irreversible land uses that would preclude mineral extraction. The SMGB may designate certain of these areas as either significant regional or statewide resources, for which SMARA provides additional protection. Pub. Res. Code §§ 2761(a), (b) (2), 2790.

Although SMARA is mostly known for its regulation of surface mine regulation, it also plays an important role in preventing mineral resources from being lost through incompatible urban development.

CLASSIFICATION AND DESIGNATION OF SIGNIFICANT MINERAL DEPOSITS

Classification and designation process. CGS classifies mineral deposits as "significant" using marketability and economic criteria. The SMGB may further designate mineral deposits as areas of regional significance (of prime importance in meeting future regional minerals needs) or statewide significance (of prime importance in meeting future state minerals needs). These designations must be preceded by a public hearing and must be made by regulation. Pub. Res. Code §§ 2726, 2727, 2790. The SMGB has published guidelines explaining how it designates and classifies mineral lands, and prepares mineral classification reports. (SMGB 1999).

Mineral resource management policies. Cities and counties must adopt MRMPs when they receive the SMGB mineral classification report or when the SMGB designates land within their boundaries as an area of regional or statewide significance. Local agencies must include these policies in their general plans and submit then to SMGB for review. SMGB has developed an MRMP review checklist that lead agencies can use as a resource in developing or updating their MRMPs (*see* www.conservation.ca.gov/smgb/Guidelines/Pages/guidelines.aspx). The MMRPs must recognize mineral classifications, assist in managing land uses affecting areas of regional or statewide significance, and emphasize the conservation and development of mineral deposits identified by

CEQA = California Environmental Quality Act

the classification process. Pub. Res. Code § 2762(a). To protect classified or designated areas, cities and counties must implement at least one of the following measures (14 Cal. Code Regs. § 3676(c)(3)):

- Place these areas into special or overlay zoning districts
- Record presence of identified mineral deposits on property titles
- Adopt general plan policies mitigating land use incompatibilities between mining and development

Project-level requirements. SMARA also imposes project-level requirements when cities and counties review an individual project that "threatens the potential to extract minerals" from classified or designated areas. Typically, these projects include projects proposed on mineral lands, as well as projects adjacent to these lands. A city or county proposing to approve such a project must prepare a statement of reasons, include the statement in California Environmental Quality Act (CEQA) documents, and submit the statement to the State Geologist and SMGB. Pub. Res. Code §§ 2762, 2763.

SMARA places further requirements on cities and counties for a project "involving" lands designated as significant mineral resources. These projects include mining projects as well as development projects. SMARA requires that a decision to approve such a project must be consistent with the city or county mineral resource management policies, and must balance mineral values against alternative land uses. Pub. Res. Code § 2763. Also, for lands designated as significant mineral resources, SMGB may hear appeals of city or county decisions approving or denying mining permits. Pub. Res. Code § 2775.

Large gravel mines eventually require reclamation under SMARA.

SURFACE MINE RECLAMATION

SMARA APPLICABILITY

Surface mining operations. SMARA generally applies to all surface mining operations. "Surface mining operations" involve the mining of minerals on mined lands by any of these methods (Pub. Res. Code § 2735):

- Mining of minerals on mined lands by removing overburden and mining directly from the mineral deposits
- Open-pit mining of naturally exposed minerals
- Auger mining, dredging, and quarrying
- Surface work incident to an underground mine

Surface mining operations include exploratory activities, and production and disposal of mining waste. Pub. Res. Code § 2735.

Open-pit mining is the most common surface mining method. It is used for sand and gravel operations and rock quarries. Excavations are usually opened by the removal of overburden (noneconomic material), followed by excavation in step-like layers (termed benching).

Mined lands. Mined lands subject to SMARA's reclamation requirements are defined broadly as "the surface, subsurface, and ground water of an area in which surface mining operations will be, are being, or have been conducted." Reclamation requirements may also extend to "affected lands" surrounding mined lands. Pub. Res. Code §§ 2729, 2733.

Operators. A mining project operator is a person or entity that directly conducts surface mining operations, or who contracts with others to conduct mining on their behalf. Once a reclamation plan is approved, it is binding on successor operators. Pub. Res. Code §§ 2731, 2779.

Exemptions. Activities exempt from SMARA's reclamation requirements include the following (Pub. Res. Code § 2714):

- Excavation and earth-moving activities that are an integral and necessary part of a construction project
- Extraction of less than 1000 cubic yards of material
- Operations that exclusively process mined material
- Earthmoving activities in oil and gas fields necessary for ongoing oil or gas extraction

STATE POLICY AND PERMIT PROCEDURES

SMARA was enacted to prevent the historic practice of mining operators abandoning mines and leaving them in a dangerous and unsightly condition. SMARA requires mining operators to restore mines to a productive land use following mining in a process called reclamation.

SMARA requires SMGB to set state policy for mining operations that includes measures to be used by lead agencies in specifying grading, backfilling, resoiling, revegetation, soil compaction, and other reclamation requirements, as well as for soil erosion control, water quality and watershed control, waste disposal, and flood control. Pub. Res. Code § 2756.

The SMGB has established procedures for review and approval of reclamation plans by lead agencies (local agencies responsible for reviewing and approving surface mining operations and reclamation plans). The SMGB has developed a model SMARA ordinance that was updated in June 2015 (State Mining and Geology Board 2015) for use by lead agencies. *See* sidebar. While this model contains each of the elements required to be included in a SMARA ordinance, as well as some additional elements common to ordinances in use statewide, SMARA recommends that it be appropriately modified to reflect local conditions and practices. The use of the model by a lead agency is discretionary, and its form is not mandated by law.

Surface Mining and Reclamation Act Model Ordinance—Sections

1. Purpose and Intent
2. Definitions
3. Incorporation by Reference
4. Scope
5. Vested Rights
6. Process
7. Standards for Reclamation
8. Statement of Responsibility
9. Findings for Approval
10. Financial Assurances
11. Interim Management Plans
12. Annual Report Requirements
13. Inspections
14. Violations and Penalties
15. Appeals
16. Fees
17. Mineral Resource Protection
18. Severability
19. Effective Date

Source: State Mining and Geology Board. 2015. Model SMARA Ordinance

Reclamation Plan Contents

- Name and address of surface mining operation
- Anticipated quantity and types of mineral to be mined
- Initiation and termination dates for the mining operation
- Maximum anticipated depth of the operation
- Detailed geologic, geographic, topographic, and property information
- Timing of mining phases
- Proposed or potential end uses
- Description of how reclamation will be accomplished
- Effect of reclamation plan on future mining in area
- Applicant acceptance of responsibility for reclamation
- Environmental setting of site
- Impacts of reclamation alternatives on uses of surrounding land uses
- Public health and safety concerns
- Slope and stability information
- Backfilling, grading, and settlement information
- Disposition of old equipment
- Temporary stream or watershed diversions

Source: Pub. Res. Code § 2772 and 14 Cal. Code Regs. § 3502(b)

Lead agencies must adopt ordinances for land use permitting and reclamation procedures to provide the regulatory framework for conducting local mining and reclamation activities. The SMGB reviews lead agency ordinances to determine whether each ordinance is in accordance with state policy. The SMGB certifies the ordinance as being in accordance with state policy if it adequately meets, or imposes requirements more stringent than, the California surface mining and reclamation policies and procedures established by the SMGB. If SMGB determines that a lead agency is not in compliance with SMARA, it has the authority to exercise any powers of that lead agency with respect to surface mining and reclamation, except for permitting. Pub. Res. Code § 2774.3.

RECLAMATION PLANS AND FINANCIAL ASSURANCES

Reclamation plan content. Before surface mining operations are conducted, the lead agency must grant a permit, approve a reclamation plan, and approve financial assurances for the reclamation. Pub. Res. Code §§ 2770, 2774. The purposes of a reclamation plan are to restore the mined lands to a useable condition amenable to alternative land uses, minimize adverse impacts on the environment, and protect public health and safety. Pub. Res. Code §§ 2711(a), 2712(a).

The reclamation plan must be applicable to a specific property and must be based on the character of the surrounding area and property, including overburden type, soil stability, topography, geology, climate, streams, and mineral commodities; specific content requirements are found at Pub. Res. Code § 2772 and 14 Cal. Code Regs. § 3502(b). *See* sidebar. The final step in this process is often topsoil replacement and revegetation with suitable plant species.

The reclamation plan must establish site-specific criteria for evaluating plan compliance, usually based on performance standards adopted by SMGB. Pub. Res. Code § 2773. A lead agency may allow an exception to SMGB performance standards if necessary based on the approved end use, and only if the alternative standard is not less stringent than the SMGB standard. 14 Cal. Code Regs. § 3700(b).

Reclamation plan process. Each lead agency must adopt a surface mining ordinance that establishes the process for reclamation plan approval. The hearing and approval process for reclamation plans is integrated into the lead agency's general processes for land use entitlements and CEQA compliance. The lead agency must approve amendments to the reclamation plan if activities substantially deviate from the approved plan. 14 Cal. Code Regs. § 3502(d). Special reclamation plan approval process requirements apply to surface mining within the boundaries of the San Gabriel Basin Water Authority and to metallic mineral mining within one mile of certain Native American sacred sites. Pub. Res. Code §§ 2772.5, 2772.6.

Before approving a reclamation plan, the lead agency must submit the reclamation plan and financial assurances to the director of DOC. The director may prepare written comments, and the lead agency must prepare a written response describing the disposition of significant issues raised. Pub. Res. Code § 2774(d). Also, operators may appeal actions or inactions of the lead agency under SMARA to SMGB. Pub. Res. Code § 2770(e).

Financial assurances. Surface mining operators must provide financial assurances that reclamation will be performed consistent with the reclamation plan. The SMGB has established guidelines for establishing these financial assurances. SMGB 2004.

The amount of the financial assurance must be sufficient to complete reclamation under the proposed reclamation plan, as well as agency administrative costs for overseeing reclamation. Assurance may include bonds, irrevocable letters of credit, or trust funds, and must stay in effect until reclamation is complete. Pub. Res. Code §§ 2770(d), 2773.1(a).

The financial assurance must be payable to both the lead agency and DOC. It must remain in effect for the duration of the mining operation and until reclamation is completed. Pub. Res. Code § 2773.1(a).

ENFORCEMENT

Operators must file annual reports on the status of mining and reclamation activities. The lead agency must inspect a surface mining operation within six months of receiving the surface mining operator's report, to determine whether the operation complies with SMARA. Thereafter, the lead agency must conduct annual inspections. Pub. Res. Code §§ 2207, 2774(b).

Operators must file annual reports on the status of mining and reclamation activities.

SMARA establishes a comprehensive administrative framework for determining whether a SMARA violation has occurred and for imposing fines. Pub. Res. Code § 2774. Remedies for a SMARA violation include a compliance order or a cease-and-desist order, with administrative penalties of up to $5,000 per day if an order is violated. Pub. Res. Code § 2774.1. Also, the director of DOC has standing to file a lawsuit alleging illegal or inadequate reclamation plans and financial assurances for surface mining operations. *People ex rel. Dept. of Conservation v. El Dorado County* (2005) 36 Cal. 4th 971.

Lead agencies are responsible for enforcing SMARA. The SMGB is authorized to hear appeals from local permits to conduct surface mining activities in an area of statewide or regional significance. The SMGB may not invalidate or set aside a challenged permit or reclamation plan. *Friends of Kings River v. County of Fresno* (2014) 232 Cal. App. 4th 105. If it finds the lead agency decision is not supported by substantial evidence, the SMGB must remand the appeal back to the lead agency for reconsideration.

Under certain circumstances, SMGB may take over the lead agency's enforcement powers. For example, SMGB may take over these powers when it finds that the lead agency has approved reclamation plans that do not comply with SMARA, or has failed to take appropriate enforcement actions. Pub. Res. Code § 2774.4(a).

for more information...

Clinkenbeard, J., 2013. California Non-Fuel Mineral Production. California Geological Survey.

Cole, D. F., 2007. California Surface Mining Law. Solano Press. Point Arena, Calif.

Manaster, K. A. and D. P. Selmi (eds.), ND. Chapter 82 of California Environmental Law and Land Use Practice. Matthew Bender. San Francisco, Calif.

State Mining and Geology Board, 1999. Guidelines for Classification and Designation of Mineral Lands.

State Mining and Geology Board, 2004. SMARA Financial Assurance Guidelines.

State Mining and Geology Board, 2015. Model SMARA Ordinance.

glossary

Auger mining—removal of minerals from the walls of mined-out strips using special machines.

Mined land—the surface, subsurface, and groundwater of an area where a surface mining operation is conducted.

Open-pit mining—mining of mineral deposits located at or near the earth's surface from surface openings.

Overburden—soil, rock, or other minerals that lie above a natural mineral deposit or in between mineral deposits before or after their removal by surface mining operations.

Reclamation—process of land treatment that minimizes adverse environmental effects of surface mining operations, so that mined lands are reclaimed to a usable condition that is readily adaptable to alternative land uses and creates no danger to public health and safety.

Reclamation plan*—a plan filed by a surface mining operator that, together with financial assurances, must be approved by a lead agency before mining activities commence.

Surface mining operation—mining of minerals on mined lands by removing overburden and mining directly from the mineral deposits; open-pit mining of naturally exposed minerals; auger mining; dredging and quarrying; or surface work incident to an underground mine. Surface mining operations include exploratory activities, and production and disposal of mining waste.

* equals permits and approvals

PART 4

PERMITTING AND ENVIRONMENTAL COMPLIANCE AUDITING GUIDES

CHAPTER 18

Permitting Guide

related Solano Press titles

CEQA Deskbook. Ronald E. Bass, Kenneth M. Bogdan, and Terry Rivasplata. 2012.

Guide to the California Environmental Quality Act. Michael H. Remy et al. 2007.

The NEPA Book. Ronald E. Bass, Albert I. Herson, and Kenneth M. Bogdan. 2000.

in this chapter...

CEQA = California Environmental Quality Act

INTRODUCTION

The preceding chapters provided an overview of California environmental law and reviewed specific regulatory programs for different resources and environmental media. How does a project applicant navigate this regulatory maze successfully? The purpose of this chapter is to describe comprehensive approaches to obtaining multiple environmental permits.

PERMITTING FUNDAMENTALS

WHAT IS A PERMIT?

To obtain a permit, the applicant must demonstrate, through a permit application, compliance with the permitting agency's substantive and procedural requirements.

Environmental permits are required for projects involving new construction or changes to existing facilities. For purposes of this chapter, the term permit is used to mean all environmental approvals, including certifications, licenses, and plan and specification approvals. As the name implies, a permit reflects a privilege to engage in a regulated activity. To obtain a permit, the applicant must demonstrate, through a permit application, compliance with the permitting agency's substantive and procedural requirements.

Some permits are required before project construction commences (such as a building permit, a stormwater construction permit, or an air quality permit to construct). Other permits are required as a condition of operation (such as an air quality permit to operate and a stormwater industrial permit).

Typically, permits last for a limited period of time. Before a permit lapses, the permit owner or operator must renew the permit or obtain a new or renewed permit to continue the regulated activity. Also, permits are sometimes subject to modification before they expire as a result of new information, an operational change, or regulatory requirements.

TYPES OF PERMITS

Discretionary versus ministerial. Permits may be characterized as discretionary or ministerial. A discretionary permit, such as a typical conditional use permit, requires an agency to exercise deliberation and analysis before issuing a permit. A ministerial permit, such as a typical building permit, involves a straightforward decision judging against standardized, objective criteria, and is not subject to California Environmental Quality Act (CEQA) requirements.

Site-specific versus permit by rule. Some permits require submission of a detailed and prescriptive site-specific application. In this instance an individualized permit may be issued governing operations at a particular facility address with specified permit conditions and limitations.

In other situations, a permit application is more generalized. In this situation, the permit applicant submits a Notice of Intent to comply with pre-set permit conditions that are not site-specific. This type of permit is known as a permit by rule.

Agencies issue permits by rule for activities such as stormwater management, discharges to municipal wastewater treatment plants, hazardous waste treatment, and air quality management (including new source performance standards, local prohibitory rules, and hazardous air pollutant emissions).

Cal/EPA = California Environmental Protection Agency

COMPREHENSIVE PERMITTING LAWS

LAWS REVIEWED IN PREVIOUS CHAPTERS

The Legislature has enacted several laws designed to integrate and streamline environmental permitting requirements. Many of these are reviewed in earlier chapters:

- CEQA (*see* chapter 2) is designed to streamline the permitting process by encouraging all permitting agencies to use a single CEQA document for their project approvals.
- The Permit Streamlining Act (*see* chapter 3) requires local and state agencies to follow standardized time limits and procedures for certain types of land use decisions.
- The Warren-Alquist State Energy Resources Conservation and Development Act (*see* chapter 4) establishes a "one-stop" certification process for new or modified thermal power plants with generating capacity of 50 megawatts or more.
- Assembly Bill 2948 of 1986 (Chapter 1504, Statutes of 1986) coordinates the issuance of multiple permits, licenses, land use approvals, and other authorizations in support of an off-site hazardous waste treatment, storage, or disposal facility. (*See* chapter 8.)

PERMIT REFORM ACT

The Environmental Protection Permit Reform Act of 1993 (Permit Reform Act, Pub. Res. Code § 71000 *et seq.*) is an additional law occasionally used to expedite the environmental permitting process where more than one permitting authority is involved. Through consolidated permitting, the program is intended to reduce the number of agencies directly involved in the permitting process and to reduce confusing and redundant layers of agency requirements.

To initiate a request for a consolidated permit, an applicant must first complete a consolidated permit notification that, among other things, describes the activities being permitted at the facility, lists the environmental permits anticipated, and identifies the lead permitting agency for purposes of the Permit Streamlining Act and CEQA. The consolidated permit notification also allows the applicant to identify the agency believed to have the "greatest overall jurisdiction" for the project and to name the agency it wants to be the consolidated permit agency. Pub. Res. Code § 71021.

The consolidated permit notification also allows the applicant to identify the agency believed to have the "greatest overall jurisdiction" for the project and to name the agency it wants to be the consolidated permit agency.

The program requires that the California Environmental Protection Agency (Cal/EPA) designate a consolidated permit agency to coordinate permitting for a project within 30 days of receipt of the notification. First and second preference is given to lead agencies under CEQA and lead agencies pursuant to the Permit Streamlining Act, respectively. Where the first and second priority agencies do not apply, Cal/EPA must use specified criteria to determine the agency with the greatest overall jurisdiction. Pub. Res. Code § 71020(b). Consolidated permit agencies facilitate and coordinate the multimedia permitting effort. Their duties include (Pub. Res. Code § 71022):

- Contacting the applicant and all environmental permit agencies identified by the applicant
- Informing the applicant and participating permit agencies of the time, date, and location of the pre-application meeting to determine the environmental permits required for the project and to review the permit application forms and scheduling
- Providing all information necessary for the applicant to submit appropriate permit applications, including provisions of relevant guidance documents, permit applications, and schedules for technical review
- Coordinating the review of all participating agency permits
- Ensuring that permit decisions made by the participating permit agencies are made in a timely manner
- Assisting in promptly resolving any conflicts
- Compiling all participating agency permits into one consolidated permit

Under the Permit Reform Act, participating agencies retain their respective authority to issue permits. Participating agencies are responsible for technical review of their permit renewals and permit modifications. Pub. Res. Code § 71020(d).

PERMITTING STRATEGIES

The California environmental permitting process can be complex and often frustrating. The following strategies should be used to facilitate the permitting process. Project applicants should consider retaining qualified environmental consultants or attorneys to develop and implement these strategies. This section presents strategies from the perspective of a private project applicant, although most strategies can be used by a public agency applicant as well.

PREPARE PERMIT INVENTORY AND CONDUCT PRELIMINARY SITE EVALUATION

When undertaking a development project that requires one or more environmental permits before construction or operation, it is essential to determine which permits and approvals federal, state, and local agencies will require.

When undertaking a development project that requires one or more environmental permits before construction or operation, it is essential to determine which permits and approvals federal, state, and local agencies will require. This book can serve as a useful starting point for developing a comprehensive permit inventory. In particular, Table 18-2, presented at the end of this chapter, summarizes common environmental permits and approvals. In addition, since most projects require some type of local permit, local governments typically should be contacted first—they often can preliminarily identify other permits required for a proposed project.

PSP = permitting strategy plan

NEPA = National Environmental Policy Act

When developing the permit inventory, the applicant should consider:

- The location of the proposed project, e.g., city, county, and coastal zone boundaries
- Resources affected by the proposed project, e.g., agricultural lands, waters of the United States
- Construction and operation activities associated with the proposed project
- The specific federal, state, regional, and local agencies with potential regulatory authority over the proposed project

The applicant should conduct a preliminary site evaluation and constraints analysis to identify potential permits and possible project redesigns to avoid or streamline permitting requirements. Reconnaissance-level investigations are usually adequate at this step in the permitting process. The investigations should focus on the presence of regulatory triggers such as wetlands and waters of the United States, endangered species, cultural resources, air quality non-attainment status, and hazardous waste and toxic substances.

PREPARE PERMITTING STRATEGY PLAN

The primary goal of a permitting strategy plan (PSP) is to define the regulatory approval processes for a proposed project, develop preliminary compliance approaches, and identify any potential inconsistent permitting requirements or other fatal flaws that could jeopardize permit approval.

The PSP may include descriptions of some or all of the following:

- The proposed project's construction and operation features that could trigger an environmental permit
- Relevant permitting agencies and their jurisdiction and permitting issues
- Possible lead agencies for CEQA and National Environmental Policy Act (NEPA) documents
- Specific permits and approvals required for construction and operation
- Applicable design, operational, and pollution control standards
- Application process for each permit
- Fees and financial obligations (e.g., surety bonds) required for each permit
- Baseline studies (e.g., seismic, soils, air quality monitoring, screening health risk assessment, wetland delineation, endangered species surveys) required by each permit
- Standard plans required before construction or operations begin (e.g., spill prevention control and countermeasure plans, stormwater pollution prevention plans)

Complex projects such as windfarms can benefit from preparation of a permitting strategy plan.

EIR = Environmental Impact Report

USACE = U.S. Army Corps of Engineers

DFW = California Department of Fish and Wildlife

MOU = memoranda of understanding

MOA = memoranda of agreement

EPA = U.S. Environmental Protection Agency

- Common technical studies or permitting steps among multiple agencies, and methods to facilitate consolidated permit processing
- Comprehensive schedules for the permitting process, permitting milestones, pre-application studies, application preparation, agency decision-making, and statutes of limitation
- Prioritization of permitting activities based on their importance or critical path schedule
- Potential permitting hurdles and strategies to address them
- A comprehensive contacts list that identifies individuals on the project applicant team and in permitting agencies responsible for each permitting task, together with their contact information
- An integrated public involvement or community relations plan

USE CEQA AND NEPA DOCUMENTS AS THE UMBRELLA PROCESSES FOR PERMITTING DECISIONS

Many environmental regulatory programs require state or local agencies to prepare CEQA documents, and federal permitting agencies to prepare NEPA documents. CEQA and NEPA both strongly encourage the integration of related federal, state, and local environmental review and consultation requirements into CEQA and NEPA documents. For example, CEQA requires that the Environmental Impact Report (EIR) project description include a list of related environmental reviews and consultations required by federal, state, or local laws, regulations, or policies. CEQA also requires the lead agency, to the fullest extent possible, to integrate CEQA review with these related environmental requirements. 14 Cal. Code Regs. § 15124(d).

Project applicants should strive to achieve the goal of "one project/one document." A CEQA or CEQA/NEPA joint document prepared for a local government land use entitlement often serves as the umbrella document for other permits and approvals needed for a project. When possible, technical studies supporting CEQA and NEPA documents should be prepared to satisfy the needs of multiple permitting agencies. For example, a wetlands technical study for a land development project should satisfy the information requirements not just of the local CEQA lead agency, but also the U.S. Army Corps of Engineers (USACE) Section 404 regulatory program and Department of Fish and Wildlife (DFW) streambed alteration agreement program.

Project applicants should strive to achieve the goal of "one project/one document."

Using CEQA and NEPA documents as "umbrellas" for related environmental review and consultation requirements reduces the potential for multiple duplicative or inconsistent environmental reviews for individual permits. Table 18-1 illustrates a simplified model approach to integrating selected environmental review requirements with CEQA and NEPA. As shown by this table, to reduce the potential for

Table 18-1. Integrating Selected Environmental Review Requirements with CEQA and NEPA

Requirement	Scoping process	Draft document	Final document	Decisionmaking
NEPA	Notice of Intent	Draft EIS	Final EIS	Lead agency decision and Record of Decision
CEQA	Notice of Preparation	Draft EIR	Final EIR	Lead agency decision and Notice of Determination
Endangered Species Act, Section 7	Request species list	Biological assessment	Biological opinion	
Clean Water Act, Section 404 (individual permit)	Define objectives, screen alternatives, submit permit application	Draft Section 404(b)(1) analysis	Final Section 404(b)(1) analysis	USACE issues Section 404 permit (after Section 401 certification or waiver)
National Historic Preservation Act, Section 106	Identify and evaluate historic and archaeological properties	Draft effects assessment	Memorandum of agreement	
Clean Air Act Conformity (non-transportation project)	Determine whether conformity requirement applies	Preliminary analysis (comparison to de minimis levels)	Detailed modeling analysis if necessary	Federal agency issues conformity determination

Source: Bass, R.E. et al. 2012. *CEQA Deskbook*. Solano Press. Reprinted with permission.

inconsistent public and agency comments, schedules should be coordinated for public and agency review of draft environmental and permitting documents.

EIS = Environmental Impact Statement

Integrated environmental review is sometimes guided by interagency programmatic memoranda of understanding or agreement (MOUs or MOAs) that already have been adopted, and also may be guided by project-specific MOUs/MOAs. For example, local agency transportation project applicants may take advantage of a programmatic agreement among Caltrans, the Federal Highway Administration (FHWA)/Federal Transit Administration (FTA), and the Environmental Protection Agency (EPA) (FHWA et al. 2006) integrating the requirements of Section 404 permitting and NEPA for projects funded by the FHWA or FTA. The project applicant should identify any programmatic MOUs/MOAs that may apply to the proposed project, and should assist in the development of project-specific MOUs/MOAs.

Also, several federal agencies have issued the "2015 Red Book," a very useful handbook for "synchronizing" agency environmental reviews for transportation and other infrastructure projects requiring environmental reviews. The Red Book offers practical advice and tools for integrating these reviews.

PREPARE COMPLETE PERMIT APPLICATIONS AND USE PRE-APPLICATION CONSULTATION

The project design and project description should be substantially complete and final before applications are prepared and filed. The applicant should consider building environmental protection or mitigation measures into the project description to increase the chances for exemptions, variances, or other permit streamlining processes. Applications should be prepared with strict adherence to the agency guidelines. Complete and legally adequate applications can minimize delays caused by return of incomplete or deficient applications. Significantly deficient applications or frequent post-application project description design changes could result in significant delays in obtaining permits as well as increased costs associated with permitting.

Pre-application meetings with each relevant regulatory agency are essential, especially because federal, state, and local agencies do not always talk to each other. These meetings will enable the applicant to build relationships with agency staff, identify agency concerns, procedures, and schedules early on, and allow an opportunity to adjust permitting strategies accordingly. During the pre-application process, the applicant can seek permitting agency input on project design and mitigation approaches, and when appropriate can incorporate these agency suggestions into the project description to facilitate the permitting process.

Before the pre-application meeting, the applicant should research the range of possible permitting actions the agency might take, and how the agency has addressed previous similar projects. For example, when seeking an exemption, variance, or other streamlined permit approach, it is helpful for the applicant to identify similar projects the agency has treated the same way.

Multiple permit applications requiring redundant information to be sent to individual agencies can be frustrating and time consuming. One promising effort to streamline the permit application process is the Joint Aquatic Resource Permit Application, which integrates environmental permitting for projects affecting coastal resources and streams in the San Francisco Bay Region (www.sfestuary.org/wp-content/uploads/2012/12/JARPA1106-final.pdf).

PROACTIVELY MANAGE THE PERMITTING PROCESS

Project applicants should communicate openly and continuously with regulatory agency staff throughout the permitting process. Meetings should be scheduled with permitting agencies at key milestones (e.g., completion of baseline studies, submittal of administrative draft documents for review) or if the project description changes. Project changes are sometimes needed, but should be minimized when possible, as they often result in significant delays in the permitting process.

Frequent agency staff turnover is a fact of life. For that reason, it is essential for project applicants to maintain detailed written documentation of discussions and decisions at every step of the permitting process. When new agency staff is assigned to a project, the applicant should schedule a meeting with the new staff and review the record of previous permitting discussions and decisions. Orienting new permitting staff in this way will reduce the chances for the new staff to reverse previous permitting decisions.

It is essential for project applicants to maintain detailed written documentation of discussions and decisions at every step of the permitting process.

Proposed permits often include boilerplate conditions. Applicants should renegotiate boilerplate conditions as needed to best fit the needs and circumstances on their projects. Mitigation requirements included in permits should be clearly written, with objective performance standards.

BEST PRACTICES FOR WORKING WITH PERMITTING STAFF

Project applicants often get frustrated with the time, cost, and inefficiencies of the environmental permitting process in California. Regulatory agency staff typically are stretched very thin, and agencies sometimes change their permitting policies and procedures when the permitting process is well underway. However, maintaining good relationships with permitting staff at all times (or retaining consultants or attorneys with these relationships) increases the probability of an expedited permitting process and favorable permitting decisions.

Applicants should remember that permitting agency staff are guided by their mission and regulatory objectives, which typically are not the same as the applicant's objectives. Applicants are more likely to get through the permitting process more smoothly if they have the ability to understand and work with the permitting agency's regulatory objectives, permit process, and political environment.

A "win–win" approach to permitting, in which agencies achieve some of their objectives through mitigation or project conditions, is generally more likely to succeed than a "win–lose" approach, in which the agency is pressured to do what the applicant wants while ignoring regulatory objectives. Applicants seldom get 100 percent of what they want.

A "win–win" approach to permitting, in which agencies achieve some of their objectives through mitigation or project conditions, is generally more likely to succeed than a "win–lose" approach, in which the agency is pressured to do what the applicant wants while ignoring regulatory objectives.

When faced with a non-responsive or difficult regulator, applicants sometimes go directly to an agency head or an elected official's office to overrule the regulator and get their needs met. While this political approach is sometimes necessary and sometimes successful, it should be used judiciously because it can not only fail, but actually backfire and result in even more onerous demands by the regulator for the applicant's current and subsequent projects.

Applicant assistance is sometimes available if agencies have insufficient staff for permit processing. Some agencies' policies allow applicants to fund staff positions. In the absence of such opportunities, applicants can still volunteer to assist agencies by preparing administrative drafts of regulatory notices and documents.

COMPREHENSIVE PERMIT LIST

Table 18-2 on the following pages lists common federal, state, regional, and local environmental permits and other approvals in California. Use this table as a starting point to prepare a comprehensive permit inventory. The table shows the name of the permit or approval, the activity triggering the permit, the permitting agency, and the chapter in this book where the permit is described in further detail. Because many specialized permits are not included in this book or table, applicants should conduct project-specific research to identify additional specialized permits.

Table 18-2. Summary of Environmental Permits and Other Approvals

Topic	Permit or approval	Activity triggering permit or approval	Regulatory agency	Chapter
California Environmental Quality Act and National Environmental Policy Act	Environmental Impact Report	Project that may have a significant environmental impact	State or local lead and responsible agencies	2
	Environmental Impact Statement	Project that may have a significant environmental impact	Federal lead and cooperating agencies	2
	Finding of no significant impact	Project with no significant environmental impact	Federal lead and cooperating agencies	2
	Negative Declaration	Project with no significant environmental impact	State or local lead and responsible agencies	2
Local Land Use and Planning Regulation	Annexation	Incorporating land into existing city or special district boundaries	Local agency formation commission	3
	Conditional use permit	Proposed use not routinely allowed by zoning of a project site	City or county	3
	Dedication	Offering of private land for public use as a condition of project approval	City or county	3
	Development agreement	Developer concessions in return for an agreement that future changes in land use regulations will not apply to proposed project	City or county	3
	Exaction	Offering of fees or dedications as a condition of project approval	City or county	3
	Final subdivision map	Satisfaction of conditions imposed on tentative subdivision map	City or county	3
	General plan amendment	Proposed project-specific change in general plan text or land use diagram	City or county	3
	Impact fee	Offering of monetary exaction to defray costs of public facilities impacts of proposed project	City or county	3
	Planned unit development	Proposed development standards specific to a proposed project	City or county	3
	Specific plan	Proposed land use and infrastructure for a portion of a community	City or county	3
	Tentative subdivision map	Subdivision of land into five or more lots	City or county	3
	Variance	Proposed project-specific waiver of development standards in a zoning ordinance	City or county	3
	Zoning amendment	Proposed project-specific change in land use zones and allowable uses	City or county	3
State and Regional Land Use Controls	Application for certification	Power plant with 50 megawatts or more of generating capacity	California Energy Commission	4
	Certificate of Public Convenience and Necessity	Construction of certain energy facilities by a regulated public utility	Public Utilities Commission	4
	Coastal development permit	Development in coastal zone	Local coastal agencies or Coastal Commission	4
	Land use lease	Use of state-owned Sovereign Lands	State Lands Commission	4

Table 18-2. Summary of Environmental Permits and Other Approvals *continued*

Topic	Permit or approval	Activity triggering permit or approval	Regulatory agency	Chapter
Air Quality	Air toxics inventory	Activity involving the manufacture, use, or release of specified air toxics and specified criteria pollutants	Local air pollution control district (APCD)	5
	Authority to construct (also known as permit to construct)	Proposed stationary activity with potential to emit air emissions	Local APCD	5
	Non-attainment new source review	Activity with the potential to release major volumes of non-attainment pollutants in a non-attainment area	Local APCD	5
	Permit by rule or prohibitory rule	Activities involving releases of organic or inorganic chemicals, particulate matter, and visible emissions	Local APCD	5
	Permit to operate	Constructed stationary activity with potential to emit air emissions	Local APCD	5
	Prevention of significant deterioration permit	Activity with the potential to release major volumes of attainment pollutants in an attainment area	Local APCD	5
	Permit by rule imposing maximum achievable control technology	Major source of hazardous air pollutants	EPA	5
	Permit by rule imposing generally achievable control technology	Minor source of hazardous air pollutants	EPA	5
	Risk management plan	Storage or use of highly hazardous and flammable chemicals	Office of Emergency Services or Certified Unified Program Agency (CUPA)	5
	Title V operating permit	"Major sources" defined by the Clean Air Act	Local APCD	5
	New source performance standards	Technology and operational controls for specified new, modified, and reconstructed sources	Local APCD	5
Hazardous Materials and Toxic Substances	Asbestos management plan	Public schools and non-profit private schools (collectively called local educational agencies)	Environmental Protection Agency (EPA)	7
	Hazardous materials business plan	Storage of specified volumes of hazardous materials	CUPA or local administering agency	7
	Prop. 65 compliance	Businesses that expose employees and the public to known carcinogens and reproductive toxins	Office of Environmental Health hazard assessment	7
	Pre-manufacture notice	Manufacturers, processors, or importers who produce or introduce a chemical product into commerce	EPA	7
	Toxic release inventory	Those who manufacture or process 25,000 pounds of chemicals annually or store or use 10,000 pounds of chemicals each year	CUPA or local administering agency	7
	Underground storage tank permit	Storage of petroleum and other hazardous substances in an underground storage tank	CUPA or local administering agency	7

Table 18-2. Summary of Environmental Permits and Other Approvals *continued*

Topic	Permit or approval	Activity triggering permit or approval	Regulatory agency	Chapter
Hazardous Wastes	Biennial report	Generating large quantities of hazardous waste	Department of Toxic Substances Control (DTSC)	8
	Conditionally authorized	On-site treatment of "California-only" hazardous waste using specified treatment methodologies on specified wastes	CUPA	8
	Conditionally exempt	On-site treatment of "California-only" hazardous waste using specified treatment methodologies on specified wastes	CUPA	8
	County hazardous waste management plan conformity	Applicant for an off-site hazardous waste treatment, storage, or disposal facility	City or county and DTSC	8
	EPA's generator identification number	Generating, transporting, treating, storing, or disposing of hazardous waste	DTSC	8
	Hazardous Materials Transportation Act shipping papers	Shipping or receiving hazardous material or hazardous waste on public roads	U.S. Department of Transportation	8
	Permit by rule	On-site treatment of "California-only" hazardous waste using specified treatment methodologies on specified wastes	CUPA	8
	Resource Conservation and Recovery Act Part B treatment, storage, and disposal facility permit	On- or off-site facilities that treat, store, or dispose of hazardous waste	DTSC	8
	Standardized permit (Class I)	On-site treatment of "California-only" hazardous waste	DTSC	8
	Hazardous waste contingency plan	Large quantity hazardous waste generator	CUPA	8
Solid Wastes	Waste discharge requirements for municipal solid waste landfill (Class III)	Owning or operating a Class III landfill disposing of solid, non-hazardous waste	Regional water quality control board (RWQCB)	9
	Construction/demolition and debris facility permit	Storing or disposing of construction debris	RWQCB	9
	Municipal solid waste transfer station permit	Owning or operating a temporarily stored solid, non-hazardous waste	Local enforcement agency and RWQCB	9
	Waste tire facility permit	Owning or operating a facility that stores or disposes of tires	California integrated waste management board	9
	Medical waste treatment permit	Treatment of medical waste	County	9
	Medical waste management plan	Major generators of hazardous waste	County	9

Table 18-2. Summary of Environmental Permits and Other Approvals *continued*

Topic	Permit or approval	Activity triggering permit or approval	Regulatory agency	Chapter
Water Quality	General stormwater construction permit	Disturbing at least one acre of soil	RWQCB	10
	General stormwater industrial permit	Industrial activity with materials potentially exposed to stormwater	RWQCB	10
	General stormwater municipal permit	Operators of municipal separate storm sewer systems serving over 100,000 people	State Water Resource Control Board (SWRCB)	10
	Stormwater pollution prevention plan	Discharge of construction, municipal, or industrial stormwater	SWRCB and RWQCB	10
	National Pollutant Discharge Elimination System permit	Discharges of pollutants to navigable waters from a point source	EPA and RWQCB	10
	Permit by rule for wastewater discharge to POTWs	Wastewater discharge to POTW	POTW	10
	Well stimulation permit	Oil and gas well stimulation	Division of Oil, Gas, & Geothermal Resources	10
	Spill prevention control and countermeasure plan	Storing at least 1,320 gallons of oil in vessels of 55 gallons or more	CUPA and EPA	10
	Waste discharge requirements	Discharges of waste that could affect the quality of the waters of the state	RWQCB	10
	Facility response plan	Facilities that could cause "substantial harm" to environment by discharging oil	EPA	10
	Spill control and countermeasure plan	Non-transportation facilities that could discharge oil into navigable waters	EPA	10
Drinking Water	Consumer confidence report	Public water system operators supplying potable water	Public water system operators supplying potable water	11
	Drinking water permit	Operating a domestic water supply	SWRCB	11
Agriculture	Conservation easement	Retention of land in agricultural or open space use	City or county	12
	Williamson Act contract	Reduced property tax assessment in return for keeping land in agricultural or open space use	City or county	12
Water Resources	Certificate of approval	Dam construction	Department of Water Resources	13
	Long-term water transfer	Transfer of water or water rights lasting more than one year	SWRCB	13
	Temporary change	Water transfer lasting one year or less involving a change in point of diversion, place of use, or purpose of use	SWRCB	13
	Temporary urgency change	Water transfer lasting one year or less to meet an urgent need involving a change in point of diversion, place of use, or purpose of use	SWRCB	13
	Water right permit	Obtaining post-1914 appropriative water right	SWRCB	13
	Water right license	Completion of project with water right permit	SWRCB	13

Table 18-2. Summary of Environmental Permits and Other Approvals *continued*

Topic	Permit or approval	Activity triggering permit or approval	Regulatory agency	Chapter
Fish and Wildlife	Biological opinion	Completion of Endangered Species Act (ESA) Section 7 formal consultation	U.S. Fish and Wildlife Service (USFWS) or National Oceanic and Atmospheric Administration (NOAA) Fisheries	14
	Habitat conservation plan	Proposed plan to conserve habitat needed to obtain ESA incidental take permit	USFWS or NOAA Fisheries	14
	Incidental take permit	Take of ESA-listed species that is incidental to otherwise lawful activities	USFWS or NOAA Fisheries	14
	Natural community conservation plan	Proposed plan to conserve a natural community that authorizes take of California Endangered Species Act (CESA)-listed species	Department of Fish and Wildlife (DFW)	14
	Section 7 consultation	Activity authorized, funded, or carried out by federal agency that may affect an ESA-listed species or critical habitat	USFWS or NOAA Fisheries	14
	Section 2081 incidental take permit	Take of CESA-listed species that is incidental to otherwise lawful activities	DFW	14
Wetlands	General Section 404 permit	Class of activities requiring Section 404 permit	U.S. Army Corps of Engineers (USACE)	15
	Lake or streambed alteration agreement	Activities involving alteration of a lake or stream zone	DFW	15
	Nationwide Section 404 permit	Activities falling within one of the nationwide permit categories	USACE	15
	Pre-construction notification	Intent to perform fill activities authorized by a nationwide permit	USACE	15
	Section 10 permit	Activities involving construction of, excavation in, or filling of navigable waters	USACE	15
	Section 401 certification	Federal activities affecting waters of the state	RWQCB and SWRCB	15
	Section 404 Permit	Discharge of dredged or fill materials into waters of the United States	USACE	15
	Standard Section 404 permit	Individual activities requiring formal Section 404 permit review	USACE	15
Forestry	Professional forester license	Engaging in timber harvest activities or preparing a timber harvest plan (THP)	Board of Forestry	16
	Program Timber Harvest Plan	THP prepared after completing a program timber Environmental Impact Report	CAL FIRE	16
	Timber harvest plan	Timber harvesting on non-federal land	CAL FIRE	16
	Timberland conversion permit	Converting timberland to non-timber uses	Board of Forestry	16
Surface Mining	Reclamation plan	Commencing surface mining activities	Local lead agencies	17
Climate Change	Greenhouse gas inventory	Facilities generating 25,000 MT CO_2e/yr	Air Resources Board (ARB) and EPA	20
	Cap-and-trade allowance	Greenhouse gas emissions for capped industrial sectors	ARB	20

for more information...

Federal Highway Administration, Federal Transit Administration, U.S. Army Corps of Engineers, and U.S. Environmental Protection Agency, 2006. Memorandum of Understanding, National Environmental Policy Act and Clean Water Act Section 404 Integration Process for Federal Aid Surface Transportation Projects in California.

U.S. Army Corps of Engineers, U.S. Coast Guard, U.S. Department of Transportation. U.S. Fish and Wildlife Service, and National Oceanic and Atmospheric Administration, 2015. 2015 Red Book: Synchronizing Environmental Reviews for Transportation and Other Infrastructure Projects. Publication No. FHWA-HEP-15-047.

glossary

Discretionary permit—requires an agency to exercise a higher level of deliberation and a higher level of analysis before issuing a permit.

Ministerial permit—involves a straight-forward decision judging against standardized, objective criteria.

Permit—for purposes of this chapter, all environmental approvals, including certifications, licenses, and plan and specification approvals.

Permit by rule—a permit in which the applicant submits a Notice of Intent to comply with pre-set permit conditions that are not site-specific.

CHAPTER 19

Environmental Compliance Auditing*

*This chapter is excerpted from the environmental auditing chapter of Matthew Bender and Company's *California Environmental Law and Land Use Practice* treatise, written by Gary A. Lucks. Reproduced with permission.

in this chapter...

EPA = U.S. Environmental Protection Agency

Cal/EPA = California Environmental Protection Agency

SOX = Sarbanes-Oxley Act

CEO = chief executive officer

CFO = chief financial officer

ISO = International Organization for Standardization

EMS = environmental management system

INTRODUCTION

This chapter ties together the substantive and procedural requirements of the environmental regulatory programs discussed in this book by describing how compliance audits can be used to manage environmental liability. Audits actively help manage the risk of noncompliance with environmental standards. Specifically, an environmental audit is an independent assessment of facility performance against environmental regulatory standards or requirements.

KEY LAWS

ENVIRONMENTAL PROTECTION AGENCY AUDIT PRIVILEGE

The federal EPA audit privilege is a self-disclosure policy designed to encourage regulated entities to voluntarily discover, promptly notify the EPA, and correct violations of federal environmental requirements. To take advantage of policy benefits (penalty reduction), entities must disclose their violations within 21 days of discovery and correct them within 60 days.

CALIFORNIA ENVIRONMENTAL PROTECTION AGENCY AUDIT PRIVILEGE

The California Environmental Protection Agency (Cal/EPA) adopted a more stringent version of the federal EPA audit privilege with more comprehensive policies for penalty reduction, criminal referrals, and fee-for-service certification. Similar to the EPA audit privilege, the Cal/EPA audit privilege allows regulated facilities that meet all nine conditions to be eligible for 100 percent mitigation of gravity-based penalties. For more information, *see* the Cal/EPA website (www.calepa.ca.gov/Enforcement/policy/VolDisclosure.pdf).

SARBANES-OXLEY ACT OF 2002

Chief executive officers and chief financial officers must personally certify that the company's financial report does not contain false information on material facts and that it accurately identifies the financial condition of the company.

The Sarbanes-Oxley Act of 2002 (SOX) (PL 107–204, 116 Stat. 745) requires publicly traded companies to provide individual audit reports detailing their internal operations. Chief executive officers (CEOs) and chief financial officers (CFOs) must personally certify that the company's financial report does not contain false information on material facts and that it accurately identifies the financial condition of the company.

INTERNATIONAL ORGANIZATION FOR STANDARDIZATION 14001

The International Organization for Standardization (ISO) 14001 standards govern the creation of Environmental Management Systems (EMSs). An EMS is a set of management processes and procedures that allows an organization to analyze, control, and reduce the environmental impacts of its activities, products, and services, and to operate with greater efficiency and control. Facilities must conduct EMS internal audits to determine whether the EMS conforms to ISO standards. EMSs often commit an organization to conducting environmental audits to demonstrate compliance.

REASONS TO CONDUCT AUDITS

Corporate officers are required to undertake all possible means to discover, prevent, or remedy criminal violations. *People v. Matthews* (1992) 7 Cal. App. 4th 1052. Audits primarily help a facility's officers and environmental manager identify and correct deficiencies before they result in agency enforcement actions. Additionally, audits can serve as management tools to help managers more effectively administer compliance programs and implement best management practices (BMPs) that are not required but can optimize environmental compliance. However, audit programs are not limited to regulatory requirements and BMPs. They can evaluate compliance against a variety of standards ranging from the full panoply of federal, state, regional, and local environmental regulations to the prescriptions of the ISO 14001 standards governing the implementation of EMSs.

BMP = best management practice

SEP = supplemental environmental project

CFEMS = compliance-focused environmental management system

COMPLIANCE MANAGEMENT

The primary incentive to develop and implement an environmental compliance audit program is to avoid administrative, civil, or criminal fines, penalties, or injunctions. Particularly in California, a state known for rigorous environmental compliance standards, an audit is a tool that provides an independent, third-party review of a facility's environmental regulatory programs. The mission of the auditor is to investigate gaps and deficiencies in a facility's compliance programs and correct them before experiencing an announced or unannounced inspection from a regulatory agency. This not only helps the environmental manager assess the health of the facility's programs, but also assists in deploying limited resources to the weakest programs presenting the largest exposure. Audits additionally provide assurance to corporate officers concerning the status of environmental compliance.

Inspections of oil tanks during environmental audits can prevent later problems.

ENFORCEMENT DISCRETION

The existence of an audit program can be a mitigating factor influencing whether and how to prosecute a violator and the ultimate criminal penalties assessed.

SUPPLEMENTAL ENVIRONMENTAL PROJECTS

Agencies have authority to offset a portion of the penalty assessed to violators and to allow implementation of an SEP—which can include an audit, a compliance-focused EMS (CFEMS), or a standard EMS. A SEP is more focused on "beyond compliance"—improved environmental performance that in many cases exceeds environmental regulatory requirements. This type of EMS is modeled after ISO 14001, which defines an EMS as:

> [T]hat part of the overall management system which includes organizational structure, planning activities, responsibilities, practices, procedures, processes

GAGAS = generally accepted government auditing standards

GAAP = generally accepted accounting principles

and resources for developing, implementing, archiving, reviewing, and maintaining [the organization's] environmental policy.

SEPs are offered by the EPA, Cal/EPA, and local agencies. For more information, *see* Cal/EPA (2003b). Federal and state SEPs include an "Other Types of Projects" category that allows violating companies to examine their operations for pollution prevention opportunities and to determine if they can reduce the use, production, or generation of hazardous materials and other wastes. These audits go well beyond standard business practices.

TYPES OF AUDITS

GOVERNMENT AUDIT

Governments engage in the audit process and base their standards on generally accepted government auditing standards (GAGAS) to foster competency, integrity, and objectivity in their reporting work. These standards are the foundation for using fieldwork and reporting standards to perform quality work.

Governmental audits include financial and performance audits, and attestation engagement. Financial audits mainly provide reasonable assurance about whether financial statements are presented accurately in conformity with generally accepted accounting principles (GAAP) or another comprehensive basis for accounting. Performance audits are objective, systematic, and independent evaluations of material to independently examine program performance and management versus objective criteria; they also potentially focus on or summarize BMPs or multidimensional issues. The main goals of performance audits are to improve a facility's operations, to encourage corrective action, and to improve public accountability. Attestation engagement entails examining or performing agreed-upon procedures about a topic, or involves making an assertion about a topic and then reporting the results.

ENVIRONMENTAL COMPLIANCE AUDIT

Facilities may benefit from engaging a third-party audit team staffed with individuals from a sister company or division or by using a third-party consultant or accounting firm.

Facilities may benefit from engaging a third-party audit team staffed with individuals from a sister company or division (*see* below) or by using a third-party consultant or accounting firm. Such an "external" audit has the advantage of taking the viewpoint of an environmental agency inspector. Typically, external third-party audit programs entail audits every two to five years at individual facilities, buildings, or programs—those that perform well can be scheduled for longer intervals between external audits, while those showing significant weaknesses or gaps may be scheduled more frequently. External audits need not comprehensively review all relevant environmental areas; instead, external audits can focus on the weakest environmental areas (e.g., air quality and hazardous wastes).

COMPLIANCE-FOCUSED ENVIRONMENTAL MANAGEMENT SYSTEM

SOP = standard operating procedure

Compliance audits are important tools for managing a facility's compliance risks. However, a facility could repeat the same compliance-based finding at the next audit, unless the root cause behind the finding is addressed. To proactively manage environmental compliance, facility managers are advised to build on their audit programs by developing and implementing CFEMSs. Because compliance assurance can be heavily dependent on the individual rather than the position, the CFEMS should include uniform, clear, and consistent schedules and standards. As a result, a CFEMS helps provide a reliable platform for ensuring more accurate compliance performance.

A CFEMS can help ensure ongoing compliance with environmental laws by clearly documenting responsibilities and establishing standard operating procedures (SOPs). SOPs establish staff accountability by laying out roles and expectations. In addition, a CFEMS helps a facility to manage change and to preserve institutional knowledge and continuity with environmental programs and responsibilities. A CFEMS also establishes an environmental awareness and regulatory training program (including scheduled regulatory and legislative updates).

A CFEMS helps a facility to manage change and to preserve institutional knowledge and continuity with environmental programs and responsibilities.

The CFEMS should include a tickler system to forecast and plan for upcoming deadlines to submit required agency reports, permit and license renewals, and other submittals. The tickler system helps management and staff to better anticipate and respond to regulatory obligations and to manage priorities more effectively. Finally, the CFEMS should include a robust self-inspection program to address compliance gaps between third-party audit intervals.

ENVIRONMENTAL MANAGEMENT SYSTEM AUDIT

An EMS represents a management framework that assists businesses and government agencies in improving environmental performance and shrinking their "environmental footprint." Some facility managers choose to develop EMSs to decrease costs and environmental impacts (e.g., pollution) associated with energy, water, and raw materials usage and waste, while increasing operational efficiency. In many cases, the EMS goes "beyond compliance" and exceeds environmental regulatory requirements. Additionally, the EMS can be a tool to enhance compliance management. Thus, an EMS can turn environmental management from a perceived "cost center" into an integrated strategic advantage.

Some businesses and facilities choose to develop and implement an EMS in accordance with ISO 14001, as described above. For others, having a certified EMS is a condition of doing business. For example, Ford Motor Company requires ISO 14001 certification from all of its suppliers with manufacturing facilities.

AUDITING PROCESS

When performing a multimedia environmental compliance audit, federal, state, regional, and local regulatory requirements are typically evaluated for the following topics:

- Air quality and climate change
- Wastewater and stormwater
- Drinking water
- Spill prevention
- Tanks (above and underground)
- Hazardous waste management
- Hazardous materials management
- Chemical transport
- Toxics (polychlorinated biphenyls, asbestos, lead, and radon)
- Historic and cultural resources
- Solid waste
- Pesticides
- Pollution prevention
- Brownfields and hazardous substances cleanup
- Internal policies and procedures

The principle objective of a regulatory compliance audit, a CFEMS, or an EMS conformity audit is to obtain an accurate assessment of site conditions and compliance status at a given facility. An auditor's ability to gather relevant information hinges on proper planning, facility cooperation, qualified auditors, and involvement of senior management. Senior management participation helps ensure that relevant staff attends audit meetings and participates as needed throughout the data-gathering phase as well as in later phases to ensure that corrective and preventive actions are implemented expeditiously. Senior management can also assist by directing resources to respond to environmental findings and observations.

An auditor's ability to gather relevant information hinges on proper planning, facility cooperation, qualified auditors, and involvement of senior management.

An audit consists of three phases: pre-audit activities, on-site audit, and post-audit activities. Each phase is discussed below and further illustrated in Figure 19-1.

PRE-AUDIT ACTIVITIES

The audit team leader begins the process by sending a commitment letter to the environmental manager. The commitment letter is intended to commit the facility to specified dates and audit milestones, as well as to provide knowledgeable escorts and logistical support for the audit team.

FIGURE 19-1
Environmental Compliance Auditing Process in California

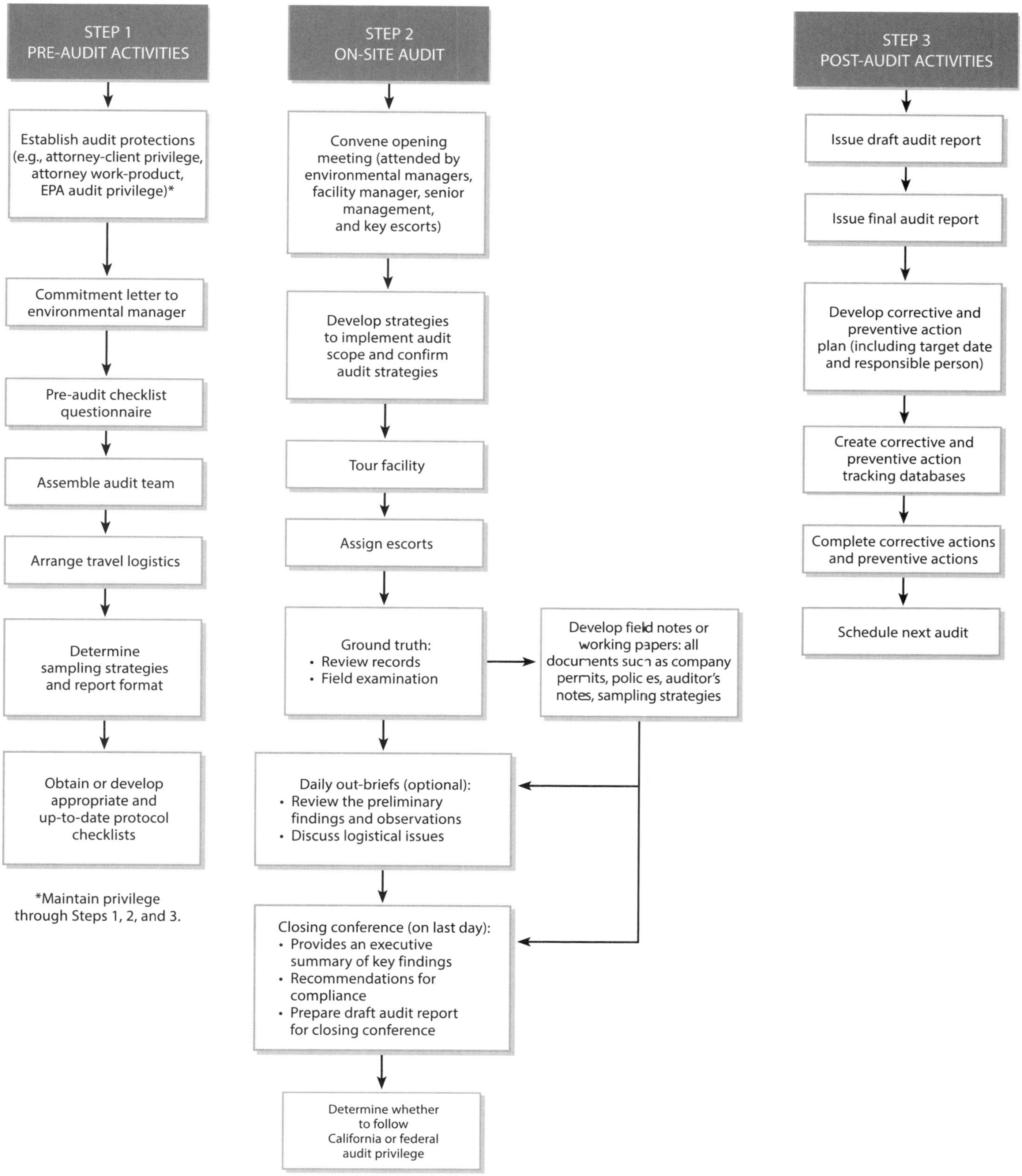

A completed pre-audit questionnaire assists the audit team leader in visualizing the level of effort necessary to complete the on-site audit by knowing the scope of the regulated programs.

Before scheduling the audit and deploying the audit team, the audit team leader should obtain as much information as possible about the size of the facility, the number and types of regulated emissions sources and units, and the types of permits, plans, and other regulated environmental programs applicable to the facility. This usually is accomplished by submitting a pre-audit checklist or questionnaire to be completed by the on-site environmental manager with the assistance of staff. The pre-audit questionnaire is designed to clarify the number and type of regulated emission units and the applicability of regulatory programs. It also identifies the records to be reviewed. Typically, the pre-audit questionnaire should be submitted a few months prior to the scheduled on-site audit and completed at least a month before the scheduled visit. Alternatively, the audit team leader can review the contents of the pre-audit checklist over a phone call with facility personnel.

A completed pre-audit questionnaire assists the audit team leader in visualizing the level of effort necessary to complete the on-site audit by knowing the scope of the regulated programs. The team leader will be in a position to:

- Determine the "fence line" of the facility (i.e., which physical aspects of the facility or programs are subject to the audit)
- Determine where and how to deploy resources to address relevant environmental programs
- Craft an appropriate sampling strategy
- Assemble appropriate regulatory checklists and protocols for use by auditors on-site
- Assess what personal protective equipment to bring
- Assemble a team of subject matter experts to review relevant environmental programs. Audit teams should include subject matter experts from all applicable regulatory topics: air quality, climate change, water quality, hazardous waste, hazardous materials, oil management, tank management, chemical transport, and toxic materials (e.g., polychlorinated biphenyls, lead, and asbestos) management
- Review the relevant EPA industry sector notebooks, which provide industry-specific manufacturing processes, typical types and amounts of pollution associated with a given industrial sector, and typical regulatory compliance considerations

ON-SITE AUDIT

On-site data gathering represents the heart of the audit. The on-site phase typically begins with a scheduled opening meeting attended by the environmental manager, facility operations manager, senior management (e.g., Vice President for Environmental Affairs), facility manager, and key escorts. The opening meeting lays out the objectives of the audit, the expectations of participants, logistical considerations, and the schedule for on-site and post-audit activities. This meeting usually is followed by a facility tour to familiarize the auditors with the nature and extent of environmental activities and existing programs.

Facility escorts are paired with auditors either before or after the facility tour. After completing the facility tour, the audit team begins to collect the "ground truth," by conducting staff interviews, reviewing records, and examining field conditions (e.g., viewing regulated equipment and emissions units, walking the site). The results of the ground truth are included in the auditor's field notes or more formalized "working papers," which serve as the evidentiary basis for drafting findings and observations. Working papers include all documents such as company permits, policies, the auditor's rough notes, and sampling strategies.

On-site data gathering represents the heart of an environmental audit.

Depending on the schedule for on-site activities, a schedule for daily meetings or "out-briefs" may be helpful to review preliminary findings and observations and to discuss logistical issues. A final, closing conference, attended by facility management, escorts, and the audit team is held on the last day. This meeting provides an executive summary of key findings, along with strategic recommendations to assist the facility in coming into compliance.

Typically, compliance audits focus on assessing facility operations to determine compliance with:

- Prescriptive multimedia environmental regulatory requirements
- Specific permit conditions (e.g., air quality permits, emissions limitations, or maintaining chemical usage logs)
- Environmental plans and inventories (e.g., spill prevention control and countermeasure plans, hazardous materials business plans, stormwater pollution prevention plans, and air toxic hotspots inventories)
- Training requirements (e.g., mandatory annual hazardous waste generator and hazardous communication trainings)
- Inspection obligations (e.g., weekly inspections for hazardous waste long-term accumulation areas)
- Reporting obligations (e.g., Title V Operating Permit annual compliance certifications, waste discharge requirements daily monitoring reports and permits, and release reporting obligations)
- Emergency response procedures
- Corporate or divisional policies and procedures
- Facility-specific standard operating procedures or BMPs

The scope of a compliance audit often includes assessing equipment calibration to demonstrate that emissions controls, treatment devices, and other mechanical equipment are functioning properly. In addition, audits typically evaluate

GMP = good management practice

NOV = notice of violation

preventive maintenance schedules for emissions controls, alarms, and tank integrity testing.

POST-AUDIT ACTIVITIES

When facility operations do not meet environmental standards, the auditor documents the noncompliant issue and characterizes it as either a "finding" or "observation." A finding represents an exceedance or violation of a regulatory standard, whereas an observation may include either an exemplary activity (i.e., a positive observation) or a condition that violates a non-regulated, internal policy or a recommended good or best management practice (GMP or BMP). In addition, an observation can identify a condition representing prospective noncompliance (e.g., a regulated emissions unit such as an underground storage tank is subject to a forthcoming schedule of compliance requiring an equipment retrofit or upgrade); the observation then can allow the facility to begin corrective action before the condition becomes a true regulatory finding.

Observations can enhance the value of the audit by bringing other non-regulated but salient issues to the attention of management. Positive observations highlight effective programs that can be shared with other facilities. Findings and observations can be handwritten on a form, entered into a handheld device, or entered into a database. Later, the findings and observations are captured in a written report, verbal closing conference, or both.

With a prioritization scheme, the audit team leader can advise the facility management and its legal representative on the most efficient way to deploy resources to respond to the findings and observations.

To provide more meaning to the audit results, it is advisable to develop a prioritization scheme for findings and observations. With a prioritization scheme, the audit team leader can advise the facility management and its legal representative on the most efficient way to deploy resources to respond to the findings and observations.

There are several approaches to assigning priorities to findings and observations. One type of scheme labels findings as significant, major, or minor, while characterizing observations as positive (for exemplary performance) or negative. Another example of a prioritization scheme is:

- **Priority 1.** Should be remedied immediately, due to actual or likely substantial endangerment to the environment or serious violation of federal, state, or local law
- **Priority 2.** Should be remedied as soon as practicable (e.g., 30 days), due to reasonable likelihood of endangerment to the environment or possibility of a future notice of violation (NOV) of law or company policy
- **Priority 3.** Should be remedied within 30 to 180 days, due to reasonable likelihood of endangerment to the environment or possibility of a future NOV of law or company policy
- **Priority 4.** Should be documented and referred for corrective action, but is not driven by a regulatory or company policy

Regardless of the prioritization scheme, the auditor can further characterize findings as repeat findings, carryover findings, and new findings. A repeat finding is one from an earlier audit observed again in a later audit. A carryover finding is one from an earlier audit not corrected prior to the subsequent audit. Finally, a new finding is one not previously observed.

Findings and observations may be summarized in a draft report that describes the conditions observed, along with documentary evidence consisting of photographs or other written evidence. The draft audit report can be as minimal as a table depicting each regulatory requirement, supporting citation, finding description, and recommended corrective action, or it may include narrative text describing these same elements. It may be advisable to protect the audit report with a confidentiality tool described below.

The report may document which facility activities were assessed (e.g., "10 of 25 hazardous waste satellite accumulation areas" or "all manifests for the past two years"). In addition to describing the basis for the findings and observations, the report should recommend corrective and preventive actions along with a suggested time frame for each. An audit report optionally can include the root cause or causes of the findings.

If the facility plans to take advantage of the audit privileges discussed below, the timing of the corrective actions and agency notifications will be affected. The facility manager then will be responsible for tracking and closing findings and observations.

Facility management is given an opportunity to review a draft of the audit report. The facility manager has discretion to assess the compliance risk of each finding and prioritize individual corrective and preventive actions. The facility manager is ultimately responsible for developing corrective and preventive actions and tracking progress.

AUDIT PROTECTIONS AND PRIVILEGES

Establishing confidentiality is crucial in the audit process. Because audits uncover potential regulatory violations, this information could be used against the facility if obtained by a regulatory agency or other parties. Establishing confidentiality also protects proprietary information, involving industrial processes or other sensitive corporate information, from disclosure to competitors. Facilities therefore should plan for and make resources available to remedy non-compliance findings. If such findings remain uncorrected, a facility risks involuntary disclosure, which could prompt administrative, civil, or criminal liability.

Establishing confidentiality is crucial in the audit process.

Audit reports prepared without establishing confidentiality cannot retroactively gain protection. The methods described below are designed to protect disclosure of sensitive information identified during an audit. However, these methods cannot prevent disclosure of evidence when employees knowingly violated regulations.

ATTORNEY-CLIENT PRIVILEGE

Attorney-client privilege promotes complete and full disclosure of information between an attorney and client, by relieving the parties from having statements used against them or the company.

Attorney-client privilege (Calif. Code of Evid. § 952 *et seq.*) promotes complete and full disclosure of information between an attorney and client, by relieving the parties from having statements used against them or the company. If clients knew that sensitive information conveyed to their attorney could be disclosed, they might be less willing to communicate such information to counsel.

Under the attorney-client privilege, the courts protect information from disclosure if all of the following are met:

- The information is communicated to obtain or render legal services.
- The information is confidential.
- The attorney or client asserts the attorney-client privilege.

The attorney-client privilege protects only information communicated between the parties for the purpose of rendering or obtaining legal advice. Because the underlying facts associated with the privileged communication are not protected, adversaries may independently uncover the same information.

Documents and reports required by public agencies as part of the permitting or compliance process (e.g., self-monitoring reports, incident reports) cannot be protected because they are a matter of public record.

If information is intentionally or inadvertently disclosed to individuals or organizations without an appropriate confidentiality agreement, then the privilege is waived, and evidence can be discovered through agency disclosure or civil discovery. For example, the privilege can be inadvertently waived by disclosing the audit report to prospective lenders or purchasers.

Today, more executives are turning to in-house counsel for legal advice. In this situation, defining and maintaining the attorney-client privilege becomes tricky, and often involves risks and difficulties that would not arise with outside counsel. In California, the state courts and Ninth Circuit Court of Appeals have held that the attorney-client privilege applies to communications between a client and in-house counsel just as it applies to communications between a client and outside counsel. *See State Farm Fire and Casualty Co. v. Superior Court* (1997) 54 Cal. App. 4th 625; *U.S. v. Rowe* (1996) 96 F. 3d 1294. Though the privilege applies to confidential communications relating strictly to legal advice, the privilege is lost when communications are made for business purposes.

Owners or operators that are required to develop and implement a Risk Management Plan (RMP) must certify that they have evaluated compliance at least every three years to verify that the procedures and practices developed under the RMP standard are adequate and are being followed. 40 C.F.R. § 68.79(a); 19 Cal.

Code Regs. § 2760.8. Audits performed to validate compliance in support of these certifications cannot be protected by the attorney-client privilege.

ATTORNEY WORK-PRODUCT DOCTRINE

The work-product doctrine protects information prepared by an attorney or his representative in anticipation of litigation. The purpose of the protection is to withhold from a client's adversary those materials prepared for the defense of that client. Protected materials under the work-product doctrine are more diverse than those under the attorney-client privilege. Protected materials may include lawyer's notes, interviews, witness statements, memoranda, photographs, drawings, and computer-generated data. Furthermore, protected materials include those generated by persons working under the direction of the attorney (e.g., consultants).

The protected materials must be collected and prepared in anticipation of litigation. While litigation need not have commenced, it must be more than a remote prospect. In other words, materials likely will be protected if litigation is "fairly obvious," "probable," or "imminent." Disclosure of materials may be required if the adversary can show sufficient need and the prospect of suffering undue hardship in obtaining the information through other means. The greatest protection under the doctrine pertains to the attorney's "opinion" work. In California, the doctrine is defined broadly and protects "any writing that reflects an attorney's impressions, conclusions, opinions, or legal research or theories" used by the lawyer in anticipation of litigation.

ENVIRONMENTAL PROTECTION AGENCY AUDIT PRIVILEGE

The EPA Audit Policy encourages regulated entities to voluntarily discover, promptly disclose to EPA, and expeditiously correct violations of federal environmental requirements. This self-disclosure policy encourages regulated entities to audit their facilities with an expectation that violations will be identified and corrected. EPA 2015. In addition, the policy states that EPA will refrain from routine requests for voluntary audit reports.

In exchange for prompt notification and correction of environmental violations, an entity can eliminate or substantially reduce gravity-based civil penalties and avoid criminal prosecution. A gravity-based penalty reflects the portion of the penalty over and above the economic advantage an entity gains as a result of noncompliance.

In exchange for prompt notification and correction of environmental violations, an entity can eliminate or substantially reduce gravity-based civil penalties and avoid criminal prosecution.

To take advantage of policy benefits, regulated entities must disclose all non-EPCRA violations within 21 days of discovery and correct them within 60 days or up to 90 days for small businesses. Disclosures may be submitted on EPA's centralized web-based "eDisclosure" portal. 80 Fed. Reg. 76476 (December 9, 2015).

Regulated entities are eligible for 100 percent mitigation of gravity-based penalties if they meet all nine of the policy's conditions described below. They are eligible for a 75 percent reduction if they meet all nine of the policy's conditions except for detecting the violation through a systematic discovery process. With some exceptions, all EPCRA violators and small businesses with non-EPCRA violations can also take advantage of the EPA audit policy where the violations were not systematically discovered. EPA 2000.

EPA generally will not recommend criminal prosecution if entities meet all nine conditions except for the systematic discovery process.

EPA reserves the right to collect any economic benefit that resulted from noncompliance, even when the entity meets all other policy conditions. EPA generally will not recommend criminal prosecution if entities meet all nine conditions except for the systematic discovery process. This "no recommendation for criminal prosecution" incentive is available unless EPA determines there was culpable behavior. The nine conditions necessary to receive penalty mitigation include the following (EPA 2015):

Condition 1. The entity must realize the violation through a systematic discovery process, such as an environmental audit or a compliance management system (e.g., a CFEMS), that reflects due diligence in preventing, detecting, and correcting violations.

Condition 2. The entity cannot discover the violation through legally required monitoring, sampling, or auditing.

Condition 3. The entity must disclose the violation in writing to EPA within 21 days of discovery or such shorter time as may be required by law.

Condition 4. The entity must independently discover and disclose the violation before EPA or another regulator likely would identify the violation through its own investigation or through third-party information.

Condition 5. The entity must correct and remediate the violation within 60 calendar days from the date of discovery and must certify that the violation was corrected (this time frame may be negotiable).

Condition 6. The entity must prevent recurrence of the violation, through such possible steps as improving environmental auditing efforts or compliance management systems.

Condition 7. Repeat violations are ineligible.

Condition 8. Certain types of violations are ineligible, including violations that result in serious actual harm to the environment or that may have presented imminent and substantial endangerment to the public health or environment.

Condition 9. The entity must cooperate.

For new owners wanting to make a clean start at recently acquired facilities, EPA has established an interim approach to applying its Audit Policy (www.epa.gov/compliance/epas-interim-approach-applying-audit-policy-new-owners). This approach contains Audit Policy incentives tailored to addressing environmental noncompliance that began prior to acquisition. It is designed to encourage new owners to audit their facilities, and to promote self-disclosure of violations. For new owners, the following five Audit Policy conditions are modified to make more violations eligible for mitigation of penalties:

Condition 1. Systemic discovery
Condition 2. Voluntary discovery
Condition 3. Prompt disclosure
Condition 8. Other violations excluded
Condition 9. Cooperation condition

CALIFORNIA ENVIRONMENTAL PROTECTION AGENCY AUDIT PRIVILEGE

Cal/EPA adopted a self-disclosure audit policy more comprehensive than the federal EPA policy. The Cal/EPA policy is referred to as the Cal/EPA Recommended Guidance on Incentives for Voluntary Disclosure (Cal/EPA 2003a). As with EPA's policy, the same nine conditions must be met for a regulated entity to enjoy reduction or elimination of state gravity-based penalties.

Cal/EPA's policy is more comprehensive than the federal policy in three major areas: penalty reduction, criminal referrals, and fee-for-service certification. Like the penalty reduction provisions of the EPA Audit Policy, by fulfilling all nine conditions, regulated entities are relieved of all gravity-based penalties. Similarly, if an entity meets all conditions except the first, gravity-based penalties will be reduced by 75 percent. However, under the California audit policy, gravity-based penalties may be reduced by an additional 15 percent for entities that invest in pollution prevention programs for up to a combined 90 percent reduction in gravity-based fees.

Like the EPA Audit Policy, Cal/EPA will not recommend criminal prosecution if all nine conditions are met.

Although EPA encourages businesses to initiate self-audit or due diligence programs, its policy provides minimal guidance as to the types of procedures that qualify. The Cal/EPA policy attempts to provide regulated entities with greater certainty by waiving a portion of penalties for violations discovered through due diligence or environmental audits. Cal/EPA defines "due diligence" to mean a "regulated entity's systematic efforts, appropriate to the size and nature of the business, to prevent, detect, disclose, and correct violations" through various efforts and mechanisms. Entities that have implemented an audit or due diligence program will be able to receive certification from Cal/EPA prior to any reporting of a violation discovered through the audit or due diligence. Businesses with audit programs can, for a fee, invite Cal/EPA to certify the adequacy of their audit programs. Certification does not guarantee immunity from an enforcement action, but will likely result in businesses receiving the full advantage of the policy.

Certification does not guarantee immunity from an enforcement action, but will likely result in businesses receiving the full advantage of the policy.

for more information...

Cal/EPA. 2003a. Recommended Guidance on Incentives for Voluntary Disclosure.

Cal/EPA.2003b. Recommended Guidance on Supplemental Environmental Projects.

Environmental Protection Agency, 2000. Final Policy Statement: Incentives for Self-Policing: Discovery, Disclosure, Correction and Prevention of Violations.

Environmental Protection Agency, 2001. Beyond Compliance: Supplemental Environmental Projects. Office of Enforcement and Compliance Assurance.

Environmental Protection Agency, 2004. Achieving Environmental Excellence: An Environmental Management Systems (EMS) Handbook for Wastewater Utilities.

Environmental Protection Agency, 2015. EPA's Audit Policy (www.epa.gov/compliance/epas-audit-policy).

Manaster, K. A. and D. P. Selmi (eds.), ND. Sections 54.13(2) and 56.20(2) of California Environmental Law and Land Use Practice. Matthew Bender. San Francisco, Calif.

Schrey, S. G., J. M. Tanenbaum, and T. M. Rudolph, February 24, 2005. Risk and Reward: Avoiding Pitfalls When Conducting Compliance Audits (www.nixonpeabody.com/116756).

glossary

Best management practices—methods determined to be the most effective, practical means for preventing or reducing pollution from nonpoint sources.

Compliance-focused environmental management system—models from which environmental management system requirements are based. CFEMS must clearly illustrate management's commitment to comply with relevant federal, state and local statutes and regulations, while continuing to make improvements regarding environmental programs.

Due diligence—a regulated entity's systematic efforts, appropriate to the size and nature of the business, to prevent, detect, disclose, and correct violations through various efforts and mechanisms.

Environmental management system—procedures allowing an organization to decrease its environmental impact and increase its operating efficiencies.

International Organization for Standardization—the world's largest developer of technical standards, ISO is a non-governmental organization and consists of a network of the national standards institutes of 157 countries. ISO standards contribute to enabling the manufacture and development of products more efficiently and also provide a safeguard for consumers.

Standard operating procedure—a set of written instructions that document a routine or repetitive activity followed by an organization.

Supplemental environmental projects—pollution prevention efforts that exceed the existing statutory obligations of dischargers and achieve an environmental benefit.

PART 5

CLIMATE CHANGE LAW AND POLICY

CHAPTER 20

Climate Change

related Solano Press title

California Land Use and Planning Law. Cecily Talbert Barclay and Matthew S. Gray. 35th Edition. 2016.

in this chapter...

Climate Models and Uncertainty in Climate Change Projections

Climate models are computer programs that use equations to represent relevant processes in the atmosphere, ocean, land and ice that make up the Earth's climate system. Different global climate models (GCMs) are run at several international centers to explore past, present and future climate conditions. GCMs are "driven" by known or assumed climate influences (forcings), including fluctuations in solar energy, volcanic activity, changing greenhouse gas concentrations, aerosols, and land use changes. Based on these forcings, GCMs project how global climate conditions might change over time.

Climate change simulations are affected by uncertainty in assumed future emissions of aerosols and greenhouse gases, the model's representation of the real climate system, rates of sea ice melting, and natural variability. Because of these uncertainties, climate scientists consider ensembles (groups) of climate simulations from several GCMs to investigate different scenarios and a range of possible future variations and changes. Also, climate change impacts are typically presented as a range rather than a single number.

INTRODUCTION

SCIENCE

Increased levels of carbon dioxide and other gases released into the atmosphere as a result of human industrial activity have increased the physical capacity of air to trap and retain energy. Gases that contribute to climate change are known as greenhouse gases (GHGs).

Since 1880, global temperatures have risen approximately 1.53°F. (UNIPCC 2013). Heat records are being broken every year. For example, in 2015 as this book was being written, the Earth's surface temperatures were the warmest since modern recordkeeping began in 1880, according to independent analyses by NASA and the National Oceanic and Atmospheric Administration (NOAA). Globally-averaged temperatures in 2015 increased the previous mark set in 2014 by 0.23°F. Fifteen of the 16 warmest years had occurred since 2001 (www.nasa.gov/press-release/nasa-noaa-analyses-reveal-record-shattering-global-warm-temperatures-in-2015).

GHGs include carbon dioxide (CO_2), methane, nitrous oxide, hydrofluorocarbons, perfluorocarbons and sulfur hexafluoride. Except for short-lived climate pollutants, these gases remain in the atmosphere for hundreds of years.

GLOBAL IMPACT

The increase in atmospheric temperature has the potentially devastating effect of raising global sea levels, thus increasing the risk, range, and strength of natural disasters worldwide. Over the period 1901 to 2010, global mean sea level rose by about 7.5 inches. A rise in global average sea level by 10 to 39 inches is projected by the year 2100 (relative to mean sea level from 1985 to 2005). UNIPCC 2013. The ranges in climate change impact projections reflect uncertainties in future GHG emissions, climate science, and natural variability. *See* sidebar.

Climate change involves significant shifts in natural weather patterns which are projected to produce drier conditions in the subtropics and wetter weather at higher latitudes. Elevated temperatures are causing heat waves, precipitation is shifting with heavy rains intensifying, coral reefs are dying, and a number of species are under significant pressure for survival and are either going extinct or migrating to higher latitudes.

The United Nations Intergovernmental Panel on Climate Change (UNIPCC) warns that climate change impacts will likely substantially worsen. In 2014 the IPCC issued a dire warning about how heat-trapping GHGs have contributed to increased global temperatures, extreme weather, and are threatening food and water resources. According to UNIPCC (2014), "Throughout the 21st century, climate-change impacts are projected to slow economic growth, make poverty reduction more difficult, further erode food security, and prolong existing and create new poverty traps, the latter particularly in urban areas and emerging hot spots of hunger."

GCM = global climate model

GHG = greenhouse gas

UNIPCC = United Nations Intergovernmental Panel on Climate Change

NOAA = National Oceanic and Atmospheric Administration

CO_2 = carbon dioxide

CALIFORNIA IMPACT

California temperatures have shown a warming trend in the past century. The state has experienced an increase of 1.1 to 2°F in mean temperature in the past century. Both minimum and maximum annual temperatures have increased, but the minimum temperatures (+1.6 to 2.5°F) have increased more than maximums (+0.4 to 1.6°F). Future projections of temperatures across California indicate that by 2060 to 2069 mean temperatures will be 3.4 to 4.9°F higher across the state than they were in the period 1985 to 1994. Seasonal trends indicate a greater increase in the summer months (4.1 to 6.5°F) than in winter months (2.7 to 3.6°F) by 2060 to 2069. DWR 2015.

In the future, climate change will lead to a number of hydrologic impacts for California. In recent decades, there has been a trend toward more rain than snow in the total precipitation volume, reducing total snowpack, which represents up to one-third of the state's water supply. More intense dry periods are likely. By the end of the century, the Sierra snowpack is projected to experience a 48 to 65 percent loss from its average at the end of the previous century. Extremes on the wet end of the spectrum are also expected to increase, due to more frequent warm, wet atmospheric river events and a higher proportion of precipitation falling as rain instead of snow. Most climate model precipitation projections for the state anticipate drier conditions in Southern California, with heavier and warmer winter precipitation in Northern California. DWR 2015.

Regarding sea level rise, during the last century, sea level at the Golden Gate in San Francisco has shown a 7-inch rise, similar to global measurements. Sea level is projected to increase by 17 to 66 inches along much of the California coast by 2100. Sea level rise is projected to be higher south of Cape Mendocino (compared to north of Cape Mendocino). National Research Council 2012.

KEY LAWS AND AGENCIES

INTERNATIONAL

United Nations Framework Convention on Climate Change. In 1992 The United Nations Conference on Environment and Development (also known as the Earth Summit) took place in Rio de Janeiro in 1992. That conference produced an international environmental treaty which set the stage for the first binding treaty on climate change in 1995, the Kyoto Protocol.

UN Intergovernmental Panel on Climate Change. The purpose of the IPCC is to assess information in the scientific and technical literature related to all significant components of the issue of climate change. The IPCC draws upon hundreds of the world's expert scientists as authors and thousands as expert reviewers. With its capacity for reporting on climate change, its consequences, and the

The IPCC draws upon hundreds of the world's expert scientists as authors and thousands as expert reviewers.

CAA = Clean Air Act

NEPA = National Environmental Policy Act

EO = Executive Order

EPA = U.S. Environmental Protection Agency

DOE = Department of Energy

viability of adaptation and mitigation measures, the IPCC is looked to as the official advisory body to the world's governments on the state of the science of the climate change issue.

FEDERAL LAWS AND AGENCIES

Global Change Research Act of 1990. This act (15 U.S.C. § 2933 *et seq.*) authorizes the 13 federal department and agencies to undertake scientific research to evaluate strategies to manage the impacts of climate change.

Kyoto Protocol. The United States did not ratify the Kyoto Protocol. In 2001, George W. Bush rejected the Kyoto Protocol and instead adopted the "Global Climate Change Policy" in 2002 which established a voluntary program intended to reduce GHG intensity in the United States by 18 percent from 2002 to 2012.

Clean Air Act. The United States Supreme Court in *Massachusetts v. EPA* (2007) 549 U.S. 497 declared that the federal CAA, as amended, gave EPA the authority to regulate GHGs as air pollutants if they "endanger public health or welfare."

National Environmental Policy Act. Council on Environmental Quality (CEQ) guidance issued in 2016 (CEQ 2016) confirmed that federal agencies must consider climate change in their NEPA documents. The guidance describes approaches for NEPA document analysis of GHG emissions, as well as the effects of climate change.

Executive Order 13653. Under EO 13653 ("Preparing the U.S. for the Impacts of Climate Change," issued in 2013), federal agencies must undertake a number of activities described later in this chapter to help the nation adapt to the impacts of climate change.

Executive Order 13693. This EO ("Federal Leadership on Climate Change and Environmental Sustainability," issued in 2015) sets a target of reducing the federal government's GHG emissions 40 percent by 2025, relative to 2008 levels. It directs federal agencies to undertake many measures to reduce GHG emissions, including ensuring that 25 percent of their total energy consumption is from clean energy sources by 2025. The EO revoked an earlier EO (13514) issued in 2009 that covered many of the same topics.

Environmental Protection Agency. EPA is responsible for implementing the CAA GHG regulatory program, including the mandatory GHG Reporting Program. EPA regulation of GHGs under the CAA is discussed in detail in this chapter.

DOE implements many research, development and demonstration programs to promote cleaner-burning fossils fuels, renewable energy, vehicle efficiency, transportation fuels, and energy efficiency.

Department of Energy. DOE implements many research, development and demonstration programs to promote cleaner-burning fossils fuels, renewable energy, vehicle efficiency, transportation fuels, and energy efficiency.

Department of Interior. The Department of Interior has established a Climate Change Response Council which coordinates response to the impacts of climate change within the various Bureaus within the Department. The Department also operates eight Regional Climate Science Centers that synthesize existing climate-change-impact data and management strategies. These centers are regional entities that extend from the National Climate Change and Wildlife Science Center, located at U.S. Geological Survey (USGS) headquarters.

U.S. Department of Agriculture. The Global Change Program Office coordinates the rural and forestry-related climate change programs for the USDA.

National Oceanic and Atmospheric Administration. NOAA provides timely and authoritative information about climate change, including providing data through the National Centers for Environmental Information. NOAA implements a global observing system to study and predict the effects of climate change, and helps plan for, and respond to climate change by exploring mitigation measures. It also helps coordinate preparation of the National Climate Assessment.

Department of State. Among other responsibilities, the Department of State must approve oil and gas pipelines crossing national boundaries. In 2015, in a highly publicized decision after years of study, it decided not to approve the proposed Keystone XL pipeline, which would have conveyed GHG-intensive tar sands oil from Canada.

U.S. Global Change Research Program. Congress in the Global Change Research Act of 1990 (PL 101-606) mandated this program to help the nation understand and respond to global change. Among other activities, the program coordinates preparation of the National Climate Assessment, a series of reports that assess the status of climate science and national climate change impacts. The Third National Climate Assessment was issued in 2014. Melillo et al. 2014.

The Climate Registry. The Climate Registry designed and operates the main voluntary GHG registry in North America. Hundreds of organizations report their emissions to this program, including leading corporations, universities, and local and state government agencies.

USGS = U.S. Geological Survey

USDA = U.S. Department of Agriculture

NOAA = National Oceanic and Atmospheric Administration

MWh = megawatt hour

RTP = regional transportation plan

SCS = Sustainable Communities Strategy

The Climate Registry designed and operates the main voluntary GHG registry in North America. Hundreds of organizations report their emissions to this program, including leading corporations, universities, and local and state government agencies.

STATE LAWS AND AGENCIES

Assembly Bill 32. AB 32 of 2006 (The California Global Warming Solutions Act, Health & Safety Code § 38500 *et seq.*) established a target of reducing California's GHG emissions to 1990 levels by 2020, and a regulatory program to achieve this target. Regulation of GHGs under AB 32 is discussed in detail in this chapter.

Senate Bill 1368. SB 1368 of 2006 (Chapter 598, Statutes of 2006) required the CEC and CPUC to establish a GHG emissions performance standard for "baseload" electricity generation of 1,100 lbs CO_2/megawatt hour (MWh).

Senate Bill 375. 375 of 2008 (Chapter 728, Statutes of 2008) requires Metropolitan Planning Organizations preparing regional transportation plans (RTPs) to adopt Sustainable Communities Strategies (SCSs) to designed to achieve specified GHG emissions reductions for cars and light trucks.

Senate Bill 350. SB 350 of 2015 (Chapter 547, Statutes of 2015) revises the state's Renewable Portfolio Standards Program by requiring utilities to procure at least 50 percent of the retail electricity from renewable sources by 2030. The law requires

CEC = California Energy Commission

CEQA = California Environmental Quality Act

NRA = Natural Resources Agency

WCI = Western Climate Initiative

the California Energy Commission (CEC) to establish annual energy efficiency standards designed to double the electricity and natural gas savings for existing buildings by 2030.

Senate Bill 32. SB 32 of 2016 (Chapter 249, Statutes of 2016) requires the ARB to ensure that statewide GHG emissions are reduced to a least 40 percent below 1990 levels by 2030.

Assembly Bill 197. AB 197 of 2016 (Chapter 250, Statutes of 2016) provides greater legislative oversight of ARB's GHG regulatory programs, requires ARB to account for the social costs of GHG emissions, and establishes a legislative preference for direct reductions of GHG emissions.

Green Building Standards. The 2013 California Green Building Standards Code (24 Cal. Code Regs. Part 11) took effect January 1, 2014. These comprehensive regulations are intended to achieve major reductions in GHG emissions, energy consumption, and water use.

California Environmental Quality Act. CEQA documents must analyze GHG impacts. SB 97 of 2007 (Pub. Res. Code § 21083.05) required the Natural Resources Agency (NRA) to adopt CEQA Guidelines amendments explaining how CEQA documents should analyze GHG impacts. The agency adopted these Guidelines amendments in late 2009. See chapter 2 for further information.

Western Climate Initiative. The WCI is a regional cap-and-trade program linked to AB 32; it includes California, British Columbia, Ontario, and Québec.

EO S-3-05, among other things, established the following GHG-emission reduction goals for California: reduction to 2000 levels by 2010; to 1990 levels by 2020; and to 80 percent below 1990 levels by 2050.

Executive Order S-3-05. EO S-3-05, among other things, established the following GHG-emission reduction goals for California: reduction to 2000 levels by 2010; to 1990 levels by 2020; and to 80 percent below 1990 levels by 2050.

Executive Order S-13-08. EO S-13-08 ordered preparation of a sea level rise assessment report, and ordered the California Natural Resources Agency (NRA) to prepare a state Climate Adaptation Strategy.

Executive Order B-16-12. EO B-16-12 orders state agencies to support the rapid commercialization of zero-emission vehicles. It directs these entities to achieve various benchmarks related to zero-emission vehicles. It also sets a state GHG emissions reduction target for the transportation sector of 80 percent below 1990 levels by 2050.

Executive Order B-18-12. EO B-18-12 requires California agencies to reduce their GHG emissions by at least 10 percent by 2015 and 20 percent by 2020 from a 2010 baseline. Agencies must also reduce overall water use at the facilities they operate by 10 percent by 2015 and by 20 percent by 2020 compared to a 2010 baseline. The EO also requires state agencies to take specific steps to increase the use of renewable energy and increase energy efficiency for new buildings.

Executive Order B-30-15. EO B-30-15, among other things, establishes a new interim statewide GHG reduction target to reduce emissions to 40 percent below

1990 levels by 2030 in order to ensure California meets its target of reducing GHG emissions to 80 percent below 1990 levels by 2050. It directs all state agencies with jurisdiction over sources of GHG emissions to implement measures to meet the 2030 and 2050 targets. The EO also establishes significant new climate adaptation policies including identification of vulnerabilities to climate change by sector or regions. Finally, it requires the NRA to update the state's climate adaptation strategy, Safeguarding California, every three years, and to ensure that its provisions are fully implemented.

CAT = Climate Action Team

ARB = Air Resources Board

CEC = California Energy Commission

CPUC = California Public Utilities Commission

CAPCOA = California Air Pollution Control Officers Association

Climate Action Team. The Governor's CAT is comprised of state agency secretaries and the heads of agencies, boards and departments, and is led by the Secretary of Cal/EPA. The CAT is authorized to coordinate statewide efforts to implement GHG emission reduction programs and the California Climate Adaptation strategy. These agencies also contribute to California Climate Change Assessment reports. The third Assessment was published in 2012 (California Climate Change Center 2012), and the fourth Assessment was under preparation when this book was published.

Air Resources Board. The ARB is the state's principle agency authorized to implement AB 32 and the mandatory GHG reporting program. It also sets motor vehicle emission standards that reduce GHGs. Under SB 375, ARB sets regional GHG reduction targets for cars and light trucks, and reviews SCSs for their ability to meet these targets.

California Energy Commission. The CEC is responsible for implementing Renewable Portfolio Standards (RPS), energy efficiency, and transportation fuels programs.

California Public Utilities Commission. The CPUC is responsible for implementing RPS and energy efficiency programs for investor-owned utilities, which it regulates.

The CPUC is responsible for implementing RPS and energy efficiency programs for investor-owned utilities, which it regulates.

Natural Resources Agency. The NRA is charged with preparing and updating the state's Climate Adaptation Strategy. It is also active in coordinating research for the California Climate Change Assessments.

REGIONAL AND LOCAL LAWS AND AGENCIES

Air districts. Local air districts are responsible for implementing the new source review permitting requirements and the Title V permitting program for GHG and criteria pollutant emissions. Many air districts also issue guidance for analyzing and mitigating GHG impacts under CEQA, and some have established other innovative programs for GHG reductions.

California Air Pollution Control Officers Association. CAPCOA has been active in issuing guidance for CEQA analysis of GHG impacts, mitigation of GHG impacts, and development of general plan policies to reduce GHG emissions. It also has established a GHG reduction exchange for purchase of GHG offsets.

MPO = Metropolitan Planning Organization

CAP = Climate Action Plan

Metropolitan Planning Organizations. Under SB 375, MPOs are regional planning agencies responsible for preparing SCSs and integrating them into their regional transportation plans.

Cities and counties. Many cities and counties have prepared or are preparing Climate Action Plans (CAPs). The scope of these plans typically includes setting GHG reduction targets and developing action plans for reducing both municipal and community-wide GHG emissions. Some CAPs also address climate adaptation strategies.

INTERNATIONAL PROGRAMS*

Pre-Kyoto. The1992 Earth Summit Treaty that was intended to stabilize GHG concentrations to "a level that would prevent dangerous anthropogenic interference with the climate system." Although the treaty did not set binding GHG emissions limits, it set a framework (known as "protocols") for establishing international agreements with binding GHG limits.

Kyoto Protocol. Parties to the UNFCC came together in 1997 to produce the Kyoto Protocol which established binding GHG limits for developed countries. The Kyoto Protocol required that the developed countries commit to reducing their GHG emissions to 5.2 percent below a 1990 baseline by 2012. The Kyoto Protocol was criticized for not including emissions from developing countries, and it was not ratified by the United States.

Cancun agreements. The world came together in 2010 in anticipation of the terms of the Kyoto Protocol expiring. This convention yielded a more modest agreement establishing a target to limit projected warming to no more than 2.0°C (3.6°F) above the pre-industrial temperature. This limit was intended to avoid the most severe impacts of future climate change. The developed countries agreed to GHG emissions targets by 2020, while developing countries committed to Nationally Appropriate Mitigation Actions to reduce GHG emissions below their business-as-usual projected emissions

Almost two hundred nations came together in Paris, France in December, 2015 for the United Nations Climate Change Conference and reached agreement on a revised global strategy to significantly reduce GHGs.

Paris 2015 United Nations Climate Change Conference (COP21). Almost two hundred nations came together in Paris, France in December, 2015 for the United Nations Climate Change Conference and reached agreement on a revised global strategy to significantly reduce GHGs. In an effort to keep global warming below an increase of 2.0°C (with an aspirational goal of below 1.5°C), the developed and developing countries pledged to rein in their GHGs, based on 188 previously submitted national climate plans. Implementation of all of these plans will still not accomplish the 2.0°C objective, thereby requiring further national commitments to reduce GHG emissions.

The United States and China COP21 plans were similar to those included in a 2014 U.S.-China joint announcement on climate change. In its climate plan, the

*For more information on these and other international programs, see the UNFCC website: unfccc.int/essential_background/items/6031.php

United States committed to reducing its GHG emissions by up to 28 percent by 2025 from 2005 levels. (This commitment was primarily based on EPA's Clean Power Plan, described below, which was promulgated in August 2015, and whose implementation was stayed by the Supreme Court in February 2016.) China pledged to peak its GHG emissions by 2030. China also agreed to increase its renewable energy goal to 20 percent by 2030 in order to displace energy generated by fossil fuels. Most of the displaced GHG emission reductions in China were to come through a national cap-and-trade system modeled somewhat on the California cap-and-trade program.

EU = European Union

HFC = hydrofluorocarbons

In addition, the signatories agreed that future national plans will be no less ambitious than existing ones, which means these 188 climate plans will provide the baseline for further necessary reductions. Countries are thus required to submit updated climate plans—called nationally determined contributions—every five years in order to close the gap between the national commitments and the 2.0°C objective. The signatories are also required to develop adaptation strategies which would be financed by an adaptation fund of $100 billion. Finally, the signatories agreed to develop an international system of transparency and accountability to track and report implementation efforts. The Paris Agreement entered into force November 4, 2016.

In addition, the signatories agreed that future national plans will be no less ambitious than existing ones, which means these 188 climate plans will provide the baseline for further necessary reductions.

The state of California was intensively engaged at all levels of the conference with the ultimate objective of integrating the California climate change program into a worldwide network of emissions trading and technology exchange.

European Union HFC limits. Fluorinated gases are potent GHGs that trap heat at a rate of 23,000 times that of CO_2. The EU limits the use of fluorinated gases by establishing a cap and reducing, by 2030, fluorinated gases by two-thirds from 2014 levels. The EU also established rules to prohibit HFCs in new refrigeration systems involving specified business sectors by 2022. Finally, EU issued a directive to replace these refrigerants with natural non-synthetic alternatives such as ammonia.

FEDERAL PROGRAMS

MASSACHUSETTS V. EPA

The United States Supreme Court in *Massachusetts v. EPA* (2007) 549 U.S. 497 ruled that EPA had the statutory authority under the CAA to regulate emissions of GHGs, because GHGs fit well within the Act's definition of "air pollutant." The court rejected as arbitrary and capricious EPA's refusal to decide whether GHGs cause climate change or should be regulated under the CAA. EPA subsequently issued endangerment findings under the CAA and began the regulatory program for GHGs described below. The endangerment findings and GHG regulatory program were upheld in *Coalition for Responsible Regulation v. EPA* (D.C. Cir. 2012) 684 F, 3d 102. EPA's CAA

CH_4 = methane

N_2O = nitrous oxide

HFC = hydrofluorocarbons

PFC = perfluorocarbons

SF_6 = sulfur hexafluoride

NF_3 = nitrogen trifluoride

HFE = hydro fluorinated ethers

PSD = prevention of significant deterioration

TPY = tons per year

"Carbon dioxide equivalent" (CO_2e) is a reference to the global warming potential of various GHGs compared to the global warming potential of CO_2. For example, the global warming potential for methane over 100 years is 20 to 23 times that of CO_2 on a per pound basis.

Used in the manufacture of consumer goods ranging from photovoltaic solar panels, LCD television screens, and microprocessors, NF_3 is a particularly potent GHG. Its global warming potential is 17,000 times greater than CO_2, and it persists in the atmosphere for 550 years.

regulatory authority displaces federal common law nuisance claims related to climate change. *American Electric Power Co. v. Connecticut* (2011) 135 S. Ct. 2537.

MANDATORY GHG REPORTING

An estimated 85 percent of the total U.S. GHG emissions are emitted from approximately 10,000 facilities. Major sources of GHGs that emit 25,000 metric tons or more per year of CO_2e must annually complete a GHG inventory and submit it to EPA. 49 C.F.R. Part 98. The annual GHG inventories are due by March 31 and must account for the actual GHGs emitted from the prior year. Facilities must quantify CO_2, methane (CH_4), nitrous oxide (N_2O), hydrofluorocarbons (HFC), perfluorocarbons (PFC), sulfur hexafluoride (SF_6), and other fluorinated gases including nitrogen trifluoride (NF_3) and hydro fluorinated ethers (HFE) in metric tons. EPA does not require third party verification validating the accuracy of the data; reporters are instead required to self-certify the accuracy of the data they submit to EPA.

This mandatory reporting obligation applies to suppliers of fossil fuels or industrial GHGs and manufacturers of vehicles and engines. EPA has established industry-specific reporting methodologies for calculating emissions sources including electronics manufacturing, ethanol production, fluorinated GHG production, food processing, industrial landfills, magnesium production, oil and natural gas systems, suppliers of coal, underground coal mines, wastewater treatment, and electrical equipment.

NEW SOURCE REVIEW AND TITLE V PERMITTING

EPA in 2010 issued regulations to require GHG emissions from the largest stationary sources to be covered by the prevention of significant deterioration (PSD) and Title V Operating Permit Programs beginning January 2, 2011. These CAA programs are described in chapter 5. The thresholds established in the CAA for determining when emissions of pollutants make a source subject to these permitting programs, 100 and 250 tons per year, were based on traditional ("criteria") pollutants and were not designed to be applied to GHGs.

EPA's GHG tailoring rule set initial emission thresholds—known as Steps 1 and 2 of the Tailoring Rule—for PSD and Title V permitting based on CO_2e emissions. 75 Fed. Reg. 31514 (June 3, 2010). Major new sources of GHGs emitting 100,000 TPY of CO_2e and modifications to existing major sources emitting 75,000 tons per year (TPY) of CO_2e were regulated. These major emitters of GHGs were required to install BACT, which is determined on a plant-wide basis.

The U.S. Supreme Court in *Utility Air Regulatory Group v. EPA* (2014) 134 S. Ct. 2427 revisited the tailoring rule and invalidated the major source GHG threshold definitions of 100,000 TPY of CO_2e and 75,000 TPY of CO_2e; however, it upheld EPA's authority to regulate GHG emissions for those facilities subject to PSD permitting for criteria pollutants ("anyway sources"). Thus, new source construction or modifications involving "major" emitters already subject to PSD due to emissions criteria pollutants are subject to PSD and Title V permitting that requires BACT to reduce GHG emissions.

The Supreme Court ruled that EPA may require an "anyway source" to comply with GHG BACT only if the source emits more than a *de minimis* amount of GHGs. It is estimated that EPA will still be able to regulate 83 percent of stationary source GHG emissions under the PSD and Title V permitting processes, because almost all these sources also emit significant quantities of criteria air pollutants.

Consistent with the Supreme Court decision, the D.C. Circuit issued an amended judgment in *Coalition for Responsible Regulation, Inc. v. Environmental Protection Agency* (D.C. Cir. April 10, 2015) Nos. 09-1322, 10-073, 10-1092 and 10-116. The amended judgment vacated the PSD and Title V tailoring regulations to the extent that they required a stationary source to obtain a PSD or Title V permit solely because the source emits GHGs above the applicable major source thresholds. EPA subsequently issued new regulations in 2015 removing several provisions of the PSD and Title V permitting regulations that were vacated by the D.C. Circuit amended judgment. 80 Fed. Reg. 50199 (August 19, 2015). It also issued regulations allowing the rescission of PSD permits under Step 2 of the tailoring rule. 80 Fed. Reg. 26183 (May 7, 2015).

NSPS = new source performance standards

VOC = volatile organic compound

CPP = EPA's Clean Power Plan

OIL AND GAS SECTOR NEW SOURCE PERFORMANCE STANDARDS

In 2016, EPA amended the new source performance standards (NSPS) for the oil and natural gas source category by setting standards for both GHGs and volatile organic compounds (VOC) for certain equipment, processes and activities. 81 Fed. Reg. 35824 (June 3, 2016). Regulated facilities include natural gas well sites, oil well sites, natural gas production gathering and boosting stations, gas processing plants, and natural gas transmission compressor stations.

POWER PLANT REGULATION

Approximately 40 percent of the electricity generated in the United States is derived from coal. The EPA's Clean Power Plan (CPP) established national limits on GHG emissions from existing and future coal-fired future power plants and generating units. 80 Fed. Reg. 64661 (October 23, 2015). By 2030, the CPP is targeted to reduce GHG emissions from the power sector by 32 percent below 2005 levels. The CPP is expected to yield co-benefits of reducing sulfur dioxide from power plants by 90 percent from 2005 levels and 72 percent lower emissions of nitrogen oxides.

Approximately 40 percent of the electricity generated in the United States is derived from coal.

The CPP requires each state to develop goals reflecting its unique energy portfolio and emissions targets for new, modified, and reconstructed power plants. The CPP establishes interim and final CO_2 emission performance rates for coal- and oil-fired power plants (known as fossil fuel-fired electric steam generating units) and natural gas-fired combined cycle generating units. States are required to design and implement plans enabling power plants within their state to meet interim CO_2 emissions performance rates from 2022 to 2029 and final CO_2 emission performance rates by 2030.

This rule requires states to reduce carbon emissions by an average of 32 percent below 2005 levels by 2030 and is premised on establishing a CO_2 emission performance rate for fossil fuel-fired electric SGUs and stationary combustion turbines. These power plants must adopt the "best system of emissions reduction...adequately demonstrated" for CO_2. State emission standards plans must establish requirements for all affected power plants within the state to meet state-wide emissions performance standards. A state measures plan can include a variety of performance measures such as renewable energy standards, switching to natural gas, improving the heat rate of existing coal-fired power plants, and establishing programs to improve residential energy efficiency. Alternatively, states can collaborate with other states to, among other strategies, trade emissions. 40 C.F.R. § 60.22 *et seq.*

The Clean Power Plan requires states to limit GHG emissions from fossil-fueled power plants.

In California, SB 1368 of 2006 (Chapter 598, Statutes of 2006) already required new base-load power plants by California's investor-owned utilities to comply with an emissions performance standard in line with emissions from combined cycle gas turbine plant (i.e., 1,100 pounds of CO_2 per megawatt-hour). In future implementation of the CPP in California, ARB anticipates that the state's cap-and-trade program (*see* below) will play a central role in the CPP compliance plan (ARB 2015).

On February 9, 2016, in a brief order (No. 15A773) responding to an application by states opposed to the CPP, the Supreme Court stayed implementation of the Clean Power Plan pending judicial review by the D.C. Circuit in the case *West Virginia v. Environmental Protection Agency*. The Court's decision was not on the merits of the rule. The order has been criticized as without precedent because the Supreme Court granted a stay of a generally applicable regulation prior to initial judicial review in the D.C. Circuit. It also was viewed as a setback to U.S. implementation of the Paris Agreement. As this book was being written, the case was scheduled to be heard before the full *en banc* panel of the D.C. Circuit Court of Appeals.

MOTOR VEHICLE EMISSIONS STANDARDS

Federal motor vehicle emissions standards, which reduce emissions of GHGs as well as criteria air pollutants, are reviewed in chapter 5. In addition, in 2016, EPA and the National Highway Traffic Administration jointly adopted new standards for medium- and heavy-duty vehicles (such as semi-trailer trucks). These standards substantially reduce GHG emission and fuel consumption. 81 Fed. Reg. 73477 (October 25, 2016).

LANDFILL GAS REGULATION

In 2016, EPA announced final updates to its NSPS to reduce emissions of methane-rich landfill gas from new, modified and reconstructed municipal solid waste

(MSW) landfills. In a separate action, EPA also issued guidelines for reducing emissions from existing MSW landfills. 81 Fed. Reg. 59332 (August 29, 2016).

BLM = Bureau of Land Management

FEDERAL LAND MANAGEMENT

Federal land management agencies such as the Bureau of Land Management (BLM) play several roles in reducing GHG emissions. BLM manages more federal land than any other agency: about 245 million surface acres as well as 700 million sub-surface acres of mineral estate. Through its leasing program, BLM can accelerate the construction of utility-scale renewable power plants and associated transmission lines. BLM and other federal land management agencies can also control the pace of leasing federal lands for fossil fuel exploration and production; for example, in 2016, the Obama Administration imposed a moratorium on new coal leases on federal lands.

Federal land management agencies can also implement policies and programs that increase carbon sequestration. For example, the U.S. Forest Service can establish sustainable forest practices such as planting new trees and improving forest health through thinning and prescribed burning. These practices can increase forest carbon in the long run.

STATE, REGIONAL, AND LOCAL PROGRAMS

AB 32, SB 32, AND AB 197

Overview. AB 32 is a pioneering state program creating a framework designed to comprehensively limit GHG emissions. This law sets forth a regulatory strategy to reduce the state's 2020 GHG emissions to the 1990 level, which the ARB has estimated at 431 million metric tons of CO_2e. This is a reduction of approximately 15 percent below emissions expected under a "business as usual" scenario. As of this writing, the state is on track to meet this goal. ARB 2014.

AB 32 sets forth a regulatory strategy to reduce the state's 2020 GHG emissions to the 1990 level, which the ARB has estimated at 431 million metric tons of CO_2e.

Figure 20-1 on the following page shows the percentage of California GHG emissions attributable to various sectors. As shown, the transportation sector in 2014 accounted for the highest percentage, approximately 37 percent.

AB 32 required ARB to do the following:

- Adopt mandatory GHG reporting regulations
- Prepare and approve a Scoping Plan for achieving the maximum technologically feasible and cost-effective reductions in GHG emissions from sources or categories of sources of GHGs by 2020, and update the Scoping Plan every five years
- Maintain and continue reductions in emissions of GHG beyond 2020
- Identify the statewide level of GHG emissions in 1990 to serve as the emissions limit to be achieved by 2020
- Identify and adopt regulations for discrete early actions that could be enforceable on or before January 1, 2010

SLCP = short-lived climate pollutant

GWP = global warming potential

MT = metric tons

FIGURE 20-1
California 2014 GHG Inventory

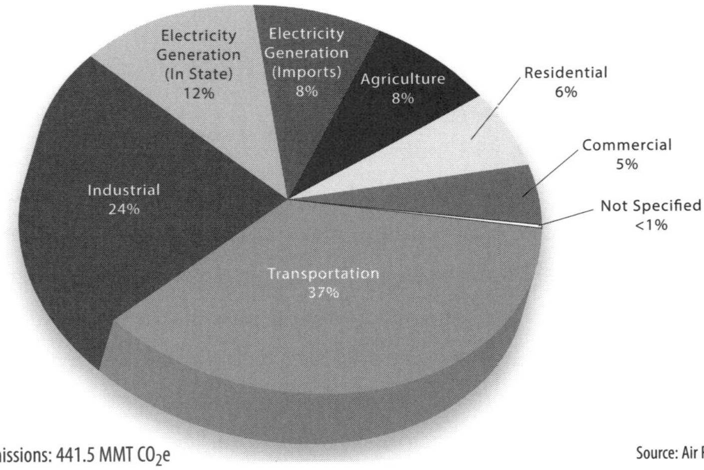

2014 Total California Emissions: 441.5 MMT CO_2e

Source: Air Resources Board

California has joined over 165 jurisdictions across the globe by signing a memorandum of understanding (the Subnational Global Climate Leader Initiative [Under2MOU.org]) that commits those governments to reducing their GHG emissions. Specifically, they agreed to limit GHG emissions by at least 80 percent of 1990 levels by 2050 or to reduce per capita CO_2 emissions to under two metric tons.

- Adopt a regulation that establishes a system of market-based declining annual aggregate emission limits for sources or categories of sources that emit GHG emissions

AB 32 and subsequent amendments define GHG as carbon dioxide, methane, nitrous oxide, hydrofluorocarbons, perfluorocarbons, sulfur hexafluoride, NF_3, and short-lived climate pollutants (SLCPs). SLCPs are a collection of pollutants that includes black carbon, methane, tropospheric ozone, and some HFCs. SLCPs are more impactful than CO_2e with respect to climate change potency and remain in the atmosphere between weeks and a few decades. This category of high GWP pollutants has a heat-trapping capacity, on a per-ton basis, of 150 times or higher than CO_2.

Mandatory GHG reporting. AB 32 required ARB to adopt mandatory GHG emission reporting regulations. Health & Safety Code § 38530 *et seq*. The regulations (17 Cal. Code Regs. § 95100 *et seq*.) requires the monitoring and annual reporting of GHG emissions from industrial facilities, fuel suppliers, and electricity importers. Beginning in 2008, facilities that emit more than 25,000 metric tons of CO_2e per year (MT CO_2e/yr) must annually report their GHG emissions. These operators must report GHG emissions from stationary combustion and process emissions including CO_2 captured and transferred off-site. Unlike the federal mandatory GHG reporting program, emission reports must be audited by third-party verifiers with specified credentials.

In the following facilities, electricity generation units that report CO_2 mass emissions throughout the year (pursuant to 40 C.F.R. Part 75) must report annual GHG emissions regardless of their emissions level:

- Cement production
- Lime manufacturing

- Nitric acid production
- Petroleum refineries
- Geologic sequestration of carbon dioxide
- Subsurface Injection of carbon dioxide

Facilities generating GHG emissions of at least 10,000 MT CO_2e/year from stationary combustion sources and process emissions must also annually report their GHG emissions. However, these emitters are not required to report the vented and fugitive emissions. This lower threshold for reporting applies to, among others, fuel suppliers, electric power entities, petroleum and natural gas system operators, and certain other operations.

Initial Scoping Plan. The AB 32 Scoping Plan serves as the blueprint to achieve the maximum technologically feasible and cost-effective reductions in GHG emissions from specific sources by 2020. The first scoping plan (ARB 2008) set forth a five-year strategy and 74 measures to help ensure that California's long-term GHG reductions are on track to meet the GHG reduction targets. Key elements of the initial Scoping Plan included the following (ARB 2014):

The AB 32 Scoping Plan serves as the blueprint to achieve the maximum technologically feasible and cost-effective reductions in GHG emissions from specific sources by 2020.

- Expand and strengthen energy efficiency programs, including building and appliance standards
- Increase electricity generation from renewable resources to at least 33 percent of the statewide electricity mix by 2020
- Establish targets for passenger vehicle-related GHG emissions for regions throughout California and pursue policies and incentives to achieve those targets
- Adopt and implement measures pursuant to existing state laws and policies, including California's clean car standards and the Low Carbon Fuel Standard
- Develop a cap-and-trade program to ensure the GHG emissions target is met, while providing flexibility to California businesses to reduce emissions at low cost

Many of these strategies have been incorporated into regulations. ARB adopted GHG rules and market mechanisms by January 1, 2012, at which time they became legally enforceable.

The Scoping Plan was legally challenged as not meeting AB 32's requirements. In *Association of Irritated Residents v. California Air Resources Board* (2012) 206 Cal. App. 4th 1487, the court held that the Scoping Plan did not improperly limit GHG reduction measures, adequately addressed cost-effectiveness determinations, and properly selected strategies for controlling industrial and agricultural sector emissions.

Scoping Plan update. ARB approved the first update to the Scoping Plan in 2014. ARB 2014. This update defines ARB's climate change priorities for the next five years.

Table 20-1. Meeting the 2020 Emissions Target

Category	2020 MMT CO_2e
AB 32 Baseline (Business as Usual) Forecast Emissions	509
Expected Reductions from Sector-Based Measures	
Energy	25
Transportation	23
High-GWP	5
Waste	2
Cap-and-Trade Reductions	23
2020 Limit	431

Source: ARB 2014

The update describes progress made to meet the near-term objectives of AB 32 and defines California's climate change priorities and activities for the next several years. It concludes that California is on track to meet the 2020 GHG limit and is well positioned to maintain and continue reductions beyond 2020. Table 20-1 shows expected reductions from different sectors necessary to achieve the 2020 limit.

The update identifies eight key focus areas comprising the major areas of California's economy and recommendations for developing additional requirements to meet the 2050 goals expressed in EO S-3-05. While the update discusses setting a mid-term target between 2020 and 2050, it does not recommend any numeric post-2020 targets, nor does it recommend a specific plan or specific actions showing how the state would meet the 2050 EO goal. The magnitude of the reductions needed to achieve the EO 2050 goal is shown in Figure 20-2.

SB 32 and second update to Scoping Plan. Executive Order B-30-15 established a mid-term GHG reduction target for California of 40 percent below 1990 levels by 2030. ARB was directed to update the AB 32 Scoping Plan to reflect the 2030 target, and at the time this book was being written, was moving forward with the update process. SB 32 of 2016 (Chapter 249, Statutes of 2016) codified the EO B-30-15 target, and requires the ARB in adopting GHG reduction rules and regulations to ensure that statewide GHG emissions are reduced to a least 40 percent below 1990 levels by 2030. SB 32 thus confirmed ARB's authority to regulate GHG emissions through 2030.

Executive Order B-30-15 established a mid-term GHG reduction target for California of 40 percent below 1990 levels by 2030.

AB 197. AB 197 of 2016 (Chapter 250, Statutes of 2016) provides greater legislative oversight of ARB's GHG regulatory programs. It established a legislative oversight committee to which the Chair of ARB must report annually, and added two ex-officio members of the legislature to the air board. Also, it required ARB, in implementing SB 32's 2030 GHG reduction target, to 1) prioritize emissions reductions to consider the "social costs" of GHG emissions and 2) prioritize "direct emission reductions" at large stationary sources and at mobile sources. These provisions responded to

FIGURE 20-2

Pre-2020 and Post-2020 GHG Emissions Trajectory

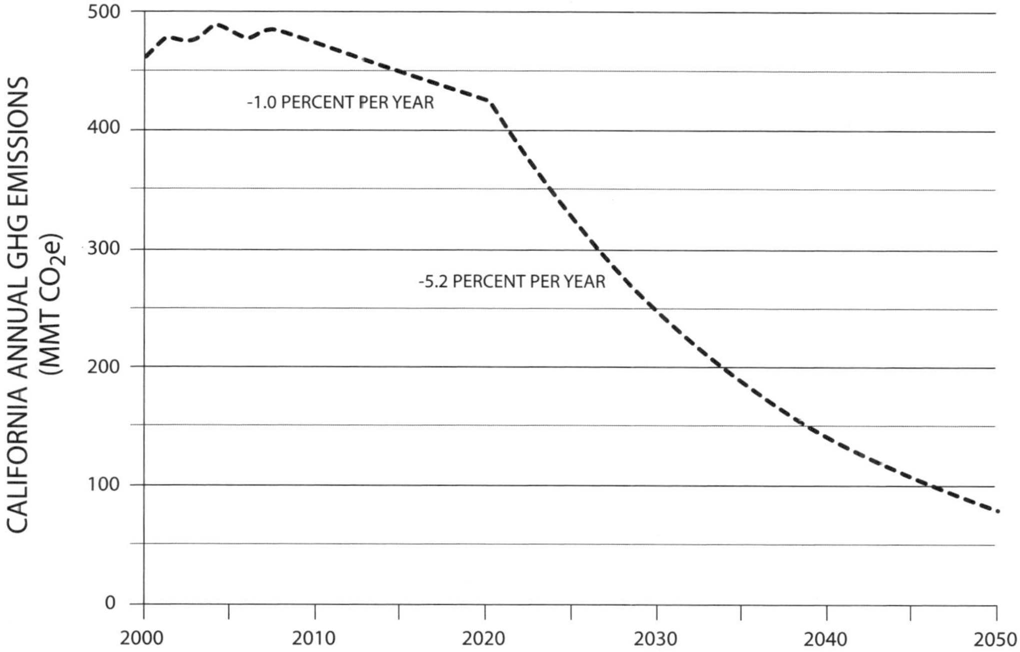

NOTE: Trajectory based on constant percentage reduction.

Source: Air Resources Board

environmental justice community concerns about the "indirect" GHG emission reductions achieved by the cap-and-trade program (*see* description below). Environmental justice groups generally oppose the cap-and trade program. The program allows large sources of both GHG and criteria pollutant emissions that are located in disadvantaged communities to continue emissions by purchasing GHG allowances.

Environmental justice groups generally oppose the cap-and trade program. The program allows large sources of both GHG and criteria pollutant emissions that are located in disadvantaged communities to continue emissions by purchasing GHG allowances.

TRANSPORTATION-RELATED MEASURES

The AB 32 Scoping Plan and Scoping Plan Update, along with other regulatory programs, target the transportation sector which contributes approximately 40 percent of the GHG emissions in California. The ARB has adopted several rules designed to diversify the state's transportation fuel mix to decrease the GHG gases generated from fossil fuels, and establish a sustainable market for cleaner-burning fuels. Specific transportation-related measures are described below.

Low-Carbon Fuel Standard. The LCFS establishes a target to reduce the carbon intensity of transportation fuel (e.g., gasoline and diesel) used in passenger vehicles by a minimum of 10 percent by 2020. This means that fuel providers (i.e., refiners, importers, and blenders of passenger vehicle fuels) in California must ensure that the mix of fuel they sell into the California market, on average, meets a declining standard for GHG emissions, taking into account upstream life cycle. Fuel producers are given flexibility on how to achieve this goal. For example, they may adopt

LCFS = low-carbon fuel standard

LEV = low-emission vehicle

strategies to incorporate increased levels of low-carbon ethanol into gasoline or instead buy credits from electric utilities that generate power from renewable sources of energy. Low carbon fuels are also subject to the cap-and-trade program. 17 Cal. Code Regs. § 95480 *et seq.*

The LCFS was upheld in *Rocky Mountain Farmers Union v. Corey* (9th Cir. 2013) 730 F3d 1070. In that case, the LCFS life cycle analysis was found not to unconstitutionally discriminate against out-of-state producers. In state court, ARB's approval of the LCFS was found to have violated certain provisions of the Administrative Procedure Act and CEQA. *Poet, LLC v. California Air Resources Board* (2013) 218 Cal. App. 4th 681. However, the Court of Appeal allowed the LCFS to remain in place while ARB took action to comply with these statutes.

AB 692 of 2015 (Chapter 588, Statutes of 2015) is intended to increase LCFS use by requiring California agencies to purchase at least three percent of "very low carbon transportation fuels," beginning January 1, 2017. State agencies must purchase an additional one percent per year thereafter until 2024.

GHG emissions standards and Advanced Clean Cars Program. As described in chapter 5, AB 1493 of 2002 (Chapter 200, Statutes of 2002) required California to establish new standards for motor vehicle GHG emissions beginning in the model year 2009. Health & Safety Code §§ 42823, 43018.5. AB 1493 mandated a 30 percent reduction in motor vehicle GHG emissions by 2016. ARB adopted implementing regulations in 2005. 13 Cal. Code Regs. §§ 1900, 1961, 1961.1. California's GHG emission standards withstood legal challenge in *Central Valley Chrysler Jeep, Inc. v. Goldstene* (2007) 529 F. Supp. 2d 1151.

A new emissions-control program for model years 2017 through 2025 combines the control of conventional air pollutants and GHGs, and requirements for greater numbers of zero-emission vehicles, into a single package of standards called Advanced Clean Cars.

In 2012, ARB approved a new emissions-control program for model years 2017 through 2025. The program combines the control of conventional air pollutants and GHGs, and requirements for greater numbers of zero-emission vehicles, into a single package of standards called Advanced Clean Cars (13 Cal. Code Regs. §§ 1962.1, 1962.2). The Advanced Clean Cars requirements include new GHG standards for model year 2017 to 2025 vehicles.

The Advanced Clean Cars Program also includes the Low Emission Vehicle (LEV) III amendments to the LEV regulations (13 Cal. Code Regs. § 1900 *et seq.*), the Zero Emission Vehicle Program, and the Clean Fuels Outlet Regulation. The Zero Emission Vehicle Program is designed to achieve California's long-term emission reduction goals by requiring manufacturers to offer for sale specific numbers of zero-emission vehicles, which include battery electric, fuel cell, and plug-in hybrid electric vehicles. The Clean Fuels Outlet regulation is intended to ensure that fuels such as electricity and hydrogen are available to meet the fueling needs of the new advanced technology vehicles as they come to market.

Executive Order B-16-12. EO B-16-12 established a goal of reducing GHG emissions from the transportation sector to 80 percent below 1990 levels by 2050. It also requires state entities to facilitate the rapid commercialization of zero-emission vehicles to achieve over 1.5 million zero-emission vehicles by 2025.

Assembly Bill 1236. AB 1236 of 2015 (Chapter 598, Statutes of 2015) removes barriers for approval of new electric vehicle (EV) charging stations and requires cities and counties to adopt ordinances creating an expedited permitting process for EV charging stations. Cities and counties may not deny an application for a use permit to install an EV charging station unless they make written findings that the proposed installation would have a specific, unavoidable adverse impact upon public health or safety.

EV = electric vehicle

ASP = automobile service provider

Heavy-duty vehicle GHG regulation. Heavy-duty vehicle regulations (13 Cal. Code Regs. § 2020 *et seq.)* reduce GHG emissions by improving the fuel efficiency of heavy-duty tractors that pull 53-foot or longer box-type trailers. Fuel efficiency is improved through improvements in tractor and trailer aerodynamics and the use of low rolling resistance tires.

Executive Order B-32-15. EO B-32-15 directs several state agencies to develop an integrated freight action plan. The integrated action plan is intended to improve freight efficiency, transition to zero-emission technologies, and increase competitiveness of California's freight system. The California Sustainable Freight Action Plan was adopted in 2016.

EO B-32-15 directs several state agencies to develop an integrated freight action plan intended to improve freight efficiency, transition to zero-emission technologies, and increase competitiveness of California's freight system.

Shore power electrification and port drayage trucks. Regulations described in chapter 5 for electrified shore power for ships at port, and for port drayage trucks, reduce GHG emissions as well as conventional pollutant emissions.

Tire pressure program. The purpose of ARB's tire pressure regulation is to reduce GHG emissions from vehicles operating with under-inflated tires by inflating them to the recommended tire pressure rating. This regulation requires automobile service providers (ASPs), when servicing passenger vehicles, to check and inflate vehicle tire pressures. 17 Cal. Code Regs. § 95550. SB 1076 of 2012 (Chapter 329, Statutes of 2012) expands upon this rule and, until January 1, 2018, requires ASPs to use tire pressure gauges that are accurate within a range of plus or minus two pounds per square inch of pressure.

Charge Ahead California Initiative. SB 1275 of 2014 (Chapter 530, Statutes of 2014) establishes the Charge Ahead California Initiative. The Initiative directs ARB to establish a funding plan and programs to achieve the goals of placing in service at least one million zero-emission and near-zero-emission vehicles by 2C13, establishing a self-sustaining market for these vehicles, and increasing access to these vehicles for disadvantaged, low-income, and moderate-income communities.

CAP-AND-TRADE PROGRAM

Overview. Most of the AB 32 emission reductions targeted by 2020 are intended to come from the regulatory programs discussed above. The remaining emissions reductions would come from a market-based cap-and-trade program modeled to a certain extent on the CAA acid rain program. This program targeted the removal of 273 million metric tons CO_2 by 2020.

The cap-and-trade program established a declining ceiling beginning on January 1, 2013 for GHG emissions for its first "capped" sector.

The cap-and-trade program established a declining ceiling beginning on January 1, 2013 for GHG emissions for its first "capped" sector. This cap applies to 360 businesses representing 600 facilities in California. The cap limits GHG emissions from large industrial facilities (that include electric generating utilities, electricity importers, and manufacturers of glass, paper, concrete and other industrial products) that annually emit over 25,000 MT CO_2e. The collective cap is set at approximately two percent below the GHG emissions forecast for 2012. That cap declined about another two percent in 2014 and will decline by three percent annually from 2015 to 2020.

This program sends a market signal that essentially requires businesses to purchase or sell GHG allowances and offsets. Businesses that were capped under the first phase were issued free allowances (one allowance equates to one metric ton of GHGs) for GHG emissions reflecting existing production levels for the facility. Some of these allowances were auctioned by the ARB.

A capped entity may meet eight percent of its compliance obligations with emissions offsets, which are emission reductions that can be purchased for certain projects not subject to the cap (e.g., forestry, rice cultivation). Offsets must be generated voluntarily and not accrue as a result of a regulatory requirement or constitute current ordinary business practice. These offsets are verified in compliance with ARB-approved offset protocols which include GHG reductions generated from forestry, urban forestry, dairy manure digesters, the destruction of ODS, rice cultivation, and the capture and destruction of fugitive mine methane and coal mine methane.

The cap and trade regulation allows ARB to approve independent offset project registries to oversee the registration of third-party GHG project verifiers. These GHG offsets can be used to comply with the offset program. Offset project registries facilitate the listing, reporting, and verification of GHG offset projects and issue registry GHG offset credits.

The three currently approved ARB registries are American Carbon Registry, Climate Action Reserve, and Verified Carbon Standard. These registries screen potential offset protocols and projects for ultimate ARB approval for the regulated carbon market. They additionally provide technical expertise and guidance to potential offset protocol and project developers. They have expanded into international initiatives in Mexico and other foreign countries which are currently outside of the California cap-and-trade program but may be linked in the future.

The second phase of the cap-and-trade program commenced on January 1, 2015 and includes distributors of transportation, natural gas and other fuels. The GHG emissions from this capped sector are set to decline approximately three percent each year between 2015 and 2020. California businesses can trade allowances within California and within the WCI which includes a regional GHG auction platform and tracking system.

RPS = Renewable Portfolio Standards

Greenhouse Gas Reduction Fund. ARB held its first auction of GHG allowances on November 14, 2012. Auctions are held every three months. All proceeds from the auction or sale of allowances must be deposited in a Greenhouse Gas Reduction Fund for appropriation by the Legislature. Gov't Code § 16428.8 *et seq.*

The Department of Finance is required to develop and submit to the Legislature a three-year investment plan for the Greenhouse Gas Reduction Fund every three years, starting in fiscal year 2013. Gov't Code § 39716. A minimum of 25 percent of the available funds must be used to fund projects located within and benefiting disadvantaged communities, with additional smaller set-asides for low-income households or communities. Gov't Code § 39713. Disadvantaged communities include urban communities located near maritime ports, major industrial sources, freeways, rail yards, and densely populated communities in the Central Valley.

A minimum of 25 percent of the Greenhouse Gas Reduction Fund must be used to fund projects located within and benefiting disadvantaged communities, with additional smaller set-asides for low-income households or communities.

SB 862 of 2014 (Chapter 36, Statutes of 2014) makes the following continuous appropriations of Greenhouse Gas Reduction Funds:

- 25 percent to the California high-speed rail project
- 20 percent to the Affordable Housing and Sustainable Communities Program, administered by the Strategic Growth Council
- 15 percent to the transit capital and operations programs

The remaining 40 percent of the funds are allocated by the Legislature annually.

ENERGY-RELATED MEASURES

The Legislature and state agencies have adopted many policies and programs that promote use of renewable energy, energy efficiency, or otherwise have the effect of reducing GHG emissions from the energy sector. Some of the most important of these are described below.

Performance standard for baseline power generation. SB 1368 of 2006 (Chapter 598, Statutes of 2006) required the CPUC to establish a GHG emissions performance standard for "baseload" generation from investor-owned utilities of 1,100 lbs/MWh. The CEC established a similar standard for local publicly owned utilities. All electricity provided to California, including imported electricity, must be generated from plants that meet or exceed this standard.

Renewable energy. The California Solar Initiative (SB 1, Chapter 132, Statutes of 2006, also known as the "Million Solar Roofs" legislation) set a goal of installing 3,000 megawatts of new solar capacity by 2017.

SB 350 of 2015 (Chapter 547, Statutes of 2015) revises the state's Renewable Portfolio Standards (RPS) Program by requiring utilities to procure at least 50 percent of the retail electricity from renewable sources by 2030; interim targets are 40 percent by 2024 and 45 percent by 2027. The former target was 33 percent by 2020. Technologies eligible for the RPS include photovoltaics; solar thermal electric; wind; certain biomass resources; geothermal electric; certain hydroelectric facilities; ocean wave, thermal and tidal energy; fuel cells using renewable fuels; landfill gas; and municipal solid waste conversion. The bill allows compliance flexibility for publicly owned utilities that satisfy 50 percent or more of their retail sales from specified large hydropower.

In addition, in 2013 the Legislature enacted the Green Tariff Shared Renewables Program. Pub. Util. Code § 2831 *et seq*. Participating utilities were required to file an application for a green tariff shared renewable program with the CPUC, which enables ratepayers to participate directly in off-site electricity generation facilities that use eligible renewable energy resources. CPUC is required to approve the application if consistent with the legislation establishing the program.

Energy efficiency. The CEC has for many years established energy efficiency standards for buildings (24 Cal. Code Regs. Part 6) and appliances (20 Cal. Code Regs. § 1601 *et seq*.). California's Building Energy Efficiency Standards are updated on an approximate three-year cycle. SB 350 of 2016 requires the CEC to establish annual energy efficiency standards designed to double the electricity and natural gas savings for existing buildings in the state by 2030, and develop a comprehensive program to achieve those standards.

The California Green Building Standards (25 Cal. Code Regs. Part 11) establish mandatory performance standards addressing the design and construction of buildings designed to maximize energy efficiency, conserve water, and reduce waste. These standards apply to new construction for low-rise and high-rise structures and to additions or alterations to existing residential buildings.

SB 17 of 2009 (Chapter 327, Statutes of 2009) established a state "smart grid," and required each electrical corporation to develop and submit a smart grid deployment plan to CPUC for approval by July 1, 2011. "Smart grid" means a distribution system that allows for the flow of information from a customer's meter in two directions, and modernizes the electric distribution. For a customer to take full advantage of their smart meter's capabilities, the customer must acquire energy management technologies so they may monitor their energy consumption in real time and respond to local control signals. AB 793 of 2015 (Chapter 589, Statutes of 2015) requires electrical corporations to develop an incentive program for customers to acquire energy management technology, and to educate customers to better understand and control their electricity use.

"Smart grid" means a distribution system that allows for the flow of information from a customer's meter in two directions, and modernizes the electric distribution.

For industrial facilities, the initial AB 32 Scoping Plan prompted a rule requiring the state's largest industrial facilities to complete a one-time (by December 15, 2011) fuel and energy efficiency assessment. 17 Cal. Code Regs. § 95600 *et seq*. ARB subsequently received assessment reports from 43 industrial facilities covering five industrial sectors: refinery, cement, hydrogen production, power generation, and oil and gas/mineral production. ARB will use these reports to identify the best approaches to secure energy efficiency improvements and the associated emission reductions at California's largest facilities. ARB 2014.

Executive Order B-18-12 orders all new state buildings and major renovations beginning design after 2025 be constructed as Zero Net Energy (ZNE) facilities. The EO sets an interim target for 50 percent of new facilities beginning design after 2020 to be ZNE. It directs state agencies to take measures toward achieving ZNE for 50 percent of the square footage of existing state-owned building area by 2025.

ZNE = Zero Net Energy

CFC = chlorofluorocarbons

HCFC = hydrochlorofluorocarbons

N_2O = nitrous oxide

MMT = million metric tons

OTHER INDUSTRIAL EMISSIONS

Overview. Industrial sources account for approximately 20 percent of California's total GHG emissions. Most emission reductions from industry under AB 32 will be realized through the cap-and-trade program. ARB has also assessed the potential for direct regulation measures that could be implemented at the industrial facilities. In addition, fugitive emissions from industrial facilities (primarily methane emissions) are not part of the cap-and-trade program. Therefore, ARB has considered direct regulations for industrial sources with significant fugitive GHG emissions—oil and gas extraction, natural gas transmission, and refineries. ARB 2014.

Fluorinated gas limits. High-technology chip manufacturers are required to reduce fluorinated gas emissions by 56 percent. Owners or operators of semiconductor operations and related device operations using fluorinated gases or heat transfer fluids must annually submit reports to their local air district quantifying emissions of fluorinated gases along with CO_2e emissions by March 1 annually. 17 Cal. Code Regs. § 95320 *et seq.*

Sulfur hexafluoride rules. Individuals who use, possess, purchase, distribute, manufacture, offer for sale or sell SF_6 or products containing SF_6 in California are also regulated and subject to reductions. The SF_6 rules prohibit intentionally emitting SF_6 in California and further prohibit the sale, supply and distribution of SF_6 in California. Owners of SF_6 gas-insulated switch gear, or electrical power equipment insulated with SF_6 gas (such as switches, fuses, electrical transmission lines, transformers and/or circuit breakers) are subject to specified SF_6 emission rate limitations. The limits drop to no more than one percent by 2020.17 Cal. Code Regs. § 95350 *et seq.*

SF_6 is a particularly strong GHG which is 23,000 times more potent in trapping heat than carbon dioxide and remains in the atmosphere for hundreds of years.

High GWP refrigerant use. In an effort to limit high (GWP) gases and remove five million tons of CO_2e (MMT CO_2e) of GHG by 2020, the ARB requires lower GWP alternatives in consumer products and in new motor vehicle air conditioning systems. These chemicals and refrigerants include propellants, chlorofluorocarbons (CFC), hydrochlorofluorocarbons (HCFCs), certain HFC refrigerants, and nitrous oxide (N_2O). The ARB restricts high GWP chemicals used in foam insulation along with products including boat horns, dusters, and tire inflators.

MVAC = motor vehicle air conditioner

Most of the high GWP emissions come from HFCs. ARB regulations, among other requirements, limit high-GWP refrigerant leaks from stationary refrigeration equipment and minimize emissions resulting from installation, maintenance, servicing, repair, and disposal of appliances containing high-GWP refrigerants. 17 Cal. Code Regs.. § 95380 *et seq*.

The ARB also regulates retailers who sell and companies that package, distribute or market small cans of motor vehicle air conditioner (MVAC) refrigerants. These include the highly potent R-134a GHG used by "do-it-yourself" consumers who recharge MVAC systems. Self-sealing valves are required on all containers, including specified labeling instructions, a recycling program for used containers, and an education program emphasizing best practices for vehicle recharging. 17 Cal. Code Regs. § 95361 *et seq*.

Gas pipeline facilities. SB 1371 of 2014 (Chapter 525, Statutes of 2014) requires the CPUC to adopt regulations for intrastate gas pipelines under its jurisdiction to minimize leaks. Methane, a potent GHG, is the primary component of natural gas.

WASTE MANAGEMENT

The primary source of GHG emissions from the waste and materials management sector includes direct methane emissions associated with the decomposition of organic materials in landfills.

The primary source of GHG emissions from the waste and materials management sector includes direct methane emissions associated with the decomposition of organic materials in landfills. The initial Scoping Plan focused on reducing fugitive methane emissions from landfills, reducing waste generation, and beneficially reusing wastes. Landfill owners or operators of active landfills (having less than 450,000 tons of waste-in-place) may be required to install a methane collection and control system to manage methane emissions from municipal solid waste landfills for those landfills that were previously unregulated. 17 Cal. Code Regs. § 95460.

The initial Scoping Plan also called for mandatory commercial recycling, which the Legislature later codified in AB 341 (Chapter 476, Statutes of 2011). That law increases California's solid waste diversion goal to no less than 75 percent by 2020 and requires local governments to develop and implement solid waste recycling programs to divert solid waste from businesses. Specifically, businesses, public entities, and multifamily residential buildings (with five or more units) that generate more than four cubic yards of solid waste weekly must arrange for recycling.

WATER

A considerable amount of energy is used moving water throughout California. Approximately 19 percent of the electricity and 30 percent of non-power plant natural gas consumption is used by the water sector (ARB 2014). To reduce GHG emissions from the water sector, the Scoping Plan Update calls for three basic strategies: prioritizing investments in conservation, adopting rate structures and pricing that maximize conservation, and promoting less energy-intensive water management.

The Water Conservation Act (SB X7-7 Stats. 2009) was enacted to conserve urban and agricultural water in California. This law established a goal to reduce per capita water use in California by 20 percent by 2020. Executive Order B-18-12 requires California agencies to reduce overall water use at the facilities they operate by 10 percent by 2015 and by 20 percent by 2020 compared to a 2010 baseline. Chapter 13 reviews additional water conservation and water supply planning programs.

SLCP = short-lived climate pollutant

NATURAL AND WORKING LANDS.

Three-quarters of California's landmass comprises biologically diverse landscapes such as forests, woodlands, shrublands, grasslands and wetlands. Although natural lands serve as a source of GHG emissions, they also have the capacity to remove or sequester CO_2 from the atmosphere. The initial Scoping Plan included a Sustainable Forest Target, whose goal was to maintain net carbon sequestration on forest lands. The Scoping Plan Update calls for a Forest Carbon Plan designed to establish longer term carbon reduction and sequestration strategies involving forestry, and identify funding recommendations to implement these strategies.

AGRICULTURE

Agricultural sources of GHG emissions account for approximately eight percent of California's carbon footprint. California's agricultural GHG emissions include on-site emissions from enteric fermentation (by animals), manure management, rice cultivation, energy use (including fuel combustion), crop residue burning, and soil management practices (fertilizer and manure applications).

Agricultural sources of GHG emissions account for approximately eight percent of California's carbon footprint.

The initial Scoping plan called for several voluntary GHG reduction measures rather than regulation due primarily to costs and scientific uncertainty in measuring GHGs in many agricultural systems. GHG reduction strategies from the agricultural sector include carbon sequestration on agricultural land, anaerobic digestion at dairies, increasing water use efficiency, electrifying agricultural water pumps, expanding the use of biomass-based fuels, and increasing fuel efficiency of farm equipment. The Scoping Plan Update, among other actions, recommends establishing interim and 2050 agricultural sector GHG reduction targets, methane capture standards for dairies, and possible modifications to a statewide GHG nitrous oxide inventory for fertilizer.

SHORT-LIVED CLIMATE POLLUTANTS

SB 605 of 2014 (Chapter 523, Statutes of 2014) calls for ARB to develop a Short-Lived Climate Pollutant (SLCP) Strategy. SLCPs include black carbon (soot), methane, and fluorinated gases (F-gases, including HFCs). ARB issued an initial proposed SLCP Strategy in April 2016.

Also, AB 1496 of 2015 (Chapter 604, Statutes of 2015) expands upon SB 605 by requiring ARB to monitor high-emission hot spots of methane. The ARB must

BAAQMD = Bay Area Air Quality Management District

SCAQMD = Southern California Air Quality Management District

GHG Rx = Greenhouse Gas Reduction Exchange

CAP = Climate Action Plan

also consult with federal and state agencies to gather information for performing life-cycle analysis of GHG emissions from natural gas imports.

SB 1383 of 2016 (Chapter 395, Statutes of 2016) sets forth more specific legislative direction for control of SLCPs. It requires ARB, no later than January 1, 2018, to approve and begin implementing its SLCP strategy to achieve the following reductions in emissions by 2030 compared to 2013 levels: methane by 40 percent, hydrofluorocarbons by 40 percent, and black carbon (non-forest) by 50 percent. The bill also specifies targets for reducing organic waste in landfills. SB 1383 also requires ARB to adopt regulations to be implemented on or after January 1, 2024 specific to the dairy and livestock industry, requiring a 40 percent reduction in methane emissions below 2013 levels by 2030, if certain conditions are met. Lastly, the bill requires CalRecycle to adopt regulations to take effect on or after January 1, 2022 to achieve specified targets for reducing organic waste in landfills.

In November 2016, ARB issued a revised SLCP Strategy. This strategy is consistent with SB 1383's legislative direction.

REGIONAL AND LOCAL PROGRAMS

Air districts. In addition to regulating stationary source GHG emissions and setting CEQA GHG thresholds of significance, some California air districts have pioneered other innovative local climate change programs. For example, the Bay Area Air Quality Management District (BAAQMD) collects a fee of 4.4¢ per ton of carbon dioxide emitted. This was the first program of its kind in the country. Also, the Southern California Air Quality Management District's (SCAQMD) SoCal Climate Solutions Exchange (Rule 270) allows individuals and companies to voluntarily reduce their GHG emissions from a given source and register those reductions. These businesses may sell reduction certificates to those seeking compliance with CEQA or another purpose.

In addition to regulating stationary source GHG emissions and setting CEQA GHG thresholds of significance, some California air districts have pioneered other innovative local climate change programs.

Also, in 2014, the CAPCOA launched a Greenhouse Gas Reduction Exchange (GHG Rx). The GHG Rx is a secure, web-based platform that features locally generated and properly validated GHG emission reduction credits from voluntary projects within California and facilitates communication between those who create the credits, potential buyers and funding organizations.

Senate Bill 375. SB 375 (Chapter 728, Statutes of 2008) requires RTPs prepared by 18 regional transportation planning agencies to incorporate an SCS in their RTPs that demonstrates how the region would achieve regional GHG emission reduction targets for 2020 and 2035 set by the ARB. Chapter 4 describes SB 375 implementation in detail.

Local climate action plans. Many cities and counties have prepared Climate Action Plans (CAPs). CAPs typically set forth measures to reduce community GHG emissions, as well as specific GHG reduction measures for government to reduce GHG emissions associated with government operations. Some CAPs also present assessment of community vulnerabilities to climate change impacts (known as vulnerability assessments), and adaptation measures to respond to climate change impacts. OPR has prepared a list of plans and initiatives adopted by California jurisdictions to address climate change (www.opr.ca.gov/docs/2016_California_Jurisdictions_Addressing_Climate_Change_Summary.pdf).

CAPs can serve to mitigate the GHG impacts of general plans. In addition, CAPs meeting certain CEQA Guidelines criteria for GHG reduction plans can streamline CEQA compliance for projects consistent with the CAP. Cal. Code Regs. § 15183.5. GHG impacts from projects consistent with these GHG reduction plans may be considered less than cumulatively considerable, and therefore less than significant. Qualified GHG reduction plans must quantify future community GHG emissions, define a threshold below which a project's GHG emissions would be less than cumulatively considerable, analyze the GHG emissions from specific covered projects, and present GHG reduction measures to reduce project GHG emissions below the threshold. Qualified GHG reduction plans must be adopted in a public process following environmental review, and include monitoring and amendment processes.

The first generation of CAPs typically used AB 32's 2020 GHG reduction target to develop local targets. In the future, they will have to grapple with setting longer-term targets, probably based on SB 32's GHG reduction target of 40 percent below 1990 levels.

The first generation of CAPs typically used AB 32's 2020 GHG reduction target to develop local targets. In the future, they will have to grapple with setting longer-term targets, probably based on SB 32's GHG reduction target of 40 percent below 1990 levels.

CAPS have been judicially challenged. For example, in *Sierra Club v. County of San Diego* (2014) 231 Cal. App. 4th 1152, the court ruled that a CAP called for in a General Plan EIR did not adopt enforceable GHG reduction measures, deadlines, and continued GHG emission reductions, as called for in the General Plan EIR. The court ordered preparation of a Supplemental EIR for the CAP.

CLIMATE CHANGE IMPACTS AND ADAPTATION

Climate change impacts in California are reviewed at the beginning of this chapter. In addition to programs to reduce GHG emissions, all levels of government are taking steps to adapt to the inevitable impacts of climate change.

FEDERAL ADAPTATION PROGRAMS

Executive Order 13653. EO 13853 requires all federal agencies to modernize their programs to support "climate resilient investments" at the federal, state and local level. It also requires federal land management agencies to modify their plans and programs to increase climate resilience, at the same time promoting carbon sequestration where possible.

The EO orders federal agencies to prepare updated Agency Adaptation Plans; these plans must assess climate risks to the agency's mission and operations, and describe how the agency will improve climate adaptation and resilience with respect to agency suppliers, supply chain, real property investments, and capital equipment

FEMA = Federal Emergency Management Agency

purchases. The EO establishes an interagency Council on Climate Preparedness and Resilience to, among other responsibilities, develop and coordinate interagency efforts on climate preparedness and resilience. It also establishes a State, Local, and Tribal Leaders Task Force on Climate Preparedness and Resilience to recommend to the President steps the federal government can take to increase climate preparedness and resilience in their communities.

The EO provides definitions of key terms that are useful for understanding climate adaptation programs at all levels of government

"Preparedness" means actions taken to plan, organize, equip, train, and exercise to build, apply, and sustain the capabilities necessary to prevent, protect against, ameliorate the effects of, respond to, and recover from climate-change-related damages.

"Adaptation" means adjustment in natural or human systems in anticipation of or response to a changing environment in a way that effectively uses beneficial opportunities or reduces negative effects.

"Adaptation" means adjustment in natural or human systems in anticipation of or response to a changing environment in a way that effectively uses beneficial opportunities or reduces negative effects.

"Resilience" means the ability to anticipate, prepare for, and adapt to changing conditions and withstand, respond to, and recover rapidly from disruptions.

Federal Emergency Management Agency Policy. The FEMA State Mitigation Plan Review Guide (FEMA 2015) requires state hazard mitigation plans to consider the impacts of climate change in order to be eligible for disaster preparedness funding. The Guide notes that the challenges posed by climate change, such as more intense storms, frequent heavy precipitation, heat waves, drought, extreme flooding and higher sea levels, could significantly alter the types and magnitudes of hazards impacting states in the future.

STATE ADAPTATION PROGRAMS

California Climate Adaptation Strategy. Executive Order S-13-08 required the NRA to prepare a California Climate Adaptation Strategy, which it did in 2009. The Agency updated the Strategy in 2014, in a report titled "Safeguarding California: Reducing Climate Risk" (Natural Resources Agency 2014). In 2016, the Agency released another report, "Safeguarding California: Implementation Action Plans" (Natural Resources Agency 2016). This latest report describes state agency actions taken to date and next steps for 10 sectors: agriculture, biodiversity and habitat, emergency management, energy, forestry, land use and community development, oceans and coastal resources and ecosystems, public health, transportation, and water. It establishes the following seven "cross sector principles:"

- Make the risks Californians face from a changing climate an integral part of all core functions of government
- Provide risk reduction measures for California's most vulnerable populations

Table 20-2. Sea Level Rise Projections Using 2000 as the Baseline

Time Period	North of Cape Mendocino*	South of Cape Mendocino*
2000 to 2030	–4 to 23 cm (–0.13 to 0.75 ft)	4 to 30 cm (0.13 to 0.98 ft)
2000 to 2050	–3 to 48 cm (–0.1 to 1.57 ft)	12 to 61 cm (0.39 to 2.0 ft)
2000 to 2100	10 to 143 cm (0.3 to 4.69 ft)	42 to 167 cm (1.38 to 5.48 ft)

*Differences in sea level rise projections north and south of Cape Mendocino are due mainly to vertical land movement. North of Cape Mendocino, geologic forces are causing much of the land to uplift, resulting in a lower rise in sea level, relative to the land, than has been observed farther south.

Source: OPC 2013

- Identify significant and sustainable funding sources for investments that reduce climate risks, human loss, and disaster spending
- Support continued climate research and data tools to inform policy and risk reduction activities
- Maximize returns to investments by prioritizing projects that produce multiple benefits and promote sustainable stewardship of California's resources
- Promote collaborative and iterative processes for crafting and refining climate risk management strategies
- Support regional and local approaches to integrate sectors and address priorities across California's diverse regions

AB 1482 of 2015 (Chapter 603, Statutes of 2015) requires the Climate Adaptation Strategy to be updated every three years, and to achieve certain statutory objectives.

California responses to sea level rise. The Ocean Protection Council led a multi-agency effort to prepare a California Sea Level Rise Guidance Document (OPC 2013). This guidance recommends use of the Natural Research Council's sea level rise projections discussed earlier in this chapter and shown in Table 20-2. Other OPC recommendations include considering time frames, adaptive capacity, and risk tolerance when selecting estimates of sea level rise; considering storms and other extreme weather events; and considering changes in shorelines and earthquakes.

The California Coastal Commission in 2015 adopted a Sea Level Rise Policy Guidance document to guide coastal planning and permitting. Earlier, in 2011, the San Francisco Bay Conservation and Development Commission had amended the San Francisco Bay Plan to address sea level rise.

The Coastal Commission's Sea Level Rise Policy Guidance recognizes three broad categories of sea level rise adaptations strategies: protection (e.g., seawalls), accommodation (e.g., elevating structures), and retreat (e.g., moving development out of hazard areas). Managed coastal retreat is an emerging strategy that is especially controversial. *See* sidebar.

Managed Coastal Retreat

Managed coastal retreat adaptation strategies relocate or remove existing development out of hazard areas and limit the construction of new development in vulnerable areas. These strategies include land use controls that encourage building in more resilient areas, and gradually removing and relocating existing development. Examples include acquisition and buyout programs, transfer of development rights programs, and removal of structures where the right to protection was waived via permit condition (California Coastal Commission 2015). Other examples include setbacks, "rolling easements," and rebuilding restrictions. These strategies may be unpopular with property owners, and may lead to regulatory takings challenges.

Integrated Climate Adaptation and Resiliency Program. SB 246 of 2015 (Chapter 606, Statutes of 2015) creates the Integrated Climate Adaptation and Resiliency Program within OPR. OPR is charged with coordinating statewide planning by connecting with regional and local governments and establishing a climate adaptation informational clearinghouse. The bill creates an advisory council to advise OPR on these activities.

LOCAL ADAPTATION PROGRAMS

California Adaptation Planning Guide. The California Adaptation Planning Guide was issued in 2012 (Governor's Office of Emergency Services and Natural Resources Agency 2012). It provides a flexible step-by-step process for local and regional climate vulnerability assessment and adaptation strategy development. The process of developing climate change adaptation strategies can vary from a short, initial qualitative process to a much more detailed, lengthy, comprehensive approach. The basic adaptation guide is supported by three companion documents with in-depth guidance on defining climate impacts, understanding regional characteristics, and developing adaptation strategies. The California Office of Emergency Services is required to update the Adaptation Planning Guide within one year of an update to the Safeguarding California plan. Pub. Res. Code § 71356.

The process of developing climate change adaptation strategies can vary from a short, initial qualitative process to a much more detailed, lengthy, comprehensive approach.

Local public trustee agencies. Scores of California local public agencies have public trust authority over commerce, navigation, and fisheries connected to tidelands and submerged lands (e.g., the ports of Los Angeles, Long Beach, San Diego, San Francisco, Oakland, Richmond, Benicia, and Eureka). Under AB 691 of 2013 (Chapter 592, Statutes of 2013), these agencies are required to evaluate the impacts of sea level rise impacting public trust lands, to identify mitigation measures to avoid impacts to these lands, and to prepare and submit an assessment of how they propose to manage sea level rise to the State Lands Commission.

SB 379 of 2015 (Chapter 608, Statutes of 2015) (Jackson) requires cities and counties to modify, as appropriate, their general plans to incorporate climate change considerations. Local governments must review and update their general plan safety elements to assess climate change risks such as fire and flood risk. This vulnerability assessment must, among other things, include feasible strategies to avoid or minimize climate change impacts arising from new land uses and essential public facilities (e.g., hospitals, emergency shelters, and emergency command centers). When considering adaptation alternatives, the general plan must adopt existing natural features and ecosystem processes such as urban tree planting, floodplain and wetlands restoration.

ENFORCEMENT

EPA authority to enforce the federal CAA is discussed in chapter 5. The ARB is authorized to enforce regulations, orders, emission limitations, and emissions reduction measures, including market-based compliance mechanisms, pursuant to AB 32. Health & Safety Code § 38580 (a).

Local governments must review and update their general plan safety elements to assess climate change risks such as fire and flood risk.

for more information...

California Air Resources Board, 2008. Climate Change Scoping Plan.

California Air Resources Board, 2014. First Update to Climate Change Scoping Plan

California Air Resources Board, 2015. Clean Power Plan Compliance Discussion Paper.

California Air Resources Board, 2016. Revised Proposed Short-Lived Climate Pollutant Strategy.

California Climate Change Center, 2012. Our Changing Climate 2012: Vulnerability & Adaptation to the Increasing Risks from Climate Change in California.

California Department of Water Resources, 2015. California Climate Science and Data for Water Resources Management.

California Ocean Protection Council, 2013. State of California Sea-Level Rise Guidance Document.

California Office of Emergency Services and Natural Resources Agency, 2012. Adaptation Planning Guide: Planning for Adaptive Communities.

Council on Environmental Quality, 2016. Final Guidance for Federal Departments and Agencies on Consideration of Greenhouse Gas Emissions and the Effects of Climate Change in National Environmental Policy Act Reviews.

Federal Emergency Management Agency, 2015. State Mitigation Plan Review Guide.

Manaster, K. A. and D. P. Selmi (eds.), ND. California Environmental Law and Land Use Practice, Chapter 85. Matthew Bender, San Francisco, Calif.

Melillo, Jerry M., Terese (T. C.) Richmond, and Gary W. Yohe (eds.), 2014. Climate Change Impacts in the United States: The Third National Climate Assessment. U.S. Global Change Research Program.

National Research Council, 2012. Sea-Level Rise for the Coasts of California, Oregon, and Washington: Past, Present, and Future.

Natural Resources Agency, 2014. Safeguarding California: Reducing Climate Risk.

Natural Resources Agency, 2016. Safeguarding California: Implementation Action Plans.

United Nations Intergovernmental Panel on Climate Change, 2013. Climate Change 2013: The Physical Science Basis. Summary for Policymakers.

United Nations Intergovernmental Panel on Climate Change, 2014. Climate Change 2014: Impacts, Adaptation, and Vulnerability. Working Group II Contribution to the Fifth Assessment Report of the Intergovernmental Panel on Climate Change.

glossary

Adaptation—adjustment or preparation of natural or human systems to a new or changing environment which moderates harm or exploits beneficial opportunities.

Anthropogenic—made by people or resulting from human activities. Usually used in the context of emissions that are produced as a result of human activities.

Biofuels—gas or liquid fuel made from plant material (biomass). Includes wood, wood waste, wood liquors, peat, railroad ties, wood sludge, spent sulfite liquors, agricultural waste, straw, tires, fish oils, tall oil, sludge waste, waste alcohol, municipal solid waste, landfill gases, other waste, and ethanol blended into motor gasoline.

Biomass—materials that are biological in origin, including organic material (both living and dead) from above and below ground, for example, trees, crops, grasses, tree litter, roots, and animals and animal waste.

Black carbon—the most strongly light-absorbing component of particulate matter (PM), and is formed by the incomplete combustion of fossil fuels, biofuels, and biomass. It is emitted directly into the atmosphere in the form of fine particles ($PM_{2.5}$).

Carbon dioxide—a naturally occurring gas, and also a by-product of burning fossil fuels and biomass, as well as land-use changes and other industrial processes. It is the principal human-caused greenhouse gas that affects the Earth's radiative balance. It is the reference gas against which other greenhouse gases are measured and therefore has a Global Warming Potential of 1.

Carbon dioxide equivalent—metric measure used to compare the emissions from various greenhouse gases based upon their global warming potential (GWP). Carbon dioxide equivalents are commonly expressed as "million metric tons of carbon dioxide equivalents (MMT CO_2eq)." The carbon dioxide equivalent for a gas is derived by multiplying the tons of the gas by the associated GWP.

Carbon sequestration—terrestrial, or biologic, carbon sequestration is the process by which trees and plants absorb carbon dioxide, release the oxygen, and store the carbon.

Chlorofluorocarbons (CFCs)—gases used for refrigeration, air conditioning, packaging, insulation, solvents, or aerosol propellants. Since they are not destroyed in the lower atmosphere, CFCs drift into the upper atmosphere where, given suitable conditions, they break down ozone.

Climate change—any significant change in the measures of climate lasting for an extended period of time. In other words, climate change includes major changes in temperature, precipitation, or wind patterns, among others, that occur over several decades or longer.

Fluorinated gases—powerful synthetic greenhouse gases such as hydrofluorocarbons, perfluorocarbons, and sulfur hexafluoride that are emitted from a variety of industrial processes. Fluorinated gases are sometimes used as substitutes for stratospheric ozone-depleting substances (e.g., chlorofluorocarbons, hydrochlorofluorocarbons, and halons) and are often used in coolants, foaming agents, fire extinguishers, solvents, pesticides, and aerosol propellants.

Fluorocarbons—carbon-fluorine compounds that often contain other elements such as hydrogen, chlorine, or bromine.

Global warming—the recent and ongoing global average increase in temperature near the Earth's surface.

Global warming potential—a measure of the total energy that a gas absorbs over a particular period of time (usually 100 years), compared to carbon dioxide.

Greenhouse effect—trapping and build-up of heat in the atmosphere (troposphere) near the Earth's surface.

Greenhouse gas (GHG)—any gas that absorbs infrared radiation in the atmosphere. Greenhouse gases include carbon dioxide, methane, nitrous oxide, ozone, chlorofluorocarbons, hydrochlorofluorocarbons, hydrofluorocarbons, perfluorocarbons, and sulfur hexafluoride.

Hydrochlorofluorocarbons (HCFCs)—compounds containing hydrogen, fluorine, chlorine, and carbon atoms. Although ozone-depleting substances, they are less potent at destroying stratospheric ozone than chlorofluorocarbons (CFCs). They have been introduced as temporary replacements for CFCs and are also greenhouse gases.

Hydrofluorocarbons (HFCs)—compounds containing only hydrogen, fluorine, and carbon atoms. They were introduced as alternatives to ozone-depleting substances in serving many industrial, commercial, and personal needs. HFCs are emitted as by-products of industrial processes and are also used in manufacturing. They do not significantly deplete the stratospheric ozone layer, but they are powerful greenhouse gases.

Methane (CH_4)—a hydrocarbon that is a greenhouse gas with a global warming potential most recently estimated at 25 times that of carbon dioxide (CO_2). Methane is produced through anaerobic (without oxygen) decomposition of waste in landfills, animal digestion, decomposition of animal wastes, production and distribution of natural gas and petroleum, coal production, and incomplete fossil fuel combustion.

Metric ton—common international measurement for the quantity of greenhouse gas emissions. A metric ton is equal to 2205 lbs or 1.1 short tons.

Ocean acidification—increased concentrations of carbon dioxide in sea water causing a measurable increase in acidity (i.e., a reduction in ocean pH). This may lead to reduced calcification rates of calcifying organisms such as corals, mollusks, algae and crustaceans.

Storm surge—an abnormal rise in sea level accompanying a hurricane or other intense storm, whose height is the difference between the observed level of the sea surface and the level that would have occurred in the absence of the storm.

Vulnerability—the degree to which a system is susceptible to, or unable to cope with, adverse effects of climate change, including climate variability and extremes. Vulnerability is a function of the character, magnitude, and rate of climate variation to which a system is exposed; its sensitivity; and its adaptive capacity.

Acronyms

ACHP = Advisory Council on Historic Preservation

AFC = application for certification

AFT = American Farmland Trust

AHERA = Asbestos Hazard Emergency Response Act

ALUC = airport land use commission

ALUCP = airport land use compatibility plan

ANSI = American National Standards Institute

APCD = air pollution control district

AQIA = air quality impact analysis

AQMD = air quality management district

ARAR = applicable or relevant and appropriate requirement

ARB = California Air Resources Board

ASP = automobile service provider

AST = aboveground storage tank

ATC = authority to construct

ATCM = airborne toxic control measure

BAAQMD = Bay Area Air Quality Management District

BACT = best available control technology

BAT = best available technology economically achievable

BCDC = San Francisco Bay Conservation and Development Commission

BCT = best conventional pollutant control technology

BDACT = best demonstrated available control technology

BDCP = Bay Delta Conservation Plan

BLM = Bureau of Land Management

BMP = best management practice

BOD = biochemical oxygen demand

BPT = best practicable control technology currently available

C.F.R. = Code of Federal Regulations

CAA = Clean Air Act

CAAQS = California ambient air quality standards

CAL FIRE = California Department of Forestry and Fire Protection

Cal. Code Regs. = California Code of Regulations

Cal/EPA = California Environmental Protection Agency

Cal/OSHA = California Occupational Safety and Health Administration

CalARP = California Accidental Release Prevention program

CAM = compliance assurance monitoring

CAP = Climate Action Plan

CAPCOA = California Air Pollution Control Officers Association

CASGEM = California State Groundwater Elevation Monitoring Program

CAT = Climate Action Team

CEC = California Energy Commission

CED = covered electronic device

CEO = chief executive officer

CEQ = President's Council on Environmental Quality

CEQA = California Environmental Quality Act

CERCLA = Comprehensive Environmental Response, Compensation, and Liability Act

CERES = California Environmental Resources Evaluation System

CERS = California Environmental Reporting System

CESA = California Endangered Species Act

CFC = chlorofluorocarbons

CFCP = California Farmland Conservancy Program

CFEMS = compliance-focused environmental management system

CFO = chief financial officer

cfs = cubic feet per second

CGS = California Geological Survey

CH_4 = methane

CLEAN = Cleanup Loan and Environmental Assistance to Neighborhoods

CLRRA = California Land Restoration and Reuse Act

CMS = corrective measures study

CNEL = community noise equivalent level

CO_2 = carbon dioxide

COC = chemicals of concern

COC = conditions of certification

COG = Council of Governments

CPP = EPA's Clean Power Plan

CPUC = California Public Utilities Commission

CSE = county-wide siting element

CTR = California toxics rule

CUP = conditional use permit

CUPA = Certified Unified Program Agency

CVP = Central Valley Project

CWA = Clean Water Act

CZMA = Coastal Zone Management Act

DAP = district attainment plan

dB = decibel

dbA = A-weighted decibel

DFW = California Department of Fish and Wildlife

DHS = Department of Homeland Security

DLRP = Division of Land Resource Protection

DMR = discharge monitoring report

DOC = California Department of Conservation

DOE = Department of Energy

DOGGR = Division of Oil, Gas, and Geothermal Resources

DOT = Department of Transportation

DPC = Delta Protection Commission

DPH = California Department of Public Health

DPR = Department of Pesticide Regulation

DSC = Delta Stewardship Council

DTSC = Department of Toxic Substances Control

DWR = California Department of Water Resources

EGPR = Environmental Goals and Policy Report

EHS = extremely hazardous substance

EIR = Environmental Impact Report

EIS = Environmental Impact Statement

EJ = environmental justice

ELGs = effluent limitation guidelines and standards

EMS = environmental management system

EMSW = engineered municipal solid waste

EO = Executive Order

EPA = U.S. Environmental Protection Agency

EPCRA = Emergency Planning and Community Right-to-Know Act

ERA = Exceedance Response Action

ERM = excluded recyclable material

ESA = Endangered Species Act

ESHA = Environmentally Sensitive Habitat Area

EU = European Union

EV = electric vehicle

FAA = Federal Aviation Administration

FAIR = Financial Assurance and Insurance for Redevelopment

FAST = Fixing America's Surface Transportation

FEMA = Federal Emergency Management Agency

FERC = Federal Energy Regulatory Commission

FHWA = Federal Highway Administration

FIFRA = Federal Insecticide, Fungicide, and Rodenticide Act

FONSI = finding of no significant impact

FRP = facility response plan

FS = feasibility study

FSZ = Farmland Security Zone

GAAP = generally accepted accounting principles

GACT = generally achievable control technology

GAGAS = generally accepted government auditing standards

GCM = global climate model

GHG = greenhouse gas

GHG Rx = Greenhouse Gas Reduction Exchange

GHS = Global Harmonized Standard

GMP = good management practice

GPO = Government Printing Office

GSAs = Groundwater Sustainability Agencies

GSP = Groundwater Sustainability Plan

GVWR = Gross Vehicle Weight Rating

GWP = global warming potential

HAP = hazardous air pollutant

HAZCOM = written hazard communication

HCD = Department of Housing and Community Development

HCFC = hydrochlorofluorocarbons

HCP = Habitat Conservation Plan (federal)

HESIS = Hazard Evaluation System and Information Service

HFC = hydrofluorocarbons

HFE = hydro fluorinated ethers

HHWE = household hazardous waste element

HRA = health risk assessment

HSAA = Carpenter-Presley-Tanner Hazardous Substance Account Act

HSAA = Hazardous Substances Account Act

HSITA = California Hazardous Substances Information and Training Act

HUD = U.S. Department of Housing and Urban Development

HWCL = Hazardous Waste Control Law

IDW = investigation-derived waste

IGP = Industrial General Permit

IIPP = Injury and Illness Prevention Program

ILRP = Irrigated Lands Regulatory Program

IOU = investor-owned utility

ISO = International Organization for Standardization

ITP = incidental take permit

IWMA = Integrated Waste Management Act

IWMP = Integrated Waste Management Plan

JD = jurisdictional determination

L_{10} = the A-weighted noise level that is exceeded 10 percent of the time

LAER = lowest achievable emission rate

LAFCO = Local Agency Formation Commission

LCFS = low-carbon fuel standard

LCP = local coastal program

Ldn = day-night average level

LDR = land disposal requirement

LEA = local enforcement agency

LEPC = local emergency planning committee

Leq = equivalent energy level

LESA = California Agricultural Land Evaluation and Site Assessment

LEV = low-emission vehicle

LOP = letter of permission

LORS = laws, ordinances, regulations, and standards

LQG = large quantity generator

LQH = large quantity handler

MACT = maximum achievable control technology

MAF = million acre-feet

MCL = maximum contaminant level

MCLG = maximum contaminant level goal

MMRP = Mitigation Monitoring or Reporting Program

MMT = million metric tons

MND = Mitigated Negative Declaration

MOA = memorandum of agreement

MOU = memorandum of understanding

MPO = Metropolitan Planning Organization

MRMP = mineral resource management policy

MS4 = municipal separate storm sewer system

MSDS = material safety data sheet

MSWLF = municipal solid waste landfill

MT = metric tons

MVAC = motor vehicle air conditioner

MW = megawatt

MWh = megawatt hour

N_2O = nitrous oxide

NAAQS = national ambient air quality standards

NAGPRA = Native American Graves Protection and Repatriation Act

NAHC = California Native American Heritage Commission

NAL = numeric action level

NCCP = Natural Communities Conservation Plan (state)

NCCPA = Natural Communities Conservation Planning Act

ND = Negative Declaration

NDFE = non-disposal facility element

NEC = No Exposure Certification

NEPA = National Environmental Policy Act

NESHAP = National Emissions Standards for Hazardous Air Pollutants

NF_3 = nitrogen trifluoride

NFIP = National Flood Insurance Program

NFPA = National Fire Protection Association

NOAA = National Oceanic and Atmospheric Administration

NOAA Fisheries = National Oceanic and Atmospheric Administration Fisheries Service

NOD = Notice of Determination

NOE = Notice of Exemption

NOI = Notice of Intent or notice of intention

NONA = notice of non-applicability

NOP = Notice of Preparation

NOV = notice of violation

NPDES = National Pollutant Discharge Elimination System

NPL = National Priorities List

NRA = Natural Resources Agency

NRC = National Response Center

NRCS = Natural Resources Conservation Service

NSPS = new source performance standards

NSR = new source review

NWP = nationwide permit

OAL = Office of Administrative Law

OEHHA = Office of Environmental Health Hazard Assessment

OES = Governor's Office of Emergency Services

OHP = Office of Historic Preservation

ONC = Office of Noise Control

OPR = Governor's Office of Planning and Research

OSHA = Occupational Safety and Health Administration; Occupational Safety and Health Act

PA = preliminary assessment

PBDE = polybrominated diphenyl ether

PCBs = polychlorinated biphenyls

PCN = pre-construction notification

PEL = permissible exposure level

PFC = perfluorocarbons

PHG = public health goals

PHI = pre-harvest inspection

PICs = products of incomplete combustion

PM = particulate matter

PMN = premanufacture notice

POTWs = publicly-owned treatment works

PRD = Permit Registration Document

PRP = potentially responsible party

PSA = Permit Streamlining Act

PSD = prevention of significant deterioration

PSES = pretreatment standards for existing sources

PSIP = Periodic Smoke Inspection Program

PSM = process safety management

PSNS = pretreatment standards for new sources

PSP = permitting strategy plan

PTE = potential to emit

PTEIR = Program Timber Environmental Impact Report

PTHP = Program Timber Harvest Plan

PTO = permit to operate

PUC = Public Utilities Commission

PUD = planned unit development

PWS = public water system

QISP = Qualified Industrial Stormwater Practitioner

QPO = qualifying property owner

RACT = reasonably available control technology

RAP = remedial action plan

RCD = resource conservation district

RCRA = Resource Conservation and Recovery Act

RD/RA = remedial design/ remedial action

RDSI = report of disposal site information

RFA = RCRA facility assessment

RFI = RCRA facility investigation

RHNA = Regional Housing Needs Assessment

RI = remedial investigation

RMP = risk management plan

ROD = Record of Decision

RPF = registered professional forester

RPPC = rigid plastic packaging container

RPS = Renewable Portfolio Standards

RQ = reportable quantity

RTP = regional transportation plan

RTPA = Regional Transportation Planning Agency

RWQCB = regional water quality control board

SARA = Superfund Amendments and Reauthorization Act

SCAQMD = Southern California Air Quality Management District

SCS = Sustainable Communities Strategy

SDS = safety data sheet

SDWA = Safe Drinking Water Act

SEP = supplemental environmental project

SERC = State Emergency Response Commission

SF6 = sulfur hexafluoride

SGC = Strategic Growth Council

SGMA = Sustainable Groundwater Management Act

SHPO = State Historic Preservation Officer

SI = site inspection

SIC = Standard Industrial Classification

SIP = State Implementation Plan

SIU = significant industrial user

SLC = State Lands Commission

SLCP = short-lived climate pollutant

SMARA = Surface Mining and Reclamation Act

SMARTS = Stormwater Multiple Application and Report Tracking System

SMGB = State Mining and Geology Board

SNEI = significant net emissions increase

SNUR = Significant New Use Rule

SOI = sphere of influence

SOP = standard operating procedure

SOX = Sarbanes-Oxley Act

SPCC = spill prevention control and countermeasure

SPPE = small power plant exemption

SQG = small quantity generator

SQH = small quantity handler

SRA = state responsibility area

SRRE = source reduction and recycling element

SSC = species of special concern

SWAT = solid waste assessment test

SWD = solid waste disposal

SWDA = Solid Waste Disposal Act and Resource Conservation and Recovery Act

SWMU = solid waste management unit

SWP = State Water Project

SWPPP = stormwater pollution prevention plan

SWRCB = State Water Resources Control Board

SYP = sustained yield plan

T-BACT = best available control technology for toxics

TAC = toxic air contaminant

THP = timber harvest plan

TIP = transportation improvement plan

TMDL = total maximum daily load

TOGs = toxic organic gases

TPQ = threshold planning quantity

TPY = tons per year

TPZ = timberland production zone

TRPA = Tahoe Regional Planning Agency

TSCA = Toxic Substances Control Act

TWW = treated waste wood

U.S.C. = United States Code

U.F.C. = Uniform Fire Code

UIC = underground injection control

UNIPCC = United Nations Intergovernmental Panel on Climate Change

UPA = unified program agency

USACE = U.S. Army Corps of Engineers

USDA = U.S. Department of Agriculture

USFWS = U.S. Fish and Wildlife Service

USGS = U.S. Geological Survey

UST = underground storage tank

UWMP = Urban Water Management Plan

VA = vulnerability assessment

VCP = Voluntary Cleanup Program

VOC = volatile organic compound

VSQG = very small quantity generator

WCI = Western Climate Initiative

WDR = waste discharge requirement

WLA = waste load allocation

WMU = waste management unit

WOTUS = waters of the United States

WQBEL = water quality-based effluent limitation

WQO = water quality objective

WQS = water quality standards

WSA = water supply assessment

WTE = waste to energy

ZNE = Zero Net Energy

Index

Note: Page numbers in *italics* indicate information in figures, maps, and tables.

B

C

D

E

F

G

H

I

O

P

S

T

U

V

W

Y

Z